## BUSINESS PLUG-INS

| | | | |
|---|---|---|---|
| B1 | BUSINESS BASICS | B12 | GLOBAL TRENDS |
| B2 | BUSINESS PROCESS | B13 | STRATEGIC OUTSOURCING |
| B3 | HARDWARE AND SOFTWARE | B14 | SYSTEMS DEVELOPMENT |
| B4 | ENTERPRISE ARCHITECTURES | B15 | PROJECT MANAGEMENT |
| B5 | NETWORKS AND TELECOMMUNICATIONS | B16 | OPERATIONS MANAGEMENT |
| B6 | INFORMATION SECURITY | B17 | ORGANIZATIONAL ARCHITECTURE TRENDS |
| B7 | ETHICS | B18 | BUSINESS INTELLIGENCE |
| B8 | SUPPLY CHAIN MANAGEMENT | B19 | GLOBAL INFORMATION SYSTEMS |
| B9 | CUSTOMER RELATIONSHIP MANAGEMENT | B20 | INNOVATION, SOCIAL ENTREPRENEURSHIP, SOCIAL NETWORKING, AND VIRTUAL WORLDS |
| B10 | ENTERPRISE RESOURCE PLANNING | | |
| B11 | EBUSINESS | B21 | MOBILE TECHNOLOGY |

## TECHNOLOGY PLUG-INS

| | | | |
|---|---|---|---|
| T1 | PERSONAL PRODUCTIVITY USING IT | T8 | DECISION MAKING USING ACCESS |
| T2 | BASIC SKILLS USING EXCEL | T9 | DESIGNING WEB PAGES |
| T3 | PROBLEM SOLVING USING EXCEL | T10 | CREATING WEB PAGES USING HTML |
| T4 | DECISION MAKING USING EXCEL | T11 | CREATING WEB PAGES USING DREAMWEAVER |
| T5 | DESIGNING DATABASE APPLICATIONS | | |
| T6 | BASIC SKILLS USING ACCESS | T12 | CREATING GANTT CHARTS WITH EXCEL AND MICROSOFT PROJECT |
| T7 | PROBLEM SOLVING USING ACCESS | | |

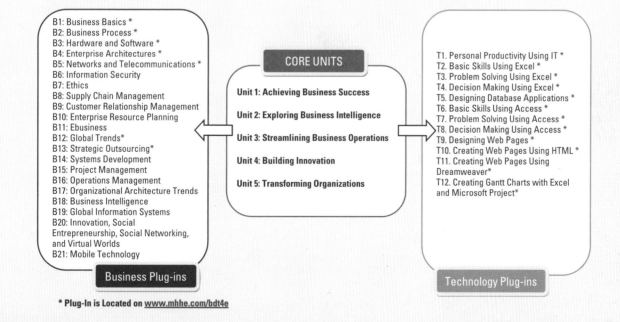

**Business Plug-ins**

B1: Business Basics *
B2: Business Process *
B3: Hardware and Software *
B4: Enterprise Architectures *
B5: Networks and Telecommunications *
B6: Information Security
B7: Ethics
B8: Supply Chain Management
B9: Customer Relationship Management
B10: Enterprise Resource Planning
B11: Ebusiness
B12: Global Trends*
B13: Strategic Outsourcing*
B14: Systems Development
B15: Project Management
B16: Operations Management
B17: Organizational Architecture Trends
B18: Business Intelligence
B19: Global Information Systems
B20: Innovation, Social Entrepreneurship, Social Networking, and Virtual Worlds
B21: Mobile Technology

**CORE UNITS**

Unit 1: Achieving Business Success

Unit 2: Exploring Business Intelligence

Unit 3: Streamlining Business Operations

Unit 4: Building Innovation

Unit 5: Transforming Organizations

**Technology Plug-ins**

T1. Personal Productivity Using IT *
T2. Basic Skills Using Excel *
T3. Problem Solving Using Excel *
T4. Decision Making Using Excel *
T5. Designing Database Applications *
T6. Basic Skills Using Access *
T7. Problem Solving Using Access *
T8. Decision Making Using Access *
T9. Designing Web Pages *
T10. Creating Web Pages Using HTML *
T11. Creating Web Pages Using Dreamweaver*
T12. Creating Gantt Charts with Excel and Microsoft Project*

* Plug-In is Located on www.mhhe.com/bdt4e

# Business Driven Technology

**FOURTH EDITION**

**Paige Baltzan**

Daniels College of Business

University of Denver

**Amy Phillips**

Daniels College of Business

University of Denver

McGraw-Hill Irwin

# McGraw-Hill
# Irwin

BUSINESS DRIVEN TECHNOLOGY

Published by McGraw-Hill/Irwin, a business unit of The McGraw-Hill Companies, Inc., 1221
Avenue of the Americas, New York, NY, 10020. Copyright © 2010, 2009, 2008, 2006 by The McGraw-Hill
Companies, Inc. All rights reserved. No part of this publication may be reproduced or distributed
in any form or by any means, or stored in a database or retrieval system, without the prior written
consent of The McGraw-Hill Companies, Inc., including, but not limited to, in any network or other
electronic storage or transmission, or broadcast for distance learning.

Some ancillaries, including electronic and print components, may not be available to customers
outside the United States.

This book is printed on acid-free paper.

1 2 3 4 5 6 7 8 9 0 WCK/WCK 0 9

ISBN 978-0-07-337679-0
MHID 0-07-337679-5

Vice president and editor-in-chief:  *Brent Gordon*
Publisher:  *Paul Ducham*
Director of development:  *Ann Torbert*
Development editor II:  *Trina Hauger*
Vice president and director of marketing:  *Robin J. Zwettler*
Marketing manager:  *Natalie Zook*
Vice president of editing, design and production:  *Sesha Bolisetty*
Manager, design & publishing services:  *Mary Conzachi*
Lead production supervisor:  *Carol A. Bielski*
Senior designer:  *Mary Kazak Sander*
Senior photo research coordinator:  *Jeremy Cheshareck*
Media project manager :  *Jennifer Lohn*
Typeface:  *10/12 Utopia*
Compositor:  *Laserwords Private Limited*
Printer:  *Quebecor World Versailles Inc.*

Library of Congress Cataloging-in-Publication Data

Baltzan, Paige.
    Business driven technology/Paige Baltzan, Amy Phillips.—4th ed.
        p. cm.
    Includes bibliographical references and index.
    ISBN-13: 978-0-07-337679-0 (alk. paper)
    ISBN-10: 0-07-337679-5 (alk. paper)
    1.   Information technology—Management. 2.   Management information systems.
3.   Information resources management. 4.   Industrial management—Technological
innovations. I. Phillips, Amy (Amy L.) II. Title.
HD30.2.H32 2010
658.4'038—dc22
                                                                    2009028544

## DEDICATION

In memory of Allan R. Biggs, my father, my
mentor, and my inspiration.
**Paige**

To my mother, Jane E. Phillips, with much love
and affection. Without you, I would not be here.
**Amy**

# TABLE OF CONTENTS

### Paige Baltzan

Paige Baltzan teaches in the Department of Information Technology and Electronic Commerce at the Daniels College of Business at the University of Denver. She holds a B.S.B.A specializing in Accounting/MIS from Bowling Green State University and an M.B.A. specializing in MIS from the University of Denver. Paige also teaches online at Strayer University. She is a coauthor of several books including *Business Driven Information Systems, Essentials of Business Driven Information Systems, I-Series,* and is a contributor to *Management Information Systems for the Information Age.*

Before joining the Daniels College faculty in 1999, Paige spent several years working for a large telecommunications company and an international consulting firm where she participated in client engagements in the United States as well as South America and Europe. Paige lives in Lakewood, Colorado, with her husband, Tony, and daughters Hannah and Sophie.

### Amy Phillips

Amy Phillips teaches in the Department of Information Technology and Electronic Commerce in the Daniels College of Business at the University of Denver. Amy's main teaching and research areas involve Internet and mobile technologies. With her MCT certification, Amy works with developing training material for Microsoft's Web Services platform, .NET. Amy has been teaching for 25 years and has coauthored several textbooks, including *Business Driven Information Systems, Management Information Systems for the Information Age 6e, Internet Explorer 6.0,* and *PowerPoint 2003.*

The overall goal of the Technology Plug-Ins is to provide additional information not covered in the text such as personal productivity using information technology, problem solving using Excel, and decision making using Access. These plug-ins also offer an all-in-one text to faculty, avoiding their having to purchase an extra book to support Microsoft Office. These plug-ins offer integration with the core chapters and provide critical knowledge using essential business applications, such as Microsoft Excel, Microsoft Access, and Microsoft Project with hands-on tutorials for comprehension and mastery. Plug-Ins T1 to T12 are located on this textbook's website at www.mhhe.com/bdt4e.

| Plug-In | Description |
|---|---|
| **T1. Personal Productivity Using IT** | This plug-in covers a number of things to do to keep a personal computer running effectively and efficiently. The 12 topics covered in this plug-in are:<br>■ Creating strong passwords.<br>■ Performing good file management.<br>■ Implementing effective backup and recovery strategies.<br>■ Using Zip files.<br>■ Writing professional emails.<br>■ Stopping spam.<br>■ Preventing phishing.<br>■ Detecting spyware.<br>■ Threads to instant messaging.<br>■ Increasing PC performance.<br>■ Using anti-virus software.<br>■ Installing a personal firewall. |
| **T2. Basic Skills Using Excel** | This plug-in introduces the basics of using Microsoft Excel, a spreadsheet program for data analysis, along with a few fancy features. The six topics covered in this plug-in are:<br>■ Workbooks and worksheets.<br>■ Working with cells and cell data.<br>■ Printing worksheets.<br>■ Formatting worksheets.<br>■ Formulas.<br>■ Working with charts and graphics. |
| **T3. Problem Solving Using Excel** | This plug-in provides a comprehensive tutorial on how to use a variety of Microsoft Excel functions and features for problem solving. The five areas covered in this plug-in are:<br>■ Lists<br>■ Conditional Formatting<br>■ AutoFilter<br>■ Subtotals<br>■ PivotTables |
| **T4. Decision Making Using Excel** | This plug-in examines a few of the advanced business analysis tools used in Microsoft Excel that have the capability to identify patterns, trends, and rules, and create "what-if" models. The four topics covered in this plug-in are:<br>■ IF<br>■ Goal Seek<br>■ Solver<br>■ Scenario Manager |
| **T5. Designing Database Applications** | This plug-in provides specific details on how to design relational database applications. One of the most efficient and powerful information management computer-based applications is the relational database. The four topics covered in this plug-in are:<br>■ Entities and data relationships.<br>■ Documenting logical data relationships.<br>■ The relational data model.<br>■ Normalization. |

| Plug-in | Description |
|---|---|
| **T6. Basic Skills Using Access** | This plug-in focuses on creating a Microsoft Access database file. One of the most efficient information management computer-based applications is Microsoft Access. Access provides a powerful set of tools for creating and maintaining a relational database. The two topics covered in this plug-in are:<br>■ Create a new database file.<br>■ Create and modify tables. |
| **T7. Problem Solving Using Access** | This plug-in provides a comprehensive tutorial on how to query a database in Microsoft Access. Queries are essential for problem solving, allowing a user to sort information, summarize data (display totals, averages, counts, and so on), display the results of calculations on data, and choose exactly which fields are shown. The three topics in this plug-in are:<br>■ Create simple queries using the simple query wizard.<br>■ Create advanced queries using calculated fields.<br>■ Format results displayed in calculated fields. |
| **T8. Decision Making Using Access** | This plug-in provides a comprehensive tutorial on entering data in a well-designed form and creating functional reports using Microsoft Access. A form is essential to use for data entry and a report is an effective way to present data in a printed format. The two topics in this plug-in are:<br>■ Creating, modifying, and running forms.<br>■ Creating, modifying, and running reports. |
| **T9. Designing Web Pages** | This plug-in provides a comprehensive assessment into the functional aspects of web design. Websites are beginning to look more alike and to employ the same metaphors and conventions. The web has now become an everyday thing whose design should not make users think. The six topics in this plug-in are:<br>■ The World Wide Web.<br>■ Designing for the unknown(s).<br>■ The process of web design.<br>■ HTML basics.<br>■ Web fonts.<br>■ Web graphics. |
| **T10. Creating Web Pages Using HTML** | This plug-in provides an overview of creating web pages using the HTML language. HTML is a system of codes that you use to create interactive web pages. It provides a means to describe the structure of text-based information in a document—by denoting certain text as headings, paragraphs, lists, and so on. The seven topics in this plug-in are:<br>■ An introduction to HTML.<br>■ HTML tools.<br>■ Creating, saving, and viewing HTML documents.<br>■ Apply style tags and attributes.<br>■ Using fancy formatting.<br>■ Creating hyperlinks.<br>■ Displaying graphics. |
| **T11. Creating Web Pages Using Dreamweaver** | This plug-in provides a tour of using Dreamweaver to create web pages. Dreamweaver allows anyone with limited web page design experience to create, modify, and maintain full-featured, professional-looking pages without having to learn how to code all the functions and features from scratch. The five topics in this plug-in are:<br>■ Navigation in Dreamweaver.<br>■ Adding content.<br>■ Formatting content.<br>■ Using cascading style sheets.<br>■ Creating tables. |
| **T12. Creating Gantt Charts with Excel and Microsoft Project** | This plug-in offers a quick and efficient way to manage projects. Excel and Microsoft Project are great for managing all phases of a project, creating templates, collaborating on planning processes, tracking project progress, and sharing information with all interested parties. The two topics in this plug-in are:<br>■ Creating Gantt Charts with Excel.<br>■ Creating Gantt Charts with Microsoft Project. |

## FEATURES

Unlike any other MIS text, *Business Driven Technology* discusses various business initiatives first and how technology supports those initiatives second. The premise for this unique approach is that business initiatives should drive technology choices. Every discussion in the text first addresses the business needs and then addresses the technology that supports those needs.

*Business Driven Technology* offers you the flexibility to customize courses according to your needs and the needs of your students by covering only essential concepts and topics in the five core units, while providing additional in-depth coverage in the business and technology plug-ins.

*Business Driven Technology*, 4e, contains 20 chapters (organized into five units), 21 business plug-ins, and 12 technology plug-ins offering you the ultimate flexibility in tailoring content to the exact needs of your MIS or IT course. The unique construction of this text allows you to cover essential concepts and topics in the five core units while providing you with the ability to customize a course and explore certain topics in greater detail with the business and technology plug-ins.

Plug-ins are fully developed modules of text that include student learning outcomes, case studies, business vignettes, and end-of-chapter material such as key terms, individual and group questions and projects, and case study exercises.

We realize that instructors today require the ability to cover a blended mix of topics in their courses. While some instructors like to focus on networks and infrastructure throughout their course, others choose to focus on ethics and security. *Business Driven Technology* was developed to easily adapt to your needs. Each chapter and plug-in is independent so you can:

- Cover any or all of the *chapters* as they suit your purpose.
- Cover any or all of the *business plug-ins* as they suit your purpose.
- Cover any or all of the *technology plug-ins* as they suit your purpose.
- Cover the plug-ins in any order you wish.

**LESS MANAGING. MORE TEACHING. GREATER LEARNING.**

McGraw-Hill *Connect MIS* is an online assignment and assessment solution that connects students with the tools and resources they'll need to achieve success.

McGraw-Hill *Connect MIS* helps prepare students for their future by enabling faster learning, more efficient studying, and higher retention of knowledge.

**MCGRAW-HILL *CONNECT MIS* FEATURES**

*Connect MIS* offers a number of powerful tools and features to make managing assignments easier, so faculty can spend more time teaching. With *Connect MIS*, students can engage with their coursework anytime and anywhere, making the learning process more accessible and efficient. *Connect MIS* offers you the features described below.

## Simple assignment management

With *Connect MIS,* creating assignments is easier than ever, so you can spend more time teaching and less time managing. The assignment management function enables you to:

- Create and deliver assignments easily with selectable interactive exercises, scenario-based questions, and test bank items.
- Streamline lesson planning, student progress reporting, and assignment grading to make classroom management more efficient than ever.
- Go paperless with the eBook and online submission and grading of student assignments.

## Smart grading

When it comes to studying, time is precious. *Connect MIS* helps students learn more efficiently by providing feedback and practice material when they need it, where they need it. When it comes to teaching, your time also is precious. The grading function enables you to:

- Have assignments scored automatically, giving students immediate feedback on their work and side-by-side comparisons with correct answers.
- Access and review each response; manually change grades or leave comments for students to review.
- Reinforce classroom concepts with practice tests and instant quizzes.

## Instructor library

The *Connect MIS* Instructor Library is your repository for additional resources to improve student engagement in and out of class. You can select and use any asset that enhances your lecture. The *Connect MIS* Instructor Library includes:

- Instructor's Manual with
    - Classroom openers and exercises for each chapter
    - Case discussion points and solutions
    - Answers to all chapter questions and cases
    - Video guides–discussion points, questions and answers
- PowerPoint Presentations with detail lecture notes
- Animated step-by-step solutions to the Apply Your Knowledge problems, narrated by the author
- Instructor Course Guide–a topical organization of all the instructor content, material and resources available

## Student study center

- The *Connect MIS* Student Study Center is the place for students to access additional data files, student versions of the PowerPoint slides and more.

## Student progress tracking

*Connect MIS* keeps instructors informed about how each student, section, and class is performing, allowing for more productive use of lecture and office hours. The progress-tracking function enables you to:

- View scored work immediately and track individual or group performance with assignment and grade reports.
- Access an instant view of student or class performance relative to learning objectives.
- Collect data and generate reports required by many accreditation organizations, such as AACSB.

**Lecture capture**

Increase the attention paid to lecture discussion by decreasing the attention paid to note taking. For an additional charge Lecture Capture offers new ways for students to focus on the in-class discussion, knowing they can revisit important topics later. Lecture Capture enables you to:

■ Record and distribute your lecture with a click of button.

■ Record and index PowerPoint presentations and anything shown on your computer so it is easily searchable, frame by frame.

■ Offer access to lectures anytime and anywhere by computer, iPod, or mobile device.

■ Increase intent listening and class participation by easing students' concerns about note-taking. Lecture Capture will make it more likely you will see students' faces, not the tops of their heads.

**McGraw-Hill *Connect Plus MIS***

McGraw-Hill reinvents the textbook learning experience for the modern student with *Connect Plus MIS.* A seamless integration of an eBook and *Connect MIS, Connect Plus MIS* provides all of the *Connect MIS* features plus the following:

■ An integrated eBook, allowing for anytime, anywhere access to the textbook.

■ A powerful search function to pinpoint and connect key concepts in a snap.

In short, *Connect MIS* offers you and your students powerful tools and features that optimize your time and energies, enabling you to focus on course content, teaching, and student learning. *Connect MIS* also offers a wealth of content resources for both instructors and students. This state-of-the-art, thoroughly tested system supports you in preparing students for the world that awaits.

For more information about Connect, go to **www.mcgrawhillconnect.com,** or contact your local McGraw-Hill sales representative.

# Tegrity Campus: Lectures 24/7

 Tegrity Campus is a service that makes class time available 24/7 by automatically capturing every lecture in a searchable format for students to review when they study and complete assignments. With a simple one-click start-and-stop process, you capture all computer screens and corresponding audio. Students can replay any part of any class with easy-to-use browser-based viewing on a PC or Mac.

Educators know that the more students can see, hear, and experience class resources, the better they learn. In fact, studies prove it. With Tegrity Campus, students quickly recall key moments by using Tegrity Campus's unique search feature. This search helps students efficiently find what they need, when they need it, across an entire semester of class recordings. Help turn all your students' study time into learning moments immediately supported by your lecture.

To learn more about Tegrity watch a 2-minute Flash demo at **http://tegritycampus.mhhe.com.**

# Assurance of Learning Ready

Many educational institutions today are focused on the notion of *assurance of learning,* an important element of some accreditation standards. *Business Driven Technology,* 4e, is designed specifically to support your assurance of learning initiatives with a simple, yet powerful solution.

Each test bank question for *Business Driven Technology* maps to a specific chapter learning outcome/objective listed in the text. You can use our test bank software, EZ Test and EZ Test Online, or in *Connect MIS* to easily query for learning outcomes/objectives that directly relate to the learning objectives for your course. You can then use the reporting features of EZ Test to aggregate student results in similar fashion, making the collection and presentation of assurance of learning data simple and easy.

## AACSB Statement

The McGraw-Hill Companies is a proud corporate member of AACSB International. Understanding the importance and value of AACSB accreditation, *Business Driven Technology,* 4e, recognizes the curricula guidelines detailed in the AACSB standards for business accreditation by connecting selected questions in the text and/or the test bank to the six general knowledge and skill guidelines in the AACSB standards.

The statements contained in *Business Driven Technology,* 4e, are provided only as a guide for the users of this textbook. The AACSB leaves content coverage and assessment within the purview of individual schools, the mission of the school, and the faculty. While *Business Driven Technology,* 4e, and the teaching package make no claim of any specific AACSB qualification or evaluation, we have within *Business Driven Technology,* 4e, labeled selected questions according to the six general knowledge and skills areas.

## McGraw-Hill Customer Care Contact Information

At McGraw-Hill, we understand that getting the most from new technology can be challenging. That's why our services don't stop after you purchase our products. You can email our Product Specialists 24 hours a day to get product-training online. Or you can search our knowledge bank of Frequently Asked Questions on our support website. For Customer Support, call **800-331-5094, email hmsupport@mcgraw-hill.com**, or visit **www.mhhe.com/support**. One of our Technical Support Analysts will be able to assist you in a timely fashion.

# Walkthrough

This text is organized around the traditional sequence of topics and concepts in information technology; however, the presentation of this material is nontraditional. That is to say, the text is divided into four major sections: (1) units, (2) chapters, (3) business plug-ins, and (4) technology plug-ins. This represents a substantial departure from existing traditional texts. The goal is to provide both students and faculty with only the most essential concepts and topical coverage in the text, while allowing faculty to customize a course by choosing from among a set of plug-ins that explore topics in more detail. All of the topics that form the core of the discipline are covered, including CRM, SCM, Porter's Five Forces model, value chain analysis, competitive advantage, information security, and ethics.

*Business Driven Technology*
includes four major components:

- 5 Core Units
- 20 Chapters
- 21 Business Plug-Ins
- 12 Technology Plug-Ins

# Format, Features, and Highlights

*Business Driven Technology, 4e,* is state of the art in its discussions, presents concepts in an easy-to-understand format, and allows students to be active participants in learning. The dynamic nature of information technology requires all students, more specifically business students, to be aware of both current and emerging technologies. Students are facing complex subjects and need a clear, concise explanation to be able to understand and use the concepts throughout their careers. By engaging students with numerous case studies, exercises, projects, and questions that enforce concepts, *Business Driven Technology* creates a unique learning experience for both faculty and students.

- **Logical Layout.** Students and faculty will find the text well organized with the topics flowing logically from one unit to the next and from one chapter to the next. The definition of each term is provided before it is covered in the chapter and an extensive glossary is included at the back of the text. Each core unit offers a comprehensive opening case study, introduction, learning outcomes, unit summary, closing case studies, key terms, and making business decision questions. The plug-ins follow the same pedagogical elements with the exception of the exclusion of opening case and closing case studies in the technology plug-ins.

- **Thorough Explanations.** Complete coverage is provided for each topic that is introduced. Explanations are written so that students can understand the ideas presented and relate them to other concepts presented in the core units and plug-ins.

- **Solid Theoretical Base.** The text relies on current theory and practice of information systems as they relate to the business environment. Current academic and professional journals and websites upon which the text is based are found in the References at the end of the book—a road map for additional, pertinent readings that can be the basis for learning beyond the scope of the unit, chapter, or plug-in.

- **Material to Encourage Discussion.** All units contain a diverse selection of case studies and individual and group problem-solving activities as they relate to the use of information technology in business. Two comprehensive cases at the end of each unit reflect the concepts from the chapters. These cases encourage students to consider what concepts have been presented and then apply those concepts to a situation they might find in an organization. Different people in an organization can view the same facts from different points of view and the cases will force students to consider some of those views.

- **Flexibility in Teaching and Learning.** While most textbooks that are "text only" leave faculty on their own when it comes to choosing cases, *Business Driven Technology* goes much further. Several options are provided to faculty with case selections from a variety of sources including *CIO, Harvard Business Journal, Wired, Forbes, Business 2.0,* and *Time,* to name just a few. Therefore, faculty can use the text alone, the text and a complete selection of cases, or anything in between.

- **Integrative Themes.** Several themes recur throughout the text, which adds integration to the material. Among these themes are value-added techniques and methodologies, ethics and social responsibility, globalization, and gaining a competitive advantage. Such topics are essential to gaining a full understanding of the strategies that a business must recognize, formulate, and in turn implement. In addition to addressing these in the chapter material, many illustrations are provided for their relevance to business practice. These include brief examples in the text as well as more detail presented in the corresponding plug-in(s) (business or technical).

# Visual Content Map

## Introduction

Information is everywhere. Most organizations value information as a strategic asset. Consider Apple and its iPod, iPod accessories, and iTunes Music Store. Apple's success depends heavily on information about its customers, suppliers, markets, and operations for each of these product lines. For example, Apple must be able to predict the number of people who will purchase an iPod to help estimate iPod accessory and iTunes sales within the next year. Estimating too many buyers will lead Apple to produce an excess of inventory; estimating too few buyers will potentially mean lost sales due to lack of product (resulting in even more lost revenues).

Understanding the direct impact information has on an organization's bottom line is crucial to running a successful business. This text focuses on information, business, technology, and the integrated set of activities used to run most organizations. Many of these activities are the hallmarks of business today—supply chain management, customer relationship management, enterprise resource planning, outsourcing, integration, ebusiness, and others. The five core units of this text cover these important activities in detail. Each unit is divided into chapters that provide individual learning outcomes and case studies. In addition to the five core units, there are technology and business "plug-ins" (see Figure Unit 1.1) that further explore topics presented in the five core units.

The chapters in Unit 1 are:

- **Chapter One**—Business Driven Technology.
- **Chapter Two**—Identifying Competitive Advantages.
- **Chapter Three**—Strategic Initiatives for Implementing Competitive Advantages.
- **Chapter Four**—Measuring the Success of Strategic Initiatives.
- **Chapter Five**—Organizational Structures That Support Strategic Initiatives.

**FIGURE UNIT 1.1**

The Format and Approach of This Text

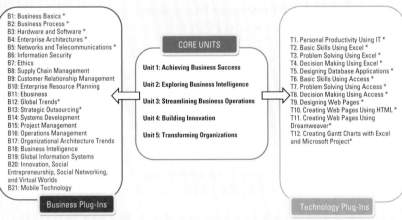

B1: Business Basics *
B2: Business Process *
B3: Hardware and Software *
B4: Enterprise Architectures *
B5: Networks and Telecommunications *
B6: Information Security
B7: Ethics
B8: Supply Chain Management
B9: Customer Relationship Management
B10: Enterprise Resource Planning
B11: Ebusiness
B12: Global Trends*
B13: Strategic Outsourcing*
B14: Systems Development
B15: Project Management
B16: Operations Management
B17: Organizational Architecture Trends
B18: Business Intelligence
B19: Global Information Systems
B20: Innovation, Social Entrepreneurship, Social Networking, and Virtual Worlds
B21: Mobile Technology

**CORE UNITS**

Unit 1: Achieving Business Success
Unit 2: Exploring Business Intelligence
Unit 3: Streamlining Business Operations
Unit 4: Building Innovation
Unit 5: Transforming Organizations

T1. Personal Productivity Using IT *
T2. Basic Skills Using Excel *
T3. Problem Solving Using Excel *
T4. Decision Making Using Excel *
T5. Designing Database Applications *
T6. Basic Skills Using Access *
T7. Problem Solving Using Access *
T8. Decision Making Using Access *
T9. Designing Web Pages *
T10. Creating Web Pages Using HTML *
T11. Creating Web Pages Using Dreamweaver*
T12. Creating Gantt Charts with Excel and Microsoft Project*

**Business Plug-Ins**

**Technology Plug-Ins**

* Plug-In is Located on www.mhhe.com/bdt4e

# Learning Outcomes and Introduction

**Introduction.** Located after the Unit Opening Case, the introduction familiarizes students with the overall tone of the chapters. Thematic concepts are also broadly defined.

**Learning Outcomes.** These outcomes focus on what students should learn and be able to answer upon completion of the chapter or plug-in.

## Introduction

Decision making and problem solving in today's electronic world encompass large-scale, opportunity-oriented, strategically focused solutions. The traditional "cookbook" approach to decisions simply will not work in the ebusiness world. Decision-making and problem-solving abilities are now the most sought-after traits in up-and-coming executives, according to a recent survey of 1,000 executives by Caliper Associates, as reported in *The Wall Street Journal.* To put it mildly, decision makers and problem solvers have limitless career potential.

***Ebusiness*** is the conducting of business on the Internet, not only buying and selling, but also serving customers and collaborating with business partners. (Unit Four discusses ebusiness in detail.) With the fast growth of information technology and the accelerated use of the Internet, ebusiness is quickly becoming standard. This unit focuses on technology to help make decisions, solve problems, and find new innovative opportunities. The unit highlights how to bring people together with the best IT processes and tools in complete, flexible solutions that can seize business opportunities (see Figure Unit 3.1). The chapters in Unit 3 are:

- **Chapter Nine**—Enabling the Organization—Decision Making.
- **Chapter Ten**—Extending the Organization—Supply Chain Management.
- **Chapter Eleven**—Building a Customer-centric Organization—Customer Relationship Management.
- **Chapter Twelve**—Integrating the Organization from End to End—Enterprise Resource Planning.

### LEARNING OUTCOMES

**9.1.** Define the systems organizations use to make decisions and gain competitive advantages.

**9.2.** Describe the three quantitative models typically used by decision support systems.

**9.3.** Describe the relationship between digital dashboards and executive information systems.

**9.4.** List and describe four types of artificial intelligence systems.

# Unit Opening Case and Opening Case Study Questions

**Unit Opening Case.** To enhance student interest, each unit begins with an opening case study that highlights an organization that has been time-tested and value-proven in the business world. This feature serves to fortify concepts with relevant examples of outstanding companies. Discussion of the case is threaded throughout the chapters in each unit.

**Opening Case Study Questions.** Located at the end of each chapter, pertinent questions connect the Unit Opening Case with important chapter concepts.

## UNIT THREE OPENING CASE

### Second Life: Succeeding in Virtual Times

Second Life is a virtual world built and owned by its residents. It opened to the public in 2003, and today is inhabited by millions of residents from around the world. The three main parts to Second Life are:

- **The World:** The world of Second Life is constantly changing and growing. It is filled with hundreds of games, from multi-player role-playing games to puzzles and grid-wide contests. There are also dance clubs, shopping malls, space stations, vampire castles' and movie theaters. To find something to do at any time of the day or night, residents simply open the Search menu and click on Events for a listing of discussions, sports, commercial, entertainment, games, pageants, education, arts and culture, and charity/support groups.
- **The Creations:** Second Life is dedicated to creativity. Everything in Second Life is resident-created, from the strobe lights in the nightclubs to the cars (or spaceships) in driveways. Imagine tinkering with the steering and handling program of a motorcycle while a friend tweaks the shape of the fuel tank and gives it a wicked flame paint job,

### OPENING CASE STUDY QUESTIONS

1. How could companies use Second Life for new product or service decision making?
2. How could financial companies use neural networks in Second Life to help their businesses?
3. How could a company such as Nike use decision support systems on Second Life to help its business?
4. How could an apparel company use Second Life to enhance decision making for a new product or service offering?

# Projects and Case Studies

**Case Studies.** This text is packed with case studies illustrating how a variety of prominent organizations and businesses have successfully implemented many of this text's concepts. All cases promote critical thinking. Company profiles are especially appealing and relevant to your students, helping to stir classroom discussion and interest. For a full list of cases explored in *Business Driven Technology*, turn to the inside back cover.

Apply Your Knowledge Project Overview

| Project Number | Project Name | Project Type | Plug-In | Focus Area | Project Level | Skill Set | Page Number |
|---|---|---|---|---|---|---|---|
| 1 | Financial Destiny | Excel | T2 | Personal Budget | Introductory | Formulas | 536 |
| 2 | Cash Flow | Excel | T2 | Cash Flow | Introductory | Formulas | 536 |
| 3 | Technology Budget | Excel | T1, T2 | Hardware and Software | Introductory | Formulas | 536 |
| 4 | Tracking Donations | Excel | T2 | Employee Relationships | Introductory | Formulas | 537 |
| 5 | Convert Currency | Excel | T2 | Global Commerce | Introductory | Formulas | 537 |
| 6 | Cost Comparison | Excel | T2 | Total Cost of Ownership | Introductory | Formulas | 537 |
| 7 | Time Management | Excel or Project | T12 | Project Management | Introductory | Gantt Charts | 538 |
| 8 | Maximize Profit | Excel | T2, T4 | Strategic Analysis | Intermediate | Formulas or Solver | 538 |
| 9 | Security Analysis | Excel | T3 | Filtering Data | Intermediate | Conditional Formatting, Autofilter, Subtotal | 539 |
| 10 | Gathering Data | Excel | T3 | Data Analysis | Intermediate | Conditional Formatting, PivotTable | 540 |

## Chapter One Case: The World Is Flat—Thomas Friedman

In his book, *The World is Flat,* Thomas Friedman describes the unplanned cascade of technological and social shifts that effectively leveled the economic world, and "accidentally made Beijing, Bangalore, and Bethesda next-door neighbors." Chances are good that Bhavya in Bangalore will read your next X-ray, or as Friedman learned firsthand, "Grandma Betty in her bathrobe" will make your JetBlue plane reservation from her Salt Lake City home.

Friedman believes this is Globalization 3.0. "In Globalization 1.0, which began around 1492, the world went from size large to size medium. In Globalization 2.0, the era that introduced us to multinational companies, it went from size medium to size small. And then around 2000 came Globalization 3.0, in which the world went from being small to tiny. There is a difference between being able to make long-distance phone calls cheaper on the Internet and walking around Riyadh with a PDA where you can have all of Google in your pocket. It is a difference in degree that's so enormous it becomes a difference in kind," Friedman states. Figure 1.10 displays Friedman's list of "flatteners."

Friedman says these flatteners converged around the year 2000 and "created a flat world: a global, Web-enabled platform for multiple forms of sharing knowledge and work, irrespective of time, distance, geography, and increasingly, language." At the very moment this platform emerged, three huge economies materialized—those of India, China, and the former Soviet Union—"and 3 billion people who were out of the game, walked onto the playing field." A final convergence may determine the fate of the United States in this chapter of globalization. A "political perfect storm," as Friedman describes it—the dot-com bust, the attacks of 9/11, and the Enron scandal—"distract us completely as a country." Just when we need to face the fact of globalization and the need to compete in a new world, "we're looking totally elsewhere."

Friedman believes that the next great breakthrough in bioscience could come from a 5-year-old who downloads the human genome in Egypt. Bill Gates's view is similar: "Twenty years ago, would you rather have been a B-student in Poughkeepsie or a genius in Shanghai?

**FIGURE 1.10**

Thomas Friedman's 10 Forces That Flattened the World

| 1. Fall of the Berlin Wall | The events of November 9, 1989, tilted the worldwide balance of power toward democracies and free markets. |
|---|---|
| 2. Netscape IPO | The August 9, 1995, offering sparked massive investment in fiber-optic cables. |
| 3. Work flow software | The rise of applications from PayPal to VPNs enabled faster, closer coordination among far-flung employees. |
| 4. Open-sourcing | Self-organizing communities, such as Linux, launched a collaborative revolution. |
| 5. Outsourcing | Migrating business functions to India saved money *and* a Third World economy. |

**Apply Your Knowledge.** At the end of this text is a set of 35 projects aimed at reinforcing the business initiatives explored in the text. These projects help to develop the application and problem-solving skills of your students through challenging and creative business-driven scenarios.

# Making Decisions

**Making Business Decisions.**
Small scenario-driven projects help students focus on decision making as they relate to the topical elements in the chapters and plug-ins.

## MAKING BUSINESS DECISIONS

### 1. Improving Information Quality

HangUps Corporation designs and distributes closet organization structures. The company operates five different systems: order entry, sales, inventory management, shipping, and billing. The company has severe information quality issues including missing, inaccurate, redundant, and incomplete information. The company wants to implement a data warehouse containing information from the five different systems to help maintain a single customer view, drive business decisions, and perform multidimensional analysis. Identify how the organization can improve its information quality when it begins designing and building its data warehouse.

### 2. Information Timeliness

Information timeliness is a major consideration for all organizations. Organizations need to decide the frequency of backups and the frequency of updates to a data warehouse. In a team, describe the timeliness requirements for backups and updates to a data warehouse for

- Weather tracking systems.
- Car dealership inventories.
- Vehicle tire sales forecasts.
- Interest rates.
- Restaurant inventories.
- Grocery store inventories.

### 3. Entities and Attributes

Martex Inc. is a manufacturer of athletic equipment and its primary lines of business include running, tennis, golf, swimming, basketball, and aerobics equipment. Martex currently supplies four primary vendors including Sam's Sports, Total Effort, The Underline, and Maximum Workout. Martex wants to build a database to help it organize its products. In a group, identify the different types of entity classes and the related attributes that Martex will want to consider when designing the database.

### 4. Integrating Information

You are currently working for the Public Transportation Department of Chatfield. The department controls all forms of public transportation including buses, subways, and trains. Each department has about 300 employees and maintains its own accounting, inventory, purchasing, and human resource systems. Generating reports across departments is a difficult

# End-of-Unit Elements

Each unit contains complete pedagogical support in the form of:

- **Unit Summary.** Revisiting the unit highlights in summary format.
- **Key Terms.** With page numbers referencing where they are discussed in the text.
- **Two Closing Case Studies.** Reinforcing important concepts with prominent examples from businesses and organizations. Discussion questions follow each case study.
- **Making Business Decisions.** Small scenario-driven projects that help students focus individually on decision making as they relate to the topical elements in the chapters.
- **Apply Your Knowledge.** In-depth projects that help students focus on applying the skills and concepts they have learned throughout the unit.
- **Business Driven Best Sellers.** Several books that discuss the unit topics are provided with a brief overview of the text. Great for graduate classes or students looking for additional materials.

# About the Plug-Ins

The plug-ins are designed to allow faculty to customize their course and cover selected topics in more detail. Students will read core material related to all of the plug-ins in the five units.

As an example, students will learn about various facets of customer relationship management (CRM) most notably in Chapter 11. However, customer relationship management has its own business plug-in. The CRM business plug-in gives both faculty and students the ability to cover CRM in more detail if desired. Likewise, students will receive an introduction to decision making in Unit 3. The Excel technology plug-ins allow coverage of decision-making tools such as PivotTables, Goal Seek, and Scenario Manager.

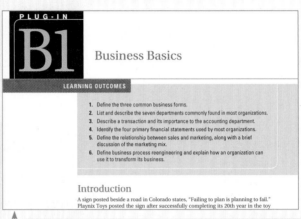

**PLUG-IN**
## B1 Business Basics

**LEARNING OUTCOMES**

1. Define the three common business forms.
2. List and describe the seven departments commonly found in most organizations.
3. Describe a transaction and its importance to the accounting department.
4. Identify the four primary financial statements used by most organizations.
5. Define the relationship between sales and marketing, along with a brief discussion of the marketing mix.
6. Define business process reengineering and explain how an organization can use it to transform its business.

### Introduction

A sign posted beside a road in Colorado states, "Failing to plan is planning to fail." Playnix Toys posted the sign after successfully completing its 20th year in the toy

**Management Focus.** By focusing on the business plug-ins, your course will take on a managerial approach to MIS.
Business plug-ins include:

| | | | |
|---|---|---|---|
| B1 | Business Basics | B13 | Strategic Outsourcing |
| B2 | Business Process | B14 | Systems Development |
| B3 | Hardware and Software | B15 | Project Management |
| B4 | Enterprise Architectures | B16 | Operations Management |
| B5 | Networks and Telecommunications | B17 | Organizational Architecture Trends |
| B6 | Information Security | B18 | Business Intelligence |
| B7 | Ethics | B19 | Global Information Systems |
| B8 | Supply Chain Management | B20 | Innovation, Social Entrepreneurship, Social Networking, and Virtual Worlds |
| B9 | Customer Relationship Management | | |
| B10 | Enterprise Resource Planning | B21 | Mobile Technology |
| B11 | Ebusiness | | |
| B12 | Global Trends | | |

**PLUG-IN**
## T7 Problem Solving Using Access 2007

**LEARNING OUTCOMES**

1. Describe the process of using the Query Wizard using Access.
2. Describe the process of using the Design view for creating a query using Access.
3. Describe the process of adding a calculated field to a query using Access.
4. Describe the process of using aggregate functions to calculate totals in queries using Access.
5. Describe how to format results displayed in calculated fields using Access.

### Introduction

A *query* is a tool for extracting, combining, and displaying data from one or more tables, according to criteria you specify. For example, in a book inventory database, you could create a query to view a list of all hardcover books with more than 500 pages that you purchased in the past five months. In a query, you can sort information, summarize data (display totals, averages, counts, and so on), display the results of calculations on data, and choose exactly which fields are shown. You can view the results of a query in a tabular format, or you can view the query's data through a form or on a report (which is covered in Plug-In T8, "Decision Making Using Access 2007"). In this plug-in, you will learn how to use the Query Wizard and Query-By-Example (QBE) tool to solve problems using Microsoft Access 2007.

**Technical Focus.** If hands-on, technical skills are more important, include technical plug-ins in your MIS course.
Technology plug-ins include:

| | | | |
|---|---|---|---|
| T1 | Personal Productivity Using IT | T7 | Problem Solving Using Access 2007 |
| T2 | Basic Skills Using Excel 2007 | T8 | Decision Making Using Access 2007 |
| T3 | Problem Solving Using Excel 2007 | T9 | Designing Web Pages |
| T4 | Decision Making Using Excel 2007 | T10 | Creating Web Pages Using HTML |
| T5 | Designing Database Applications | T11 | Creating Web Pages Using Dreamweaver |
| T6 | Basic Skills and Tools Using Access 2007 | T12 | Creating Gantt Charts with Excel and Microsoft Project |

# End-of-Plug-In Elements

Each business plug-in contains complete pedagogical support in the form of:
- **Plug-in Summary.** Revisiting the plug-in highlights in summary format.
- **Key Terms.** With page numbers referencing where they are discussed in the text.
- **Two Closing Case Studies.** Reinforcing important concepts with prominent examples from businesses and organizations. Discussion questions follow each case study.
- **Making Business Decisions.** Small scenario-driven projects that help students focus individually on decision making as they relate to the topical elements in the chapters.

---

## ✳ PLUG-IN SUMMARY

The study of business begins with understanding the different types of busine including a sole proprietorship, partnership, or a corporation. Figure B1.15 highli seven departments found in a typical business.

All of these departments must be able to execute activities specific to their business f tion and also be able to work with the other departments to create synergies throughou entire business.

- **Accounting** provides quantitative information about the finances of the business including recording, measuring, and describing financial information.
- **Finance** deals with the strategic financial issues associated with increasing the value of the business, while observing applicable laws and social responsibilities.
- **Human resources (HR)** includes the policies, plans, and procedures for the effective manag
- **Sales** which
- **Marke** marke the co
- **Opera** or pro

---

## ✳ KEY TERMS

| | | |
|---|---|---|
| Accounting, 000 | and profit-and-loss (P&L) | Partnership, 000 |
| Accounting department, 000 | statement), 000 | Partnership agreement, 000 |
| Asset, 000 | Information technology (IT), 000 | Product life cycle, 000 |
| Balance sheet, 000 | Liability, 000 | Profit, 000 |
| Bookkeeping, 000 | Limited liability, 000 | Revenue, 000 |
| Break-even point, 000 | Limited | |
| Business process, 000 | (LLC | |
| Business process reengineering | Limited | |
| (BPR), 000 | Loss, 0 | |
| Capital, 000 | Manage | |
| Corporation (also called, | syst | |

---

## ✳ CLOSING CASE ONE

### Battle of the Toys—FAO Schwarz Is Back!

German immigrant Frederick Schwarz established FAO Schwarz, a premier seller of fine toys, in 1862. After moving between several store locations in Manhattan, the growing company settled at 745 Fifth Avenue in 1931. FAO Schwarz soon became a toy institution, despite the impending Depression.

Unfortunately, the New York institution closed its doors in 2004 after its owner, FAO Inc., filed for bankruptcy twice in 2003. The company ran into trouble because it could not compete with the deep discounts offered on toys at chain stores like Wal-Mart and Target. All the stores in the FAO chain were closed.

Some people believe that FAO Schwarz was its own worst enemy. The company sold Sesame Street figures for $9 while the same figure at a discount store went for less than $3.

In 2004, the New York investment firm D. E. Shaw & Co. bought the rights to the FAO Schwarz name and reopened the Manhattan and Las Vegas stores. The grand reopening of the New York store occurred on November 25, 2004, during the Macy's Thanksgiving Day parade. It appears that the company has learned from its previous mistakes and is moving forward with a new business strategy of offering high-end, hard-to-find toys and products along with outstanding customer service.

Jerry Welch, FAO chief executive officer, states the company based its new business strategy on offering customers—local, visitors, and Internet—a unique shopping experience in

# Support and Supplemental Material

All of the supplemental material supporting *Business Driven Technology* was developed by the author team to ensure you receive accurate, high-quality, and in-depth content. Included are a complete set of materials that will assist students and faculty in accomplishing course objectives.

For a complete author-narrated overview of the support and supplemental materials of this text, please visit the Online Learning Center.

**Online Learning Center** (www.mhhe.com/bdt4e) The McGraw-Hill website for *Business Driven Technology* includes support for students and faculty. All supplements will be available exclusively on the OLC. This will allow the authors to continually update and add to the instructor support materials. The following materials will be available on the OLC:

**Video Exercises.** Each of the videos that accompany the text is supported by detailed teaching notes on how to turn the videos into classroom exercises where your students can apply the knowledge they are learning after watching the videos.

**Test Bank.** This computerized package allows instructors to custom design, save, and generate tests. The test program permits instructors to edit, add, or delete questions from the test banks; analyze test results; and organize a database of tests and students results. In addition to the traditional test bank material, a new test bank will offer Excel and Access questions for testing purposes.

- **Instructor's Manual (IM).** The IM, written by the authors, includes suggestions for designing the course and presenting the material. Each chapter is supported by answers to end-of-chapter questions and problems, and suggestions concerning the discussion topics and cases.
- **PowerPoint Presentations.** A set of PowerPoint slides, created by the authors, accompanies each chapter that features bulleted items that provide a lecture outline, plus key figures and tables from the text, and detailed teaching notes on each slide.
- **Sample Syllabi.** Several syllabi have been developed according to different course lengths—quarters and semesters, as well as different course concentrations such as a business emphasis or a technology focus.
- **Classroom Exercises.** Choose from over 30 detailed classroom exercises that engage and challenge students. For example, if you are teaching systems development, start the class with the "Skyscraper Activity" where the students build a prototype that takes them through each phase of the systems development life cycle. All classroom exercises can be found in the IM.
- **Business Driven Teaching Notes.** The Business Driven Teaching Notes is a comprehensive Excel spreadsheet containing over 150 additional classroom activities, discussion questions, and video clips. You can also turn any of the classroom activities into additional assignments and use the discussion

---

**Supplements:**
- Business Driven Teaching Notes
- Online Learning Center
- Instructor's Manual
- PowerPoint Presentations.
- Sample Syllabi
- Classroom Exercises
- Image Library
- Project Files
- Internet Links
- Captivate Files
- Cohesion Case

questions for your online courses. You can use the business driven teaching notes to customize your lectures. Each topic in the text is represented by a tab in the workbook. Simply choose the activities you wish to use, reorder based on your lecture, and hide any you do not want. Then you can easily print your detailed lecture notes straight from the worksheet.

- **Image Library.** Text figures and tables, as permission allows, are provided in a format by which they can be imported into PowerPoint for class lectures.
- **Project Files.** The authors have provided files for all projects that need further support, such as data files.
- **Internet Links.** Throughout the text are website addresses where related material can be obtained from the web. These sites provide valuable information that, when used with the text, provides a complete, up-to-date coverage of information technology and business.
- **Captivate Files.** A complete set of narrated solution files for all Excel, Access, and web development projects provide narrated step-by-step detail for each project. These are a great aid to help instructors quickly understand questions and can be posted for students to review, saving instructor time with case reviews.
- **Cohesion Case.** The Broadway Cafe is a running case instructors can use to reinforce core material such as customer relationship management, supply chain management, business intelligence, and decision making. The case has 15 sections that challenge students to develop and expand their grandfather's coffee shop. Students receive hands-on experience in business and learn technology's true value of enabling business. Please note that the Cohesion Case is not a McGraw-Hill product but a Baltzan and Phillips direct product. The case can be found at www.cohesioncase.com.

## Media Content

**MP3 Content.** Harness the power of one of the most popular technology tools students use today—the MP3 player. Our innovative approach allows students to download audio and video presentations right into their MP3 players and take learning materials with them wherever they go. The content is also available in Shockwave files so you can watch it on a computer if you choose not to use an MP3 player. This text offers more than 40 MP3 downloads with MP3 IMs to help the instructors turn the MP3s into classroom discussions and exercises.

**Video Content.** Twenty videos accompany this text and cover topics from entrepreneurship to disaster recovery. Video content icons are placed throughout the text highlighting where we recommend watching the videos. Video IMs are also available so you can turn the videos into engaging classroom activities.

**Use our EZ Test Online to help your students prepare to succeed with Apple iPod® iQuiz.** Using our EZ Test Online you can make test and quiz content available for a student's Apple iPod®. Students must purchase the iQuiz game application from Apple for 99¢ in order to use the iQuiz content. It works on fifth generation iPods and better. Instructors only need EZ Test Online to produce iQuiz-ready content. Instructors take their existing tests and quizzes and export them to a file that can then be made available to the student to take as a self-quiz on their iPods.

# Empowered Instruction

**Classroom Performance System**
Engage students and assess real-time lecture retention with this simple yet powerful wireless application. You can even deliver tests that instantly grade themselves.

**PowerPoint Presentations**
Robust, detailed, and designed to keep students engaged. Detailed teaching notes are also included on every slide.

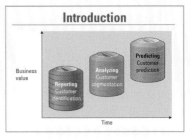

- Walk the students through the systems development life cycle:
  - *Planning phase*—involves establishing a high-level plan of the intended project and determining project goals
  - *Analysis phase*—involves analyzing end-user business requirements and refining project goals into defined functions and operations of the intended system
  - *Design phase*—involves describing the desired features and operations of the system including screen layouts, business rules, process diagrams, pseudo code, and other documentation
  - *Development phase*—involves taking all of the detailed design documents form the design phase and transforming them into the actual system
  - *Testing phase*—involves bringing all the project pieces together into a special testing environment to test for errors, bugs, and interoperability, in order to verify that the system meets all the business requirements defined in the analysis phase
  - *Implementation phase*—involves placing the system into production so users can begin to perform actual business operations with the system
  - *Maintenance phase*—involves performing changes, corrections, additions, and upgrades to ensure the system continues to meet the business goals

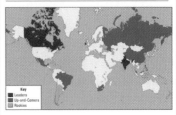

# MI**S**OURCE

**Software Skills & Computer Concepts**
MISource provides animated tutorials and simulated practice of the core skills in Microsoft Office 2007 Excel, Access, and PowerPoint.

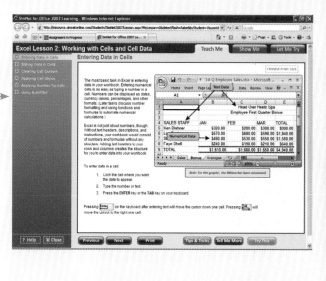

Spend less time reviewing software skills and computer literacy.

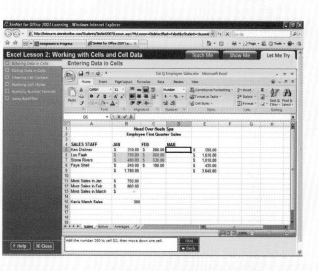

## VIDEOS

Videos will be downloadable from the instructor side of the OLC. Selections from our archive of videos from previous years will be delivered upon request.

## MBA MIS CASES

Developed by Richard Perle of Loyola Marymount University, these 14 comprehensive cases allow you to add MBA-level analysis to your course. Visit our website to review a sample case.

## ONLINE LEARNING CENTER

Visit www.mhhe.com/bdt4e for additional instructor and student resources.

## ONLINE COURSES

Content for *Business Driven Technology* is available in WebCT, Blackboard, and PageOut formats to accommodate virtually any online delivery platform.

There are numerous people whom we want to heartily thank for their hard work, enthusiasm, and dedication on the fourth edition of *Business Driver Technology*.

This text draws from the efforts of a number of people at McGraw-Hill/Irwin. Paul Ducham, our Publisher, thank you for your insight, your intellect, and your continuous support and belief in our abilities—we simply could not have succeeded without you! Trina Hauger, our Development Editor, thank you for always taking the extra time to ask those all-important questions that everyone else seemed to miss. Mary Conzachi, our Manager of Publishing Services, thank you for making the difficult production process smooth and effortless.

We also thank Brent Gordon (Editorial Director), Natalie Zook (Marketing Manager), Mary Sander (Designer), Jennifer Lohn (Media Project Manager), Carol Bielski (Production Supervisor), and Jeremy Cheshareck (Photo Coordinator), for your support and dedication to the success of this text.

To the faculty at the Daniels College of Business at the University of Denver— Richard Scudder, Don McCubbrey, Paul Bauer, Hans Hultgren, Daivd Paul, Dan Connolly, and Ked Davisson—thank you. Your feedback, advice, and support is truly valued and greatly appreciated.

Last, but certainly not least, we offer our sincerest gratitude and deepest appreciation to our valuable reviewers whose feedback was instrumental.

Dennis Adams
*University of Houston*

Kamal Agarwal
*Howard University*

Syed Imtiaz Ahmad
*Eastern Michigan University*

Lawrence Andrew
*Western Illinois University*

Antonio Arreola-Risa
*Texas A&M University*

Jean-Pierre Auffret
*George Mason University*

Kristi-Ann L. Berg
*Minot State University*

Nora M. Braun
*Augsburg College*

James Cappel
*Central Michigan University*

Judith P. Carlisle
*Dowling College*

Gerald J. Carvalho
*University of Utah*

Casey Cegielski
*Auburn University*

Elia Chepaltis
*Fairfield University*

Edward J. Cherian
*George Washington University*

Beom-Jin Choi
*California State University– Sacramento*

Joobin Choobineh
*Texas A&M University*

Phillip D. Coleman
*Western Kentucky University*

Samuel Coppage
*Old Dominion University*

Joanna DeFranco-Tommarello
*New Jersey Institute of Technology*

Roy Dejoie
*Purdue University*

Robert Denker
*Baruch College–CUNY*

Charles Downing
*Northern Illinois University*

Uldarico Rex Dumdum
*Marywood University*

Richard Egan
*New Jersey Institute of Technology*

Roland Eichelberger
*Baylor University*

Michael Eierman
*University of Wisconsin–Oshkosh*

Juan Esteva
*Eastern Michigan University*

David Fitoussi
*University of California–Irvine*

Jerry Fjermestad
*New Jersey Institute of Technology*

Roger Flynn
*University of Pittsburgh*

Janet Formichelli
*Kent State University*

Janos T. Fustos
*Metropolitan State College of Denver*

Sharyn Hardy Gallagher
*University of Massachusetts–Lowell*

Michael Gendron
*Central Connecticut State University*

Edward J. Glantz
*Pennsylvania State University*

Marvin L. Golland
*Polytechnic University, Brooklyn*

Robert Gordon
*Hofstra University*

Diane Graf
*Northern Illinois University*

Dale D. Gust
*Central Michigan University*

Don Hardaway
*Saint Louis University*

Jun He
*University of Pittsburgh*

Gerald L. Hershey
*University of North Carolina, Greensboro*

Fred H. Hughes
*Faulkner University*

Surinder Kahai
*SUNY, Binghamton*

Rex Karsten
*University of Northern Iowa*

Joseph Kasten
*Dowling College*

Yong Jin Kim
*Binghamton University*

Tracie Kinsley
*George Mason University*

Elias Kirche
*Florida Gulf Coast University*

Fred L. Kitchens
*Ball State University*

Brian J. Klas
*Montclair State University*

Barbara D. Klein
*University of Michigan–Dearborn*

Richard Klein
*Clemson University*

Chang E. Koh
*University of North Texas*

Gerald Kohers
*Sam Houston State University*

Rebecca Berens Koop
*University of Dayton*

Brett J. L. Landry
*University of New Orleans*

William Lankford
*University of West Georgia*

Robert Lawton
*Western Illinois University*

Al Lederer
*University of Kentucky*

John D. (Skip) Lees
*California State University, Chico*

Bingguang Li
*Albany State University*

Shin-Jeng Lin
*Le Moyne College*

Steve Loy
*Eastern Kentucky University*

Cindy Joy Marcelis
*Temple University*

Prosenjit Mazumdar
*George Mason University*

Dana McCann
*Central Michigan University*

Charlotte McConn
*Pennsylvania State University*

Matthew McGowan
*Bradley University*

Earl McKinney
*Bowling Green State University*

John Melrose
*University of Wisconsin–Eau Claire*

Jim Mensching
*California State University, Chico*

Pam Milstead
*Louisiana Tech University*

Ellen F. Monk
*University of Delaware*

Philip F. Musa
*The University of Alabama at Birmingham*

George Nezlek
*Grand Valley State University*

Jennifer Nightingale
*Duquesne University*

Peter Otto
*Dowling College*

Barry Pasternack
*California State University–Fullerton*

Gerald Peppers
*Howard University*

Floyd D. Ploeger
*Texas State University–San Marcos*

Patricia Quirin
*Robert Morris University*

T. S. Ragu-Nathan
*University of Toledo*

Mahesh S. Raisinghani
*University of Dallas*

Alan Rea
*Western Michigan University*

Brent Reeves
*Abilene Christian University*

Paula Ruby
*Arkansas State University*

Werner Schenk
*University of Rochester*

Roy Schmidt
*Bradley University*

David Schroeder
*Valparaiso University*

Scott Serich
*George Washington University*

Sherri Shade
*Kennesaw State University*

Nancy C. Shaw
*George Mason University*

Betsy Page Sigman
*Georgetown University*

Marcos P. Sivitanides
*Texas State University*

Marion S. Smith
*Texas Southern University*

Ute H. St. Clair
*Binghamton University*

Robert Szymanski
*University of Central Florida*

Suzanne Testerman
*University of Akron*

Amrit Tiwana
*Emory University*

Yung-Chin Alex Tung
*University of Connecticut*

Douglas E. Turner
*State University of West Georgia*

David A. Vance
*Mississippi State University*

B. Vijayaraman
*The University of Akron*

Linda Wallace
*Virginia Tech*

Barbara Warner
*University of South Florida*

John Wee
*University of Mississippi*

Rick Weible
*Marshall University*

Nilmini Wickramsinghe
*Cleveland State University*

Anita Whitehill
*Foothill College*

Dennis Williams
*California Polytechnic State University*

Karen Williams
*University of Texas at San Antonio*

G. W. K. Willis
*Baylor University*

Kathleen Wright
*Salisbury University*

Judy Wynekoop
*Florida Gulf Coast University*

Ruben Xing
*Montclair State University*

James E. Yao
*Montclair State University*

Shu Zou
*Temple University*

Robert Zwick
*Baruch College–CUNY*

Dane Cornelius
*Georgia Perimeter College*

Sergio Davalos
*University of Washington–Tacoma*

Kenneth Griggs
*California Polytechnic State University*

April Heltsley
*Indiana University*

Nenad Jukic
*Loyola University*

Gerald Karush
*Southern New Hampshire University*

Amy Kinser
*Indiana University*

James Eric Kinser
*Indiana University*

Brian Kovar
*Kansas State University*

John Quigley
*East Tennessee State University*

Muhammad Razi
*Western Michigan University*

Andrew Targowski
*Western Michigan University*

Rosemary Wild
*California Polytechnic State University*

Wita Wojtkowski
*Boise State University*

Alexander Yap
*Elon University*

Jeanne Zucker
*East Tennessee State University*

# Business
# Driven
# Technology

## What's in IT for Me?

This unit sets the stage for diving into *Business Driven Technology*. It starts from the ground floor by providing a clear description of what information technology is and how IT fits into business strategies and organizational activities. It then provides an overview of how organizations operate in competitive environments and must continually define and redefine their business strategies to create competitive advantages. Doing so allows organizations to not only survive, but also thrive. Individuals who understand and can access and analyze the many different enterprisewide information systems dramatically improve their decision-making and problem-solving abilities. Most importantly, information technology is shown as a key enabler to help organizations operate successfully in highly competitive environments.

You, as a business student, must recognize the tight correlation between business and technology. You must first understand information technology's role in daily business activities, and then understand information technology's role in supporting and implementing enterprisewide initiatives and global business strategies. After reading this unit, you should have acquired a solid grasp of business driven information systems, technology fundamentals, and business strategies. You should also have gained an appreciation of the various kinds of information systems employed by organizations and how you can use them to help make strategically informed decisions. All leaders must appreciate the numerous ethical and security concerns voiced by customers today. These concerns directly influence a customer's likelihood to embrace electronic technologies and conduct business over the web. In this sense, these concerns affect a company's bottom line. You can find evidence in recent news reports about how the stock price of organizations dramatically falls when information privacy and security breaches are publicized. Further, organizations face potential litigation if they fail to meet their ethical, privacy, and security obligations concerning the handling of information in their companies.

## Apple—Merging Technology, Business, and Entertainment

Apple Inc., back from near oblivion, is setting the pace in the digital world with innovation and creativity that have been missing from the company for the past 20 years. The introduction of the iPod and the iPhone, brilliant mergers of technology, business, and entertainment, catapulted Apple back into the mainstream. Now the company is using customers to take it to the next level.

### Capitalizing on New Trends

In 2000, Steve Jobs was fixated on developing video editing software for the Macintosh. But then he realized millions of people were using computers and CD burners to make audio CDs and to download digital songs called MP3s from illegal online services like Napster. Jobs was worried that he was looking in the wrong direction and had missed the MP3 bandwagon.

Jobs moved fast. He began by purchasing SoundStep from Jeff Robbin, a 28-year-old software engineer and former Apple employee. SoundStep was developing software that simplified the importing and compression of MP3 songs. Robbin and a couple of other programmers began writing code from scratch and developed the first version of iTunes for the Mac in less than four months. This powerful and ingenious database could quickly sort tens of thousands of songs in a multitude of ways and find particular tracks in nanoseconds.

Jobs next challenged the team to make iTunes portable. He envisioned a Walkman-like player that could hold thousands of songs and be taken anywhere. The idea was to modify iTunes and build a tiny new system for what was basically a miniature computer, along with a user interface that could sort and navigate music files with the same sophistication as iTunes on the Mac. The iPod was born nine months later.

Jobs noticed that one last key element was missing, an online store for buying downloadable songs. Such a store would need an ebusiness infrastructure that could automatically deliver songs and track billing and payments for conceivably millions of purchases. In the spring of 2003, 18 months after the launch of the iPod, Apple's iTunes Music Store opened for business. The company's goal was to sell 1 million songs in the first six months. It hit this goal in six days.

## Capitalizing on the iPod

With millions of iPods in the hands of consumers, other companies are noticing the trend and finding ways to capitalize on the product. John Lin created a prototype of a remote control for the iPod. Lin took his prototype to *Macworld* where he found success. A few months later, Lin's company had Apple's blessing and a commitment for shelf space in its retail stores. "This is how Apple supports the iPod economy," Lin said.

In the iPod-dominated market, hundreds of companies have been inspired to develop more than 500 accessories—everything from rechargers for the car to $1,500 Fendi bags. Eric Tong, vice president at Belkin, a cable and peripheral manufacturer, believes that 75 percent of all iPod owners purchase at least one accessory—meaning that 30 million accessories have been sold. With most of the products priced between $10 and $200, that puts the iPod economy well over $300 million and perhaps as high as $6 billion. Popular iPod accessories include:

- Altec Lansing Technologies—iPod speakers and recharger dock ($150).
- Belkin—TuneCast mobile FM transmitter ($40).
- Etymotic Research—high-end earphones ($150).
- Griffin Technology—iTrip FM transmitter ($35).
- Kate Spade—Geneva faux-croc mini iPod holder ($55).
- Apple—socks set in six colors, green, purple, blue, orange, pink, and gray ($29).
- Apple—digital camera connector ($29).

## iPod's Impact on the Music Business

In the digital era, the unbundling of CDs through the purchase of individual tracks lets consumers pay far less to get a few of their favorite songs rather than buying an entire album. Many analysts predicted that the iPod's success coupled with the consumer's ability to choose individual song downloads would lead to increased revenues for music businesses. However, the industry is seeing individual downloads cannibalizing album profits and failing to attract new music sales. "I've still never bought a download," said Eneka Iriondo-Coysh, a 21-year-old graphic-design student in London who has owned a 10,000 song–capacity iPod for more than two years. "I do it all from my CDs," mostly hip-hop and soul.

The global music industry has been under siege for years amid declining sales. Record companies suffer from piracy, including billions of dollars in lost revenue due to bootlegged CDs. At the same time, music faces new competition for consumer time and money from video games, DVDs, and mobile phones. At traditional record stores, DVDs and games are taking an increasing amount of shelf space, squeezing out CDs. The music download numbers suggest that the iPod's iconic success is not translating into new music sales the way the evolution from vinyl albums to cassettes and then CDs did. For many users, the portable devices are just another way of stocking and listening to music, not an incentive to buy new music.

## Capitalizing on the iPhone

The Apple iPhone is a disruptive mobile phone that allows customers to make a call by simply touching a name or number in an address book, a favorites list, or a call log. It also automatically syncs all contacts from a PC, Mac, or Internet services, and it allows customers to select voice-mail messages in any order—just like email. Customers can easily construct a favorites list for frequently made calls and can quickly merge calls to create conference calls.

The iPhone's most impressive feature is a rich email client. With its advanced Safari browser iPhone allows customers see web pages the way they were designed to be seen, then easily zoom in by simply tapping on the multi-touch display with a finger. Safari also includes built-in Google and Yahoo! search capabilities. The iPhone can multitask, allowing customers to read a web page while downloading email in the background over wireless networks. Expect the iPhone accessory business to be as powerful and vast as the iPod accessory business. A few of the new iPhone accessories include:

- iPhone Bluetooth headset—$149.
- iPhone doc—$49.
- iPhone stereo headset—$29.
- Apple Doc Connector to USB—$29.

## Apple Applications

Looking at someone using an iPhone is an interesting experience because there is a good chance they are not making a phone call. They could be doing a number of things from playing a game, to trading stocks, watching a TV show, or even conducting serious business with a mobile version of Salesforce.com's customer-management software. In a brilliant strategic move Apple began letting outsiders offer software for the iPhone and in less than six months more than 10,000 applications have been created. In fact, there are more than 15,000 applications available at its App Store section of iTunes and they have been downloaded a total of 500 million times. This is up from 10,000 applications and 300 million downloads just a month ago.

This is truly astonishing advancement and incredibly dire news for Apple's smart-phone rivals. Already, the iPhone/App Store market is getting so huge relative to other smart-phone markets that some smart developers argue that there is no point in adapting applications for the new Google's Android or any other iPhone competitor. According to Jeff Holden, CEO of Pelago Inc., when he created his social networking company he fully intended to follow the conventional wisdom for how to build a sizeable, fast-growing software company: get your programs on as many platforms and devices as possible. But when he crunched the numbers he came to an interesting business conclusion: the 13 million iPhone owners had already downloaded as much software as 1.1 billion other cell-phone owners! To entrepreneurs, developing a program for the iPhone automatically provides a significantly larger market—almost 94 times larger than its competitors. "Why would I ever build for anything but the iPhone?" says Holden.

# Introduction

Information is everywhere. Most organizations value information as a strategic asset. Consider Apple and its iPod, iPod accessories, and iTunes Music Store. Apple's success depends heavily on information about its customers, suppliers, markets, and operations for each of these product lines. For example, Apple must be able to predict the number of people who will purchase an iPod to help estimate iPod accessory and iTunes sales within the next year. Estimating too many buyers will lead Apple to produce an excess of inventory; estimating too few buyers will potentially mean lost sales due to lack of product (resulting in even more lost revenues).

Understanding the direct impact information has on an organization's bottom line is crucial to running a successful business. This text focuses on information, business, technology, and the integrated set of activities used to run most organizations. Many of these activities are the hallmarks of business today—supply chain management, customer relationship management, enterprise resource planning, outsourcing, integration, ebusiness, and others. The five core units of this text cover these important activities in detail. Each unit is divided into chapters that provide individual learning outcomes and case studies. In addition to the five core units, there are technology and business "plug-ins" (see Figure Unit 1.1) that further explore topics presented in the five core units.

The chapters in Unit 1 are:

- **Chapter One**—Business Driven Technology.
- **Chapter Two**—Identifying Competitive Advantages.
- **Chapter Three**—Strategic Initiatives for Implementing Competitive Advantages.
- **Chapter Four**—Measuring the Success of Strategic Initiatives.
- **Chapter Five**—Organizational Structures That Support Strategic Initiatives.

**FIGURE UNIT 1.1**

The Format and Approach of This Text

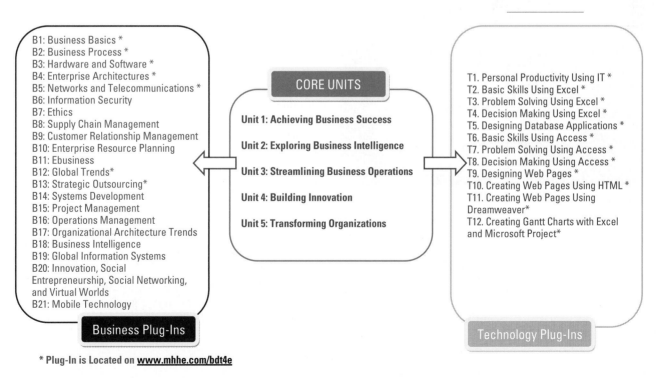

B1: Business Basics *
B2: Business Process *
B3: Hardware and Software *
B4: Enterprise Architectures *
B5: Networks and Telecommunications *
B6: Information Security
B7: Ethics
B8: Supply Chain Management
B9: Customer Relationship Management
B10: Enterprise Resource Planning
B11: Ebusiness
B12: Global Trends*
B13: Strategic Outsourcing*
B14: Systems Development
B15: Project Management
B16: Operations Management
B17: Organizational Architecture Trends
B18: Business Intelligence
B19: Global Information Systems
B20: Innovation, Social Entrepreneurship, Social Networking, and Virtual Worlds
B21: Mobile Technology

**Business Plug-Ins**

**CORE UNITS**

**Unit 1: Achieving Business Success**

**Unit 2: Exploring Business Intelligence**

**Unit 3: Streamlining Business Operations**

**Unit 4: Building Innovation**

**Unit 5: Transforming Organizations**

T1. Personal Productivity Using IT *
T2. Basic Skills Using Excel *
T3. Problem Solving Using Excel *
T4. Decision Making Using Excel *
T5. Designing Database Applications *
T6. Basic Skills Using Access *
T7. Problem Solving Using Access *
T8. Decision Making Using Access *
T9. Designing Web Pages *
T10. Creating Web Pages Using HTML *
T11. Creating Web Pages Using Dreamweaver*
T12. Creating Gantt Charts with Excel and Microsoft Project*

**Technology Plug-Ins**

* Plug-In is Located on **www.mhhe.com/bdt4e**

# Business Driven Technology

## Information Technology's Role in Business

Students frequently ask, "Why do we need to study information technology?" The answer is simple: Information technology is everywhere in business. Understanding information technology provides great insight to anyone learning about business.

It is easy to demonstrate information technology's role in business by reviewing a copy of popular business magazines such as *BusinessWeek, Fortune,* or *Fast Company.* Placing a marker (such as a Post-it Note) on each page that contains a technology-related article or advertisement indicates that information technology is everywhere in business (see Figure 1.1). These are *business* magazines, not *technology* magazines, yet they are filled with technology. Students who understand technology have an advantage in business, and gaining a detailed understanding of information technology is important to all students regardless of their area of expertise.

The magazine articles typically discuss such topics as databases, customer relationship management, web services, supply chain management, security, ethics, business intelligence, and so on. They also focus on companies such as Siebel, Oracle, Microsoft, and

**FIGURE 1.1**

Technology in *BusinessWeek* and *Fortune*

IBM. This text explores these topics in detail, along with reviewing the associated business opportunities and challenges.

### INFORMATION TECHNOLOGY'S IMPACT ON BUSINESS OPERATIONS

Figure 1.2 highlights the business functions receiving the greatest benefit from information technology, along with the common business goals associated with information technology projects according to *CIO* magazine.

Achieving the results outlined in Figure 1.2, such as reducing costs, improving productivity, and generating growth, is not easy. Implementing a new accounting system or marketing plan is not likely to generate long-term growth or reduce costs across an entire organization. Businesses must undertake enterprisewide initiatives to achieve broad general business goals such as reducing costs. Information technology plays a critical role in deploying such initiatives by facilitating communication and increasing business intelligence. For example instant messaging and WiMAX allow people across an organization to communicate in new and innovative ways.

Understanding information technology begins with gaining an understanding of how businesses function and IT's role in creating efficiencies and effectiveness across the organization. Typical businesses operate by functional areas (often called functional silos). Each functional area undertakes a specific core business function (see Figure 1.3).

Functional areas are anything but independent in a business. In fact, functional areas are *interdependent* (see Figure 1.4). Sales must rely on information from operations to understand inventory, place orders, calculate transportation costs, and gain insight into product availability based on production schedules. For an organization to succeed, every department or functional area must work together sharing common information and not be a "silo." Information technology can enable departments to more efficiently and effectively perform their business operations.

Any individual anticipating a successful career in business whether it is in accounting, finance, human resources, or operation management must understand the basics of information technology.

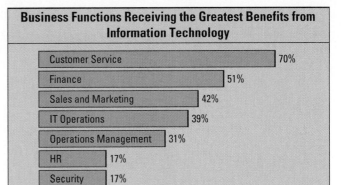

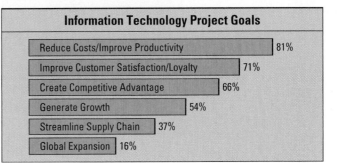

**FIGURE** 1.2

Business Benefits and Information Technology Project Goals

# Information Technology Basics

*Information technology (IT)* is a field concerned with the use of technology in managing and processing information. Today, the term *information technology* has ballooned to encompass many aspects of computing and technology, and the term is more recognizable than ever. The information technology umbrella can be quite large, covering many fields that deal with the use of electronic computers and computer software to convert, store, protect, process, transmit, and retrieve information securely. Information technology can be an important enabler of business success and innovation. This is not to say that IT *equals* business success and innovation or that IT *represents* business success and innovation. Information technology is most useful when it leverages the talents of people. Information technology in and of itself is not useful unless the right people know how to use and manage it effectively.

Management information systems is a business function just as marketing, finance, operations, and human resources are business functions. Formally defined, *management information systems (MIS)* is a general name for the business function and academic discipline covering the application of people, technologies, and procedures—collectively called information systems—to solve business problems.

**FIGURE 1.3**

Departmental Structure of
a Typical Organization

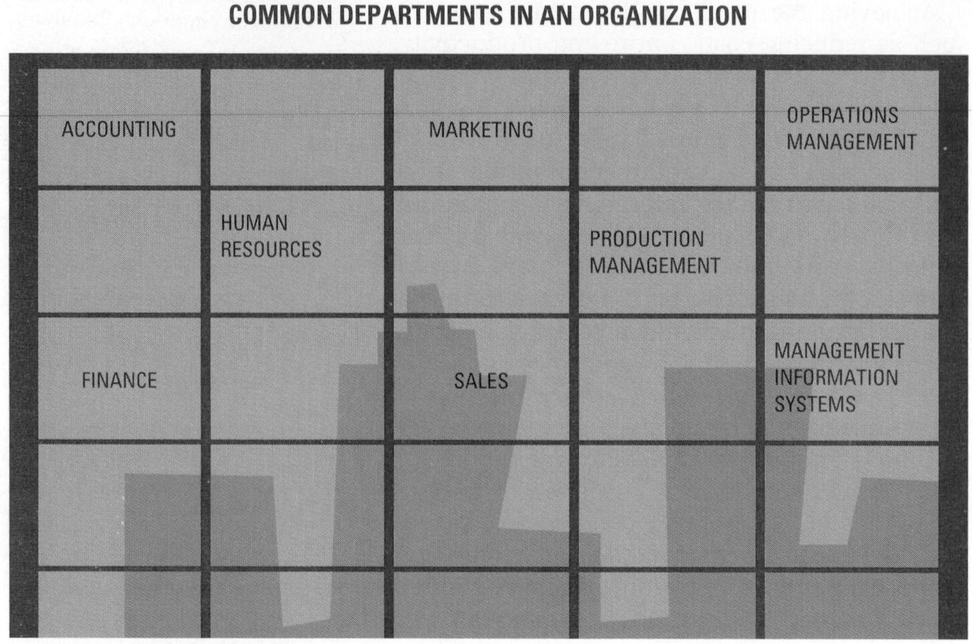

**COMMON DEPARTMENTS IN AN ORGANIZATION**

- **Accounting** provides quantitative information about the finances of the business including recording, measuring, and describing financial information.

- **Finance** deals with the strategic financial issues associated with increasing the value of the business, while observing applicable laws and social responsibilities.

- **Human resources (HR)** includes the policies, plans, and procedures for the effective management of employees (human resources).

- **Sales** is the function of selling a good or service and focuses on increasing customer sales, which increases company revenues.

- **Marketing** is the process associated with promoting the sale of goods or services. The marketing department supports the sales department by creating promotions that help sell the company's products.

- **Operations management** (also called **production management**) is the management of systems or processes that convert or transform resources (including human resources) into goods and services.

- **Management information systems (MIS)** is the academic discipline covering the application of people, technologies, and procedures—collectively called information systems—to solve business problems.

When beginning to learn about management information systems it is important to understand the following:

- Data, information, and business intelligence.
- IT resources.
- IT cultures.

## DATA, INFORMATION, AND BUSINESS INTELLIGENCE

It is important to distinguish between data, information, and business intelligence. *Data* are raw facts that describe the characteristics of an event. Characteristics for a sales event could include the date, item number, item description, quantity ordered, customer name, and shipping details. *Information* is data converted into a meaningful and useful context. Information from sales events could include best-selling

FIGURE 1.4

Marketing Working with
Other Organizational
Departments

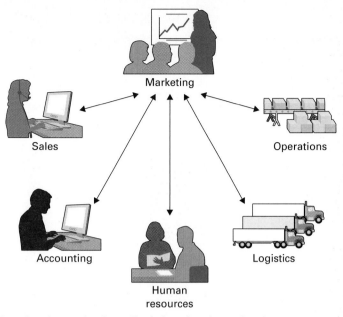

Functional organization—Each functional area has its own systems and communicates with every other functional area (diagram displays Marketing communicating with all other functional areas in the organization).

item, worst-selling item, best customer, and worst customer. ***Business intelligence*** refers to applications and technologies that are used to gather, provide access to, and analyze data and information to support decision-making efforts. Business intelligence helps companies gain a more comprehensive knowledge of the factors affecting their business, such as metrics on sales, production, and internal operations, which help companies make better business decisions (see Figures 1.5, 1.6, 1.7).

## IT RESOURCES

The plans and goals of the IT department must align with the plans and goals of the organization. Information technology can enable an organization to increase efficiency in manufacturing, retain key customers, seek out new sources of supply, and introduce effective financial management.

It is not always easy for managers to make the right choices when using IT to support (and often drive) business initiatives. Most managers understand their business initiatives well, but are often at a loss when it comes to knowing how to use

FIGURE 1.5

Data in an Excel
Spreadsheet

| OrderDate | ProductName | Quantity | Unit Price | Total Sales | Unit Cost | Total Cost | Profit | Customer | SalesRep |
|---|---|---|---|---|---|---|---|---|---|
| 04-Jan-10 | Mozzarella cheese | 41 | 24 | 984 | 18 | 738 | 246 | The Station | Debbie Fernand |
| 04-Jan-10 | Romaine lettuce | 90 | 15 | 1,350 | 14 | 1,260 | 90 | The Station | Roberta Cross |
| 05-Jan-10 | Red onions | 27 | 12 | 324 | 8 | 216 | 108 | Bert's Bistro | Loraine Schultz |
| 06-Jan-10 | Romaine lettuce | 67 | 15 | 1,005 | 14 | 938 | 67 | Smoke House | Roberta Cross |
| 07-Jan-10 | Black olives | 79 | 12 | 948 | 6 | 474 | 474 | Flagstaff House | Loraine Schultz |
| 07-Jan-10 | Romaine lettuce | 46 | 15 | 690 | 14 | 644 | 46 | Two Bitts | Loraine Schultz |
| 07-Jan-10 | Romaine lettuce | 52 | 15 | 780 | 14 | 728 | 52 | Pierce Arrow | Roberta Cross |
| 08-Jan-10 | Red onions | 39 | 12 | 468 | 8 | 312 | 156 | Mamm'a Pasta Palace | Loraine Schultz |
| 09-Jan-10 | Romaine lettuce | 66 | 15 | 990 | 14 | 924 | 66 | The Dandelion | Loraine Schultz |
| 10-Jan-10 | Romaine lettuce | 58 | 15 | 870 | 14 | 812 | 58 | Carmens | Loraine Schultz |
| 10-Jan-10 | Pineapple | 40 | 33 | 1,320 | 28 | 1,120 | 200 | The Station | Loraine Schultz |

*Rows of data in an Excel spreadsheet.*

**FIGURE** 1.6

Data Turned into
Information

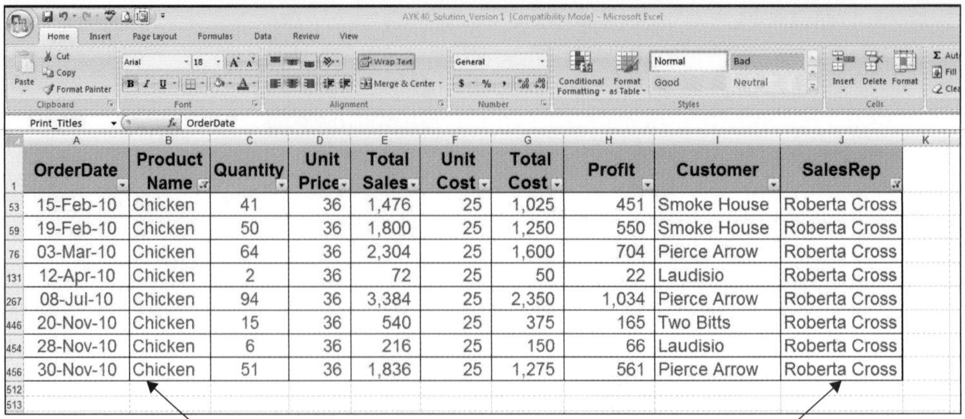

| | OrderDate | Product Name | Quantity | Unit Price | Total Sales | Unit Cost | Total Cost | Profit | Customer | SalesRep |
|---|---|---|---|---|---|---|---|---|---|---|
| 53 | 15-Feb-10 | Chicken | 41 | 36 | 1,476 | 25 | 1,025 | 451 | Smoke House | Roberta Cross |
| 59 | 19-Feb-10 | Chicken | 50 | 36 | 1,800 | 25 | 1,250 | 550 | Smoke House | Roberta Cross |
| 76 | 03-Mar-10 | Chicken | 64 | 36 | 2,304 | 25 | 1,600 | 704 | Pierce Arrow | Roberta Cross |
| 131 | 12-Apr-10 | Chicken | 2 | 36 | 72 | 25 | 50 | 22 | Laudisio | Roberta Cross |
| 267 | 08-Jul-10 | Chicken | 94 | 36 | 3,384 | 25 | 2,350 | 1,034 | Pierce Arrow | Roberta Cross |
| 446 | 20-Nov-10 | Chicken | 15 | 36 | 540 | 25 | 375 | 165 | Two Bitts | Roberta Cross |
| 454 | 28-Nov-10 | Chicken | 6 | 36 | 216 | 25 | 150 | 66 | Laudisio | Roberta Cross |
| 456 | 30-Nov-10 | Chicken | 51 | 36 | 1,836 | 25 | 1,275 | 561 | Pierce Arrow | Roberta Cross |

*Data features, such as Autofilter, turn data into information.
This view shows all of Roberta Cross's chicken sales.*

**FIGURE** 1.7

Information Turned into
Business Intelligence

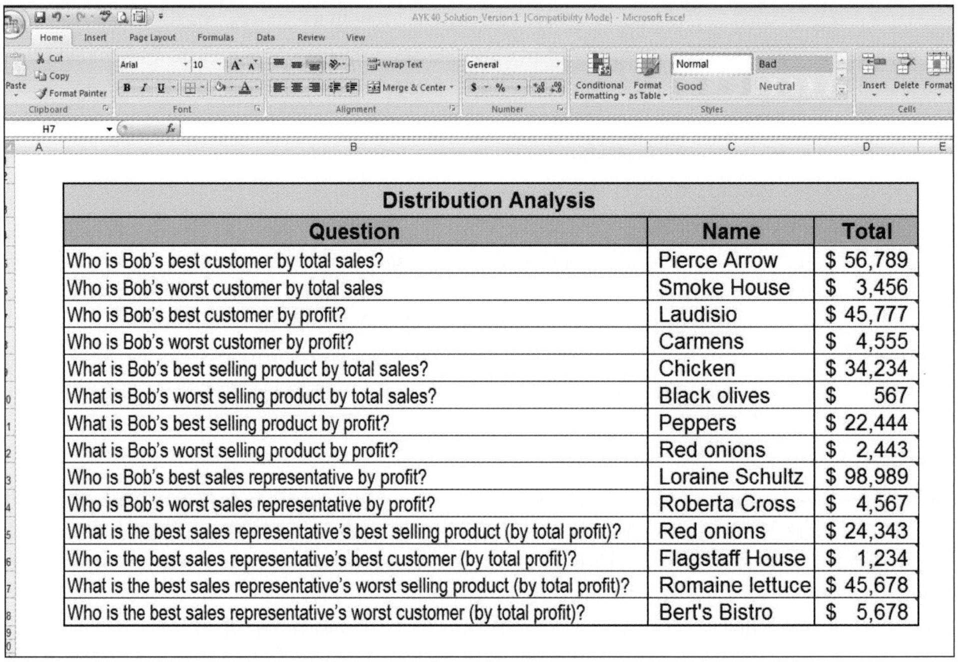

| Distribution Analysis | | |
|---|---|---|
| **Question** | **Name** | **Total** |
| Who is Bob's best customer by total sales? | Pierce Arrow | $ 56,789 |
| Who is Bob's worst customer by total sales | Smoke House | $ 3,456 |
| Who is Bob's best customer by profit? | Laudisio | $ 45,777 |
| Who is Bob's worst customer by profit? | Carmens | $ 4,555 |
| What is Bob's best selling product by total sales? | Chicken | $ 34,234 |
| What is Bob's worst selling product by total sales? | Black olives | $ 567 |
| What is Bob's best selling product by profit? | Peppers | $ 22,444 |
| What is Bob's worst selling product by profit? | Red onions | $ 2,443 |
| Who is Bob's best sales representative by profit? | Loraine Schultz | $ 98,989 |
| Who is Bob's worst sales representative by profit? | Roberta Cross | $ 4,567 |
| What is the best sales representative's best selling product (by total profit)? | Red onions | $ 24,343 |
| Who is the best sales representative's best customer (by total profit)? | Flagstaff House | $ 1,234 |
| What is the best sales representative's worst selling product (by total profit)? | Romaine lettuce | $ 45,678 |
| Who is the best sales representative's worst customer (by total profit)? | Bert's Bistro | $ 5,678 |

*Advanced analytical tools, such as Pivot Tables, uncover business
intelligence in the data. For example, best customer, worst
customer, and best sales representative's best-selling product.*

and manage IT effectively in support of those initiatives. Managers who understand what IT is, and what IT can and cannot do, are in the best position for success.

**Putting It All Together**

In essence,

- *People* use
- *information technology* to work with
- *information* (see Figure 1.8).

Those three key resources—people, information, and information technology (in that order of priority)—are inextricably linked. If one fails, they all fail. Most important, if one fails, then chances are the business will fail.

## IT CULTURES

An organization's culture plays a large role in determining how successfully it will share information. Culture will influence the way people use information (their information behavior) and will reflect the importance that company leaders attribute to the use of information in achieving success or avoiding failure. Four common information-sharing cultures exist in organizations today: information-functional, information-sharing, information-inquiring, and information-discovery (see Figure 1.9).

An organization's IT culture can directly affect its ability to compete in the global market. If an organization operates with an information-functional culture it will have a great degree of difficulty operating. Getting products to market quickly and creating a view of its end-to-end (or entire) business from sales to billing will be a challenge. If an organization operates with an information-discovery culture it will be able to get products to market quickly and easily see a 360-degree view of its entire organization. Employees will be able to use this view to better understand the market and create new products that offer a competitive advantage.

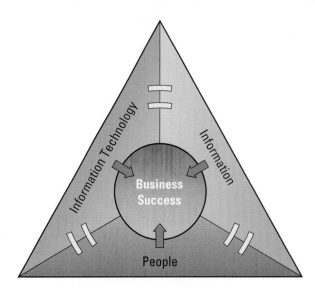

**FIGURE 1.8**

The Relationship among People, Information, and Information Technology

**FIGURE 1.9**

Different Information Cultures Found in Organizations

| Organizational Information Cultures | |
| --- | --- |
| **Information-Functional Culture** | Employees use information as a means of exercising influence or power over others. For example, a manager in sales refuses to share information with marketing. This causes marketing to need the sales manager's input each time a new sales strategy is developed. |
| **Information-Sharing Culture** | Employees across departments trust each other to use information (especially about problems and failures) to improve performance. |
| **Information-Inquiring Culture** | Employees across departments search for information to better understand the future and align themselves with current trends and new directions. |
| **Information-Discovery Culture** | Employees across departments are open to new insights about crises and radical changes and seek ways to create competitive advantages. |

## OPENING CASE STUDY QUESTIONS

1. Explain how Apple achieved business success through the use of information, information technology, and people.

2. Describe the types of information employees at an Apple store require and compare it to the types of information the executives at Apple's corporate headquarters require. Are there any links between these two types of information?

3. Identify the type of information culture that would have the greatest negative impact on Apple's operations.

In his book, *The World is Flat,* Thomas Friedman describes the unplanned cascade of technological and social shifts that effectively leveled the economic world, and "accidentally made Beijing, Bangalore, and Bethesda next-door neighbors." Chances are good that Bhavya in Bangalore will read your next X-ray, or as Friedman learned firsthand, "Grandma Betty in her bathrobe" will make your JetBlue plane reservation from her Salt Lake City home.

Friedman believes this is Globalization 3.0. "In Globalization 1.0, which began around 1492, the world went from size large to size medium. In Globalization 2.0, the era that introduced us to multinational companies, it went from size medium to size small. And then around 2000 came Globalization 3.0, in which the world went from being small to tiny. There is a difference between being able to make long-distance phone calls cheaper on the Internet and walking around Riyadh with a PDA where you can have all of Google in your pocket. It is a difference in degree that's so enormous it becomes a difference in kind," Friedman states. Figure 1.10 displays Friedman's list of "flatteners."

Friedman says these flatteners converged around the year 2000 and "created a flat world: a global, Web-enabled platform for multiple forms of sharing knowledge and work, irrespective of time, distance, geography, and increasingly, language." At the very moment this platform emerged, three huge economies materialized—those of India, China, and the former Soviet Union—"and 3 billion people who were out of the game, walked onto the playing field." A final convergence may determine the fate of the United States in this chapter of globalization. A "political perfect storm," as Friedman describes it—the dot-com bust, the attacks of 9/11, and the Enron scandal—"distract us completely as a country." Just when we need to face the fact of globalization and the need to compete in a new world, "we're looking totally elsewhere."

Friedman believes that the next great breakthrough in bioscience could come from a 5-year-old who downloads the human genome in Egypt. Bill Gates's view is similar: "Twenty years ago, would you rather have been a B-student in Poughkeepsie or a genius in Shanghai?"

**FIGURE** 1.10

Thomas Friedman's 10 Forces That Flattened the World

| | |
|---|---|
| **1. Fall of the Berlin Wall** | The events of November 9, 1989, tilted the worldwide balance of power toward democracies and free markets. |
| **2. Netscape IPO** | The August 9, 1995, offering sparked massive investment in fiber-optic cables. |
| **3. Work flow software** | The rise of applications from PayPal to VPNs enabled faster, closer coordination among far-flung employees. |
| **4. Open-sourcing** | Self-organizing communities, such as Linux, launched a collaborative revolution. |
| **5. Outsourcing** | Migrating business functions to India saved money *and* a Third World economy. |
| **6. Offshoring** | Contract manufacturing elevated China to economic prominence. |
| **7. Supply-chaining** | Robust networks of suppliers, retailers, and customers increased business efficiency. |
| **8. Insourcing** | Logistics giants took control of customer supply chains, helping mom-and-pop shops go global. |
| **9. Informing** | Power searching allowed everyone to use the Internet as a "personal supply chain of knowledge." |
| **10. Wireless** | Wireless technologies pumped up collaboration, making it mobile and personal. |

Twenty years ago you'd rather be a B-student in Poughkeepsie. Today, it is not even close. You'd much prefer to be the genius in Shanghai because you can now export your talents anywhere in the world."

## Questions

1. Do you agree or disagree with Friedman's assessment that the world is flat? Be sure to justify your answer.
2. What are the potential impacts of a flat world for a student performing a job search?
3. What can students do to prepare themselves for competing in a flat world?
4. Identify a current flattener not mentioned on Friedman's list.

# 2 Identifying Competitive Advantages

**2.1.** Explain why competitive advantages are typically temporary.

**2.2.** List and describe each of the five forces in Porter's Five Forces Model.

**2.3.** Compare Porter's three generic strategies.

**2.4.** Describe the relationship between business processes and value chains.

## Identifying Competitive Advantages

To survive and thrive, an organization must create a competitive advantage. A ***competitive advantage*** is a product or service that an organization's customers place a greater value on than similar offerings from a competitor. Unfortunately, competitive advantages are typically temporary because competitors often seek ways to duplicate the competitive advantage. In turn, organizations must develop a strategy based on a new competitive advantage.

When an organization is the first to market with a competitive advantage, it gains a first-mover advantage. The ***first-mover advantage*** occurs when an organization can significantly impact its market share by being first to market with a competitive advantage. FedEx created a first-mover advantage several years ago when it developed its customer self-service software allowing people and organizations to request a package pick-up, print mailing slips, and track packages online. Other parcel delivery services quickly followed with their own versions of the software. Today, customer self-service on the Internet is a standard for doing business in the parcel delivery industry.

As organizations develop their competitive advantages, they must pay close attention to their competition through environmental scanning. ***Environmental scanning*** is the acquisition and analysis of events and trends in the environment external to an organization. Information technology has the opportunity to play an important role in environmental scanning. For example, Frito-Lay, a premier provider of snack foods such as Cracker Jacks and Cheetos, does not just send its representatives into grocery stores to stock shelves—they carry handheld computers and record the product offerings, inventory, and even product locations of competitors. Frito-Lay uses this information to gain business intelligence on everything from how well competing products are selling to the strategic placement of its own products.

Organizations use three common tools to analyze and develop competitive advantages: (1) the Five Forces Model, (2) the three generic strategies, and (3) value chains.

## The Five Forces Model—Evaluating Business Segments

For a business to prosper it must be able to quickly respond to all forms of competition from its rivals. To remain competitive businesses face decisions such as offering new products, entering new markets, and even competing in new industries

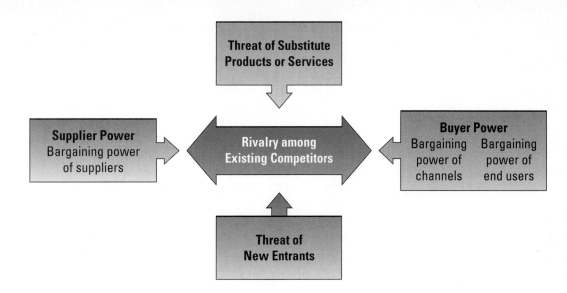

**FIGURE** 2.1

Porter's Five Forces Model

or industry segments. Michael Porter, a university professor at Harvard Business School, identified four competitive forces that can hurt potential sales:

1. Knowledgeable customers can force down prices by pitting rivals against each another.
2. Influential suppliers can drive down profits by charging higher prices for supplies.
3. New market entrants can steal potential investment capital.
4. Substitute products can steal customers.

To combat these competitive forces Porter developed the Five Forces Model, which is a useful tool to aid in understanding competition and its implications for business strategy. Understanding Porter's five forces can help a company identify potential opportunities and create a competitive advantage while deterring potential rivals. The **Five Forces Model** helps determine the relative attractiveness of an industry and includes the following five forces (see Figure 2.1).

1. Buyer power
2. Supplier power
3. Threat of substitute products or services
4. Threat of new entrants
5. Rivalry among existing competitors

## BUYER POWER

**Buyer power** is assessed by analyzing the ability of buyers to directly impact the price they are willing to pay for an item. Factors used to assess buyer power include number of customers, size of orders, differences between competitors, sensitivity of price, and availability of substitute products. If buyer power is high they can force a company and its competitors to compete on price, which typically drives prices down. One way to reduce buyer power is by using switching costs. **Switching costs** are costs that can make customers reluctant to switch to another product or service. A switching cost need not have an associated monetary cost. For example, switching doctors is difficult because the new doctor will not have the patient's history and the relationship with the patient. This is a great example of using a switching cost to reduce buyer power, as switching doctors has an associated intangible cost.

Another way a company can reduce buyer power—and create a competitive advantage—is to expand and improve services so it is harder for customers to leave. One common tool companies use to reduce buyer power is a loyalty program. *Loyalty programs* reward customers based on the amount of business they do with a particular organization. The travel industry is famous for its loyalty programs such as frequent-flyer programs for airlines and frequent-stayer programs for hotels. Keeping track of the activities and accounts of many thousands or millions of customers covered by loyalty programs is not practical without large-scale IT systems. Loyalty programs are a good example of using IT to reduce buyer power. Because of the rewards (e.g., free airline tickets, upgrades, or hotel stays) travelers receive, they are more likely to be loyal to or give most of their business to a single organization.

## SUPPLIER POWER

A *supply chain* consists of all parties involved, directly or indirectly, in the procurement of a product or raw material. In a typical supply chain, an organization will probably be both a supplier (to customers) and a customer (of other supplier organizations) as illustrated in Figure 2.2. *Supplier power* is assessed by the suppliers' ability to directly impact the price they are charging for supplies (including materials, labor, and services). Factors used to assess supplier power include number of suppliers, size of suppliers, uniqueness of services, and availability of substitute products. If supplier power is high the supplier can directly influence the industry by:

- Charging higher prices
- Limiting quality or services
- Shifting costs to industry participants

Typically, when a supplier raises prices the buyers will pass on the increase in price to their customers by raising prices on the end-product. When supplier power is high, buyers lose revenue because they cannot pass on the raw material price increase to their customers. For example, if Microsoft (supplier with high power) raises the price of its operating system it will decrease the profitability of its buyers (PC manufacturers such as Dell, Gateway, HP). The PC market is fierce and customers frequently purchase PCs based on price. If Microsoft increases the price of operating systems and the PC manufacturers cannot raise prices without jeopardizing sales, then the PC manufacturers have no choice—they must pay more for raw materials while selling their end-products at the same price thereby shrinking their profits. One tactic a company can use to decrease the power of its suppliers is to use standardized parts so it can easily switch suppliers.

## THREAT OF SUBSTITUTE PRODUCTS OR SERVICES

The *threat of substitute products or services* is high when there are many alternatives to a product or service and low when there are few alternatives from which to choose. For example, there are many substitute products in the airline industry. Buyers have numerous substitute products for transportation including automobiles, trains, and boats. Technology has even created substitute products to the airline industry including videoconferencing and virtual meetings. Many individuals use collaboration meeting software such as WebEx instead of traveling.

**FIGURE 2.2**

An Organization within the Supply Chain

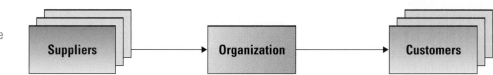

Ideally, an organization would like to be in a market in which there are few substitutes for the products or services it offers. Polaroid had this unique competitive advantage for many years until it forgot to continuously scan the competitive environment and soon went bankrupt when people began taking pictures with everything from their video cameras to their cell phones. A company can reduce the threat of substitute products by offering added-value through wider product availability. Soft-drink manufacturers reduced the threat of substitute products by introducing product availability through vending machines, gas stations, and convenience stores, which dramatically increased the availability of soft drinks relative to other beverages. Companies can also offer various add-on services making the substitute product less of a threat. For example, cellular phones could also include GPS and digital video capabilities making the landline phone less of a substitute.

## THREAT OF NEW ENTRANTS

The *threat of new entrants* is high when it is easy for new competitors to enter a market and low when there are significant entry barriers to entering a market. An *entry barrier* is a product or service feature that customers have come to expect from organizations in a particular industry and must be offered by an entering organization to compete and survive. For example, a new bank must offer its customers an array of IT-enabled services, including ATMs, online bill paying, and online account monitoring. These are significant barriers to entering the banking market. At one time, the first bank to offer such services gained a valuable first-mover advantage, but only temporarily, as other banking competitors developed their own IT systems.

## RIVALRY AMONG EXISTING COMPETITORS

*Rivalry among existing competitors* is high when competition is fierce in a market and low when competition is more complacent. Although competition is always more intense in some industries than in others, the overall trend is toward increased competition in almost every industry. The retail grocery industry is intensively competitive. While Kroger, Safeway, and Albertson's in the United States compete in many different ways, essentially they try to beat or match the competition on price. Most implement loyalty programs to provide customers special discounts while the store gathers valuable information on purchasing habits. In the future, expect to see grocery stores using wireless technologies to track customer movement throughout the store and match it to products purchased to determine purchasing sequences.

*Product differentiation* occurs when a company develops unique differences in its products with the intent to influence demand. Companies can use product differentiation to reduce rivalry. For example, there are many companies that sell books and videos on the Internet. Amazon differentiates its products by using customer profiling. When a customer visits Amazon.com repeatedly, Amazon begins to offer products tailored to that particular customer based on the customer's profile. In this way Amazon has reduced its rivals' power by offering its customers a differentiated product.

## USING THE FIVE FORCES MODEL TO ANALYZE THE AIRLINE INDUSTRY

Taking a look at all five of the competitive forces can provide a company with a comprehensive picture of its industry including business strategies it can implement to remain competitive. A company that was contemplating entering the airline industry could use the five forces model to quickly understand that this might be a risky move because it is an unprofitable industry as all of the five forces are strong.

- **Buyer power:** Buyer power is high as customers have many airlines to choose from and typically make purchases based on price, not carrier.
- **Supplier power:** Supplier power is high as there are limited plane and engine manufacturers to choose from and unionized workforces squeeze the airline's profitability.
- **Threat of substitute products or services:** Threat of substitute products is high as there are numerous transportation alternatives including automobiles, trains, and boats. There are even substitutes to travel such as video conferencing and virtual meetings.
- **Threat of new entrants:** Threat of new entrants is high as new airlines are continuously entering the market including the new sky taxies which offer low-cost on-demand air taxi service.
- **Rivalry among existing competitors:** Rivalry in the airline industry is high—just search Travelocity.com and see how many choices are offered. For this reason airlines are forced to compete on price.

# The Three Generic Strategies—Creating a Business Focus

Once the relative attractiveness of an industry is determined and an organization decides to enter that market, it must formulate a strategy for entering the new market. An organization can follow Porter's three generic strategies when entering a new market: (1) broad cost leadership, (2) broad differentiation, or (3) a focused strategy. Broad strategies reach a large market segment, while focused strategies target a niche market. A focused strategy concentrates on either cost leadership or differentiation. Trying to be all things to all people, however, is a recipe for disaster, since it is difficult to project a consistent image to the entire marketplace. Porter suggests that an organization is wise to adopt only one of the three generic strategies. (See Figure 2.3.)

To illustrate the use of the three generic strategies, consider Figure 2.4. The matrix shown demonstrates the relationships among strategies (cost leadership versus differentiation) and market segmentation (broad versus focused).

**FIGURE 2.3**

Porter's Three Generic Strategies

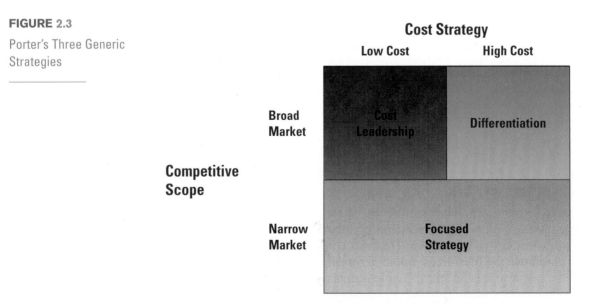

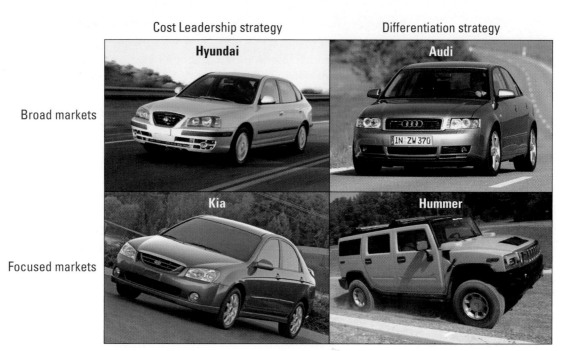

**FIGURE** 2.4

Three Generic Strategies in the Auto Industry

- **Hyundai** is following a broad cost leadership strategy. Hyundai offers low-cost vehicles, in each particular model stratification, that appeal to a large audience.

- **Audi** is pursuing a broad differentiation strategy with its Quattro models available at several price points. Audi's differentiation is safety, and it prices its various Quattro models (higher than Hyundai) to reach a large, stratified audience.

- **Kia** has a more focused cost leadership strategy. Kia mainly offers low-cost vehicles in the lower levels of model stratification.

- **Hummer** offers the most focused differentiation strategy of any in the industry (including Mercedes-Benz).

# Value Chain Analysis—Targeting Business Processes

Once an organization enters a new market using one of Porter's three generic strategies, it must understand, accept, and successfully execute its business strategy. Every aspect of the organization contributes to the success (or failure) of the chosen strategy. The business processes of the organization and the value chain they create play an integral role in strategy execution. Figure 2.5 combines Porter's Five Forces and his three generic strategies creating business strategies for each segment.

## VALUE CREATION

A *business process* is a standardized set of activities that accomplish a specific task, such as processing a customer's order. To evaluate the effectiveness of its business processes, an organization can use Michael Porter's value chain approach. An organization creates value by performing a series of activities that Porter identified as the value chain. The *value chain* approach views an organization as a series of processes, each of which adds value to the product or service for each

| | Generic Strategies | | |
|---|---|---|---|
| **Industry Force** | **Cost Leadership** | **Differentiation** | **Focused** |
| **Entry Barriers** | Ability to cut price in retaliation deters potential entrants. | Customer loyalty can discourage potential entrants. | Focusing develops core competencies that can act as an entry barrier. |
| **Buyer Power** | Ability to offer lower price to powerful buyers. | Large buyers have less power to negotiate because of few close alternatives. | Large buyers have less power to negotiate because of few alternatives. |
| **Supplier Power** | Better insulated from powerful suppliers. | Better able to pass on supplier price increases to customers. | Suppliers have power because of low volumes, but a differentiation-focused firm is better able to pass on supplier price increases. |
| **Threat of Substitutes** | Can use low price to defend against substitutes. | Customers become attached to differentiating attributes, reducing threat of substitutes. | Specialized products and core competency protect against substitutes. |
| **Rivalry** | Better able to compete on price. | Brand loyalty to keep customers from rivals. | Rivals cannot meet differentiation-focused customer needs. |

**FIGURE 2.5**

Generic Strategies and
Industry Forces

customer. To create a competitive advantage, the value chain must enable the organization to provide unique value to its customers. In addition to the firm's own value-creating activities, the firm operates in a value system of vertical activities including those of upstream suppliers and downstream channel members. To achieve a competitive advantage, the firm must perform one or more value-creating activities in a way that creates more overall value than do competitors. Added value is created through lower costs or superior benefits to the consumer (differentiation).

Organizations can add value by offering lower prices or by competing in a distinctive way. Examining the organization as a value chain (actually numerous distinct but inseparable value chains) leads to the identification of the important activities that add value for customers and then finding IT systems that support those activities. Figure 2.6 depicts a value chain. Primary value activities, shown at the bottom of the graph, acquire raw materials and manufacture, deliver, market, sell, and provide after-sales services. Support value activities, along the top of

**FIGURE 2.6**

A Graphical Depiction of a
Value Chain

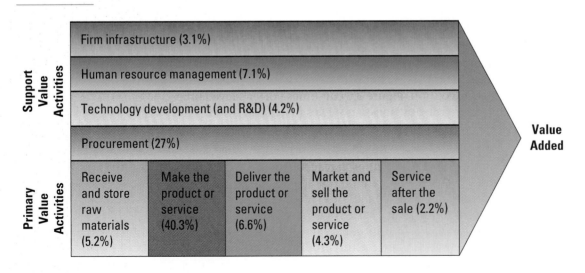

the graph, such as firm infrastructure, human resource management, technology development, and procurement, support the primary value activities.

The goal here is to survey the customers and ask them the extent to which they believe each activity adds value to the product or service. This generates a quantifiable metric, displayed in percentages in Figure 2.6, for how each activity adds value (or reduces value). The competitive advantage decision then is to (1) target high value-adding activities to further enhance their value, (2) target low value-adding activities to increase their value, or (3) perform some combination of the two.

Organizations should attempt to use information technology to add value to both primary and support value activities. One example of a primary value activity facilitated by IT is the development of a marketing campaign management system that could target marketing campaigns more efficiently, thereby reducing marketing costs. The system would also help the organization better pinpoint target market needs, thereby increasing sales. One example of a support value activity facilitated by IT is the development of a human resources system that could more efficiently reward employees based on performance. The system could also identify employees who are at risk of leaving their jobs, allowing the organization to find additional challenges or opportunities that would help retain these employees and thus reduce turnover costs.

Value chain analysis is a highly useful tool in that it provides hard and fast numbers for evaluating the activities that add value to products and services. An organization can find additional value by analyzing and constructing its value chain in terms of Porter's Five Forces (see Figure 2.7). For example, if an organization wants to decrease its buyers' or customers' power it can construct its value chain activity of "service after the sale" by offering high levels of quality customer service.

**FIGURE** 2.7

The Value Chain and Porter's Five Forces

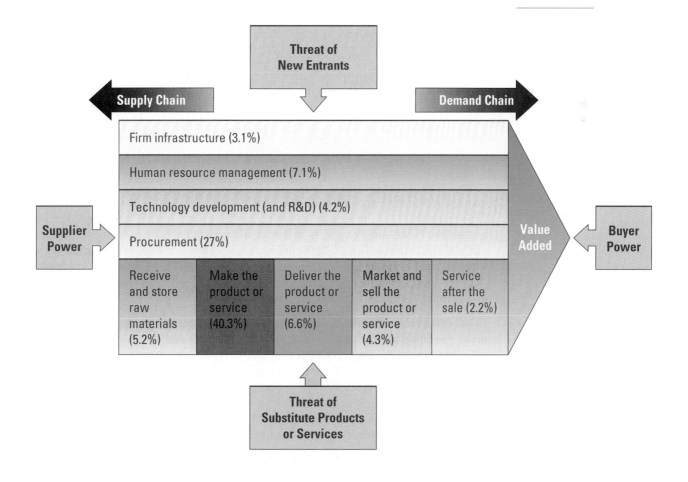

This will increase the switching costs for its customers, thereby decreasing their power. Analyzing and constructing its support value activities can help an organization decrease the threat of new entrants. Analyzing and constructing its primary value activities can help an organization decrease the threat of substitute products or services.

A company can implement its selected strategy by means of programs, budgets, and procedures. Implementation involves organization of the firm's resources and motivation of the employees to achieve objectives. How the company implements its chosen strategy can have a significant impact on its success. In a large company, the personnel implementing the strategy are usually different from those formulating the strategy. For this reason, proper communication of the strategy is critical. Failure can result if the strategy is misunderstood or if lower-level managers resist its implementation because they do not understand the process for selecting the particular strategy.

An organization must continually adapt to its competitive environment, which can cause its business strategy to change. To remain successful, an organization should use Porter's Five Forces, the three generic strategies, and value chain analysis to adopt new business strategies.

## OPENING CASE STUDY QUESTIONS

1. How can Apple use environmental scanning to gain business intelligence?

2. Using Porter's Five Forces Model, analyze Apple's buyer power and supplier power.

3. Which of the three generic strategies is Apple following?

4. Which of Porter's Five Forces did Apple address through the introduction of the iPhone and customer developed iPhone applications?

## Chapter Two Case: *BusinessWeek* Interview with Michael Porter

The Harvard professor and popular author explains the "location paradox" and talks about the competitive challenges facing the United States. Ever since his 1990 book *The Competitive Advantage of Nations,* Harvard Business School professor Michael Porter has been regarded as a leading authority on the economic development of nations, regions, and cities. Both as an academic and consultant, Porter is best known for his work on the importance of developing a specialty in industrial clusters—high concentrations of companies in a sector such as semiconductors, cars, or textiles. In an interview with Senior Writer Pete Engardio, Porter explains why he believes globalization has actually made industry clusters and local advantages even more important, rather than weakened them.

**If globalization means that work, technology, and money can now move anywhere over the Internet, does the physical location of an industry still really matter?**
"I call it the location paradox. If you think of globalization, your first reaction is to think that location doesn't matter anymore. There are no barriers to investment. But the paradox is that location still matters. The U.S. is still the most important space in the world, for example, and regions have tremendous specialization. Anything that can be easily accessed from a distance no longer is a competitive advantage. But the more there are no barriers, the more things are mobile, the more decisive location becomes. This point has tripped up a lot of really smart people.

As a result, the bottom half of U.S. locations are facing more stress. Many cities used to have a natural advantage just because they were in the U.S. But that is not such an advantage anymore. We are finding a tendency for the rich regions to get richer."

### How has globalization affected the idea of regional clusters?

"Now that globalization continues to power forward, what has happened is that clusters must become more specialized in individual locations. The global economy is speeding up the process by which clusters get more focused. There is a footwear cluster in Italy, for example, where they still produce very advanced products. The design, marketing, and technology still are in Italy. But much of the production has shifted to Romania, where the Italians have developed another cluster. All of the production companies actually are Italian-owned. Taiwan has done the same by shifting production to China. The innovation is in Taiwan, but its companies are moving aspects of their cluster that don't need to be in Taiwan."

### What are the big differences in the way communities approach development today compared to 1990, when you wrote *The Competitive Advantage of Nations?*

"There has been tremendous change in the last 15 or 20 years. Before *Competitive Advantage* was published, the dominant view was that you need to get costs down, offer incentives, and have a development department that hunts for investment. I think the level of sophistication has risen at the state and local level. They now understand that competitiveness does not just mean low costs.

Another big change from 20 years ago is that the notion of industry clusters is now pretty much ubiquitous. Many regions now look at development in these terms, and have identified hundreds and hundreds of different clusters. I think that the fact that productivity growth has risen dramatically shows that economic development has been a big success over the past few years."

### If every community is developing the same industry clusters, how do they stand out?

"I think it's very important to understand that the bar has risen substantially. Everything matters now. The schools matter. The roads matter. You have to understand this is a marathon. Also, you can't try to build clusters across the board and be into everything. You have to build on your strengths."

### Many local officials in the U.S. talk a lot about collaboration among universities, companies, and governments across an entire region. Is this new?

"There is a growing recognition that the interaction between one region or metropolitan area and its neighbors is important. The overlap between clusters is very important in stimulating growth. Isolated clusters are less powerful than integrated clusters. That's because new clusters often grow out of old clusters. I also think there is more recognition that you need a lot of cross-company collaboration in a region. Companies realize they have a lot of shared issues. Meanwhile, universities used to be seen as standalone institutions. Now, more regional economies see universities as players and are integrating them into industrial clusters."

### Does the U.S. have a competitiveness problem?

"I think the U.S. is facing some very serious challenges. But the most important drivers of competitiveness are not national. They are regional and local. National policies and circumstances explain about 20 percent to 25 percent of why a regional economy is doing well. What really matters is where the skills and highly competitive institutions are based. Some of these assets take a very long time to build. But competitiveness essentially is in the hands of regions."

## Questions

1. In today's global business environment, does the physical location of a business matter?
2. Why is collaboration among universities important?
3. Is there a competitiveness problem in the United States?
4. What are the big differences in the way communities approach development today compared to 1990, when Porter wrote *The Competitive Advantage of Nations?*

# Strategic Initiatives for Implementing Competitive Advantages

**3.1.** List and describe the four basic components of supply chain management.

**3.2.** Explain customer relationship management systems and how they can help organizations understand their customers.

**3.3.** Summarize the importance of enterprise resource planning systems.

**3.4.** Identify how an organization can use business process reengineering to improve its business.

## Strategic Initiatives

Trek, a leader in bicycle products and accessories, gained more than 30 percent of the worldwide market by streamlining operations through the implementation of several IT systems. According to Jeff Stang, director of IT and operational accounting, the most significant improvement realized from the new systems was the ability to obtain key management information to drive business decisions in line with the company's strategic goals. Other system results included a highly successful website developed for the 1,400 Trek dealers where they could enter orders directly, check stock availability, and view accounts receivable and credit summaries. Tonja Green, Trek channel manager for North America, stated, "We wanted to give our dealers an easier and quicker way to enter their orders and get information. Every week the number of web orders increases by 25 to 30 percent due to the new system."

This chapter introduces high-profile strategic initiatives that an organization can undertake to help it gain competitive advantages and business efficiencies—supply chain management, customer relationship management, business process reengineering, and enterprise resource planning. Each of these strategic initiatives is covered in detail throughout this text. This chapter provides a brief introduction only.

## Supply Chain Management

To understand a supply chain, consider a customer purchasing a Trek bike from a dealer. On one end, the supply chain has the customer placing an order for the bike with the dealer. The dealer purchases the bike from the manufacturer, Trek. Trek purchases raw materials such as packaging material, metal, and accessories from many different suppliers to make the bike. The supply chain for Trek encompasses every activity and party involved in the process of fulfilling the order from the customer for the new bike.

***Supply chain management (SCM)*** involves the management of information flows between and among stages in a supply chain to maximize total supply chain effectiveness and profitability. The four basic components of supply chain management are:

1. **Supply chain strategy**—the strategy for managing all the resources required to meet customer demand for all products and services.
2. **Supply chain partners**—the partners chosen to deliver finished products, raw materials, and services including pricing, delivery, and payment processes along with partner relationship monitoring metrics.
3. **Supply chain operation**—the schedule for production activities including testing, packaging, and preparation for delivery. Measurements for this component include productivity and quality.
4. **Supply chain logistics**—the product delivery processes and elements including orders, warehouses, carriers, defective product returns, and invoicing.

Dozens of steps are required to achieve and carry out each of the above components. SCM software can enable an organization to generate efficiencies within these steps by automating and improving the information flows throughout and among the different supply chain components.

Wal-Mart and Procter & Gamble (P&G) implemented a tremendously successful SCM system. The system linked Wal-Mart's distribution centers directly to P&G's manufacturing centers. Every time a Wal-Mart customer purchases a P&G product, the system sends a message directly to the factory alerting P&G to restock the product. The system also sends an automatic alert to P&G whenever a product is running low at one of Wal-Mart's distribution centers. This real-time information allows P&G to efficiently make and deliver products to Wal-Mart without having to maintain large inventories in its warehouses. The system also generates invoices and receives payments automatically. The SCM system saves time, reduces inventory, and decreases order-processing costs for P&G. P&G passes on these savings to Wal-Mart in the form of discounted prices.

Figure 3.1 diagrams the stages of the SCM system for a customer purchasing a product from Wal-Mart. The diagram demonstrates how the supply chain is dynamic and involves the constant flow of information between the different parties. For example, the customer generates order information by purchasing a product from Wal-Mart. Wal-Mart supplies the order information to its warehouse or distributor. The warehouse or distributor transfers the order information to the manufacturer, who provides pricing and availability information to the store and replenishes the product to the store. Payment funds among the various partners are transferred electronically.

**FIGURE 3.1**

Supply Chain for a Product Purchased from Wal-Mart

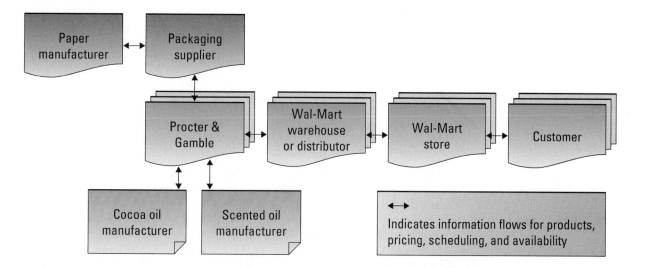

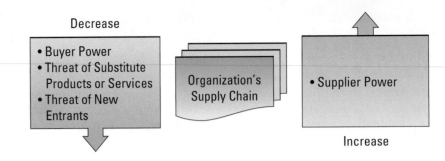

Effective and efficient supply chain management systems can enable an organization to:

- Decrease the power of its buyers.
- Increase its own supplier power.
- Increase switching costs to reduce the threat of substitute products or services.
- Create entry barriers thereby reducing the threat of new entrants.
- Increase efficiencies while seeking a competitive advantage through cost leadership (see Figure 3.2).

# Customer Relationship Management

Today, most competitors are simply a mouse-click away. This intense marketplace has forced organizations to switch from being sales focused to being customer focused.

Charles Schwab recouped the cost of a multimillion-dollar customer relationship management system in less than two years. The system, developed by Siebel, allows the brokerage firm to trace each interaction with a customer or prospective customer and then provide services (retirement planning, for instance) to each customer's needs and interests. The system gives Schwab a better and more complete view of its customers, which it can use to determine which customers are serious investors and which ones are not. Automated deposits from paychecks, for example, are a sign of a serious investor, while stagnant balances signal a nonserious investor. Once Schwab is able to make this determination, the firm allocates its resources accordingly, saving money by not investing time or resources in subsidizing nonserious investors.

***Customer relationship management (CRM)*** involves managing all aspects of a customer's relationship with an organization to increase customer loyalty and retention and an organization's profitability. CRM allows an organization to gain insights into customers' shopping and buying behaviors in order to develop and implement enterprisewide strategies. Kaiser Permanente undertook a CRM strategy to improve and prolong the lives of diabetics. After compiling CRM information on 84,000 of its diabetic patients among its 2.4 million northern California members, Kaiser determined that only 15 to 20 percent of its diabetic patients were getting their eyes checked routinely. (Diabetes is the leading cause of blindness.) As a result, Kaiser is now enforcing more rigorous eye-screening programs for diabetics and creating support groups for obesity and stress (two more factors that make diabetes even worse). This CRM-based "preventive medicine" approach is saving Kaiser considerable sums of money and saving the eyesight of diabetic patients.

Figure 3.3 provides an overview of a typical CRM system. Customers contact an organization through various means including call centers, web access, email, faxes, and direct sales. A single customer may access an organization multiple times through many different channels. The CRM system tracks every communication between the customer and the organization and provides access to CRM information within different systems from accounting to order fulfillment. Understanding all customer communications allows the organization to communicate effectively with each customer. It gives the organization a detailed understanding

**FIGURE** 3.3

CRM Overview

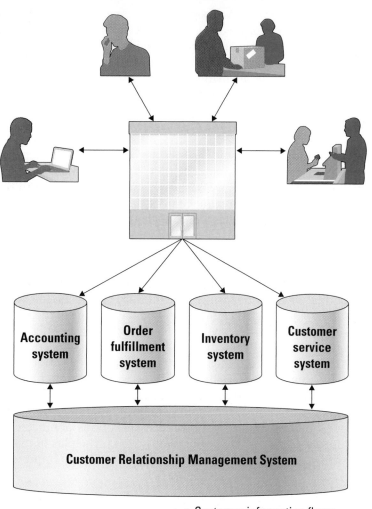

Customer information flows
are represented by arrows.

of each customer's products and services record regardless of the customer's preferred communication channel. For example, a customer service representative can easily view detailed account information and history through a CRM system when providing information to a customer such as expected delivery dates, complementary product information, and customer payment and billing information.

## CRM STRATEGY

Eddie Bauer ships 110 million catalogs a year, maintains two websites, and has over 600 retail stores. The company collects information through customer transactions and analyzes the information to determine the best way to market to each individual customer. Eddie Bauer discovered that customers who shop across all three of its distribution channels—catalogs, websites, and stores—spend up to five times more than customers who shop through only one channel.

Michael Boyd, director of CRM at Eddie Bauer, stated, "Our experience tells us that CRM is in no way, shape, or form a software application. Fundamentally, it is a business strategy to try to optimize profitability, revenue, and satisfaction at an individual customer level. Everything in an organization, every single process, every single application, is a tool that can be used to serve the CRM goal."

It is important to realize that CRM is not just technology, but also a strategy that an organization must embrace on an enterprise level. Although there are many technical components of CRM, it is actually a process and business goal simply enhanced by technology. Implementing a CRM system can help an organization identify customers and design specific marketing campaigns tailored to each customer, thereby increasing customer spending. A CRM system also allows an organization to treat customers as individuals, gaining important insights into their buying preferences and behaviors and leading to increased sales, greater profitability, and higher rates of customer loyalty.

# Business Process Reengineering

A *business process* is a standardized set of activities that accomplish a specific task, such as processing a customer's order. *Business process reengineering (BPR)* is the analysis and redesign of workflow within and between enterprises. The concept of BPR traces its origins to management theories developed as early as the 19th century. The purpose of BPR is to make all business process the best-in-class. Frederick Taylor suggested in the 1880s that managers could discover the best processes for performing work and reengineer the processes to optimize productivity. BPR echoes the classical belief that there is one best way to conduct tasks. In Taylor's time, technology did not allow large companies to design processes in a cross-functional or cross-departmental manner. Specialization was the state-of-the-art method to improve efficiency given the technology of the time.

BPR reached its heyday in the early 1990s when Michael Hammer and James Champy published their best-selling book, *Reengineering the Corporation.* The authors promoted the idea that radical redesign and reorganization of an enterprise (wiping the slate clean) sometimes was necessary to lower costs and increase quality of service and that information technology was the key enabler for that radical change. Hammer and Champy believed that the workflow design in most large corporations was based on invalid assumptions about technology, people, and organizational goals. They suggested seven principles of reengineering to streamline the work process and thereby achieve significant improvement in quality, time management, and cost (see Figure 3.4).

## FINDING OPPORTUNITY USING BPR

Companies frequently strive to improve their business processes by performing tasks faster, cheaper, and better. Figure 3.5 displays different ways to travel the same road. A company could improve the way that it travels the road by moving from foot to horse and then from horse to car. However, true BPR would look at taking a different path. A company could forget about traveling on the same old road and use an airplane to get to its final destination. Companies often follow the same indirect path for doing business, not realizing there might be a different, faster, and more direct way of doing business.

Creating value for the customer is the leading factor for instituting BPR, and information technology often plays an important enabling role. Radical and fundamentally

**FIGURE** 3.4

Seven Principles of Business Process Reengineering

| Seven Principles of Business Process Reengineering |
|---|
| 1  Organize around outcomes, not tasks. |
| 2  Identify all the organization's processes and prioritize them in order of redesign urgency. |
| 3  Integrate information processing work into the real work that produces the information. |
| 4  Treat geographically dispersed resources as though they were centralized. |
| 5  Link parallel activities in the workflow instead of just integrating their results. |
| 6  Put the decision point where the work is performed, and build control into the process. |
| 7  Capture information once and at the source. |

new business processes enabled Progressive Insurance to slash the claims settlement from 31 days to four hours. Typically, car insurance companies follow this standard claims resolution process: The customer gets into an accident, has the car towed, and finds a ride home. The customer then calls the insurance company to begin the claims process, which usually takes over a month (see Figure 3.6).

Progressive Insurance improved service to its customers by offering a mobile claims process. When a customer has a car accident he or she calls in the claim on the spot. The Progressive claims adjustor comes to the accident and performs a mobile claims process, surveying the scene and taking digital photographs. The adjustor then offers the customer on-site payment, towing services, and a ride home (see Figure 3.6).

A true BPR effort does more for a company than simply improve it by performing a process better, faster, and cheaper. Progressive Insurance's BPR effort redefined best practices for its entire industry. Figure 3.7 displays the different types of change an organization can achieve, along with the magnitude of change and the potential business benefit.

**FIGURE** 3.5

Better, Faster, Cheaper or BPR

## PITFALLS OF BPR

One hazard of BPR is that the company becomes so wrapped up in fighting its own demons that it fails to keep up with its competitors in offering new products or services. While American Express tackled a comprehensive reengineering of its credit card business, MasterCard and Visa introduced a new product—the corporate procurement card. American Express lagged a full year behind before offering its customers the same service.

# Enterprise Resource Planning

Today's business leaders need significant amounts of information to be readily accessible with real-time views into their businesses so that decisions can be made when they need to be, without the added time of tracking data and generating reports. ***Enterprise resource planning (ERP)*** integrates all departments and functions throughout an organization into a single IT system (or integrated set of IT systems) so that employees can make decisions by viewing enterprisewide information on all business operations.

Many organizations fail to maintain consistency across business operations. If a single department, such as sales, decides to implement a new system without considering the other departments, inconsistencies can occur throughout the company. Not all systems are built to talk to each other and share data, and if sales

**FIGURE** 3.6

Auto Insurance Claims Processes

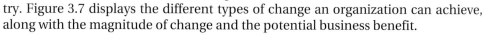

Company A: Claims Resolution Process

Progressive Insurance: Claims Resolution Process

ACME Insurance Agency

Resolution Cycle Time: 3–8 weeks

Resolution Cycle Time: 30 min–3 hours

FIGURE 3.7

The Benefits and
Magnitude of Change

**Process Change Spectrum**

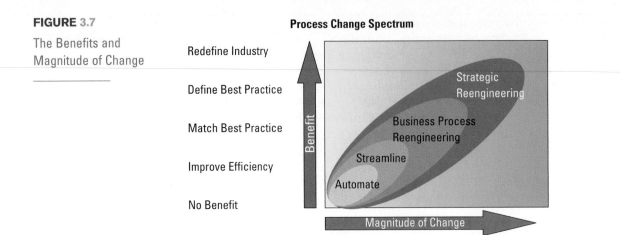

suddenly implements a new system that marketing and accounting cannot use or is inconsistent in the way it handles information, the company's operations become siloed. Figure 3.8 displays sample data from a sales database, and Figure 3.9 displays samples from an accounting database. Notice the differences in data formats, numbers, and identifiers. Correlating this data would be difficult, and the inconsistencies would cause numerous reporting errors from an enterprisewide perspective.

Los Angeles is a city of 3.5 million, with 44,000 city employees, and a budget of $4 billion. Yet a few years ago each department conducted its own purchasing. That meant 2,000 people in 600 city buildings and 60 warehouses were ordering material. Some 120,000 purchase orders (POs) and 50,000 checks per year went to more than 7,000 vendors. Inefficiency was rampant.

"There was a lack of financial responsibility in the old system, and people could run up unauthorized expenditures," said Bob Jensen, the city's ERP project manager. Each department maintained its own inventories on different systems. Expense-item mismatches piled up. One department purchased one way, others preferred a different approach. Mainframe-based systems were isolated. The city

FIGURE 3.8

Sales Information Sample

| | OrderDate | ProductName | Quantity | Unit Price | Unit Cost | Customer ID | SalesRep ID |
|---|---|---|---|---|---|---|---|
| 2 | Monday, January 04, 2010 | Mozzarella cheese | 41.5 | $ 24.15 | $ 15.35 | AC45 | EX-107 |
| 3 | Monday, January 04, 2010 | Romaine lettuce | 90.65 | $ 15.06 | $ 14.04 | AC45 | EX-109 |
| 4 | Tuesday, January 05, 2010 | Red onions | 27.15 | $ 12.08 | $ 10.32 | AC67 | EX-104 |
| 5 | Wednesday, January 06, 2010 | Romaine lettuce | 67.25 | $ 15.16 | $ 10.54 | AC96 | EX-109 |
| 6 | Thursday, January 07, 2010 | Black olives | 79.26 | $ 12.18 | $ 9.56 | AC44 | EX-104 |
| 7 | Thursday, January 07, 2010 | Romaine lettuce | 46.52 | $ 15.24 | $ 11.54 | AC32 | EX-104 |
| 8 | Thursday, January 07, 2010 | Romaine lettuce | 52.5 | $ 15.26 | $ 11.12 | AC84 | EX-109 |
| 9 | Friday, January 08, 2010 | Red onions | 39.5 | $ 12.55 | $ 9.54 | AC103 | EX-104 |
| 10 | Saturday, January 09, 2010 | Romaine lettuce | 66.5 | $ 15.98 | $ 9.56 | AC4 | EX-104 |
| 11 | Sunday, January 10, 2010 | Romaine lettuce | 58.26 | $ 15.87 | $ 9.50 | AC174 | EX-104 |
| 12 | Sunday, January 10, 2010 | Pineapple | 40.15 | $ 33.54 | $ 22.12 | AC45 | EX-104 |
| 13 | Monday, January 11, 2010 | Pineapple | 71.56 | $ 33.56 | $ 22.05 | AC4 | EX-104 |
| 14 | Thursday, January 14, 2010 | Romaine lettuce | 18.25 | $ 15.00 | $ 10.25 | AC174 | EX-104 |
| 15 | Thursday, January 14, 2010 | Romaine lettuce | 28.15 | $ 15.26 | $ 10.54 | AC44 | EX-107 |
| 16 | Friday, January 15, 2010 | Pepperoni | 33.5 | $ 15.24 | $ 10.25 | AC96 | EX-109 |
| 17 | Friday, January 15, 2010 | Parmesan cheese | 14.26 | $ 8.05 | $ 4.00 | AC96 | EX-104 |
| 18 | Saturday, January 16, 2010 | Parmesan cheese | 72.15 | $ 8.50 | $ 4.00 | AC103 | EX-109 |
| 19 | Monday, January 18, 2010 | Parmesan cheese | 41.5 | $ 24.15 | $ 15.35 | AC45 | EX-107 |
| 20 | Monday, January 18, 2010 | Romaine lettuce | 90.65 | $ 15.06 | $ 14.04 | AC45 | EX-109 |
| 21 | Wednesday, January 20, 2010 | Tomatoes | 27.15 | $ 12.08 | $ 10.32 | AC67 | EX-104 |
| 22 | Thursday, January 21, 2010 | Peppers | 67.25 | $ 15.16 | $ 10.54 | AC96 | EX-109 |
| 23 | Thursday, January 21, 2010 | Mozzarella cheese | 79.26 | $ 12.18 | $ 9.56 | AC44 | EX-104 |
| 24 | Saturday, January 23, 2010 | Black olives | 46.52 | $ 15.24 | $ 11.54 | AC32 | EX-104 |
| 25 | Sunday, January 24, 2010 | Mozzarella cheese | 52.5 | $ 15.26 | $ 11.12 | AC84 | EX-109 |
| 26 | Tuesday, January 26, 2010 | Romaine lettuce | 39.5 | $ 12.55 | $ 9.54 | AC103 | EX-104 |
| 27 | Wednesday, January 27, 2010 | Parmesan cheese | 66.5 | $ 15.98 | $ 9.56 | AC4 | EX-104 |
| 28 | Thursday, January 28, 2010 | Peppers | 58.26 | $ 15.87 | $ 9.50 | AC174 | EX-104 |
| 29 | Thursday, January 28, 2010 | Mozzarella cheese | 40.15 | $ 33.54 | $ 22.12 | AC45 | EX-104 |
| 30 | Friday, January 29, 2010 | Tomatoes | 71.56 | $ 33.56 | $ 22.05 | AC4 | EX-104 |
| 31 | Friday, January 29, 2010 | Peppers | 18.25 | $ 15.00 | $ 10.25 | AC174 | EX-104 |

FIGURE 3.9

Accounting Information
Sample

| OrderDate | ProductName | Quantity | Unit Price | Total Sales | Unit Cost | Total Cost | Profit | Customer | SalesRep |
|---|---|---|---|---|---|---|---|---|---|
| 04-Jan-10 | Mozzarella cheese | 41 | 24 | 984 | 18 | 738 | 246 | The Station | Debbie Fernandez |
| 04-Jan-10 | Romaine lettuce | 90 | 15 | 1,350 | 14 | 1,260 | 90 | The Station | Roberta Cross |
| 05-Jan-10 | Red onions | 27 | 12 | 324 | 8 | 216 | 108 | Bert's Bistro | Loraine Schultz |
| 06-Jan-10 | Romaine lettuce | 67 | 15 | 1,005 | 14 | 938 | 67 | Smoke House | Roberta Cross |
| 07-Jan-10 | Black olives | 79 | 12 | 948 | 6 | 474 | 474 | Flagstaff House | Loraine Schultz |
| 07-Jan-10 | Romaine lettuce | 46 | 15 | 690 | 14 | 644 | 46 | Two Bitts | Loraine Schultz |
| 07-Jan-10 | Romaine lettuce | 52 | 15 | 780 | 14 | 728 | 52 | Pierce Arrow | Roberta Cross |
| 08-Jan-10 | Red onions | 39 | 12 | 468 | 8 | 312 | 156 | Mamm'a Pasta Palace | Loraine Schultz |
| 09-Jan-10 | Romaine lettuce | 66 | 15 | 990 | 14 | 924 | 66 | The Dandelion | Loraine Schultz |
| 10-Jan-10 | Romaine lettuce | 58 | 15 | 870 | 14 | 812 | 58 | Carmens | Loraine Schultz |
| 10-Jan-10 | Pineapple | 40 | 33 | 1,320 | 28 | 1,120 | 200 | The Station | Loraine Schultz |
| 11-Jan-10 | Pineapple | 71 | 33 | 2,343 | 28 | 1,988 | 355 | The Dandelion | Loraine Schultz |
| 14-Jan-10 | Romaine lettuce | 18 | 15 | 270 | 14 | 252 | 18 | Carmens | Loraine Schultz |
| 14-Jan-10 | Romaine lettuce | 28 | 15 | 420 | 14 | 392 | 28 | Flagstaff House | Debbie Fernandez |
| 15-Jan-10 | Pepperoni | 33 | 53 | 1,749 | 35 | 1,155 | 594 | Smoke House | Roberta Cross |
| 15-Jan-10 | Parmesan cheese | 14 | 8 | 112 | 4 | 56 | 56 | Smoke House | Loraine Schultz |
| 16-Jan-10 | Parmesan cheese | 72 | 8 | 576 | 4 | 288 | 288 | Mamm'a Pasta Palace | Roberta Cross |
| 18-Jan-10 | Parmesan cheese | 10 | 8 | 80 | 4 | 40 | 40 | Mamm'a Pasta Palace | Loraine Schultz |
| 18-Jan-10 | Romaine lettuce | 42 | 15 | 630 | 14 | 588 | 42 | Smoke House | Roberta Cross |
| 20-Jan-10 | Tomatoes | 48 | 9 | 432 | 7 | 336 | 96 | Two Bitts | Loraine Schultz |
| 21-Jan-10 | Peppers | 29 | 21 | 609 | 12 | 348 | 261 | The Dandelion | Roberta Cross |
| 21-Jan-10 | Mozzarella cheese | 10 | 24 | 240 | 18 | 180 | 60 | Mamm'a Pasta Palace | Debbie Fernandez |
| 23-Jan-10 | Black olives | 98 | 12 | 1,176 | 6 | 588 | 588 | Two Bitts | Roberta Cross |
| 24-Jan-10 | Mozzarella cheese | 45 | 24 | 1,080 | 18 | 810 | 270 | Carmens | Loraine Schultz |
| 26-Jan-10 | Romaine lettuce | 58 | 15 | 870 | 14 | 812 | 58 | Two Bitts | Loraine Schultz |
| 27-Jan-10 | Parmesan cheese | 66 | 8 | 528 | 4 | 264 | 264 | Flagstaff House | Loraine Schultz |
| 28-Jan-10 | Peppers | 85 | 21 | 1,785 | 12 | 1,020 | 765 | Pierce Arrow | Loraine Schultz |
| 28-Jan-10 | Mozzarella cheese | 12 | 24 | 288 | 18 | 216 | 72 | The Dandelion | Debbie Fernandez |
| 29-Jan-10 | Tomatoes | 40 | 9 | 360 | 7 | 280 | 80 | Pierce Arrow | Roberta Cross |

chose an ERP system as part of a $22 million project to integrate purchasing and financial reporting across the entire city. The project resulted in cutting the check processing staff in half, processing POs faster than ever, reducing the number of workers in warehousing by 40 positions, decreasing inventories from $50 million to $15 million, and providing a single point of contact for each vendor. In addition, $5 million a year has been saved in contract consolidation.

Figure 3.10 shows how an ERP system takes data from across the enterprise, consolidates and correlates the data, and generates enterprisewide organizational reports. Original ERP implementations promised to capture all information onto one true "enterprise" system, with the ability to touch all the business processes within the organization. Unfortunately, ERP solutions have fallen short of these promises, and typical implementations have penetrated only 15 to 20 percent of the organization. The issue ERP intends to solve is that knowledge within a majority of organizations currently resides in silos that are maintained by a select few, without the ability to be shared across the organization, causing inconsistency across business operations.

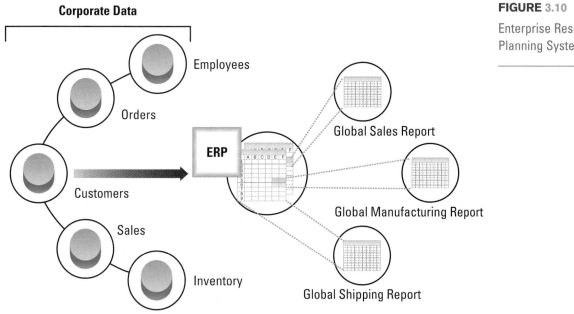

**Corporate Data**

Employees

Orders

Customers

Sales

Inventory

ERP

Global Sales Report

Global Manufacturing Report

Global Shipping Report

FIGURE 3.10

Enterprise Resource
Planning System

1. Evaluate how Apple can gain business intelligence through the implementation of a customer relationship management system.

2. Create an argument against the following statement: "Apple should not invest any resources to build a supply chain management system."

3. Why would a company like Apple invest in BPR?

## Chapter Three Case: Got Milk? It's Good for You— Unless It Is Contaminated!

Dong Lizhong, a farmer and migrant worker dairy farmer in China, bet that being a dairy farmer was his golden ticket out of a factory job. Unfortunately, a contamination crisis shattered his dairy business when babies mysteriously started developing kidney stones from contaminated baby formula. A chemical called melamine—an additive used to make plastic—was discovered in the milk supply of China's third-largest dairy producer. Tragically, four infants died from the contamination and at least 53,000 fell ill. According to the official Xinhua news agency, officials knew about problems with the milk for months before informing the public.

China's four largest dairy organizations, accounting for nearly half the country's milk market, pulled their goods off shelves. More than 20 countries, including France, India, and South Korea, banned not only dairy products from China, but also candies, cookies, and chocolates. "This is a disastrous setback. I estimate that it will take one or two years to rebuild confidence in dairy products," says Luo Yunbo, dean of the College of Food Science and Nutritional Engineering at China Agricultural University.

The local milk-collection station in Dong Lizhong's village has discontinued purchasing milk. Farmers are continuing to milk their cows, but they now drink the milk themselves or "feed the cabbages"—pour the milk in their cabbage fields. Dong estimates that he has already lost $1,461, or a quarter of his annual income last year, in expenses to feed corn and fresh grass to his 20 dairy cows. "Unless someone starts buying milk, we're going to see a lot of cows being slaughtered very soon," states Dong.

### Cutting Corners

Chinese do not traditionally drink milk. However, as the country has grown more affluent over the past few decades, the domestic dairy industry has skyrocketed. China's two largest dairy companies have greatly benefited from this new trend: China Mengniu Dairy and Inner Mongolia Yili Industrial Group. Simultaneously, numerous entrepreneurs—from dairy farmers to milk-collection station owners to milk distributors—have jumped into the supply chain of dairy products to make their fortunes. Due to the fierce competition within China's dairy industry a few companies decided to cut corners to reduce costs, regardless of the consequences.

As Mengniu and Yili expanded at breathtaking speed, they found themselves in the unique position where supply could not keep up with demand. According to KPMG, China consumes 25 million tons of milk yearly, putting its dairy market ahead of France and Germany. In their quest for more raw milk, Mengniu and Yili have expanded outside their base in the northern province of Inner Mongolia and set up milk production facilities in other parts of China. Not surprisingly, most of the quality problems in milk have been found in dairy farms in Hebei and Inner Mongolia provinces, where the competition for raw milk supplies has been the fiercest.

Most dairy farmers in Hebei province traditionally sold their milk to milk-collection stations established by local heavyweight Sanlu. In recent years, new privately owned milk-collection stations to buy raw milk for Mengniu and Yili started popping up next to existing stations. These new entrants captured raw milk supplies by offering dairy farmers slightly higher prices. "This competition broke the rules. As milk buyers fought over milk supplies, their standards for quality fell," says Roger Liu, vice-chairman of American Dairy (ADY), a Heilongjiang province-based powdered milk company.

### Additives to Boost Protein

Many of the milking stations do not have the equipment to test milk for additives. At the Nanxincheng station, 16 households bring their dairy cows in the area to be milked in the red brick farmhouse. The farmers hook up the cows up to a milking machine, which pumps the milk directly into a big vat. "They didn't test the milk here. They sent it to Sanlu for testing," says Du Yanjun, a government inspector posted to monitor the Nanxincheng station after the contamination crisis broke.

The milk is collected from the stations and shipped by middlemen to big dairy companies like Sanlu, which do their own testing and grading. It now appears that unscrupulous middlemen commonly add melamine into the raw milk to increase protein levels in their milk samples, so their milk will be graded higher. Ingesting melamine can cause kidney stones or kidney failure, especially in infants.

Matthew Estes, president and CEO of BabyCare, had looked into switching from Australian and New Zealand sources of milk for the company's infant-formula business in China. BabyCare did extensive testing of possible suppliers and realized it could not locate a suitable supplier in China. "We couldn't the find quality that met our standards. We chose to not sell rather than take the risk," he says.

### Going to Jail

A Chinese court sentenced two of the primary middlemen to death and a dairy boss to life in prison for their roles in the milk contamination scandal. The swift trial and harsh sentences show Beijing's resolve in tackling the country's stubborn food safety problems and an eagerness by the communist leadership to move past the embarrassing scandal.

### Going to Starbucks

Starbucks Corp. has launched a new brand of coffee grown by farmers in China and says it hopes to bring the blend to stores all over the world. The Seattle-based company, which has been closing stores in the U.S. to cut costs, says its new blend is made in China's southwestern province of Yunnan, bordering Vietnam, Laos and Myanmar. "Our intention is to work with the officials and the farmers in Yunnan province to bring Chinese coffee not (only) to China, but Chinese coffee to the world," Martin Coles, president of Starbucks Coffee International, told the Associated Press. "Ultimately I'd love to see our coffees from China featured on the shelves of every one of our stores in 49 countries around the world," he said. A launch date for foreign distribution hasn't been announced and will depend on how soon farmers can grow enough beans to ensure local and overseas supply.

The company has been working for three years with farmers and officials in the province before the launch, and the coffee will initially combine Arabica beans from Latin America and the Asia-Pacific with local Yunnan beans. But Coles said they hope to develop a source of superpremium Arabica coffee from the province, expanding it to new brand offerings in China, and then internationally. The new blend will be called "South of the Clouds," the meaning of Yunnan in Chinese.

### Questions

1. Explain why the supply chain can dramatically impact a company's base performance.
2. List all of the products that could possibly be affected by a problem in the U.S. milk supply chain.
3. How can a CRM system help communicate issues in the supply chain?
4. How could BPR help uncover issues in a company's supply chain?
5. What are the pros and cons for Starbucks of outsourcing the growing of its coffee beans to Chinese farmers?

# 4

# Measuring the Success of Strategic Initiatives

**4.1.** Compare efficiency IT metrics and effectiveness IT metrics.

**4.2.** List and describe five common types of efficiency IT metrics.

**4.3.** List and describe four types of effectiveness IT metrics.

**4.4.** Explain customer metrics and their importance to an organization.

## Measuring Information Technology's Success

IT has become an important part of organizations' strategy, competitive advantage, and profitability. There is management pressure to build systems faster, better, and at minimum cost. The return on investment that an organization can achieve from the money it spends on IT has come under increased scrutiny from senior business executives and directors. Consequently, IT now has to operate like other parts of the organization, being aware of its performance and its contribution to the organization's success and opportunities for improvement. So what is it that managers need to know about measuring the success of information technology?

The first thing managers need to understand about IT success is that it is incredibly difficult to measure. Determining the return on investment (ROI) of new computer equipment is difficult. For example, what is the ROI of a fire extinguisher? If the fire extinguisher is never used, the return on the investment is low. If the extinguisher puts out a fire that could destroy the entire building, then its ROI is high. This is similar to IT systems. If a company implements a $5,000 firewall to virus attacks on the computer systems and it never stops a virus, the company lost $5,000. If the firewall stops viruses that could have cost the company millions of dollars, then the ROI of that firewall is significantly greater than $5,000. A few questions banking executives recently raised regarding their IT systems include:

- Is the internal IT operation performing satisfactorily?
- Should the company outsource some or all of the IT operations?
- How is the outsourcing company performing?
- What are the risk factors to consider in an IT project?
- What questions should be asked to ensure an IT project proposal is realistic?
- What are the characteristics of a healthy project?
- Which factors are most critical to measure to ensure the project achieves success?

Peter Drucker, a famous management guru, once stated that if you cannot measure it, you cannot manage it. Managers need to ask themselves how they are going to manage IT projects if they cannot find a way to measure the projects.

IT professionals know how to install and maintain information systems. Business professionals know how to run a successful business. But how does a company decide if an information system helps make a business successful?

The answer lies in the metrics. Designing metrics requires an expertise that neither IT nor business professionals usually possess. Metrics are about neither technology nor business strategy. The questions that arise in metrics design are almost philosophical: How do you define success? How do you apply quantifiable measures to business processes, especially qualitative ones like customer service? What kind of information best reflects progress, or the lack of it?

*Key performance indicators (KPIs)* are the measures that are tied to business drivers. Metrics are the detailed measures that feed those KPIs. Performance metrics fall into a nebulous area of business intelligence that is neither technology- nor business-centered, but this area requires input from both IT and business professionals to find success. Cisco Systems implemented a cross-departmental council to create metrics for improving business process operations. The council developed metrics to evaluate the efficiency of Cisco's online order processing and discovered that due to errors, more than 70 percent of online orders required manual input and were unable to be automatically routed to manufacturing. By changing the process and adding new information systems, within six months the company doubled the percentage of orders that went directly to manufacturing.

## Efficiency and Effectiveness

Organizations spend enormous sums of money on IT to compete in today's fast-paced business environment. Some organizations spend up to 50 percent of their total capital expenditures on IT. To justify these expenditures, an organization must measure the payoff of these investments, their impact on business performance, and the overall business value gained.

Efficiency and effectiveness metrics are two primary types of IT metrics. *Efficiency IT metrics* measure the performance of the IT system itself including throughput, speed, and availability. *Effectiveness IT metrics* measure the impact IT has on business processes and activities including customer satisfaction, conversion rates, and sell-through increases. Peter Drucker offers a helpful distinction between efficiency and effectiveness. Drucker states that managers "Do things right" and/or "Do the right things." Doing things right addresses efficiency—getting the most from each resource. Doing the right things addresses effectiveness—setting the right goals and objectives and ensuring they are accomplished.

Effectiveness focuses on how well an organization is achieving its goals and objectives, while efficiency focuses on the extent to which an organization is using its resources in an optimal way. The two—efficiency and effectiveness—are definitely interrelated. However, success in one area does not necessarily imply success in the other.

## Benchmarking—Baseline Metrics

Regardless of what is measured, how it is measured, and whether it is for the sake of efficiency or effectiveness, there must be *benchmarks,* or baseline values the system seeks to attain. *Benchmarking* is a process of continuously measuring system results, comparing those results to optimal system performance (benchmark values), and identifying steps and procedures to improve system performance.

| Efficiency | Effectiveness |
|---|---|
| 1. United States (3.11) | 1. Canada |
| 2. Australia (2.60) | 2. Singapore |
| 3. New Zealand (2.59) | 3. United States |
| 4. Singapore (2.58) | 4. Denmark |
| 5. Norway (2.55) | 5. Australia |
| 6. Canada (2.52) | 6. Finland |
| 7. United Kingdom (2.52) | 7. Hong Kong |
| 8. Netherlands (2.51) | 8. United Kingdom |
| 9. Denmark (2.47) | 9. Germany |
| 10. Germany (2.46) | 10. Ireland |

**FIGURE 4.1**

Comparing Efficiency IT and Effectiveness IT Metrics for Egovernment Initiatives

Consider egovernment worldwide as an illustration of benchmarking efficiency IT metrics and effectiveness IT metrics (see survey results in Figure 4.1). From an effectiveness point of view, Canada ranks number one in terms of egovernment satisfaction of its citizens. (The United States ranks third.) The survey, sponsored by Accenture, also included such attributes as CRM practices, customer-service vision, approaches to offering egovernment services through multiple-service delivery channels, and initiatives for identifying services for individual citizen segments. These are all benchmarks at which Canada's government excels.

In contrast, the *United Nations Division for Public Economics and Public Administration* ranks Canada sixth in terms of efficiency IT metrics. (It ranked the United States first.) This particular ranking based purely on efficiency IT metrics includes benchmarks such as the number of computers per 100 citizens, the number of Internet hosts per 10,000 citizens, the percentage of the citizen population online, and several other factors. Therefore, while Canada lags behind in IT efficiency, it is the premier egovernment provider in terms of effectiveness.

Governments hoping to increase their egovernment presence would benchmark themselves against these sorts of efficiency and effectiveness metrics. There is a high degree of correlation between egovernment efficiency and effectiveness, although it is not absolute.

# The Interrelationships of Efficiency and Effectiveness IT Metrics

Efficiency IT metrics focus on the technology itself. Figure 4.2 highlights the most common types of efficiency IT metrics.

While these efficiency metrics are important to monitor, they do not always guarantee effectiveness. Effectiveness IT metrics are determined according to an organization's goals, strategies, and objectives. Here, it becomes important to consider the strategy an organization is using, such as a broad cost leadership strategy (Wal-Mart, for example), as well as specific goals and objectives such as increasing new customers by 10 percent or reducing new-product development

**FIGURE 4.2**

Common Types of Efficiency IT Metrics

| Efficiency IT Metrics | |
|---|---|
| *Throughput* | The amount of information that can travel through a system at any point. |
| *Transaction speed* | The amount of time a system takes to perform a transaction. |
| *System availability* | The number of hours a system is available for users. |
| *Information accuracy* | The extent to which a system generates the correct results when executing the same transaction numerous times. |
| *Web traffic* | Includes a host of benchmarks such as the number of page views, the number of unique visitors, and the average time spent viewing a web page. |
| *Response time* | The time it takes to respond to user interactions such as a mouse click. |

FIGURE 4.3

Common Types of
Effectiveness IT Metrics

| Effectiveness IT Metrics | |
| --- | --- |
| Usability | The ease with which people perform transactions and/or find information. A popular usability metric on the Internet is degrees of freedom, which measures the number of clicks required to find desired information. |
| Customer satisfaction | Measured by such benchmarks as satisfaction surveys, percentage of existing customers retained, and increases in revenue dollars per customer. |
| Conversion rates | The number of customers an organization "touches" for the first time and persuades to purchase its products or services. This is a popular metric for evaluating the effectiveness of banner, pop-up, and pop-under ads on the Internet. |
| Financial | Such as return on investment (the earning power of an organization's assets), cost-benefit analysis (the comparison of projected revenues and costs including development, maintenance, fixed, and variable), and break-even analysis (the point at which constant revenues equal ongoing costs). |

cycle times to six months. Broad, general effectiveness metrics are outlined in Figure 4.3.

In the private sector, eBay constantly benchmarks its information technology efficiency and effectiveness. Maintaining constant website availability and optimal throughput performance is critical to eBay's success. Jupiter Media Metrix ranked eBay as the website with the highest visitor volume (efficiency) for the fourth year in a row, with an 80 percent growth from the previous year. The eBay site averaged 8 million unique visitors during each week of the holiday season that year with daily peaks exceeding 12 million visitors. To ensure constant availability and reliability of its systems, eBay implemented ProactiveNet, a performance measurement and management-tracking tool. The tool allows eBay to monitor its environment against baseline benchmarks, which helps the eBay team keep tight control of its systems. The new system has resulted in improved system availability with a 150 percent increase in productivity as measured by system uptime.

Be sure to consider the issue of security while determining efficiency and effectiveness IT metrics. When an organization offers its customers the ability to purchase products over the Internet it must implement the appropriate security—such as encryption and Secure Sockets Layers (SSLs; denoted by the lock symbol in the lower right corner of a browser window and/or the "s" in https). It is actually inefficient for an organization to implement security measures for Internet-based transactions as compared to processing nonsecure transactions. However, an organization will probably have a difficult time attracting new customers and increasing web-based revenue if it does not implement the necessary security measures. Purely from an efficiency IT metric point of view, security generates some inefficiency. From an organization's business strategy point of view, however, security should lead to increases in effectiveness metrics.

Figure 4.4 depicts the interrelationships between efficiency and effectiveness. Ideally, an organization should operate in the upper right-hand corner of the graph, realizing both significant increases in efficiency and effectiveness.

FIGURE 4.4

The Interrelationships
between Efficiency and
Effectiveness

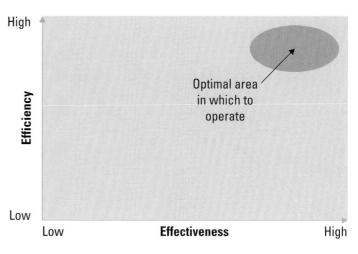

However, operating in the upper left-hand corner (minimal effectiveness with increased efficiency) or the lower right-hand corner (significant effectiveness with minimal efficiency) may be in line with an organization's particular strategies. In general, operating in the lower left-hand corner (minimal efficiency and minimal effectiveness) is not ideal for the operation of any organization.

# Metrics for Strategic Initiatives

What is a metric? A metric is nothing more than a standard measure to assess performance in a particular area. Metrics are at the heart of a good, customer-focused management system and any program directed at continuous improvement. A focus on customers and performance standards shows up in the form of metrics that assess the ability to meet customers' needs and business objectives.

Business leaders want to monitor key metrics in real time to actively track the health of their business. Most business professionals are familiar with financial metrics. Different financial ratios are used to evaluate a company's performance. Companies can gain additional insight into their performance by comparing financial ratios against other companies in their industry. A few of the more common financial ratios include:

- Internal rate of return (IRR)—the rate at which the net present value of an investment equals zero.
- Return on investment (ROI)—indicates the earning power of a project and is measured by dividing the benefits of a project by the investment.
- Payback method—number of years to recoup the cost of an initiative based on projected annual net cash flow.
- Break-even analysis—determines the volume of business required to make a profit at the current prices charged for the products or services. For example, if a promotional mailing costs $1,000 and each item generates $50 in revenue, the company must generate 20 sales to break even and cover the cost of the mailing. The break-even point is the point at which revenues equal costs. The point is located by performing a break-even analysis. All sales over the break-even point produce profits; any drop in sales below that point will produce losses (see Figure 4.5).

Most managers are familiar with financial metrics but unfamiliar with information system metrics. The following metrics will help managers measure and manage their strategic initiatives:

- Website metrics.
- Supply chain management (SCM) metrics.
- Customer relationship management (CRM) metrics.
- Business process reengineering (BPR) metrics.
- Enterprise resource planning (ERP) metrics.

## WEBSITE METRICS

Most companies measure the traffic on a website as the primary determinant of the website's success. However, heavy website traffic does not necessarily indicate large sales. Many organizations with lots of website traffic have minimal sales. A company can use web traffic analysis or web analytics to determine the revenue generated, the number of new customers acquired, any reductions in customer service calls, and

**FIGURE** 4.5

Break-Even Analysis

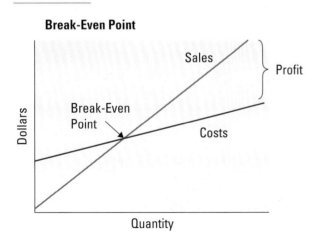

**FIGURE** 4.6

Website Metrics

**Website Metrics**

- **Abandoned registrations:** Number of visitors who start the process of completing a registration page and then abandon the activity.

- **Abandoned shopping carts:** Number of visitors who create a shopping cart and start shopping and then abandon the activity before paying for the merchandise.

- **Click-through:** Count of the number of people who visit a site, click on an ad, and are taken to the site of the advertiser.

- **Conversion rate:** Percentage of potential customers who visit a site and actually buy something.

- **Cost-per-thousand (CPM):** Sales dollars generated per dollar of advertising. This is commonly used to make the case for spending money to appear on a search engine.

- **Page exposures:** Average number of page exposures to an individual visitor.

- **Total hits:** Number of visits to a website, many of which may be by the same visitor.

- **Unique visitors:** Number of unique visitors to a site in a given time. This is commonly used by Nielsen/Net ratings to rank the most popular websites.

**FIGURE** 4.7

Supply Chain Management Metrics

**Supply Chain Management Metrics**

- **Back order:** An unfilled customer order. A back order is demand (immediate or past due) against an item whose current stock level is insufficient to satisfy demand.

- **Customer order promised cycle time:** The anticipated or agreed upon cycle time of a purchase order. It is a gap between the purchase order creation date and the requested delivery date.

- **Customer order actual cycle time:** The average time it takes to actually fill a customer's purchase order. This measure can be viewed on an order or an order line level.

- **Inventory replenishment cycle time:** Measure of the manufacturing cycle time plus the time included to deploy the product to the appropriate distribution center.

- **Inventory turns (inventory turnover):** The number of times that a company's inventory cycles or turns over per year. It is one of the most commonly used supply chain metrics.

so on. The Yankee Group reports that 66 percent of companies determine website success solely by measuring the amount of traffic. New customer acquisition ranked second on the list at 34 percent, and revenue generation ranked third at 23 percent. Figure 4.6 displays a few metrics managers should be familiar with to help measure website success along with an organization's strategic initiatives. A web-centric metric is a measure of the success of web and ebusiness initiatives. Of the hundreds of web-centric metrics available, some are general to almost any web or ebusiness initiative and others are dependent on the particular initiative.

## SUPPLY CHAIN MANAGEMENT (SCM) METRICS

Supply chain management metrics can help an organization understand how it's operating over a given time period. Supply chain measurements can cover many areas including procurement, production, distribution, warehousing, inventory, transportation, and customer service. However, a good performance in one part of the supply chain is not sufficient. A supply chain is only as strong as its weakest link. The solution is to measure all key areas of the supply chain. Figure 4.7 displays common supply chain management metrics.

**FIGURE** 4.8

CRM Metrics

| Sales Metrics | Service Metrics | Marketing Metrics |
| --- | --- | --- |
| Number of prospective customers | Cases closed same day | Number of marketing campaigns |
| Number of new customers | Number of cases handled by agent | New customer retention rates |
| Number of retained customers | Number of service calls | Number of responses by marketing campaign |
| Number of open leads | Average number of service requests by type | Number of purchases by marketing campaign |
| Number of sales calls | Average time to resolution | Revenue generated by marketing campaign |
| Number of sales calls per lead | Average number of service calls per day | Cost per interaction by marketing campaign |
| Amount of new revenue | Percentage compliance with service-level agreement | Number of new customers acquired by marketing campaign |
| Amount of recurring revenue | Percentage of service renewals | Customer retention rate |
| Number of proposals given | Customer satisfaction level | Number of new leads by product |

## CUSTOMER RELATIONSHIP MANAGEMENT (CRM) METRICS

Wondering what CRM metrics to track and monitor using reporting and real-time performance dashboards? Best practice is no more than seven (plus or minus two) metrics out of the hundreds possible should be used at any given management level. Figure 4.8 displays common CRM metrics tracked by organizations.

## BUSINESS PROCESS REENGINEERING (BPR) AND ENTERPRISE RESOURCE PLANNING (ERP) METRICS

Business process reengineering and enterprise resource planning are large, organizationwide initiatives. Measuring these types of strategic initiatives is extremely difficult. One of the best methods is the balanced scorecard. This approach to strategic management was developed in the early 1990s by Drs. Robert Kaplan of the Harvard Business School and David Norton. Addressing some of the weaknesses and vagueness of previous measurement techniques, the balanced scorecard approach provides a clear prescription as to what companies should measure in order to balance the financial perspective.

The *balanced scorecard* is a management system, in addition to a measurement system, that enables organizations to clarify their vision and strategy and translate them into action. It provides feedback around both the internal business processes and external outcomes in order to continuously improve strategic performance and results. When fully deployed, the balanced scorecard transforms strategic planning from an academic exercise into the nerve center of an enterprise. Kaplan and Norton describe the innovation of the balanced scorecard as follows:

> The balanced scorecard retains traditional financial measures. But financial measures tell the story of past events, an adequate story for industrial age companies for which

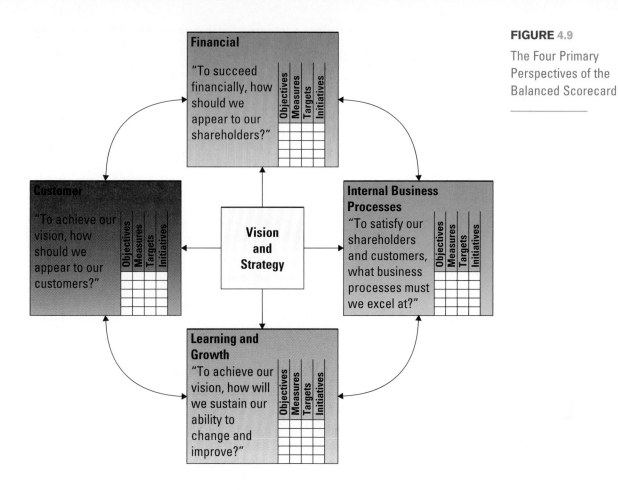

**FIGURE** 4.9

The Four Primary
Perspectives of the
Balanced Scorecard

investments in long-term capabilities and customer relationships were not critical for success. These financial measures are inadequate, however, for guiding and evaluating the journey that information age companies must make to create future value through investment in customers, suppliers, employees, processes, technology, and innovation. (Kaplan, Robert, Norton, David, "The BSC: Translating Strategy into Action" (Vintage Books: 1998))

The balanced scorecard views the organization from four perspectives, and users should develop metrics, collect data, and analyze their business relative to each of these perspectives:

- The learning and growth perspective.
- The internal business process perspective.
- The customer perspective.
- The financial perspective (see Figure 4.9).

Recall that companies cannot manage what they cannot measure. Therefore, metrics must be developed based on the priorities of the strategic plan, which provides the key business drivers and criteria for metrics that managers most desire to watch.

One warning regarding metrics—do not go crazy. The trick is to find a few key metrics to track that provide significant insight. Remember to tie metrics to other financial and business objectives in the firm. The key is to get good insight without becoming a slave to metrics. The rule of thumb is to develop seven key metrics, plus or minus two.

1. Formulate a strategy describing how Apple can use efficiency IT metrics to improve its business.

2. Formulate a strategy describing how Apple can use effectiveness IT metrics to improve its business.

3. List three CRM metrics Apple should track, along with the reasons these metrics will add value to Apple's business strategy.

4. List three SCM metrics Apple should track, along with the reasons these metrics will add value to Apple's business strategy.

5. How can Apple use the balanced scorecard to make its business more efficient?

## Chapter Four Case: How Do You Value Friendster?

Jonathan Abrams is keeping quiet about how he is going to generate revenue from his website, Friendster, which specializes in social networking. Abrams was a 33-year-old Canadian software developer whose experiences included being laid off by Netscape and then moving from one start-up to another. Abrams was unemployed, not doing well financially, and certainly not looking to start another business, when he developed the idea for Friendster. He quickly coded a working prototype and watched in amazement as his website took off.

The buzz around social networking start-ups has been on the rise. A number of high-end venture capital (VC) firms, including Sequoia and Mayfield, have invested more than $40 million into social networking start-ups such as LinkedIn, Spoke, and Tribe Networks. Friendster received over $13 million in venture capital from Kleiner, Perkins, Caufield, Byers, and Benchmark Capital, which reportedly valued the company at $53 million—a startling figure for a company that had yet to generate even a single dime in revenue.

A year after making its public debut, Friendster was one of the largest social networking websites, attracting over 5 million users and receiving more than 50,000 page views per day. The question is how do efficiency metrics, such as web traffic and page views, turn into cash flow? Everyone is wondering how Friendster is going to begin generating revenue.

The majority of Abrams's competitors make their money by extracting fees from their subscribers. Friendster is going to continue to let its subscribers meet for free but plans to charge them for premium services such as the ability to customize their profile page. The company also has plans to extend beyond social networking to an array of value-added services such as friend-based job referrals and classmate searches. Abrams is also looking into using his high-traffic website to tap into the growing Internet advertising market.

Abrams does not appear concerned about generating revenue or about potential competition. He states, "Match.com has been around eight years, has 12 million users, and has spent many millions of dollars on advertising to get them. We're a year old, we've spent zero dollars on advertising, and in a year or less, we'll be bigger than them—it's a given."

The future of Friendster is uncertain. Google offered to buy Friendster for $30 million even though there are signs, both statistical and anecdotal, that Friendster's popularity may have peaked.

## Questions

1. How could you use efficiency IT metrics to help place a value on Friendster?

2. How could you use effectiveness IT metrics to help place a value on Friendster?

3. Explain how a venture capital company can value Friendster at $53 million when the company has yet to generate any revenue.

4. Explain why Google would be interested in buying Friendster for $30 million when the company has yet to generate any revenue.

5. Google purchased You-Tube for $1.65 billion. Do you think this was a smart investment? Why or why not?

# Organizational Structures That Support Strategic Initiatives

**LEARNING OUTCOMES**

**5.1.** Compare the responsibilities of a chief information officer (CIO), chief technology officer (CTO), chief privacy officer (CPO), chief security officer (CSO), and chief knowledge officer (CKO).

**5.2.** Explain the gap between IT people and business people and the primary reason this gap exists.

**5.3.** Define the relationship between security and ethics.

## Organizational Structures

Employees across the organization must work closely together to develop strategic initiatives that create competitive advantages. Understanding the basic structure of a typical IT department including titles, roles, and responsibilities will help an organization build a cohesive enterprisewide team.

## IT Roles and Responsibilities

Information technology is a relatively new functional area, having been around formally in most organizations only for about 40 years. Job titles, roles, and responsibilities often differ dramatically from organization to organization. Nonetheless, clear trends are developing toward elevating some IT positions within an organization to the strategic level.

Most organizations maintain positions such as chief executive officer (CEO), chief financial officer (CFO), and chief operations officer (COO) at the strategic level. Recently there are more IT-related strategic positions such as chief information officer (CIO), chief technology officer (CTO), chief security officer (CSO), chief privacy officer (CPO), and chief knowledge officer (CKO).

J. Greg Hanson is proud to be the first CIO of the U.S. Senate. Contrary to some perceptions, the technology found in the Senate is quite good, according to Hanson. Hanson's responsibilities include creating the Senate's technology vision, leading the IT department, and deploying the IT infrastructure. Hanson must work with everyone from the 137 network administrators to the senators themselves to ensure that everything is operating smoothly. Hanson is excited to be the first CIO of the U.S. Senate and proud of the honor and responsibility that come with the job.

The **chief information officer (CIO)** is responsible for (1) overseeing all uses of information technology and (2) ensuring the strategic alignment of IT with business goals and objectives. The CIO often reports directly to the CEO. (See Figure 5.1 for the average CIO compensation.) CIOs must possess a solid and detailed understanding of every aspect of an organization coupled with tremendous insight into the capability of IT. Broad functions of a CIO include:

1. *Manager*—ensure the delivery of all IT projects, on time and within budget.

2. *Leader*—ensure the strategic vision of IT is in line with the strategic vision of the organization.

3. *Communicator*—advocate and communicate the IT strategy by building and maintaining strong executive relationships.

Although CIO is considered a position within IT, CIOs must be concerned with more than just IT. According to a recent survey (see Figure 5.2), most CIOs ranked "enhancing customer satisfaction" ahead of their concerns for any specific aspect of IT. CIOs with the broad business view that customer satisfaction is more crucial and critical than specific aspects of IT should be applauded.

The *chief technology officer (CTO)* is responsible for ensuring the throughput, speed, accuracy, availability, and reliability of an organization's information technology. CTOs are similar to CIOs, except that CIOs take on the additional responsibility for effectiveness of ensuring that IT is aligned with the organization's strategic initiatives. CTOs have direct responsibility for ensuring the *efficiency* of IT systems throughout the organization. Most CTOs possess well-rounded knowledge of all aspects of IT, including hardware, software, and telecommunications.

The *chief security officer (CSO)* is responsible for ensuring the security of IT systems and developing strategies and IT safeguards against attacks from hackers and viruses. The role of a CSO has been elevated in recent years because of the number of attacks from hackers and viruses. Most CSOs possess detailed knowledge of networks and telecommunications because hackers and viruses usually find their way into IT systems through networked computers.

The *chief privacy officer (CPO)* is responsible for ensuring the ethical and legal use of information within an organization. CPOs are the newest senior executive position in IT. Recently, 150 of the Fortune 500 companies added the CPO position to their list of senior executives. Many CPOs are lawyers by training, enabling them to understand the often complex legal issues surrounding the use of information.

The *chief knowledge officer (CKO)* is responsible for collecting, maintaining, and distributing the organization's knowledge. The CKO designs programs and systems that make it easy for people to reuse knowledge. These systems create repositories of organizational documents, methodologies, tools, and practices, and they establish methods for filtering the information. The CKO must continuously encourage employee contributions to keep the systems up-to-date. The CKO can contribute directly to the organization's bottom line by reducing the learning curve for new employees or employees taking on new roles.

Danny Shaw was the first CKO at Children's Hospital in Boston. His initial task was to unite information from disparate systems to enable analysis of both the efficiency and effectiveness of the hospital's care. Shaw started by building a series of small, integrated information systems that quickly demonstrated value. He then gradually built on those successes, creating a knowledge-enabled organization one layer at a time. Shaw's information systems have enabled administrative and clinical operational analyses.

With the election of President Barack Obama comes the appointment of the first-ever national chief technology officer (CTO). The job description, as listed on Change.gov, states that the first CTO must "ensure the safety of our networks and lead an interagency effort, working with chief technology and chief information officers of each of the federal agencies, to ensure that they use best-in-class technologies and share best practices." A federal level CTO demonstrates the ongoing growth of technology positions outside corporate America. In the future expect to see many

| Industry | Average CIO Compensation |
|---|---|
| Wholesale/Retail/Distribution | $243,304 |
| Finance | $210,547 |
| Insurance | $197,697 |
| Manufacturing | $190,250 |
| Medical/Dental/Health Care | $171,032 |
| Government | $118,359 |
| Education | $ 93,750 |

**FIGURE** 5.1

Average CIO Compensation by Industry

**FIGURE** 5.2

What Concerns CIOs the Most?

| Percentage | CIOs' Concerns |
|---|---|
| 94% | Enhancing customer satisfaction |
| 92 | Security |
| 89 | Technology evaluation |
| 87 | Budgeting |
| 83 | Staffing |
| 66 | ROI analysis |
| 64 | Building new applications |
| 45 | Outsourcing hosting |

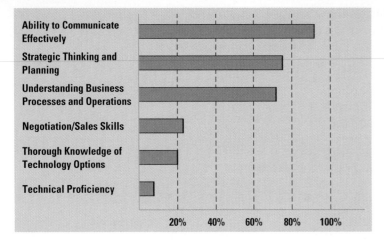

Ability to Communicate Effectively

Strategic Thinking and Planning

Understanding Business Processes and Operations

Negotiation/Sales Skills

Thorough Knowledge of Technology Options

Technical Proficiency

20%    40%    60%    80%    100%

**FIGURE 5.3**

Skills Pivotal for Success in Executive IT Roles

more technology positions in government and nonprofit organizations.

All the above IT positions and responsibilities are critical to an organization's success. While many organizations may not have a different individual for each of these positions, they must have leaders taking responsibility for all these areas of concern. The individuals responsible for enterprisewide IT and IT-related issues must provide guidance and support to the organization's employees. Figure 5.3 displays the personal skills pivotal for success in an executive IT role.

# The Gap between Business Personnel and IT Personnel

One of the greatest challenges today is effective communication between business personnel and IT personnel. Business personnel possess expertise in functional areas such as marketing, accounting, sales, and so forth. IT personnel have the technological expertise. Unfortunately, a communications gap often exists between the two. Business personnel have their own vocabularies based on their experience and expertise. IT personnel have their own vocabularies consisting of acronyms and technical terms. Effective communication between business and IT personnel should be a two-way street with each side making the effort to better understand the other (including through written and oral communication).

## IMPROVING COMMUNICATIONS

Business personnel must seek to increase their understanding of IT. Although they do not need to know every technical detail, it will benefit their careers to understand what they can and cannot accomplish using IT. Business managers and leaders should read business-oriented IT magazines, such as *InformationWeek* and *CIO,* to increase their IT knowledge.

At the same time, an organization must develop strategies for integrating its IT personnel into the various business functions. Too often, IT personnel are left out of strategy meetings because of the belief they do not understand the business so they will not add any value. That is a dangerous position to take. IT personnel must understand the business if the organization is going to determine which technologies can benefit (or hurt) the business. With a little effort to communicate, IT personnel, by providing information on the functionality available in CRM systems, might add tremendous value to a meeting about how to improve customer service. Working together, business and IT personnel have the potential to create customer-service competitive advantages.

It is the responsibility of the CIO to ensure effective communications between business and IT personnel. While the CIO assumes the responsibility on an enterprisewide level, it is also each employee's responsibility to communicate effectively on a personal level.

# Organizational Fundamentals—Ethics and Security

Ethics and security are two fundamental building blocks that organizations must base their businesses on. Such events as the Enron and Bernie Madoff scandals along with 9/11 have shed new light on the meaning of ethics and security. When the behavior of a few individuals can destroy billion-dollar organizations because of a lapse in ethics or security, the value of highly ethical and highly secure organizations should be evident. Review the Ethics and Security plug-ins to gain a detailed understanding of these topics. Due to the importance of these topics, they will be readdressed throughout this text.

# Ethics

Ian Clarke, the inventor of a file-swapping service called Freenet, decided to leave the United States for the United Kingdom, where copyright laws are more lenient. Wayne Rosso, the inventor of a file-sharing service called Grokster, left the United States for Spain, again saying goodbye to tough U.S. copyright protections. File sharing encourages a legal network of shared thinking that can improve drug research, software development, and flow of information. The United States copyright laws, designed decades before the Internet was invented, make file sharing and many other Internet technologies illegal.

The ethical issues surrounding copyright infringement and intellectual property rights are consuming the ebusiness world. Advances in technology make it easier and easier for people to copy everything from music to pictures. Technology poses new challenges for our *ethics*—the principles and standards that guide our behavior toward other people. Review Figure 5.4 for an overview of concepts, terms, and ethical issues stemming from advances in technology.

In today's electronic world, privacy has become a major ethical issue. *Privacy* is the right to be left alone when you want to be, to have control over your own personal possessions, and to not be observed without your consent. Some of the most problematic decisions organizations face lie in the murky and turbulent waters of privacy. The burden comes from the knowledge that each time employees make a decision regarding issues of privacy, the outcome could sink the company some day.

The Securities and Exchange Commission (SEC) began inquiries into Enron's accounting practices on October 22, 2001. David Duncan, the Arthur Andersen partner in charge of Enron, instructed his team to begin destroying paper and electronic Enron-related records on October 23, 2001. Kimberly Latham, a subordinate to Duncan, sent instructions on October 24, 2001, to her entire team to follow Duncan's orders and even compiled a list of computer files to delete. Arthur Andersen blames Duncan for destroying thousands of Enron-related documents. Duncan blames the Arthur Andersen attorney, Nancy Temple, for sending him a memo instructing him to destroy files. Temple blames Arthur Andersen's document deletion policies.

Regardless of who is to blame, the bigger issue is that the destruction of files after a federal investigation has begun is both unethical and illegal. A direct corporate order to destroy information currently under federal investigation poses a dilemma for any professional. Comply, and you participate in potentially criminal activities; refuse, and you might find yourself looking for a new job.

Privacy is one of the biggest ethical issues facing organizations today. Trust between companies, customers, partners, and suppliers is the support structure of

| Intellectual property | Intangible creative work that is embodied in physical form. |
| --- | --- |
| Copyright | The legal protection afforded an expression of an idea, such as a song, video game, and some types of proprietary documents. |
| Fair use doctrine | In certain situations, it is legal to use copyrighted material. |
| Pirated software | The unauthorized use, duplication, distribution, or sale of copyrighted software. |
| Counterfeit software | Software that is manufactured to look like the real thing and sold as such. |

**FIGURE** 5.4

Issues Affected by Technology Advances

**FIGURE** 5.5

Primary Reasons Privacy
Issues Reduce Trust for
Ebusiness

| | |
|---|---|
| 1. | Loss of personal privacy is a top concern for Americans in the 21st century. |
| 2. | Among Internet users, 37 percent would be "a lot" more inclined to purchase a product on a website that had a privacy policy. |
| 3. | Privacy/security is the number one factor that would convert Internet researchers into Internet buyers. |

the ebusiness world. One of the main ingredients in trust is privacy. Widespread fear about privacy continues to be one of the biggest barriers to the growth of ebusiness. People are concerned their privacy will be violated as a consequence of interactions on the web. Unless an organization can effectively address this issue of privacy, its customers, partners, and suppliers may lose trust in the organization, which hurts its business. Figure 5.5 displays the results from a *CIO* survey as to how privacy issues reduce trust for ebusiness.

## Security—How Much Will Downtime Cost Your Business?

The old business axiom "time is money" needs to be updated to more accurately reflect the crucial interdependence between IT and business processes. To reflect the times, the phrase should be "uptime is money." The leading cause of downtime is a software failure followed by human error, according to Infonetics research. Unplanned downtime can strike at any time from any number of causes, ranging from tornadoes to sink overflows to network failures to power outages. Although natural disasters may appear to be the most devastating causes of IT outages, they are hardly the most frequent or biggest threats to uptime. Figure 5.6 highlights sources of unplanned downtime.

**FIGURE** 5.6

Sources of Unplanned
Downtime

| Sources of Unplanned Downtime | | |
|---|---|---|
| Bomb threat | Hacker | Snowstorm |
| Burst pipe | Hail | Sprinkler malfunction |
| Chemical spill | Hurricane | Static electricity |
| Construction | Ice storm | Strike |
| Corrupted data | Insects | Terrorism |
| Earthquake | Lightning | Theft |
| Electrical short | Network failure | Tornado |
| Epidemic | Plane crash | Train derailment |
| Equipment failure | Frozen pipe | Smoke damage |
| Evacuation | Power outage | Vandalism |
| Explosion | Power surge | Vehicle crash |
| Fire | Rodents | Virus |
| Flood | Sabotage | Water damage (various) |
| Fraud | Shredded data | Wind |

FIGURE 5.7

The Cost of Downtime

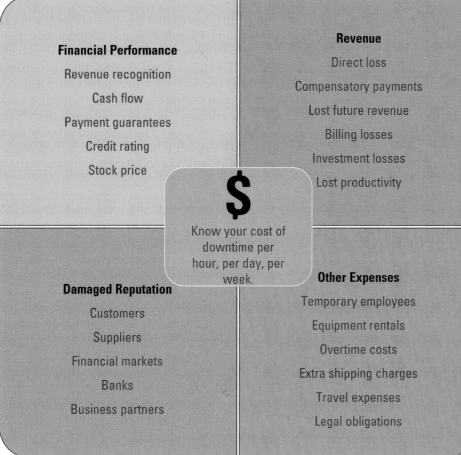

According to Gartner Group, on average, enterprises lose $108,000 of revenue every hour their IT infrastructure is down. Figure 5.7 displays the four categories of costs associated with downtime, according to the Gartner Group. A few questions companies should ask when determining the cost of downtime include:

- How many transactions can the company afford to lose without significantly impacting business?
- Does the company depend upon one or more mission-critical applications to conduct business?
- How much revenue will the company lose for every hour a critical application is unavailable?
- What is the productivity cost associated with each hour of downtime?
- How will collaborative business processes with partners, suppliers, and customers be affected by an unexpected IT outage?
- What is the total cost of lost productivity and lost revenue during unplanned downtime?

The reliability and resilience of IT systems have never been more essential for success as businesses cope with the forces of globalization, 24 × 7 operations, government and trade regulations, and overextended IT budgets and resources. Any unexpected IT downtime in today's business environment has the potential to cause both short- and long-term costs with far-reaching consequences. Understanding information security's role in a business is critical to keeping downtime to a minimum and uptime to a maximum.

## PROTECTING INTELLECTUAL ASSETS

Smoking is not just bad for a person's health; it seems that it is also bad for company security, according to a new study. With companies banning smoking inside their offices, smokers are forced outside—usually to specific smoking areas in the back of the building. The doors leading out to them are a major security hole, according to a study undertaken by NTA Monitor Ltd., a U.K.-based Internet security tester.

NTA's tester was able to easily get inside a corporate building through a back door that was left open so smokers could easily and quickly get out and then back in, according to the company. Once inside, the tester asked an employee to take him to a meeting room, claiming that the IT department had sent him. Even without a pass, he reportedly gained access unchallenged and was then able to connect his laptop to the company's network.

Organizational information is intellectual capital. Just as organizations protect their assets—keeping their money in an insured bank or providing a safe working environment for employees—they must also protect their intellectual capital. An organization's intellectual capital includes everything from its patents to its transactional and analytical information. With security breaches on the rise and computer hackers everywhere, an organization must put in place strong security measures to survive.

The Health Insurance Portability and Accountability Act (HIPAA) protects the privacy and security of personal health records and has the potential to impact every business in the United States. HIPAA affects all companies that use electronic data interchange (EDI) to communicate personal health records. HIPAA requires health care organizations to develop, implement, and maintain appropriate security measures when sending electronic health information. Most important, these organizations must document and keep current records detailing how they are performing security measures for all transmissions of health information. On April 21, 2005, security rules for HIPAA became enforceable by law.

According to recent Gartner polls, less than 10 percent of all health care organizations have begun to implement the security policies and procedures required by HIPAA. The Health Information Management Society estimates that 70 percent of all health care providers failed to meet the April 2005 deadline for privacy rule compliance. Health care organizations need to start taking HIPAA regulations seriously since noncompliance can result in substantial fines and even imprisonment.

Beyond the health care industry, all businesses must understand the importance of information security, even if it is not enforceable by law. *Information security* is a broad term encompassing the protection of information from accidental or intentional misuse by persons inside or outside an organization. With current advances in technologies and business strategies such as CRM, organizations are able to determine valuable information—such as who are the top 20 percent of their customers who produce 80 percent of their revenues. Most organizations view this type of information as valuable intellectual capital, and they are implementing security measures to prevent the information from walking out the door or falling into the wrong hands.

Adding to the complexity of information security is the fact that organizations must enable employees, customers, and partners to access all sorts of information electronically to be successful. Doing business electronically automatically creates tremendous information security risks for organizations. There are many technical aspects of security, but the biggest information security issue is not technical, but human. Most information security breaches result from people misusing an organization's information either intentionally or inadvertently. For example, many individuals freely give up their passwords or leave them on sticky notes next to their computers, leaving the door wide open to intruders.

Figure 5.8 displays the typical size of an organization's information security budget relative to the organization's overall IT budget from the CSI/FBI Computer Crime and Security Survey. Forty-six percent of respondents indicated that their

**Percentage of IT Budget Spent on Information Security**

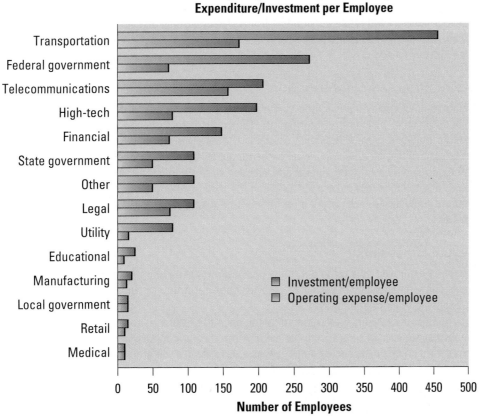

**FIGURE** 5.8

Organizational Spending
on Information Security

organization spent between 1 and 5 percent of the total IT budget on security. Only 16 percent indicated that their organization spent less than 1 percent of the IT budget on security.

Figure 5.9 displays the spending per employee on computer security broken down by both public and private industries. The highest average computer security investment per employee was found in the transportation industry.

Security is perhaps the most fundamental and critical of all the technologies/disciplines an organization must have squarely in place to execute its business strategy. Without solid security processes and procedures, none of the other technologies can develop business advantages.

**Average Reported Computer Security
Expenditure/Investment per Employee**

**FIGURE** 5.9

Computer Security
Expenditures/Investments
by Industry

1. Predict what might have happened to Apple if its top executives had not supported investments in IT.

2. Explain why it would be unethical for Apple to allow its customers to download free music from iTunes.

3. Evaluate the effects on Apple's business if it failed to secure its customer information and all of it was accidentally posted to an anonymous website.

4. Explain why Apple should have a CIO, CTO, CPO, CSO, and CKO.

## Chapter Five Case: Executive Dilemmas in the Information Age

The vast array of business initiatives from supply chain management, to customer relationship management, business process reengineering, and enterprise resource planning makes it clear that information technology has evolved beyond the role of mere infrastructure to the support of business strategy. Today, in more and more industries, IT is a business strategy and is quickly becoming a survival issue.

Board and executive team agendas are increasingly peppered with, or even hijacked by, a growing range of IT issues from compliance to ethics and security. In most companies today, computers are key business tools. They generate, process, and store the majority of critical business information. Executives must understand how IT can affect a business by successfully addressing a wide range of needs—from large electronic discovery projects to the online review of document collections by geographically dispersed teams. A few examples of executive IT issues follow.

### Stolen Proprietary Information

A computer company investigated to determine if an executive who accepted a job with a competitor stole proprietary information. The hard drive from the executive's laptop and desktop machine were forensically imaged. The analysis established that the night before the executive left, he downloaded all of the company's process specifications and distributor agreements, which he then zipped and emailed to the competitor. Additionally, reconstruction of deleted files located emails between the executive and the competitor discussing his intent to provide the proprietary information if he was offered additional options in the new company.

### Sexual Harassment

A woman employed by a large defense contractor accused her supervisor of sexual harassment. The woman was fired from her job for poor performance and subsequently sued her ex-boss and the former employer.

A computer company was retained by the plaintiff's attorneys to investigate allegations of the former supervisor's harassing behavior. After making a forensic image backup of the ex-boss's hard drive, the forensic company was able to recover deleted electronic messages that showed the ex-boss had a history of propositioning women under his supervision for "special favors." A situation that might have been mired in a "he said/she said" controversy was quickly resolved; the woman got her job back, and the real culprit was terminated.

## Stolen Trade Secrets

The board of directors of a technical research company demoted the company's founder and CEO. The executive, disgruntled because of his demotion, was later terminated. It was subsequently determined that the executive had planned to quit about the same time he was fired and establish a competitive company. Upon his termination, the executive took home two computers; he returned them to the company four days later, along with another company computer that he had previously used at home. Suspicious that critical information had been taken, the company's attorneys sent the computers to a computer forensic company for examination.

After making a forensic image backup of the hard drives, the forensic analysis identified a file directory that had been deleted during the aforementioned four-day period that had the same name as the competing company the executive had established. A specific search of the deleted files in this directory identified the executive's "to do list" file. This file indicated the executive planned to copy the company's database (valued at $100 million) for his personal use. Another item specified the executive was to "learn how to destroy evidence on a computer."

The computer forensic company's examination also proved that the executive had been communicating with other competing companies to establish alliances, in violation of the executive's nondisclosure agreement with the company. It was also shown that numerous key company files were located on removable computer storage media that had not been turned over by the executive to the company.

## Questions

1. Explain why understanding technology, especially in the areas of security and ethics, is important for a CEO. How do a CEO's actions affect the organizational culture?

2. Identify why executives in nontechnological industries need to worry about technology and its potential business ramifications.

3. Describe why continuously learning about technology allows an executive to better analyze threats and opportunities.

4. Identify three things that a CTO, CPO, or CSO could do to prevent the above issues.

U nderstanding and working with technology have become an integral part of life in the 21st century. Most students take courses in various disciplines in their educational careers, such as in marketing, operations management, management, finance, accounting, and information technology, each of which is designed to provide insight into the tasks of each functional area. In the business world, these are all intertwined and inextricably linked.

Information technology can be an important enabler of business success and innovation and is most useful when it leverages the talents of people. Technology in and of itself is not useful unless the right people know how to use and manage it effectively.

Organizations use information technology to capture, process, organize, distribute, and massage information. Information technology enables an organization to:

- Integrate all functional areas and the tasks they perform.

- Gain an enterprisewide view of its operations.

- Efficiently and effectively utilize resources.

- Realize tremendous market and industry growth by gaining insight into the market at large (through environmental scanning) and insight into internal operations.

★ **KEY TERMS**

Balanced scorecard,   42
Benchmark,   37
Benchmarking,   37
Business intelligence,   11
Business process,   21, 30
Business process
   reengineering (BPR),   30
Buyer power,   17
Chief information officer
   (CIO),   46
Chief knowledge officer
   (CKO),   47
Chief privacy officer
   (CPO),   47
Chief security officer
   (CSO),   47
Chief technology officer
   (CTO),   47
Competitive advantage,   16
Copyright,   49
Counterfeit software,   49

Customer relationship
   management (CRM),   28
Data,   10
Effectiveness IT metrics,   37
Efficiency IT metrics,   37
Enterprise resource planning
   (ERP),   31
Entry barrier,   19
Environmental scanning,   16
Ethics,   49
Fair use doctrine,   49
First-mover advantage,   16
Five Forces Model,   17
Information,   10
Information accuracy,   38
Information security,   52
Information technology (IT),   9
Intellectual property,   49
Key performance indicator
   (KPI),   37
Loyalty program,   18

Management information
   systems (MIS), 9
Pirated software,   49
Privacy,   49
Product differentiation,   19
Response time,   38
Rivalry among existing
   competitors,   19
Supplier power,   18
Supply chain,   18
Supply chain management
   (SCM),   26
System availability,   38
Switching cost,   17
Threat of new entrants,   19
Threat of substitute products or
   services,   18
Throughput,   38
Transaction speed,   38
Value chain,   21
Web traffic,   38

## Major League Baseball–The Real Competitive Advantages

The bases are empty and the game is tied as Jayson Werth steps into the batter's box at the end of the eighth inning for the Philadelphia Phillies. Werth, the right fielder, faces Steven Shell, relief pitcher for the Washington Nationals. On Shell's fourth pitch, he leaves a sluggish curveball hanging over the plate. Werth smashes it into the stands for a game-winning home run.

As the stadium goes wild, an incredibly sophisticated information system swings into action as 60 people in a downtown Manhattan office begin slicing and dicing the video of Werth's home run. The clips are sent to thousands of computers and cell phones around the world and a few minutes after the hit a commuter on the local train to Philadelphia's Main Line watches it for free on his cell phone and stadium visitors quickly learn that Shell's pitch was a mere 74 miles per hour and that it broke 14 inches.

The brains behind the business is the Major League Baseball Advanced Media (MLBAM), which generates around $450 million a year. Fifty percent of MLBAM's revenues come from fans who pay $120 a season to watch games live over the Internet and the remainder is generated from advertising next to its online content. The business has grown into a significant revenue source for Major League Baseball, which has total revenues of about $6 billion. "They have a passionate base that they went after in a smart way," says Bobby Tulsiani, analyst with the market research firm JupiterResearch.

MLBAM's strategy is enlightening for other sports franchises and, undeniably, for other companies in the online content business. While most leagues limit what they put on the web and avoid streaming live video online out of fear that their television ratings could be hurt, MLB's experience suggests that such concerns might be misplaced. "Rights fees are up, attendance is up, viewership is up," says Bob Bowman, chief executive at MLBAM. "Somehow the strategy of putting [baseball games] on every device that has a plug or a battery has worked for the business partners. Even more important, it's worked for our fans."

## Staggering Amount of Stats

The biggest draw for fans to MLBAM's online content is the amount of information the company provides that is unavailable anywhere else or on any other type of device. Without the online content fans simply would not know that Werth's home run came on Shell's 18th pitch of the evening or that his first and third pitches to Werth were both 89 mph fastballs, while the fateful curveball was 15 mph slower.

One pitfall is that a truly obsessive fan could easily become lost in so much data including clips of each major event in the league's games this season, statistics on how particular players have done against a starting pitcher, and final standings for every season back to 2001. "It's much more than what you can get on television," says Jupiter's Tulsiani. "It taps into the base by offering multiple camera angles, stats, and on-demand video."

MLBAM's New York offices are like an adolescent's idea of a dream job. On one recent summer day, dozens of workers sat at desks watching hour after hour of baseball live. There was a flurry of activity when something important happened in a game, like Werth's homer or a crucial strikeout.

## Generating Revenue

MLBAM's primary competitive advantage lies in the unique video editing information system it created that allows employees to produce highlights in just a few minutes, which is important because the group is sending out about 200 highlights a day during the regular season. The system works by playing each game on a computer in a small window and as soon as something important happens, an MLBAM employee rewinds the game in the computer and marks, then saves, the highlight. It is then passed along through two supervisors who send the highlight out over the Internet to thousands of paying customers.

"The program took about two months to make," says MLBAM's Joe Inzerillo, senior vice president for multimedia and distribution. Would MLBAM ever consider licensing its program? "We've had inquiries about people wanting to buy the program, but it is so tethered to our back end that we'd have to address compatibility issues. It's unlikely it would make sense to sell it."

Instead, the company uses its technological competitive advantages to work with other sports. This year the NCAA paid between six and seven figures to run its live streaming of the men's college basketball tournament through MLBAM's servers. They also run Major League Soccer's web operation. MLBAM thinks it is unlikely other sports will want to swallow their pride and ask baseball to run their Internet operations.

## Big Revenue Opportunity

MLBAM sees mobile phones as the next big revenue opportunity. It is already creating customized applications for a number of phones, including BlackBerries and iPhones, allowing customers to tap into the statistics from the Gameday website. "The one device we all rely on is our cell phone," says Bowman. "It is with us, sadly perhaps, as many as 24 hours a day." As technology continues to improve, and streaming video becomes more portable on all devices, some fear television will disappear. It will be interesting to see how the future for MLBAM unfolds.

## Questions

1. Using Porter's Five Forces Model, analyze MLBAM's buyer power and supplier power. What could MLBAM do to increase customer loyalty?
2. Which of Porter's three generic strategies is MLBAM following?
3. How can MLBAM use efficiency IT metrics and effectiveness IT metrics to improve its business?
4. Predict what might happen to MLBAM if it failed to secure its subscriber information and all personal information—including credit card numbers—was accidentally posted to an anonymous website.
5. How could MLBAM use a customer relationship management system to improve revenue growth?

## Business 2.0: Bad Business Decisions

*Business 2.0* magazine looked at the top 100 bad business decisions of all time including bungled layoffs, customer-service snafus, executive follies, and other madness. Five of the top 10 bad business decisions of all time were made because business personnel did not understand information technology; these five are highlighted below. Perhaps one good reason to pay attention in this course is so that you will not end up on *Business 2.0*'s bad business decisions!

## Bad Business Decision 3 of 10: Starbucks

### Winner: Dumbest Moment—Marketing

Starbucks directs baristas in the southeastern United States to email a coupon for a free iced coffee to friends and family members. But email knows no geographic boundaries and, worse, can be printed repeatedly.

After the email spreads to every corner of the country and is reproduced en masse, Starbucks yanks the offer, leading disgruntled customer Kelly Coakley to file a $114 million class-action lawsuit.

## Bad Business Decision 4 of 10: Radioshack

### Winner: Dumbest Moment—Human Resources

*From: RadioShack*
*To: RadioShack employees*
*Subject: Your former job*
RadioShack fires 400 staffers via email. Affected employees receive a message that reads, "The work force reduction notification is currently in progress. Unfortunately your position is one that has been eliminated."

## Bad Business Decision 7 of 10: AOL

### Winner: Dumbest Moment—Data Security

In an "attempt to reach out to the academic community with new research tools," AOL releases the search queries of 657,000 users.

Though AOL insists that the information contains no personally identifiable data, *The New York Times* and other news outlets promptly identify a number of specific users, including searcher No. 4417749, soon-to-be-ex-AOL-subscriber Thelma Arnold of Lilburn, Georgia, whose queries include "women's underwear" and "dog that urinates on everything."

The gaffe leads to the resignation of AOL's chief technology officer and a half-billion-dollar class-action lawsuit.

### Bad Business Decision 8 of 10: UCLA

#### Winner: Dumbest Moment—Ecommerce

On the morning of April 3, 2006, Amazon.com sends an email headed "UCLA Wins!" to virtually everyone to whom it has ever sold a sports-related item, attempting to hawk a cap celebrating the Bruins' stirring victory in college basketball's championship game.

Just one problem: The game isn't scheduled to be played until later that night. When it is, UCLA is trounced by Florida, 73–57.

### Bad Business Decision 9 of 10: Bank of America

#### Winner: Dumbest Moment—Outsourcing

After Bank of America announces plans to outsource 100 tech support jobs from the San Francisco Bay Area to India, the American workers are told that they must train their own replacements in order to receive their severance payments.

Here are a few other bad ones that did not make the top 10, but are worth mentioning.

### Bad Business Decision: McDonald's

Guess the translator took the phrase "viral marketing" a bit too literally. McDonald's runs a promotional contest in Japan in which it gives away 10,000 Mickey D's-branded MP3 players.

The gadgets come preloaded with 10 songs—and, in some cases, a version of the QQPass family of Trojan horse viruses, which, when uploaded to a PC, seek to capture passwords, user names, and other data and then forward them to hackers.

### Bad Business Decision: General Motors

Then again, viral marketing can be messed up in English too. As part of a cross promotion with the NBCTV show *The Apprentice,* GM launches a contest to promote its Chevy Tahoe SUV. At Chevyapprentice.com, viewers are given video and music clips with which to create their own 30-second commercials.

Among the new Tahoe ads that soon proliferate across the web are ones with taglines like "Yesterday's technology today" and "Global warming isn't a pretty SUV ad—it's a frightening reality."

### Bad Business Decision: New York Times Company

We were wondering how Billy the paperboy could afford that gold-plated Huffy. News carriers and retailers in Worcester, Massachusetts, get an unexpected bonus with their usual shipment of the *Telegram & Gazette:* the credit and debit card numbers of 240,000 subscribers to the paper and its sister publication, the *Boston Globe,* both owned by the New York Times Co.

The security breach is the result of a recycling program in which paper from the *Telegram & Gazette*'s business office is reused to wrap bundles of newspapers.

### Bad Business Decision: Sony

PC-B-Q. Defects in batteries made by Sony for portable computing cause a handful of notebooks to burst into spectacularly photogenic flames.

The end result is the biggest computer-related recall ever, as Dell replaces the batteries in more than 4 million laptops. In short order, Apple (1.8 million), Lenovo/IBM (500,000), and others do the same.

### QUESTION

1. Explain why understanding information technology and management information systems can help you achieve business success—or more importantly, help you avoid business disasters—regardless of your major.

## 1. Competitive Analysis

Cheryl O'Connell is the owner of a small, high-end retailer of women's clothing called Excelus. Excelus's business has been successful for many years, largely because of Cheryl's ability to anticipate the needs and wants of her loyal customer base and provide them with personalized service. Cheryl does not see any value in IT and does not want to invest any capital in something that will not directly affect her bottom line. Develop a proposal describing the potential IT-enabled competitive opportunities or threats Cheryl might be missing by not embracing IT. Be sure to include a Porter's Five Forces analysis and discuss which one of the three generic strategies Cheryl should pursue.

## 2. Using Efficiency and Effectiveness Metrics

You are the CEO of a 500-bed acute care general hospital. Your internal IT department is responsible for running applications that support both administrative functions (e.g., patient accounting) as well as medical applications (e.g., medical records). You need assurance that your IT department is a high quality operation in comparison to similar hospitals. What metrics should you ask your CIO to provide you to give the assurance you seek? Provide the reasoning behind each suggested metric. Also, determine how the interrelationship between efficiency metrics and effectiveness metrics can drive your business's success.

## 3. Building Business Relationships

Synergistics Inc. is a start-up company that specializes in helping businesses build successful internal relationships. You have recently been promoted to senior manager of the Business and IT Relationship area. Sales for your new department have dwindled over the last two years for a variety of reasons including the burst of the technological stock bubble, recent economic conditions, and a poorly communicated business strategy. Your first task on the job is to prepare a report detailing the following:

■ Fundamental reasons for the gap between the IT and business sides.

■ Strategies you can take to convince your customers that this is an area that is critical to the success of their business.

■ Strategies your customers can follow to ensure that synergies exist between the two sides.

## 4. Acting Ethically

Assume you are an IT manager and one of your projects is failing. You were against the project from the start; however, the project had powerful sponsorship from all of the top executives. You know that you are doomed and that the project is doomed. The reasons for the failure are numerous including the initial budget was drastically understated, the technology is evolving and not stable, the architecture was never scaled for growth, and your resources do not have the necessary development skills for the new technology. One of your team leads has come to you with a plan to sabotage the project that would put the project out of its misery without assigning any blame to the individuals on the project. Create a document detailing how you would handle this situation.

## 5. Determining IT Organizational Structures

You are the chief executive officer for a start-up telecommunications company. The company currently has 50 employees and plans to ramp up to 3,000 by the end of the year. Your first task is to determine how you are going to model your organization. You decide to address the IT department's organizational structure first. You need to consider if you want to have a CIO, CPO, CSO, CTO, and CKO, and if so, what their reporting structure will look like and why. You also need to determine the different roles and responsibilities for each executive position. Once you have compiled this information, put together a presentation describing your IT department's organizational structure.

### 6. Comparing CRM Vendors

As a team, search the Internet for at least one recent and authoritative article that compares or ranks customer relationship management systems. Select two packages from the list and compare their functions and features as described in the article(s) you found as well as on each company's website. Find references in the literature where companies that are using each package have reported their experiences, both good and bad. Draw on any other comparisons you can find. Prepare a presentation for delivery in class on the strengths and weaknesses of each package, which one you favor, and why.

### 7. Applying the Three Generic Strategies

The unit discussed examples of companies that pursue differentiated strategies so that they are not forced into positions where they must compete solely on the basis of price. Pick an industry and have your team members find and compare two companies, one that is competing on the basis of price and another that has chosen to pursue a differentiated strategy enabled by the creative use of IT. Some industries you may want to consider are clothing retailers, grocery stores, airlines, and personal computers. Prepare a presentation for the class on the ways that IT is being used to help the differentiating company compete against the low-cost provider. Before you begin, spend some class time to make sure each team selects a different industry if at all possible.

### 8. The Five Forces Model

Your team is working for a small investment company that specializes in technology investments. A new company, Geyser, has just released an operating system that plans to compete with Microsoft's operating systems. Your company has a significant amount of capital invested in Microsoft. Your boss, Jan Savage, has asked you to compile a Porter's Five Forces analysis for Microsoft to ensure that your company's Microsoft investment is not at risk.

---

## ★ APPLY YOUR KNOWLEDGE

### 1. Capitalizing on Your Career

Business leaders need to be involved in information technology—any computer-based tool that people use to work with information and support the information and information-processing needs of an organization—for the following (primary) reasons:

- The sheer magnitude of the dollars spent on IT must be managed to ensure business value.

- Research has consistently shown that when business leaders are involved in information technology, it enables a number of business initiatives, such as gaining a competitive advantage, streamlining business processes, and even transforming entire organizations.

- Research has consistently shown that when business leaders are not involved in IT, systems fail, revenue is lost, and even entire companies can fail as a result of poorly managed IT.

One of the biggest challenges facing organizations is, "How do we get general business leaders involved in IT?" Research has shown that involvement is highly correlated with personal experience with IT and IT education, including university classes and IT executive seminars. Once general business leaders understand IT through experience and education, they are more likely to be involved in IT, and more likely to lead their organizations in achieving business success through IT.

### Project Focus

1. Search the Internet to find examples of the types of technologies that are currently used in the field or industry that you plan to pursue. For example, if you are planning on a career in accounting or finance, you should become familiar with financial systems such as Oracle Financials. If you are planning a career in logistics or distribution, you should research supply chain management systems. If you are planning a career in marketing, you should research customer relationship management systems, blogs, and emarketing.
2. IT is described as an enabler/facilitator of competitive advantage, organizational effectiveness, and organizational efficiency. As a competitive tool, IT can differentiate an organization's products, services, and prices from its competitors by improving product quality, shortening product development or delivery time, creating new IT-based products and services, and improving customer service before, during, and after a transaction. Search the Internet and find several examples of companies in the industry where you plan to work that have achieved a competitive advantage through IT.
3. Create a simple report of your findings; include a brief overview of the type of technologies you found and how organizations are using them to achieve a competitive advantage.

## 2. Achieving Alignment

Most companies would like to be in the market-leading position of JetBlue, Dell, or Wal-Mart, all of which have used information technology to secure their respective spots in the marketplace. These companies have a relentless goal of keeping the cost of technology down by combining the best of IT and business leadership.

It takes more than a simple handshake between groups to start on the journey toward financial gains; it requires operational discipline and a linkage between business and technology units. Only recently have companies not on the "path for profits" followed the lead of their successful counterparts, requiring more operational discipline from their IT groups as well as more IT participation from their business units. Bridging this gap is one of the greatest breakthroughs a company can make.

Companies that master the art of finely tuned, cost-effective IT management will have a major advantage. Their success will force their competitors to also master the art or fail miserably. This phenomenon has already occurred in the retail and wholesale distribution markets, which have had to react to Wal-Mart's IT mastery, as one example. Other industries will follow. This trend will change not only the face of IT, but also the future of corporate America.

As world markets continue to grow, the potential gains are greater than ever. However, so are the potential losses. The future belongs to those who are perceptive enough to grasp the significance of IT and resourceful enough to synchronize business management and information technology.

### Project Focus

1. Use any resource to answer the question, "Why is business-IT alignment so difficult?" Use the following questions to begin your analysis:
   a. How do companies prioritize the demands of various business units as they relate to IT?
   b. What are some of the greatest IT challenges for the coming year?

    *c.* What drives IT decisions?

    *d.* Who or what is the moving force behind IT decisions?

    *e.* What types of efficiency metrics and effectiveness metrics might these companies use to measure the impact of IT?

    *f.* How can a company use financial metrics to monitor and measure IT investments?

    *g.* What are some of the issues with using financial metrics to evaluate IT?

## 3. Market Dissection

To illustrate the use of the three generic strategies, consider Figure AYK.1. The matrix shown demonstrates the relationships among strategies (cost leadership versus differentiation) and market segmentation (broad versus focused).

- Hyundai is following a broad cost leadership strategy. Hyundai offers low-cost vehicles, in each particular model stratification, that appeal to a large audience.

- Audi is pursuing a broad differentiation strategy with its Quattro models available at several price points. Audi's differentiation is safety and it prices its various Quattro models (higher than Hyundai) to reach a large, stratified audience.

- Kia has a more focused cost leadership strategy. Kia mainly offers low-cost vehicles in the lower levels of model stratification.

- Hummer offers the most focused differentiation strategy of any in the industry (including Mercedes-Benz).

### Project Focus

Create a similar graph displaying each strategy for a product of your choice. The strategy must include an example of the product in each of the following markets: (1) cost leadership, broad market, (2) differentiation, broad market, (3) cost leadership, focused market, and (4) differentiation, focused market. Potential products include:

**FIGURE** AYK.1

Porter's Three Generic Strategies

- Cereal
- Dog food
- Soft drinks

Cost Leadership strategy        Differentiation strategy

Broad market

Focused market

- Computers
- Shampoo
- Snack foods
- Jeans
- Sneakers
- Sandals
- Mountain bikes
- TV shows
- Movies

## 4. Grading Security

Making The Grade is a nonprofit organization that helps students learn how to achieve better grades in school. The organization has 40 offices in 25 states and more than 2,000 employees. The company wants to build a website to offer its services online. Making The Grade's online services will provide parents seven key pieces of advice for communicating with their children to help them achieve academic success. The website will offer information on how to maintain open lines of communication, set goals, organize academics, regularly track progress, identify trouble spots, get to know their child's teacher, and celebrate their children's successes.

### Project Focus

You and your team work for the director of information security. Your team's assignment is to develop a document discussing the importance of creating information security polices and an information security plan. Be sure to include the following:

- The importance of educating employees on information security.
- A few samples of employee information security policies specifically for Making The Grade.
- Other major areas the information security plan should address.
- Signs the company should look for to determine if the website is being hacked.
- The major types of attacks the company should expect to experience.

## 5. Eyes Everywhere

The movie *Minority Report* chronicled a futuristic world where people are uniquely identifiable by their eyes. A scan of each person's eyes gives or denies them access to rooms, computers, and anything else with restrictions. The movie portrayed a black market in new eyeballs to help people hide from the authorities. (Why did they not just change the database entry instead? That would have been much easier, but a lot less dramatic.)

The idea of using a biological signature is entirely plausible since biometrics is currently being widely used and is expected to gain wider acceptance in the near future because forging documents has become much easier with the advances in computer graphics programs and color printers. The next time you get a new passport, it may incorporate a chip that has your biometric information encoded on it. Office of Special Investigations agents with fake documents found that it was relatively easy to enter the United States from Canada, Mexico, and Jamaica, by land, sea, and air.

The task of policing the borders is daunting. Some 500 million foreigners enter the country every year and go through identity checkpoints. More than 13 million permanent-resident and border-crossing cards have been issued by the U.S. government. Also, citizens of 27 countries do not need visas to enter this country. They are expected to have passports that comply with U.S. specifications that will also be readable at the border.

In the post-9/11 atmosphere of tightened security, unrestricted border crossing is not acceptable. The Department of Homeland Security is charged with securing the nation's borders, and as part of this plan, new entry/exit procedures were instituted at the beginning of 2003. An integrated system, using biometrics, will be used to identify foreign visitors to the United States and reduce the likelihood of terrorists entering the country.

Early in 2003, after 6 million biometric border-crossing cards had been issued, a pilot test conducted at the Canadian border detected more than 250 imposters. The testing started with two biometric identifiers: photographs for facial recognition and fingerprint scans. As people enter and leave the country, their actual fingerprints and facial features are compared to the data on the biometric chip in the passport.

## Project Focus

In a group, discuss the following:

1. How do you feel about having your fingerprints, facial features, and perhaps more of your biometric features encoded in documents like your passport? Explain your answer.
2. Would you feel the same way about having biometric information on your driver's license as on your passport? Why or why not?
3. Is it reasonable to have different biometric identification requirements for visitors from different nations? Explain your answer. What would you recommend as criteria for deciding which countries fall into what categories?
4. The checkpoints U.S. citizens pass through upon returning to the country vary greatly in the depth of the checks and the time spent. The simplest involves simply walking past the border guards who may or may not ask you your citizenship. The other end of the spectrum requires that you put up with long waits in airports where you have to line up with hundreds of other passengers while each person is questioned and must produce a passport to be scanned. Would you welcome biometric information on passports if it would speed the process, or do you think that the disadvantages of the reduction in privacy, caused by biometric information, outweigh the advantages of better security and faster border processing? Explain your answer.

## 6. Setting Boundaries

Even the most ethical people sometimes face difficult choices. Acting ethically means behaving in a principled fashion and treating other people with respect and dignity. It is simple to say, but not so simple to do since some situations are complex or ambiguous. The important role of ethics in our lives has long been recognized. As far back as 44 B.C., Cicero said that ethics are indispensable to anyone who wants to have a good career. Having said that, Cicero, along with some of the greatest minds over the centuries, struggled with what the rules of ethics should be.

Our ethics are rooted in our history, culture, and religion, and our sense of ethics may shift over time. The electronic age brings with it a new dimension in the ethics debate—the amount of personal information that we can collect and store, and the speed with which we can access and process that information.

## Project Focus

In a group, discuss how you would react to the following situations:

1. A senior marketing manager informs you that one of her employees is looking for another job and she wants you to give her access to look through her email.
2. A vice president of sales informs you that he has made a deal to provide customer information to a strategic partner, and he wants you to burn all of the customer information onto a DVD.

3. You are asked to monitor your employee's email to discover if he is sexually harassing another employee.

4. You are asked to install a video surveillance system in your office to watch if employees are taking office supplies home with them.

5. You are looking on the shared network drive and discover that your boss's entire hard drive has been copied to the network for everyone to view. What do you do?

6. You have been accidentally copied on an email from the CEO, which details who will be the targets of the next round of layoffs. What would you do?

## 7. Porter's Five Forces

Porter's Five Forces Model is an easy framework with which to understand market forces. Break into groups and choose two products from the list below on which to perform a Porter's Five Forces analysis.

- Laptop computer and desktop computer.
- PDA and laptop computer.
- iPod and Walkman.
- DVD player and VCR player.
- Digital camera and Polaroid camera.
- Cell phone and Blackberry PDA.
- Coca-Cola plastic bottle and Coca-Cola glass bottle.
- GPS device and a road atlas.
- Roller skates and Rollerblades.
- Digital books and printed books.
- Digital paper and paper.

## 8. Measuring Efficiency and Effectiveness

In a group, create a plan to measure the efficiency and effectiveness of this course and recommendations on how you could improve the course to make it more efficient and more effective. You must determine ways to benchmark current efficiency and effectiveness and ways to continuously monitor and measure against the benchmarks to determine if the course is becoming more or less efficient and effective (class quizzes and exams are the most obvious benchmarks). Be sure your plan addresses the following:

- Design of the classroom.
- Room temperature.
- Lighting and electronic capabilities of the classroom.
- Technology available in the classroom.
- Length of class.
- Email and instant messaging.
- Students' attendance.
- Students' preparation.
- Students' arrival time.
- Quizzes and exams (frequency, length, grades).

### 9. Discovering Reengineering Opportunities

In an effort to increase efficiency, your college has hired you to analyze its current business processes for registering for classes. Analyze the current business processes from paying tuition to registering for classes and determine which steps in the process are:

- Broken
- Redundant
- Antiquated

Be sure to define how you would reengineer the processes for efficiency.

### 10. Reorganizing an Organization

The AAA Management Company specializes in the management of rental properties and generates over $20 million in revenues each year and has more than 2,000 employees throughout the United States, Canada, and Mexico. The company has just hired a new CEO, David Paul. David is planning to reorganize the company so that it operates more efficiently and effectively. Next is the new organizational structure that he plans to present to the board of directors on Monday. Break into groups and explain the advantages and disadvantages of such a reporting structure. Reorganize the reporting structure in the way that will be most beneficial to the operations of the company, being sure to justify the new structure.

### 11. Contemplating Sharing

Bram Cohen is the creator of one of the most successful peer-to-peer (P2P) programs ever developed, BitTorrent. BitTorrent allows users to quickly upload and download

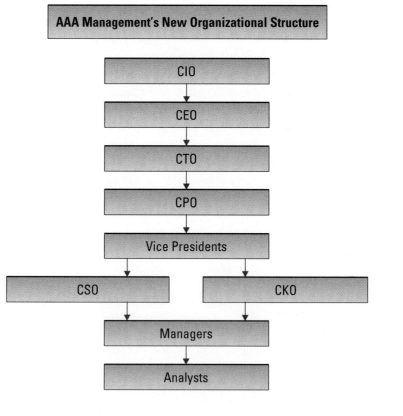

**AAA Management's New Organizational Structure**

CIO

CEO

CTO

CPO

Vice Presidents

CSO          CKO

Managers

Analysts

enormous amounts of data, including files that are hundreds or thousands of times bigger than a single MP3. BitTorrent's program is faster and more efficient than traditional P2P networking.

Cohen showed his code to the world at a hacker conference, as a free, open source project aimed at computer users who need a cheap way to swap software online. But the real audience turns out to be TV and movie fanatics. It takes hours to download a ripped episode of *Alias* or *Monk* off Kazaa, but BitTorrent can do it in minutes. As a result, more than 20 million people have downloaded the BitTorrent application. If any one of them misses a favorite TV show, no worries. Surely, someone has posted it as a "torrent." As for movies, if you can find it at Blockbuster, you can probably find it online somewhere—and use BitTorrent to download it. "Give and ye shall receive" became Cohen's motto, which he printed on T-shirts and sold to supporters.

### Project Focus

There is much debate surrounding the ethics of peer-to-peer networking. Do you believe BitTorrent is ethical or unethical? Justify your answer.

## ★ BUSINESS DRIVEN BEST SELLERS

### *Why Most Things Fail: Evolution, Extinction, and Economics.* By Paul Ormerod (John Wiley and Sons, 2005).

Failure is the most fundamental feature of biological, social, and economic systems. Just as species fail—and become extinct—so do companies, brands, and public policies. And while failure may be hard to handle, understanding the pervasive nature of failure in the world of human societies and economies is essential for those looking to succeed. Linking economic models with models of biological evolution, *Why Most Things Fail* identifies the subtle patterns that comprise the apparent disorder of failure and analyzes why failure arises. Throughout the book, author Paul Ormerod exposes the flaws in some of today's most basic economic assumptions, and examines how professionals in both business and government can help their organizations survive and thrive in a world that has become too complex. Along the way, Ormerod discusses how the Iron Law of Failure applies to business and government and reveals how you can achieve optimal social and economic outcomes by properly adapting to a world characterized by constant change, evolution, and disequilibrium. Filled with in-depth insight, expert advice, and illustrative examples, *Why Most Things Fail* will show you why failure is so common and what you can do to become one of the few who succeed.

### *Reengineering the Corporation.* By Michael Hammer and James Champy (Harper-Collins Publishing, 2003).

Business process reengineering reached its heyday in the early 1990s when Michael Hammer and James Champy published their best-selling book, *Reengineering the Corporation.* The authors promoted the idea that radical redesign and reorganization of an enterprise (wiping the slate clean) sometimes was necessary to lower costs and increase quality of service and that information technology was the key enabler for that radical change. Hammer and Champy believed that workflow design in most large corporations was based on invalid assumptions about technology, people, and organizational goals.

**The First 90 Days. By Michael Watkins (Harvard Business School Press, 2003).**

In *The First 90 Days,* Harvard Business School professor Michael Watkins presents a road map for taking charge in your first 90 days in a management job. The first days in a new position are critical because a small difference in your actions can have a huge impact on long-term results. Leaders at all levels are very vulnerable in their first few months in a new job because they lack in-depth knowledge of the challenges they will face and what it will take to succeed with their new company. Failure to create momentum in the first 90 days virtually guarantees an uphill battle for the rest of an executive's tenure. *The First 90 Days* will equip you with strategies and tools to get up to speed faster and achieve more sooner. It will show you how to diagnose your situation and understand its challenges and opportunities. You will also learn how to assess your own strengths and weaknesses, how to quickly establish priorities, and how to manage key relationships that will help you succeed.

**Execution. By Larry Bossidy and Ram Charan (Random House, 2002).**

Organizations face many challenges in today's shaky economy—competitive battles, increased costs, decreased margins, and a host of other internal and external forces. To shore up their companies' responses to these factors, today's leaders must be able to take the goals they set for their organizations and turn them into results. Unfortunately, too many companies struggle to bridge the gap between goals and results—they create solid, logical, even bold plans, but are unable to execute properly. Honeywell CEO Larry Bossidy and management adviser Ram Charan contend that the reason for this gap is that businesspeople do not think about execution as a discipline or a cornerstone of a business's culture—and they must. From middle management all the way up to CEO, a company's leaders must recognize execution as the most important collective set of activities in which they can engage. No more is there room for leaders who rely merely on their vision to get from goals to results; to survive, they must get more involved in the details of execution. There is much work to be done, and *Execution* shows you how to do it.

**The Dumbest Moments in Business History: Useless Products, Ruinous Deals, Clueless Bosses, and Other Signs of Unintelligent Life in the Workplace. By Adam Horowitz and the editors of *Business 2.0* (Portfolio, 2004).**

In *The Dumbest Moments in Business History,* the editors of *Business 2.0* have compiled the best of their first four annual issues plus great (or not so great, if you happen to be responsible) moments from the past. Grouped by theme—bosses gone bad, criminally creative accounting, etc.—*The Dumbest Moments in Business History* is a fun and funny look at the big-time ways that big-time companies have screwed up through the decades. Featuring numerous funny anecdotes, each reveals a person or organization that should have known better, but just did not. If you are interested in learning how not to conduct business take a look at the valuable lessons provided in this book. From New Coke to the Edsel, from *Rosie* magazine to Burger King's "Herb the Nerd," the book's highlights include:

- A Romanian car plant whose workers banded together to eliminate the company's debt by donating sperm and giving the proceeds to their employer.

- The Heidelberg Electric Belt, a sort of low-voltage jockstrap sold in 1900 to cure impotence, kidney disorders, insomnia, and many other complaints.

- The time Beech-Nut sold "100% pure apple juice" that contained nary a drop of apple juice.
- The Midas ad campaign featuring an elderly customer ripping open her blouse and showing her "mufflers" to the guys in the shop.
- A London video game maker that sought volunteers who would allow the company to place ads on the headstones of deceased relatives.

# Exploring Business Intelligence

## What's in IT for me?

This unit introduces the concept of information and its relative importance to organizations. It distinguishes between data stored in transactional databases and information housed in enterprise data warehouses. This unit also provides an overview of database fundamentals and the steps required to integrate various bits of data stored across multiple, operational data stores into a comprehensive and centralized repository of summarized information, which can be turned into powerful business intelligence.

You, as a business student, must understand the difference between transactional data and summarized information and the different types of questions you would use a transactional database or enterprise data warehouse to answer. You need to be aware of the complexity of storing data in databases and the level of effort required to transform operational data into meaningful, summarized information. You need to realize the power of information and the competitive advantage a data warehouse brings an organization in terms of facilitating business intelligence. Understanding the power of information will help you prepare to compete in a global marketplace. Armed with the power of information, you will make smart, informed, and data-supported managerial decisions.

## It Takes a Village to Write an Encyclopedia

The concept of gathering all the world's knowledge in a single place goes back to the ancient Library of Alexandria, but the modern concept of a general-purpose, widely distributed, printed encyclopedia dates from shortly before the 18th century. The Internet has expanded on the concept with the development of Wikipedia. Founded by Jimmy Wales, Wikipedia is a project to produce a free content encyclopedia that can have thousands of contributors and be edited by anyone, and it now contains millions of articles and pages worldwide. Wikipedia ranks among the top 15 online destinations worldwide.

A wiki is a type of website connected to a database that allows users to easily add and edit content and is especially suited for collaborative writing. The name is based on the Hawaiian term *wiki,* meaning quick, fast, or to hasten. In essence, wiki is a simplification of the process of creating web pages combined with a database that records each individual change, so that at any time, a page can be reverted to any of its previous states. A wiki system may also provide tools that allow users to easily monitor the constantly changing state of the wiki and discuss the issues that emerge in trying to achieve a general consensus about wiki content.

### Wikipedia Tightens the Reins

Wikipedia is exploding with information. The site originally allowed unrestricted access so that people could contribute without registering. As with any database management system, governance is a key issue. Without governance, there is no control over how information is published and maintained.

When you research Wikipedia, you find stories about how competing companies are removing and editing each other's entries in Wikipedia to gain market share. The *Washington Post* reported that Capitol Hill is playing "WikiPolitics" by editing representatives' and senators' biographies and speeches. Wikipedia had to temporarily block certain Capitol Hill web addresses from altering entries.

Wikipedia recently began tightening its rules for submitting entries following the disclosure that it ran a piece falsely implicating a man in the Kennedy assassinations.

John Seigenthaler Sr., who was Robert Kennedy's administrative assistant in the early 1960s, wrote an article revealing that Wikipedia had run a biography claiming Seigenthaler had been suspected in the assassinations of the former attorney general and his brother, President John F. Kennedy. Wikipedia now requires users to register before they can create and edit articles.

Wikipedia has grown into a storehouse of pieces on topics ranging from medieval art to nanotechnology. The volume of content is possible because the site relies on volunteers, including many experts in their fields, to submit entries and edit previously submitted articles. The website hopes that the registration requirement will limit the number of stories being created. "What we're hopeful to see is that by slowing that down to 1,500 a day from several thousand, the people who are monitoring this will have more ability to improve the quality," Wales said. "In many cases the types of things we see going on are impulse vandalism."

## The Future of Wiki

Can the wisdom of crowds trump the genius of Google? Wales believes that it not only can, but it will. Wales plans to launch a new search engine called Wikiasari, and hopes that it could someday overtake Google as the web search leader.

Like Wikipedia, Wikiasari will rely on the support of a volunteer community of users. The idea is that web surfers and programmers will be able to bring their collective intelligence to bear, to fine-tune search results and make the experience more effective for everyone. "If you search in Google, a lot of the results are very, very good and a lot of the results are very, very bad," Wales says. What that shows, Wales says, is that mathematical formulas alone do not produce consistently relevant results. "Human intelligence is still a very important part of the process," he says.

People can contribute to Wikiasari in one of two ways. The first is by enabling ordinary computer users to rerank search results. When a user performs a search on Wikiasari, the engine will return results based on a formula akin to Google's Page-Rank system, which determines relevance by counting the number of times other web pages link to a specific page, among other things. Unlike Google, however, users will then be able to reorder the results based on which links they find most useful by selecting an edit function. Wikiasari's servers will then store the new results along with the original query. When the same query is made in the future, Wikiasari will return the results in the order saved by most users.

Potential web users with programming knowledge have a second way to contribute. Wikiasari's technology is based on Apache's open-source web search software Lucene and Nutch, and Wales plans to unveil all the company's computer code to the outside world. This kind of open-source development is in sharp contrast to the approach of the leading search engines, which do not release their search ranking formulas. Yet Wales contends that his open approach will ultimately prevail, because anyone any place in the world can weigh in with tweaks to Wikiasari's code to help return more relevant results.

## A Fly in the Wiki

Wikipedia will fail in four years, crushed under the weight of an automated assault by marketers and others seeking online traffic. So says law professor Eric Goldman, who predicts Wikipedia's downfall. Goldman, a professor at the Santa Clara University School of Law, argues that Wikipedia will see increasingly vigorous efforts to subvert its editorial process, much as Digg.com has seen. As marketers become more determined and turn to automated tools to alter Wikipedia entries to generate online traffic, Goldman predicts Wikipedians will burn out trying to keep entries clean.

"Thus, Wikipedia will enter a death spiral where the rate of junkiness will increase rapidly until the site becomes a wasteland," Goldman writes. "Alternatively, to prevent this death spiral, Wikipedia will change its core open-access architecture, increasing the database's vitality by changing its mission somewhat."

As precedent, Goldman cites the fate of the Open Directory Project, a user-edited web directory, which he says "is now effectively worthless." "I love Wikipedia," Goldman concludes. "I use it every day. Based on the stats from my Google personalized search, Wikipedia is the Number one site I click on from Google search results. So I'm not rooting for it to fail. But the very architecture of Wikipedia contains the seeds of its own destruction. Without fame or fortune, I don't think Wikipedia's incentive system is sustainable."

# Introduction

Information is powerful. Information is useful in telling an organization how its current operations are performing and estimating and strategizing how future operations might perform. New perspectives open up when people have the right information and know how to use it. The ability to understand, digest, analyze, and filter information is a key to success for any professional in any industry. Unit Two demonstrates the value an organization can uncover and create by learning how to manage, access, analyze, and protect organizational information. The chapters in Unit Two are:

- **Chapter Six**—Valuing Organizational Information.
- **Chapter Seven**—Storing Organizational Information—Databases.
- **Chapter Eight**—Accessing Organizational Information—Data Warehouse.

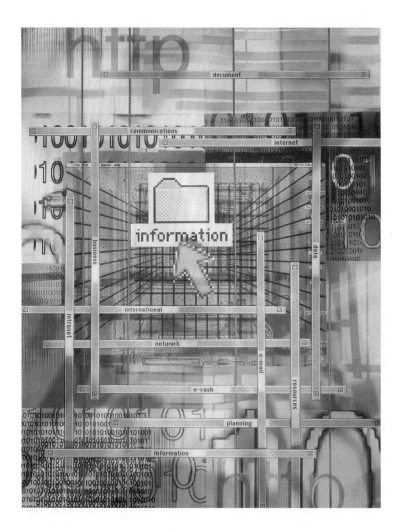

# Valuing Organizational Information

**LEARNING OUTCOMES**

**6.1.** Describe the broad levels, formats, and granularities of information.

**6.2.** Differentiate between transactional and analytical information.

**6.3.** List, describe, and provide an example of each of the five characteristics of high quality information.

**6.4.** Assess the impact of low quality information on an organization and the benefits of high quality information on an organization.

## Organizational Information

Google recently reported a 200 percent increase in sales of its new Enterprise Search Appliance tool. Companies use the tool within an enterprise information portal (EIP) to search corporate information for answers to customer questions and to fulfill sales orders. Hundreds of Google's customers are already using the tool—Xerox, Hitachi Data Systems, Nextel Communications, Procter & Gamble, Discovery Communications, Cisco Systems, Boeing. The ability to search, analyze, and comprehend information is vital for any organization's success. The incredible 200 percent growth in sales of Google's Search Appliance tool is a strong indicator that organizations are coveting technologies that help organize and provide access to information.

Information is everywhere in an organization. When addressing a significant business issue, employees must be able to obtain and analyze all the relevant information so they can make the best decision possible. Organizational information comes at different levels and in different formats and "granularities." *Information granularity* refers to the extent of detail within the information (fine and detailed or coarse and abstract). Employees must be able to correlate the different levels, formats, and granularities of information when making decisions. For example, if employees are using a supply chain management system to make decisions, they might find that their suppliers send information in different formats and granularity at different levels. One supplier might send detailed information in a spreadsheet, another supplier might send summary information in a Word document, and still another might send aggregate information from a database. Employees will need to compare these different types of information for what they commonly reveal to make strategic SCM decisions. Figure 6.1 displays types of information found in organizations.

Successfully collecting, compiling, sorting, and finally analyzing information from multiple levels, in varied formats, exhibiting different granularity can provide tremendous insight into how an organization is performing. Taking a hard look at organizational information can yield exciting and unexpected results such as potential new markets, new ways of reaching customers, and even new ways of doing business.

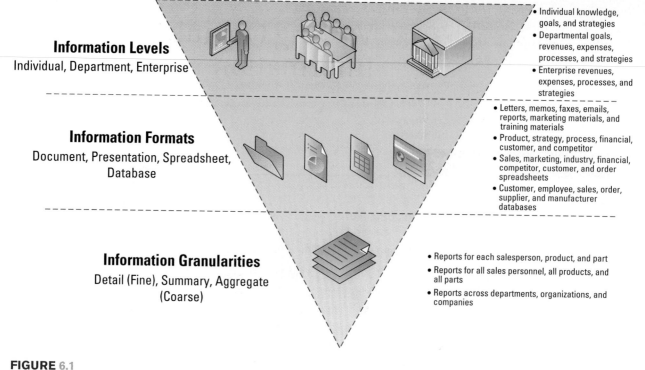

**Information Levels**
Individual, Department, Enterprise

- Individual knowledge, goals, and strategies
- Departmental goals, revenues, expenses, processes, and strategies
- Enterprise revenues, expenses, processes, and strategies

**Information Formats**
Document, Presentation, Spreadsheet, Database

- Letters, memos, faxes, emails, reports, marketing materials, and training materials
- Product, strategy, process, financial, customer, and competitor
- Sales, marketing, industry, financial, competitor, customer, and order spreadsheets
- Customer, employee, sales, order, supplier, and manufacturer databases

**Information Granularities**
Detail (Fine), Summary, Aggregate (Coarse)

- Reports for each salesperson, product, and part
- Reports for all sales personnel, all products, and all parts
- Reports across departments, organizations, and companies

**FIGURE 6.1**

Levels, Formats, and Granularities of Organizational Information

Samsung Electronics took a detailed look at over 10,000 reports from its resellers to identify "lost deals" or orders lost to competitors. The analysis yielded the enlightening result that 80 percent of lost sales occurred in a single business unit, the health care industry. Furthermore, Samsung was able to identify that 40 percent of its lost sales in the health care industry were going to one particular competitor. Before performing the analysis, Samsung was heading into its market blind. Armed with this valuable information, Samsung is changing its selling strategy in the health care industry by implementing a new strategy to work more closely with hardware vendors to win back lost sales.

Not all companies are successful at managing information. Staples, the office-supplies superstore, opened its first store in 1986 with state-of-the-art technology. The company experienced rapid growth and soon found itself overwhelmed with the resulting volumes of information. The state-of-the-art technology quickly became obsolete, and the company was unable to obtain any insight into its massive volumes of information. A simple query such as identifying the customers who purchased a computer, but not software or peripherals, took hours. Some queries required several days to complete and by the time the managers received answers to their queries it was too late for action.

After understanding the different levels, formats, and granularities of information, it is important to look at a few additional characteristics that help determine the value of information. These characteristics are type (transactional and analytical), timeliness, and quality.

## The Value of Transactional and Analytical Information

*Transactional information* encompasses all of the information contained within a single business process or unit of work, and its primary purpose is to support the performing of daily operational tasks. Examples of transactional information are withdrawing cash from an ATM, making an airline reservation, or purchasing stocks. Organizations capture and store transactional information in databases, and they use it when performing operational tasks and repetitive decisions such as analyzing daily sales reports and production schedules to determine how much inventory to carry.

*Analytical information* encompasses all organizational information, and its primary purpose is to support the performing of managerial analysis tasks. Analytical information includes transactional information along with other information such as market and industry information. Examples of analytical information are trends, sales, product statistics, and future growth projections. Analytical information is used when making important ad hoc decisions such as whether the organization should build a new manufacturing plant or hire additional sales personnel. Figure 6.2 displays different types of transactional and analytical information.

## The Value of Timely Information

The need for timely information can change for each business decision. Some decisions require weekly or monthly information while other decisions require daily information. Timeliness is an aspect of information that depends on the situation. In some industries, information that is a few days or weeks old can be relevant while in other industries information that is a few minutes old can be almost worthless. Some organizations, such as 911 centers, stock traders, and banks, require consolidated, up-to-the-second information, 24 hours a day, seven days a week. Other organizations, such as insurance and construction companies, require only daily or even weekly information.

*Real-time information* means immediate, up-to-date information. *Real-time systems* provide real-time information in response to query requests. Many organizations use real-time systems to exploit key corporate transactional information. In a survey of 700 IT executives by Evans Data Corp., 48 percent of respondents said they were already analyzing information in or near real-time, and another 25 percent reported plans to add real-time systems.

The growing demand for real-time information stems from organizations' need to make faster and more effective decisions, keep smaller inventories, operate more efficiently, and track performance more carefully. But timeliness is relative. Organizations need fresh, timely information to make good decisions. Information also needs to be timely in the sense that it meets employees' needs—but no more. If employees can absorb information only on an hourly or daily basis, there is no need to gather real-time information in smaller increments. For example, MBIA Insurance Corp. uses overnight updates to feed its real-time systems. Employees use this information to make daily risk decisions for mortgages, insurance policies, and

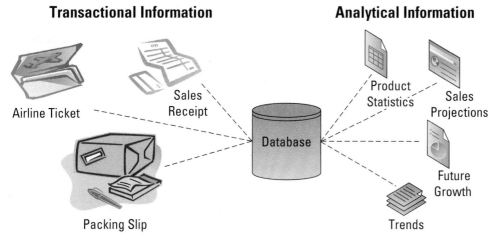

**Transactional Information**

Airline Ticket

Sales Receipt

Packing Slip

Database

**Analytical Information**

Product Statistics

Sales Projections

Future Growth

Trends

**FIGURE** 6.2

Transactional versus Analytical Information

**Chapter 6** Valuing Organizational Information ⁎ **79**

other services. The company found that overnight updates were sufficient, as long as users could gain immediate access to the information they needed to make business decisions during the day.

Most people request real-time information without understanding one of the biggest pitfalls associated with real-time information—continual change. Imagine the following scenario: Three managers meet at the end of the day to discuss a business problem. Each manager has gathered information at different times during the day to create a picture of the situation. Each manager's picture may be different because of this time discrepancy. Their views on the business problem may not match since the information they are basing their analysis on is continually changing. This approach may not speed up decision making, and may actually slow it down.

The timeliness of the information required must be evaluated for each business decision. Organizations do not want to find themselves using real-time information to make a bad decision faster.

# The Value of Quality Information

Westpac Financial Services (WFS), one of the four major banks in Australia, serves millions of customers from its many core systems, each with its own database. The databases maintain information and provide users with easy access to the stored information. Unfortunately, the company failed to develop information-capturing standards, which led to inconsistent organizational information. For example, one system had a field to capture email addresses while another system did not. Duplicate customer information among the different systems was another major issue, and the company continually found itself sending conflicting or competing messages to customers from different operations of the bank. A customer could also have multiple accounts within the company, one representing a life insurance policy and one representing a credit card. WFS had no way to identify that the two different customer accounts were for the same customer.

WFS had to solve its information quality problems immediately if it was to remain competitive. The company purchased NADIS (Name & Address Data Integrity Software), a software solution that filters customer information, highlighting missing, inaccurate, and redundant information. Customer service ratings are on the rise for WFS now that the company can operate its business with a single and comprehensive view of each one of its customers.

Business decisions are only as good as the quality of the information used to make the decisions. Figure 6.3 reviews five characteristics common to high quality information: accuracy, completeness, consistency, uniqueness, and timeliness. Figure 6.4 highlights several issues with low quality information including:

1. The first issue is *missing* information. The customer's first name is missing. (See #1 in Figure 6.4.)

**FIGURE** 6.3

Five Common Characteristics of High Quality Information

| Accuracy | Are all the values correct? For example, is the name spelled correctly? Is the dollar amount recorded properly? |
|---|---|
| Completeness | Are any of the values missing? For example, is the address complete including street, city, state, and zip code? |
| Consistency | Is aggregate or summary information in agreement with detailed information? For example, do all total fields equal the true total of the individual fields? |
| Uniqueness | Is each transaction, entity, and event represented only once in the information? For example, are there any duplicate customers? |
| Timeliness | Is the information current with respect to the business requirements? For example, is information updated weekly, daily, or hourly? |

| ID | Last Name | First Name | Street | City | State | Zip | Phone | Fax | Email |
|----|-----------|-----------|--------|------|-------|-----|-------|-----|-------|
| 113 | Smith | ▼ | 123 S. Main | Denver | CO | 80210 | (303) 777-1258 | (303) 777-5544 | ssmith@aol.com |
| 114 | Jones | Jeff | 12A ▼ | Denver | CO | 80224 | (303) 666-6868 | (303) 666-6868 | ▼(303) 666-6868 |
| 115 | Roberts | Jenny | 1244 Colfax | Denver | CO | 85231 | 759-5654 | 853-6584 | jr@msn.com |
| 116 | Robert | Jenny | 1244 Colfax | Denver | CO | 85231 | 759-5654 | 853-6584 | jr@msn.com |

1. Missing information (no first name)
2. Incomplete information (no street)
5. Inaccurate information (invalid email)
3. Probable duplicate information (similar names, same address, phone number)
4. Potential wrong information (are the phone and fax numbers the same or is this an error?)
6. Incomplete information (missing area codes)

**FIGURE 6.4**

Low Quality Information Example

2. The second issue is *incomplete* information since the street address contains only a number and not a street name.

3. The third issue is a probable *duplication* of information since the only slight difference between the two customers is the spelling of the last name. Similar street addresses and phone numbers make this likely.

4. The fourth issue is potential *wrong* information because the customer's phone and fax numbers are the same. Some customers might have the same number for phone and fax line, but the fact that the customer also has this number in the email address field is suspicious.

5. The fifth issue is definitely an example of *inaccurate* information since a phone number is located in the email address field.

6. The sixth issue is *incomplete* information since there is not a valid area code for the phone and fax numbers.

Recognizing how low quality information issues occur will allow organizations to begin to correct them. The four primary sources of low quality information are:

1. Online customers intentionally enter inaccurate information to protect their privacy.

2. Different systems have different information entry standards and formats.

3. Call center operators enter abbreviated or erroneous information by accident or to save time.

4. Third-party and external information contains inconsistencies, inaccuracies, and errors.

Addressing the above sources of information inaccuracies will significantly improve the quality of organizational information and the value that can be extracted from the information.

## UNDERSTANDING THE COSTS OF POOR INFORMATION

Using the wrong information can lead to making the wrong decision. Making the wrong decision can cost time, money, and even reputations. Every business decision is only as good as the information used to make the decision. Bad information can cause serious business ramifications such as:

■ Inability to accurately track customers, which directly affects strategic initiatives such as CRM and SCM.

■ Difficulty identifying the organization's most valuable customers.

- Inability to identify selling opportunities and wasted revenue from marketing to nonexisting customers and nondeliverable mail.
- Difficulty tracking revenue because of inaccurate invoices.
- Inability to build strong relationships with customers—which increases buyer power.

## UNDERSTANDING THE BENEFITS OF GOOD INFORMATION

High quality information can significantly improve the chances of making a good decision and directly increase an organization's bottom line. Lillian Vernon Corp., a catalog company, used web analytics to discover that men preferred to shop at Lillian Vernon's website instead of looking through its paper catalog. Based on this information, the company began placing male products more prominently on its website and soon realized a 15 percent growth in sales to men.

Another company discovered that Phoenix, Arizona, is not a good place to sell golf clubs, even with its high number of golf courses. An analysis revealed that typical golfers in Phoenix are either tourists or conventioneers. These golfers usually bring their clubs with them while visiting Phoenix. The analysis further revealed that two of the best places to sell golf clubs in the United States are Rochester, New York, and Detroit, Michigan.

There are numerous examples of companies that have used their high quality information to make solid strategic business decisions. High quality information does not automatically guarantee that every decision made is going to be a good one, since people ultimately make decisions. But such information ensures that the basis of the decisions is accurate. The success of the organization depends on appreciating and leveraging the true value of timely and high quality information.

### OPENING CASE STUDY QUESTIONS

1. Determine if an entry in Wikipedia is an example of transactional information or analytical information.

2. Describe the impact to Wikipedia if the information contained in its database is of low quality.

3. Review the five common characteristics of high quality information and rank them in order of importance to Wikipedia.

4. Explain how Wikipedia is resolving the issue of poor information.

## Chapter Six Case:  Political Microtargeting: What Data Crunchers Did for Obama

In his Presidential Inauguration speech President Barack Obama spoke a word rarely expressed—*data*—referencing indicators of economic and other crises. It is not surprising that the word *data* was spoken in his inauguration speech as capturing and analyzing data has been crucial to Obama's rise to power. Throughout Obama's historic campaign he used the Internet not only for social networking and fund raising, but also to identify potential swing voters. Obama's team carefully monitored contested states and congressional districts, since one to two thousand voters could prove decisive—meaning the focus was on only a tiny fraction of the voting public. Both political parties hired technology wizards to help sift through the mountains of consumer and demographic details to recognize these important voters.

## Ten "Tribes"

Spotlight Analysis, a Democratic consultancy, used political microtargeting to analyze neighborhood details, family sizes, and spending patterns to categorize every American of voting age—175 million of us—into 10 "values tribes." Individual tribe members do not necessarily share the same race, religion, or income bracket, but they have common mind-sets about political issues: God, community, responsibility, opportunity. Spotlight identified a particular morally guided (but not necessarily religious) tribe of some 14 million voters that it dubbed "Barn Raisers." Barn Raisers comprise many races, religions, and ethnic groups and around 40 percent of Barn Raisers favor Democrats and 27 percent favor Republicans. Barn Raisers are slightly less likely to have a college education than Spotlight's other swing groups. They are active in community organizations, ambivalent about government, and care deeply about "playing by the rules" and "keeping promises," to use Spotlight's definitions. Spotlight believed that the Barn Raisers held the key to the race between Obama and his Republican challenger, Arizona Senator John McCain.

Not typically seen outside of such corporate American icons as Google, Amazon, and eBay, political microtargeting, which depends on data, databases, and data analysis techniques, is turning political parties into sophisticated, intelligent, methodical machines. In nanoseconds, computers sort 175 million voters into segments and quickly calculate the potential that each individual voter has to swing from red or purple to blue or vice versa.

For some, political microtargeting signals the dehumanization of politics. For others, this type of sophisticated analysis is a highly efficient way of pinpointing potential voters. For example, analyzing a voter in Richmond, Virginia, traditionally simply identifies the number of school-age children, type of car, zip code, magazine subscriptions, and mortgage balance. But data crunching could even indicate if the voter has dogs or cats. (Cat owners lean slightly for Democrats, dog owners trend Republican.) After the analysis the voter is placed into a political tribe and analyzers can draw conclusions about the issues that matter to this particular voter. Is that so horrible?

## Behavioral Grouping

For generations, governments lacked the means to study individual behaviors and simply placed all citizens into enormous groupings such as Hispanics, Jews, union members, hunters, soccer moms, etc. With the use of sophisticated databases and data analysis techniques companies such as Spotlight can group individuals based more on specific behavior and choices, and less on the names, colors, and clans that mark us from birth.

When Spotlight first embarked on its research the company interviewed thousands of voters the old-fashioned way. At first, the Barn Raisers did not seem significant and the tribe represented about 9 percent of the electorate. However, when Spotlight's analysts dug deeper, they discovered that Barn Raisers stood at the epicenter of America's political swing. In 2004, 90 percent of them voted for President Bush, but then the group's political leanings shifted, with 64 percent of them saying they voted for Democrats in the 2006 election. Spotlight surveys showed that political scandals, tax-funded boondoggles like Alaska's Bridge to Nowhere, and the botched job on Hurricane Katrina sent them packing.

Suddenly, Spotlight identified millions of potential swing voters. The challenge then became locating the swing voters by states. For this, the company analyzed the demographics and buying patterns of the Barn Raisers they surveyed personally. Then it began correlating data from the numerous commercially available databases with matching profiles. By Spotlight's count, this approach nailed Barn Raisers three times out of four. So Democrats could bet that at least three-quarters of them would be likely to welcome an appeal stressing honesty and fair play.

### Still Swing Voters

It is still undetermined to what extent Spotlight's strategy worked and the company has not correlated the Barn Raisers to their actual votes. However, it is reasonable to presume that amid that sea of humanity stretched out before Obama on Washington's Mall on January 20, at least some were moved by microtargeted appeals. And if Obama and his team fail to honor their mathematically honed vows, the Barn Raisers may abandon them in droves. They are swing voters, after all.

### Questions

1. Describe the difference between transactional and analytical information and determine which types Spotlight used to identify its 10 tribes.

2. Explain the importance of high quality information for political microtargeting.

3. Review the five common characteristics of high quality information and rank them in order of importance for political microtargeting.

4. In terms of political microtargeting explain the following sentence: It is never possible to have all of the information required to make a 100 percent accurate prediction.

5. Do you agree that political microtargeting signals the dehumanization of politics?

# Storing Organizational Information—Databases

**7.1.** Define the fundamental concepts of the relational database model.

**7.2.** Evaluate the advantages of the relational database model.

**7.3.** Compare relational integrity constraints and business-critical integrity constraints.

**7.4.** Describe the benefits of a data-driven website.

**7.5.** Describe the two primary methods for integrating information across multiple databases.

## Storing Organizational Information

Organizational information is stored in a database. Applications and programs, such as supply chain management systems, and customer relationship management systems, access the data in the database so the program can consult it to answer queries. The records retrieved in answer to questions become information that can be used to make decisions. The computer program used to manage and query a database is known as a database management system (DBMS). The properties and design of database systems are included in the study of information science.

The central concept of a database is that of a collection of records, or pieces of information. Typically, a given database has a structural description of the type of facts held in that database: This description is known as a *schema*. The schema describes the objects that are represented in the database and the relationships among them. There are a number of different ways of organizing a schema, that is, of modeling the database structure: These are known as database models (or data models). The most commonly used model today is the relational model, which represents all information in the form of multiple related tables each consisting of rows and columns. This model represents relationships by the use of values common to more than one table. Other models, such as the hierarchical model, and the network model, use a more explicit representation of relationships.

Many professionals consider a collection of data to constitute a database only if it has certain properties, for example, if the data are managed to ensure integrity and quality, if it allows shared access by a community of users, if it has a schema, or if it supports a query language. However, there is no definition of these properties that is universally agreed upon.

# Relational Database Fundamentals

There are many different models for organizing information in a database, including the hierarchical database, network database, and the most prevalent—the relational database model. Broadly defined, a ***database*** maintains information about various types of objects (inventory), events (transactions), people (employees), and places (warehouses). In a ***hierarchical database model,*** information is organized into a tree-like structure that allows repeating information using parent/child relationships in such a way that it cannot have too many relationships. Hierarchical structures were widely used in the first mainframe database management systems. However, owing to their restrictions, hierarchical structures often cannot be used to relate to structures that exist in the real world. The ***network database model*** is a flexible way of representing objects and their relationships. Where the hierarchical model structures data as a tree of records, with each record having one parent record and many children, the network model allows each record to have multiple parent and child records, forming a lattice structure. The ***relational database model*** is a type of database that stores information in the form of logically related two-dimensional tables. This text focuses on the relational database model.

Consider how the Coca-Cola Bottling Company of Egypt (TCCBCE) implemented an inventory-tracking database to improve order accuracy by 27 percent, decrease order response time by 66 percent, and increase sales by 20 percent. With over 7,400 employees, TCCBCE owns and operates 11 bottling plants and 29 sales and distribution centers, making it one of the largest companies in Egypt.

Traditionally, the company sent distribution trucks to each customer's premises to take orders and deliver stock. Many problems were associated with this process including numerous information entry errors, which caused order-fulfillment time to take an average of three days. To remedy the situation, Coca-Cola decided to create presales teams equipped with handheld devices to visit customers and take orders electronically. On returning to the office, the teams synchronized orders with the company's inventory-tracking database to ensure automated processing and rapid dispatch of accurate orders to customers.

## ENTITIES AND ATTRIBUTES

Figure 7.1 illustrates the primary concepts of the relational database model—entities, entity classes, attributes, keys, and relationships. An ***entity*** in the relational database model is a person, place, thing, transaction, or event about which information is stored. A table in the relational database model is a collection of similar entities. The tables of interest in Figure 7.1 are *CUSTOMER, ORDER, ORDER LINE, PRODUCT,* and *DISTRIBUTOR.* Notice that each entity class (the collection of similar entities) is stored in a different two-dimensional table. ***Attributes,*** also called fields or columns, are characteristics or properties of an entity class. In Figure 7.1 the attributes for *CUSTOMER* include *Customer ID, Customer Name, Contact Name,* and *Phone.* Attributes for *PRODUCT* include *Product ID, Product Description,* and *Price.* Each specific entity in an entity class (e.g., Dave's Sub Shop in the *CUSTOMER* table) occupies one row in its respective table. The columns in the table contain the attributes.

## KEYS AND RELATIONSHIPS

To manage and organize various entity classes within the relational database model, developers must identify primary keys and foreign keys and use them to create logical relationships. A ***primary key*** is a field (or group of fields) that uniquely identifies a given entity in a table. In *CUSTOMER,* the *Customer ID* uniquely identifies each entity (customer) in the table and is the primary key. Primary keys are important because they provide a way of distinguishing each entity in a table.

**FIGURE 7.1**

Potential Relational Database for Coca-Cola Bottling Company of Egypt (TCCBCE)

**Order Number: 34562**

Coca-Cola Bottling Company of Egypt
Sample Sales Order

| Customer: Dave's Sub Shop | Date: 8/6/2008 |
|---|---|

| Quantity | Product | Price | Amount |
|---|---|---|---|
| 100 | Vanilla Coke | $0.55 | $55 |
| | | | |
| | | | |

Distributor Fee $12.95
Order Total $67.95

**CUSTOMER**

| Customer ID | Customer Name | Contact Name | Phone |
|---|---|---|---|
| 23 | Dave's Sub Shop | David Logan | (555)333-4545 |
| 43 | Pizza Palace | Debbie Fernandez | (555)345-5432 |
| 765 | T's Fun Zone | Tom Repicci | (555)565-6655 |

**ORDER**

| Order ID | Order Date | Customer ID | Distributor ID | Distributor Fee | Total Due |
|---|---|---|---|---|---|
| 34561 | 7/4/2008 | 23 | DEN8001 | $22.00 | $145.75 |
| 34562 | 8/6/2008 | 23 | DEN8001 | $12.95 | $67.95 |
| 34563 | 6/5/2008 | 765 | NY9001 | $29.50 | $249.50 |

**ORDER LINE**

| Order ID | Line Item | Product ID | Quantity |
|---|---|---|---|
| 34561 | 1 | 12345AA | 75 |
| 34561 | 2 | 12346BB | 50 |
| 34561 | 3 | 12347CC | 100 |
| 34562 | 1 | 12349EE | 100 |
| 34563 | 1 | 12345AA | 100 |
| 34563 | 2 | 12346BB | 100 |
| 34563 | 3 | 12347CC | 50 |
| 34563 | 4 | 12348DD | 50 |
| 34563 | 5 | 12349EE | 100 |

**DISTRIBUTOR**

| Distributor ID | Distributor Name |
|---|---|
| DEN8001 | Hawkins Shipping |
| CHI3001 | ABC Trucking |
| NY9001 | Van Distributors |

**PRODUCT**

| Product ID | Product Description | Price |
|---|---|---|
| 12345AA | Coca-Cola | $0.55 |
| 12346BB | Diet Coke | $0.55 |
| 12347CC | Sprite | $0.55 |
| 12348DD | Diet Sprite | $0.55 |
| 12349EE | Vanilla Coke | $0.55 |

A *foreign key* in the relational database model is a primary key of one table that appears as an attribute in another table and acts to provide a logical relationship between the two tables. Consider Hawkins Shipping, one of the distributors appearing in the *DISTRIBUTOR* table. Its primary key, *Distributor ID,* is DEN8001. Notice that *Distributor ID* also appears as an attribute in the ORDER table. This establishes the fact that Hawkins Shipping (*Distributor ID* DEN8001) was responsible for delivering orders 34561 and 34562 to the appropriate customer(s). Therefore, *Distributor ID* in the *ORDER* table creates a logical relationship (who shipped what order) between *ORDER* and *DISTRIBUTOR*.

## Relational Database Advantages

From a business perspective, database information offers many advantages, including:

- Increased flexibility.
- Increased scalability and performance.
- Reduced information redundancy.
- Increased information integrity (quality).
- Increased information security.

### INCREASED FLEXIBILITY

Databases tend to mirror business structures, and a good database can handle changes quickly and easily, just as any good business needs to be able to handle changes quickly and easily. Equally important, databases provide flexibility in allowing each user to access the information in whatever way best suits his or her needs. The distinction between logical and physical views is important in understanding flexible database user views. The *physical view* of information deals with the physical storage of information on a storage device such as a hard disk. The *logical view* of information focuses on how users logically access information to meet their particular business needs. This separation of logical and physical views is what allows each user to access database information differently. That is, while a database has only one physical view, it can easily support multiple logical views. In the previous database illustration, for example, users could perform a query to determine which distributors delivered shipments to Pizza Palace last week. At the same time, another person could perform some sort of statistical analysis to determine the frequency at which Sprite and Diet Coke appear on the same order. These represent two very different logical views, but both views use the same physical view.

Consider another example—a mail-order business. One user might want a CRM report presented in alphabetical format, in which case last name should appear before first name. Another user, working with a catalog mailing system, would want customer names appearing as first name and then last name. Both are easily achievable, but different logical views of the same physical information.

### INCREASED SCALABILITY AND PERFORMANCE

The official website of The American Family Immigration History Center, www.ellisisland.org, generated over 2.5 billion hits in its first year of operation. The site offers easy access to immigration information about people who entered America through the Port of New York and Ellis Island between 1892 and 1924. The database contains over 25 million passenger names correlated to 3.5 million images of ships' manifests.

Only a database could "scale" to handle the massive volumes of information and the large numbers of users required for the successful launch of the Ellis Island website. *Scalability* refers to how well a system can adapt to increased demands. *Performance* measures how quickly a system performs a certain process or transaction. Some organizations must be able to support hundreds or thousands of online users including employees, partners, customers, and suppliers, who all want to access and share information. Databases today scale to exceptional levels, allowing all types of users and programs to perform information-processing and information-searching tasks.

## REDUCED INFORMATION REDUNDANCY

*Redundancy* is the duplication of information, or storing the same information in multiple places. Redundant information occurs because organizations frequently capture and store the same information in multiple locations. The primary problem with redundant information is that it is often inconsistent, which makes it difficult to determine which values are the most current or most accurate. Not having correct information is confusing and frustrating for employees and disruptive to an organization. One primary goal of a database is to eliminate information redundancy by recording each piece of information in only one place in the database. Eliminating information redundancy saves space, makes performing information updates easier, and improves information quality.

## INCREASED INFORMATION INTEGRITY (QUALITY)

*Information integrity* is a measure of the quality of information. Within a database environment, *integrity constraints* are rules that help ensure the quality of information. Integrity constraints can be defined and built into the database design. The database (more appropriately, the database management system, which is discussed below) ensures that users can never violate these constraints. There are two types of integrity constraints: (1) relational integrity constraints and (2) business-critical integrity constraints.

*Relational integrity constraints* are rules that enforce basic and fundamental information-based constraints. For example, an operational integrity constraint would not allow someone to create an order for a nonexistent customer, provide a markup percentage that was negative, or order zero pounds of raw materials from a supplier. *Business-critical integrity constraints* enforce business rules vital to an organization's success and often require more insight and knowledge than relational integrity constraints. Consider a supplier of fresh produce to large grocery chains such as Kroger. The supplier might implement a business-critical integrity constraint stating that no product returns are accepted after 15 days past delivery. That would make sense because of the chance of spoilage of the produce. These types of integrity constraints tend to mirror the very rules by which an organization achieves success.

The specification and enforcement of integrity constraints produce higher quality information that will provide better support for business decisions. Organizations that establish specific procedures for developing integrity constraints typically see a decline in information error rates and an increase in the use of organizational information.

## INCREASED INFORMATION SECURITY

Information is an organizational asset. Like any asset, the organization must protect its information from unauthorized users or misuse. As systems become increasingly complex and more available over the Internet, security becomes an even bigger issue. Databases offer many security features including passwords, access levels, and access controls. Passwords provide authentication of the user who is gaining access to the system. Access levels determine who has access to the different types of information, and access controls determine what type of access they have to the information. For example, customer service representatives might need read-only access to customer order information so they can answer customer order inquiries; they might not have or need the authority to change or delete order information. Managers might require access to employee files, but they should have access only to their own employees' files, not the employee files for the entire company. Various security features of databases can ensure that individuals have only certain types of access to certain types of information.

Databases can increase personal security as well as information security. The Chicago Police Department (CPD) has relied on a crime-fighting system called Citizen and Law Enforcement Analysis and Reporting (CLEAR). CLEAR electronically streamlines the way detectives enter and access critical information to help them solve crimes, analyze crime patterns, and ultimately promote security in a proactive manner. The CPD enters 650,000 new criminal cases and 500,000 new arrests into CLEAR each year.

## Database Management Systems

Ford's European plant manufactures more than 5,000 vehicles a day and sells them in over 100 countries worldwide. Every component of every model must conform to complex European standards, including passenger safety standards and pedestrian and environmental protection standards. These standards govern each stage of Ford's manufacturing process from design to final production. The company needs to obtain many thousands of different approvals each year to comply with the standards. Overlooking just one means the company cannot sell the finished vehicle, which brings the production line to a standstill and could potentially cost Ford up to 1 million euros per day. Ford built the Homologation Timing System (HTS), based on a relational database, to help it track and analyze these standards. The reliability and high performance of the HTS have helped Ford substantially reduce its compliance risk.

A database management system is used to access information from a database. A ***database management system (DBMS)*** is software through which users and application programs interact with a database. The user sends requests to the DBMS and the DBMS performs the actual manipulation of the information in the database. There are two primary ways that users can interact with a DBMS: (1) directly and (2) indirectly, as displayed in Figure 7.2. In either case, users access the DBMS and the DBMS accesses the database.

**FIGURE** 7.2

Interacting Directly and Indirectly with a Database through a DBMS

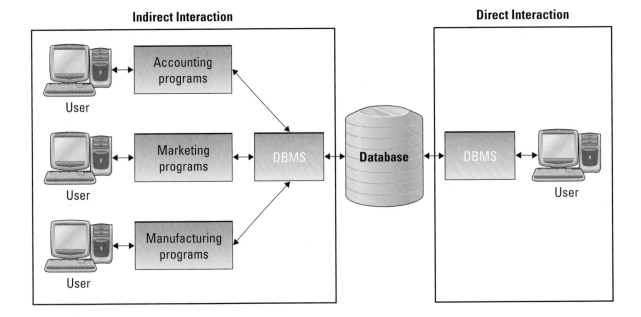

## DATA-DRIVEN WEBSITES

The pages on a website must change according to what a site visitor is interested in browsing. Consider for example, a company selling sports cars. A database is created with information on each of the currently available cars (e.g., make, model, engine details, year, a photograph, etc.). A visitor to the website clicks on Porsche, for example, enters the price range he or she is interested in, and hits "Go." The visitor is presented with information on available cars within the price range and an invitation to purchase or request more information from the company. Via a secure administration area on the website, the company has the ability to modify, add, or remove cars to the database.

A ***data-driven website*** is an interactive website kept constantly updated and relevant to the needs of its customers through the use of a database. Data-driven websites are especially useful when the site offers a great deal of information, products, or services. Website visitors are frequently angered if they are buried under an avalanche of information when searching a website. A data-driven website invites visitors to select and view what they are interested in by inserting a query. The website analyzes the query and then custom builds a web page in real-time that satisfies the query. Figure 7.3 displays a Wikipedia user querying business intelligence and the database sending back the appropriate web page that satisfies the user's request.

### Data-Driven Website Business Advantages

When building a website, ask two primary questions to determine if the website needs a database:

1. How often will the content change?
2. Who will be making the content changes?

**FIGURE** 7.3

Wikipedia—Data-Driven Website

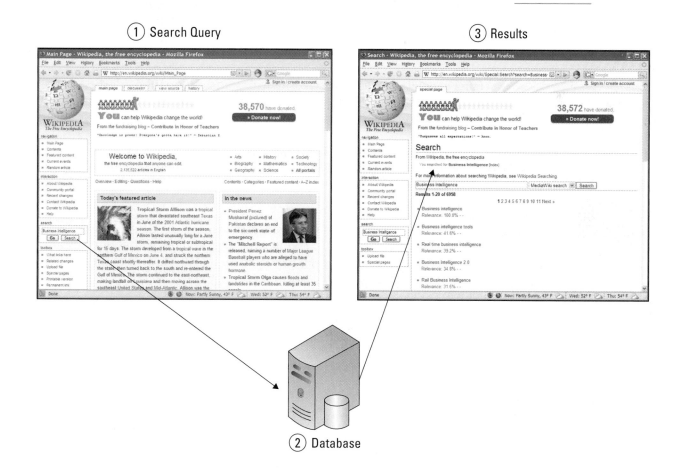

① Search Query　　　　③ Results

② Database

| Data-Driven Website Advantages |
| --- |
| ■ Development: Allows the website owner to make changes any time—all without having to rely on a developer or knowing HTML programming. A well-structured, data-driven website enables updating with little or no training. |
| ■ Content management: A static website requires a programmer to make updates. This adds an unnecessary layer between the business and its web content, which can lead to misunderstandings and slow turnarounds for desired changes. |
| ■ Future expandability: Having a data-driven website enables the site to grow faster than would be possible with a static site. Changing the layout, displays, and functionality of the site (adding more features and sections) is easier with a data-driven solution. |
| ■ Minimizing human error: Even the most competent programmer charged with the task of maintaining many pages will overlook things and make mistakes. This will lead to bugs and inconsistencies that can be time consuming and expensive to track down and fix. Unfortunately, users who come across these bugs will likely become irritated and may leave the site. A well-designed, data-driven website will have "error trapping" mechanisms to ensure that required information is filled out correctly and that content is entered and displayed in its correct format. |
| ■ Cutting production and update costs: A data-driven website can be updated and "published" by any competent data-entry or administrative person. In addition to being convenient and more affordable, changes and updates will take a fraction of the time that they would with a static site. While training a competent programmer can take months or even years, training a data-entry person can be done in 30 to 60 minutes. |
| ■ More efficient: By their very nature, computers are excellent at keeping volumes of information intact. With a data-driven solution, the system keeps track of the templates, so users do not have to. Global changes to layout, navigation, or site structure would need to be programmed only once, in one place, and the site itself will take care of propagating those changes to the appropriate pages and areas. A data-driven infrastructure will improve the reliability and stability of a website, while greatly reducing the chance of "breaking" some part of the site when adding new areas. |
| ■ Improved stability: Any programmer who has to update a website from "static" templates must be very organized to keep track of all the source files. If a programmer leaves unexpectedly, it could involve re-creating existing work if those source files cannot be found. Plus, if there were any changes to the templates, the new programmer must be careful to use only the latest version. With a data-driven website, there is peace of mind, knowing the content is never lost—even if your programmer is. |

**FIGURE 7.4**

Data-Driven Website
Advantages

For a general informational website with static information, it is best to build a "static" website—one that a developer can update on an as-needed basis, perhaps a few times a year. A static website is less expensive to produce and typically meets business needs.

For a website with continually changing information—press releases, new product information, updated pricing, etc.—it is best to build a data-driven website. Figure 7.4 displays the many advantages associated with a data-driven website.

### Data-Driven Business Intelligence

Companies can gain business intelligence by viewing the data accessed and analyzed from their website. Figure 7.5 displays how running queries or using analytical tools, such as a Pivot Table, on the database that is attached to the website can offer insight into the business, such as items browsed, frequent requests, items bought together, etc.

## Integrating Information among Multiple Databases

Until the 1990s, each department in the United Kingdom's Ministry of Defense (MOD) and Army headquarters had its own systems, each system had its own database, and sharing information among the departments was difficult. Manually

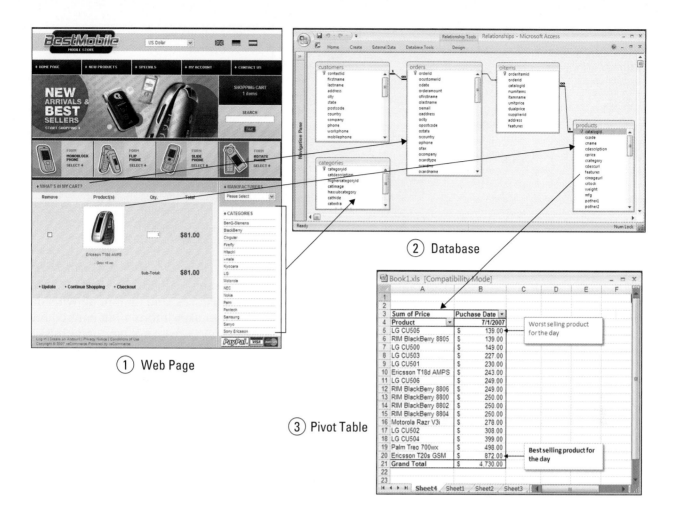

① Web Page

② Database

③ Pivot Table

**FIGURE** 7.5

BI in a Data-Driven Website

inputting the same information multiple times into the different systems was also time consuming and inefficient. In many cases, management could not even compile the information it required to answer questions and make decisions.

The Army solved the problem by integrating its systems, or building connections between its many databases. These integrations allow the Army's multiple systems to automatically communicate by passing information between the databases, eliminating the need for manual information entry into multiple systems because after entering the information once, the integrations send the information immediately to all other databases. The integrations not only enable the different departments to share information, but have also dramatically increased the quality of the information. The Army can now generate reports detailing its state of readiness and other vital issues, nearly impossible tasks before building the integrations among the separate systems.

An **_integration_** allows separate systems to communicate directly with each other. Similar to the UK's Army, an organization will probably maintain multiple systems, with each system having its own database. Without integrations, an organization will (1) spend considerable time entering the same information in multiple systems and (2) suffer from the low quality and inconsistency typically embedded in redundant information. While most integrations do not completely eliminate redundant information, they can ensure the consistency of it across multiple systems.

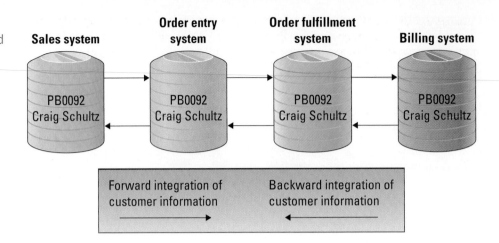

An organization can choose from two integration methods. The first is to create forward and backward integrations that link processes (and their underlying databases) in the value chain. A *forward integration* takes information entered into a given system and sends it automatically to all downstream systems and processes. A *backward integration* takes information entered into a given system and sends it automatically to all upstream systems and processes.

Figure 7.6 demonstrates how this method works across the systems or processes of sales, order entry, order fulfillment, and billing. In the order entry system, for example, an employee can update the information for a customer. That information, via the integrations, would be sent upstream to the sales system and downstream to the order fulfillment and billing systems.

Ideally, an organization wants to build both forward and backward integrations, which provide the flexibility to create, update, and delete information in any of the systems. However, integrations are expensive and difficult to build and maintain and most organizations build only forward integrations (sales through billing in Figure 7.6). Building only forward integrations implies that a change in the initial system (sales) will result in changes occurring in all the other systems. Integration of information is not possible for any changes occurring outside the initial system, which again can result in inconsistent organizational information. To address this issue, organizations can enforce business rules that all systems, other than the initial system, have read-only access to the integrated information. This will require users to change information in the initial system only, which will always trigger the integration and ensure that organizational information does not get out of sync.

**FIGURE** 7.7

Integrating Customer
Information among
Databases

The second integration method builds a central repository for a particular type of information. Figure 7.7 provides an example of customer information integrated using this method across four different systems in an organization. Users can create, update, and delete customer information only in the central customer information database. As users perform these tasks on the central customer information database, integrations automatically send the

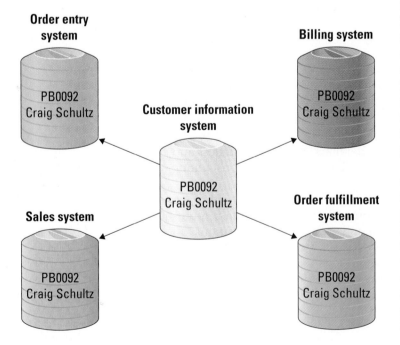

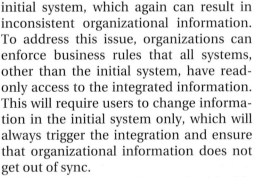

new and/or updated customer information to the other systems. The other systems limit users to read-only access of the customer information stored in them. Again, this method does not eliminate redundancy—but it does ensure consistency of the information among multiple systems.

## OPENING CASE STUDY QUESTIONS

1. Identify the different types of entity classes that might be stored in Wikipedia's database.

2. Explain why database technology is so important to Wikipedia's business model.

3. Explain the difference between logical and physical views and why logical views are important to Wikipedia's customers.

## Chapter Seven Case: Keeper of the Keys

More than 145,000 consumers nationwide were placed at risk by a data theft at database giant ChoicePoint. Criminals tricked the company by posing as legitimate businesses to gain access to the various ChoicePoint databases, which contain a treasure trove of consumer data, including names, addresses, Social Security numbers, credit reports, and other information. At least 50 suspicious accounts had been opened in the name of nonexistent debt collectors, insurance agencies, and other companies, according to the company.

Without a doubt, databases are one of the most important IT tools that organizations use today. Databases contain large repositories of detailed data. When a transaction occurs, a sale, for example, a database stores every detail of the transaction including customer name, customer address, credit card number, products purchased, discounts received, and so on.

Organizations must carefully manage their databases. This management function includes properly organizing the information in these repositories in the most efficient way, ensuring that no erroneous information ever enters the databases, and—most important—protecting the information from thieves and hackers.

Information is a valuable commodity, and, sadly, this makes it a target for theft. Organizations store large amounts of customer information including Social Security numbers, credit card numbers, and bank account numbers—just think of the information stored at eBay, Amazon, or the IRS. When someone steals personal information (not necessarily by taking it from the person, but rather stealing it from a company), that person becomes a victim of identity theft. Consider this short list of organizations that have lost information and the huge numbers of customers affected.

- Bank of America: 1.2 million customers.

- CardSystems: 40 million customers.

- Citigroup: 3.9 million customers.

- DSW Shoe Warehouse: 1.4 million customers.

- TJX Companies: 45.6 million customers.

- Wachovia: 676,000 customers.

Adding up the numbers, over 90 million people had their personal information either stolen or lost through organizations.

## Business Accountability in Data Security

Companies may soon face stiff penalties for wayward data security practices. Massachusetts is considering legislation that would require companies to pay for any costs associated with a data breach of their IT systems. This move to protect customer data in Massachusetts comes at a fitting time, as two prominent retailers in the area, TJX Companies and Stop & Shop, wrestle with the aftermath of significant breaches that have exposed some of their customers to fraud.

Much of the expense associated with stopping fraudulent activity, such as canceling or reissuing credit or debit cards, stopping payment, and refunding customers, has been absorbed by the banks issuing credit or debit cards to the victims. The merchant banks that allow businesses such as TJX and Stop & Shop stores to accept credit and debit card transactions are penalized with fines from Visa, MasterCard, and other credit card organizations if the merchants they work with are found to violate the payment card industry's data security standards.

But the businesses who have had customer data stolen have largely suffered only from the costs to offer customers free credit-monitoring services and to repair a tarnished public image. In the case of popular retailers, this tarnish is easily polished away when juicy sales incentives are offered to get customers back.

Massachusetts House Bill 213, sponsored by Rep. Michael Costello, proposes to amend the Commonwealth's general laws to include a section that would require any corporation or other commercial entity whose sensitive customer information is stolen to notify customers about the data breach and also make companies liable to card-issuing banks for the costs those banks incur because of the breach and any subsequent fraudulent activity. This would include making businesses cover the costs to cancel or reissue cards, stop payments or block transactions with respect to any such account, open or reopen an account, and issue any refund or credit made to any customer of the bank as a result of unauthorized transactions.

The Massachusetts legislation is a key step in compelling companies to invest in better data security. Passage of this bill would put Massachusetts ahead of other states in terms of protecting customer data and spreading out the penalties so that both financial institutions and retailers have incentives to improve security. Security vendors are likely to be watching Massachusetts very closely, as the bill also would create an urgent need for companies doing business in that state to invest in ways to improve their ability to protect customer data. If the companies will not do this on their own, then holding them accountable for their customers' financial losses may be just what is needed to stop the next data breach from occurring.

## Questions

1. How many organizations have your personal information, including your Social Security number, bank account numbers, and credit card numbers?

2. What information is stored at your college? Is there a chance your information could be hacked and stolen from your college?

3. What can you do to protect yourself from identity theft?

4. Do you agree or disagree with changing laws to hold the company where the data theft occurred accountable? Why or why not?

5. What impact would holding the company liable where the data theft occurred have on large organizations?

6. What impact would holding the company liable where the data theft occurred have on small businesses?

# 8

# Accessing Organizational Information—Data Warehouse

**8.1.** Describe the roles and purposes of data warehouses and data marts in an organization.

**8.2.** Compare the multidimensional nature of data warehouses (and data marts) with the two-dimensional nature of databases.

**8.3.** Identify the importance of ensuring the cleanliness of information throughout an organization.

**8.4.** Explain the relationship between business intelligence and a data warehouse.

## Accessing Organizational Information

Applebee's Neighborhood Grill & Bar posts annual sales in excess of $3.2 billion and is actively using information from its data warehouse to increase sales and cut costs. The company gathers daily information for the previous day's sales into its data warehouse from 1,500 restaurants located in 49 states and seven countries. Understanding regional preferences, such as patrons in Texas preferring steaks more than patrons in New England, allows the company to meet its corporate strategy of being a neighborhood grill appealing to local tastes. The company has found tremendous value in its data warehouse by being able to make business decisions about customers' regional needs. The company also uses data warehouse information to perform the following:

■ Base labor budgets on actual number of guests served per hour.

■ Develop promotional sale item analysis to help avoid losses from overstocking or understocking inventory.

■ Determine theoretical and actual costs of food and the use of ingredients.

## History of Data Warehousing

In the 1990s as organizations began to need more timely information about their business, they found that traditional operational information systems were too cumbersome to provide relevant data efficiently and quickly. Operational systems typically include accounting, order entry, customer service, and sales and are not appropriate for business analysis for the following reasons:

■ Information from other operational applications is not included.

■ Operational systems are not integrated, or not available in one place.

■ Operational information is mainly current—does not include the history that is required to make good decisions.

■ Operational information frequently has quality issues (errors)—the information needs to be cleansed.

- Without information history, it is difficult to tell how and why things change over time.
- Operational systems are not designed for analysis and decision support.

During the latter half of the 20th century, the numbers and types of databases increased. Many large businesses found themselves with information scattered across multiple platforms and variations of technology, making it almost impossible for any one individual to use information from multiple sources. Completing reporting requests across operational systems could take days or weeks using antiquated reporting tools that were designed to execute the business rather than run the business. From this idea, the data warehouse was born as a place where relevant information could be held for completing strategic reports for management. The key here is the word *strategic* as most executives were less concerned with the day-to-day operations than they were with a more overall look at the model and business functions.

A key idea within data warehousing is to take data from multiple platforms/technologies (as varied as spreadsheets, databases, and word files) and place them in a common location that uses a common querying tool. In this way operational databases could be held on whatever system was most efficient for the operational business, while the reporting/strategic information could be held in a common location using a common language. Data warehouses take this a step further by giving the information itself commonality by defining what each term means and keeping it standard. An example of this would be gender, which can be referred to in many ways (Male, Female, M/F, 1/0), but should be standardized on a data warehouse with one common way of referring to each sex (M/F).

This design makes decision support more readily available without affecting day-to-day operations. One aspect of a data warehouse that should be stressed is that it is *not* a location for *all* of a business's information, but rather a location for information that is interesting, or information that will assist decision makers in making strategic decisions relative to the organization's overall mission.

Data warehousing is about extending the transformation of data into information. Data warehouses offer strategic level, external, integrated, and historical information so businesses can make projections, identify trends, and decide key business issues. The data warehouse collects and stores integrated sets of historical information from multiple operational systems and feeds them to one or more data marts. It may also provide end-user access to support enterprisewide views of information.

## Data Warehouse Fundamentals

A **data warehouse** is a logical collection of information—gathered from many different operational databases—that supports business analysis activities and decision-making tasks. The primary purpose of a data warehouse is to aggregate information throughout an organization into a single repository in such a way that employees can make decisions and undertake business analysis activities. Therefore, while databases store the details of all transactions (for instance, the sale of a product) and events (hiring a new employee), data warehouses store that same information but in an aggregated form more suited to supporting decision-making tasks. Aggregation, in this instance, can include totals, counts, averages, and the like. Because of this sort of aggregation, data warehouses support only analytical processing.

The data warehouse modeled in Figure 8.1 compiles information from internal databases or transactional/operational databases and external databases through **extraction, transformation, and loading (ETL),** which is a process that extracts information from internal and external databases, transforms the information using a common set of enterprise definitions, and loads the information into a data warehouse. The data warehouse then sends subsets of the information to data marts. A **data mart** contains a subset of data warehouse information. To distinguish between

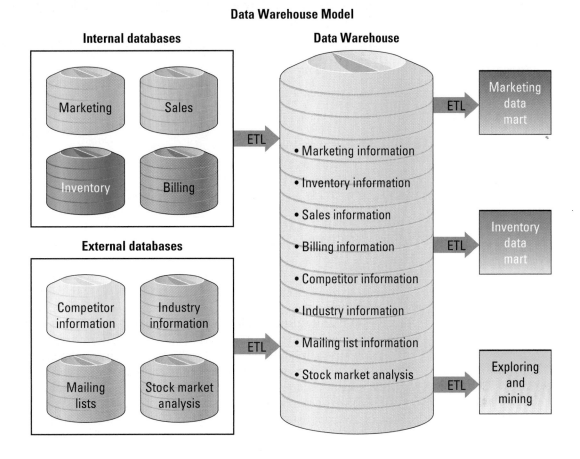

**Data Warehouse Model**

FIGURE 8.1

Model of a Typical Data Warehouse

data warehouses and data marts, think of data warehouses as having a more organizational focus and data marts as having focused information subsets particular to the needs of a given business unit such as finance or production and operations.

Lands' End created an organizationwide data warehouse so all its employees could access organizational information. Lands' End soon found out that there could be "too much of a good thing." Many of its employees would not use the data warehouse because it was simply too big, too complicated, and had too much irrelevant information. Lands' End knew there was valuable information in its data warehouse, and it had to find a way for its employees to easily access the information. Data marts were the perfect solution to the company's information overload problem. Once the employees began using the data marts, they were ecstatic at the wealth of information. Data marts were a huge success for Lands' End.

## MULTIDIMENSIONAL ANALYSIS AND DATA MINING

A relational database contains information in a series of two-dimensional tables. In a data warehouse and data mart, information is multidimensional, meaning it contains layers of columns and rows. For this reason, most data warehouses and data marts are *multidimensional databases*. A *dimension* is a particular attribute of information. Each layer in a data warehouse or data mart represents information according to an additional dimension. A *cube* is the common term for the representation of multidimensional information. Figure 8.2 displays a cube (cube *a*) that represents store information (the layers), product information (the rows), and promotion information (the columns).

Once a cube of information is created, users can begin to slice and dice the cube to drill down into the information. The second cube (cube *b*) in Figure 8.2 displays a slice representing promotion II information for all products, at all stores. The third

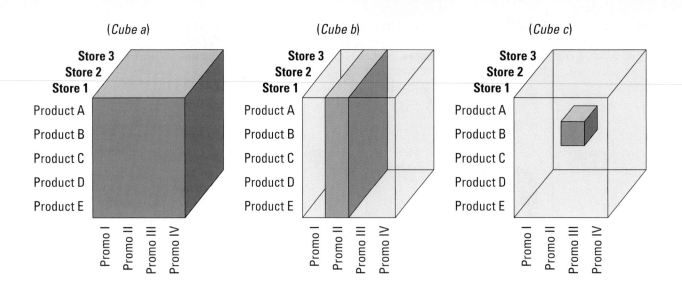

(Cube a)   (Cube b)   (Cube c)

**FIGURE** 8.2

A Cube of Information
for Performing a
Multidimensional Analysis
on Three Different Stores,
for Five Different Products,
and Four Different
Promotions

cube (cube *c*) in Figure 8.2 displays only information for promotion III, product B, at store 2. By using multidimensional analysis, users can analyze information in a number of different ways and with any number of different dimensions. For example, users might want to add dimensions of information to a current analysis including product category, region, and even forecasted versus actual weather. The true value of a data warehouse is its ability to provide multidimensional analysis that allows users to gain insights into their information.

Data warehouses and data marts are ideal for off-loading some of the querying against a database. For example, querying a database to obtain an average of sales for product B at store 2 while promotion III is under way might create a considerable processing burden for a database, essentially slowing down the time it takes another person to enter a new sale into the same database. If an organization performs numerous queries against a database (or multiple databases), aggregating that information into a data warehouse could be beneficial.

***Data mining*** is the process of analyzing data to extract information not offered by the raw data alone. For example, Ruf Strategic Solutions helps organizations employ statistical approaches within a large data warehouse to identify customer segments that display common traits. Marketers can then target these segments with specially designed products and promotions.

Data mining can also begin at a summary information level (coarse granularity) and progress through increasing levels of detail (drilling down), or the reverse (drilling up). To perform data mining, users need data-mining tools. ***Data-mining tools*** use a variety of techniques to find patterns and relationships in large volumes of information and infer rules from them that predict future behavior and guide decision making. Data-mining tools for data warehouses and data marts include query tools, reporting tools, multidimensional analysis tools, statistical tools, and intelligent agents.

Sega of America, one of the largest publishers of video games, uses a data warehouse and statistical tools to distribute its annual advertising budget of more than $50 million. With its data warehouse, product line specialists and marketing strategists "drill" into trends of each retail store chain. Their goal is to find buying trends that help them determine which advertising strategies are working best and how to reallocate advertising resources by media, territory, and time.

## INFORMATION CLEANSING OR SCRUBBING

Maintaining quality information in a data warehouse or data mart is extremely important. The Data Warehousing Institute estimates that low quality information costs U.S. businesses $600 billion annually. That number may seem high, but it is not. If an organization is using a data warehouse or data mart to allocate dollars across advertising strategies (such as in the case of Sega of America), low quality information will definitely have a negative impact on its ability to make the right decision.

To increase the quality of organizational information and thus the effectiveness of decision making, businesses must formulate a strategy to keep information clean. This is the concept of information cleansing or scrubbing. ***Information cleansing or scrubbing*** is a process that weeds out and fixes or discards inconsistent, incorrect, or incomplete information.

Specialized software tools use sophisticated algorithms to parse, standardize, correct, match, and consolidate data warehouse information. This is vitally important because data warehouses often contain information from several different databases, some of which can be external to the organization. In a data warehouse, information cleansing occurs first during the ETL process and second on the information once it is in the data warehouse. Companies can choose information cleansing software from several different vendors including Oracle, SAS, Ascential Software, and Group 1 Software. Ideally, scrubbed information is error free and consistent.

Dr Pepper/Seven Up, Inc., was able to integrate its myriad databases in a data warehouse (and subsequently data marts) in less than two months, giving the company access to consolidated, clean information. Approximately 600 people in the company regularly use the data marts to analyze and track beverage sales across multiple dimensions, including various distribution routes such as bottle/can sales, fountain food-service sales, premier distributor sales, and chain and national accounts. The company is now performing in-depth analysis of up-to-date sales information that is clean and error free.

Looking at customer information highlights why information cleansing is necessary. Customer information exists in several operational systems. In each system all details of this customer information could change from the customer ID to contact information (see Figure 8.3). Determining which contact information is accurate and correct for this customer depends on the business process that is being executed.

Figure 8.4 displays a customer name entered differently in multiple operational systems. Information cleansing allows an organization to fix these types of inconsistencies and cleans the information in the data warehouse. Figure 8.5 displays the typical events that occur during information cleansing.

Achieving perfect information is almost impossible. The more complete and accurate an organization wants its information to be, the more it costs (see Figure 8.6). The trade-off for perfect information lies in accuracy versus completeness. Accurate information means it is correct, while complete information means there are no blanks. A birth date of 2/31/10 is an example of complete but inaccurate information

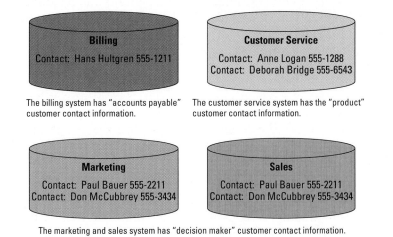

**FIGURE** 8.3

Contact Information in Operational Systems

**Billing**

Contact: Hans Hultgren 555-1211

The billing system has "accounts payable" customer contact information.

**Customer Service**

Contact: Anne Logan 555-1288
Contact: Deborah Bridge 555-6543

The customer service system has the "product" customer contact information.

**Marketing**

Contact: Paul Bauer 555-2211
Contact: Don McCubbrey 555-3434

**Sales**

Contact: Paul Bauer 555-2211
Contact: Don McCubbrey 555-3434

The marketing and sales system has "decision maker" customer contact information.

**FIGURE** 8.4

Standardizing Customer
Name from Operational
Systems

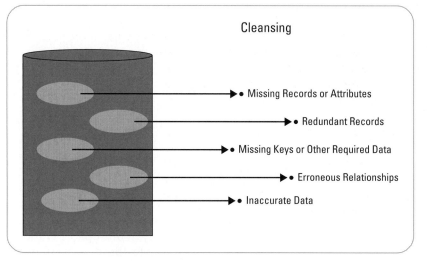

**Sales**

Customers:
| JD0021 | Jane Doe |
| BL0557 | Bob Lake |
| JS0288 | Judy Smith |
| **PB0092** | **Pat Burton** |

**Customer Service**

Customers:
| 10622FA | Susan Brown |
| 10472FB | Judie R Smithe |
| **10772FA** | **Patti Burten** |
| 10922MC | Larry Trump |

**Billing**

Customers:
| 000980 | Burton, Tricia |
| 002670 | Smith, Judie |
| 000466 | Burton, Patricia |
| 006777 | Lake, RobertP. |

**Customer Information**

Customers:
| 10001 | Jane Doe |
| 10002 | Robert P. Lake |
| 10003 | Judie R. Smith |
| 10004 | Patricia Burton |

**FIGURE** 8.5

Information Cleansing
Activities

Cleansing

- Missing Records or Attributes
- Redundant Records
- Missing Keys or Other Required Data
- Erroneous Relationships
- Inaccurate Data

**FIGURE** 8.6

Accurate and Complete
Information

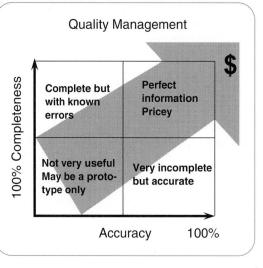

Quality Management

100% Completeness (vertical axis)

| Complete but with known errors | Perfect information Pricey |
| Not very useful May be a proto-type only | Very incomplete but accurate |

Accuracy     100%

(February 31 does not exist). An address containing Denver, Colorado, without a ZIP code is an example of incomplete information that is accurate. For their information, most organizations determine a percentage high enough to make good decisions at a reasonable cost, such as 85 percent accurate and 65 percent complete.

# Business Intelligence

***Business intelligence (BI)*** refers to applications and technologies that are used to gather, provide access to, and analyze data and information to support decision-making efforts. An early reference to business intelligence occurs in Sun Tzu's book titled *The Art of War*. Sun Tzu claims that to succeed in war, one should have full knowledge of one's own strengths and weaknesses and full knowledge of the enemy's strengths and weaknesses. Lack of either one might result in defeat. A certain school of thought draws parallels between the challenges in business and those of war, specifically:

- Collecting information.
- Discerning patterns and meaning in the information.
- Responding to the resultant information.

Before the start of the information age in the late 20th century, businesses sometimes collected information from nonautomated sources. Businesses then lacked the computing resources to properly analyze the information and often made commercial decisions based primarily on intuition.

As businesses started automating more and more systems, more and more information became available. However, collection remained a challenge due to a lack of infrastructure for information exchange or to incompatibilities between systems. Reports sometimes took months to generate. Such reports allowed informed long-term strategic decision making. However, short-term tactical decision making continued to rely on intuition.

In modern businesses, increasing standards, automation, and technologies have led to vast amounts of available information. Data warehouse technologies have set up repositories to store this information. Improved ETL has increased the speedy collecting of information. Business intelligence has now become the art of sifting through large amounts of data, extracting information, and turning that information into actionable knowledge.

## ENABLING BUSINESS INTELLIGENCE

Competitive organizations accumulate business intelligence to gain sustainable competitive advantage, and they may regard such intelligence as a valuable core competence in some instances. The principal BI enablers are technology, people, and corporate culture.

### Technology

Even the smallest company with BI software can do sophisticated analyses today that were unavailable to the largest organizations a generation ago. The largest companies today can create enterprisewide BI systems that compute and monitor metrics on virtually every variable important for managing the company. How is this possible? The answer is technology—the most significant enabler of business intelligence.

### People

Understanding the role of people in BI allows organizations to systematically create insight and turn these insights into actions. Organizations can improve their decision making by having the right people making the decisions. This usually means a manager who is in the field and close to the customer rather than an analyst rich in data but poor in experience. In recent years "business intelligence for the masses" has been an important trend, and many organizations have made great strides in providing sophisticated yet simple analytical tools and information to a much larger user population than was previously possible.

## Culture

A key responsibility of executives is to shape and manage corporate culture. The extent to which the BI attitude flourishes in an organization depends in large part on the organization's culture. Perhaps the most important step an organization can take to encourage BI is to measure the performance of the organization against a set of key indicators. The actions of publishing what the organization thinks are the most important indicators, measuring these indicators, and analyzing the results to guide improvement display a strong commitment to BI throughout the organization.

### OPENING CASE STUDY QUESTIONS

1. Determine how Wikipedia could use a data warehouse to improve its business operations.

2. Explain why Wikipedia must cleanse or scrub the information in its data warehouse.

3. Explain how a company could use information from Wikipedia to gain business intelligence.

## Chapter Eight Case: Mining the Data Warehouse

According to a Merrill Lynch survey in 2006, business intelligence software and data-mining tools were at the top of CIOs' technology spending list. Following are a few examples of how companies are using data warehousing and data-mining tools to gain valuable business intelligence.

### Ben & Jerry's

These days, when we all scream for ice cream, Ben & Jerry's cuts through the din by using integrated query, reporting, and online analytical processing technology from BI software vendor Business Objects. Through an Oracle database and with BI from Business Objects, Ben & Jerry's tracks the ingredients and life of each pint. If a consumer calls in with a complaint, the consumer affairs staff matches the pint with which supplier's milk, eggs, cherries, or whatever did not meet the organization's near-obsession with quality.

The BI tools let Ben & Jerry's officials access, analyze, and act on customer information collected by the sales, finance, purchasing, and quality-assurance departments. The company can determine what milk customers prefer in the making of the ice cream. The technology helped Ben & Jerry's track more than 12,500 consumer contacts in 2005. The information ranged from comments about the ingredients used in ice cream to queries about social causes supported by the company.

### California Pizza Kitchen

California Pizza Kitchen (CPK) is a leading casual dining chain in the premium pizza segment with a recognized consumer brand and an established, loyal customer base. Founded in 1985, there are currently more than 130 full-service restaurants in over 26 states, the District of Columbia, and five foreign countries.

Before implementing its BI tool, Cognos, CPK used spreadsheets to plan and track its financial statements and line items. The finance team had difficulty managing the volumes of data, complex calculations, and constant changes to the spreadsheets. It took several weeks of two people working full time to obtain one version of the financial statements and future forecast. In addition, the team was limited by the software's inability to link cells and calculations across multiple spreadsheets, so updating other areas of corporate records became a time-consuming task. With Cognos, quarterly forecasting cycles have been reduced from eight days to two days. The finance team can now spend more time reviewing the results rather than collecting and entering the data.

## Noodles & Company

Noodles & Company has more than 70 restaurants throughout Colorado, Illinois, Maryland, Michigan, Minnesota, Texas, Utah, Virginia, and Wisconsin. The company recently purchased Cognos BI tools to help implement reporting standards and communicate real-time operational information to field management throughout the United States.

Before implementing the first phase of the Cognos solution, IT and finance professionals spent days compiling report requests from numerous departments including sales and marketing, human resources, and real estate. Since completing phase one, operational Cognos reports are being accessed on a daily basis through the Noodles & Company website. This provides users with a single, 360-degree view of the business and consistent reporting throughout the enterprise.

Noodles & Company users benefit from the flexible query and reporting capabilities, allowing them to see patterns in the data to leverage new business opportunities. Cognos tools can pull information directly from a broad array of relational, operational, and other systems.

## Questions

1. Explain how Ben & Jerry's is using business intelligence tools to remain successful and competitive in a saturated market.

2. Identify why information cleansing is critical to California Pizza Kitchen's business intelligence tool's success.

3. Illustrate why 100 percent accurate and complete information is impossible for Noodles & Company to obtain.

4. Describe how each of the companies above is using BI to gain a competitive advantage.

The five common characteristics of quality information include accuracy, completeness, consistency, uniqueness, and timeliness. The costs to an organization of having low quality information can be enormous and could result in revenue losses and ultimately business failure. Databases maintain information about various types of objects, events, people, and places and help to alleviate many of the problems associated with low quality information such as redundancy, integrity, and security.

A data warehouse is a logical collection of information—gathered from many different operational databases—that supports business analysis activities and decision-making tasks. Data marts contain a subset of data warehouse information. Organizations gain tremendous insight into their business by mining the information contained in data warehouses and data marts.

Understanding the value of information is key to business success. Employees must be able to optimally access and analyze organizational information. The more knowledge employees have concerning how the organization stores, maintains, provides access to, and protects information the better prepared they will be when they need to use that information to make critical business decisions.

## ★ KEY TERMS

Analytical information, 79
Attribute, 86
Backward integration, 94
Business Intelligence (BI), 103
Business-critical integrity constraint, 89
Cube, 99
Database, 86
Database management system (DBMS), 90
Data-driven website, 91
Data mart, 98
Data mining, 100
Data-mining tools, 100

Data warehouse, 98
Entity, 86
Extraction, transformation, and loading (ETL), 98
Foreign key, 88
Forward integration, 94
Hierarchical database model, 86
Information cleansing or scrubbing, 101
Information granularity, 77
Information integrity, 89
Integration, 93
Integrity constraint, 89

Logical view, 88
Network database model, 86
Performance, 89
Physical view, 88
Primary key, 86
Real-time information, 79
Real-time system, 79
Redundancy, 89
Relational database model, 86
Relational integrity constraint, 89
Scalability, 89
Transactional information, 78

Harrah's—Gambling Big on Technology

The large investment made by Harrah's Entertainment Inc. in its information technology strategy has been tremendously successful. The results of Harrah's investment include:

- 10 percent annual increase in customer visits.
- 33 percent increase in gross market revenue.
- Yearly profits of over $208 million.
- Highest three-year ROI (return on investment) in the industry.
- A network that links over 42,000 gaming machines in 26 casinos across 12 states.
- Rated number six of the 100 best places to work in IT for 2003 by *ComputerWorld* magazine.
- Recipient of 2000 Leadership in Data Warehousing Award from the Data Warehousing Institute (TDWI), the premier association for data warehousing.

The casino industry is highly competitive. Bill Harrah was a man ahead of his time when he opened his first bingo parlor in 1937 with the commitment of getting to know each one of his customers. In 1984, Phil Satre, president and CEO of Harrah's, continued a commitment to customers. In search of its competitive advantage, Harrah's invested in an enterprisewide technology infrastructure to maintain Bill Harrah's original conviction: "Serve your customers well and they will be loyal."

## Harrah's Commitment to Customers

Harrah's recently implemented its patented Total Rewards™ program to help build strong relationships with its customers. The program rewards customers for their loyalty by tracking their gaming habits across its 26 properties and currently maintains information on over 19 million customers, information the company uses to analyze, predict, and maximize each customer's value.

One major reason for the company's success is Harrah's implementation of a service-oriented strategy. Total Rewards allows Harrah's to give every customer the appropriate amount of personal attention, whether it's leaving sweets in the hotel room or offering free meals. Total Rewards works by providing each customer with an account and a corresponding card that the player swipes each time he or she plays a casino game. The program collects information on the amount of time the customers gamble, their total winnings and losses, and their betting strategies. Customers earn points based on the amount of time they spend gambling, which they can then exchange for comps such as free dinners, hotel rooms, tickets to shows, and even cash.

Total Rewards helps employees determine which level of service to provide each customer. When a customer makes a reservation at Harrah's, the service representative taking the call can view the customer's detailed information including the customer's loyalty level, games typically played, past winnings and losses, and potential net worth. If the service representative notices that the customer has a Diamond loyalty level, for example, the service representative knows that customer should never have to wait in line and should always receive free upgrades to the most expensive rooms.

"Almost everything we do in marketing and decision making is influenced by technology," says Gary Loveman, Harrah's chief operating officer. "The prevailing wisdom in this business is that the attractiveness of property drives customers. Our approach is different. We stimulate demand by knowing our customers. For example, if one of our customers always vacations at Harrah's in April, they will receive a promotion in February redeemable for a free weekend in April."

## Gaining Business Intelligence with a Data Warehouse

Over 90 million customers visit Harrah's each year, and tracking a customer base larger than the population of Australia is a challenge. To tackle it, Harrah's began developing a system called WINet (Winner's Information Network). WINet links all Harrah's properties, allowing the company to collect and share customer information on an enterprisewide basis. WINet collects customer information from all the company transactions, game machines, and hotel management and reservations systems and places the information in a central data warehouse. Information in the data warehouse includes both customer and gaming information recorded in hourly increments. The marketing department uses the data warehouse to analyze customer information for patterns and insights, which allows it to create individualized marketing programs for each customer based on spending habits. Most important, the data warehouse allows the company to make business decisions based on information, not intuition.

Casinos traditionally treat customers as though they belong to a single property, typically the place the customer most frequently visits. Harrah's was the first casino to realize the potential of rewarding customers for visiting more than one property. Today, Harrah's has found that customers who visit more than one of its properties represent the fastest growing revenue segment. In the first two years of the Total Rewards program, the company received a $100 million increase in revenue from customers who gambled at more than one casino.

Harrah's also uses business intelligence to determine gaming machine performance. Using the data warehouse, Harrah's examines the performance and cost structure of each individual gaming machine. The company can quickly identify games that do not deliver optimal operational performance and can make a decision to move or replace the games. The capability to assess the performance of each individual slot machine has provided Harrah's with savings in the tens of millions of dollars. CIO Tim Stanley stated, "As we leverage more data from our data warehouse and increase the use and sophistication of our decision science analytical tools, we expect to have many new ways to improve customer loyalty and satisfaction, drive greater revenues, and decrease our costs as part of our ongoing focus on achieving sustainable profitability and success."

## Information Security and Privacy

Some customers have concerns about Harrah's information collection strategy since they want to keep their gambling information private. The good news for these customers is that casinos are actually required to be more mindful of privacy concerns than most companies. For example, casinos cannot send marketing material to any underage persons. To adhere to strict government regulations, casinos must ensure that the correct information security and restrictions are in place. Many other companies actually make a great deal of money by selling customer information. Harrah's will not be joining in this trend since its customer information is one of its primary competitive advantages.

## The Future of Harrah's

Harrah's current systems support approximately $140,000 in revenue per hour (that's almost $25 million weekly). In the future, Harrah's hopes to become device-independent by allowing employees to access the company's data warehouse via PDAs, handheld computers, and even cell phones. "Managing relationships with customers is incredibly important to the health of our business," Stanley says. "We will apply whatever technology we can to do that."

## Questions

1. Identify the effects poor information might have on Harrah's service-oriented business strategy.
2. Summarize how Harrah's uses database technologies to implement its service-oriented strategy.
3. Harrah's was one of the first casino companies to find value in offering rewards to customers who visit multiple Harrah's locations. Describe the effects on the company if it did not build any integrations among the databases located at each of its casinos.
4. Estimate the potential impact to Harrah's business if there is a security breach in its customer information.
5. Explain the business effects if Harrah's fails to use data-mining tools to gather business intelligence.
6. Identify three different types of data marts Harrah's might want to build to help it analyze its operational performance.
7. Predict what might occur if Harrah's fails to clean or scrub its information before loading it into its data warehouse.
8. How could Harrah's use data mining to increase revenue?

## ✱ UNIT CLOSING CASE TWO

### Searching for Revenue—Google

Google founders Sergey Brin and Larry Page recently made *Forbes* magazine's list of world billionaires. The company is famous for its highly successful search engine.

### How Google Works

Figure Unit 2.1 displays the life of an average Google query. The web server sends the query to the index servers. The content inside the index server is similar to the index at the back of a book—it tells which pages contain the words that match any particular query term. Then the query travels to the document servers, which actually retrieve the stored documents and generate snippets to describe each search result. Finally, the search engine returns the results to the user. All these activities occur within a fraction of a second.

Google consists of three distinct parts:

1. The web crawler, known as Googlebot, finds and retrieves web pages and passes them to the Google indexer. Googlebot functions much like a web browser. It sends a request for a web page to a web server, downloads the entire page, and then hands it off to Google's indexer. Googlebot can request thousands of different web pages simultaneously.
2. The indexer indexes every word on each page and stores the resulting index of words in a huge database. This index is sorted alphabetically by search term, with each index entry

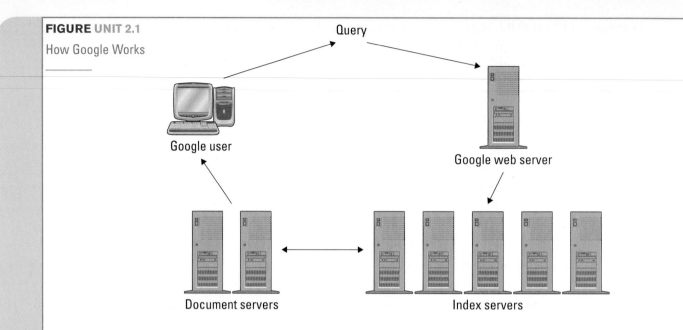

**FIGURE** UNIT 2.1

How Google Works

Query

Google user

Google web server

Document servers

Index servers

storing a list of documents in which the term appears and the location within the text where it occurs. Indexing the full text of web pages allows Google to go beyond simply matching single search terms. Google gives more priority to pages that have search terms near each other and in the same order as the query. Google can also match multi-word phrases and sentences.

3. The query processor compares the search query to the index and recommends the documents that it considers most relevant. Google considers over a hundred factors in determining which documents are most relevant to a query, including the popularity of the page, the position and size of the search terms within the page, and the proximity of the search terms to one another. The query processor has several parts, including the user interface (search box), the "engine" that evaluates queries and matches them to relevant documents, and the results formatter.

## Selling Words

Google's primary line of business is its search engine; however, the company does not generate revenue from people using its site to search the Internet. It generates revenue from the marketers and advertisers that are paying to place their ads on the site.

Around 200 million times each day, people from all over the world access Google to perform searches. AdWords, a part of the Google site, allows advertisers to bid on common search terms. The advertisers simply enter in the keywords they want to bid on and the maximum amounts they want to pay per click, per day. Google then determines a price and a search ranking for those keywords based on how much other advertisers are willing to pay for the same terms. Pricing for keywords can range from 5 cents to $3 a click. A general search term like "tropical vacation" costs less than a more specific term like "Hawaiian vacation." Whoever bids the most for a term appears in a sponsored advertisement link either at the top or along the side of the search-results page.

Paid search is the ultimate in targeted advertising because consumers type in exactly what they want. One of the primary advantages of paid search web programs such as AdWords is that customers do not find it annoying, as is the problem with some forms of web advertising such as banner ads and pop-up ads. According to the Interactive Advertising Bureau, overall industry revenues from paid search surpassed banner ads in the third quarter of 2003.

"A big percentage of queries we get are commercial in nature," confirms Salar Kamangar, Google's director of product management. "It is a marketplace where the advertisers tell us about themselves by telling us how much each lead is worth. They have an incentive to bid how much they really want to pay, because if they underbid, their competitors will get more traffic."

Kamangar came up with the AdWords concept and oversees that part of the business today. AdWords, which launched in 2005, accounts for the vast majority of Google's annual revenue and the company has over 150,000 advertisers in its paid-search program, up from zero in 2002.

## Expanding Google

Google has a secret weapon working for its research and development department—hackers. Hackers actually develop many of the new and unique ways to expand Google. The company elicits hacker ideas through its application program interface (API), a large piece of the Google code. The API enables developers to build applications around the Google search engine. By making the API freely available, Google has inspired a community of programmers that are extending Google's capabilities. "It's working," states Nelson Minar, who runs the API effort. "We get clever hacks, educational uses, and wacky stuff. We love to see people do creative things with our product." A few of the successful user-developed applications include:

- **Banana Slug**—www.bananaslug.com. For customers who hit a dead end with Google search, the site adds a random word to search text that generates surprising results.
- **Cookin' with Google**—www.researchbuzz.org. Enter the ingredients that are in the fridge and the site returns potential recipes for those ingredients.
- **Google Alert**—www.googlealert.com. Google Alert automatically searches the web for information on a topic and returns the results by email.
- **RateMyProfessors.com**—www.ratemyprofessors.com. The goal of this site was to create a place where students could rank their teachers. However, too many jokesters typing in false professor names such as "Professor Harry Leg" and "Professor Ima Dog" left the information on the site questionable. The developers turned to the Google API to create an automatic verification tool. If Google finds enough mentions in conjunction with a professor or university then it considers the information valid and posts it to the website.

## Stopping Google

As part of its Google Print Library Project, the company is working to scan all or parts of the book collections of the University of Michigan, Harvard University, Stanford University, the New York Public Library, and Oxford University. It intends to make those texts searchable on Google and to sell advertisements on the web pages.

The Authors Guild filed a lawsuit against Google, alleging that its scanning and digitizing of library books constitutes a massive copyright infringement. "This is a plain and brazen violation of copyright law," Nick Taylor, president of the New York-based Authors Guild, said in a statement about the lawsuit, which is seeking class-action status. "It's not up to Google or anyone other than the authors, the rightful owners of these copyrights, to decide whether and how their works will be copied."

In response, Google defended the program in a company blog posting. "We regret that this group chose to sue us over a program that will make millions of books more discoverable to the world—especially since any copyright holder can exclude their books from the program," wrote Susan Wojcicki, vice president of product management. "Google respects copyright. The use we make of all the books we scan through the Library Project is fully consistent with both the fair use doctrine under U.S. copyright law and the principles underlying copyright law itself, which allow everything from parodies to excerpts in book reviews."

## Questions

1. Determine if Google's search results are examples of transactional or analytical information.
2. Describe the impact on Google's business if the search information it presented to its customers was of low quality.

3. Explain how the website RateMyProfessors.com solved its problem of poor information.

4. Identify how Google might use a data warehouse to improve its business.

5. Explain why Google would need to cleanse the information in its data warehouse.

6. Identify a data mart that Google's marketing and sales department might use to track and analyze its AdWords revenue.

## ★ MAKING BUSINESS DECISIONS

### 1. Improving Information Quality

HangUps Corporation designs and distributes closet organization structures. The company operates five different systems: order entry, sales, inventory management, shipping, and billing. The company has severe information quality issues including missing, inaccurate, redundant, and incomplete information. The company wants to implement a data warehouse containing information from the five different systems to help maintain a single customer view, drive business decisions, and perform multidimensional analysis. Identify how the organization can improve its information quality when it begins designing and building its data warehouse.

### 2. Information Timeliness

Information timeliness is a major consideration for all organizations. Organizations need to decide the frequency of backups and the frequency of updates to a data warehouse. In a team, describe the timeliness requirements for backups and updates to a data warehouse for

- Weather tracking systems.
- Car dealership inventories.
- Vehicle tire sales forecasts.
- Interest rates.
- Restaurant inventories.
- Grocery store inventories.

### 3. Entities and Attributes

Martex Inc. is a manufacturer of athletic equipment and its primary lines of business include running, tennis, golf, swimming, basketball, and aerobics equipment. Martex currently supplies four primary vendors including Sam's Sports, Total Effort, The Underline, and Maximum Workout. Martex wants to build a database to help it organize its products. In a group, identify the different types of entity classes and the related attributes that Martex will want to consider when designing the database.

### 4. Integrating Information

You are currently working for the Public Transportation Department of Chatfield. The department controls all forms of public transportation including buses, subways, and trains. Each department has about 300 employees and maintains its own accounting, inventory, purchasing, and human resource systems. Generating reports across departments is a difficult task and usually involves gathering and correlating the information from the many different systems. It typically takes about two weeks to generate the quarterly balance sheets and profit and loss statements. Your team has been asked to compile a report recommending what the Public Transportation Department of Chatfield can do to alleviate its information and system issues. Be sure that your report addresses the various reasons departmental reports are presently difficult to obtain as well as how you plan to solve this problem.

### 5. Explaining Relational Databases

You have been hired by Vision, a start-up recreational equipment company. Your manager, Holly Henningson, is unfamiliar with databases and their associated business value. Holly has asked you to create a report detailing the basics of databases. Holly would also like you to provide a detailed explanation of relational databases along with their associated business advantages.

---

## ★ APPLY YOUR KNOWLEDGE

### 1. Determining Information Quality Issues

*Real People* is a magazine geared toward working individuals that provides articles and advice on everything from car maintenance to family planning. *Real People* is currently experiencing problems with its magazine distribution list. Over 30 percent of the magazines mailed are returned because of incorrect address information, and each month it receives numerous calls from angry customers complaining that they have not yet received their magazines. Below is a sample of *Real People*'s customer information. Create a report detailing all of the issues with the information, potential causes of the information issues, and solutions the company can follow to correct the situation.

| ID | First Name | Middle Name | Last Name | Street | City | State | ZIP Code |
|-----|------------|-------------|------------|----------------|---------------|-------|----------|
| 433 | M | J | Jones | 13 Denver | Denver | CO | 87654 |
| 434 | Margaret | J | Jones | 13 First Ave. | Denver | CO | 87654 |
| 434 | Brian | F | Hoover | Lake Ave. | Columbus | OH | 87654 |
| 435 | Nick | H | Schweitzer | 65 Apple Lane | San Francisco | OH | 65664 |
| 436 | Richard | A | | 567 55th St. | New York | CA | 98763 |
| 437 | Alana | B | Smith | 121 Tenny Dr. | Buffalo | NY | 142234 |
| 438 | Trevor | D | Darrian | 90 Fresrdestil | Dallas | TX | 74532 |

### 2. Mining the Data Warehouse

Alana Smith is a senior buyer for a large wholesaler that sells different types of arts and crafts to greeting card stores such as Hallmark. Alana's latest marketing strategy is to send all of her customers a new line of hand-made picture frames from Russia. Alana's data support her decision for the new line. Her analysis predicts that the frames should sell an average of 10 to 15 per store, per day. Alana is excited about the new line and is positive it will be a success.

One month later Alana learns that the frames are selling 50 percent below expectations and averaging between five and eight frames sold daily in each store. Alana decides to access the company's data warehouse to determine why sales are below expectations. Identify several different dimensions of data that Alana will want to analyze to help her decide what is causing the problems with the picture frame sales.

### 3. Cleansing Information

You are working for BI, a start-up business intelligence consulting company. You have a new client that is interested in hiring BI to clean up its information. To determine how good your work is, the client would like your analysis of the following spreadsheet.

| CUST ID | First Name | Last Name | Address | City | State | ZIP | Phone | Last Order Date |
|---------|-----------|-----------|---------|------|-------|-----|-------|-----------------|
| 233620 | Christopher | Lee | 12421 W Olympic Blvd | Los Angeles | CA | 75080-1100 | (972)680-7848 | 4/18/2002 |
| 233621 | Bruce | Brandwen | 268 W 44th St | New York | PA | 10036-3906 | (212)471-6077 | 5/3/2002 |
| 233622 | Glr | Johnson | 4100 E Dry Creek Rd | Littleton | CO | 80122-3729 | (303)712-5461 | 5/6/2002 |
| 233623 | Dave | Owens | 466 Commerce Rd | Staunton | VA | 24401-4432 | (540)851-0362 | 3/19/2002 |
| 233624 | John | Coulbourn | 124 Action St | Maynard | MA | 1754 | (978)987-0100 | 4/24/2002 |
| 233629 | Dan | Gagliardo | 2875 Union Rd | Cheektowaga | NY | 14227-1461 | (716)558-8191 | 5/4/2002 |
| 23362 | Damanceee | Allen | 1633 Broadway | New York | NY | 10019-6708 | (212)708-1576 | |
| 233630 | Michael | Peretz | 235 E 45th St | New York | NY | 10017-3305 | (212)210-1340 | 4/30/2002 |
| | | | | | | | (608)238-9690 | |
| 233631 | Jody | Veeder | 440 Science Dr | Madison | WI | 53711-1064 | X227 | 3/27/2002 |
| 233632 | Michael | Kehrer | 3015 SSE Loop 323 | Tyler | TX | 75701 | (903)579-3229 | 4/28/ |
| 233633 | Erin | Yoon | 3500 Carillon Pt | Kirkland | WA | 98033-7354 | (425)897-7221 | 3/25/2002 |
| 233634 | Madeline | Shefferly | 4100 E Dry Creek Rd | Littleton | CO | 80122-3729 | (303)486-3949 | 3/33/2002 |
| 233635 | Steven | Conduit | 1332 Enterprise Dr | West Chester | PA | 19380-5970 | (610)692-5900 | 4/27/2002 |
| 233636 | Joseph | Kovach | 1332 Enterprise Dr | West Chester | PA | 19380-5970 | (610)692-5900 | 4/28/2002 |
| 233637 | Richard | Jordan | 1700 N | Philadelphia | PA | 19131-4728 | (215)581-6770 | 3/19/2002 |
| 233638 | Scott | Mikolajczyk | 1655 Crofton Blvd | Crofton | MD | 21114-1387 | (410)729-8155 | 4/28/2002 |
| 233639 | Susan | Shragg | 1875 Century Park E | Los Angeles | CA | 90067-2501 | (310)785-0511 | 4/29/2002 |
| 233640 | Rob | Ponto | 29777 Telegraph Rd | Southfield | MI | 48034-1303 | (810)204-4724 | 5/5/2002 |
| 233642 | Lauren | Butler | 1211 Avenue Of The Americas | New York | NY | 10036-8701 | (212)852-7494 | 4/22/2002 |
| 233643 | Christopher | Lee | 12421 W Olympic Blvd | Los Angeles | CA | 90064-1022 | (310)689-2577 | 3/25/2002 |
| 233644 | Michelle | Decker | 6922 Hollywood Blvd | Hollywood | CA | 90028-6117 | (323)817-4655 | 5/8/2002 |
| 233647 | Natalia | Galeano | 1211 Avenue Of The Americas | New York | NY | 10036-8701 | (646)728-6911 | 4/23/2002 |
| 233648 | Bobbie | Orchard | 4201 Congress St | Charlotte | NC | 28209-4617 | (704)557-2444 | 5/11/2002 |
| 233650 | Ben | Konfino | 1111 Stewart Ave | Bethpage | NY | 11714-3533 | (516)803-1406 | 3/19/2002 |
| 233651 | Lenee | Santana | 1050 Techwood Dr NW | Atlanta | GA | 30318-KKRR | (404)885-2000 | 3/22/2002 |
| 233652 | Lauren | Monks | 7700 Wisconsin Ave | Bethesda | MD | 20814-3578 | (301)771-4772 | 3/19/2005 |
| 233653 | Mark | Woolley | 10950 Washington Blvd | Culver City | CA | 90232-4026 | (310)202-2900 | 4/20/2002 |
| 233654 | Stan | Matthews | 1235 W St NE | Washington | DC | 20018-1107 | (202)608-2000 | 3/25/2002 |

## 4. Different Dimensions

The focus of data warehousing is to extend the transformation of data into information. Data warehouses offer strategic level, external, integrated, and historical information so businesses can make projections, identify trends, and make key business decisions. The data warehouse collects and stores integrated sets of historical information from multiple operational systems and feeds them to one or more data marts. It may also provide end-user access to support enterprisewide views of information.

### Project Focus

You are currently working on a marketing team for a large corporation that sells jewelry around the world. Your boss has asked you to look at the following dimensions of data to determine which ones you want in your data mart for performing sales and market analysis (see Figure AYK.1). As a team, categorize the different dimensions ranking them from 1 to 5, with 1 indicating that the dimension offers the highest value and must be in your data mart and 5 indicating that the dimension offers the lowest value and does not need to be in your data mart.

## 5. Understanding Search

Pretend that you are a search engine. Choose a topic to query. It can be anything such as your favorite book, movie, band, or sports team. Search your topic on Google, pick three or four pages from the results, and print them out. On each printout, find the individual words

**FIGURE** AYK.1

Data Warehouse Data

| Dimension | Value (1–5) | Dimension | Value (1–5) |
|---|---|---|---|
| Product number | | Season | |
| Store location | | Promotion | |
| Customer net worth | | Payment method | |
| Number of sales personnel | | Commission policy | |
| Customer eating habits | | Manufacturer | |
| Store hours | | Traffic report | |
| Salesperson ID | | Customer language | |
| Product style | | Weather | |
| Order date | | Customer gender | |
| Product quantity | | Local tax information | |
| Ship date | | Local cultural demographics | |
| Current interest rate | | Stock market closing | |
| Product cost | | Customer religious affiliation | |
| Customer's political affiliation | | Reason for purchase | |
| Local market analysis | | Employee dress code policy | |
| Order time | | Customer age | |
| Customer spending habits | | Employee vacation policy | |
| Product price | | Employee benefits | |
| Exchange rates | | Current tariff information | |
| Product gross margin | | | |

from your query (such as "Boston Red Sox" or "The Godfather") and use a highlighter to mark each word with color. Do that for each of the documents that you print out. Now tape those documents on a wall, step back a few feet, and review your documents. If you did not know what the rest of a page said and could only judge by the colored words, which document do you think would be most relevant? Is there anything that would make a document look more relevant? Is it better to have the words be in a large heading or to occur several times in a smaller font? Do you prefer it if the words are at the top or the bottom of the page? How often do the words need to appear? Come up with two or three things you would look for to see if a document matched a query well. This exercise mimics search engine processes and should help you understand why a search engine returns certain results over others.

## ★ BUSINESS DRIVEN BEST SELLERS

*Business @ The Speed of Thought.* **By Bill Gates (Grand Central Publishing, 1999).**

*Business @ The Speed of Thought* was written by Bill Gates to inspire you to demand—and get—more from technology, enabling you and your company to respond faster to your customers, adapt to changing business demands, and prosper in the digital economy. "How you gather, manage, and use information will determine whether you win or lose" is Bill Gates's simple message. *Business @ The Speed of Thought* is not a technical book. It shows how business and technology are now inextricably linked. Each chapter is structured around a business or management issue, showing how digital processes can dramatically improve your results.

*Why Smart Executives Fail.* **By Sydney Finkelstein. (Penguin Putnam, 2003).**

In *Why Smart Executives Fail,* Sydney Finkelstein, a professor of management at Dartmouth's Tuck School of Business, explains why leadership fails and how company leaders can get back on track. This book shows examples from GM, Mattel, Motorola, Rite Aid, Webvan, and other companies as well as the results of six years of research on the issue of leadership failure. Finkelstein explains that the causes of failed management are surprisingly few, and they are not ineptitude or greed. Even the brightest executives fail because:

- They choose not to cope with innovation, change, and management.
- They misread the competition.
- They brilliantly fulfill the wrong vision.
- They cling to an inaccurate view of reality.
- They ignore vital information.
- They identify too closely with the company.

# 3

# Streamlining Business Operations

## What's in IT for Me?

Information is a powerful asset. It is a key organizational asset that enables companies to carry out business initiatives and strategic plans. Companies that manage information are primed for competitive advantage and success. Information systems provide the key tools allowing access to and flow of information across enterprises. This unit emphasizes the important role strategic decision-making information systems play in increasing efficiency and effectiveness across global enterprises and providing the infrastructure required for supply chain management, customer relationship management, and enterprise resource planning. These systems facilitate interactions among customers, suppliers, partners, and employees providing new communication channels beyond those traditionally used by organizations such as face-to-face or paper-based methods.

A supply chain consists of all direct and indirect parties involved in the procurement of products and raw material. These parties can be internal groups or departments within an organization or external partner companies and end customers. You, as a business student, need to know the significance of a supply chain to organizational success and the critical role information technology plays in ensuring smooth operations of a supply chain.

You, as a business student, must understand the critical relationship your business will have with its customers. You must understand how to analyze your organizational data to ensure you are not just meeting, but exceeding your customers' expectations. Business intelligence is the best way to understand your customers' current—and more importantly—future needs. Like never before, enterprises are technologically empowered to reach their goals of integrating, analyzing, and making intelligent business decisions based on their data.

You, as a business student, must understand how to give employees, customers, and business partners access to information by means of newer technologies such as enterprise resource planning systems and enterprise portals. Creating access to information with the help of information systems facilitates completion of current tasks while encouraging the sharing and generation of new ideas that lead to the development of innovations, improved work habits, and best practices.

## Second Life: Succeeding in Virtual Times

Second Life is a virtual world built and owned by its residents. It opened to the public in 2003, and today is inhabited by millions of residents from around the world. The three main parts to Second Life are:

- **The World:** The world of Second Life is constantly changing and growing. It is filled with hundreds of games, from multi-player role-playing games to puzzles and grid-wide contests. There are also dance clubs, shopping malls, space stations, vampire castles' and movie theaters. To find something to do at any time of the day or night, residents simply open the Search menu and click on Events for a listing of discussions, sports, commercial, entertainment, games, pageants, education, arts and culture, and charity/support groups.

- **The Creations:** Second Life is dedicated to creativity. Everything in Second Life is resident-created, from the strobe lights in the nightclubs to the cars (or spaceships) in driveways. Imagine tinkering with the steering and handling program of a motorcycle while a friend tweaks the shape of the fuel tank and gives it a wicked flame paint job, in-world and in real-time, before taking it for a spin down a newly created road to look for land to buy. Have you ever wondered what it would be like to have a pair of black leather wings? Build them and give it a go.

- **The Marketplace:** The Marketplace currently supports millions of U.S. dollars in monthly transactions. This commerce is handled with the in-world unit of trade, the Linden dollar, which can be converted to U.S. dollars at several thriving online Linden dollar exchanges. Users can make real money in a virtual world because Second Life has a fully integrated economy designed to reward risk, innovation, and craftsmanship. Residents create their own virtual goods and services. Residents retain the intellectual property rights of their creations and can sell them at various in-world venues. Businesses succeed by the ingenuity, artistic ability, entrepreneurial acumen, and good reputation of their owners. Residents who have amassed lots of Linden dollars are matched with residents who want to buy Linden dollars at LindeX (the official Linden dollar exchange) or at other unaffiliated third-party exchanges.

## Businesses on Second Life

Second Life is an exciting new venue for collaboration, business ventures, distance learning, new media studies, and marketing. Business possibilities on Second Life are endless; a few examples include:

- Hold a virtual meeting with sales managers located in Europe and Asia.
- Present new sales initiatives and discuss them with the team real-time.
- Build a new world that allows Second Life residents to interact with company products or services and test new designs and concepts before introducing them to the real world.
- Sell products and services in Second Life by creating an event to promote the product: a concert, a class, a famous speaker, a party, a contest. Many companies are excited about the numerous ways they can use Second Life to support their business. A few companies paving the way on Second Life include:

| | | |
|---|---|---|
| 1-800-flowers.com | H&R Block | Sony |
| Adidas | IBM | Sprint |
| Amazon | Intel | Student Travel Association |
| American Apparel | Kraft Food | Starwood Hotels |
| American Cancer Society | Lacoste | Sundance Channel |
| BBC Radio 1 | Major League Baseball | Toyota |
| Best Buy Co. Inc. | Mazda | Universal Motown Records |
| BMW | Mercedes-Benz | Visa |
| Calvin Klein | Microsft | Warner bros. Music |
| Circuit City | MTV | Weather Channel |
| Cisco | NASA | *Wired* magazine |
| Coca-cola | National Basketball | Xerox |
| Coldwell Banker | Assocation | Yahoo |
| Comcast | NBC | Yankee Stadium |
| Crayola | Nissan | |
| Dell | NPR | |

## Second Life Success Stories

### Virtual Dublin

John Mahon, known as Ham Rambler in Second Life, created the popular city of Dublin. His company, PickSL.net, builds community-based businesses in Second Life. Dublin, as John explains, started with an Irish bar, some great barmen, and plenty of good-spirited conversation. Since then, it has become a destination location in Second Life. "I joined Second Life more than two years ago," John says. "I felt what was missing was a comfortable, easygoing place to meet, talk, and interact. In other words: a good Irish bar. Everyone knows what a good Irish bar is. It needs no marketing. So I built the bar, and it was incredibly successful. I streamed in Irish music. There were lots of friendly people. I didn't start Dublin as a commercial project. It started as a bar where people could gather, hang out, and bring their friends. And then it became clear that people wanted more and that I should build a city around the bar. Build a larger context, in other words. That's where Dublin came from. It's a place people will go," John says.

### Infinite Vision Media

The interactive marketing agency Infinite Vision Media specializes in 3D web spaces. Once part of the original team that created the lovely Dublin region, IVM now uses its deep real-world experience in advertising, branding, architecture, and programming to create immersive experiences for Second Life residents.

### Neo-Realms Entertainment

As a game and content developer, Neo-Realms Entertainment has hooked the big one in Second Life. The flagship game, Neo-Realms Fishing, can be played at three different fishing camps in-world. "We created the first fishing camp in 2004," says co-founder and designer Steven McCall (known as Sweegy Manilow in Second Life). Steve and his fellow Neo-Realmers, Thanh Ha and Bryan King, were casting in real-world ponds when they realized the dearth of fishing games online. "We thought, 'All MMPGs really need fishing,'" Steve says, laughing. Although it sounded a little esoteric, it turned out that the threesome had their fingers on the pulse of consumer taste. Their little fishing expedition became a huge hit. Featuring various rod and bait types, their system offers fishing quests, reward points redeemable for prizes, and daily multiplayer tournaments for prizes and money. "It's also just a good place to hang out with your friends and socialize," says Steve.

### Crescendo Design

In the real world of Wisconsin, architect Jon Brouchoud and his team at Crescendo Design create custom homes and sell plans for Springboard Homes. Their goal is to make energy-efficient, green design features more affordable. Jon and his team have found Second Life to be a great architectural tool. They use Second Life both within their company and among long-distance clients to create virtual designs and structures.

### Global Kids

Global Kids is a nonprofit group working to prepare urban youth to become global citizens and community leaders. With help from Main Grid content creators and consultants like The Magicians and the Electric Sheep Company, Global Kids created a program where students in New York City collaborate with Teen Grid Residents from around the world. The teens had to finish the interactive adventure to participate in a real-world essay contest. Winners of the contest received cash prizes (in U.S. dollars) and were part of an awards ceremony co-broadcast into the Teen Grid and on stage in New York City.

### American Apparel

American Apparel opened a store in Second Life on Lerappa Island (Lerappa is apparel spelled backward). Resident Aimee Weber was responsible for the build. What makes this opening so special is that it makes an exclusive offer for Second Life residents. Purchasers at the in-world American Apparel store will get a notecard with a promotional code offering a real life discount at American Apparel's online store.

### Sire Records/Regina Spektor

Recently, Sire Records and musician Regina Spektor launched an interactive, virtual listening party for her fourth album, *Begin to Hope,* inside Second Life. Songs from the album were available at six listening posts in a virtual New York City loft in-world.

### Marvin the Robot

When Rivers Run Red was asked to create Marvin the Robot for the film *Hitchhikers Guide to the Galaxy,* Justin Bovington headed for Second Life. Rivers Run Red is an innovative marketing and communication firm located in the United Kingdom, and Justin is Fizik Baskerville, a developer in Second Life where he creates his ideas and makes them real. With Marvin, Justin successfully demonstrated Second Life's viability as a development platform—blurring the line between Second Life and real life.

# Introduction

Decision making and problem solving in today's electronic world encompass large-scale, opportunity-oriented, strategically focused solutions. The traditional "cookbook" approach to decisions simply will not work in the ebusiness world. Decision-making and problem-solving abilities are now the most sought-after traits in up-and-coming executives, according to a recent survey of 1,000 executives by Caliper Associates, as reported in *The Wall Street Journal*. To put it mildly, decision makers and problem solvers have limitless career potential.

***Ebusiness*** is the conducting of business on the Internet, not only buying and selling, but also serving customers and collaborating with business partners. (Unit Four discusses ebusiness in detail.) With the fast growth of information technology and the accelerated use of the Internet, ebusiness is quickly becoming standard. This unit focuses on technology to help make decisions, solve problems, and find new innovative opportunities. The unit highlights how to bring people together with the best IT processes and tools in complete, flexible solutions that can seize business opportunities (see Figure Unit 3.1). The chapters in Unit 3 are:

- **Chapter Nine**—Enabling the Organization—Decision Making.
- **Chapter Ten**—Extending the Organization—Supply Chain Management.
- **Chapter Eleven**—Building a Customer-centric Organization—Customer Relationship Management.
- **Chapter Twelve**—Integrating the Organization from End to End—Enterprise Resource Planning.

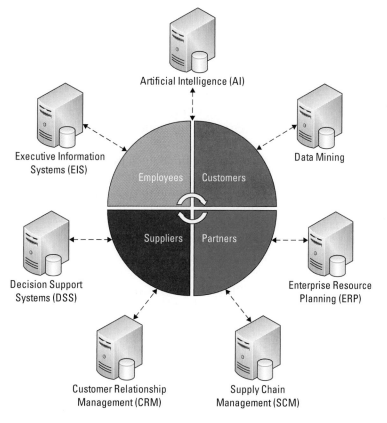

**FIGURE UNIT 3.1**

Decision-Enabling, Problem-Solving, and Opportunity-Seizing Systems

# 9

# Enabling the Organization—Decision Making

**9.1.** Define the systems organizations use to make decisions and gain competitive advantages.

**9.2.** Describe the three quantitative models typically used by decision support systems.

**9.3.** Describe the relationship between digital dashboards and executive information systems.

**9.4.** List and describe four types of artificial intelligence systems.

## Decision Making

What is the value of information? The answer to this important question varies. Karsten Solheim would say that the value of information is its ability to lower a company's handicap. Solheim, an avid golfer, invented a putter, one with a "ping," that led to a successful golf equipment company and the Ping golf clubs. Ping Inc., a privately held corporation, was the first to offer customizable golf clubs. And Ping thanks information technology for the explosion of its business over the past decade.

Ping prides itself on being a just-in-time manufacturer that depends on a highly flexible information system to make informed production decisions. The system scans Ping's vast amounts of order information and pulls orders that meet certain criteria such as order date, order priority, and customer type. Ping then places the appropriate inventory orders allowing the company to maintain only 5 percent of its inventory in its warehouse. Ping depends on its flexible information systems for both decision support and operational problem solving.

Business is accelerating at a breakneck pace. The more information a business acquires, the more difficult it becomes to make decisions. Hence, the amount of information people must understand to make good decisions is growing exponentially. In the past, people could rely on manual processes to make decisions because they had only limited amounts of information to deal with. Today, with massive volumes of available information it is almost impossible for people to make decisions without the aid of information systems. Figure 9.1 highlights the primary reasons dependence on information systems to make decisions and solve problems is growing and will continue to grow.

A *model* is a simplified representation or abstraction of reality. Models can calculate risks, understand uncertainty, change variables, and manipulate time. Decision-making information systems work by building models out of organizational information to lend insight into important business issues and opportunities. Figure 9.2 displays three common types of decision-making information systems used in organizations today. Each system uses different models to assist in decision making, problem solving, and opportunity capturing. These systems include:

- Transaction Processing Systems.
- Decision Support Systems.
- Executive Information Systems.

| Reasons for Growth of Decision-Making Information Systems |
|---|
| 1. **People need to analyze large amounts of information**—Improvements in technology itself, innovations in communication, and globalization have resulted in a dramatic increase in the alternatives and dimensions people need to consider when making a decision or appraising an opportunity. |
| 2. **People must make decisions quickly**—Time is of the essence and people simply do not have time to sift through all the information manually. |
| 3. **People must apply sophisticated analysis techniques, such as modeling and forecasting, to make good decisions**—Information systems substantially reduce the time required to perform these sophisticated analysis techniques. |
| 4. **People must protect the corporate asset of organizational information**—Information systems offer the security required to ensure organizational information remains safe. |

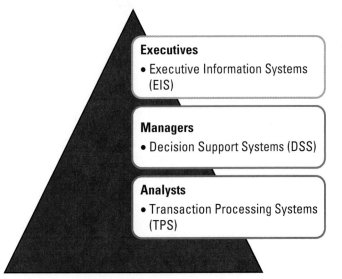

**Organizational Levels**

**FIGURE 9.2**

IT Systems in an
Enterprise

# Transaction Processing Systems

The structure of a typical organization is similar to a pyramid. Organizational activities occur at different levels of the pyramid. People in the organization have unique information needs and thus require various sets of IT tools (see Figure 9.3). At the lower levels of the pyramid, people perform daily tasks such as processing transactions. ***Online transaction processing (OLTP)*** is the capturing of transaction and event information using technology to (1) process the information according to defined business rules, (2) store the information, and (3) update existing information to reflect the new information. During OLTP, the organization must capture every detail of transactions and events. A ***transaction processing system (TPS)*** is the basic business system that serves the operational level (analysts) in an organization. The most common example of a TPS is an operational accounting system such as a payroll system or an order-entry system.

Moving up through the organizational pyramid, people (typically managers) deal less with the details ("finer" information) and more with meaningful aggregations of information ("coarser" information) that help them make broader decisions for the organization. (Granularity means "fine" and detailed or "coarse" and abstract information.) ***Online analytical processing (OLAP)*** is the manipulation of information to create business intelligence in support of strategic decision making.

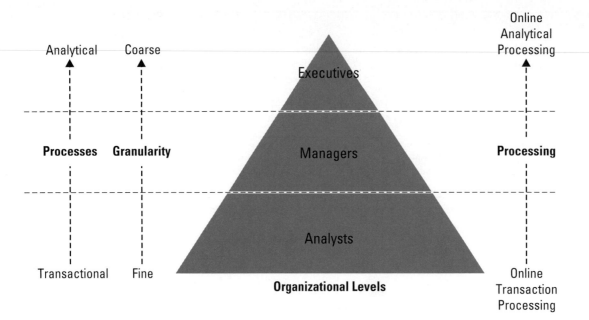

**FIGURE** 9.3

Enterprise View of Information and Information Technology

# Decision Support Systems

At limousine and transportation company BostonCoach, the most critical process for managers is dispatching a fleet of hundreds of vehicles as efficiently as possible. BostonCoach requires a real-time dispatching system that considers inventory, customer needs, and soft dimensions such as weather and traffic. Researchers at IBM's Thomas J. Watson Research Center built BostonCoach a mathematical algorithm for a custom dispatch system that combines information about weather, traffic conditions, driver locations, and customer pickup requests and tells BostonCoach dispatchers which cars to assign to which customers. The system is so efficient that, after launching it in Atlanta, BostonCoach experienced a 20 percent increase in revenues.

A *decision support system (DSS),* such as BostonCoach's, models information to support managers and business professionals during the decision-making process. Three quantitative models are typically used by DSSs: (1) sensitivity analysis, (2) what-if analysis, and (3) goal-seeking analysis.

1. *Sensitivity analysis* is the study of the impact that changes in one (or more) parts of the model have on other parts of the model. Users change the value of one variable repeatedly and observe the resulting changes in other variables.

2. *What-if analysis* checks the impact of a change in an assumption on the proposed solution. For example, "What will happen to the supply chain if a hurricane in South Carolina reduces holding inventory from 30 percent to 10 percent?" Users repeat this analysis until they understand all the effects of various situations. Figure 9.4 displays an example of what-if analysis using Microsoft Excel. The tool is calculating the net effect of a 20 percent increase in sales on the company's bottom line.

3. *Goal-seeking analysis* finds the inputs necessary to achieve a goal such as a desired level of output. Instead of observing how changes in a variable affect other variables as in what-if analysis, goal-seeking analysis sets a target value (a goal) for a variable and then repeatedly changes other variables until the target value is achieved. For example, "How many customers are required to purchase our new product line to increase gross profits to $5 million?" Figure 9.5 displays a goal-seeking scenario using Microsoft Excel. The model is seeking the monthly mortgage payment needed to pay off the remaining balance in 130 months.

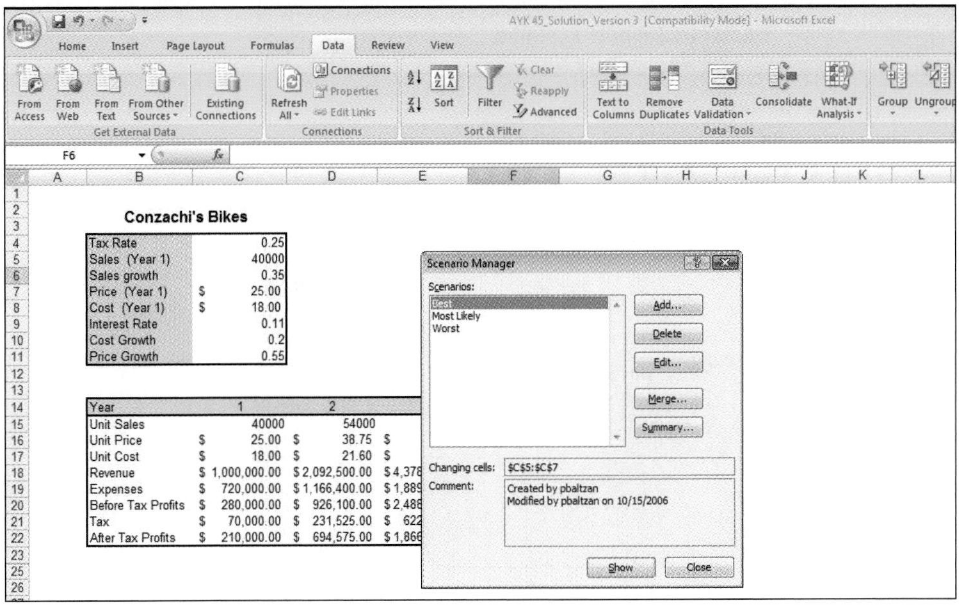

**FIGURE** 9.4

Example of What-If
Analysis in Microsoft
Excel

**FIGURE** 9.4

Example of What-If
Analysis in Microsoft
Excel

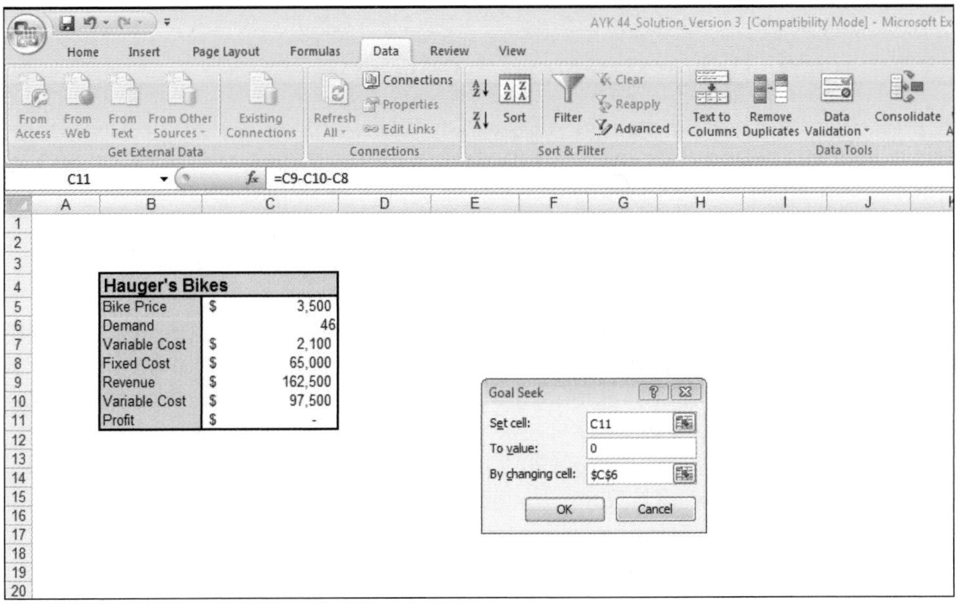

**FIGURE** 9.5

Examples of Goal-Seeking
Analysis in Microsoft
Excel

One national insurance company uses DSSs to analyze the amount of risk the company is undertaking when it insures drivers who have a history of driving under the influence of alcohol. The DSS discovered that only 3 percent of married male homeowners in their forties received more than one DUI. The company decided to lower rates for customers falling into this category, which increased its revenue while mitigating its risk.

Figure 9.6 displays how a TPS is used within a DSS. The TPS supplies transaction-based data to the DSS. The DSS summarizes and aggregates the information from the many different TPS systems, which assists managers in making informed decisions. Burlington Northern and Santa Fe Railroad (BNSF) regularly tests its railroad tracks. Each year hundreds of train derailments result from defective tracks. Using a DSS to schedule train track replacements helped BNSF decrease its rail-caused derailments by 33 percent.

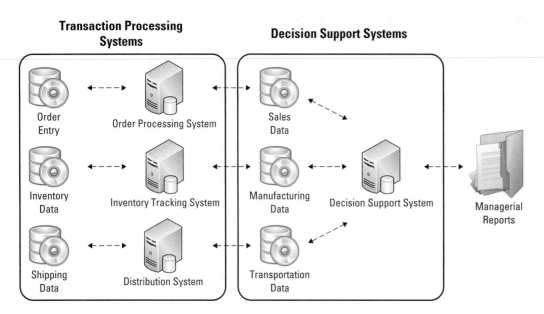

**Transaction Processing Systems**

Order Entry

Order Processing System

Inventory Data

Inventory Tracking System

Shipping Data

Distribution System

**Decision Support Systems**

Sales Data

Manufacturing Data

Decision Support System

Transportation Data

Managerial Reports

**FIGURE 9.6**

Interaction Between TPSs and DSSs

# Executive Information Systems

An *executive information system (EIS)* is a specialized DSS that supports senior-level executives within the organization. An EIS differs from a DSS because an EIS typically contains data from external sources as well as data from internal sources (see Figure 9.7).

Consolidation, drill-down, and slice-and-dice are a few of the capabilities offered in most EISs.

- *Consolidation* involves the aggregation of information and features simple roll-ups to complex groupings of interrelated information. Many organizations track financial information at a regional level and then consolidate the information at a single global level.

- *Drill-down* enables users to get details, and details of details, of information. Viewing monthly, weekly, daily, or even hourly information represents drill-down capability.

- *Slice-and-dice* is the ability to look at information from different perspectives. One slice of information could display all product sales during a given promotion. Another slice could display a single product's sales for all promotions.

## DIGITAL DASHBOARDS

A common feature of an EIS is a digital dashboard. *Digital dashboards* integrate information from multiple components and tailor the information to individual preferences. Digital dashboards commonly use indicators to help executives quickly identify the status of key information or critical success factors. Following is a list of potential features included in a dashboard designed for a senior executive of an oil refinery:

- A hot list of key performance indicators, refreshed every 15 minutes.

- A running line graph of planned versus actual production for the past 24 hours.

- A table showing actual versus forecasted product prices and inventories.

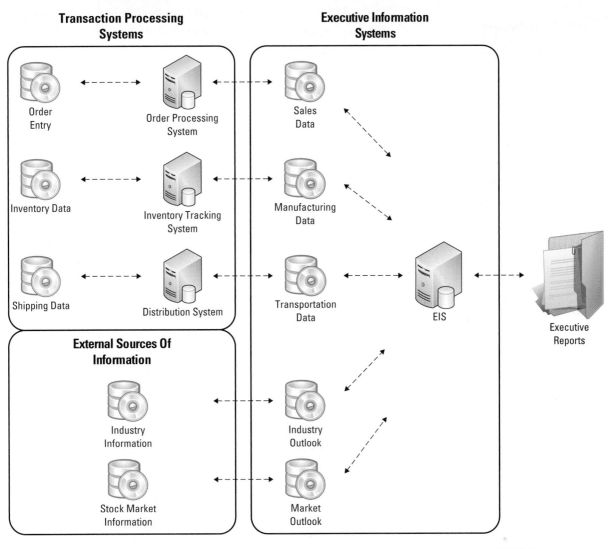

**Transaction Processing Systems**

Order Entry

Order Processing System

Inventory Data

Inventory Tracking System

Shipping Data

Distribution System

**External Sources Of Information**

Industry Information

Stock Market Information

**Executive Information Systems**

Sales Data

Manufacturing Data

Transportation Data

Industry Outlook

Market Outlook

EIS

Executive Reports

**FIGURE 9.7**

Interaction Between TPSs and EISs

- A list of outstanding alerts and their resolution status.
- A graph of crude-oil stock market prices.
- A scroll of headline news from Petroleum Company news, an industry news service.

Digital dashboards, whether basic or comprehensive, deliver results quickly. As digital dashboards become easier to use, more executives can perform their own analysis without inundating IT personnel with questions and requests for reports. According to an independent study by Nucleus Research, there is a direct correlation between use of digital dashboards and companies' return on investment (ROI). Figure 9.8 and Figure 9.9 display two different digital dashboards from Visual Mining.

EIS systems, such as digital dashboards, allow executives to move beyond reporting to using information to directly impact business performance. Digital dashboards help executives react to information as it becomes available and make decisions, solve problems, and change strategies daily instead of monthly.

Verizon Communications CIO Shaygan Kheradpir tracks 100-plus major IT systems on a single screen called "The Wall of Shaygan." Every 15 seconds, a new set of charts communicating Verizon's performance flashes onto a giant LCD screen in Kheradpir's office. The 44 screen shots cycle continuously, all day long, every

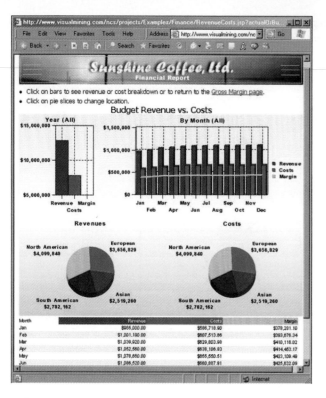

day. The dashboard includes more than 300 measures of business performance that fall into one of three categories:

1. **Market pulse**—examples include daily sales numbers, market share, and subscriber turnover.

2. **Customer service**—examples include problems resolved on the first call, call center wait times, and on-time repair calls.

3. **Cost driver**—examples include number of repair trucks in the field, repair jobs completed per day, and call center productivity.

Kheradpir has memorized the screens and can tell at a glance when the lines on the charts are not trending as expected. The system informs him of events such as the percentage of customer calls resolved by voice systems, number of repair trucks in the field, and amount of time to resolve an IT system issue. The dashboard works the same way for 400 managers at every level of Verizon. There are two primary types of executive informative system: artificial intelligence and data mining.

**FIGURE 9.8**

Visual Mining, NetCharts Corporate Financial Dashboard

# Artificial Intelligence (AI)

Executive information systems are starting to take advantage of artificial intelligence to help executives make strategic decisions. RivalWatch, based in Santa Clara, California, offers a strategic business information service using artificial intelligence that enables organizations to track the product offerings, pricing policies, and promotions of online competitors. Clients can determine the competitors they want to watch and the specific information they wish to gather, ranging from

**FIGURE 9.9**

Visual Mining, NetCharts Marketing Communications Dashboard

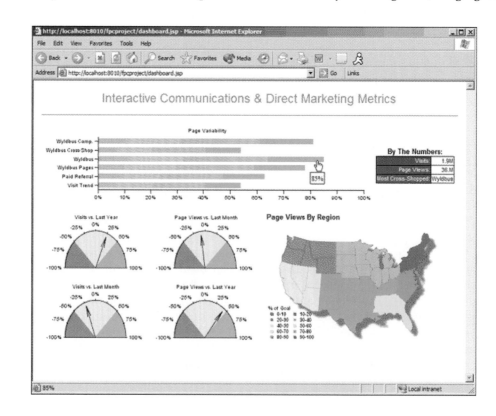

products added, removed, or out of stock to price changes, coupons offered, and special shipping terms. Clients can check each competitor, category, and product either daily, weekly, monthly, or quarterly.

"Competing in the Internet arena is a whole different ballgame than doing business in the traditional brick-and-mortar world because you're competing with the whole world rather than the store down the block or a few miles away," said Phil Lumish, vice president of sales and marketing at RivalWatch.com. "With new products and campaigns being introduced at a breakneck pace, ebusinesses need new tools to monitor the competitive environment, and our service is designed specifically to meet that need."

***Intelligent systems*** are various commercial applications of artificial intelligence. ***Artificial intelligence (AI)*** simulates human intelligence such as the ability to reason and learn. AI systems can learn or understand from experience, make sense of ambiguous or contradictory information, and even use reasoning to solve problems and make decisions effectively. AI systems can perform such tasks as boosting productivity in factories by monitoring equipment and signaling when preventive maintenance is required. The ultimate goal of AI is the ability to build a system that can mimic human intelligence. AI systems are beginning to show up everywhere:

- At Manchester Airport in England, the Hefner AI Robot Cleaner alerts passengers to security and nonsmoking rules while it scrubs up to 65,600 square feet of floor per day. Laser scanners and ultrasonic detectors keep it from colliding with passengers.

- Shell Oil's SmartPump keeps drivers in their cars on cold, wet winter days. It can service any automobile built after 1987 that has been fitted with a special gas cap and a windshield-mounted transponder that tells the robot where to insert the pump.

- Matsushita's courier robot navigates hospital hallways, delivering patient files, X-ray films, and medical supplies.

- The FireFighter AI Robot can extinguish flames at chemical plants and nuclear reactors with water, foam, powder, or inert gas. The robot puts distance between the human operator and the fire.

AI systems dramatically increase the speed and consistency of decision making, solve problems with incomplete information, and resolve complicated issues that cannot be solved by conventional computing. There are many categories of AI systems; four of the most familiar are: (1) expert systems, (2) neural networks, (3) genetic algorithms, and (4) intelligent agents.

## EXPERT SYSTEMS

***Expert systems*** are computerized advisory programs that imitate the reasoning processes of experts in solving difficult problems. Human expertise is transferred to the expert system and users can access the expert system for specific advice. Most expert systems reflect expertise from many humans and can therefore perform better analysis than any single expert. Typically, the system includes a knowledge

*Examples of AI Systems*

base containing various accumulated experience and a set of rules for applying the knowledge base to each particular situation. The best-known expert systems play chess and assist in medical diagnosis. Expert systems are the most commonly used form of AI in the business arena because they fill the gap when human experts are difficult to find, hard to retain, or too expensive.

## NEURAL NETWORKS

A *neural network,* also called an *artificial neural network,* is a category of AI that attempts to emulate the way the human brain works. The types of decisions for which neural networks are most useful are those that involve pattern or image recognition because a neural network can learn from the information it processes. Neural networks analyze large quantities of information to establish patterns and characteristics in situations where the logic or rules are unknown.

The finance industry is a veteran in neural network technology and has been relying on various forms of it for over two decades. The industry uses neural networks to review loan applications and create patterns or profiles of applications that fall into two categories: approved or denied. One neural network has become the standard for detecting credit card fraud. Since 1992, this technology has slashed fraud by 70 percent for U.S. Bancorp. Now, even small credit unions are required to use the software in order to qualify for debit-card insurance from Credit Union National Association. Additional examples of neural networks include:

- Citibank uses neural networks to find opportunities in financial markets. By carefully examining historical stock market data with neural network software, Citibank financial managers learn of interesting coincidences or small anomalies (called market inefficiencies). For example, it could be that whenever IBM stock goes up, so does Unisys stock. Or it might be that a U.S. Treasury note is selling for 1 cent less in Japan than it is in the United States. These snippets of information can make a big difference to Citibank's bottom line in a very competitive financial market.

- In Westminster, California, a community of 87,000 people, police use neural network software to fight crime. With crime reports as input, the system detects and maps local crime patterns. Police say that with this system they can better predict crime trends, improve patrol assignments, and develop better crime prevention programs.

- Fingerhut, the mail-order company based in Minnesota, has 6 million people on its customer list. To determine which customers were and were not likely to order from its catalog, Fingerhut recently switched to neural network software. The company finds that the new software is more effective and expects to generate millions of dollars by fine-tuning its mailing lists.

- Fraud detection widely uses neural networks. Visa, MasterCard, and many other credit card companies use a neural network to spot peculiarities in individual accounts. MasterCard estimates neural networks save it $50 million annually.

- Many insurance companies (Cigna, AIG, Travelers, Liberty Mutual, Hartford) along with state compensation funds and other carriers use neural network software to identify fraud. The system searches for patterns in billing charges, laboratory tests, and frequency of office visits. A claim for which the diagnosis was a sprained ankle but included an electrocardiogram would be flagged for the account manager.

- FleetBoston Financial Corporation uses a neural network to watch transactions with customers. The neural network can detect patterns that may indicate a customer's growing dissatisfaction with the company. The neural network looks for signs like decreases in the number of transactions or in the account balance of one of FleetBoston's high-value customers.

Neural networks' many features include:

- Learning and adjusting to new circumstances on their own.
- Lending themselves to massive parallel processing.

- Functioning without complete or well-structured information.
- Coping with huge volumes of information with many dependent variables.
- Analyzing nonlinear relationships in information (they have been called fancy regression analysis systems).

The biggest problem with neural networks to date has been that the hidden layers are hidden. It is difficult to see how the neural network is learning and how the neurons are interacting. Newer neural networks no longer hide the middle layers. With these systems, users can manually adjust the weights or connections, giving them more flexibility and control.

*Fuzzy logic* is a mathematical method of handling imprecise or subjective information. The basic approach is to assign values between 0 and 1 to vague or ambiguous information. The higher the value, the closer it is to 1. For instance, the value zero is used to represent nonmembership, and the value one is used to represent membership. Fuzzy logic is used in washing machines that determine by themselves how much water to use or how long to wash (they continue washing until the water is clean). In accounting and finance, fuzzy logic allows people to analyze information with subjective financial values (like intangibles such as goodwill) that are very important considerations in economic analysis. Fuzzy logic and neural networks are often combined to express complicated and subjective concepts in a form that makes it possible to simplify the problem and apply rules that are executed with a level of certainty.

## GENETIC ALGORITHMS

A *genetic algorithm* is an artificial intelligence system that mimics the evolutionary, survival-of-the-fittest process to generate increasingly better solutions to a problem. A genetic algorithm is essentially an optimizing system: It finds the combination of inputs to yield the best outputs.

Genetic algorithms are best suited to decision-making environments in which thousands, or perhaps millions, of solutions are possible. Genetic algorithms can find and evaluate solutions with many more possibilities, faster and more thoroughly than a human. Organizations face decision-making environments for all types of problems that require optimization techniques such as the following:

- Business executives use genetic algorithms to help them decide which combination of projects a firm should invest in, taking complicated tax considerations into account.
- Investment companies use genetic algorithms to help in trading decisions.
- Telecommunication companies use genetic algorithms to determine the optimal configuration of fiber-optic cable in a network that may include as many as 100,000 connection points. The genetic algorithm evaluates millions of cable configurations and selects the one that uses the least amount of cable.

## INTELLIGENT AGENTS

An *intelligent agent* is a special-purpose knowledge-based information system that accomplishes specific tasks on behalf of its users. Intelligent agents use their knowledge base to make decisions and accomplish tasks in a way that fulfills the intentions of a user. Intelligent agents usually have a graphical representation such as "Sherlock Holmes" for an information search agent.

One of the simplest examples of an intelligent agent is a shopping bot. A *shopping bot* is software that will search several retailer websites and provide a comparison of each retailer's offerings including price and availability. Increasingly, intelligent agents handle the majority of a company's Internet buying and selling and handle such processes as finding products, bargaining over prices, and executing transactions. Intelligent agents also have the capability to handle all supply chain buying and selling.

Another application for intelligent agents is in environmental scanning and competitive intelligence. For instance, an intelligent agent can learn the types of competitor information users want to track, continuously scan the web for it, and alert users when a significant event occurs.

By 2010, some 4 million AI robots are expected to populate homes and businesses, performing everything from pumping gas to delivering mail. According to a new report by the United Nations and the International Federation of Robotics, more than half the AI robots will be toys and the other half will perform services. Bots will deactivate bombs, clean skyscraper windows, and vacuum homes.

### Multi-Agent Systems and Agent-Based Modeling

What do cargo transport systems, book distribution centers, the video game market, a flu epidemic, and an ant colony have in common? They are all complex adaptive systems and thus share some common characteristics. By observing parts of the ecosystem, like ant or bee colonies, artificial intelligence scientists can use hardware and software models that incorporate insect characteristics and behavior to (1) learn how people-based systems behave; (2) predict how they will behave under a given set of circumstances; and (3) improve human systems to make them more efficient and effective. This concept of learning from ecosystems and adapting their characteristics to human and organizational situations is called *biomimicry.*

In the last few years, AI research has made much progress in modeling complex organizations as a whole with the help of *multi-agent systems.* In a multi-agent system, groups of intelligent agents have the ability to work independently and to interact with each other. The simulation of a human organization using a multi-agent system is called *agent-based modeling.* Agent-based modeling is a way of simulating human organizations using multiple intelligent agents, each of which follows a set of simple rules and can adapt to changing conditions.

Agent-based modeling systems are being used to model stock market fluctuations, predict the escape routes that people seek in a burning building, estimate the effects of interest rates on consumers with different types of debt, and anticipate how changes in conditions will affect the supply chain, to name just a few. Examples of companies that have used agent-based modeling to their advantage include:

- Southwest Airlines—to optimize cargo routing.
- Procter & Gamble—to overhaul its handling of what the company calls its "supply network" of 5 billion consumers in 140 countries.
- Air Liquide America—to reduce production and distribution costs of liquefied industrial gases.
- Merck & Co.—to find more efficient ways of distributing anti-AIDS drugs in Africa.
- Ford Motor Co.—to build a model of consumer preferences and find the best balance between production costs and customers' demands.
- Edison Chouest Offshore LLC—to find the best way to deploy its service and supply vessels in the Gulf of Mexico.

# Data Mining

Wal-Mart consolidates point-of-sale details from its 3,000 stores and uses AI to transform the information into business intelligence. Data-mining systems sift instantly through the information to uncover patterns and relationships that would elude an army of human researchers. The results enable Wal-Mart to predict sales of every product at each store with uncanny accuracy, translating into huge savings in inventories and maximum payoff from promotional spending. Figure 9.10 displays the average organizational spending on data-mining tools.

Data-mining software typically includes many forms of AI such as neural networks and expert systems. Data-mining tools apply algorithms to information sets to uncover inherent trends and patterns in the information, which analysts use to develop new business strategies. Analysts use the output from data-mining tools to build models that, when exposed to new information sets, perform a variety of data analysis functions. The analysts provide business solutions by putting together the analytical techniques and the business problem at hand, which often reveals important new correlations, patterns, and trends in information.

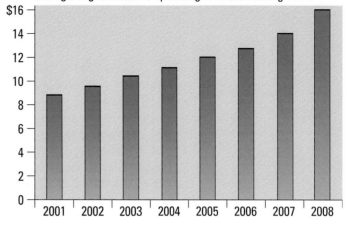

Average Organizational Spending on Data-Mining Tools*

**FIGURE 9.10**

Data-Mining Tools Investment Forecast

--------------------

\* In millions of dollars

---

## OPENING CASE STUDY QUESTIONS

1. How could companies use Second Life for new product or service decision making?
2. How could financial companies use neural networks in Second Life to help their businesses?
3. How could a company such as Nike use decision support systems on Second Life to help its business?
4. How could an apparel company use Second Life to enhance decision making for a new product or service offering?

---

## Chapter Nine Case: Defense Advanced Research Projects Agency (DARPA) Grand Challenge

The DARPA Grand Challenge was designed to leverage American ingenuity to develop autonomous vehicle technologies that can be used by the military. Created in response to a Congressional and U.S. Department of Defense (DoD) mandate with the goal of saving lives on the battlefield, the DARPA Grand Challenge brings together individuals and organizations from industry, the R&D community, government, the armed services, and academia, and includes students, backyard inventors, and automotive enthusiasts.

### DARPA Grand Challenge 2004

The DARPA Grand Challenge 2004 field test of autonomous ground vehicles ran from Barstow, California, to Primm, Nevada, and offered a $1 million prize. From the qualifying round at the

California Speedway, 15 finalists emerged to attempt the Grand Challenge. However, the prize went unclaimed as no vehicles were able to complete the difficult desert route.

## DARPA Grand Challenge 2005

The DARPA Grand Challenge 2005 was held on October 8, 2005, in the Mojave Desert and offered a $2 million prize to the team that completed the course the fastest in under 10 hours. Five teams completed the Grand Challenge course of 132 miles over desert terrain, and Stanley, the Stanford Racing Team's car, garnered the $2 million prize with a winning time of 6 hours, 53 minutes.

The Grand Challenge demonstrated that autonomous ground vehicles can travel long distances across difficult terrain at militarily relevant rates of speed. DARPA Director Dr. Tony Tether said, "When the Wright brothers flew their little plane, they proved it could be done, and just as aviation 'took off' after those achievements, so will the very exciting and promising robotics technologies displayed here today."

## Questions

1. Describe how the DoD is using AI to improve its operations and save lives.
2. Explain why the DoD would use an event, such as the DARPA Grand Challenge, to further technological innovation.
3. Describe how autonomous vehicles could be used by organizations around the world to improve business efficiency and effectiveness.
4. The Ansari X is another technological innovation competition focusing on spacecraft. To win the $10 million Ansari X Prize, a private spacecraft had to be the first to carry the weight equivalent of three people to an altitude of 62.14 miles twice within two weeks. SpaceShipOne, a privately built spacecraft, won the $10 million Ansari X Prize on October 4, 2004. Describe the potential business impacts of the Ansari X competition.

# Extending the Organization—Supply Chain Management

**10.1.** List and describe the components of a typical supply chain.

**10.2.** Define the relationship between decision making and supply chain management.

**10.3.** Describe the four changes resulting from advances in IT that are driving supply chains.

**10.4.** Summarize the best practices for implementing a successful supply chain management system.

## Supply Chain Management

Companies that excel in supply chain operations perform better in almost every financial measure of success, according to a report from Boston-based AMR Research Inc. When supply chain excellence improves operations, companies experience a 5 percent higher profit margin, 15 percent less inventory, 17 percent stronger "perfect order" ratings, and 35 percent shorter cycle times than their competitors. "The basis of competition for winning companies in today's economy is supply chain superiority," says Kevin O'Marah, vice president of research at AMR Research. "These companies understand that value chain performance translates to productivity and market-share leadership. They also understand that supply chain leadership means more than just low costs and efficiency; it requires a superior ability to shape and respond to shifts in demand with innovative products and services."

## Basics of Supply Chain

The average company spends nearly half of every dollar that it earns on production needs—goods and services it needs from external suppliers to keep producing. A *supply chain* consists of all parties involved, directly or indirectly, in the procurement of a product or raw material. *Supply chain management (SCM)* involves the management of information flows between and among stages in a supply chain to maximize total supply chain effectiveness and profitability.

In the past, companies focused primarily on manufacturing and quality improvements within their four walls; now their efforts extend beyond those walls to influence the entire supply chain including customers, customers' customers, suppliers, and suppliers' suppliers. Today's supply chain is a complex web of suppliers, assemblers, logistic firms, sales/marketing channels, and other business partners linked primarily through information networks and contractual relationships. SCM systems enhance and manage the relationships. The supply chain has three main links (see Figure 10.1):

1. Materials flow from suppliers and their upstream suppliers at all levels.
2. Transformation of materials into semi-finished and finished products, or the organization's own production processes.
3. Distribution of products to customers and their downstream customers at all levels.

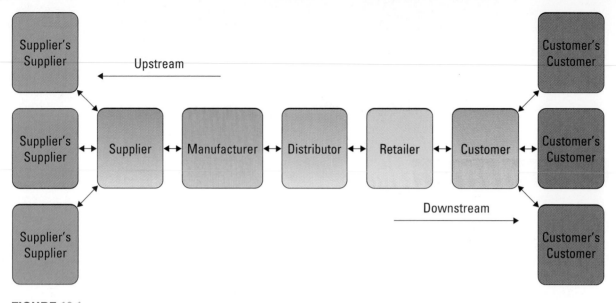

**FIGURE** 10.1

A Typical Supply Chain

Organizations must embrace technologies that can effectively manage and oversee their supply chains. SCM is becoming increasingly important in creating organizational efficiencies and competitive advantages. Best Buy checks inventory levels at each of its 750 stores in North America as often as every half-hour with its SCM system, taking much of the guesswork out of inventory replenishment. Supply chain management improves ways for companies to find the raw components they need to make a product or service, manufacture that product or service, and deliver it to customers. Figure 10.2 highlights the five basic components for supply chain management.

Technology advances in the five SCM components have significantly improved companies' forecasting and business operations in the last few years. Businesses today have access to modeling and simulation tools, algorithms, and applications that can combine information from multiple sources to build forecasts for days, weeks, and months in advance. Better forecasts for tomorrow result in better preparedness today.

Mattel Inc. spent several years investing heavily in software and processes that simplify its supply chain, cut costs, and shorten cycle times. Using supply chain management strategies the company cut weeks out of the time it takes to design, produce, and ship everything from Barbies to Hot Wheels. Mattel installed optimization software that measures, tweaks, and validates the operations of its seven distribution centers, seven manufacturing plants, and other facilities that make up its vast worldwide supply chain. Mattel improved forecasting from monthly to weekly. The company no longer produces more inventory than stores require and delivers inventory upon request. Mattel's supply chain moves quickly to make precise forecasts that help the company meet demand.

# Information Technology's Role in the Supply Chain

As companies evolve into extended organizations, the roles of supply chain participants are changing. It is now common for suppliers to be involved in product development and for distributors to act as consultants in brand marketing. The notion of virtually seamless information links within and between organizations is an essential element of integrated supply chains.

Information technology's primary role in SCM is creating the integrations or tight process and information linkages between functions within a firm—such as

FIGURE 10.2

The Five Basic Supply
Chain Management
Components

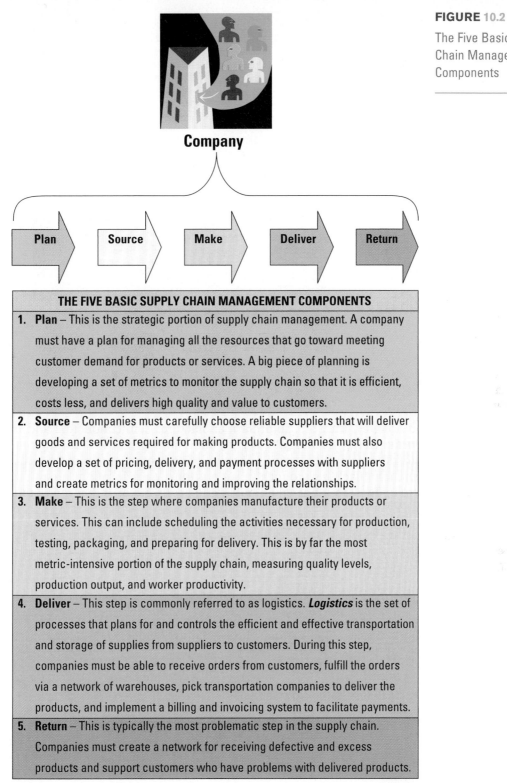

**THE FIVE BASIC SUPPLY CHAIN MANAGEMENT COMPONENTS**

1. **Plan** – This is the strategic portion of supply chain management. A company must have a plan for managing all the resources that go toward meeting customer demand for products or services. A big piece of planning is developing a set of metrics to monitor the supply chain so that it is efficient, costs less, and delivers high quality and value to customers.

2. **Source** – Companies must carefully choose reliable suppliers that will deliver goods and services required for making products. Companies must also develop a set of pricing, delivery, and payment processes with suppliers and create metrics for monitoring and improving the relationships.

3. **Make** – This is the step where companies manufacture their products or services. This can include scheduling the activities necessary for production, testing, packaging, and preparing for delivery. This is by far the most metric-intensive portion of the supply chain, measuring quality levels, production output, and worker productivity.

4. **Deliver** – This step is commonly referred to as logistics. *Logistics* is the set of processes that plans for and controls the efficient and effective transportation and storage of supplies from suppliers to customers. During this step, companies must be able to receive orders from customers, fulfill the orders via a network of warehouses, pick transportation companies to deliver the products, and implement a billing and invoicing system to facilitate payments.

5. **Return** – This is typically the most problematic step in the supply chain. Companies must create a network for receiving defective and excess products and support customers who have problems with delivered products.

marketing, sales, finance, manufacturing, and distribution—and between firms, which allow the smooth, synchronized flow of both information and product between customers, suppliers, and transportation providers across the supply chain. Information technology integrates planning, decision-making processes, business operating processes, and information sharing for business performance management (see Figure 10.3). Considerable evidence shows that this type of supply chain integration results in superior supply chain capabilities and profits.

**FIGURE** 10.3

The Integrated Supply
Chain

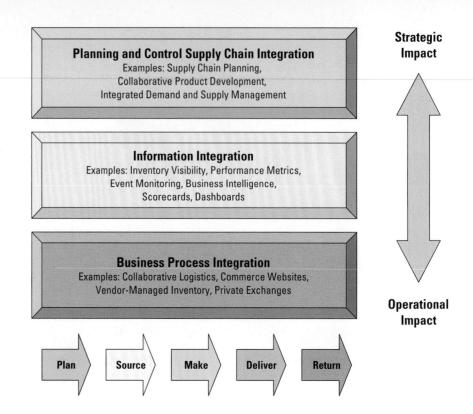

**FIGURE** 10.4

Factors Driving Supply
Chain Management

Adaptec, Inc., of California manufactures semiconductors and markets them to the world's leading PC, server, and end-user markets through more than 115 distributors and thousands of value-added resellers worldwide. Adaptec designs and manufactures products at various third-party locations around the world. The company uses supply chain integration software over the Internet to synchronize planning. Adaptec personnel at the company's geographically dispersed locations communicate in real time and exchange designs, test results, and production and shipment information. Internet-based supply chain collaboration software helped the company reduce inventory levels and lead times.

Although people have been talking about the integrated supply chain for a long time, it has only been recently that advances in information technology have made it possible to bring the idea to life and truly integrate the supply chain. Visibility, consumer behavior, competition, and speed are a few of the changes resulting from information technology advances that are driving supply chains (see Figure 10.4).

## VISIBILITY

**Supply chain visibility** is the ability to view all areas up and down the supply chain. Changing supply chains requires a comprehensive strategy buoyed by information technology. Organizations can use technology tools that help them integrate upstream and downstream, with both customers and suppliers.

To make a supply chain work most effectively, organizations must create visibility in real time. Organizations must know about customer events triggered downstream, but so must their suppliers and their suppliers' suppliers. Without this information, partners throughout the supply chain can experience a bullwhip effect, in which disruptions intensify throughout the chain. The **bullwhip effect** occurs when distorted product demand information passes from one entity to the next throughout the supply chain. The misinformation regarding a slight rise in demand for

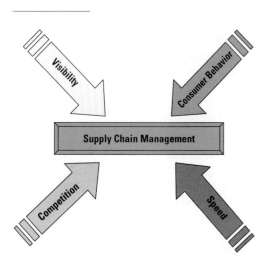

a product could cause different members in the supply chain to stockpile inventory. These changes ripple throughout the supply chain, magnifying the issue and creating excess inventory and costs.

Today, information technology allows additional visibility in the supply chain. Electronic information flows allow managers to view their suppliers' and customers' supply chains. Some organizations have completely changed the dynamics of their industries because of the competitive advantage gained from high visibility in the supply chain. Dell is the obvious example. The company's ability to get product to the customer and the impact of the economics have clearly changed the nature of competition and caused others to emulate this model.

## CONSUMER BEHAVIOR

The behavior of customers has changed the way businesses compete. Customers will leave if a company does not continually meet their expectations. They are more demanding because they have information readily available, they know exactly what they want, and they know when and how they want it. **Demand planning software** generates demand forecasts using statistical tools and forecasting techniques. Companies can respond faster and more effectively to consumer demands through supply chain enhancements such as demand planning software. Once an organization understands customer demand and its effect on the supply chain it can begin to estimate the impact that its supply chain will have on its customers and ultimately the organization's performance. The payoff for a successful demand planning strategy can be tremendous. A study by Peter J. Metz, executive director of the MIT Center for ebusiness, found that companies have achieved impressive bottom-line results from managing demand in their supply chains, averaging a 50 percent reduction in inventory and a 40 percent increase in timely deliveries.

## COMPETITION

Supply chain management software can be broken down into (1) supply chain planning software and (2) supply chain execution software—both increase a company's ability to compete. **Supply chain planning (SCP) software** uses advanced mathematical algorithms to improve the flow and efficiency of the supply chain while reducing inventory. SCP depends entirely on information for its accuracy. An organization cannot expect the SCP output to be accurate unless correct and up-to-date information regarding customer orders, sales information, manufacturing capacity, and delivery capability is entered into the system.

An organization's supply chain encompasses the facilities where raw materials, intermediate products, and finished goods are acquired, transformed, stored, and sold. These facilities are connected by transportation links, where materials and products flow. Ideally, the supply chain consists of multiple organizations that function as efficiently and effectively as a single organization, with full information visibility. **Supply chain execution (SCE) software** automates the different steps and stages of the supply chain. This could be as simple as electronically routing orders from a manufacturer to a supplier. Figure 10.5 details how SCP and SCE software correlate to the supply chain.

General Motors, Ford, and DaimlerChrysler made history when the three automotive giants began working together to create a unified supply chain planning/execution system that all three companies and their suppliers could leverage. The combined automotive giants' purchasing power is tremendous with GM spending $85 billion per year, Ford spending $80 billion per year, and DaimlerChrysler spending $73 billion per year. The ultimate goal is to process automotive production from ordering materials and forecasting demand to making cars directly to consumer specifications through the web. The automotive giants understand the impact strategic supply chain planning and execution can have on their competition.

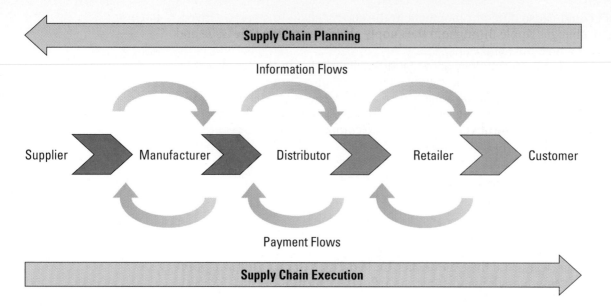

Supply Chain Planning

Information Flows

Supplier → Manufacturer → Distributor → Retailer → Customer

Payment Flows

Supply Chain Execution

**FIGURE** 10.5

Supply Chain Planning and Supply Chain Execution: Software's Correlation to the Supply Chain

## SPEED

During the past decade, competition has focused on speed. New forms of servers, telecommunications, wireless applications, and software are enabling companies to perform activities that were once never thought possible. These systems raise the accuracy, frequency, and speed of communication between suppliers and customers, as well as between internal users. Another aspect of speed is the company's ability to satisfy continually changing customer requirements efficiently, accurately, and quickly. Timely and accurate information is more critical to businesses than ever before. Figure 10.6 displays the three factors fostering this change.

# Supply Chain Management Success Factors

To succeed in today's competitive markets, companies must align their supply chains with the demands of the markets they serve. Supply chain performance is now a distinct competitive advantage for companies proficient in the SCM area. Perdue Farms excels at decision making based on its supply chain management system. Perdue Farms moves roughly 1 million turkeys, each within 24 hours of processing, to reach holiday tables across the nation yearly. The task is no longer as complicated as it was before Perdue Farms invested $20 million in SCM technology. SCM makes Perdue more adept at delivering the right number of turkeys, to the right customers, at the right time.

**FIGURE** 10.6

Three Factors Fostering Speed

To achieve success such as reducing operating costs, improving asset productivity, and compressing order cycle time, an organization should follow the seven principles of supply chain management outlined in Figure 10.7.

These seven principles run counter to previous built-in functional thinking of how companies organize, operate, and serve customers. Old concepts of supply chains are typified by discrete manufacturing, linear structure, and a focus on buy-sell transactions ("I buy from my suppliers, I sell to my customers"). Because the traditional supply chain is spread out linearly, some suppliers are removed from the end customer. Collaboration adds the value of visibility for these companies. They benefit by knowing

### Factors Fostering Supply Chain Speed

1. Pleasing customers has become something of a corporate obsession. Serving the customer in the best, most efficient, and most effective manner has become critical, and information about issues such as order status, product availability, delivery schedules, and invoices has become a necessary part of the total customer service experience.

2. Information is crucial to managers' abilities to reduce inventory and human resource requirements to a competitive level.

3. Information flows are essential to strategic planning for and deployment of resources.

**FIGURE** 10.7

Seven Principles of Supply
Chain Management

| Seven Principles of Supply Chain Management |
|---|
| 1. Segment customers by service needs, regardless of industry, and then tailor services to those particular segments. |
| 2. Customize the logistics network and focus intensively on the service requirements and on the profitability of the preidentified customer segments. |
| 3. Listen to signals of market demand and plan accordingly. Planning must span the entire chain to detect signals of changing demand. |
| 4. Differentiate products closer to the customer, since companies can no longer afford to hold inventory to compensate for poor demand forecasting. |
| 5. Strategically manage sources of supply, by working with key suppliers to reduce overall costs of owning materials and services. |
| 6. Develop a supply chain information technology strategy that supports different levels of decision making and provides a clear view (visibility) of the flow of products, services, and information. |
| 7. Adopt performance evaluation measures that apply to every link in the supply chain and measure true profitability at every stage. |

immediately what is being transacted at the customer end of the supply chain (the end customer's activities are visible to them). Instead of waiting days or weeks (or months) for the information to flow upstream through the supply chain, with all the potential pitfalls of erroneous or missing information, suppliers can react in near real-time to fluctuations in end-customer demand.

Dell Inc. offers one of the best examples of an extremely successful SCM system. Dell's highly efficient build-to-order business model enables it to deliver customized computer systems quickly. As part of the company's continual effort to improve its supply chain processes, Dell deploys supply chain tools to provide global views of forecasted product demand and materials requirements, as well as improved factory scheduling and inventory management.

Organizations should study industry best practices to improve their chances of successful implementation of SCM systems. The following are keys to SCM success.

### MAKE THE SALE TO SUPPLIERS

The hardest part of any SCM system is its complexity because a large part of the system extends beyond the company's walls. Not only will the people in the organization need to change the way they work, but also the people from each supplier that is added to the network must change. Be sure suppliers are on board with the benefits that the SCM system will provide.

### WEAN EMPLOYEES OFF TRADITIONAL BUSINESS PRACTICES

Operations people typically deal with phone calls, faxes, and orders scrawled on paper and will most likely want to keep it that way. Unfortunately, an organization cannot disconnect the telephones and fax machines just because it is implementing a supply chain management system. If the organization cannot convince people that using the software will be worth their time, they will easily find ways to work around it, which will quickly decrease the chances of success for the SCM system.

### ENSURE THE SCM SYSTEM SUPPORTS THE ORGANIZATIONAL GOALS

It is important to select SCM software that gives organizations an advantage in the areas most crucial to their business success. If the organizational goals support highly efficient strategies, be sure the supply chain design has the same goals.

## DEPLOY IN INCREMENTAL PHASES AND MEASURE AND COMMUNICATE SUCCESS

Design the deployment of the SCM system in incremental phases. For instance, instead of installing a complete supply chain management system across the company and all suppliers at once, start by getting it working with a few key suppliers, and then move on to the other suppliers. Along the way, make sure each step is adding value through improvements in the supply chain's performance. While a big-picture perspective is vital to SCM success, the incremental approach means the SCM system should be implemented in digestible bites, and also measured for success one step at a time.

## BE FUTURE ORIENTED

The supply chain design must anticipate the future state of the business. Because the SCM system likely will last for many more years than originally planned, managers need to explore how flexible the systems will be when (not if) changes are required in the future. The key is to be certain that the software will meet future needs, not only current needs.

# SCM Success Stories

Figure 10.8 depicts the top reasons more and more executives are turning to SCM to manage their extended enterprises. Figure 10.9 lists several companies using supply chain management to drive operations.

Apple Computer initially distributed its business operations over 16 legacy applications. Apple quickly realized that it needed a new business model centered around an integrated supply chain to drive performance efficiencies. Apple devised an implementation strategy that focused on specific SCM functions—finance, sales, distribution, and manufacturing—that would most significantly help its business. The company decided to deploy leading-edge functionality with a new business model that provided:

- Build-to-order and configure-to-order manufacturing capabilities.
- Web-enabled configure-to-order order entry and order status for customers buying directly from Apple at Apple.com.
- Real-time credit card authorization.
- Available-to-promise and rules-based allocations.
- Integration to advanced planning systems.

**FIGURE** 10.8

Top Reasons Executives Use SCM to Manage Extended Enterprises

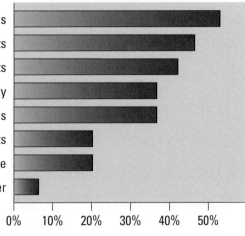

SCM Bottom-Line Benefits

Since its SCM system went live, Apple has experienced substantial benefits in many areas including measurable improvements in its manufacturing processes, a decrease by 60 percent in its build-to-order and configure-to-order cycle times, and the ability to process more than 6,000 orders daily.

| Companies Using Supply Chain to Drive Operations | |
|---|---|
| Dell | Business grows 17 percent per year with a $40 billion revenue base. |
| Nokia | Supply chain best practices are turning ideas into profitable businesses. |
| Procter & Gamble | Consumer-driven supply chain is the defining architecture for large consumer companies. Best practices in product innovation and supply chain effectiveness are tops. |
| IBM | Hardware supply chain product-development processes overhauled to the tune of 70 percent better, faster, and cheaper. |
| Wal-Mart Stores | Everyday low prices define the customer demand driving Wal-Mart's partner integrated supply chain. |
| Toyota Motor | Lean is one of the top three best practices associated with benchmarked supply chain excellence. |
| The Home Depot | Cutting-edge supply chain management improved logistics and innovative services. |
| Best Buy | SCM has radically thinned inventories and delivered enviable business positions. |
| Marks & Spencer | A pioneer in the use of radio frequency identification (RFID) in stores, Marks & Spencer manages to grow and stay lean. |

## OPENING CASE STUDY QUESTIONS

1. Would you need supply chain management systems in a virtual world such as Second Life? Why or why not?

2. How could a real company augment its supply chain management system through Second Life?

3. If you were an apparel company, such as Nike or REI, what would your virtual SCM system look like? Create a drawing of this system and be sure to include all upstream and downstream participants.

## Chapter Ten Case: RFID—Future Tracking the Supply Chain

One of the hottest new technologies in the supply chain is a radio frequency identification (RFID) tag. These tags are tiny and can carry large amounts of data tracking everything from price to temperature. Supply chains around the globe are being revamped with RFID tags. However, some people might be taking the ability to track the supply chain with RFID tags a bit too far.

## Tracking People

The elementary school that required students to wear RFID tags to track their movements ended the program because the company that developed the technology pulled out. "I'm disappointed; that's about all I can say at this point," stated Ernie Graham, the superintendent and principal of Brittan Elementary School. "I think I let my staff down."

Students were required to wear identification cards around their necks with their picture, name, and grade and a wireless transmitter that beamed ID numbers to a teacher's handheld computer when the children passed under an antenna posted above a classroom door. The school instituted the system, without parental input, to simplify attendance-taking and potentially reduce vandalism and improve student safety. "I'm happy for now that kids are not being tagged, but I'm still fighting to keep it out of our school system," said parent Dawn Cantrall, who filed a complaint with the American Civil Liberties Union. "It has to stop here."

While many parents criticized the tags for violating privacy and possibly endangering children's health, some parents supported the plan. "Technology scares some people; it's a fear of the unknown," parent Mary Brower said. "Any kind of new technology has the potential for misuse, but I feel confident the school is not going to misuse it."

## Tracking Children

Children's sleepwear with radio frequency identification tags sewn into the seams hit stores in early 2006. Made by Lauren Scott California, the nightgowns and pajamas will be one of the first commercial RFID-tagged clothing lines sold in the United States. The PJs are designed to keep kids safe from abductions, says proprietor Lauren Scott, who licensed the RFID technology from SmartWear Technologies Inc., a maker of personal security systems. Readers positioned in doorways and windows throughout a house scan tags within a 30-foot radius and trigger an alarm when boundaries are breached.

A pamphlet attached to the garment informs customers that the sleepwear is designed to help prevent child abductions. It directs parents to a website that explains how to activate and encode the RFID tag with a unique digital identification number. The site also provides information on a $500 home-installed system that consists of RFID readers and a low-frequency encoder that connects through a USB port to a computer. Parents can sign up to include data about their children, including photos, in the SmartWear database. That information can be shared with law enforcement agencies or the Amber Alert system if a child disappears.

SmartWear has several other projects in the works including an extended-range RFID tag that can transmit signals up to 600 feet. The tag could be inserted into law enforcement and military uniforms or outerwear, such as ski jackets, and used to find a missing or lost person or to recover and identify a body.

## Plastic RFID

A typical RFID tag costs 40 cents, making price a barrier for many potential applications. Start-up OrganicID is creating a plastic RFID tag that it expects will reduce the price to a penny or less. CEO Klaus Dimmler hopes to market the plastic tags, which will operate in the 13.56-MHz range, by 2008.

## Questions

1. What are some advantages and disadvantages of tagging students with RFID tags?

2. What are some advantages and disadvantages of tagging children's pajamas with RFID tags?

3. Do you agree or disagree that tagging students with RFID tags is a violation of privacy rights? Explain why.

4. Do you agree or disagree that tagging children's pajamas with RFID tags is a violation of privacy rights? Explain why.

5. Describe the relationship between privacy rights and RFID.

6. Determine a way that schools could use RFID tags without violating privacy rights.

# Building a Customer-centric Organization—Customer Relationship Management

**11.1.** Compare operational and analytical customer relationship management.

**11.2.** Identify the primary forces driving the explosive growth of customer relationship management.

**11.3.** Define the relationship between decision making and analytical customer relationship management.

**11.4.** Summarize the best practices for implementing a successful customer relationship management system.

## Customer Relationship Management (CRM)

After 1-800-Flowers.com achieved operational excellence in the late 1990s, it turned to building customer intimacy to continue to improve profits and business growth. The company turned brand loyalty into brand relationships by using the vast amounts of information it collected to better understand customers' needs and expectations. The floral delivery company adopted SAS Enterprise Miner to analyze the information in its CRM systems. Enterprise Miner sifts through information to reveal trends, explain outcomes, and predict results so that businesses can increase response rates and quickly identify their profitable customers. With the help of Enterprise Miner, 1-800-Flowers.com is continuing to thrive, with 27 percent annual increases in revenue.

CRM is a business philosophy based on the premise that those organizations that understand the needs of individual customers are best positioned to achieve sustainable competitive advantage in the future. Many aspects of CRM are not new to organizations; CRM is simply performing current business better. Placing customers at the forefront of all thinking and decision making requires significant operational and technology changes, however.

A customer strategy starts with understanding who the company's customers are and how the company can meet strategic goals. *The New York Times* understands this and has spent the past decade researching core customers to find similarities among groups of readers in cities outside the New York metropolitan area. Its goal is to understand how to appeal to those groups and make *The New York Times* a national newspaper, expanding its circulation and the "reach" it offers to advertisers. *The New York Times* is growing in a relatively flat publishing market and has achieved a customer retention rate of 94 percent in an industry that averages roughly 60 percent.

As the business world increasingly shifts from product focus to customer focus, most organizations recognize that treating existing customers well is the best source of profitable and sustainable revenue growth. In the age of ebusiness, however, an organization is challenged more than ever before to truly satisfy its customers. CRM will allow an organization to:

- Provide better customer service.
- Make call centers more efficient.

- Cross-sell products more effectively.
- Help sales staff close deals faster.
- Simplify marketing and sales processes.
- Discover new customers.
- Increase customer revenues.

The National Basketball Association's New York Knicks are becoming better than ever at communicating with their fans. Thanks to a CRM solution, the New York Knicks' management now knows which season-ticket holders like which players, what kind of merchandise they buy, and where they buy it. Management is finally able to send out fully integrated email campaigns that do not overlap with other marketing efforts.

## Recency, Frequency, and Monetary Value

An organization can find its most valuable customers by using a formula that industry insiders call RFM—recency, frequency, and monetary value. In other words, an organization must track:

- How recently a customer purchased items (recency).
- How frequently a customer purchases items (frequency).
- How much a customer spends on each purchase (monetary value).

Once a company has gathered this initial customer relationship management (CRM) information, it can compile it to identify patterns and create marketing campaigns, sales promotions, and services to increase business. For example, if Ms. Smith buys only at the height of the season, then the company should send her a special offer during the off-season. If Mr. Jones always buys software but never computers, then the company should offer him free software with the purchase of a new computer.

CRM technologies can help organizations track RFM and answer tough questions such as who are their best customers and which of their products are the most profitable. This chapter details the different operational and analytical CRM technologies an organization can use to strengthen its customer relationships and increase revenues.

## The Evolution of CRM

Knowing the customer, especially knowing the profitability of individual customers, is highly lucrative in the financial services industry. Its high transactional nature has always afforded the financial services industry more access to customer information than other industries have, but it has embraced CRM technologies only recently.

Barclays Bank is a leading financial services company operating in more than 70 countries. In the United Kingdom, Barclays has over 10 million personal customers and about 9.3 million credit cards in circulation, and it serves 500,000 small-business customers. Barclays decided to invest in CRM technologies to help gain valuable insights into its business and customers.

With its new CRM system, Barclays' managers are better able to predict the financial behavior of individual customers and assess whether a customer is likely to pay back a loan in full and within the agreed upon time period. This helps Barclays manage its profitability with greater precision because it can charge its customers a more appropriate rate of interest based on the results of the customer's risk assessment. Barclays also uses a sophisticated customer segmentation system to identify groups of profitable customers, both on a corporate and a personal level, which it can then target for new financial products. One of the most valuable pieces of

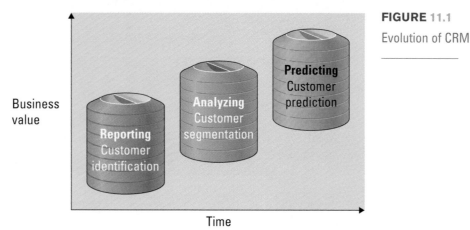

**FIGURE** 11.1

Evolution of CRM

Business value

Time

information Barclays discovered was that about 50 percent of its customers are not profitable and that less than 30 percent of its customers provide 90 percent of its profits.

There are three phases in the evolution of CRM: (1) reporting, (2) analyzing, and (3) predicting (see Figure 11.1). CRM reporting technologies help organizations identify their customers across other applications. CRM analysis technologies help organizations segment their customers into categories such as best and worst customers. CRM predicting technologies help organizations make predictions regarding customer behavior such as which customers are at risk of leaving.

Both operational and analytical CRM technologies can assist in customer reporting (identification), customer analysis (segmentation), and customer prediction. Figure 11.2 highlights a few of the important questions an organization can answer using CRM technologies.

## The Ugly Side of CRM: Why CRM Matters More Now than Ever Before

*Business 2.0* ranked "You—the customer" as number one in the top 50 people who matter most in business. It has long been said that the customer is always right, but for a long time companies never really meant it. Now, companies have no choice as the power of the customer grows exponentially as the Internet grows. You—or

**FIGURE** 11.2

Reporting, Analyzing, and Predicting Examples

| REPORTING "Asking What Happened" | ANALYZING "Asking Why It Happened" | PREDICTING "Asking What Will Happen" |
|---|---|---|
| What is the total revenue by customer? | Why did sales not meet forecasts? | What customers are at risk of leaving? |
| How many units did we manufacture? | Why was production so low? | What products will the customer buy? |
| Where did we sell the most products? | Why did we not sell as many units as last year? | Who are the best candidates for a mailing? |
| What were total sales by product? | Who are our customers? | What is the best way to reach the customer? |
| How many customers did we serve? | Why was customer revenue so high? | What is the lifetime profitability of a customer? |
| What are our inventory levels? | Why are inventory levels so low? | What transactions might be fraudulent? |

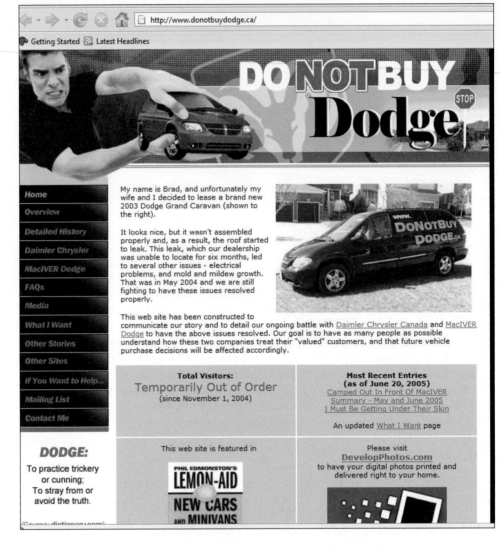

rather, the collaborative intelligence of tens of millions of people, the networked you—continually create and filter new forms of content, anointing the useful, the relevant, and the amusing and rejecting the rest. You do it on websites like Amazon, Flickr, and YouTube, via podcasts and SMS polling, and on millions of self-published blogs. In every case, you have become an integral part of the action as a member of the aggregated, interactive, self-organizing, auto-entertaining audience. But the "You Revolution" goes well beyond user-generated content. Companies as diverse as Delta Air Lines and T-Mobile are turning to you to create their ad slogans. Procter & Gamble and Lego are incorporating your ideas into new products. You constructed open-source software and are its customer and its caretaker. None of this should be a surprise, since it was you—your crazy passions and hobbies and obsessions—that built out the web in the first place. And somewhere out there, you are building web 3.0. We do not yet know what that is, but one thing is for sure: It will matter. Figure 11.3 displays a few examples of the power of the people.

## Customer Relationship Management's Explosive Growth

Brother International Corporation experienced skyrocketing growth in its sales of multifunction centers, fax machines, printers, and labeling systems in the late 1990s. Along with skyrocketing sales growth came a tremendous increase in customer service calls. When Brother failed to answer the phone fast enough, product returns started to increase. The company responded by increasing call center capacity, and the rate of returns began to drop. However, Dennis Upton, CIO of Brother International, observed that all the company was doing was answering the phone. He quickly realized that the company was losing a world of valuable market intelligence (business intelligence) about existing customers from all those telephone calls. The company decided to deploy SAP's CRM solution. The 1.8 million calls Brother handled dropped to 1.57 million, which reduced call center staff from 180 agents to 160 agents. Since customer demographic information is now stored and displayed on the agent's screen based on the incoming telephone number, the company has reduced call duration by an average of one minute, saving the company $600,000 per year.

In the context of increasing business competition and mature markets, it is easier than ever for informed and demanding customers to defect since they are just a click away from migrating to an alternative. When customers buy on the Internet, they see, and they steer, entire value chains. The Internet is a "looking glass," a two-way mirror, and its field of vision is the entire value chain. While the Internet cannot totally replace the phone and face-to-face communication with customers, it can strengthen these interactions and all customer touch points. Customer web interactions become conversations, interactive dialogs with shared knowledge, not just business transactions. Web-based customer care can actually become the focal point of customer relationship management and provide breakthrough benefits for both the enterprise and its customers, substantially reducing costs while improving service.

According to an AMR Research survey of more than 500 businesses in 14 key vertical markets, half of all current CRM spending is by manufacturers. Current users are allocating 20 percent of their IT budgets to CRM solutions. Those who have not invested in CRM may soon come on board: Of the respondents in the study who are not currently using CRM, roughly one-third plan to implement these types of technology solutions within the next year. Figure 11.4 displays the top CRM business drivers.

**FIGURE** 11.4

CRM Business Drivers

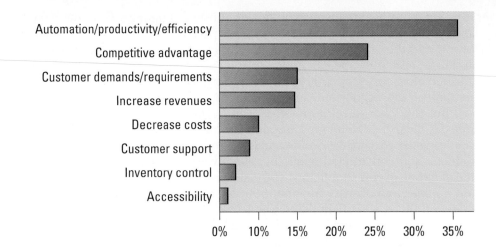

# Using Analytical CRM to Enhance Decisions

Joe Guyaux knows the best way to win customers is to improve service. Under his leadership and with the help of Siebel CRM, the PNC retail banking team increased new consumer checking customers by 19 percent in 2003. Over two years, PNC retained 21 percent more of its consumer checking households as well as improved customer satisfaction by 9 percent.

The two primary components of a CRM strategy are operational CRM and analytical CRM. *Operational CRM* supports traditional transactional processing for day-to-day front-office operations or systems that deal directly with the customers. *Analytical CRM* supports back-office operations and strategic analysis and includes all systems that do not deal directly with the customers. The primary difference between operational CRM and analytical CRM is the direct interaction between the organization and its customers. See Figure 11.5 for an overview of operational CRM and analytical CRM.

Maturing analytical CRM and behavioral modeling technologies are helping numerous organizations move beyond "legacy benefits" like enhanced customer service and retention to systems that can truly improve business profitability. Unlike operational CRM that automates call centers and sales forces with the aim

**FIGURE** 11.5

Operational CRM and Analytical CRM

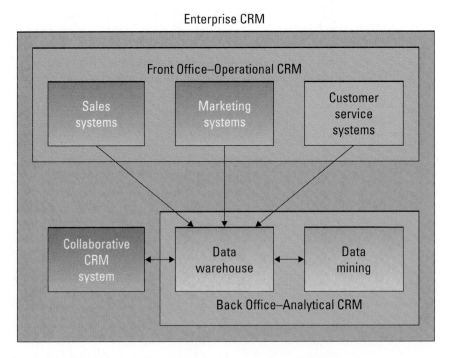

of enhancing customer transactions, analytical CRM solutions are designed to dig deep into a company's historical customer information and expose patterns of behavior on which a company can capitalize. Analytical CRM is primarily used to enhance and support decision making and works by identifying patterns in customer information collected from the various operational CRM systems.

For many organizations, the power of analytical CRM solutions provides tremendous managerial opportunities. Depending on the specific solution, analytical CRM tools can slice-and-dice customer information to create made-to-order views of customer value, spending, product affinities, percentile profiles, and segmentations. Modeling tools can identify opportunities for cross-selling, up-selling, and expanding customer relationships.

*Personalization* occurs when a website can know enough about a person's likes and dislikes that it can fashion offers that are more likely to appeal to that person. Many organizations are now utilizing CRM to create customer rules and templates that marketers can use to personalize customer messages.

The information produced by analytical CRM solutions can help companies make decisions about how to handle customers based on the value of each and every one. Analytical CRM can help make decisions as to which customers are worth investing in, which should be serviced at an average level, and which should not be invested in at all.

# Customer Relationship Management Success Factors

CRM solutions make organizational business processes more intelligent. This is achieved by understanding customer behavior and preferences, then realigning product and service offerings and related communications to make sure they are synchronized with customer needs and preferences. If an organization is implementing a CRM system, it should study the industry best practices to help ensure a successful implementation (see Figure 11.6).

**FIGURE** 11.6

CRM Implementation Strategies

| **CRM Implementation Strategies** |
|---|
| 1. **Clearly Communicate the CRM Strategy**—Boise Office Solutions spent $25 million implementing a successful CRM system. One primary reason for the system's success was that Boise started with a clear business objective for the system: to provide customers with greater economic value. Only after establishing the business objective did Boise Office Solutions invest in CRM technology to help meet the goal. Ensuring that all departments and employees understand exactly what CRM means and how it will add value to the organization is critical. Research by Gartner Dataquest indicates that enterprises that attain success with CRM have interested and committed senior executives who set goals for what CRM should achieve, match CRM strategies with corporate objectives, and tie the measurement process to both goals and strategies. |
| 2. **Define Information Needs and Flows**—People who perform successful CRM implementations have a clear understanding of how information flows in and out of their organization. Chances are information comes into the organization in many different forms over many different touchpoints. |
| 3. **Build an Integrated View of the Customer**—Essential to a CRM strategy is choosing the correct CRM system that can support organizational requirements. The system must have the corresponding functional breadth and depth to support strategic goals. Remember to take into account the system's infrastructure including ease of integration to current systems, discussed in greater detail later in this unit. |
| 4. **Implement in Iterations**—Implement the CRM system in manageable pieces—in other words avoid the "big bang" implementation approach. It is easier to manage, measure, and track the design, building, and deployment of the CRM system when it is delivered in pieces. Most important, this allows the organization to find out early if the implementation is headed for failure and thus either kill the project and save wasted resources or change direction to a more successful path. |
| 5. **Scalability for Organizational Growth**—Make certain that the CRM system meets the organization's future needs as well as its current needs. Estimating future needs is by far one of the hardest parts of any project. Understanding how the organization is going to grow, predicting how technology is going to change, and anticipating how customers are going to evolve are very difficult challenges. Taking the time to answer some tough questions up front will ensure the organization grows into, instead of out of, its CRM system. |

CRM is critical to business success. It is the key competitive strategy to stay focused on customer needs and to integrate a customer-centric approach throughout an organization. CRM can acquire enterprisewide knowledge about customers and improve the business processes that deliver value to an organization's customers, suppliers, and employees. Using the analytical capabilities of CRM can help a company anticipate customer needs and proactively serve customers in ways that build relationships, create loyalty, and enhance bottom lines.

## OPENING CASE STUDY QUESTIONS

1. Why is it important for any company to use CRM strategies to manage customer information?

2. How are CRM strategies in Second Life different from CRM strategies in the real world?

3. If the virtual world is the first point of contact between a company and its customers, how might that transform the entire shopping experience?

4. How could companies use Second Life to connect with customers that would be difficult or too expensive in the real world?

## Chapter Eleven Case:  Can You Find Your Customers?

Entrepreneurship is all about finding niche markets, which arise from an untapped potential in a corner of an existing market ignored by major companies. Finding customers for a specialized or niche business is no longer an arduous manual task. Somewhere there is a list of names that will allow a business, no matter how "niche," to locate its specific target customers.

Vinod Gupta was working for a recreational vehicle (RV) manufacturer in Omaha, Nebraska, in 1972. One day his boss requested a list of all the RV dealers in the country. Of course, at this time no such list existed. Gupta decided to create one. Gupta ordered every Yellow Pages phone book in the country, 4,500 total, took them home to his garage, and started manually sorting through each book one-by-one, compiling the RV list that his boss coveted. After providing the list Gupta told his boss he could have it for free if he could also sell it to other RV manufacturers. Gupta's boss agreed, and his company—infoUSA, Inc.—was launched.

Today infoUSA no longer sells lists on yellow pieces of paper, but maintains one of the nation's largest databases, including 14 million businesses and 220 million consumers. Over 4 million customers access this resource. More than 90 percent are entrepreneurial companies and have only one or two employees. These small businesses account for 60 percent of infoUSA's annual revenue of $311 million.

The point is that entrepreneurial businesses that want to thrive in specialty markets can use databases for reaching customers. While this resource does not do the whole job, it can and should comprise the core of a marketing program which also includes publicity, word-of-mouth recommendations, or "buzz," savvy geographical placement of the company's physical outlets, such as retail stores and offices, and, if affordable, advertising.

## Slicing and Dicing

Put another way, databases, which slice-and-dice lists to pinpoint just the right prospects for products or services, enable entrepreneurs to find the proverbial needle in the haystack. An entrepreneur might target a market of only 200 companies or a select universe of individuals who might have use for a specific product or service—such as feminist-oriented prayer books for Lutheran women ministers in their 20s, or seeds for gardeners who grow vegetables native to Sicily, or, like one of infoUSA's own customers, jelly beans for companies with employee coffee-break rooms.

Databases have the ability to take the legwork out of locating specialized customers and make the job as easy as one, two, three. According to infoUSA, to use databases effectively, company owners must take three distinct steps:

## Step 1: Know Your Customers

"In any business, there is no substitute for retaining existing customers. Make these people happy, and they become the base from which you add others. As a niche marketer, you have at least an idea who might want what you have to sell, even if those prospects aren't yet actually buying. Get to know these people. Understand what they are looking for. Consider what they like and don't like about your product or service."

## Step 2: Analyze Your Customers

"Your current customers or clients have all of the information you need to find other customers. Analyze them to find common characteristics. If you are selling to businesses, consider revenue and number of employees. If you are selling to consumers, focus on demographics, such as age, as well as income levels. Armed with this information about your customers, you are ready to make use of a database to look for new ones."

## Step 3: Find New Customers Just Like Your Existing Customers

"In a niche business, you find new customers by cloning your existing customers. Once you know and understand your current customers, you can determine the types of businesses or customers to target."

"An online brokerage, for example, was seeking to build its business further and needed a list of names of people 'with a propensity to invest' just like its current clients. Our company used proprietary modeling to provide a set of names of individuals from throughout the U.S. with the required level of income."

"You should buy a database-generated list only if you have analyzed your current customers. In addition, you should wait to buy until you are ready to use the list, because lists do have a short shelf life—about 30 to 60 days if you are selling to consumers and six to nine months if you are selling to businesses. Indeed, about 70 percent of infoUSA's entire database changes over annually."

## No Magic Bullet

The magic of databases is that there is no magic. Every entrepreneur has a product or service to sell. The trick is to match what you are selling with people who are buying. Used effectively, databases serve as the resource for making that happen. Do not make the mistake of expecting a database to perform the entire job of securing customers for products or services. An entrepreneur must be ever vigilant about prospecting—and not only when business is slow. Entrepreneurs must encourage sales representatives to call on customers even when business is booming and they do not require their revenues to keep the company afloat. Once customers are secured, make servicing them a top priority.

**Questions**

1. Explain how technology has dramatically impacted the efficiency and effectiveness of finding customers.

2. Explain the two different types of CRM systems and explain how a company can use infoUSA's database for creating a CRM strategy.

3. Describe three ways a new small business can extend its customer reach by performing CRM functions from an infoUSA database.

4. infoUSA discussed three distinct steps company owners must take to use databases effectively. Rank these steps in order of importance to a CRM strategy.

# Integrating the Organization from End to End—Enterprise Resource Planning

**12.1.** Describe the role information plays in enterprise resource planning systems.

**12.2.** Identify the primary forces driving the explosive growth of enterprise resource planning systems.

**12.3.** Explain the business value of integrating supply chain management, customer relationship management, and enterprise resource planning systems.

## Enterprise Resource Planning (ERP)

Enterprise resource planning systems serve as the organization's backbone in providing fundamental decision-making support. In the past, departments made decisions independent of each other. ERP systems provide a foundation for collaboration between departments, enabling people in different business areas to communicate. ERP systems have been widely adopted in large organizations to store critical knowledge used to make the decisions that drive performance.

To be competitive, organizations must always strive for excellence in every business process enterprisewide, a daunting challenge if the organization has multisite operations worldwide. To obtain operational efficiencies, lower costs, improve supplier and customer relations, and increase revenues and market share, all units of the organization must work together harmoniously toward congruent goals. An ERP system will help an organization achieve this.

One company that has blazed a trail with ERP is Atlanta-based United Parcel Service of America, Inc. (UPS). UPS has developed a number of web-based applications that track information such as recipient signatures, addresses, time in transit, and other shipping information. These services run on an SAP foundation that UPS customers can connect to using real-time ERP information obtained from the UPS website. Currently, 6.2 million tracking requests pass through the company's website each day. By automating the information delivery process, UPS has dramatically reduced the demand on its customer service representatives. Just as important, UPS has improved relationships with its business partners—in effect integrating its business with theirs—by making it easier for consumers to find delivery information without leaving the website of the merchant.

The heart of an ERP system is a central database that collects information from and feeds information into all the ERP system's individual application components (called modules), supporting diverse business functions such as accounting, manufacturing, marketing, and human resources. When a user enters or updates information in one module, it is immediately and automatically updated throughout the entire system, as illustrated in Figure 12.1.

ERP automates business processes such as order fulfillment—taking an order from a customer, shipping the purchase, and then billing for it. With an ERP system, when a customer service representative takes an order from a customer, he or she has all the information necessary to complete the order (the customer's credit rating and order history, the company's inventory levels, and the delivery schedule).

**FIGURE** 12.1

ERP Integration Data Flow

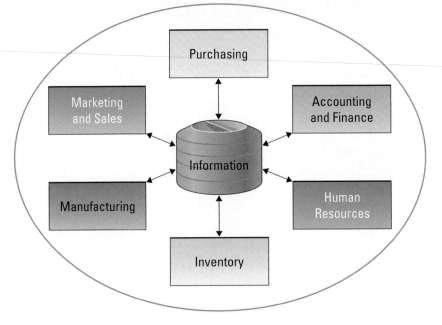

Everyone else in the company sees the same information and has access to the database that holds the customer's new order. When one department finishes with the order, it is automatically routed via the ERP system to the next department. To find out where the order is at any point, a user need only log in to the ERP system and track it down, as illustrated in Figure 12.2. The order process moves like a bolt of lightning through the organization, and customers get their orders faster and with fewer errors than ever before. ERP can apply that same magic to the other major business processes, such as employee benefits or financial reporting.

## Bringing the Organization Together

In most organizations, information has traditionally been isolated within specific departments, whether on an individual database, in a file cabinet, or on an employee's PC. ERP enables employees across the organization to share information across

**FIGURE** 12.2

ERP Process Flow

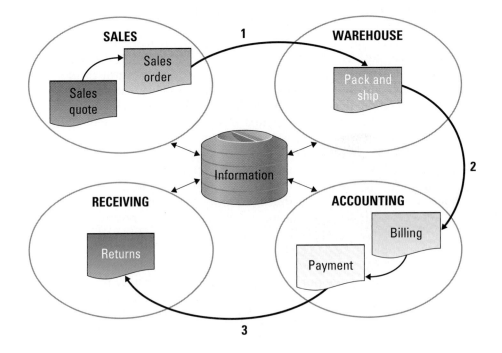

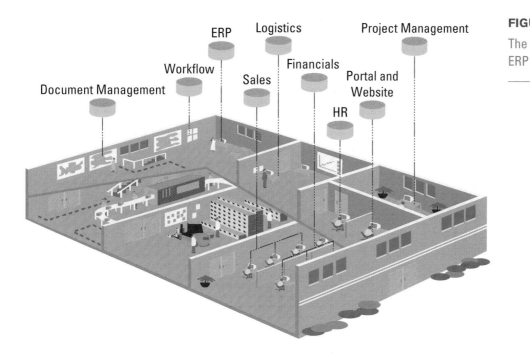

**FIGURE** 12.3

The Organization before ERP

Document Management · Workflow · ERP · Logistics · Sales · Financials · Project Management · Portal and Website · HR

a single, centralized database. With extended portal capabilities, an organization can also involve its suppliers and customers to participate in the workflow process, allowing ERP to penetrate the entire value chain, and help the organization achieve greater operational efficiency (see Figures 12.3 and 12.4).

## The Evolution of ERP

Originally, ERP solutions were developed to deliver automation across multiple units of an organization, to help facilitate the manufacturing process and address issues such as raw materials, inventory, order entry, and distribution. However,

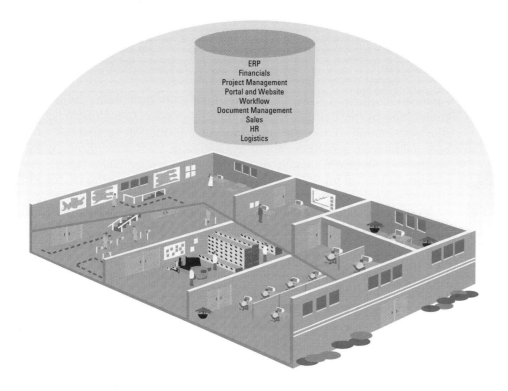

**FIGURE** 12.4

ERP—Bringing the Organization Together

ERP
Financials
Project Management
Portal and Website
Workflow
Document Management
Sales
HR
Logistics

FIGURE 12.5

The Evolution of ERP

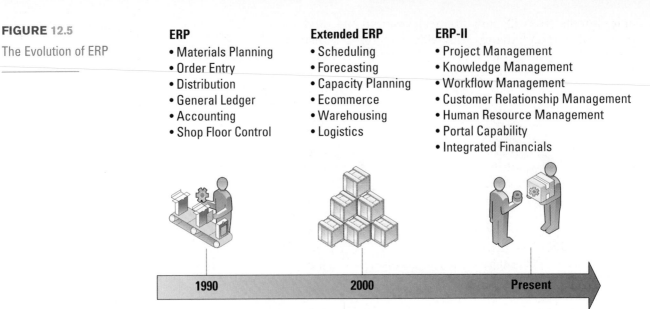

| ERP | Extended ERP | ERP-II |
|---|---|---|
| • Materials Planning | • Scheduling | • Project Management |
| • Order Entry | • Forecasting | • Knowledge Management |
| • Distribution | • Capacity Planning | • Workflow Management |
| • General Ledger | • Ecommerce | • Customer Relationship Management |
| • Accounting | • Warehousing | • Human Resource Management |
| • Shop Floor Control | • Logistics | • Portal Capability |
| | | • Integrated Financials |

1990          2000          Present

ERP was unable to extend to other functional areas of the company such as sales, marketing, and shipping. It could not tie in any CRM capabilities that would allow organizations to capture customer-specific information, nor did it work with websites or portals used for customer service or order fulfillment. Call center or quality assurance staff could not tap into the ERP solution, nor could ERP handle document management, such as cataloging contracts and purchase orders.

ERP has grown over the years to become part of the extended enterprise. From its beginning as a tool for materials planning, it has extended to warehousing, distribution, and order entry. With its next evolution, ERP expands to the front office including CRM. Now administrative, sales, marketing, and human resources staff can share a tool that is truly enterprisewide. To compete on a functional level today, companies must adopt an enterprisewide approach to ERP that utilizes the Internet and connects to every facet of the value chain. Figure 12.5 shows how ERP has grown since the 1990s to accommodate the needs of the entire organization.

FIGURE 12.6

SCM Market Overview

# Integrating SCM, CRM, and ERP

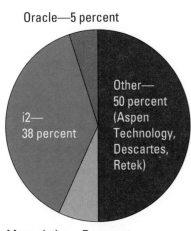

Oracle—5 percent

i2—38 percent

Other—50 percent (Aspen Technology, Descartes, Retek)

Manugistics—7 percent

Applications such as SCM, CRM, and ERP are the backbone of ebusiness. Integration of these applications is the key to success for many companies. Integration allows the unlocking of information to make it available to any user, anywhere, anytime. Originally, there were three top ERP vendors—PeopleSoft, Oracle, and SAP. In December 2004, Oracle purchased PeopleSoft for $10 billion, leaving two main competitors in the ERP market—Oracle and SAP.

Most organizations today have no choice but to piece their SCM, CRM, and ERP applications together since no one vendor can respond to every organizational need; hence, customers purchase applications from multiple vendors. Oracle and SAP both offer CRM and SCM components. However, these modules are not as functional or flexible as the modules offered by industry leaders of SCM and CRM such as Siebel and i2 Technologies, as depicted in Figures 12.6 and 12.7. As a result, organizations face the challenge of integrating their systems. For example, a single organization might choose its CRM components from Siebel, SCM components from i2, and financial components and HR management components from Oracle. Figure 12.8 displays the general audience and purpose for each of these applications that have to be integrated.

From its roots in the California Gold Rush era, San Francisco–based Del Monte Foods has grown to become the nation's largest producer and distributor of premium quality processed fruits, vegetables, and tomato products. With annual sales of over $3 billion, Del Monte is also one of the country's largest producers, distributors, and marketers of private-label food and pet products with a powerful portfolio of brands including Del Monte, StarKist, Nature's Goodness, 9Lives, and Kibbles 'n Bits.

Del Monte's acquisition of StarKist, Nature's Goodness, 9Lives, and Kibbles 'n Bits from the H. J. Heinz Company required an integration between Del Monte's and H. J. Heinz's business processes. Del Monte needed to overhaul its IT infrastructure, migrating from multiple platforms including UNIX and mainframe systems and consolidating applications centrally on a single system. The work required integration of business processes across manufacturing, financial, supply chain, decision support, and transactional reporting areas.

The revamp of Del Monte's architecture stemmed from a strategic decision. Del Monte decided to implement an ERP system to support its entire U.S. operations, with headquarters in San Francisco, operations in Pittsburgh, and distribution centers and manufacturing facilities across the country. The company concluded that the only way it could unite its global operations and open its system to its customers, which are mainly large retailers, was through the use of an ERP system. Among other key factors was the need to embrace an ebusiness strategy. The challenge facing Del Monte was to select an ERP system to merge multiple systems quickly and cost effectively. If financial and customer service targets were to be achieved, Del Monte needed to integrate new businesses that more than doubled

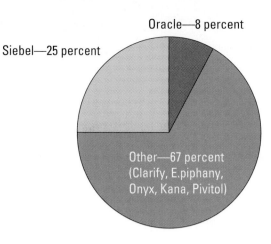

**FIGURE** 12.7

CRM Market Overview

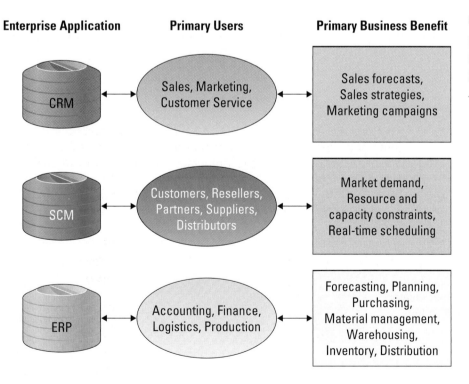

**FIGURE** 12.8

Primary Users and Business Benefits of Strategic Initiatives the size of the company. Since implementing the ERP system, customers and trading partners are now provided with a single, consistent, and integrated view of the company.

## Integration Tools

Effectively managing the transformation to an integrated enterprise will be critical to the success of the 21st century organization. The key is the integration of the disparate IT applications. An integrated enterprise infuses support areas, such as finance and human resources, with a strong customer orientation. Integrations are achieved using *middleware*—several different types of software that sit in the middle of and provide connectivity between two or more software applications. Middleware translates information between disparate systems. *Enterprise application integration (EAI) middleware* represents a new approach to middleware by packaging together commonly used functionality, such as providing prebuilt links to popular enterprise applications, which reduces the time necessary to develop solutions that integrate applications from multiple vendors. A few leading vendors of EAI middleware include Active Software, Vitria Technology, and Extricity. Figure 12.9 displays the data points where these applications integrate and illustrates the underlying premise of architecture infrastructure design.

Companies run on interdependent applications, such as SCM, CRM, and ERP. If one application performs poorly, the entire customer value delivery system is affected. For example, no matter how great a company is at CRM, if its SCM system does not work and the customer never receives the finished product, the company will lose that customer. The world-class enterprises of tomorrow must be built on the foundation of world-class applications implemented today.

Coca-Cola's business model is a common one among well-known franchisers. Coca-Cola gets the majority of its $18 billion in annual revenue from franchise fees it earns from bottlers all over the world. Bottlers, along with the franchise, license Coke's secret recipe and many others including recipes for Odwalla, Nestea, Minute Maid, and Sprite. Now Coca-Cola hopes that bottlers will also buy into adopting common business practices using a service-oriented architecture ERP system.

The target platform chosen by Coca-Cola is mySAP enterprise resource planning (ERP) by SAP. If it works, Coca-Cola and its bottlers stand to make and save a lot of money, and SAP will be able to position itself as one of the dominant ERP

**FIGURE 12.9**

Integrations between SCM, CRM, and ERP Applications

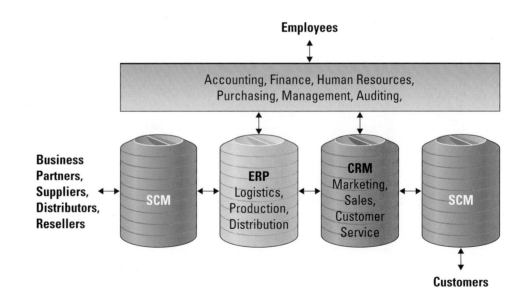

players. Already, Coca-Cola and many of its bottlers use versions of SAP for finance, manufacturing, and a number of administrative functions. But Coca-Cola wants everyone to move to a "services" architecture environment.

Coca-Cola hopes that this services standardization will make its supply chain more efficient and reduce costs. In explaining why a services approach is so vitally important, Jean-Michel Ares, CIO of Coca-Cola, stated, "That will allow bottlers to converge one step at a time, one process area at a time, one module at a time, at a time that's right for the bottler. We can march across the bottling world incrementally."

# Enterprise Resource Planning's Explosive Growth

Cisco Systems Inc., a $22 billion producer of computer-network equipment, is using an ERP system to create a consolidated trial balance sheet and a consolidated income statement within a half day of a fiscal quarter's close, compared with two weeks more than five years ago when Cisco was a $4 billion company. What's more, during those years, the time devoted to transaction processing has fallen from 65 percent to 35 percent, and finance group expenses, as a percentage of the total company revenues, have fallen from 2 percent to 1.3 percent. All that has occurred even as Cisco added people to its finance department to keep pace with the company's growth. The ERP system gives Cisco executives a look at revenues, expenses, margins, and profits every day of every month.

Business in the 21st century is complex, fluid, and customer-centric. It requires stringent, yet flexible processes and communications systems that extend globally and respond instantaneously. The processes and systems must be integrated. No part of the enterprise can escape the pressure to deliver measurable results. Here are a few reasons ERP solutions have proven to be such a powerful force:

- ERP is a logical solution to the mess of incompatible applications that had sprung up in most businesses.
- ERP addresses the need for global information sharing and reporting.
- ERP is used to avoid the pain and expense of fixing legacy systems.

To qualify as a true ERP solution, the system not only must integrate various organization processes, but also must be:

- **Flexible**—An ERP system should be flexible in order to respond to the changing needs of an enterprise.
- **Modular and open**—An ERP system has to have an open system architecture, meaning that any module can be interfaced with or detached whenever required without affecting the other modules. The system should support multiple hardware platforms for organizations that have a heterogeneous collection of systems. It must also support third-party add-on components.
- **Comprehensive**—An ERP system should be able to support a variety of organizational functions and must be suitable for a wide range of business organizations.
- **Beyond the company**—An ERP system must not be confined to organizational boundaries but rather support online connectivity to business partners or customers.

ERP as a business concept resounds as a powerful internal information management nirvana: Everyone involved in sourcing, producing, and delivering the company's product works with the same information, which eliminates redundancies, cuts wasted time, and removes misinformation.

1. If you operated a business entirely on Second Life would you require an ERP system? Why or why not?

2. How would an ERP system be used in Second Life to support a global organization?

## Chapter Twelve Case: Shell Canada Fuels Productivity with ERP

Shell Canada is one of the nation's largest integrated petroleum companies and is a leading manufacturer, distributor, and marketer of refined petroleum products. The company, headquartered in Calgary, produces natural gas, natural gas liquids, and bitumen. Shell Canada is also the country's largest producer of sulphur. There is a Canada-wide network of 1,809 Shell-branded retail gasoline stations and convenience food stores from coast-to-coast.

To run such a complex and vast business operation successfully, the company relies heavily on the use of a mission-critical enterprise resource planning (ERP) system. The use of such a system is a necessity in helping the company integrate and manage its daily operations—operations that span from wells and mines, to processing plants, to oil trucks and gas pumps.

For example, the ERP system has helped the company immensely in terms of reducing and streamlining the highly manual process of third-party contractors submitting repair information and invoices. On average, there are between 2,500 and 4,000 service orders handled by these contractors per month on a nationwide basis.

Before implementation of the ERP system, contractors had to send Shell Canada monthly summarized invoices that listed maintenance calls the contractors made at various Shell gasoline stations. Each one of these invoices would take a contractor between 8 and 20 hours to prepare. Collectively, the contractors would submit somewhere between 50 and 100 invoices every month to Shell Canada. This involved each invoice being reviewed by the appropriate territory manager and then forwarded to the head office for payment processing. This alone consumed another 16 to 30 hours of labor per month. At the head office, another 200 hours of work was performed by data entry clerks who had to manually enter batch invoice data into the payment system.

And this would be the amount of time needed if things went smoothly! More hours of labor were required to decipher and correct errors if any mistakes were introduced from all the manual invoice generation and data reentry involved. Often errors concerning one line item on an invoice would deter payment of the whole invoice. This irritated the contractors and did not help foster healthy contractor relationships.

To make matters worse, despite the hours involved and the amount of human data-handling required, detailed information about the service repairs that contractors did was often not entered into the payment system. And if it was entered, the information was not timely—it was often weeks or even months old by the time it made it into the payment processing system. As a result, Shell was not collecting sufficient information about what repairs were being done, what had caused the problem, and how it had been resolved.

Fortunately, the ERP solution solved these inadequacies by providing an integrated web-based service order, invoicing, and payment submission system. With this tool, third-party contractors can enter service orders directly into Shell's ERP system via the web. When this is done, the contractors can also enter detailed information about the work that was performed—sometimes even attaching photos and drawings to help describe the work that was done. With the ERP system, it takes only a few minutes for a contractor to enter details about a service order. Further, this information can be transmitted through a wireless PDA to the appropriate Shell manager for immediate approval—shaving off more time in unnecessary delays.

Another bonus of the ERP system is that the contractor's monthly summarized invoices can now be generated automatically and fed directly into the ERP system's account payables application for processing. No rekeying of data required! Even better, if there is an issue or concern with one invoice item, the other items on the invoice can still be processed for payment.

Shell Canada's ERP system also handles other operational tasks. For example, the system can help speed up maintenance and repair operations at the company's refineries. With the ERP system in place, rather than trying to utilize a variety of disparate internal systems to access blueprints, schematics, spare parts lists, and other tools and information, workers at the refineries can now use the ERP system to access these things directly from a centralized database.

An added benefit of the ERP system is its ease of use. Past systems used by refinery workers were complex and difficult to search for information. The ERP system in place now has a portal-like interface that allows refinery workers to access the functions and information they need to keep operations running. The web interface allows workers access to this information with one or two clicks of a mouse.

An important part of any successful ERP implementation is training end users to learn how to utilize the system and to teach them about the functions and abilities of the ERP system. Recognizing this, Shell Canada offered its personnel both formal and informal ERP training. These proved to be invaluable in teaching end users the mechanics of the system and raising awareness of the benefits of the system and the efficiencies that the ERP system could offer Shell Canada. This not only helped promote end-user acceptance of the ERP system, but also greatly increased employees' intentions to use the system in their daily work.

Shell Canada executives are pleased and optimistic about the advantages of the ERP system. With this new system, employees across the company have gained fast and easy access to the tools and information they need to conduct their daily operations.

## Questions

1. How did ERP help improve business operations at Shell?
2. How important was training in helping roll out the system to Shell personnel?
3. How could extended ERP components help improve business operations at Shell?
4. What advice would you give Shell if it decided to choose a different ERP software solution?
5. How can integrating SCM, CRM, and ERP help improve business operations at Shell?

Today, organizations of various sizes are proving that systems that support decision making and opportunity seizing are essential to thriving in the highly competitive electronic world. We are living in an era when information technology is a primary tool, knowledge is a strategic asset, and decision making and problem solving are paramount skills. The tougher, larger, and more demanding a problem or opportunity is, and the faster and more competitive the environment is, the more important decision-making and problem-solving skills become. This unit discussed numerous tools and strategic initiatives that an organization can take advantage of to assist in decision making:

■ Supply chain management (SCM)—managing information flows within the supply chain to maximize total supply chain effectiveness and profitability.

■ Customer relationship management (CRM)—managing all aspects of customers' relationships with an organization to increase customer loyalty and retention and an organization's profitability.

■ Enterprise resource planning (ERP)—integrating all departments and functions throughout an organization into a single IT system (or integrated set of IT systems) so that managers and leaders can make enterprisewide decisions by viewing enterprisewide information on all business operations.

## ★ KEY TERMS

Analytical CRM, 152
Artificial intelligence (AI), 131
Bullwhip effect, 140
Consolidation, 128
Decision support system
  (DSS), 126
Demand planning software, 141
Digital dashboard, 128
Drill-down, 128
Ebusiness, 123
Enterprise application integration
  (EAI) middleware, 162
Executive information system
  (EIS), 128
Expert system, 131

Fuzzy logic, 133
Genetic algorithm, 133
Goal-seeking analysis, 126
Intelligent agent, 133
Intelligent system, 131
Logistics, 139
Middleware, 162
Model, 124
Neural network or artificial
  neural network, 132
Online analytical processing
  (OLAP), 125
Online transaction processing
  (OLTP), 125
Operational CRM, 152

Personalization, 153
Sensitivity analysis, 126
Shopping bot, 133
Slice-and-dice, 128
Supply chain, 137
Supply chain execution (SCE)
  software, 141
Supply chain management
  (SCM), 137
Supply chain planning (SCP)
  software, 141
Supply chain visibility, 140
Transaction processing system
  (TPS), 125
What-if analysis, 126

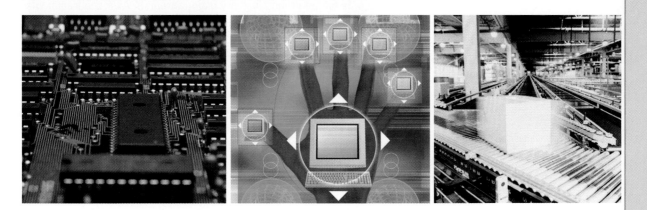

### Dell's Famous Supply Chain

Speed is at the core of everything Dell does. Dell assembles nearly 80,000 computers every 24 hours. The computer manufacturer has done more than any other company when it comes to tweaking its supply chain. More than a decade ago, Dell carried 20 to 25 days of inventory in a sprawling network of warehouses. Today, Dell does not have a single warehouse and carries only two hours of inventory in its factories and a maximum of just 72 hours across its entire operation. Dell's vast, global supply chain is in constant overdrive making the company one of the fastest, most hyperefficient organizations on the planet.

## Disaster Occurs

In 2002, a 10-day labor lockout shut down 29 West Coast ports extending from Los Angeles to Seattle, idled 10,000 union dockworkers, and blocked hundreds of cargo ships from unloading raw materials and finished goods. The port closings paralyzed global supply chains and ultimately cost U.S. consumers and businesses billions of dollars.

Analysts expected Dell, with its just-in-time manufacturing model, would be especially hard hit when parts failed to reach its two U.S.-based factories. Without warehouses filled with motherboards and hard drives the world's largest PC maker would simply find itself with nothing to sell within a matter of days. Dell knew all too well that its ultra-lean, high-speed business model left it vulnerable to just such a situation. "When a labor problem or an earthquake or a SARS epidemic breaks out, we've got to react quicker than anyone else," said Dick Hunter, the company's supply chain expert. "There's no other choice. We know these things are going to happen; we must move fast to fix them. We just can't tolerate any kind of delay."

Fortunately, the same culture of speed and flexibility that seems to put Dell at the mercy of disruptions also helps it deal with them. Dell was in constant, round-the-clock communication with its parts makers in Taiwan, China, and Malaysia and its U.S.-based shipping partners. Hunter dispatched a "tiger team" of 10 logistics specialists to Long Beach, California, and other ports; they worked with Dell's carrying and freight-forwarding networks to assemble a contingency plan.

When the tiger team confirmed that the closings were all but certain, Dell moved into high gear. It chartered 18 airplanes (747s) from UPS, Northwest Airlines, and China Airlines. A 747 holds the equivalent of 10 tractor-trailers—enough parts to manufacture 10,000 PCs. The bidding for the planes grew fierce, running as high as $1 million for a one-way flight from Asia to the West Coast. Dell got in the bidding early and kept costs around $500,000 per plane. Dell also worked with its Asia-based suppliers to ensure that its parts were always at the Shanghai and Taipei airports in time for its returning charters to land, reload, refuel, and take off. The company was consistently able to get its planes to the United States and back within 33 hours, which kept its costs down and its supply chain moving.

Meanwhile, Dell had people on the ground in every major harbor. In Asia, the freight specialists saw to it that Dell's parts were the last to be loaded onto each cargo ship so they would be unloaded first when the ship hit the West Coast. The biggest test came when the ports reopened and companies scrambled to sort through the backed-up mess of thousands of containers. Hunter's tiger team had anticipated this logistical nightmare. Even though Dell had PC components in hundreds of containers on 50 ships, it knew the exact moment when each component cycled through the harbor, and it was among the first to unload its parts and speed them to its factories in Austin, Texas, and Nashville, Tennessee. In the end, Dell did the impossible: It survived a 10-day supply chain blackout with roughly 72 hours of inventory without delaying a single customer order.

The aftershocks of the port closings reverberated for weeks. Many companies began to question the wisdom of running so lean in an uncertain world, and demand for warehouse space soared as they piled up buffer inventory to ensure against labor unrest, natural disasters, and terrorist attacks.

### Building a "Dell-like" Supply Chain

Dell's ultimate competitive weapon is speed, which gives the technical giant's bottom line a real boost. Figure Unit 3.2 displays a five-point plan for building a fast supply chain—direct from Dell.

### Questions

1. Identify a few key metrics a Dell marketing executive might want to monitor on a digital dashboard.
2. Determine how Dell can benefit from using decision support systems and executive information systems in its business.
3. Describe how Dell has influenced visibility, consumer behavior, competition, and speed though the use of IT in its supply chain.
4. Explain the seven principles of SCM in reference to Dell's business model.
5. Identify how Dell can use CRM to improve its business operations.
6. Explain how an ERP system could help Dell gain business intelligence.

**FIGURE UNIT 3.2**

How to Build a Dell-like Supply Chain

| Dell-Like Supply Chain Plan |
|---|
| 1. **The supply chain starts with the customer.** By cutting out retailers and selling directly to its customers, Dell is in a far better position to forecast real customer demand. |
| 2. **Replace inventory with information.** To operate with close to zero inventory, Dell communicates constantly with its suppliers. It sends out status updates three times a day from its assembly plants; every week it updates its quarterly demand forecasts. By making communication its highest priority, Dell ensures the lowest possible inventory. |
| 3. **If you cannot measure it, you cannot manage it.** Dell knows what works because it measures everything from days in inventory to the time it takes to build a PC. As Dell slashed those numbers, it got more efficient. |
| 4. **Complexity slows you down.** Dell cut the number of its core PC suppliers from several hundred to about 25. It standardized critical PC components, which streamlined its manufacturing. Dell got faster by making things simpler. |
| 5. **Create a watershed mind-set.** Dell is not content with incremental improvement; it demands massive change. Each year, it wants its Austin-based PC-assembly plant—already very fast—to improve production by 30 percent. "You don't get a big result if you do not challenge people with big goals," Dell CEO Kevin Rollins said. |

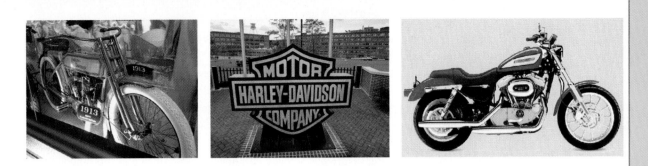

### Revving Up Sales at Harley-Davidson

Harley-Davidson produces 290,000 motorcycles and generates over $4 billion in net revenues yearly. There is a mystique associated with a Harley-Davidson motorcycle. No other motorcycle in the world has the look, feel, and sound of a Harley-Davidson, and many people consider it a two-wheeled piece of art. Demand for Harley-Davidson motorcycles outweighs supply. Some models have up to a two-year wait list. Harley-Davidson has won a number of awards including:

- Rated second in *ComputerWorld*'s Top 100 Best Places to Work in IT.
- Rated 51st in *Fortune*'s 100 Best Companies to Work For.
- Rated first in *Fortune*'s 5 Most Admired Companies in the motor vehicles industry.
- Rated first in the Top 10 Sincerest Corporations by the *Harris Interactive Report*.
- Rated second in the Top 10 Overall Corporations by the *Harris Interactive Report*.

## Harley-Davidson's Focus on Technology

Harley-Davidson's commitment to technology is paying off: In 2003 it decreased production costs and inventories by $40 million as a direct result of using technology to increase production capacity. The company's technology budget of $50 million is more than 2 percent of its revenue, which is far above the manufacturing industry average. More than 50 percent of this budget is devoted to developing new technology strategies.

Harley-Davidson focuses on implementing ebusiness strategies to strengthen its market share and increase customer satisfaction. Over 80 projects were in development in 2003, and the majority of the new projects focused on sharing information, gaining business intelligence, and enhancing decision making.

Talon, Harley-Davidson's proprietary dealer management system, is one of its most successful technology initiatives. Talon handles inventory, vehicle registration, warranties, and point-of-sale transactions for all Harley-Davidson dealerships. The system performs numerous time-saving tasks such as checking dealer inventory, automatically generating parts orders, and allowing the company to review and analyze information across its global organization. Talon gives Harley-Davidson managers a 360-degree view into enterprisewide information that supports strategic goal setting and decision making throughout all levels of the organization.

## Building Supplier Relationships

Harley-Davidson invests time, energy, and resources into continually improving its company-to-company strategic business initiatives such as supply chain management. The company understands and values the importance of building strong relationships with its suppliers. To develop these important relationships the company deployed Manugistics, an SCM system that allows it to do business with suppliers in a collaborative, web-based environment. The company plans to use the SCM software to better manage its flow of materials and improve collaboration activities with its key suppliers.

## Building Customer Relationships

Each time a customer reaches out to the company, Harley-Davidson has an opportunity to build a trusting relationship with that particular customer. Harley-Davidson realizes that it takes more than just building and selling motorcycles to fulfill the dreams of its customers. For this reason, the company strives to deliver unforgettable experiences along with its top quality products.

Harley-Davidson sells over $500 million worth of parts and accessories to its loyal followers. Ken Ostermann, Harley-Davidson's manager of electronic commerce and communications, decided that the company could increase these sales if it could offer the products online. The dilemma facing Ostermann's online strategy was that selling jackets, saddlebags, and T-shirts directly to consumers would bypass Harley-Davidson's 650 dealers, who depend on the high-margin accessories to fuel their businesses' profits. Ostermann's solution was to build an online store, Harley-Davidson.com, which prompts customers to select a participating Harley-Davidson dealership before placing any online orders. The selected dealership is then responsible for fulfilling the order. This strategy has helped ensure that the dealers remain the focal point of customers' buying experiences.

To guarantee that every customer has a highly satisfying online buying experience, the company asks the dealers to agree to a number of standards including:

- Checking online orders twice daily.
- Shipping online orders within 24 hours.
- Responding to customer inquiries within 24 hours.

The company still monitors online customer metrics such as time taken to process orders, number of returned orders, and number of incorrect orders, ensuring that Harley-Davidson delivers on its message of prompt, excellent service consistently to all its loyal customers. The company receives over 1 million visitors a month to its online store. Customer satisfaction scores for the website moved from the extremely satisfied level to the exceptional level in a year.

Another of Harley-Davidson's customer-centric strategies is its Harley's Owners Group (HOG), established in 1983. HOG is the largest factory-sponsored motorcycle club in the world with more than 600,000 members. HOG offers a wide array of events, rides, and benefits to its members. HOG is one of the key drivers helping to build a strong sense of community among Harley-Davidson owners. Harley-Davidson has built a customer following that is extremely loyal, a difficult task to accomplish in any industry.

## Harley-Davidson's Corporate Culture

Harley-Davidson employees are the engine behind its outstanding performance and the foundation of the company's overall success. Harley-Davidson believes in a strong sense of corporate ethics and values, and the company's top five core values serve as a framework for the entire corporation:

1. Tell the truth.
2. Be fair.
3. Keep your promises.
4. Respect the individual.
5. Encourage intellectual curiosity.

The company credits its core values as the primary reason it won the two prestigious awards from the *Harris Interactive Report,* one of the most respected consumer reviews for corporate sincerity, ethics, and standards. Sticking to strong ethics and values is and will continue to be a top priority for the company and its employees.

To enhance its enterprise further Harley-Davidson plans to keep taking advantage of new technologies and strategies including a web-based approach to accessing information and an enterprisewide system to consolidate procurement at its eight U.S. facilities.

## Questions

1. Explain how Talon helps Harley-Davidson employees improve their decision-making capabilities.
2. Identify a few key metrics a Harley-Davidson marketing executive might want to monitor on a digital dashboard.
3. How can Harley-Davidson benefit from using decision support systems and executive information systems in its business?
4. How would Harley-Davidson's business be affected if it decided to sell accessories directly to its online customers? Include a brief discussion of the ethics involved with this decision.
5. Evaluate the HOG CRM strategy and recommend an additional benefit Harley-Davidson could provide to its HOG members to increase customer satisfaction.
6. How could Harley-Davidson's SCM system, Manugistics, improve its business operations?
7. Provide a potential illustration of Harley-Davidson's SCM system including all upstream and downstream participants.
8. Explain how an ERP system could help Harley-Davidson gain business intelligence in its operations.

## ★ MAKING BUSINESS DECISIONS

### 1. Implementing an ERP System

Blue Dog Inc. is a leading manufacturer in the high-end sunglasses industry. Blue Dog Inc. reached record revenue levels of over $250 million last year. The company is currently deciding on the possibility of implementing an ERP system to help decrease production costs and increase inventory control. Many of the executives are nervous about making such a large investment in an ERP system due to its low success rates. As a senior manager at Blue Dog Inc. you have been asked to compile a list of the potential benefits and risks associated with implementing an ERP system along with your recommendations for the steps the company can take to ensure a successful implementation.

### 2. DSS and EIS

Dr. Rosen runs a large dental conglomerate—Teeth Doctors—that staffs over 700 dentists in six states. Dr. Rosen is interested in purchasing a competitor called Dentix that has 150 dentists in three additional states. Before deciding whether to purchase Dentix, Dr. Rosen must consider several issues:

- The cost of purchasing Dentix.
- The location of the Dentix offices.
- The current number of customers per dentist, per office, and per state.
- The merger between the two companies.
- The professional reputation of Dentix.
- Other competitors.

Explain how Dr. Rosen and Teeth Doctors can benefit from the use of information systems to make an accurate business decision in regard to the potential purchase of Dentix.

### 3. SCM, CRM, and ERP

Jamie Ash is interested in applying for a job at a large software vendor. One of the criteria for the job is a detailed understanding of strategic initiatives such as SCM, CRM, and ERP. Jamie has no knowledge of any of these initiatives and cannot even explain what the acronyms mean. Jamie has come to you for help. She would like you to compile a summary of the three initiatives including an analysis of how the three are similar and how they are different. Jamie would also like to perform some self-training via the web so be sure to provide her with several additional links to key websites that offer detailed overviews on SCM, CRM, and ERP.

### 4. Customer Relationship Management Strategies

On average, it costs an organization six times more to sell to a new customer than to sell to an existing customer. As the co-owner of a medium-sized luggage distributor, you have recently been notified by your EIS systems that sales for the past three months have decreased by an average of 17 percent. The reasons for the decline in sales are numerous, including a poor economy, people's aversion to travel because of the terrorist attacks, and some negative publicity your company received regarding a defective product line. In a group, explain how implementing a CRM system can help you understand and combat the decline in sales. Be sure to justify why a CRM system is important to your business and its future growth.

### 5. Finding Information on Decision Support Systems

You are working on the sales team for a small catering company that maintains 75 employees and generates $1 million in revenues per year. The owner, Pam Hetz, wants to understand how she can use decision support systems to help grow her business. Pam has an initial understanding of DSS systems and is interested in learning more about what types are available, how they can be used in a small business, and the cost associated with different DSS systems. In a group, research the website www.dssresources.com and compile a presentation that discusses DSS systems in detail. Be sure to answer all Pam's questions on DSS systems in the presentation.

### 6. Analyzing Dell's Supply Chain Management System

Dell's supply chain strategy is legendary. Essentially, if you want to build a successful SCM system your best bet is to model your SCM system after Dell's. In a team, research Dell's supply chain management strategy on the web and create a report discussing any new SCM updates and strategies the company is using that were not discussed in this text. Be sure to include a graphical presentation of Dell's current supply chain model.

### 7. Gaining Business Intelligence from Strategic Initiatives

You are a new employee in the customer service department at Premier One, a large pet food distributor. The company, founded by several veterinarians, has been in business for three years and focuses on providing nutritious pet food at a low cost. The company currently has 90 employees and operates in seven states. Sales over the past three years have tripled and the manual systems currently in place are no longer sufficient to run the business. Your first task is to meet with your new team and create a presentation for the president and chief executive officer describing supply chain management, customer relationship management, and enterprise resource planning systems. The presentation should highlight the main benefits Premier One can receive from these strategic initiatives along with any additional added business value that can be gained from the systems.

## 1. Great Stories

With the advent of the Internet, when customers have an unpleasant customer experience, the company no longer has to worry about them telling a few friends and family; the company has to worry about them telling everyone. Internet service providers are giving consumers frustrated with how they were treated by a company another means of fighting back. Free or low-cost computer space for Internet websites is empowering consumers to tell not only their friends, but also the world about the way they have been treated. A few examples of disgruntled customer stories from the Internet include:

- **Bad Experience with Blue Marble Biking**—Tourist on biking tour is bitten by dog, requires stitches. Company is barred from hotel because of incident, and in turn it bars the tourist from any further tours.

- **Best Buy Receipt Check**—Shopper declines to show register receipt for purchase to door guard at Lakewood Best Buy, which is voluntary. Employees attempt to seize cart, stand in shopper's path, and park a truck behind shopper's car to prevent departure.

- **Enterprise Rent-A-Car Is a Failing Enterprise**—Enterprise Rent-A-Car did not honor reservations, did not have cars ready as stated, rented cars with nearly empty tanks, and charged higher prices to corporate account holders.

### Project Focus

The Internet is raising the stakes for customer service. With the ability to create a website dedicated to a particular issue, a disgruntled customer can have nearly the same reach as a manufacturer. The Internet is making it more difficult for companies to ignore their customers' complaints. In a group, search the web for the most outrageous story of a disgruntled customer. A few places to start include:

- **Complain Complain (complaincomplain.net)**—provides professionally written, custom complaint letters to businesses.

- **The Complaint Department (www.thecomplaintdepartment.ca)**—a for-fee consumer complaint resolution and letter writing service.

- **The Complaint Station (www.thecomplaintstation.com)**—provides a central location to complain about issues related to companies' products, services, employment, and get rich quick scams.

- **Complaints.com Consumer Complaints (www.complaints.com)**—database of consumer complaints and consumer advocacy.

- **Baddealings.com (www.baddealings.com)**—forum and database on consumer complaints and scams on products and services.

## 2. Classic Car Problems

Classic Cars Inc. operates high-end automotive dealerships that offer luxury cars along with luxury service. The company is proud of its extensive inventory, top-of-the-line mechanics, and especially its exceptional service, which even includes a cappuccino bar at each dealership.

The company currently has 40 sales representatives at four locations. Each location maintains its own computer systems, and all sales representatives have their own contact management systems. This splintered approach to operations causes numerous problems including customer communication issues, pricing strategy issues, and inventory control issues. A few examples include:

- A customer shopping at one dealership can go to another dealership and receive a quote for a different price for the same car.
- Sales representatives are frequently stealing each other's customers and commissions.
- Sales representatives frequently send their customers to other dealerships to see specific cars and when the customer arrives, the car is not on the lot.
- Marketing campaigns are not designed to target specific customers; they are typically generic, such as 10 percent off a new car.
- If a sales representative quits, all of his or her customer information is lost.

### Project Focus

You are working for Customer One, a small consulting company that specializes in CRM strategies. The owner of Classic Cars Inc., Tom Repicci, has hired you to help him formulate a strategy to put his company back on track. Develop a proposal for Tom detailing how a CRM system can alleviate the company's issues and create new opportunities.

### 3. Building Visibility

Visionary companies are building extended enterprises to best compete in the new Internet economy. An extended enterprise combines the Internet's power with new business structures and processes to eliminate old corporate boundaries and geographic restrictions. Networked supply chains create seamless paths of communication among partners, suppliers, manufacturers, retailers, and customers. Because of advances in manufacturing and distribution, the cost of developing new products and services is dropping, and time to market is speeding up. This has resulted in increasing customer demands, local and global competition, and increased pressure on the supply chain.

To stay competitive, companies must reinvent themselves so that the supply chain—sourcing and procurement, production scheduling, order fulfillment, inventory management, and customer care—is no longer a cost-based back-office exercise, but rather a flexible operation designed to effectively address today's challenges.

The Internet is proving an effective tool in transforming supply chains across all industries. Suppliers, distributors, manufacturers, and resellers now work together more closely and effectively than ever. Today's technology-driven supply chain enables customers to manage their own buying experiences, increases coordination and connectivity among supply partners, and helps reduce operating costs for every company in the chain.

### Project Focus

In the past, assets were a crucial component of success in supply chain management. In today's market, however, a customer-centric orientation is key to retaining competitive advantage. Using the Internet and any other resources available, develop a strategic plan for implementing a networked, flexible supply chain management system for a start-up company of your choice. Research Netflix if you are unfamiliar with how start-up companies are changing the supply chain. Be sure that your supply chain integrates all partners—manufacturers, retailers, suppliers, carriers, and vendors—into a seamless unit and views customer relationship management as a key competitive advantage. There are several points to consider when creating your customer-centric supply chain strategy:

- Taking orders is only one part of serving customer needs.
- Businesses must fulfill the promise they make to customers by delivering products and information upon request—not when it is convenient for the company.

- Time to market is a key competitive advantage. Companies must ensure uninterrupted supply, and information about customer demands and activities is essential to this requirement.

- Cost is an important factor. Companies need to squeeze the costs from internal processes to make the final products less expensive.

- Reducing design-cycle times is critical, as this allows companies to get their products out more quickly to meet customer demand.

## 4. Netflix Your Business

Netflix reinvented the video rental business using supply chain technology. Netflix, established in 1998, is the largest online DVD rental service, offering flat-rate rental-by-mail to customers in the United States. Headquartered in Los Gatos, California, it has amassed a collection of 80,000 titles and over 6.8 million subscribers. Netflix has over 42 million DVDs and ships 1.6 million a day, on average, costing a reported $300 million a year in postage. On February 25, 2007, Netflix announced the delivery of its billionth DVD.

The company provides a monthly flat-fee service for the rental of DVD movies. A subscriber creates an ordered list, called a rental queue, of DVDs to rent. The DVDs are delivered individually via the United States Postal Service from an array of regional warehouses (44 in 29 states). A subscriber keeps a rented DVD as long as desired but has a limit on the number of DVDs (determined by subscription level) that can be checked out at any one time. To rent a new DVD, the subscriber mails the previous one back to Netflix in a prepaid mailing envelope. Upon receipt of the disc, Netflix ships another disc in the subscriber's rental queue.

### Project Focus

Netflix's business is video rental, but it used technology to revamp the supply chain to completely disrupt the entire video rental industry. Reinvent IT is a statewide contest where college students can propose a new business that they will reinvent by revamping the supply chain (such as Netflix has done). You want to enter and win the contest. Reinvent a traditional business, such as the video rental business, using supply chain technologies.

## 5. Finding Shelf Space at Wal-Mart

Wal-Mart's business strategy of being a low-cost provider by managing its supply chain down to the minutiae has paid off greatly. Each week, approximately 100 million customers, or one-third of the U.S. population, visit Wal-Mart's U.S. stores. Wal-Mart is currently the world's largest retailer and the second largest corporation behind ExxonMobil. It was founded by Sam Walton in 1962 and is the largest private employer in the United States and Mexico. Wal-Mart is also the largest grocery retailer in the United States, with an estimated 20 percent of the retail grocery and consumables business, and the largest toy seller in the United States, with an estimated 45 percent of the retail toy business, having surpassed Toys "R" Us in the late 1990s.

Wal-Mart's business model is based on selling a wide variety of general merchandise at "always low prices." The reason Wal-Mart can offer such low prices is due to its innovative use of information technology tools to create its highly sophisticated supply chain. Over the past decade, Wal-Mart has famously invited its major suppliers to jointly develop powerful supply chain partnerships. These are designed to increase product flow efficiency and, consequently, Wal-Mart's profitability.

Many companies have stepped up to the challenge, starting with the well-known Wal-Mart/Procter & Gamble alliance, which incorporated vendor-managed inventory, category management, and other intercompany innovations. Wal-Mart's CFO became a key customer as P&G's objective became maximizing Wal-Mart's internal profitability. Unlike many other retailers, Wal-Mart does not charge a slotting fee to suppliers for their products to appear in the store. Alternatively, Wal-Mart focuses on selling more popular products and often pressures store managers to drop unpopular products in favor of more popular ones, as well as pressuring manufacturers to supply more popular products.

### Project Focus

You are the owner of a high-end collectible toy company. You create everything from authentic sports figure replicas to famous musicians and movie characters including Babe Ruth, Hulk Hogan, Mick Jagger, Ozzy Osbourne, Alien, and the Terminator. It would be a huge win for your company if you could get your collectibles into Wal-Mart. Compile a strategic plan highlighting the steps required to approach Wal-Mart as your supply chain partner. Be sure to address the pros and cons of partnering with Wal-Mart, including the cost to revamp your current supply chain to meet Wal-Mart's tough supply chain requirements.

## 6. Shipping Problems

Entrepreneurship is in Alyssa Stuart's blood. Alyssa has been starting businesses since she was 10 years old, and she finally has the perfect business of custom-made furniture. Customers who visit Alyssa's shop can choose from a number of different fabrics and 50 different styles of couch and chair designs to create their custom-made furniture. Once the customer decides on a fabric pattern and furniture design, the information is sent to China where the furniture is built and shipped to the customer via the West Coast. Alyssa is excited about her business; all of her hard work has finally paid off as she has over 17,000 customers and 875 orders currently in the pipe.

### Project Focus

Alyssa's business is booming. Her high quality products and outstanding customer service have created an excellent reputation for her business. But Alyssa's business is at risk of losing everything and she has come to you for help solving her supply chain issues.

Yesterday, a dockworkers' union strike began and shut down all of the West Coast shipping docks from San Francisco to Canada. Work will resume only when the union agrees to new labor contracts, which could take months. Alyssa has asked you to summarize the impact of the dock shutdown on her business and create a strategy to keep her business running, which is especially difficult since Alyssa guarantees 30-day delivery on all products or the product is free. What strategies do you recommend for Alyssa's business to continue working while her supply chain is disrupted by the dockworkers' strike?

## 7. Political Supply Chains

The U.S. government has crafted a deal with the United Arab Emirates (UAE) that would let a UAE-based firm, Dubai Ports World (DPW), run six major U.S. ports. If the approval is unchallenged, Dubai Ports World would run the ports of New York, New Jersey, Baltimore, New Orleans, Miami, and Philadelphia. Currently, London-based Peninsular and Oriental Steam Navigation Co. (P&O), the fourth largest port operator in the world, runs the six ports. But the $6.8 billion sale of P&O to DPW would effectively turn over North American operations to the government-owned company in Dubai.

### Project Focus

Some citizens are worried that the federal government may be outsourcing U.S. port operations to a company prone to terrorist infiltration by allowing a firm from the United Arab Emirates to run port operations within the United States. You have been called in on an investigation to determine the potential effects on U.S. businesses' supply chains if these ports were shut down due to terrorist activities. The United Arab Emirates has had people involved in terrorism. In fact, some of its financial institutions laundered the money for the 9/11 terrorists. Create an argument for or against outsourcing these ports to the UAE. Be sure to detail the effect on U.S. businesses' supply chains if these ports are subjected to terrorist acts.

## 8. JetBlue on YouTube

JetBlue took an unusual and interesting CRM approach by using YouTube to apologize to its customers. JetBlue's founder and CEO, David Neeleman, apologized to customers via You-Tube after a very, very bad week for the airline: 1,100 flights canceled due to snow storms and thousands of irate passengers. Neeleman's unpolished, earnest delivery makes this apology worth accepting. But then again, we were not stuck on a tarmac for eight hours. With all of the new advances in technology and the many ways to reach customers, do you think using You-Tube is a smart approach? What else could JetBlue do to help gain back its customers' trust?

### Project Focus

You are the founder and CEO of GoodDog, a large pet food manufacturing company. Recently, at least 16 pet deaths have been tied to tainted pet food, fortunately not manu-factured by your company. A recall of potentially deadly pet food has dog and cat owners studying their animals for even the slightest hint of illness and swamping veterinarians nationwide with calls about symptoms both real and imagined. Create a strategy for using YouTube as a vehicle to communicate with your customers as they fear for their pets' lives. Be sure to highlight the pros and cons of using YouTube as a customer communication vehicle. Are there any other new technologies you could use as a customer communica-tion vehicle that would be more effective than YouTube?

## 9. Second Life CRM

The virtual world of Second Life could become the first point of contact between compa-nies and customers and could transform the whole customer experience. Since it began hosting the likes of Adidas, Dell, Reuters, and Toyota, Second Life has become technology's equivalent of India or China—everyone needs an office and a strategy involving it to keep their shareholders happy. But beyond opening a shiny new building in the virtual world, what can such companies do with their virtual real estate?

Like many other big brands, PA Consulting has its own offices in Second Life and has learned that simply having an office to answer customer queries is not enough. Real peo-ple, albeit behind avatars, must be staffing the offices—in the same way having a website is not enough if there is not a call center to back it up when a would-be customer wants to speak to a human being. The consultants believe call centers could one day ask customers to follow up a phone call with them by moving the query into a virtual world.

Unlike many corporate areas in the virtual world, the National Basketball Association incorporates capabilities designed to keep fans coming back, including real-time 3-D diagrams of games as they are being played.

### Project Focus

You are the executive director of CRM at StormPeak, an advanced AI company that devel-ops robots. You are in charge of overseeing the first virtual site being built in Second Life. Create a CRM strategy for doing business in a virtual world. Here are a few questions to get you started:

- How will customer relationships be different in a virtual world?
- What is your strategy for managing customer relationships in this new virtual environment?
- How will supporting Second Life customers differ from supporting traditional customers?
- How will supporting Second Life customers differ from supporting website customers?
- What customer security issues might you encounter in Second Life?
- What customer ethical issues might you encounter in Second Life?

*Built to Last.* **By Jim Collins (Collins Business Essentials, 1994).**

Drawing upon a six-year research project at the Stanford University Graduate School of Business, Jim Collins and Jerry I. Porras took 18 truly exceptional and long-lasting companies and studied each in direct comparison to one of its top competitors. They examined the companies from their very beginnings to the present day—as start-ups, as midsize companies, and as large corporations. Throughout, the authors asked: "What makes the truly exceptional companies different from the comparison companies and what were the common practices these enduringly great companies followed throughout their history?"

Filled with hundreds of specific examples and organized into a coherent framework of practical concepts that can be applied by managers and entrepreneurs at all levels, *Built to Last* provides a master blueprint for building organizations that will prosper long into the 21st century and beyond.

*Good to Great.* **By Jim Collins (Collins Business Essentials, 2001).**

*Built to Last,* the defining management study of the 90s showed how great companies triumph over time and how long-term sustained performance can be engineered into the DNA of an enterprise from the very beginning.

But what about the company that is not born with great DNA? How can good companies, mediocre companies, even bad companies achieve enduring greatness?

- The study: For years, this question preyed on the mind of Jim Collins. Are there companies that defy gravity and convert long-term mediocrity or worse into long-term superiority? And if so, what are the universal distinguishing characteristics that cause a company to go from good to great?

- The standards: Using tough benchmarks, Collins and his research team identified a set of elite companies that made the leap to great results and sustained those results for at least 15 years. How great? After the leap, the good-to-great companies generated cumulative stock returns that beat the general stock market by an average of seven times in 15 years, better than twice the results delivered by a composite index of the world's greatest companies, including Coca-Cola, Intel, General Electric, and Merck.

- The findings: The findings of the good-to-great study will surprise many readers and shed light on virtually every area of management strategy and practice.

- Level 5 leaders: The research team was shocked to discover the type of leadership required to achieve greatness.

- The hedgehog concept: To go from good to great requires transcending the curse of competence.

- A culture of discipline: When you combine a culture of discipline with an ethic of entrepreneurship, you get the magical alchemy of great results.

- Technology accelerators: Good-to-great companies think differently about the role of technology.

- The flywhere and the doom loop: Those who launch radical change programs and wrenching restructuring will almost certainly fail to make the leap.

*The Anatomy of Buzz.* **By Emanuel Rosen (Doubleday, 2000).**

Today's consumers are skeptical, and they suffer from information overload. The result: They'll probably ignore the expensive television and print ads your marketing team creates. So how do people decide which car to buy, or which fashions fit the image they are looking for, or what new techno-appliance is a must for their homes? The first section of this book discusses how buzz spreads and the huge social networks to which we all belong and what we know about how buzz spreads through them.

The second section identifies two factors that need to be there for buzz to spread. First, the product must be "contagious" in some way. For example, the game Trivial Pursuit was contagious because people who played it were compelled to demonstrate their knowledge to others. But contagion needs to be accelerated. That is the second factor. The marketers of this game executed a massive grassroots campaign that let people in numerous social networks get "infected" by the game and tell others.

The third part of the book describes techniques that companies have used to encourage their customers to talk: How BMW created buzz about the Z3 Roadster through a "sneak preview" in a James Bond movie. How the founders of Powerbar spread the word about their energy food by working with "network hubs" such as coaches and leading athletes.

## *Loyalty Rules!* By Frederick F. Reichheld (Bain and Company, 2001).

Loyalty is at the heart of any company that boasts high productivity, solid profits, and sustained growth. For example, Harley-Davidson recovered from near bankruptcy by building loyal relationships with all stakeholders. And Southwest Airlines, which has never had a layoff, is the only consistently profitable major airline in the United States every year since 1973.

Frederick Reichheld, author of *Loyalty Rules!,* argues that loyalty is still the fuel that drives financial success—even, and perhaps especially, in today's volatile, high-speed economy—but that most organizations are running on empty. Why? Because leaders too often confuse profits with purpose, taking the low road to short-term gains at the expense of employees, customers, and, ultimately, investors. In a business environment that thrives on networks of mutually beneficial relationships, says Reichheld, it is the ability to build strong bonds of loyalty—not short-term profits—that has become the "acid test" of leadership.

Based on extensive research into companies from online start-ups to established institutions—including Harley-Davidson, Enterprise Rent-A-Car, Cisco Systems, Dell Computer, Intuit, and more—Reichheld reveals six bedrock principles of loyalty upon which leaders build enduring enterprises. Underscoring that success requires both understanding and measuring loyalty, he couples each principle with straightforward actions that drive measurement systems, compensation, organization, and strategy:

1. Play to win/win: Never profit at the expense of partners.
2. Be picky: Membership must be a privilege.
3. Keep it simple: Reduce complexity for speed and flexibility.
4. Reward the right results: Worthy partners deserve worthy goals.
5. Listen hard and talk straight: Insist on honest, two-way communication and learning.
6. Preach what you practice: Explain your principles, then live by them.

Providing tools for implementing the timeless principles of loyalty in a volatile economy, *Loyalty Rules!* is a practical guidebook for taking the high road in business—the only road that leads to lasting success.

# 4  Building Innovation

The pace of technological change never ceases to amaze. What only a few years ago would have been considered Star Trek technology is becoming normal. What used to take hours to download over a dial-up modem connection can now transfer in a matter of seconds through an invisible, wireless network connection from a computer thousands of miles away. We are living in an increasingly wireless present and hurtling ever faster toward a wireless future. The tipping point of ubiquitous, wireless, handheld, mobile computing is not far away.

Managers must understand the importance of ebusiness and how it has revolutionized fundamental business processes. Ebusiness offers new opportunities for growth and new ways of performing business activities that were simply not possible before the Internet. As a business student, you should understand the fundamental impact of the Internet and the innovations in mobile technologies on business. As a future manager and organizational knowledge worker, you need to understand what benefits ebusiness and wireless business practices can offer an organization and your career. Furthermore, you need to understand the challenges that come along with the adoption of web technologies, how Web 2.0 is impacting communication and the limitations on the mobile worker. This unit will give you this knowledge and help prepare you for success in today's electronic wireless global marketplace.

## The Ironman

The Ironman Triathlon World Championship, one of the world's most grueling athletic contests, brings 1,700 of the world's top endurance athletes to rugged Kailua-Kona, Hawaii, for a world championship race every fall. In a single day superfit athletes attempt to swim 2.4 miles, cycle 112 miles, and run a full 26.2 mile marathon. The vast majority of athletes that compete at the Ironman each year aim simply to just finish the course, especially if they are first timers, or set a personal record time if they've raced this distance before.

In the past, it was almost impossible for family or friends to know how their son, sister, friend, or colleague was faring in the race. Those who could afford the trip to Hawaii would see the start, and then the athletes would disappear, and that was pretty much it until the finish line. However, Florida-based World Triathlon Corporation (WTC), owner of the Ironman Triathlon, has changed all that by using mobile technology, long-range WiMAX networks, wi-fi enabled hotspots, and live webcasts via the Ironman.com website.

Anyone with the interest can now follow any athlete to find out where he or she is on the course and what speed he or she is running. What makes this possible is WiMAX to provide high-speed broadband connections in various locations along the 140-mile course. The company also uses radio frequency identification (RFID) to track the athlete's progress and high-bandwidth communications to transmit professional-quality video and other data that make the information accessible over the Ironmanlive.com website.

Since the course which the athletes compete on is rough and rugged on an island with an active volcano networking the course was a real challenge. In addition Hawaii is hot and windy, and there is no existing infrastructure. Airspan Networks provided the WiMAX infrastructure, using its high-performance base stations to create a high-throughput backbone capable of transmitting data rates required for top-quality video. The WiMAX base station was set up on top of a hotel that served as the event's starting point and finish line, which also happened to be one of the lowest geographical points of the course. In addition, the Airspan team was operating in a non-line-of-sight environment and highly porous volcanic rock absorbed the wireless signals more than other types of rock would. Airspan needed to keep the fidelity of the signals strong by setting up relays on the ridge sides of the volcano, the side of the road, and the sides of buildings. There were locations without power for cameras, and therefore generators were used. This was a wireless deployment in every sense of the word, and a great demonstration of the viability of wireless technology.

Wireless-enabled video stations equipped with network video cameras filmed the athletes as they passed by. That footage was then stitched into the live webcast, along with pre-event interviews, commentary, and footage shot from cameras on motorcycles and helicopters. In a live production studio at the event site WTC produced the broadcast that streamed the video data to the global servers that run the Ironmanlive. com website.

To bring the athletes and their fans closer Ironman used other wireless technologies such as RFID to track each athlete's progress along the event route and maximize accuracy and safety. Each athlete wore an ankle bracelet with an RFID tag, and as a competitor crossed over one of 12 timing mats spread throughout the course, the RFID tag communicated to a reader that captured the athlete's times, and that information was relayed over the wireless network to a database. This information was available on the Ironmanlive.com website just seconds later, where spectators and viewers could see the athlete's pace and timing.

Eight wireless hotspots were set up, including five along the event course and at the finish line. An Internet cafe was established with notebook and handheld computers, providing convenient, wireless access to event information and the Ironmanlive.com site. Two giant-screen displays showed the live program coverage from Ironmanlive. com. WTC staff used additional notebooks and handheld devices to manage the race and access information on each athlete's progress. The health care team used PDAs to scan athletes' RFID tags if they needed medical care allowing instant access to medical records and local contact information.

The WTC earns tremendous respect for its sports broadcasting leadership in its use of wireless technology. This allows WTC to drive larger audiences and higher advertising revenues. Larger audiences and better experiences for athletes and their families ultimately lead to greater participation in and growing popularity of the Ironman Triathlon.

# Introduction

One of the biggest forces changing business is the Internet. Technology companies like Intel and Cisco were among the first to seize the Internet to overhaul their operations. Intel deployed web-based automation to liberate its 200 salesclerks from tedious order-entry positions. Instead, salesclerks concentrate on customer relationship management functions such as analyzing sales trends and pampering customers. Cisco handles 75 percent of its sales online, and 45 percent of online orders never touch employees' hands. This type of Internet-based ordering has helped Cisco hike productivity by 20 percent over the past few years.

*Ebusiness* is the conducting of business on the Internet, not only buying and selling, but also serving customers and collaborating with business partners. Organizations realize that putting up simple websites for customers, employees, and partners does not create an ebusiness. Ebusiness websites must create a buzz, much as Amazon has done in the book-selling industry. Ebusiness websites must be innovative, add value, and provide useful information. In short, the site must build a sense of community and collaboration, eventually becoming the port of entry for business. This unit focuses on the opportunities and advantages found with developing collaborative partnerships in ebusiness and includes:

- **Chapter Thirteen**—Creating Innovative Organizations.
- **Chapter Fourteen**—Ebusiness.
- **Chapter Fifteen**—Creating Collaborative Partnerships.
- **Chapter Sixteen**—Integrating Wireless Technology in Business.

# 13 Creating Innovative Organizations

**13.1.** Compare disruptive and sustaining technologies.

**13.2.** Explain how the Internet caused disruption among businesses.

**13.3.** Define the relationship between the Internet and the World Wide Web.

**13.4.** Describe the Internet's impact on information along with how these changes are affecting businesses.

## Disruptive Technology

Polaroid, founded in 1937, produced the first instant camera in the late 1940s. The Polaroid camera was one of the most exciting technological advances the photography industry had ever seen. By using a Polaroid camera, customers no longer had to depend on others to develop their pictures. The technology was innovative and the product was high-end. The company eventually went public, becoming one of Wall Street's most prominent enterprises, with its stock trading above $60 in 1997. In 2002, the stock was down to 8 cents and the company declared bankruptcy.

How could a company like Polaroid, which had innovative technology and a captive customer base, go bankrupt? Perhaps company executives failed to use Porter's Five Forces to analyze the threat of substitute products or services. If they had, would they have noticed the two threats, one-hour film processing and digital cameras, that eventually stole Polaroid's market share? Would they have understood that their customers, people who want instant access to their pictures without having a third party involved, would be the first to use one-hour film processing and the first to purchase digital cameras? Could the company have found a way to compete with one-hour film processing and the digital camera to save Polaroid?

Most organizations face the same dilemma as Polaroid—the criteria an organization uses to make business decisions for its present business could possibly create issues for its future business. Essentially, what is best for the current business could ruin it in the long term. Some observers of our business environment have an ominous vision of the future—digital Darwinism. ***Digital Darwinism*** implies that organizations that cannot adapt to the new demands placed on them for surviving in the information age are doomed to extinction.

### DISRUPTIVE VERSUS SUSTAINING TECHNOLOGY

A ***disruptive technology*** is a new way of doing things that initially does not meet the needs of existing customers. Disruptive technologies tend to open new markets and destroy old ones. A ***sustaining technology,*** on the other hand, produces an improved product customers are eager to buy, such as a faster car or larger hard drive. Sustaining technologies tend to provide us with better, faster, and cheaper products in established markets. Incumbent companies most often lead sustaining

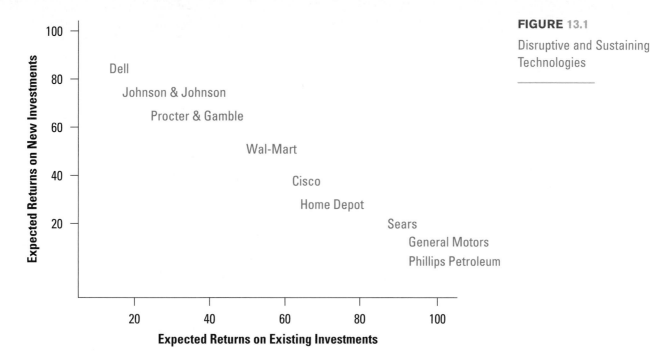

**FIGURE** 13.1

Disruptive and Sustaining
Technologies

technology to market, but virtually never lead in markets opened by disruptive technologies. Figure 13.1 displays companies that are expecting future growth to occur from new investments (disruptive technology) and companies that are expecting future growth to occur from existing investments (sustaining technology).

Disruptive technologies typically cut into the low end of the marketplace and eventually evolve to displace high-end competitors and their reigning technologies. Sony is a perfect example of a company that entered the low end of the marketplace and eventually evolved to displace its high-end competitors. Sony started as a tiny company that built portable, battery-powered transistor radios people could carry around with them. The sound quality of Sony's transistor radios was poor because the transistor amplifiers were of lower quality than traditional vacuum tubes, which produce a better sound. But customers were willing to overlook sound quality for the convenience of portability. With the experience and revenue stream from the portables, Sony improved its technology to produce cheap, low-end transistor amplifiers that were suitable for home use and used those revenues to improve the technology further, which produced better radios.

The *Innovator's Dilemma,* a book by Clayton M. Christensen, discusses how established companies can take advantage of disruptive technologies without hindering existing relationships with customers, partners, and stakeholders. Companies like Xerox, IBM, Sears, and DEC all listened to existing customers, invested aggressively in technology, had their competitive antennae up, and still lost their market-dominant positions. Christensen states that these companies may have placed too much emphasis on satisfying customers' current needs, while neglecting to adopt new disruptive technology that will meet customers' future needs, thus causing the companies to eventually fail. Figure 13.2 highlights several companies that launched new businesses by capitalizing on disruptive technologies.

## THE INTERNET—BUSINESS DISRUPTION

When the Internet was in its early days, no one had any idea how massive it would become. Computer companies did not think it would be a big deal; neither did the phone companies or cable companies. Difficult to access and operate, it seemed likely to remain an arcane tool of the Defense Department and academia. However,

**FIGURE** 13.2

Companies That
Capitalized on Disruptive
Technology

| Company | Disruptive Technology |
| --- | --- |
| Charles Schwab | Online brokerage |
| Hewlett-Packard | Microprocessor-based computers; ink-jet printers |
| IBM | Minicomputers; personal computers |
| Intel | Low-end microprocessors |
| Intuit | QuickBooks software; TurboTax software; Quicken software |
| Microsoft | Internet-based computing; operating system software; SQL and Access database software |
| Oracle | Database software |
| Quantum | 3.5-inch disks |
| Sony | Transistor-based consumer electronics |

the Internet grew, and grew, and grew. It began with a handful of users in the mid-1960s and reached 1 billion by 2005 (see Figures 13.3 and 13.4). Estimates predict there will be more than 3 billion Internet users by 2010. Already, villages in Indonesia and India have Internet access before they have electricity.

# Evolution of the Internet

During the Cold War in the mid-1960s, the U.S. military decided it needed a bomb-proof communications system, and thus the concept for the Internet was born. The system would link computers throughout the country allowing messages to get though even if a large section of the country was destroyed. In the early days, the only linked computers were at government think tanks and a few universities. The Internet was essentially an emergency military communications system operated by the Department of Defense's Advanced Research Project Agency (ARPA) and called ARPANET. Formally defined, the ***Internet*** is a global public network of computer networks that pass information from one to another using common

**FIGURE** 13.3

Internet Penetration by
World Region

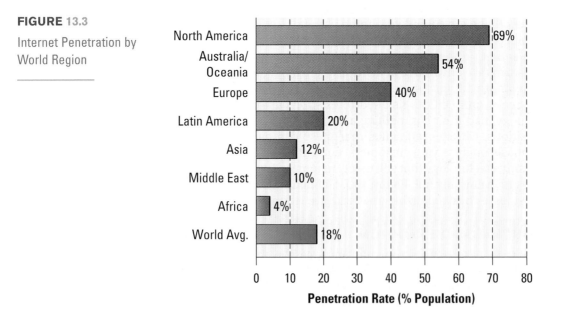

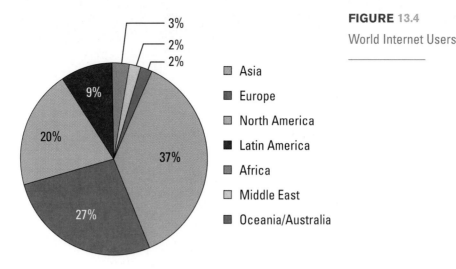

**FIGURE** 13.4

World Internet Users

- 3%
- 2%
- 2%

- Asia
- Europe
- North America
- Latin America
- Africa
- Middle East
- Oceania/Australia

9%

20%

37%

27%

computer protocols. **_Protocols_** are the standards that specify the format of data as well as the rules to be followed during transmission.

In time, every university in the United States that had defense-related funding installed ARPANET computers. Gradually, the Internet moved from a military pipeline to a communications tool for scientists. As more scholars came online, system administration transferred from ARPA to the National Science Foundation. Years later, businesses began using the Internet, and the administrative responsibilities were once again transferred. Today, no one party operates the Internet; however, several entities oversee the Internet and set standards including:

- Internet Engineering Task Force (IETF): The protocol engineering and development arm of the Internet.

- Internet Architecture Board (IAB): Responsible for defining the overall architecture of the Internet, providing guidance and broad direction to the IETF.

- Internet Engineering Steering Group (IESG): Responsible for technical management of IETF activities and the Internet standards process.

## EVOLUTION OF THE WORLD WIDE WEB

People often interchange the terms _Internet_ and the _World Wide Web,_ but these terms are not synonymous. Throughout the 1960s, 1970s, and 1980s, the Internet was primarily used by the Department of Defense to support activities such as email and transferring files. The Internet was restricted to noncommercial activities, and its users included government employees, researchers, university professors, and students. The World Wide Web changed the purpose and use of the Internet.

The **_World Wide Web (WWW)_** is a global hypertext system that uses the Internet as its transport mechanism. **_Hypertext transport protocol (HTTP)_** is the Internet standard that supports the exchange of information on the WWW. By defining universal resource locators (URLs) and how they can be used to retrieve resources anywhere on the Internet, HTTP enables web authors to embed hyperlinks in web documents. HTTP defines the process by which a web client, called a browser, originates a request for information and sends it to a web server, a program designed to respond to HTTP requests and provide the desired information. In a hypertext system, users navigate by clicking a hyperlink embedded in the current document. The action displays a second document in the same or a separate browser window. The web has quickly become the ideal medium for publishing information on the Internet and serves as the platform for the electronic economy. Figure 13.5 displays the reasons for the popularity and growth in the WWW.

**FIGURE** 13.5

Reasons for World Wide
Web Growth

| Reasons for Growth of the World Wide Web |
|---|
| ■ The microcomputer revolution made it possible for an average person to own a computer. |
| ■ Advancements in networking hardware, software, and media made it possible for business PCs to be inexpensively connected to larger networks. |
| ■ Browser software such as Microsoft's Internet Explorer and Netscape Navigator gave computer users an easy-to-use graphical interface to find, download, and display web pages. |
| ■ The speed, convenience, and low cost of email have made it an incredibly popular tool for business and personal communications. |
| ■ Basic web pages are easy to create and extremely flexible. |

The WWW remained primarily text-based until 1991 when two events occurred that would forever change the web and the amount and quality of information available (see Figure 13.6). First, Tim Berners-Lee built the first website on August 6, 1991 (http://info.cern.ch/—the site has been archived). The site provided details about the World Wide Web including how to build a browser and set up a web server. It also housed the world's first web directory, since Berners-Lee later maintained a list of other websites apart from his own.

Second, Marc Andreesen developed a new computer program called the NCSA Mosaic (National Center for Supercomputing Applications at the University of Illinois) and gave it away! The browser made it easier to access the websites that had started to appear. Soon websites contained more than just text; they also had sound and video files (see Figure 13.7). These pages, written in the hypertext markup language (HTML), have links that allow the user to quickly move from one document to another, even when the documents are stored in different computers. Web browsers read the HTML text and convert it into a web page.

By eliminating time and distance, the Internet makes it possible to perform business in ways not previously imaginable. The *digital divide* is when those with access to technology have great advantages over those without access to technology. People living in the village of Siroha, India, must bike five miles to find a telephone. For over 700 million rural people living in India, the digital divide was a way of life,

**FIGURE** 13.6

The Internet's Impact on
Information

| Internet's Impact on Information | |
|---|---|
| **Easy to compile** | Searching for information on products, prices, customers, suppliers, and partners is faster and easier when using the Internet. |
| **Increased richness** | *Information richness* refers to the depth and breadth of information transferred between customers and businesses. Businesses and customers can collect and track more detailed information when using the Internet. |
| **Increased reach** | *Information reach* refers to the number of people a business can communicate with, on a global basis. Businesses can share information with numerous customers all over the world. |
| **Improved content** | A key element of the Internet is its ability to provide dynamic relevant content. Buyers need good content descriptions to make informed purchases, and sellers use content to properly market and differentiate themselves from the competition. Content and product description establish the common understanding between both parties to the transaction. As a result, the reach and richness of that content directly affects the transaction. |

until recently. Media Lab Asia sells telephony and email services via a mobile Internet kiosk mounted on a bicycle, which is known as an "info-thelas." The kiosk has an onboard computer equipped with an antenna for Internet service and a specially designed all-day battery. Over 2,000 villages have purchased the kiosk for $1,200, and another 600,000 villages are interested.

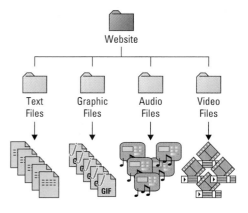

**FIGURE** 13.7

File Formats Offered over the WWW

## WEB 2.0

The impact of Web 2.0 is just starting to become apparent. **Web 2.0** is a set of economic, social, and technology trends that collectively form the basis for the next generation of the Internet—a more mature, distinctive medium characterized by user participation, openness, and network effects. The term does not mean a new version of the WWW, but refers to changes in the ways software developers and users make use of the web as a platform. According to Tim O'Reilly, "Web 2.0 is the business revolution in the computer industry caused by the move to the Internet as platform, and an attempt to understand the rules for success on that new platform." Figure 13.8 displays O'Reilly's version of the move from Web 1.0 to Web 2.0, and Figure 13.9 displays the timeline of Web 1.0 and Web 2.0.

Web 2.0 is more than just the latest technology buzzword; it is a transformative force that is catapulting companies across all industries toward a new way of performing business. Companies that take advantage of the numerous opportunities associated with Web 2.0 can achieve the coveted first-mover advantage in their

| Web 1.0 | | Web 2.0 |
|---|---|---|
| Doubleclick | --> | Google Adsense |
| Ofoto | --> | Flickr |
| Akamai | --> | Bittorrent |
| MP3.Com | --> | Napster |
| Britannica Online | --> | Wikipedia |
| Personal Websites | --> | Blogging |
| Evite | --> | Upcoming.Org And EVDB |
| Domain Name Speculation | --> | Search Engine Optimization |
| Page Views | --> | Cost Per Click |
| Screen Scraping | --> | Web Services |
| Publishing | --> | Participation |
| Content Management Systems | --> | Wikis |
| Directories (Taxonomy) | --> | Tagging ("Folksonomy") |
| Stickiness | --> | Syndication |

**FIGURE** 13.8

The Move from Web 1.0 to Web 2.0

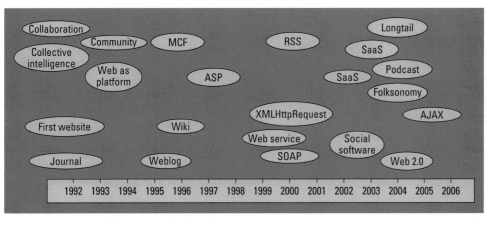

**FIGURE** 13.9

Timeline of Web 1.0

markets. A few reasons for this change include the following raw demographic and technological drivers:

- Over 1 billion individuals have Internet access.
- Mobile devices outnumber desktop computers by a factor of two.
- Always-on broadband connections account for over 50 percent of all U.S. Internet access.

Merging these drivers with the basic rules of social networking produces Web 2.0—the next-generation, user-driven, intelligent web. A few examples of Web 2.0 include:

- In the first quarter of 2006, MySpace.com signed up 280,000 new users each day and had the second most Internet traffic of any website.
- By the second quarter of 2006, 50 million blogs were created—new ones were added at a rate of two per second.
- In 2005, eBay conducted 8 billion web services transactions.

### THE FUTURE—WEB 3.0

*Web 3.0* has many different meanings and basically describes the evolution of web usage and interaction among several separate paths. Web 3.0 really transforms the web into a database, making content accessible by multiple nonbrowser applications and leveraging artificial intelligence technologies, or the semantic web. The *semantic web* is an evolving extension of the WWW in which web content can be expressed not only in natural language, but also in a format that can be read and used by software agents, thus permitting them to find, share, and integrate information more easily. It derives from W3C director Sir Tim Berners-Lee's vision of the web as a universal medium for data, information, and knowledge exchange.

### OPENING CASE STUDY QUESTIONS

1. Do you believe the Ironman has used disruptive technology to change the way athletes participate in sports? Why or why not?
2. What types of Web 2.0 technologies could WTC use on the Ironman.com website?
3. What types of ethical dilemmas might WTC face in deploying real-time video over the Internet?
4. What types of security issues does WTC need to address?

## Chapter Thirteen Case: Failing to Innovate

It is a sad but common tale—a dynamic company comes up with an innovative new product that utilizes cutting-edge technology in an exciting way that generates lots of hype and attention. But for some reason this new product fails to click with the masses and falls into oblivion, only to see other products gain massive success by following in its footsteps.

It's not always a case of right technology at the wrong time. Sometimes these first movers failed to build on their innovation, instead sitting on their initial achievements and letting more nimble competitors refine their idea into something more attractive and functional. And some just made too many mistakes to succeed.

Obtaining the first-mover advantage is critical to any business that wants to compete in the Internet economy. However, gaining a first-mover advantage is typically temporary, and without remaining innovative the company can soon fail. Here is a list of the top 10 first movers that flopped, according to Jim Rapoza of eWeek.

1. **Apple Newton PDA**—When it was launched in the early 90s, the Apple Newton was first lauded but later mocked because of its failings (it even had the honor of being spoofed on *The Simpsons*). But one can draw a straight line from the Newton to current products such as tablet PCs, smart phones, and the new Apple iPhone.

2. **PointCast**—In 1997, one of the hottest products found on the desktop of nearly every IT worker was PointCast, which delivered selected news items directly to the desktop. It quickly launched the "push" craze, which just as quickly imploded spectacularly. But today's RSS and news feeds all owe a debt to PointCast.

3. **Gopher Protocol**—It was so close. Launched just before the web itself, Gopher quickly became popular in universities and business. Using search technology, it worked very much like a website, but it could not compete with the web itself.

4. **VisiCalc**—Often lauded as the first killer application for the PC, the VisiCalc spreadsheet was a must-have for early PC-enabled businesses but quickly fell behind more polished spreadsheets from Lotus and Microsoft.

5. **Atari**—For those of a certain age, the word *Atari* is synonymous with video games. The pioneer in home gaming consoles failed to innovate in the face of more nimble competitors.

6. **Diamond Rio**—For $200 and with 32MB of RAM (with a SmartMedia slot for memory expansion), the Rio helped launch the MP3 revolution. That is, until white earbuds and a thing called the iPod took over.

7. **Netscape Navigator**—Netscape Navigator was essentially the web for users in the early to mid-1990s. But Netscape could not withstand the Microsoft onslaught, along with plenty of mistakes the company made itself, and now only lives on as the original basis of the Mozilla browsers.

8. **AltaVista**—Not the first search engine, but the first to use many of the natural language technologies common today and the first to gain real web popularity, AltaVista failed to keep up with technological changes.

9. **Ricochet Networks**—Nothing created geek lust like sitting next to someone who had a Ricochet card plugged into the laptop. Look, she is in a cab and accessing the Internet at ISDN speeds! But Ricochet never expanded to enough cities to be a serious player.

10. **IBM Simon Phone**—The iPhone's $499 price is nothing compared with the $900 price tag the IBM Simon had when it finally became available in 1994. But it pioneered most of the features found in today's smart phones and even beat the iPhone when it came to a buttonless touch-screen interface.

## Questions

1. If these companies all had a first-mover advantage, then why did the products fail?
2. For each of the above determine if the technology used was disruptive or sustaining.
3. Choose one of the products above and determine what the company could have done to prevent the product from failing.
4. Can you name another technology product that failed? Why did it fail? What could the company have done differently for it to succeed?

# 14 Ebusiness

**14.1.** Compare ecommerce and ebusiness.

**14.2.** Compare the four types of ebusiness models.

**14.3.** Describe the benefits and challenges associated with ebusiness.

**14.4.** Explain the differences among eshops, emalls, and online auctions.

## Ebusiness

Tom Anderson and Chris DeWolf started MySpace, a social networking website that offers its members information about the independent music scene around the country representing both Internet culture and teenage culture. Musicians sign up for free MySpace home pages where they can post tour dates, songs, and lyrics. Fans sign up for their own web pages to link to favorite bands and friends. MySpace is the world's second most popular English-language website with over 100 million users.

One of the biggest benefits of the Internet is how it enables organizations to perform business with anyone, anywhere, anytime. **Ecommerce** is the buying and selling of goods and services over the Internet. Ecommerce refers only to online transactions. **Ebusiness,** derived from the term *ecommerce,* is the conducting of business on the Internet, not only buying and selling, but also serving customers and collaborating with business partners. The primary difference between ecommerce and ebusiness is that ebusiness also refers to online exchanges of information, for example, a manufacturer allowing its suppliers to monitor production schedules or a financial institution allowing its customers to review their banking, credit card, and mortgage accounts.

In the past few years, ebusiness seems to have permeated every aspect of daily life. Both individuals and organizations have embraced Internet technologies to enhance productivity, maximize convenience, and improve communications globally. From banking to shopping to entertainment, the Internet has become integral to daily life. Figure 14.1 provides examples of a few of the industries using ebusiness.

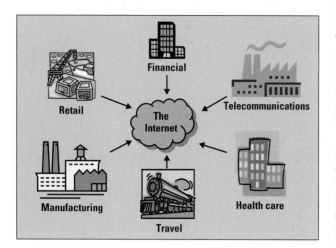

**FIGURE 14.1**

Overview of Several Industries Using Ebusiness

## Ebusiness Models

An **ebusiness model** is an approach to conducting electronic business on the Internet. Ebusiness transactions take place between two major entities—businesses and consumers. All ebusiness activities happen within the framework of two types of

| Ebusiness Term | Definition |
| --- | --- |
| *Business-to-business (B2B)* | Applies to businesses buying from and selling to each other over the Internet. |
| *Business-to-consumer (B2C)* | Applies to any business that sells its products or services to consumers over the Internet. |
| *Consumer-to-business (C2B)* | Applies to any consumer that sells a product or service to a business over the Internet. |
| *Consumer-to-consumer (C2C)* | Applies to sites primarily offering goods and services to assist consumers interacting with each other over the Internet. |

|  | Business | Consumer |
| --- | --- | --- |
| **Business** | B2B | B2C |
| **Consumer** | C2B | C2C |

**FIGURE** 14.2

Basic Ebusiness Models

business relationships: (1) the exchange of products and services between businesses (business-to-business, or B2B) and (2) the exchange of products and services with consumers (business-to-consumer, or B2C) (see Figure 14.2).

The primary difference between B2B and B2C are the customers; B2B customers are other businesses while B2C markets to consumers. Overall, B2B relations are more complex and have higher security needs; plus B2B is the dominant ebusiness force, representing 80 percent of all online business. Figure 14.3 illustrates all the ebusiness models: business-to-business, business-to-consumer, consumer-to-consumer, and consumer-to-business.

EBags is a true ebusiness success story. It is thriving as the world's leading online provider of bags and accessories for all lifestyles. With 180 brands and over 8,000 products, eBags has sold more than 4 million bags since its launch in March 1999. It carries a complete line of premium and popular brands, including Samsonite, Jan-Sport, The North Face, Liz Claiborne, and Adidas. The company has received several awards for excellence in online retailing including the Circle of Excellence Platinum Award from Bizrate.com, Web Site of the Year from *Catalog Age* magazine, and Email Marketer of the Year from ClickZ.MessageMedia. This success can

**FIGURE** 14.3

Ebusiness Models

Business-to-Business (B2B)  Business-to-Consumer (B2C)

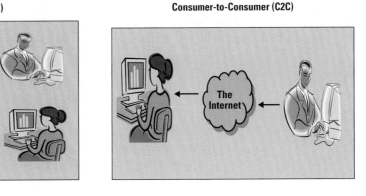

Consumer-to-Business (C2B)  Consumer-to-Consumer (C2C)

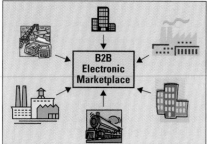

**FIGURE** 14.4

Business-to-Business
Emarketplace Overview

be attributed to eBags' commitment to providing each customer with superior service, 24 hours a day, 365 days a year, including convenient, real-time UPS order tracking. According to Jon Nordmark, CEO of eBags.com, "From a customer perspective, we've spent a great deal of time developing pioneering ways to guide our shoppers to the bags and accessories that enhance their lifestyles through function and fashion."

## BUSINESS-TO-BUSINESS (B2B)

***Business-to-business (B2B)*** applies to businesses buying from and selling to each other over the Internet. Online access to data, including expected shipping date, delivery date, and shipping status, provided either by the seller or a third-party provider, is widely supported by B2B models. Electronic marketplaces represent a new wave in B2B ebusiness models. ***Electronic marketplaces,*** or ***emarketplaces,*** are interactive business communities providing a central market space where multiple buyers and sellers can engage in ebusiness activities (see Figure 14.4). They present structures for conducting commercial exchange, consolidating supply chains, and creating new sales channels. Their primary goal is to increase market efficiency by tightening and automating the relationship between buyers and sellers. Existing emarketplaces allow access to various mechanisms in which to buy and sell almost anything, from services to direct materials.

## BUSINESS-TO-CONSUMER (B2C)

***Business-to-consumer (B2C)*** applies to any business that sells its products or services to consumers over the Internet. Carfax has been in the vehicle history report business for 20 years with an original customer base of used-car dealers. "The Internet was just a new way for us to reach the consumer market," Carfax President Dick Raines said. Carfax spent $20 million on print and TV ads to attract customers to its website. Customers can purchase a Carfax report for $14.95 or six days of reports for $19.95. Carfax has now launched a partnership program for small auto dealers' websites and a cash-back program offering customers 20 percent of revenues received for their referrals. "We continue to look for more and more ways to add value," Raines said. Common B2C ebusiness models include eshops and emalls.

### Eshop

An ***eshop,*** sometimes referred to as an ***estore*** or ***etailer,*** is a version of a retail store where customers can shop at any hour of the day without leaving their home or office. These online stores sell and support a variety of products and services. The online businesses channeling their goods and services via the Internet only, such as Amazon.com, are called *pure plays.* The others are an extension of traditional retail outlets that sell online as well as through a traditional physical store. They are generally known as "bricks and clicks" or "clicks and mortar" organizations, such as the Gap (www.gap.com) and Best Buy (www.bestbuy.com) (see Figure 14.5).

**FIGURE** 14.5

Types of Businesses

| Business Types | |
|---|---|
| *Brick-and-mortar business* | A business that operates in a physical store without an Internet presence. |
| *Pure-play (virtual) business* | A business that operates on the Internet only without a physical store. Examples include Amazon.com and Expedia.com. |
| *Click-and-mortar business* | A business that operates in a physical store and on the Internet. Examples include REI and Barnes and Noble. |

FIGURE 14.6

Online Auctions

| Online Auctions | |
|---|---|
| Electronic Auction (eauction) | Sellers and buyers solicit consecutive bids from each other and prices are determined dynamically. |
| Forward Auction | An auction that sellers use as a selling channel to many buyers and the highest bid wins. |
| Reverse Auction | An auction that buyers use to purchase a product or service, selecting the seller with the lowest bid. |

## Emall

An *emall* consists of a number of eshops; it serves as a gateway through which a visitor can access other eshops. An emall may be generalized or specialized depending on the products offered by the eshops it hosts. Revenues for emall operators include membership fees from participating eshops, advertising, and possibly a fee on each transaction if the emall operator also processes payments. Eshops in emalls benefit from brand reinforcement and increased traffic as visiting one shop on the emall often leads to browsing "neighboring" shops. An example of an emall is the Arizona emall www.1az1.com/shopping.

## CONSUMER-TO-BUSINESS (C2B)

*Consumer-to-business (C2B)* applies to any consumer that sells a product or service to a business over the Internet. One example of this ebusiness model is Priceline .com where bidders (or customers) set their prices for items such as airline tickets or hotel rooms, and a seller decides whether to supply them. The demand for C2B ebusiness will increase over the next few years due to customers' desires for greater convenience and lower prices.

## CONSUMER-TO-CONSUMER (C2C)

*Consumer-to-consumer (C2C)* applies to sites primarily offering goods and services to assist consumers interacting with each other over the Internet. The Internet's most successful C2C online auction website, eBay, links like-minded buyers and sellers for a small commission. Figure 14.6 displays the different types of online auctions.

C2C online communities, or virtual communities, interact via email groups, web-based discussion forums, or chat rooms. C2C business models are consumer-driven and opportunities are available to satisfy most consumers' needs, ranging from finding a mortgage to job hunting. They are global swap shops based on customer-centered communication. One C2C community, KazaA, allows users to download MP3 music files, enabling users to exchange files. Figure 14.7 highlights the different types of C2C communities that are thriving on the Internet.

FIGURE 14.7

C2C Communities

| C2C Communities |
|---|
| ■ **Communities of interest**—People interact with each other on specific topics, such as golfing and stamp collecting. |
| ■ **Communities of relations**—People come together to share certain life experiences, such as cancer patients, senior citizens, and car enthusiasts. |
| ■ **Communities of fantasy**—People participate in imaginary environments, such as fantasy football teams and playing one-on-one with Michael Jordan. |

# Ebusiness Benefits and Challenges

According to an NUA Internet Survey, the Internet links more than 1 billion people worldwide. Experts predict that global Internet usage will have nearly tripled between 2006 and 2010, making ebusiness a more significant factor in the global economy. As ebusiness improves, organizations will experience benefits and challenges alike. Figure 14.8 details ebusiness benefits for an organization.

The Internet is forcing organizations to refocus their information systems from the inside out. A growing number of companies are already using the Internet to streamline their business processes, procure materials, sell products, automate customer service, and create new revenue streams. Although the benefits of ebusiness systems are enticing, developing, deploying, and managing these systems is not always easy. Unfortunately, ebusiness is not something a business can just go out and buy. Figure 14.9 details the challenges facing ebusiness.

A key element of emarketplaces is their ability to provide not only transaction capabilities but also dynamic, relevant content to trading partners. The original ebusiness websites provided shopping cart capabilities built around product catalogs. As a result of the complex emarketplace that must support existing business processes and systems, content is becoming even more critical for emarketplaces. Buyers need good content description to make informed purchases, and sellers use content to properly market and differentiate themselves from the competition. Content and product description establish the common understanding between both parties to the transaction. As a result, the accessibility, usability, accuracy, and richness of that content directly affect the transaction. Figure 14.10 displays the different benefits and challenges of various emarketplace revenue models.

# Mashups

A *web mashup* is a website or web application that uses content from more than one source to create a completely new service. The term is typically used in the context of music; putting Jay-Z lyrics over a Radiohead song makes something old become new. The web version of a mashup allows users to mix map data, photos, video, news feeds, blog entries and so on. Content used in mashups is typically sourced from an *application programming interface (API),* which is a set of routines, protocols, and tools for building software applications. A good API makes

**FIGURE** 14.8

Ebusiness Benefits

| Ebusiness Benefits | |
| --- | --- |
| **Highly Accessible** | Businesses can operate 24 hours a day, 7 days a week, 365 days a year. |
| **Increased Customer Loyalty** | Additional channels to contact, respond to, and access customers helps contribute to customer loyalty. |
| **Improved Information Content** | In the past, customers had to order catalogs or travel to a physical facility before they could compare price and product attributes. Electronic catalogs and web pages present customers with updated information in real time about goods, services, and prices. |
| **Increased Convenience** | Ebusiness automates and improves many of the activities that make up a buying experience. |
| **Increased Global Reach** | Businesses, both small and large, can reach new markets. |
| **Decreased Cost** | The cost of conducting business on the Internet is substantially less than traditional forms of business communication. |

FIGURE 14.9

Ebusiness Challenges

| Ebusiness Challenges | |
|---|---|
| **Protecting Consumers** | Consumers must be protected against unsolicited goods and communication, illegal or harmful goods, insufficient information about goods or their suppliers, invasion of privacy, and cyberfraud. |
| **Leveraging Existing Systems** | Most companies already use information technology to conduct business in non-Internet environments, such as marketing, order management, billing, inventory, distribution, and customer service. The Internet represents an alternative and complementary way to do business, but it is imperative that ebusiness systems integrate existing systems in a manner that avoids duplicating functionality and maintains usability, performance, and reliability. |
| **Increasing Liability** | Ebusiness exposes suppliers to unknown liabilities because Internet commerce law is vaguely defined and differs from country to country. The Internet and its use in ebusiness have raised many ethical, social, and political issues, such as identity theft and information manipulation. |
| **Providing Security** | The Internet provides universal access, but companies must protect their assets against accidental or malicious misuse. System security, however, must not create prohibitive complexity or reduce flexibility. Customer information also needs to be protected from internal and external misuse. Privacy systems should safeguard the personal information critical to building sites that satisfy customer and business needs. A serious deficiency arises from the use of the Internet as a marketing means. Sixty percent of Internet users do not trust the Internet as a payment channel. Making purchases via the Internet is considered unsafe by many. This issue affects both the business and the consumer. However, with encryption and the development of secure websites, security is becoming less of a constraint for ebusinesses. |
| **Adhering to Taxation Rules** | The Internet is not yet subject to the same level of taxation as traditional businesses. While taxation should not discourage consumers from using electronic purchasing channels, it should not favor Internet purchases over store purchases either. Instead, a tax policy should provide a level playing field for traditional retail businesses, mail-order companies, and Internet-based merchants. The Internet marketplace is rapidly expanding, yet it remains mostly free from traditional forms of taxation. In one recent study, uncollected state and local sales taxes from ebusiness were projected to exceed $60 billion in 2008. |

it easier to develop a program by providing all the building blocks. A programmer puts the blocks together. Most operating environments, such as Microsoft Windows, provide an API so that programmers can write applications consistent with the operating environment. Many people experimenting with mashups are using Microsoft, Google, eBay, Amazon, Flickr, and Yahoo APIs, which has led to the creation of mashup editors. **Mashup editors** are WSYIWYGs (What You See Is What You Get) for mashups. They provide a visual interface to build a mashup, often allowing the user to drag and drop data points into a web application.

Whoever thought technology could help sell bananas? Dole Organic now places three-digit farm codes on each banana and creates a mashup using Google Earth and its banana database. Socially and environmentally conscious buyers can plug the numbers into Dole's website and look at a bio of the farm where the bananas were raised. The site tells the story of the farm and its surrounding community, lists its organic certifications, posts some photos, and offers a link to satellite images of the farm in Google Earth. Customers can personally monitor the production and treatment of their fruit from the tree to the grocer. The process assures customers

| Revenue Models | Advantages | Limitations |
|---|---|---|
| Transaction fees | ■ Can be directly tied to savings (both process and price savings)<br>■ Important revenue source when high level of liquidity (transaction volume) is reached | ■ If process savings are not completely visible, use of the system is discouraged (incentive to move transactions offline)<br>■ Transaction fees likely to decrease with time |
| License fees | ■ Creates incentives to do many transactions<br>■ Customization and back-end integration leads to lock-in of participants | ■ Up-front fee is a barrier to entry for participants<br>■ Price differentiation is complicated |
| Subscription fees | ■ Creates incentives to do transactions<br>■ Price can be differentiated<br>■ Possibility to build additional revenue from new user groups | ■ Fixed fee is a barrier to entry for participants |
| Fees for value-added services | ■ Service offering can be differentiated<br>■ Price can be differentiated<br>■ Possibility to build additional revenue from established and new user groups (third parties) | ■ Cumbersome process for customers to continually evaluate new services |
| Advertising fees | ■ Well-targeted advertisements can be perceived as value-added content by trading participants<br>■ Easy to implement | ■ Limited revenue potential<br>■ Overdone or poorly targeted advertisements can be disturbing elements on the website |

**FIGURE** 14.10

The Benefits and Challenges of Various Emarketplace Revenue Models

that their bananas have been raised to proper organic standards on an environmentally friendly, holistically minded plantation. Other interesting mashups include:

■ **1001 Secret Fishing Holes:** Over a thousand fishing spots in national parks, wildlife refuges, lakes, campgrounds, historic trails, etc. (Google Maps API).

■ **25 Best Companies to Work For:** Map of the 100 best U.S. companies to work for as rated by *Fortune* magazine (Google Maps API).

■ **Album Covers:** Uses the Amazon API and an Ajax-style user interface to retrieve CD/DVD covers from the Amazon catalog (Amazon eCommerce API).

■ **Gawker:** A handy mashup for keeping up with celebrity sightings in New York City. Readers are encouraged to email as soon as the celeb is spotted (Google Maps API).

■ **Gigul8tor:** Provides a data entry page where bands can enter information about upcoming gigs and venues. Gigul8tor displays a list of possible locations depending on the venue engine and enters event information right into Eventful in an interface designed just for bands. It shows how different user interfaces could be built in front of Eventful with mashup techniques.

■ **GBlinker:** A Google pin wired to a serial port so it flashes when email arrives.

■ **OpenKapow:** Offers a platform for creating web-based APIs, feeds, and HTML snippets from any website, taking mashup possibilities way beyond the more than 300 APIs offered on ProgrammableWeb.

■ **The Hype Machine:** Combines blog posts from a set of curated music blogs with Amazon sales data and upcoming events. The Hype Machine tracks songs and discussion posted on the best blogs about music. It integrates with iTunes to take customers right from the web page to the track they are interested in. If the customer prefers buying through Amazon, The Hype Machine figures out what CD page to display.

- **Zillow:** Sophisticated home valuation tools with 65 million listings and extensive data on comparables (Microsoft Virtual Earth API).
- **ProgrammableWeb:** The favorite community website of mashup developers provides comprehensive listings of APIs available on the web and includes forums where developers can discuss how to best use them.

## OPENING CASE STUDY QUESTIONS

1. Identify the type of ebusiness model WTC is using for the Ironman and explain why it has been so successful.

2. What advantages would WTC have in opening up an Ironman emarketplace?

3. What would be an example of WTC using a mashup for the Ironman?

## Chapter Fourteen Case: eBiz

Amazing things are happening on the Internet, things nobody would believe. Here are two stories that demonstrate how innovation, creativity, and a great idea can turn the Internet into a cash cow.

### A Million Dollar Homepage

The Million Dollar Homepage is a website conceived by Alex Tew, a 21-year-old student from Cricklade, Wiltshire, England, to help raise money for his university education. Launched on August 26, 2005, the website is said to have generated a gross income of $1,037,100 and has a current Google PageRank of 7.

The index page of the site consists of a 1000 by 1000 pixel grid (1 million pixels), on which he sells image-based links for $1 per pixel, in minimum 10 by 10 blocks. A person who buys one or more of these pixel blocks can design a tiny image that will be displayed on the block, decide which URL the block will link to, and write a slogan that appears when the cursor hovers over the link. The aim of the site was to sell all of the pixels in the image, thus generating $1 million of income for the creator, which seems to have been accomplished. On January 1, 2006, the final 1,000 pixels left were put up for auction on eBay. The auction closed on January 11 with the winning bid of $38,100. This brought the final tally to $1,037,100 in gross income. See the Million Dollar Homepage on the next page.

### One Red Paperclip

The website One Red Paperclip was created by Kyle MacDonald, a Canadian blogger who bartered his way from a single paper clip to a house in a series of trades spanning almost one year. MacDonald began with one red paper clip on July 14, 2005. By July 5, 2006, a chain of bartering had ultimately led to trading a movie role for a two-story farmhouse in Kipling, Saskatchewan. On July 7, 2006—almost exactly one year after MacDonald began his experiment—the deed to the house was signed. In September, at the housewarming party where 12 of the 14 traders were present, he proposed to his girlfriend and she accepted. The wedding ring was made from the original red paper clip he got back from the first woman to have agreed to trade with him.

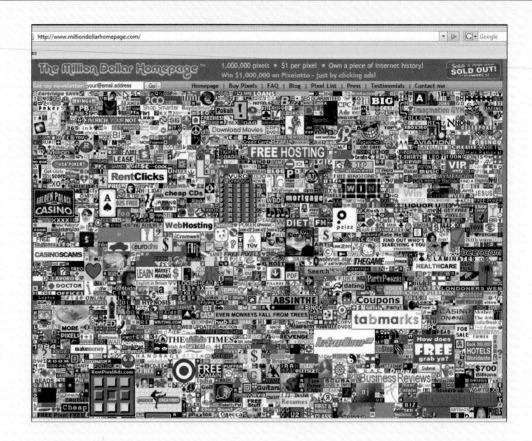

Following is the timeline, based on the website and as summarized by the BBC:

- On July 14, 2005, MacDonald went to Vancouver and traded the paper clip for a fish-shaped pen.

- MacDonald then traded the pen the same day for a hand-sculpted doorknob from Seattle, Washington, which he nicknamed Knob-T.

- On July 25, 2005, MacDonald traveled to Amherst, Massachusetts, with a friend to trade the Knob-T for a Coleman camp stove (with fuel).

- On September 24, 2005, he went to San Clemente, California, and traded the camp stove for a Honda generator, from a U.S. Marine.

- On November 16, 2005, MacDonald made a second (and successful) attempt (after having the generator confiscated by the New York City Fire Department) in Maspeth, Queens, to trade the generator for an "instant party": an empty keg, an IOU for filling the keg with the beer of the holder's choice, and a neon Budweiser sign.

- On December 8, 2005, he traded the "instant party" to Quebec comedian and radio personality Michel Barrette for a Ski-doo snowmobile.

- Within a week of that, MacDonald traded the snowmobile for a two-person trip to Yahk, British Columbia, in February 2006.

- On or about January 7, 2006, the second person on the trip to Yahk traded MacDonald a cube van for the privilege.

- On or about February 22, 2006, he traded the cube van for a recording contract with Metal Works in Toronto.

- On or about April 11, 2006, MacDonald traded the recording contract to Jody Gnant for a year's rent in Phoenix, Arizona.

- On or about April 26, 2006, he traded the one year's rent in Phoenix, Arizona, for one afternoon with Alice Cooper.

- On or about May 26, 2006, MacDonald traded the one afternoon with Alice Cooper for a KISS motorized snow globe.

- On or about June 2, 2006, he traded the KISS motorized snow globe to Corbin Bernsen for a role in the film *Donna on Demand*.

- On or about July 5, 2006, MacDonald traded the movie role for a two-story farmhouse in Kipling, Saskatchewan.

## Questions

1. How else can you use the Internet to raise money?
2. What types of businesses could benefit from trading on the Internet?
3. Can you think of any other disruptive or nontraditional ways that you could use the Internet?

# Creating Collaborative Partnerships

**15.1.** Identify the different ways in which companies collaborate using technology.

**15.2.** Compare the different categories of collaboration technologies.

**15.3.** Define the fundamental concepts of a knowledge management system.

**15.4.** Provide an example of a content management system along with its business purpose.

**15.5.** Evaluate the advantages of using a workflow management system.

**15.6.** Explain how groupware can benefit a business.

## Teams, Partnerships, and Alliances

To be successful—and avoid being eliminated by the competition—an organization must constantly undertake new initiatives, address both minor and major problems, and capitalize on significant opportunities. To support these activities, an organization often will create and utilize teams, partnerships, and alliances because the expertise needed is beyond the scope of a single individual or organization. These teams, partnerships, and alliances can be formed internally among a company's employees or externally with other organizations (see Figure 15.1).

Businesses of all sizes and in all markets have witnessed the benefits of leveraging their IT assets to create competitive advantage. Whereas information technology efforts in the past were aimed at increasing operational efficiency, the advent and proliferation of network-based computing (the Internet being the most visible, but not only, example) has enabled organizations to build systems with which all sorts of communities can interact. The ultimate result will allow organizations to do business with customers, business partners, suppliers, governments and regulatory agencies, and any other community relevant to their particular operation or activity.

**FIGURE** 15.1

Teams, Partnerships, and Alliances Within and External to an Organization

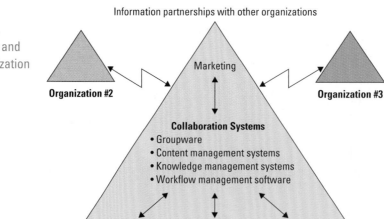

In the same way that organizations use internal teams, they are increasingly forming alliances and partnerships with other organizations. The **core competency** of an organization is its key strength, a business function that it does better than any of its competitors. Apple is highly regarded for its strength in product design, while Accenture's core competency is the design and installation of information systems. A **core competency strategy** is one in which an organization chooses to focus specifically on what it does best (its core competency) and forms partnerships and alliances with other specialist organizations to handle nonstrategic business processes. Strategic alliances enable businesses to gain competitive advantages through access to a partner's resources, including markets, technologies, and people. Teaming up with another business adds complementary resources and capabilities, enabling participants to grow and expand more quickly and efficiently, especially fast-growing companies that rely heavily on outsourcing many areas of their business to extend their technical and operational resources. In the outsourcing process, they save time and boost productivity by not having to develop their own systems from scratch. They are then free to concentrate on innovation and their core business.

Information technology makes such business partnerships and alliances easier to establish and manage. An **information partnership** occurs when two or more organizations cooperate by integrating their IT systems, thereby providing customers with the best of what each can offer. The advent of the Internet has greatly increased the opportunity for IT-enabled business partnerships and alliances. Amazon developed a profitable business segment by providing ebusiness outsourcing services to other retailers that use Amazon's website software. Some well-known retailers partnering with Amazon include Office Depot and Target.

## Collaboration Systems

Heineken USA has shortened its inventory cycle time for beer production and distribution from three months to four weeks. By using its collaborative system to forecast demand and expedite shipping, the company has dramatically cut inventory levels and shipping costs while increasing sales.

Over the past few years most business processes have changed on various dimensions (e.g., flexibility, interconnectivity, coordination style, autonomy) because of market conditions and organizational models. Frequently, information is located within physically separated systems as more and more organizations spread their reach globally. This creates a need for a software infrastructure that enables collaboration systems.

A **collaboration system** is an IT-based set of tools that supports the work of teams by facilitating the sharing and flow of information. Collaboration solves specific business tasks such as telecommuting, online meetings, deploying applications, and remote project and sales management (see Figure 15.2).

Collaboration systems allow people, teams, and organizations to leverage and build upon the ideas and talents of staff, suppliers, customers, and business partners. Collaboration systems meet unique business challenges that:

- Include complex interactions between people who may be in different locations and desire to work across function and discipline areas.
- Require flexibility in work process and the ability to involve others quickly and easily.
- Call for creating and sharing information rapidly and effortlessly within a team.

Most organizations collaborate with other companies in some capacity. Consider the supplier-customer relationship, which can be thought of in terms of a continuous life cycle of engagement, transaction, fulfillment, and service activities. Rarely do companies excel in all four life cycle areas, either from a business process or

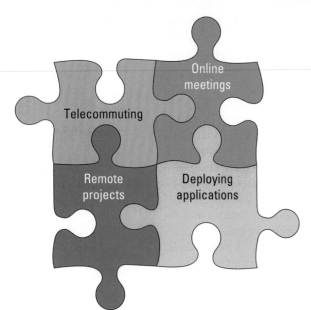

**FIGURE** 15.2

Collaborative Business Areas

**FIGURE** 15.3

Typical Collaborative Business Functions

from a technology-enabled aspect. Successful organizations identify and invest in their core competencies, and outsource or collaborate for those competencies that are not core to them. Collaboration systems fall into one of two categories:

1. **Unstructured collaboration** (sometimes referred to as **information collaboration**) includes document exchange, shared whiteboards, discussion forums, and email. These functions can improve personal productivity, reducing the time spent searching for information or chasing answers.

2. **Structured collaboration** (or **process collaboration**) involves shared participation in business processes, such as workflow, in which knowledge is hard-coded as rules. This is beneficial in terms of improving automation and the routing of information.

Regardless of location or format—be it unstructured or structured—relevant accurate information must be readily and consistently available to those who need it anytime, anywhere, and on any device. The integration of IT systems enables an organization to provide employees, partners, customers, and suppliers with the ability to access, find, analyze, manage, and collaborate on content. The collaboration can be done across a wide variety of formats, languages, and platforms. Figure 15.3 illustrates many of the typical collaborative functions within most organizations.

Lockheed Martin Aeronautics Company's ability to share complex project information across an extended supply chain in real time was key in its successful bid for a $19 billion Department of Defense (DoD) contract to build 21 supersonic stealth fighters. New government procurement rules require defense contractors to communicate effectively to ensure that deadlines are met, costs are controlled, and projects are managed throughout the life cycle of the contract.

| Function | Collaborator(s) | Business Function(s) |
|---|---|---|
| Planning and forecasting | Supplier, customer | Real-time information sharing (forecast information and sales information) |
| Product design | Supplier, customer | Document exchange, computer-aided design (CAD) |
| Strategic sourcing | Supplier | Negotiation, supplier performance management |
| Component compatibility testing | Supplier | Component compatibility |
| Pricing | Supplier, customer | Pricing in supply chain |
| Marketing | Supplier, customer | Joint/cooperative marketing campaigns, branding |
| Sales | Customer | Shared leads, presentations, configuration and quotes |
| Make-to-order | Customer | Requirements, capabilities, contract terms |
| Order processing | Supplier, customer | Order solution |
| Fulfillment: Logistics and service | Supplier, customer | Coordination of distribution |
| International trade logistics | Customer | Document exchange, import/export documents |
| Payment | Customer | Order receipt, invoicing |
| Customer service/support | Supplier, customer | Shared/split customer support |

In anticipation of the contract, the Fort Worth, Texas, unit of Lockheed Martin Corporation developed a real-time collaboration system that can tie together its partners, suppliers, and DoD customers via the Internet. The platform lets participants collectively work on product design and engineering tasks as well as supply chain and life cycle management issues. Lockheed will host all transactions and own the project information. The platform will let DoD and Lockheed project managers track the daily progress of the project in real time. This is the first major DoD project with such a requirement. The contract, awarded to the Lockheed unit and partners Northrop Grumman Corp. and BAE Systems, is the first installment in what could amount to a $200 billion program for 3,000 jet fighters over 40 years. The strengths of the collaboration process lie with the integration of many systems, namely:

- Knowledge management systems
- Content management systems
- Workflow management systems
- Groupware systems

# Knowledge Management Systems

**Knowledge management (KM)** involves capturing, classifying, evaluating, retrieving, and sharing information assets in a way that provides context for effective decisions and actions. Organizations can generate value from their intellectual and knowledge-based assets using KM. KM collects employees', partners', and customers' knowledge and distributes the aggregated information among employees, departments, and even other companies to devise best practices.

A good example of KM is a golf caddie. Golf caddies are expected to do far more than simply carry clubs; they should be able to offer detailed information on the course and provide advice such as "The wind makes the third hole play 20 yards longer." If a golf caddie can provide additional benefits such as solid advice it directly impacts their tip at the end of the game. Customers might visit certain golf courses because of the caddies, and sharing information among caddies helps the entire golf course become more profitable. Typically, course managers collect the caddie knowledge and compile it in a notebook or distribute it to a mobile device. In this same manner, developing a sophisticated KM system can improve the results for all individuals involved in an organization from customers to partners to employees.

KM is exploding throughout U.S. businesses for two primary reasons. First, the millions of baby boomers preparing to retire has spurred numerous KM initiatives as organizations attempt to glean all of the vital information about their jobs, companies, and industries that is about to walk out the door. Second, organizations that are outsourcing must address the tricky issue of transferring knowledge from their full-time employees—whose jobs are being outsourced—to the outsourcer's employees.

## KM IN BUSINESS

Knowledge is an organizational competitive advantage. Information systems can allocate an organization's knowledge base by interconnecting people and digitally collecting their knowledge. The principal purpose of KM is to ensure an organization's knowledge of work process details, sources of information, and typical solutions to problem is immediately available to all employees in real time. A **knowledge management system (KMS)** supports the capturing, organization, and dissemination of knowledge (i.e., know-how) throughout an organization. It is up to the organization to determine what information qualifies as knowledge. KMS goes beyond providing information contained in spreadsheets, databases, and documents and includes the intangible knowledge and know-how maintained in individuals' heads.

## EXPLICIT AND TACIT KNOWLEDGE

Not every piece of information has value, and organizations must determine what information qualifies as intellectual and knowledge-based assets. These fall into two categories: explicit or tacit. **Explicit knowledge** consists of anything that can be documented, archived, and codified, often with the help of IT. Patents, trademarks, business plans, marketing research, and customer lists are all examples of explicit knowledge. **Tacit knowledge** is the knowledge contained in people's heads. The issue with gathering tacit knowledge is figuring out how to recognize, generate, share, and manage knowledge that resides in people's heads. Emails and instant messaging can help identify some forms of tacit knowledge, but overall it is extremely difficult to even identify tacit knowledge. *Shadowing* and *joint problem solving* are two best practices for transferring or re-creating tacit knowledge inside an organization.

### Shadowing

With shadowing, less experienced employees examine more experienced employees to understand how their counterparts approach tasks. Dorothy Leonard and Walter Swap, two knowledge management experts, stress the importance of having the protégé discuss his or her observations with the expert to deepen the dialog and crystallize the knowledge transfer.

### Joint Problem Solving

People are frequently unaware of how they approach problems or execute tasks and therefore cannot detail how they perform their roles. In joint problem solving a novice employee and an expert employee work together on a project, which will bring out the details of how the expert handles responsibilities and work issues. The primary difference between shadowing and joint problem solving is that shadowing is far more passive, while joint problem solving is hands-on.

Information is worthless if it is not analyzed and disseminated to the right people, at the right place, and at the right time. An intellectual asset such as knowledge must be shared if an organization wants to remain competitive. Effective KMSs share the following characteristics:

■ Foster innovation by encouraging the free flow of ideas.

■ Improve customer service by streamlining response time.

■ Boost revenues by getting products and services to market faster.

■ Enhance employee retention rates by recognizing the value of employees' knowledge.

■ Streamline operations and reduce costs by eliminating redundant or unnecessary processes.

A creative approach to knowledge management can result in improved efficiency, higher productivity, and increased revenues in practically any business function. Figure 15.4 indicates the reasons organizations launch KMS.

KMS software is helping ChevronTexaco Corporation improve how it manages the assets in oil fields by enabling employees in multiple disciplines to easily access and share the information they need to make decisions. ChevronTexaco teams of 10 to 30 people are responsible for managing the assets, such as the drilling equipment, pipelines, and facilities, for a particular oil field. Within each team, earth scientists and various engineers with expertise in production, reservoirs, and facilities work together to keep the oil field up and running. Each member of the asset team needs to communicate with other members to make decisions

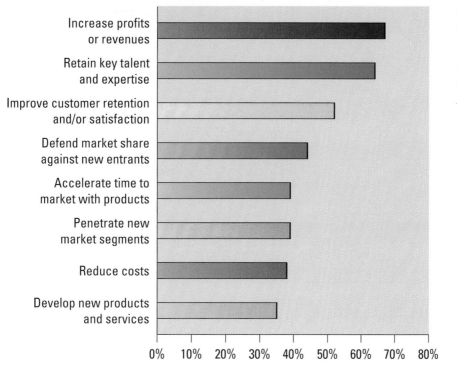

Increase profits or revenues

Retain key talent and expertise

Improve customer retention and/or satisfaction

Defend market share against new entrants

Accelerate time to market with products

Penetrate new market segments

Reduce costs

Develop new products and services

0%  10%  20%  30%  40%  50%  60%  70%  80%

based on the collection and analysis of huge amounts of information from various departments.

Individual team members can look at information from the perspective of their own department with the help of a KMS. This has helped ChevronTexaco achieve a 30 percent productivity gain, a 50 percent improvement in safety performance, and more than $2 billion in operating cost reductions. Through KMSs, Chevron-Texaco has restructured its gasoline retailing business and now drills oil and gas wells faster and cheaper.

Not every organization matches ChevronTexaco's success with KM. Numerous KM projects have failed over the past few years, generating an unwillingness to undertake—or even address—KM issues among many organizations. However, KM is an effective tool if it is tied directly to specific business needs and opportunities.

Beginning with targeted projects that deliver value quickly, companies can achieve the success that has proved elusive with many big-bang approaches. Successful KM projects typically focus on creating value in a specific process area, or even just for a certain type of transaction. Companies should start with one job at a time—preferably the most knowledge-oriented one—and build KM into a job function in a way that actually helps employees do their work better and faster, then expand to the next most knowledge-intensive job, and so on. Celebrating even small successes with KM will help build a base of credibility and support for future KM projects.

## Content Management Systems

A *content management system* provides tools to manage the creation, storage, editing, and publication of information in a collaborative environment. As a website grows in size and complexity, the business must establish procedures to ensure that things run smoothly. At a certain point, it makes sense to automate this process and use a content management system to manage this effectively. The content management system marketplace is complex, incorporating document management,

| Common Types of Content Management Systems | |
| --- | --- |
| **Document management system (DMS)** | DMS—Supports the electronic capturing, storage, distribution, archiving, and accessing of documents. A DMS optimizes the use of documents within an organization independent of any publishing medium (for example, the web). A DMS provides a document repository with information about other information. The system tracks the editorial history of each document and its relationships with other documents. A variety of search and navigation methods are available to make document retrieval easy. A DMS manages highly structured and regulated content, such as pharmaceutical documentation. |
| **Digital asset management (DAM) system** | DAM—Though similar to document management, DAM generally works with binary rather than text files, such as multimedia file types. DAM emphasizes file manipulation and conversion, for example, converting GIF files to JPEG. |
| **Web content management (WCM) system** | WCM—Adds an additional layer to document and digital asset management that enables publishing content both to intranets and to public websites. In addition to maintaining the content itself, WCM systems often integrate content with online processes like ebusiness systems. |

**FIGURE** 15.5

Common Types of Content Management Systems

digital asset management, and web content management. Figure 15.5 highlights the three primary types of content management systems. Figure 15.6 lists the major content management system vendors.

## WORKING WIKIS

*Wikis* are web-based tools that make it easy for users to add, remove, and change online content. *Business wikis* are collaborative web pages that allow users to edit documents, share ideas, or monitor the status of a project. Wikipedia, one of the largest online collaboration websites, is a good example. Many organizations offer their employees wikis for collaboration purposes; for example, Intel, Motorola, IBM, and Sony use wikis for everything from setting internal meeting agendas to posting documents related to new products. Companies also use wikis to engage customers in ongoing discussions about products and generate dialog on issues and concerns. Motorola and T-Mobile use customer wikis as continually updated user guides. TV networks including ABC and CBS are creating fan wikis that let viewers interact with each other as they unravel mysteries from such shows as *Lost* and *CSI: Crime Scene Investigation*.

**FIGURE** 15.6

Major Content Management System Vendors

| Vendors | Strengths | Weaknesses | Costs |
| --- | --- | --- | --- |
| **Documentum** www.documentum.com | Document and digital asset management | Personalization features not as strong as competitors | Major components start at less than $100,000 |
| **FatWire** www.fatwire.com | Web content management | May not scale to support thousands of users | SPARK, $25,000; Update Engine, $70,000 and up |
| **InterWoven** www.interwoven.com | Collaboration, enterprise content management | Requires significant customization | InterWoven 5 Platform, $50,000; average cost for a new customer, $250,000 |
| **Percussion** www.percussion.com | Web content management | May not scale to support thousands of users | Rhythmyx Content Manager, about $150,000 |
| **Stellent** www.stellent.com | Document conversion to Web-ready formats | Engineering for very large implementations with thousands of users | Content and Collaboration Servers, $50,000 to $250,000 each |
| **Vignette** www.vignette.com | Personalization | Document management and library services are not as robust as others | V6 Multisite Content Manager, $200,000 and up; V6 Content Suite, $450,000 and up |

Finnish handset-maker Nokia estimates at least 20 percent of its 68,000 employees use wiki pages to update schedules, check project status, trade ideas, edit files, and so on. "It's a reversal of the normal way things are done," says Stephen Johnston, senior manager for corporate strategy at Nokia, who helped pioneer the technology. Where Nokia once bought outside software to help foster collaboration, now "some of the most interesting stuff is emerging from within the company itself," says Johnston. It is a similar tale at Dresdner Kleinwort, a London-based investment bank, where a few pioneers in the IT department created a program called Socialtext to facilitate different IT tasks. The wiki program spread so quickly that Dresdner Kleinwort decided to launch its own corporate wiki and soon the bank's 5,000 employees had created more than 6,000 individual pages and logged about 100,000 hits on the company's official wiki.

The experience of Nokia and Dresdner Kleinwort offer insight into how to nurture the use of a radically new technology to change the way organizations work. Clearly, not everyone recognizes the value of wikis right way. The initial efforts at Dresdner, for example, confused employees and had to be refined to make the technology easier to use. More important than tweaking the technology was a simple edict from one of the proponents: Do not send emails, use the wiki. Gradually, employees embraced the use of the wiki, seeing how it increased collaboration and reduced time-consuming email traffic.

# Workflow Management Systems

A **workflow** defines all the steps or business rules, from beginning to end, required for a business process. Therefore, **workflow management systems** facilitate the automation and management of business processes and control the movement of work through the business process. Work activities can be performed in series or in parallel and involve people and automated computer systems. In addition, many workflow management systems allow the opportunity to measure and analyze the execution of the process because workflow systems allow the flow of work between individuals and/or departments to be defined and tracked. Workflow software helps automate a range of business tasks and electronically route the right information to the right people at the right time. Users are notified of pending work, and managers can observe status and route approvals through the system quickly.

There are two primary types of workflow systems: messaging-based and database-based. **Messaging-based workflow systems** send work assignments through an email system. The workflow system automatically tracks the order for the work to be assigned and, each time a step is completed, the system automatically sends the work to the next individual in line. For example, each time a team member completes a piece of the project, the system automatically sends the document to the next team member.

**Database-based workflow systems** store documents in a central location and automatically ask the team members to access the document when it is their turn to edit the document. Project documentation is stored in a central location and team members are notified by the system when it is their turn to log in and work on their portion of the project.

Either type of workflow system helps to present information in a unified format, improves teamwork by providing automated process support, and allows team members to communicate and collaborate within a unified environment. Figure 15.7 lists some typical features associated with workflow management systems.

New York City was experiencing a record number of claims, ranging from injuries resulting from slips on sidewalks to medical malpractice at city hospitals. The city processes over 30,000 claims and incurs $250 million in claim costs annually. Claims are generally filed with the Comptroller's Office, which investigates them

| Workflow Feature | Description |
|---|---|
| Process definition tool | A graphical or textual tool for defining a business process. Each activity within the process is associated with a person or a computer application. Rules are created to determine how the activities progress across the workflow and which controls are in place to govern each activity. |
| Simulation, prototyping, and piloting | Some systems allow workflow simulation or create prototype and/or pilot versions of a particular workflow to test systems on a limited basis before going into production. |
| Task initiation and control | The business process defined above is initiated and the appropriate resources (human and/or IT related) are scheduled and/or engaged to complete each activity as the process progresses. |
| Rules-based decision making | Rules are created for each step to determine how workflow-related information is to be processed, routed, tracked, and controlled. As an example, one rule might generate email notifications when a condition has been met. Another rule might implement conditional routing of documents and tasks based on the content of fields. |
| Document routing | In simple systems, this is accomplished by passing a file or folder from one recipient to another (e.g., an email attachment). In sophisticated systems, document routing is completed by checking the documents in and out of a central repository. Both systems might allow for "redlining" of the documents so that each person in the process can add their own comments without affecting the original document. |
| Applications to view and manipulate information | Word-processors, spreadsheets, and production systems are used to allow workers to create, update, and view information. |
| Work list | Current tasks are quickly identified along with such things as a due date, goal date, and priority by using work lists. In some systems, an anticipated workload is displayed as well. These systems analyze where jobs are in the workflow and how long each step should take, and then estimate when various tasks will reach a worker's desk. |
| Task automation | Computerized tasks are automatically invoked. These might include such things as letter writing, email notices, or execution of production systems. Task automation often requires customization of the basic workflow product. |
| Event notification | Employees can be notified when certain milestones occur or when workload increases. |
| Process monitoring | The workflow system can provide an organization with valuable information on current workload, future workload, bottlenecks (current or potential), turn-around time, or missed deadlines. |
| Tracking and logging of activities | Information about each step can be logged. This might include such things as start and completion times, worker(s) assigned to the task, and key status fields. Later, this information can be used to analyze the process or to provide evidence that certain tasks were in fact completed. |

**FIGURE** 15.7

Workflow Management
System Features

and offers to settle meritorious claims. The New York City Comptroller's Office, with the assistance of its consultants Xerox and Universal Systems Inc., utilized a workflow management system to enhance revenues and decrease operating costs. With the implementation of the Omnibus Automated Image Storage Information System (OAISIS) for processing contracts and claims, New York City will save over $20 million. Numerous city organizations were involved in the workflow management system, including Bureau of Law and Adjustment, Office of Contracts/Administration, Management and Accounting Systems, and Bureau of Information Systems.

In supporting all these organizations, the system performs many functions that were previously labor-intensive and detracted from the quality and efficiency of investigations. The workflow management system screens claims to determine accordance with statutory requirements. Acknowledgment letters are generated automatically, with little or no resource allocation involved in assignment of claims or routing of claims to specific work locations. Status letters are automatically generated by the system for certain claim types, thus allowing the Comptroller's Office to keep claimants informed two months, five months, and one year from the date of their filing. All this is done automatically by the workflow management system.

Workflow management systems allow management to schedule individual systematic claim reviews without disrupting the investigation. Management can also see the entire claim process graphically and determine bottlenecks. Deployment of additional resources to needed areas occurs without a management analysis of a particular process problem.

# Groupware Systems

*Groupware* is software that supports team interaction and dynamics including calendaring, scheduling, and videoconferencing. Organizations can use this technology to communicate, cooperate, coordinate, solve problems, compete, or negotiate. While traditional technologies like the telephone qualify as groupware, the term refers to a specific class of technologies relying on modern computer networks, such as email, newsgroups, videophones, and chat rooms. Groupware systems fall along two primary categories (see Figure 15.8):

1. Users of the groupware are working together at the same time (real-time or synchronous groupware) or different times (asynchronous groupware).

2. Users are working together in the same place (colocated or face-to-face) or in different places (non-colocated or distance).

The groupware concept integrates various systems and functionalities into a common set of services or a single (client) application. In addition, groupware can represent a wide range of systems and methods of integration. Figure 15.9 displays the advantages groupware systems offer an organization over single-user systems.

Lotus Notes is one of the world's leading software solutions for collaboration that combines messaging, groupware, and the Internet. The structure of Notes allows it to track, route, and manage documents. Systems that lend themselves to Notes involve tracking, routing, approval, document management, and organization.

Toyota developed an intranet system to promote information sharing within the company and to raise productivity. Unfortunately, the company's conventional email system became overloaded, generating problems. Users did not receive incoming messages and were not able to send messages. Individual departments had introduced their own email systems, which were not always compatible. Messages to other mail systems, including those outside the company, experienced delays. To deal with these difficulties, Toyota's information systems department reviewed the email system and restructured it so that email, now recognized as an important communication tool, is utilized more effectively in business transactions.

## VIDEOCONFERENCING

A *videoconference* is a set of interactive telecommunication technologies that allow two or more locations to interact via two-way video and audio transmissions simultaneously. It has also been called visual collaboration and is a type of groupware. Videoconferencing uses telecommunications of audio and video to bring people at different sites together for a meeting. This can be as simple as a conversation between two people in private offices (point-to-point) or involve several sites (multi-point) with more than one person in large rooms at different sites. Besides the audio and visual transmission of people, videoconferencing can be used to share documents, computer-displayed information, and whiteboards.

Simple analog videoconferences could be established as early as the invention of the television. Such videoconferencing

**FIGURE** 15.8

Groupware Systems

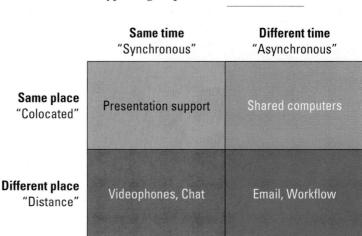

|  | **Same time** "Synchronous" | **Different time** "Asynchronous" |
|---|---|---|
| **Same place** "Colocated" | Presentation support | Shared computers |
| **Different place** "Distance" | Videophones, Chat | Email, Workflow |

FIGURE 15.9

Groupware Advantages

| Groupware System Advantages |
| --- |
| Facilitating communication (faster, easier, clearer, more persuasive) |
| Enabling telecommuting |
| Reducing travel costs |
| Sharing expertise |
| Forming groups with common interests where it would not be possible to gather a sufficient number of people face-to-face |
| Saving time and cost in coordinating group work |
| Facilitating group problem solving |

systems consisted of two closed-circuit television systems connected via cable. During the first manned space flights, NASA used two radio frequency (UHF or VHF) links, one in each direction. TV channels routinely use this kind of videoconferencing when reporting from distant locations, for instance. Then mobile links to satellites using special trucks became rather common (see Figure 15.10 for an example of videoconferencing).

Videoconferencing is now being introduced to online networking websites to help businesses form profitable relationships quickly and efficiently without leaving their place of work. Several factors support business use of videoconferencing, including:

- Over 60 percent of face-to-face communication is nonverbal. Therefore, an enriched communications tool such as videoconferencing can promote an individual's or a team's identity, context, and emotional situation.

- 56 percent of business professionals waste an estimated 30 minutes a day using inefficient communication methods, costing businesses an estimated $297 billion annually.

- The latest technology is available with reliable and easy-to-use conferencing, fostering collaboration at meetings.

- Enterprises that fail to use modern communications technologies run the very real risk of falling behind their competition.

FIGURE 15.10

Videoconferencing

## WEB CONFERENCING

*Web conferencing* blends audio, video, and document-sharing technologies to create virtual meeting rooms where people "gather" at a password-protected website. There, they can chat in conference calls or use real-time text messages. They can mark up a shared document as if it were a blackboard, and even watch live software demos or video clips.

Perhaps the biggest surprise about web conferencing is its simplicity. Users only need to set up an account and download a few small software files. The best part about a web conference is that attendees do not have to have the same hardware or software. Every participant can see what is on anyone else's screen, regardless of the application being used (see Figure 15.11 for an example of web conferencing).

Even with its video features, web conferencing is not quite like being there—or like being in a sophisticated (and pricey) videoconferencing facility. Still, professionals can accomplish more sitting at their desks than in an airport waiting to make travel connections. A growing number of companies are offering web conferencing. Leaders in this industry include WebEx, SameTime 2, and Elluminate Live.

## INSTANT MESSAGING

Email is by far the dominant collaboration application, but real-time collaboration tools like instant messaging are creating a new communication dynamic within organizations. ***Instant messaging*** (sometimes called ***IM*** or ***IMing***) is a type of communications service that enables someone to create a kind of private chat room with another individual in order to communicate in real time over the Internet. In 1992, AOL deployed IM to the consumer market, allowing users to communicate with other IMers through a buddy list. Most of the popular instant messaging programs provide a variety of features, such as:

- Web links: Share links to favorite websites.
- Images: Look at an image stored on someone else's computer.
- Sounds: Play sounds.
- Files: Share files by sending them directly to another IMer.
- Talk: Use the Internet instead of a phone to talk.
- Streaming content: Receive real-time or near-real-time stock quotes and news.
- Instant messages: Receive immediate text messages.

Commercial vendors such as AOL and Microsoft offer free instant messaging tools. Real-time collaboration, such as instant messaging, live web conferencing, and screen or document sharing, creates an environment for decision making. AOL, Microsoft's MSN, and Yahoo! have begun to sell enterprise versions of their instant messaging services that match the capabilities of business-oriented products like IBM's Lotus Sametime. Figure 15.12 demonstrates the IM application presence within IT systems.

IBM Lotus software has released new versions of its real-time collaboration platform, IBM Lotus Instant Messaging and IBM Lotus Web Conferencing, plus its mobile counterpart, IBM Lotus Instant Messaging Everyplace. These built-for-business products let an organization offer presence awareness, secure instant messaging, and web conferencing. The products give employees instant access to colleagues and company information regardless of time, place, or device.

The bigger issue in collaboration for organizations is cultural. Collaboration brings teams of people together from different regions, departments, and even companies—people who bring different skills, perceptions, and capabilities. A formal collaboration strategy helps create the right environment as well as the right systems for team members.

**FIGURE 15.11**

Web Conferencing

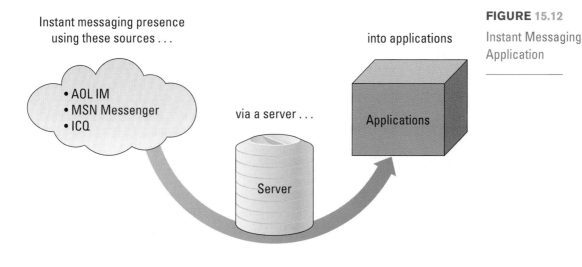

**FIGURE 15.12**

Instant Messaging Application

1. Identify which systems WTC could use to collaborate internally.

2. Explain which Internet technologies have facilitated the way in which WTC collaborates with both its participants and business partners.

3. List the four collaboration systems discussed in this chapter and rank them in order of importance to WTC's business.

4. Describe how WTC could leverage the power of a knowledge management system for its employees and for its participants.

## Chapter Fifteen Case:  Enterprise Content Management at Statoil

Statoil is the world's third largest exporter of crude oil and a substantial supplier of natural gas to the European market. The company has approximately 25,500 employees in locations scattered over 34 countries. Based in Norway, Statoil is the leading operator on the Norwegian continental shelf and experiencing strong growth in international production.

Since 2002, the company has adopted an ecollaboration strategy. The goal of the strategy is to create a corporate "knowledge reservoir" that provides global access to a common pool of digital assets and is used to support work processes and share information between Statoil and its customers, employees, and business partners.

Access to this knowledge reservoir is provided through an information portal and controlled through the assignment of end-user roles. For instance, a customer would have much more limited access to information housed in the knowledge reservoir than a Statoil employee would. The need for this strategy arose from the information overload that burdened the company. Typical for many decentralized organizations, Statoil's information was scattered across a number of different storage media and applications. The total number of databases in 2002 exceeded 5,500. The core foundation of the knowledge reservoir is content management. This involves the ability to support a content life cycle in the company that effectively deals with the capture, transformation, storage, security, distribution, retrieval, and eventual destruction of documents. Though Statoil is making great gains in facilitating such content management practices, it is also facing some challenges in getting there.

The largest problem is how content is currently maintained throughout the company. There are literally thousands of heterogeneous content databases involving stand-alone intranet and extranet applications and over 800 databases containing archived documents. Though technically all these are accessible across the enterprise, logically people are unaware of the availability of documents residing in those shared content areas, and hence, much of the material never gets loaded into a centralized, shared content management system. Having so much content resident outside of a shared, centralized content management system has negative implications on archiving, version management, publication, and workflow.

Another difficulty is that people still tend to use personal email folders to manage document attachments, rather than post documents once in a central location for others to use. Emailing attachments causes network congestion and chews up precious file storage space. If stored centrally, a document is stored just once and people can simply reference the document there if needed. Another challenge is that the storage of files in their original production format makes retrieval of these items difficult after a few years. This is because content management system technologies change and the format of these production files does not. On the flip-side, updating the format to be compatible with content management system technologies may make these files unusable for retrieval by the original application that produced them. The best solution would be to store content in application-independent formats.

Difficulties also stem from the lack of embedded routines that could potentially delete unwanted information stored across production or archiving systems. This results in the redundant storage of information and the overaccumulation of content. To clean up content, Statoil has to issue "campaigns" to encourage employees to delete unnecessary information.

Another challenge pertains to search. No single integrated search facility can retrieve documents across the thousands of other heterogeneous content-based systems. This largely is a result of different business units utilizing different taxonomies to classify their content and storing their content in different physical structures. Hence, information retrieval across business units is problematic, despite the best intentions of the company.

Though these challenges are obstacles to the effective management of corporate content, Statoil is making great strides in overcoming them. To date, the ecollaboration strategy has yielded several successes for the company, including:

- A basic content management solution.
- Automatic archiving.
- Long-term storage of content with separate data indexes.
- Automatic security levels of information based on metadata.
- Integration of existing standard office tools.
- A corporate yellow pages.
- One common portal framework.
- Training services for the content management solution.
- Implementation of content management guidelines for use by third-party solution providers (i.e., for working on projects with partners).
- The establishment of required elearning modules for employees.

Overall, Statoil is doing well in creating and managing information content, regardless of whether it is sourced internally within the organization or externally from information suppliers, and in automating the content life cycle, from creation to archival, with information delivered to the recipient independent of time, place, or media.

## Questions

1. Why do you think content management is such a critical part of Statoil's strategy?
2. Comment on the utility and importance of Statoil's use of an information portal to promote enterprisewide content management.
3. To what extent do you think Statoil's predicament of information overload is typical for organizations?
4. What lessons learned and insights from the chapter's discussion on collaboration tools could help promote Statoil's adoption and use of its content management initiative?

# Integrating Wireless Technology in Business

## Business Drivers for a Mobile Workforce

Dr Pepper/Seven Up Inc., of Plano, Texas, monitors the operation of its vending machines via wireless technology. Dr Pepper/Seven Up Inc. has installed specialized hardware and software along with wireless technology in vending machines. The software collects inventory, sales, and "machine-health" data at each vending machine, and then, on a daily basis, the Dr Pepper/Seven Up Inc. network operations center polls each machine. A dome antenna atop the vending machine allows broadcast and reception via a wireless network. The data are aggregated and stored at a separate facility. With client software installed on their PCs, managers and sales personnel at Dr Pepper/Seven Up Inc. can access the data via a secure website. Management at Dr Pepper/Seven Up Inc. is excited about the business value of the data being collected, both for daily operations and because of the potential for data mining. Information like this is helpful when considering new placements of vending machines or locations where multivendor machines might be warranted, such as in front of a Target store or high-traffic supermarket. Dr Pepper/Seven Up Inc. can use the data to plan loading of trucks and truck routes.

Rapid and widespread growth of mobile technology in the 21st century has shaped one of the largest technology markets after the PC revolution in the 1980s and 1990s. Untethered connectivity, anytime, anywhere, has fueled a major market and technology disruption, which has permeated almost every consumer market worldwide. The domino effect of the success of mobile technology has resulted in opportunities for innovation and creativity in technology, marketing, and business strategy.

Companies worldwide are going mobile to increase productivity, speed delivery to market, and reduce operating costs. Retail, distribution, and manufacturing businesses are no exception. Wireless transmissions rely on radio waves (e.g., cellular technology), microwaves, and satellites to send data across high-frequency radio ranges that later connect to wired media.

United Parcel Service and FedEx have been using mobile technologies for years, making it possible for information about dispatching and deliveries to travel between couriers and central stations. FedEx's famous tracking system, which can find a package's location from its tracking number, uses a wireless courier-management system.

The terms *mobile* and *wireless* are often used synonymously, but actually denote two different technologies. *Mobile* means the technology can travel with the user, but it is not necessarily in real-time; users can download software, email messages, and web pages onto their personal digital assistant (PDA), laptop, or other mobile

FIGURE 16.1

Wireless Drivers

| Drivers of Wireless Technology Growth | |
|---|---|
| Universal access to information and applications | People are mobile and have more access to information than ever before, but they still need to get to the point where they can access all information anytime, anywhere, anyplace. |
| The automation of business processes | Wireless technologies have the ability to centralize critical information and eliminate redundant processes. |
| User convenience, timeliness, and ability to conduct business 24 × 7 × 365 | People delayed in airports no longer have to feel cut off from the world or their office. Through wireless tools and wireless solutions such as a BlackBerry RIM device, they can access their information anytime, anywhere, anyplace. |

device for portable reading or reference. Information collected while on the road can be synchronized with a PC or corporate server.

*Wireless,* on the other hand, refers to any type of electrical or electronic operation that is accomplished without the use of a "hard wired" connection. International Data Corporation expected nearly two-thirds of handheld devices to include integrated wireless networking by 2010. Figure 16.1 displays the factors inspiring the growth of wireless technologies.

State government agencies, such as transportation departments, use wireless devices to collect field information—tracking inventory, reporting times, monitoring logistics, and completing forms—all from a mobile environment. The transportation industry is using mobile devices to help determine current locations and alternate driving routes.

Mobile technologies are transforming how we live, work, and play. Handheld devices continue to offer additional functionality, and cellular networks are advancing rapidly in their increased speed and throughput abilities. These enabling technologies fuel widespread adoption and creation of new and innovative ways to perform business. The big changes that will re-create workplaces, industries, and organizations are coming from mobile and wireless technologies. Figure 16.2 displays a few common examples of mobile technologies that are changing our world.

The retail industry is fiercely competitive. With the advent of the World Wide Web, nontraditional companies such as Amazon.com have emerged and have

FIGURE 16.2

Mobile Devices Changing Business

| Mobile Devices Changing Business |
|---|
| ■ **Wireless local area network (wLAN):** uses radio waves rather than wires to transmit information across a local area network. |
| ■ **Cellular phones and pagers:** provide connectivity for portable and mobile applications, both personal and business. |
| ■ **Cordless computer peripherals:** connect wirelessly to a computer, such as a cordless mouse, keyboard, and printer. |
| ■ **Satellite television:** allows viewers in almost any location to select from hundreds of channels. |
| ■ **WiMAX wireless broadband:** enables wireless networks to extend as far as 30 miles and transfer information, voice, and video at faster speeds than cable. It is perfect for Internet service providers (ISPs) that want to expand into sparsely populated areas, where the cost of bringing in cable wiring or DSL is too high. |
| ■ **Security sensor:** alerts customers to break-ins and errant pop flies. Its dual sensors record vibration and acoustic disturbances—a shattered window—to help avoid false alarms. |

made brick-and-mortar companies like Barnes & Noble rethink their strategy. Competition is also driving profit margins down. The success of a retailer depends on inventory management, cost control, and proactive customer service. To gain the competitive advantage, more and more retailers are turning to mobile applications to enhance worker productivity, operational efficiencies, and anytime, anywhere customer service. On the sales floor and in the warehouse, mobile solutions can help track materials and shipments from suppliers and distributors to the customers, manage inventory, and support point-of-sales activities. Since vast amounts of data can be collected in an automated fashion, analysis can be done much faster and the results can be used continuously to improve operations and customer service. Figure 16.3 briefly describes several important steps companies should take to formulate an effective mobile strategy.

# Mobile Workforce Trends

Airplane seats. Car dashboards. Digital cameras. Kiosks at shopping malls, school campuses, and hotels. Stadium bleachers. Handheld calculators. Kitchen appliances. These are just a few of the mobile devices and locations that are being wired for wireless. The visionary images of yesterday are giving way to a reality in which connectivity is nearly ubiquitous. Real-time information is now the currency of business and the enabler of groundbreaking innovations in education, entertainment, and media. The predictions help identify emerging mobile trends and indicate ways that consumers and businesses will benefit. These trends include widespread use of mobile social networks, greater choice in multifunction devices, and more wireless home entertainment options.

**FIGURE** 16.3

Steps to Take for Deploying Mobile Strategies

| Step | Description |
|---|---|
| Defining risks | Before a realistic assessment of any mobile strategy can be put in place, companies must define evaluation criteria. Many companies look at technology and applications in isolation, without defining any potential risks to the organization: risks both if the project is undertaken and if it is not. |
| Knowing the limits of technology | It is imperative that companies not only examine the abilities of any technology to provide needed functionality, but also to explore any limits of the chosen technology. Setting realistic expectations for any mobile technology, both to IT resources deploying the solution and to the ultimate users, is a necessary component of any successful mobile strategy. |
| Protecting data from loss | Companies must take concrete and immediate steps to assure protection of mobile corporate information assets. Security must be a multi-faceted approach and encompass a variety of techniques covering all areas of exposure. |
| Compliance in the mobile enterprise | The move to mobility, with far more devices "free to roam wild," will cause a major upsurge in occurrences of data breaches, some of which may not even be discovered, or not discovered for a significant period. Companies must formulate a mobile security strategy before the problem becomes overwhelming. |
| Staying flexible and embracing change | Companies should not assume that once created, a mobile strategy is a fixed and/or finished product. With the high rate of change in the marketplace (e.g., devices, connection types, applications), it is incumbent upon the organization to monitor and modify the policy on a regular basis. |

- **Social networking gets mobilized.** Mobility is added to existing Internet business models, services, and behaviors, driving traffic for wireless operators. Those in their teens and twenties accustomed to constant connectivity and habit-forming websites, such as MySpace and Facebook, lead a wave of membership in mobile social networks. Location social networking including friend and event finder services are gaining popularity, even in the professional and over-50 segments. Google, Yahoo!, and Skype are more compelling for users than wireless brands, which are hard-pressed to compete. Social networking applications initially are preloaded on many mobile devices sold and later become downloadable.

- **Mobile TV.** In the short term, wireless users are unlikely to plunk down $5.99 to $9.99 per month for mobile TV service. Instead, look for per-view or per-minute pricing for "sneaking," a consumer tendency to watch key minutes of a sports event or drama while engaged in another activity. Sneaking leads to more regular viewing, and within three to five years, mobile TV will become an indispensable service. Broadcast TV is the primary driver of revenues and consumer adoption, but peer-to-peer video is gaining interest, too. Operators are squaring off with content providers over control of the subscriber relationship and user experience.

- **Multifunction devices become cheaper and more versatile.** Intense competition and margin pressure will continue in the handset market, forcing prices of third-generation (3G) handsets below $90 and making them affordable for a wide range of users. Seeking to replicate the success of camera phones, device manufacturers will produce more multifunction units with music-playing, location, video and other capabilities. Twenty percent of all handsets sold in North America are application specific—built for a usage proposition, such as music or video consumption or business productivity.

- **Location-based services.** GPS is the location technology of choice for the wireless industry. Handset manufacturers will continue to push GPS-enabled handsets as the technology evolves from popular in-car satellite navigation systems like TomTom to a broadly accepted feature in wireless phones. With Nokia having launched its first GPS-enabled handsets in early 2007 and bandwidth available to support new multimedia services, location-based service providers are building critical mass. Since there are 10 to 20 times more mobile phones sold than any other consumer electronics device, wireless is a huge driver for GPS adoption.

- **Mobile advertising.** Major brands are shifting from basic SMS marketing to more sophisticated multimedia advertising. RBC Capital Markets expects mobile marketing revenues to balloon from $45 million in 2005 to $1.5 billion by 2010. With the technological ability to target and measure the effectiveness of mobile advertising, brands are more strategic in their approach. Rich 3G content and video services and accuracy advancements in GPS-based location services deliver further value to brands targeting existing and potential customers in innovative ways.

- **Wireless providers move into home entertainment.** Mobile makes headway against fixed broadband operators, which have dominated Internet and cheaper voice service provision in the home. Wi-fi will remain the primary wireless access technology. The fixed operators may be strengthened by wi-fi capabilities in consumer electronics devices (set-top boxes, game consoles, and MP3 players) that enable cost-effective content downloads.

- **Wireless security moves to the forefront.** There is a monumental need to put strong security measures in place. This could be the year that hackers really start paying attention to millions of wireless devices, the growth in mobile data usage, and vulnerable points between mobile and fixed networks. CIOs consistently cite security as their number one concern in extending network access to wireless devices. Attacks, viruses, and data security now exceed device loss or theft as concerns. Emerging services, such as VoIP and mobile payments, provide additional challenges. Vulnerabilities directly affect the bottom line, corporate image, regulatory compliance, and competitive advantage.

- **Enterprise mobility.** Enterprises can't resist the convenient, reliable, attractively priced, bundled mobile solutions entering the market. Corporations switch from phones to mobile computers for transactions, data collection, and messaging for a wide variety of employees. Many voice communications processes, such as order placement and delivery notifications, dispatch operations, and remote asset monitoring, continue to shift to wireless data to increase information access and field transaction volume across organizations. Many corporations will completely replace their cellular handsets with a combined voice/data device or a data-only device.

## OPENING CASE STUDY QUESTIONS

1. Why is real-time information important to the Ironman championship?
2. How is WTC using wireless technology to improve its operations?
3. List the ethical and security dilemmas that WTC faces in using the various forms of wireless technology.

## Chapter Sixteen Case:  Wireless Electricity

Imagine a future in which wireless power transfer is feasible: cell phones, MP3 players, laptop computers and other portable electronics capable of charging themselves without ever being plugged in, finally freeing us from the power cord. Some of these devices might not even need their bulky batteries to operate.

Scientists have known for nearly two centuries how to transmit electricity without wires, and the phenomenon has been demonstrated several times before. But it was not until the rise of personal electronic devices that the demand for wireless power materialized. In the past few years, at least three companies have debuted prototypes of wireless power devices, though their distance range is relatively limited. Thanks to wireless technology, researchers at MIT extended the wi-fi concept to allow the beaming of power to anything that uses electricity. The MIT scientists successfully powered a 60-watt light bulb from a power source seven feet away. The team called their invention WiTricity, short for "wireless electricity."

The first wireless powering system to market is an inductive device that looks like a mouse pad and can send power through the air, over a distance of up to a few inches. A powered coil inside the pad creates a magnetic field, which induces current to flow through a small secondary coil that's built into any portable device, such as a flashlight, a phone, or a BlackBerry. The electrical current that then flows in that secondary coil charges the device's onboard rechargeable battery. Although many portable devices, such as the iPhone, have yet to be outfitted with this tiny coil, a number of companies are about to introduce products that are.

The practical benefit of this approach is huge. You can drop any number of devices on the charging pad, and they will recharge—wirelessly. No more tangle of power cables or jumble of charging stations. What's more, because you are invisible to the magnetic fields created by the system, no electricity will flow into you if you stray between device and pad. Nor are there any exposed "hot" metal connections. And the pads are smart with built-in coils which know if the device sitting on them is authorized to receive power, or if it needs power at all. So car keys won't be charged or the flashlight overcharged.

One of the dominant players in this technology is Michigan-based Fulton Innovation. Fulton's new pad-based system, called eCoupled, will be available to police, fire-and-rescue, and contractor fleets—an initial market of as many as 700,000 vehicles annually. The system is being integrated into a truck console to allow users to charge anything from a compatible rechargeable flashlight to a PDA. The tools and other devices now in the pipeline at companies such as Bosch, Energizer, and others will look just like their conventional ancestors. Companies such as Philips Electronics, Olympus, and Logitech will create a standard for products, from flashlights to drills to cell phones to TV remotes.

## Applications

- Wireless power transfer technology can be applied in a wide variety of applications and environments. The ability of the technology to transfer power safely, efficiently, and over distance can improve products by making them more convenient, reliable, and environmentally friendly. Wireless power transfer technology can be used to provide:

- Direct wireless power—when all the power a device needs is provided wirelessly, and no batteries are required. This mode is for a device that is always used within range of its power source.

- Automatic wireless charging—when a device with rechargeable batteries charges itself while still in use or at rest, without requiring a power cord or battery replacement. This mode is for a mobile device that may be used both in and out of range of its power source.

## Consumer Electronics

- Automatic wireless charging of mobile electronics (phones, laptops, game controllers, etc.) in home, car, office, wi-fi hotspots while devices are in use and mobile.

- Direct wireless powering of stationary devices (flat screen TVs, digital picture frames, home theater accessories, wireless loud speakers, etc.) eliminating expensive custom wiring, unsightly cables and power supplies.

- Direct wireless powering of desktop PC peripherals: wireless mouse, keyboard, printer, speakers, display, etc., eliminating disposable batteries and awkward cabling.

## Industrial

- Direct wireless power and communication interconnections across rotating and moving "joints" (robots, packaging machinery, assembly machinery, machine tools) eliminating costly and failure-prone wiring.

- Direct wireless power and communication interconnections at points of use in harsh environments (drilling, mining, underwater, etc.) where it is impractical or impossible to run wires.

- Direct wireless power for wireless sensors, eliminating the need for expensive power wiring or battery replacement and disposal.

- Automatic wireless charging for mobile robots, automatic guided vehicles, cordless tools and instruments eliminating complex docking mechanisms and labor intensive manual recharging and battery replacement.

## Transportation

- Automatic wireless charging for existing electric vehicle classes: golf carts, industrial vehicles.
- Automatic wireless charging for future hybrid and all-electric passenger and commercial vehicles, at home, in parking garages, at fleet depots, and at remote kiosks.
- Direct wireless power interconnections to replace costly vehicle wiring harnesses.

## Other Applications

- Direct wireless power interconnections and automatic wireless charging for implantable medical devices (pacemaker, defibrillator, etc.).
- Automatic wireless charging for high-tech military systems (battery-powered mobile devices, covert sensors, unmanned mobile robots and aircraft, etc.).
- Direct wireless powering and automatic wireless charging of smart cards.
- Direct wireless powering and automatic wireless charging of consumer appliances, mobile robots, etc.

## Questions

1. Explain the fundamentals of wireless power transfer technology.
2. Describe the business benefits of using wireless electricity.
3. Identify two types of business opportunities companies could use to gain a competitive advantage using wireless electricity.
4. What are some other creative uses of wireless electricity not mentioned in the case?
5. How would a wireless power distribution network operate similar to cell networks?

In a remarkably short time, the Internet has grown from a virtual playground into a vital, sophisticated medium for business, more specifically, ebusiness. Online consumers are flooding to the Internet, and they come with very high expectations and a degree of control that they did not have with traditional bricks-and-mortar companies. The enticement of doing business online must be strengthened by the understanding that, to succeed online, businesses will have to be able to deliver a satisfying and consistent customer experience, building brand loyalty and guaranteeing high rates of customer retention.

Strategic alliances enable businesses to gain competitive advantage(s) through access to a partner's resources, including markets, technologies, and people. Teaming up with another business adds complementary resources and capabilities, enabling participants to grow and expand more quickly and efficiently.

**✳ KEY TERMS**

Application programming interforce (API) 196
Brick-and-mortar business, 194
Business-to-business (B2B), 194
Business-to-consumer (B2C), 194
Business wiki 208
Click-and-mortar business, 194
Collaboration system, 203
Consumer-to-business (C2B), 195
Consumer-to-consumer (C2C), 195
Content management system, 207
Core competency, 203
Core competency strategy, 203
Database-based workflow system, 209
Digital asset management system (DAM), 208
Digital Darwinism, 184
Digital divide, 188
Disruptive technology, 184

Document management system (DMS), 208
Ebusiness, 183
Ebusiness model, 192
Ecommerce, 192
Electronic marketplace (emarketplace), 194
Emall, 195
Eshop (estore, etailer), 194
Explicit knowledge, 206
Groupware, 211
Hypertext transport protocol (HTTP), 187
Information partnership, 203
Information reach, 188
Information richness, 188
Instant messaging (IM or IMing), 213
Internet, 186
Knowledge management (KM), 205
Knowledge management system (KMS), 205
Mashup editor 197

Messaging-based workflow system, 209
Protocol, 187
Pure-play (virtual) business, 194
Semantic web 190
Structured collaboration (process collaboration), 204
Sustaining technology, 184
Tacit knowledge, 206
Unstructured collaboration (information collaboration), 204
Videoconference 211
Web 2.0, 189
Web conferencing 212
Web content management system (WCM), 208
Web mashup 196
Wiki 209
Workflow, 209
Workflow management system, 209
World Wide Web (WWW), 187

### Improving Highway Safety through Collaboration

Information on traffic-related deaths and accidents is two to three years out of date in some states, making it difficult to devise new safety regulations, rebuild unsafe roads, develop safer automobiles, and improve emergency services. Systems used by federal, state, and local agencies to collect and share information need to be overhauled, and the U.S. Department of Transportation's National Highway Traffic Safety Administration said it would ask Congress for $300 million over the next six years to upgrade them.

The goal is to eliminate antiquated paper-based reporting systems and implement a nation-wide initiative to automate and synchronize the collection and sharing of information. The information will include vehicle-related injuries, associated health care costs, safety stops, driver licenses, vehicle registration, and adjudicated violations.

## Safer Driving

Federal highway safety officials want $300 million to finance:

- Wireless communications equipment to facilitate electronic information collection and transmission during traffic safety stops.
- Real-time information transfer and editing processes to update driver's license or vehicle registration information from traffic stops or crash sites.
- Centralized access to query all traffic record databases.
- Standardized search capabilities on common queries and information transmission using XML formats.

Few states have the capability to capture and transmit traffic record and crash information electronically, and those that do are limited, said Joseph Carra, director of the National Center for Statistics and Analysis at the highway safety agency. "Today, the information is written and stored in files. It's a paper process. The files are sent to the state office, whose clerks input the information into proprietary computer systems. And there it sits."

## Collaborating

Better information will save lives and money, says the federal highway safety administration. About 43,220 people were killed on the nation's highways in 2003, and another 2.9 million suffered serious injuries. Traffic accidents in 2000, the latest year for which information is available, cost the U.S. economy about $230 billion, the agency says.

The wide-ranging proposal calls for standardized formats to improve information sharing among various government agencies and private groups, more sophisticated sensors in cars and along highways to gather detailed information on crashes, and wireless handheld devices to let police officers check for outstanding warrants on drivers, among other ideas. Federal funding will encourage states to adopt federal standards. Many states, suffering from a slow economy and declining tax revenues, have not been able to fund upgrades themselves. Some, however, have projects under-way.

## Revamping Texas

Texas is about halfway done with an IT project to build a crash-records information system, a joint initiative between its Department of Public Safety and the Texas Department of Transportation. When completed, police officers will be able to file accident reports via the Web, and other state agencies will be able to electronically link their systems with it and share information.

Texas has been working on the crash-records system for several years. The state has a $9.9 million contract with IBM to build an information warehouse using a DB2 Universal Database, WebSphere Application Server, Tivoli Storage Manager, and MQ-Series, its message-queuing product. IBM says Florida, Arizona, and New Mexico are considering similar systems.

The Texas system is replacing a decades-old one that is "archaic and in need of many changes," said Carol Rawson, deputy division director for the traffic operations division with the state transportation department. The old system requires time-consuming manual entry of around 850,000 accident forms a year, as well as manual cross-checking and validation to ensure the information is correct. Because the process took so long, the state's accident information is backlogged some 30 months. "This is all about safety," Rawson said. "The way you tell if a road is safe is you look at accident information. So that information is critical."

## Questions

1. How are collaboration tools helping to save lives in Texas?
2. How could a police department use groupware to help with collaboration on accident reports?
3. Describe how a police department could use workflow systems to help with accident reports and health-care-related issues.
4. What would be the impact on lives if a state fails to implement collaboration tools to help track and analyze highway accidents?
5. How could police departments use wireless technologies to operate more efficiently and effectively?

### Social Networking

Not long ago, it seemed that four companies would forever dominate the web in traffic and ad dollars. Each of the Big Four—Google, Yahoo!, Microsoft's MSN, and Time Warner's AOL—attracts more than 100 million unique visitors a month. Collectively the group accounts for roughly 90 percent of gross ad dollars online. But now those companies are facing a threat to their dominance. Today's massive social networking systems are rapidly becoming webs within the web—one-stop shops for a wide range of services (from content to communications to commerce) that were once the unique province of the Big Four.

Facebook, MySpace, LinkedIn and other social-networking sites have been the rage of the tech industry lately. Following investments by Microsoft, News Corp. and Goldman Sachs, the companies are valued in the billions of dollars and are considered blueprints for how to build a website. Facebook has become the Web's largest social network as measured by active users, which offers bread-and-butter portal services like email and instant messaging as well as photo posting and video sharing. In addition, Facebook has partnered with Amazon.com to produce a shopping application that lets users buy items at Amazon without leaving Facebook's site, while using opt-in "news feeds" that broadcast activities on Amazon, such as product reviews and wish list updates, to Facebook friends. Additionally, Facebook now uses a chat feature that automatically populates itself with a user's Facebook "friends," that may render older instant messaging services, such as AOL's AIM, defunct.

Jumping on the wireless apps mega-trend, Facebook uses mobile alerts to deliver mobile services for traditional styled cell phones and more intelligent smartphones. Applications for popular devices, such as the iPhone or BlackBerry, deliver even richer social experiences. Video has taken off, too, with 45 million clips uploaded on Facebook including higher-resolution video formats allowing Facebook users to send video messages from the site and from mobiles devices.

Launched in 2003, MySpace became one of the most visited websites in the world within a few years. With almost a billion visits per month, MySpace is considered the most popular social network (by traffic volume). The site was originally started by musicians as a tool to help users discover new music and engage with bands. Today, MySpace members leverage the service to discover people with similar tastes or experiences. Utilizing a system of adding friends to your network, the ability to customize your profile, write blog entries, play favorite MP3 tracks, join groups and enter discussions, MySpace allows users to interact in a way unparalleled before its emergence. However, the most compelling reason to join MySpace is for fun. There are many avenues toward entertainment on the social network including browsing through musician profiles and exploring areas dedicated to television shows or movies. But MySpace isn't just for fun, as many businesses maintain MySpace profiles in order to use the social media site as a form of marketing. For musicians, actors, authors, entrepreneurs, and others that maintain a public image, a MySpace profile can be a very important connection to fans.

Since it scored a $900 million, three-year deal with Google in 2006, MySpace has been profitable. And it has given News Corp. a nice turn on its $650 million acquisition in 2005. MySpace has recently formed partnerships with major record labels Sony BMG Music Entertainment, Warner Music Group, and Vivendi's Universal Music Group to offer its 117 million members tickets, ring tones, and artist merchandise. Driving a good chunk of sales is a project launched last summer called HyperTargeting, software that mines the profiles of MySpace users to deliver ads tailored to their interests. Hundreds of advertisers are part of the program, including Toyota and Taco Bell. Another income source is the sale of mobile ring tones and ads.

When it comes to enterprise collaboration and social software, LinkedIn rules the roost. LinkedIn is more effective at meeting the requirements of social computing the enterprise environment demands. With more than 30 million users representing 150 industries around the world, LinkedIn is a fast-growing professional networking site that allows members to create business contacts, search for jobs, and find potential clients. Individuals have the ability to create their own professional profile that can be viewed by others in their network, and also view the profiles of their own contacts. While MySpace and Facebook are tailored to keeping members in touch with friends and family, LinkedIn is perceived as being "more professional" for business users.

Social networking sites are also growing at exponential rates and attracting users of all ages. Facebook's fastest-growing segment is users over 25 years of age. LinkedIn, the business-oriented social networking site, claims more than 30 million active members with an average age of 41. The social networking websites are typically divided into three categories: general interest, niche sites with a specific theme, and international sites. The following are the top sites in these three categories:

### General Interest

■ **MySpace:** Started in 2003, MySpace was a driving force in popularizing social networking and still maintains the largest userbase.

■ **Facebook:** Founded by Mark Zuckerberg, Facebook was designed as a social networking site for Harvard students. After spreading from Harvard through the university ranks and down into high school, Facebook was opened to the public in 2006.

■ **Hi5:** A fast-growing social network with a strong base in Central America, Hi5 has over 50 million users worldwide.

■ **Ning:** A social network for creating social networks, Ning takes the idea of groups to a whole new level.

### Niche Sites

■ **Flixster:** With a tagline of "stop watching bad movies," Flixster combines social networking with movie reviews.

■ **Last.fm:** Billing itself as a social music site, Last.fm allows members to create their own radio station that learns what the person likes and suggests new music based on those interests. In addition to this, you can listen to the radio stations of friends and other Last.fm members.

■ **LinkedIn:** A business-oriented social network, members invite people to be "connections" instead of "friends." LinkedIn is a contact management system as well as a social network, and has a question-and-answer section similar to Yahoo! Answers.

■ **Xanga:** A social blogging site that combines social networking elements with blogging. Members earn credits for participating in the site and can spend credits on various things such as buying mini-pictures to post in the comments of a friend's blog.

### International Sites

■ **Badoo:** Based in London, Badoo is one of the top social networking sites in Europe.

■ **Migente:** A social networking site targeted at Latin America.

■ **Orkut:** Originally created by Google to compete with MySpace and Facebook, it has mainly caught hold in Brazil.

■ **Studivz:** A German version of Facebook with a strong audience in students.

## Corporate Use of Social Networking

Corporations and smaller businesses haven't embraced online business networks with nearly the same abandon as teens and college students who have flocked to social sites. Yet companies are steadily overcoming reservations and using the sites and related technology to craft potentially powerful business tools. Recruiters at Microsoft and Starbucks, for instance, troll online networks such as LinkedIn for potential job candidates. Goldman Sachs and Deloitte run their own online alumni networks for hiring back former workers (called boomerangs) and strengthening bonds with former alums. Maintaining such networks will be critical in industries like IT and health care that are likely to be plagued by worker shortages for years to come. Social networking can also be important for organizations like IBM, where some 42 percent of employees regularly work from home or client locations. IBM's social network makes it easier to locate employee expertise within the firm, organize virtual work groups, and communicate across large distances. As another example of corporate social networks, Reuters has rolled out Reuters Space, a private online community for financial professionals. Profile pages can also contain a personal blog and news feeds (from Reuters or external services). Every profile page is accessible to the entire Reuters Space community, but members can choose which personal details are available to whom. While IBM and Reuters have developed their own social network platforms, firms are increasingly turning to third-party vendors like Select-Minds (adopted by Deloitte, Dow Chemical, and Goldman Sachs) and LiveWorld (adopted by Intuit, eBay, the NBA, and Scientific American).

## Questions

1. Are Facebook, MySpace, and LinkedIn using disruptive or sustaining technology to run their businesses?
2. What are some of the business challenges facing social networking sites?
3. What are the characteristics of a social network?
4. What security issues do social networking sites create?
5. What are some current social networking trends?
6. How can social networking sites generate revenue beyond selling banner and text ads?

## ★ MAKING BUSINESS DECISIONS

### 1. Everybody Needs an Internet Strategy

An Internet strategy addresses the reasons businesses want to "go online." "Going online" because it seems like the right thing to do now or because everyone else is doing it is not a good enough reason. A business must decide how it will best utilize the Internet for its particular needs. It must plan for where it wants to go and how best the Internet can help shape that vision. Before developing a strategy, a business should spend time on the Internet, see what similar businesses have, and what is most feasible, given a particular set of resources. Think of a new online business opportunity and answer the following questions:

a. Why do you want to put your business online?
b. What benefits will going online bring?
c. What effects will Internet connectivity have on your staff, suppliers, and customers?

### 2. Searching for Disruption

Scheduler.com is a large corporation that develops software that automates scheduling and record keeping for medical and dental practices. Scheduler.com currently holds 48 percent of its market share, has more than 8,700 employees, and operates in six countries. You are the vice president of product development at Scheduler.com. You have just finished reading *The Innovator's Dilemma* by Clayton Christensen and you are interested in determining what types of disruptive technologies you can take advantage of, or should watch out for, in your industry. Use the Internet to develop a presentation highlighting the types of disruptive technologies you have found that have the potential to give the company a competitive advantage or could cause the company to fail.

### 3. Leveraging the Competitive Value of the Internet

Physical inventories have always been a major cost component of business. Linking to suppliers in real time dramatically enhances the classic goal of inventory "turn." The Internet provides a multitude of opportunities for radically reducing the costs of designing, manufacturing, and selling goods and services. E-mango.com, a fruit emarketplace, must take advantage of these opportunities or find itself at a significant competitive disadvantage. Identify the disadvantages that confront E-mango.com if it does not leverage the competitive value of the Internet.

### 4. Assessing Internet Capabilities

Hoover's Rentals is a small privately owned business that rents sports equipment in Denver, Colorado. The company specializes in winter rentals including ski equipment, snowboarding equipment, and snowmobile equipment. Hoover's has been in business for 20 years and, for the first time, it is experiencing a decline in rentals. Brian Hoover, the company's owner, is puzzled by the recent decreases. The snowfall for the last two years has been outstanding, and the ski resorts have opened earlier and closed later than most previous years. Reports say tourism in the Colorado area is up, and the invention of loyalty programs has significantly increased the number of local skiers. Overall, business should be booming. The only reason for the decrease in sales might be the fact that big retailers such as Wal-Mart and Gart Sports are now renting winter sports equipment. Brian would like your team's help in determining how he can use the Internet to help his company increase sales and decrease costs to compete with these big retailers.

### 5. Gaining Efficiency with Collaboration

During the past year, you have been working for a manufacturing firm to help improve its supply chain management by implementing enterprise resource planning and supply chain management systems. For efficiency gains, you are recommending that the manufacturing firm should be turning toward collaborative systems. The firm has a need to share intelligent plans and forecasts with supply chain partners, reduce inventory levels, improve working capital, and reduce manufacturing changeovers. Given the technologies presented to you in this unit, what type of system(s) would you recommend to facilitate your firm's future needs?

### 6. Collaboration on Intranets

MyIntranet.com is a worldwide leader in providing online intranet solutions. The MyIntranet.com online collaboration tool is a solution for small businesses and groups inside larger organizations that need to organize information, share files and documents, coordinate calendars, and enable efficient collaboration, all in a secure, browser-based environment. MyIntranet.com has just added conferencing and group scheduling features to its suite of hosted collaboration software. Explain why infrastructure integration is critical to the suite of applications to function within this environment.

### 7. Finding Innovation

Along with disruptive technologies, there are also disruptive strategies. The following are a few examples of companies that use disruptive strategies to gain competitive advantages:

- Circuit City, Best Buy—These two disrupted the consumer electronics departments of full-service and discount department stores, which has sent them up-market into higher margin goods.
- Ford—Henry Ford's Model T was so inexpensive that he enabled a much larger population of people, who historically could not afford cars, to own one.
- JetBlue—Whereas Southwest Airlines initially followed a strategy of new-market disruption, JetBlue's approach is low-end disruption. Its long-range viability depends on

the major airlines' motivation to run away from the attack, as integrated steel mills and full-service department stores did.

- McDonald's—The fast-food industry has been a hybrid disrupter, making it so inexpensive and convenient to eat out that it created a massive wave of growth in the "eating out" industry. McDonald's earliest victims were mom-and-pop diners.

There are numerous other examples of corporations that have used disruptive strategies to create competitive advantages. In a team, prepare a presentation highlighting three additional companies that used disruptive strategies to gain a competitive advantage.

### 8. Communicating with Instant Messages

You are working for a new start-up magazine, *Jabber Inc.,* developed for information professionals that provides articles, product reviews, case studies, evaluation, and informed opinions. You need to collaborate on news items and projects, and exchange data with a variety of colleagues inside and outside the *Jabber Inc.* walls. You know that many companies are now embracing the instant messaging technology. Prepare a brief report for the CIO that will explain the reasons IM is not just a teenage fad, but also a valuable communications tool that is central to everyday business.

## ★ APPLY YOUR KNOWLEDGE

### 1. Working Together

Upon execution of a business process, a workflow system dictates the presentation of the information, tracks the information, and maintains the information's status. For example, the following highlights the common steps performed during a team project:

1. Find out what information and deliverables are required for the project and the due date.
2. Divide the work among the team members.
3. Determine due dates for the different pieces of work.
4. Compile all the completed work together into a single project.

One of the hardest parts of a team project is getting team members to complete their work on time. Often one team member cannot perform his or her work until another team member has finished. This situation causes work to sit idle waiting for a team member to pick it up to either approve it, continue working on it, or reformat it. Workflow systems help to automate the process of presenting and passing information around a team.

### Project Focus

You have just received an assignment to work on a group project with 10 other students. The project requires you to develop a detailed business plan for a business of your choice. The types of activities you will need to perform include market analysis, industry analysis, growth opportunities, Porter's Five Forces analysis, financial forecasts, competitive advantage analysis, and so on. For your project, determine the following:

1. How could you use collaboration tools to facilitate the sharing of information and the completion of the project?
2. What advantages can your group gain from using groupware?
3. What advantages can your group gain from using IM?

4. How could you use a workflow system to manage the tasks for the group members?

5. Describe a few of the biggest issues you anticipate experiencing during the group project. Identify ways that you can resolve these issues using collaboration tools.

## 2. Internet Groceries

E-Grocery, founded in 2007, is an online grocery shopping and delivery service. The company caters to thousands of customers in the Phoenix, Seattle, and Denver areas. Established on the idea that people will buy groceries over the Internet, e-Grocery offers over 25,000 items.

Ninety percent of e-Grocery's orders come in via computer; the rest are received by fax. Orders are received at the central office in Lakewood, Colorado, and then distributed by email to a local affiliate store. The store receives the order, the delivery address, and a map to the order location. A store employee designated to online orders will fill, deliver, and collect for the order. E-Grocery members are charged actual shelf prices, plus a per-order charge of $5.00 or 5 percent of the order amount, whichever is greater. Members also receive additional benefits such as electronic coupons, customer discounts, recipes, and tips.

### Project Focus

The company is using interactive technology to change the shopping experience. The success of e-Grocery lies within many areas. Analyze the e-Grocery business model using the questions below. Feel free to think outside the box to develop your own analysis of online grocery shopping and ebusiness models.

1. What is e-Grocery's ebusiness model?
2. How does e-Grocery compete with traditional retailers?
3. What value can e-Grocery offer as a true competitive advantage in this marketplace?
4. What is the threat of new entrants in this market segment?
5. How is e-Grocery using technology to change the shopping experience?
6. What are the logistics for making e-Grocery profitable?
7. How does e-Grocery profit from online customer interaction?
8. What kinds of ebusiness strategies can e-Grocery's marketing department use to help grow its business?
9. What are some of the benefits and challenges facing e-Grocery?

## 3. Getting Personal

Consider Sally Albright, the reigning queen of customization in the movie *When Harry Met Sally*. Take, for example, the scene where she orders pie a la mode: "I'd like the pie heated. And I don't want the ice cream on top; I want it on the side. And I'd like strawberry instead of vanilla if you have it. If not, then no ice cream, just whipped cream, but only if it's real." Particular, yes, but Sally knew what she liked—and was not afraid to ask for it.

### Project Focus

A growing number of online retailers are letting you have it your way, too. Choose a company highlighted in Figure AYK.1 and create your own product. Was the website easy to use? Would this service entice you as a customer to make a purchase over a generic product? If you could personalize a product what would it be and how would the website work?

| Company | Product |
|---|---|
| Tommy Hilfiger, custom.tomm.com | Premium-cotton chinos and jeans ($98) |
| Lands' End, www.landsend.com | Utilitarian jeans and chinos made of luxurious twill in traditional silhouettes ($59) |
| JCPenney, www.custom.jcpenney.com | Substantial twill pants in classic cuts ($44) |
| Ralph Lauren Polo, www.polo.com | Everything from basic polos to oxford shirts ($80) |
| TIMBUK2; www.timbuk2.com | Hip nylon messenger bags ($105) |
| L.L. Bean, www.llbean.com | Sturdy and colorful books, totes, and messenger bags ($70) |
| Nike, www.nikeid.com | Full range of athletic shoes and accessories ($90) |
| VANS, www.vans.com | Classic "Old Skool" lace-up or slip-on sneakers ($50) |
| Converse, www.converseone.com | Custom Chuck Taylors, the company's most classic style ($60) |

### 4. Express Yourself

One of the most popular websites among students is MySpace, a site that allows students to express themselves by personalizing their home page. What is your favorite band? Who is your favorite author? What is your favorite movie? You can find out a lot about a person by finding out the answers to these questions.

#### Project Focus

Build a website dedicated to your favorite band, book, or movie. Your website must contain all of the following:

- An image.
- Two different size headings.
- Different sizes and colors of text.
- Two horizontal rules.
- Text that is bolded, underlined, and/or italicized.
- A textured background.
- A link to a website.
- A link to your email.
- One numbered and one unnumbered list.

### 5. Creating a Presence

More than 1 billion people are on the Internet. Having an Internet presence is critical for any business that wants to remain competitive. Businesses need their websites to create a "buzz" to attract customers. Ebusiness websites must be innovative, stimulating, add value, and provide useful information. In short, the site must build a sense of community and collaboration, eventually becoming the "port of entry" for business.

#### Project Focus

You are applying for a job at BagEm, a start-up ebusiness devoted to selling custom book bags that does not have any physical stores and only sells bags over the Internet. You are up against several other candidates for the job. BagEm has asked you to use your business expertise and website development skills to design and build a potential website. The candidate with the best website will be awarded the job. Good luck!

## 6. GoGo Gadgets

Now that wi-fi and other types of high-speed wireless networks are becoming common, devices using that technology are multiplying rapidly. Wireless gadgets run the gamut from cell phones to kitchen appliances and digital cameras. Here are some of the hottest new wireless broadband gadgets.

- Samsung's $3,499 POPCON refrigerator will feature a wi-fi enabled, detachable screen that can function as a TV. The fridge also can be programmed to remember products' expiration dates and generate alerts when the milk is getting old.
- The Nokia 770 Internet Tablet is small enough to fit in a pocket. It comes with a 4.13-inch-wide touch screen that can be used to access the web over a wi-fi network. The $350 device can also access the web via a cell phone with a Bluetooth connection.
- Motorola's latest E815 mobile phone operates over Verizon Wireless's new EVDO (Evolution Data Optimized) wireless network, offering speeds comparable to digital subscriber line (DSL). The phone can even record and play back video clips. It also features a built-in MP3 digital music player.
- Hop-On's just-announced HOP 1515 may look like a typical cell phone, but it actually makes calls over wi-fi networks. Typically sold with a $20 to $30 monthly service plan, the phone allows for unlimited over-the-web international and long-distance calling. The $39 HOP 1515 is sold through wi-fi hotspot operators, wireless carriers, and retailers.
- Eastman Kodak's EasyShare-One is a digital camera with wi-fi capabilities, allowing users to share their snapshots wirelessly. You will be able to snap a photo and immediately show it to a friend on a wi-fi-enabled PC or TV.

### Project Focus

A dizzying array of new wireless technologies now promises to make today's wi-fi networks seem like poky dial-up connections by comparison. These new technologies will extend the reach of wireless networks, not just geographically but also into new uses in the home and office.

1. Research the Internet and discover new wireless devices that entrepreneurs and established companies can use to improve their business.
2. Explain how businesses can use these devices to create competitive advantages, streamline production, and improve productivity.

## 7. WAP

Wireless Internet access is quickly gaining popularity among people seeking high-speed Internet connections when they are away from their home or office. The signal from a typical wireless access point (WAP) only extends for about 300 feet in any direction, so the user must find a "hotspot" to be able to access the Internet while on the road. Sometimes hotspots are available for free or for a small fee.

You work for a sales company, SalesTek, which has a salesforce of 25 representatives and customers concentrated in Denver, Colorado; Salt Lake City, Utah; and Santa Fe, New Mexico. Your sales representatives are constantly on the road and they require 24 × 7 Internet access.

You have been asked to find hotspots for your colleagues to connect to while they are on the road. It is critical that your salesforce can access the Internet 24 × 7 to connect with customers, suppliers, and the corporate office. Create a document detailing how your mobile workforce will be able to stay connected to the Internet while traveling. Here are a few tips to get you started:

1. Use websites such as www.wifinder.com and www.jiwire.com to determine which commercial hotspots would be the most appropriate for your salesforce and the commercial network service that these hotspots use.

2. Research the websites of two or three commercial networks that seem most appropriate to discover more about pricing and services. (Hint: T-Mobile is one example.)

3. Use www.wifinder.com and www.wififreespot.com to determine how many free public hotspots are available in these cities. Are there enough for your company to rely on them or should you use a commercial wi-fi system. If so, which one?

4. You might also research www.fon.com to see alternative methods of using home broadband connections to stay connected.

## 8. Securing Your Home Wireless Network

These days wireless networking products are so ubiquitous and inexpensive that anyone can easily build a wireless network with less than $100 worth of equipment. However, wireless networks are exactly that—wireless—they do not stop at walls. In fact, wireless networks often carry signals more than 300 feet from the wireless router. Living in an apartment, dorm, condominium, or house means that you might have dozens of neighbors who can access your wireless network.

It is one thing to let a neighbor borrow a lawn mower, but it is another thing to allow a neighbor to access a home wireless network. There are several good reasons for not sharing a home wireless network including:

- It may slow Internet performance.

- It allows others to view files on your computers and spread dangerous software such as viruses.

- It allows others to monitor the websites you visit, read your email and instant messages as they travel across the network, and copy your user names and passwords.

- It allows others to send spam or perform illegal activities with your Internet connection.

**Project Focus**

Securing a home wireless network is invaluable and allows you to enable security features that can make it difficult for uninvited guests to connect through your wireless network. Create a document detailing all of the features you can use to secure a home wireless network.

## 9. Weather Bots

Warren Jackson, an engineering graduate student at the University of Pennsylvania, was not interested in the weather until he started investigating how the National Weather Service collected weather data. The weather service has collected most of its information using weather balloons that carry a device to measure items such as pressure, wind speed, and humidity. When the balloon reaches about 100,000 feet and pressure causes it to pop, the device falls and lands a substantial distance from its launch point. The National Weather Service and researchers sometimes look for the $200 device, but of the 80,000 sent up annually, they write off many as lost.

Convinced there had to be a better way, Warren began designing a GPS-equipped robot that launches a parachute after the balloon pops and brings the device back down to Earth, landing it at a predetermined location set by the researchers. The idea is so inventive that the Penn's Weiss Tech House, a university organization that encourages students to innovate and bring their ideas to market, awarded Warren and some fellow graduate engineering students first prize in its third annual PennVention Contest. Warren won $5,000 and access to expert advice on prototyping, legal matters, and branding.

### Project Focus

GPS and GIS can be used in all sorts of devices, in many different industries, for multiple purposes. You want to compete, and win first prize, in the PennVention next year. Create a product, using a GPS or GIS, that is not currently in the market today that you will present at the fourth annual PennVention.

## 10. Wireless Networks and Streetlamps

Researchers at Harvard University and BBN Technologies have designed CitySense, a wireless network capable of reporting real-time sensor data across the entire city of Cambridge, Massachusetts. CitySense is unique because it solves a constraint on previous wireless networks—battery life. The network mounts each node on a municipal streetlamp, where it draws power from city electricity. Researchers plan to install 100 sensors on streetlamps throughout Cambridge by 2011, using a grant from the National Science Foundation. Each node will include an embedded PC running the Linux operating system, an 802.11 wi-fi interface, and weather sensors.

One of the challenges in the design was how the network would allow remote nodes to communicate with the central server at Harvard and BBN. CitySense will do that by letting each node form a mesh with its neighbors, exchanging data through multiple-hop links. This strategy allows a node to download software or upload sensor data to a distant server hub using a small radio with only a 1-kilometer range.

### Project Focus

You are responsible for deploying a CitySense network around your city. What goals would you have for the system besides monitoring urban weather and pollution? What other benefits could a CitySense network provide? How could local businesses and citizens benefit from the network? What legal and ethical concerns should you understand before deploying the network? What can you do to protect your network and your city from these issues?

## 11. Sharptooth Incorporated

Stephen Kern is the founder and CEO of Sharptooth, a small business that buys and sells comic strips to magazines and newspapers around the country. Some of Sharptooth's artists have made it big and are syndicated in hundreds of magazines and newspapers, while others are new to the industry. Stephen started in the business as an artist and began contracting with other artists when he realized he had a knack for promoting and marketing comic materials. His artistic background is great for spotting talented young artists, but not so great for running the business.

### Project Focus

Stephen recently began selling comics to new forms of media such as blog sites, websites, and other online tools. Stephen has hired you to build him a new system to track all online comic sales. You quickly notice that Stephen has a separate system for each of his different lines of business including newspaper sources, magazine sources, billboard sources, and now online sources. You notice that each system works independently to perform its job of creating, updating, and maintaining sales information, but you are wondering how Stephen operates his business as a whole. Create a list of issues Stephen will encounter if he continues to run his business with four separate systems performing the same operations. What could happen to Stephen's business if he cannot correlate the details of each? Be sure to highlight at least 10 issues where separate systems could cause Stephen problems.

## 12. Wiki Debate

Wikipedia is a multilingual, web-based, free content encyclopedia project. Wikipedia is written collaboratively by volunteers from all around the world. With rare exceptions, its articles can be edited by anyone with access to the Internet, simply by clicking a line to edit the page. The name Wikipedia is a portmanteau of the words *wiki* (a type of collaborative website) and *encyclopedia.* Since its creation in 2001, Wikipedia has grown rapidly into one of the largest reference websites.

In every article, links guide users to associated articles, often with additional information. Anyone is welcome to add information, cross-references, or citations, as long as they do so within Wikipedia's editing policies and to an appropriate standard. One need not fear accidentally damaging Wikipedia when adding or improving information, as other editors are always around to advise or correct obvious errors, and Wikipedia's software, known as MediaWiki, is carefully designed to allow easy reversal of editorial mistakes.

### Project Focus

A group of people believe the end of Wikipedia is close as people use the tool to self-promote. Some believe that Wikipedia will fail in four years, crushed under the weight of an automated assault by marketers and others seeking online traffic. Eric Goldman, a professor at the Santa Clara University School of Law, argues that Wikipedia will see increasingly vigorous efforts to subvert its editorial process, much as Digg has seen. As marketers become more determined and turn to automated tools to alter Wikipedia entries to generate online traffic, Goldman predicts Wikipedians will burn out trying to keep entries clean. Goldman writes that Wikipedia will enter a death spiral where the rate of junkiness will increase rapidly until the site becomes a wasteland. Alternatively, to prevent this death spiral, Wikipedia will change its core open-access architecture, increasing the database's vitality by changing its mission somewhat. Create a paper discussing where you think the future of Wikipedia is headed.

## 13. Secure Collaboration

As the methods and modes of communication continue to evolve, challenges will mount for businesses trying to secure their data and for law enforcement looking to monitor communications as part of their investigations. That was the theme of the keynote speech that Sun Microsystems' chief security officer and renowned cryptographer Whitfield Diffie delivered at the AT&T Cyber Security Conference.

The growth of virtual communities across the web as a communications channel creates a double-edged sword in this respect. Second Life and other virtual communities offer a growing abundance of information, although this information will ultimately need to be protected if virtual communities are to grow as meaningful channels of business-to-business and business-to-customer communication.

Diffie believes that with millions of people joining Second Life and companies building facilities there, it may be that virtual communities become the preferred medium of human communication. This growing volume of information opens the opportunity to use virtual communities as a source of intelligence, and communications will always be spied on.

Of course, the volume of businesses present in virtual communities such as Second Life will have to grow before they become a meaningful source of information. Once this happens, though, watch out. Diffie believes that communication always outstrips the ability to protect it. Who would be interested in gathering intelligence floating through virtual communities? The answer is businesses, governments (domestic and foreign), and reporters—the same entities that have adapted every other form of communication preceding the web. Diffie feels the future will be a golden age for intelligence.

### Project Focus

As we create new and better ways to collaborate, what happens to information security?

## ★ BUSINESS DRIVEN BEST SELLERS

### The Power of Mobility. By Russell McGuire (John Wiley & Sons, 2007).

Over 80 percent of Americans above the age of five own a cell phone, most with digital cameras built in, and bundled with an email service specifically designed for sending those captured moments to friends and family. These consumer applications are just simple examples of mobility being built in to everyday products to create tremendous new value. From a business perspective, a new technology can introduce radical changes—changes so dramatic that they fundamentally shift the nature of the business, the nature of the product, and the reasons customers buy the product. When this happens, the rules of competition change. It is happening now: The age of mobility is upon us. How will it impact you and your business in the months and years to come?

The Power of Mobility shows you how to look forward, envision the power of mobility in your business, and implement the steps required to turn vision into reality. Russell McGuire, one of the telecom industry's leading strategists, details the specific actions you must take to deliver the tremendous value that mobility adds—and win customers' hearts and wallets. He presents a powerful framework for capturing the power of mobility: the seven steps. If you can digitize, connect, evaluate, limit, position, protect, and learn, you will capture the power of mobility in your products, your services, and your processes. He further clarifies the power of the seven steps with illustrative case studies of seven companies that have successfully implemented this framework and redefined the rules of competition in their industries.

The mobility age represents a great opportunity for businesses large and small to capture the power of mobility to create competitive differentiation and to take market share. Stories of businesses that have been crushed by the competition because they have denied the changes brought by technologies in the past will likely be repeated. You have a choice. You can wait for a competitor to lead and define the rules to his benefit and your demise. Or you can lead and set the rules—if you capture the power of mobility now.

### The Innovator's Solution. By Clayton Christensen and Michael Raynor (Harvard Business School Publishing, 2003).

Roughly one company in every 10 is able to sustain the kind of growth that translates into an above-average increase in shareholder returns over more than a few years. Once a company's core business has matured, the pursuit of new platforms for growth entails daunting risk. To put it simply, most companies have no idea how to grow, and pursuing growth the wrong way can be worse than no growth.

In The Innovator's Dilemma, Clayton Christensen displays how companies that focus on high-end products for profitable customers can be blindsided by "disruptive technologies" from new competitors—innovations that target low-end customers seeking cheaper products.

In *The Innovator's Solution,* Christensen and co-author Michael Raynor show how established companies can create disruptions rather than being destroyed by them and how to turn innovative ideas into new disruptive products that will lead to long-term profitable growth.

### *Purple Cow.* By Seth Godin (Penguin Group, 2003).

Following the traditional rules of marketing is not enough anymore. Consumers are simply inundated with information channels from newspapers and magazines to blogs and email. In today's competitive market, companies must create a remarkable new product to make customers take notice. According to marketing guru Seth Godin, such a product is a Purple Cow, a product or service that is worth making a remark about.

The impact of advertising in newspapers and magazines is fading as people are overwhelmed with information and have stopped paying attention to most media messages. To create a Purple Cow product, Godin advises companies to stop advertising and start innovating. Godin recommends that marketers target a niche, and he explains different ways to spread an idea to consumers who are most likely to purchase the product. Godin claims there is not a shortage of remarkable ideas—every business has opportunities to do great things—but there is a shortage of the will to execute those ideas.

### *Into the Unknown: Leadership Lessons from Lewis and Clark's Daring Westward Expedition.* By Jack Uldrich (AMACOM, 2004).

Latching onto the idea that everything old is new again, Jack Uldrich, a former naval officer and author of *The Next Big Thing Is Really Small,* puts forth Lewis and Clark as two shining examples of all that is right with leadership and management. Spotlighting the pair's many strong points, from people skills and future-thinking capabilities to optimism and an ability to see the forest as well as the trees, Uldrich (drawing on what has obviously been years of extensive research) points to modern-day companies such as Coca-Cola, General Electric, and DaimlerChrysler as entities that could all learn something from Lewis and Clark.

Whether the "project" is a westward expedition or a hostile corporate takeover, Uldrich makes the case that the past is not so different from the present—or from the future—especially when concerning new technologies. The parallels between these men and today's leaders are intriguing and well thought out. For corporate types looking for tips, there are certainly plenty to digest. The overriding messages are clear: mentor and be mentored; find a way to balance the task at hand with the overall future vision; maintain a confident and optimistic approach from the beginning.

# Transforming Organizations

This unit provides an overview of how organizations build information systems to prepare for competing in the 21st century. You as a business student need to know about this because information systems are the underlying foundation of how companies operate. A basic understanding of the principles of building information systems will make you a more valuable employee. You will be able to identify trouble spots early during the design process and make suggestions that will result in a better delivered information systems project—one that satisfies both you and your business.

Building an information system is analogous to constructing a house. You could sit back and let the developers do all the design work, construction, and testing with hopes that the house will satisfy your needs. However, participating in the house building process helps to guarantee that your needs are not only being heard, but also being met. It is good business practice to have direct user input steering the development of the finished product. The same is true for building information systems. Your knowledge of the systems development process will allow you to participate and ensure you are building flexible enterprise architectures that not only support current business needs, but also your future business needs.

Have you ever dreamed of traveling to exotic cities like Paris, Tokyo, Rio de Janeiro, or Cairo? In the past, the closest many people ever got to working in such cities was in their dreams. Today, the situation has changed. Most major companies cite global expansion as a link to future growth and a recent study noted that 91 percent of the companies doing business globally believe it is important to send employees on assignments in other countries.

If a career in global business has crossed your mind, this unit will help you understand the nature of competition in the global business world. The United States is a market of about 300 million people, but there are more than 6 billion potential customers in the 193 countries that make up the global market. Perhaps more interesting is that approximately 75 percent of the world's population lives in developing areas where technology, education, and per capita income still lag considerably behind developed (or industrialized) nations such as the United States. Developing countries are still a largely untapped market.

You, the business student, should be familiar with the potential of global business, including its many benefits and challenges. The demand for students with training in global business is almost certain to grow as the number of businesses competing in global markets increases.

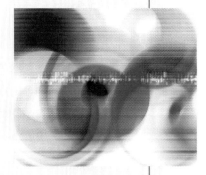

### E-espionage

*BusinessWeek* magazine recently probed the rising attacks on America's most sensitive computer networks, uncovering startling security gaps. The email message addressed to a Booz Allen Hamilton executive from the Pentagon was mundane—a shopping list of weaponry India wanted to buy. But the missive was a brilliant fake. Lurking beneath the description of aircraft, engines, and radar equipment was an insidious piece of computer code, known as Poison Ivy, designed to suck sensitive data out of the $4 billion consulting firm's computer network.

The Pentagon had not sent the email. Its origin is unknown, but the message traveled through Korea on its way to Booz Allen. Its authors knew enough about the "sender" and "recipient" to craft a message unlikely to arouse suspicion. Had the Booz Allen executive clicked on the attachment, his every keystroke would have been reported back to a mysterious master at the Internet address cybersyndrome.3322.org, which is registered through an obscure company headquartered on the banks of China's Yangtze River.

The email aimed at Booz Allen paints a vivid picture of the alarming new capabilities of America's cyberenemies. The September 5, 2007, email message was sent to John F. "Jack" Mulhern, vice president for international military assistance programs at Booz Allen. In the high-tech world of weapons sales, Mulhern's specialty, the email looked authentic enough. "Integrate U.S., Russian, and Indian weapons and avionics," the email noted, describing the Indian government's expectations for its fighter jets. "Source code given to India for indigenous computer upgrade capability." Such lingo could easily be understood by Mulhern. The 62-year-old former U.S. Naval officer and 33-year veteran of Booz Allen's military consulting business is an expert in helping to sell U.S. weapons to foreign governments.

The email was more convincing because of its apparent sender: Stephen J. Moree, a civilian who works for a group that reports to the office of Air Force Secretary Michael W. Wynne. Among its duties, Moree's unit evaluates the security of selling U.S. military aircraft to other countries. There would be little reason to suspect anything seriously amiss in Moree passing along the highly technical document with "India MRCA Request for Proposal" in the subject line. The Indian government had just released the request a week earlier, on August 28, and the language in the email closely tracked the request. Making the message appear more credible still, it referred to upcoming Air Force communiqués and a "Team Meeting" to discuss the deal.

But the missive from Moree to Jack Mulhern was a fake. An analysis of the email's path and attachment, conducted for *BusinessWeek* by three cybersecurity specialists, shows it was sent by an unknown attacker, bounced through an Internet address in South Korea, relayed through a Yahoo! server in New York, and finally made its way to Mulhern's Booz Allen in-box. The analysis also shows the code—known as malware, for malicious software—tracks keystrokes on the computers of people who open it. A separate program disables security measures such as password protection on Microsoft Access database files, a program often used by large organizations such as the U.S. defense industry to manage big batches of data.

## Global Threats

The U.S. government and its sprawl of defense contractors have been the victims of an unprecedented rash of similar attacks recently, say current and former U.S. government officials. "It's espionage on a massive scale," said Paul B. Kurtz, a former high-ranking national security official. Government agencies reported 12,986 cybersecurity incidents to the U.S. Homeland Security Department in one fiscal year, triple the number from two years earlier. Incursions on the military's networks were up 55 percent, said Lieutenant General Charles E. Croom, head of the Pentagon's Joint Task Force for Global Network Operations. Private targets such as Booz Allen are just as vulnerable and pose just as much potential security risk. "They have our information on their networks. They're building our weapon systems. You wouldn't want that in enemy hands," Croom said. Cyber attackers "are not denying, disrupting, or destroying operations—yet. But that doesn't mean they don't have the capability."

## The Monster We Created

*BusinessWeek* learned that the U.S. government launched a classified operation called Byzantine Foothold to detect, track, and disarm intrusions on the government's most critical networks. In some cases, the government's own cybersecurity experts are engaged in "hack-backs"—following the malicious code to peer into the hackers' own computer systems.

The government has yet to disclose the breaches discovered by Byzantine Foothold. *BusinessWeek* learned that intruders managed to worm into the State Department's highly sensitive Bureau of Intelligence and Research, a key channel between the work of intelligence agencies and the rest of the government. The breach posed a risk to CIA operatives in embassies around the globe, said several network security specialists familiar with the effort to cope with what is seen as an internal crisis. Teams worked around the clock in search of malware, they said, calling the White House regularly with updates.

One member of the emergency team summoned to the scene recalled that each time cybersecurity professionals thought they had eliminated the source of a "beacon" reporting back to its master, another popped up. He compared the effort to the arcade game Whack-A-Mole. The State Department said it eradicated the infection, but only after sanitizing scores of infected computers and servers and changing passwords. Microsoft's own patch, meanwhile, was not deployed until August 2006, three months after the infection. A Microsoft spokeswoman declined to comment on the episode, but said: "Microsoft has, for several years, taken a comprehensive approach to help protect people online."

## Poison Ivy

Commercial computer security firms have dubbed the malicious code hidden inside the email attachment Poison Ivy, and it has a devious—and worrisome—capability known as a RAT, a remote administration tool. RAT gives the attacker control over the host PC, capturing screen shots and perusing files. It lurks in the background of Microsoft Internet Explorer browsers while users surf the web. Then it phones home to its "master" at an Internet address currently registered under the name cybersyndrome.3322.org.

The digital trail to cybersyndrome.3322.org, followed by analysts at *BusinessWeek*'s request, leads to one of China's largest free domain-name-registration and email services. Called 3322.org, it is registered to a company called Bentium in the city of Changzhou, an industry hub outside Shanghai. A range of security experts say that 3322.org provides names for computers and servers that act as the command and control centers for more than 10,000 pieces of malicious code launched at government and corporate networks in recent years. Many of those PCs are in China; the rest could be anywhere.

The founder of 3322.org, a 37-year-old technology entrepreneur named Peng Yong, says his company merely allows users to register domain names. "As for what our users do, we cannot completely control it," Peng said. The bottom line: If Poison Ivy infected Jack Mulhern's computer at Booz Allen, any secrets inside could be seen in China. And if it spread to other computers, as malware often does, the infection opens windows on potentially sensitive information there, too.

## Internet Globalization: Good or Bad?

In just two years, thousands of highly customized attack emails have landed on the laptops and PCs of U.S. government workers and defense contracting executives. According to sources familiar with the matter, the attacks targeted sensitive information on the networks of at least seven agencies—the Defense, State, Energy, Commerce, Health and Human Services, Agriculture, and Treasury departments—and also defense contractors Boeing, Lockheed Martin, General Electric, Raytheon, and General Dynamics.

Many security experts worry the Internet has become too unwieldy to be tamed. New threats appear every day, each seemingly more sophisticated than the previous one. The Defense Department, whose Advanced Research Projects Agency (DARPA) developed the Internet in the 1960s, is beginning to think it created a monster. "You don't need an Army, a Navy, an Air Force to beat the U.S.," said General William T. Lord, commander of the Air Force Cyber Command, a unit formed in November 2006 to upgrade Air Force computer defenses. "You can be a peer force for the price of the PC on my desk."

Adding to Washington's anxiety, current and former U.S. government officials say many of the new attackers are trained professionals backed by foreign governments. "The new breed of threat that has evolved is nation-state-sponsored stuff," said Amit Yoran, a former director of Homeland Security's National Cyber Security Division. Added one of the nation's most senior military officers: "We've got to figure out how to get at it before our regrets exceed our ability to react."

# Introduction

In a competitive business climate, an organization's ability to efficiently align resources and business activities with strategic objectives can mean the difference between succeeding and just surviving. To achieve strategic alignment, organizations increasingly manage their systems development efforts and project planning activities to monitor performance and make better business decisions. Fast-growing companies outsource many areas of their business to extend their technical and operational resources. By outsourcing, they save time and boost productivity by not having to develop their own systems from scratch. They are then free to concentrate on innovation and their core business. The chapters in Unit 5 are:

- **Chapter Seventeen**—Building Software to Support an Agile Organization.
- **Chapter Eighteen**—Managing Organizational Projects.
- **Chapter Nineteen**—Outsourcing in the 21st Century.
- **Chapter Twenty**—Developing a 21st Century Organization.

# Building Software to Support an Agile Organization

**17.1.** Identify the business benefits associated with successful software development.

**17.2.** Describe the seven phases of the systems development life cycle.

**17.3.** Summarize the different software development methodologies.

**17.4.** Define the relationship between the systems development life cycle and software development.

**17.5.** Compare the waterfall methodology and the agile methodology.

**17.6** Explain why software problems are business problems.

## The Crucial Role of Software

Every type of organization in business today, from farming to pharmaceutical to franchising, is affected by technology and the software developed to operate, improve, or innovate it. Companies are impacted by software solutions that enable them to improve their cost structure, manage people better, and develop and deliver new products to market. These organizational improvements help companies sustain their competitive advantage and position in the marketplace. They can solve complex problems, dislodge competitors, or create exciting opportunities to pursue. Organizations must learn and mature in their ability to identify, build, and implement systems to remain competitive.

Essentially, software built correctly can support nimble organizations and can transform as the organization and its business transforms. Software that effectively meets employee needs will help an organization become more productive and enhance decision making. Software that does not meet employee needs might have a damaging effect on productivity and can even cause a business to fail. Employee involvement along with using the right implementation methodology when developing software is critical to the success of an organization.

## Developing Software

Nike's SCM system failure, which spun out of control to the tune of $400 million, is legendary. Nike blamed the system failure on its SCM vendor, i2 Technologies. Nike states that i2 Technologies' demand and supply planning module created serious inventory problems. The i2 deployment, part of a multimillion-dollar ebusiness upgrade, caused Nike CEO Philip Knight to famously say, "This is what we get for our $400 million?" The SCM vendor saw its stock plummet with the Nike disaster, along with its reputation. Katrina Roche, i2's chief marketing officer, asserted that Nike failed to use the vendor's implementation methodology and templates, which contributed to the problem.

Software development problems often lead to high-profile disasters. Hershey's glitch in its ERP implementation made the front page of *The Wall Street Journal* and cost the company millions. Hershey said computer problems with its SAP software system created a backlog of orders, causing slower deliveries, and resulting in lower earnings. Statistics released in 2006 by the National Research Council show that U.S. companies spent $250 billion in 2005 to repair damage caused by software defects.

If software does not work, the organization will not work. Traditional business risk models typically ignored software development, largely because most organizations considered the impact from software and software development on the business to be minor. In the digital age, however, software success, or failure, can lead directly to business success, or failure. Almost every large organization in the world relies on software, either to drive its business operations or to make its products work. As organizations' reliance on software grows, so do the business-related consequences of software successes and failures as displayed in Figure 17.1.

The lucrative advantages of successful software implementations provide significant incentives to manage software development risks. However, according to the Chaos report from the Standish Group, a Massachusetts-based consultancy, more than half the software development projects undertaken in the United States come in late or over budget and the majority of successful projects maintain fewer features and functions than originally specified. Organizations also cancel around 33 percent of these projects during development. Understanding the basics of software development, or the systems development life cycle, will help organizations avoid potential software development pitfalls and ensure that software development efforts are successful.

## The Systems Development Life Cycle (SDLC)

The *systems development life cycle (SDLC)* is the overall process for developing information systems from planning and analysis through implementation and maintenance. The SDLC is the foundation for all systems development methodologies, and literally hundreds of different activities are associated with each phase in

**FIGURE 17.1**

Business-Related Consequences of Software Success and Failure

### Business-Related Consequences of Software Success and Failure

**Increase or decrease revenues**—Organizations have the ability to directly increase profits by implementing successful IT systems. Organizations can also lose millions when software fails or key information is stolen or compromised.

Nike's poorly designed supply chain management software delayed orders, increased excess inventories, and caused earnings to fall 24 percent below expectations.

**Repair or damage brand reputation**—Technologies such as CRM can directly enhance a company's brand reputation. Software can also severely damage a company's reputation if it fails to work as advertised or has security vulnerabilities that affect its customers' trust.

H&R Block customers were furious when the company accidentally placed its customers' passwords and Social Security numbers on its website.

**Prevent or incur liabilities**—Technology such as CAT scans, MRIs, and mammograms can save lives. Faulty technology used in airplanes, automobiles, pacemakers, or nuclear reactors can cause massive damage, injury, or death.

The parent company of bankrupt pharmaceutical distributor FoxMeyer sued SAP for $500 million over ERP software failure that allegedly crippled its operations.

**Increase or decrease productivity**—CRM and SCM software can directly increase a company's productivity. Large losses in productivity can also occur when software malfunctions or crashes.

The Standish Group estimates that defective software code accounted for 45 percent of computer-system downtime and cost U.S. companies $100 billion in lost productivity.

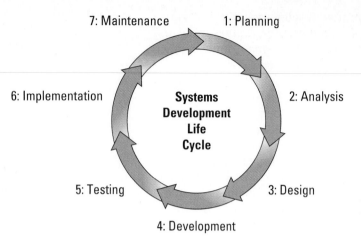

**FIGURE** 17.2

The Systems Development
Life Cycle

the SDLC. Typical activities include determining budgets, gathering system requirements, and writing detailed user documentation. The activities performed during each systems development project will vary.

The SDLC begins with a business need, followed by an assessment of the functions a system must have to satisfy the need, and ends when the benefits of the system no longer outweigh its maintenance costs. This is why it is referred to as a life cycle. The SDLC has seven distinct phases: planning, analysis, design, development, testing, implementation, and maintenance (see Figure 17.2).

1. **Planning:** The ***planning phase*** involves establishing a high-level plan of the intended project and determining project goals. Planning is the first and most critical phase of any systems development effort an organization undertakes, regardless of whether the effort is to develop a system that allows customers to order products over the Internet, determine the best logistical structure for warehouses around the world, or develop a strategic information alliance with another organization. Organizations must carefully plan the activities (and determine why they are necessary) to be successful.

2. **Analysis:** The ***analysis phase*** involves analyzing end-user business requirements and refining project goals into defined functions and operations of the intended system. ***Business requirements*** are the detailed set of business requests that the system must meet in order to be successful. The analysis phase is obviously critical. A good start is essential and the organization must spend as much time, energy, and resources as necessary to perform a detailed, accurate analysis.

3. **Design:** The ***design phase*** involves describing the desired features and operations of the system including screen layouts, business rules, process diagrams, pseudo code, and other documentation.

4. **Development:** The ***development phase*** involves taking all of the detailed design documents from the design phase and transforming them into the actual system. In this phase the project transitions from preliminary designs to the actual physical implementation.

5. **Testing:** The ***testing phase*** involves bringing all the project pieces together into a special testing environment to test for errors, bugs, and interoperability and verify that the system meets all of the business requirements defined in the analysis phase.

6. **Implementation:** The ***implementation phase*** involves placing the system into production so users can begin to perform actual business operations with the system.

7. **Maintenance:** Maintaining the system is the final sequential phase of any systems development effort. The ***maintenance phase*** involves performing changes, corrections, additions, and upgrades to ensure the system continues to meet the business goals. This phase continues for the life of the system because the system must change as the business evolves and its needs change, demanding constant monitoring, supporting the new system with frequent minor changes (for example, new reports or information capturing), and reviewing the system to be sure it is moving the organization toward its strategic goals.

# Traditional Software Development Methodology: Waterfall

Today, systems are so large and complex that teams of architects, analysts, developers, testers, and users must work together to create the millions of lines of custom-written code that drive enterprises. For this reason, developers have created a number of different systems development life cycle methodologies. A **methodology** is a set of policies, procedures, standards, processes, practices, tools, techniques, and tasks that people apply to technical and management challenges. It is used to manage the deployment of technology with work plans, requirements documents, and test plans. It is also used to deploy technology. A formal methodology could include coding standards, code libraries, development practices, and much more.

## WATERFALL METHODOLOGY

The oldest of these, and the best known, is the waterfall methodology: a sequence of phases in which the output of each phase becomes the input for the next (see Figure 17.3). The traditional **waterfall methodology** is an activity-based process in which each phase in the SDLC is performed sequentially from planning through implementation and maintenance. The traditional waterfall method no longer serves most of today's development efforts. The success rate for software development projects that follow this approach is about 1 in 10. Paul Magin, a senior executive with Part Miner, a leading supplier of technical components, states, "Waterfall is a punishing technology. It forces people to be accurate when they simply cannot. It is dangerous and least desirable in today's development environment. It does not accommodate midcourse changes; it requires that you know exactly what you want to do on the project and a steady-state until the work is done; it requires guarantees that requirements will not change. We all know that it is nearly impossible to have all requirements up front. When you use a cascading method, you end up with cascading problems that are disastrous if not identified and corrected early in the process."

Waterfall is inflexible, expensive, and requires rigid adherence to the sequentially based steps in the process. Figure 17.4 explains some issues related to the waterfall methodology.

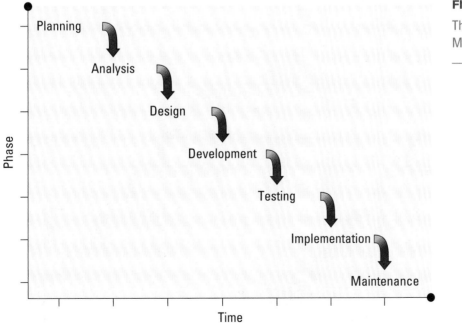

**FIGURE** 17.3

The Traditional Waterfall Methodology

FIGURE 17.4

Issues Related to the
Waterfall Methodology

| Issues Related to the Waterfall Methodology | |
| --- | --- |
| The business problem | Any flaws in accurately defining and articulating the business problem in terms of what the business users actually require flow onward to the next phase. |
| The plan | Managing costs, resources, and time constraints is difficult in the waterfall sequence. What happens to the schedule if a programmer quits? How will a schedule delay in a specific phase impact the total cost of the project? Unexpected contingencies may sabotage the plan. |
| The solution | The waterfall methodology is problematic in that it assumes users can specify all business requirements in advance. Defining the appropriate IT infrastructure that is flexible, scalable, and reliable is a challenge. The final IT infrastructure solution must meet not only current but also future needs in terms of time, cost, feasibility, and flexibility. Vision is inevitably limited at the head of the waterfall. |

Today's business environment is fierce. The desire and need to outsmart and outplay competitors remains intense. Given this drive for success, leaders push internal development teams and external vendors to deliver agreed-upon systems faster and cheaper so they can realize benefits as early as possible. Even so, systems remain large and complex. The traditional waterfall methodology no longer serves as an adequate systems development methodology in most cases. Because this development environment is the norm and not the exception anymore, development teams use a new breed of alternative development methods to achieve their business objectives.

## Agile Software Development Methodologies

Standish Group's CHAOS research clearly shows that the smaller the project, the greater the success rate. The iterative development style is the ultimate in small projects. Basically, *iterative development* consists of a series of tiny projects. Iterative has become the foundation of multiple agile types of methodologies. Figure 17.5 displays an iterative approach.

An *agile methodology* aims for customer satisfaction through early and continuous delivery of useful software components developed by an iterative process with

FIGURE 17.5

The Iterative Approach

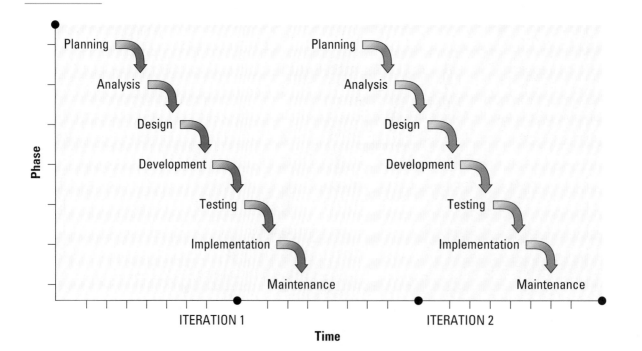

a design point that uses the bare minimum requirements. Agile is what it sounds like: fast and efficient, small and nimble, lower cost, fewer features, shorter projects. Using agile methods helps refine feasibility and supports the process for getting rapid feedback as functionality is introduced. Developers can adjust as they move along and better clarify unclear requirements.

Magin also states that the key to delivering a successful product or system is to deliver value to users as soon as possible—give them something they want and like early to create buy-in, generate enthusiasm, and, ultimately, reduce scope. Using agile methodologies helps maintain accountability and helps to establish a barometer for the satisfaction of end users. It does no good to accomplish something on time and on budget if it does not satisfy the end user. The primary forms of agile methodologies include:

- Rapid prototyping or rapid application development methodology.
- Extreme programming methodology.
- Rational unified process (RUP) methodology.
- Scrum methodology.

It is important not to get hung up on the names of the methodologies—some are proprietary brand names, others are generally accepted names. It is more important to know how these alternative methodologies are used in today's business environment and the benefits they can deliver.

## RAPID APPLICATION DEVELOPMENT (RAD) METHODOLOGY

In response to the faster pace of business, rapid application development has become a popular route for accelerating systems development. *Rapid application development (RAD)* (also called *rapid prototyping*) *methodology* emphasizes extensive user involvement in the rapid and evolutionary construction of working prototypes of a system to accelerate the systems development process. Figure 17.6 displays the fundamentals of RAD.

A *prototype* is a smaller-scale representation or working model of the users' requirements or a proposed design for an information system. The prototype is an essential part of the analysis phase when using the RAD methodology.

PHH Vehicle Management Services, a Baltimore fleet-management company with over 750,000 vehicles, wanted to build an enterprise application that opened the entire vehicle information database to customers over the Internet. To build the application quickly, the company abandoned the traditional waterfall approach. Instead, a team of 30 developers began prototyping the Internet application, and the company's customers evaluated each prototype for immediate feedback. The development team released new prototypes that incorporated the customers' feedback every six weeks. The PHH Interactive Vehicle application went into production seven months after the initial work began. Over 20,000 customers, using a common browser, can now access the PHH Interactive site at any time from anywhere in the world to review their accounts, analyze billing information, and order vehicles.

## EXTREME PROGRAMMING METHODOLOGY

*Extreme programming (XP) methodology,* like other agile methods, breaks a project into tiny phases, and developers cannot continue on to the next phase until the

| Fundamentals of RAD |
| --- |
| Focus initially on creating a prototype that looks and acts like the desired system. |
| Actively involve system users in the analysis, design, and development phases. |
| Accelerate collecting the business requirements through an interactive and iterative construction approach. |

**FIGURE** 17.6

Fundamentals of RAD

first phase is complete. XP emphasizes the fact that the faster the communication or feedback the better the results. There are basically four parts: planning, designing, coding, and testing. Unlike other methodologies, these are not phases; they work in tandem with each other. Planning includes user stories, stand-up meetings, and small releases. The design segment also stresses to not add functionality until it is needed. In the coding part, the user is always available for feedback, developers work in pairs, and the code is written to an agreed standard. In testing, the tests are written before the code. Extreme programming users are embedded into the development process. This technique is powerful because of the narrow communication gap between developers and users—it is a direct link. This saves valuable time and, again, continues to clarify needed (and unneeded) requirements.

One reason for XP's success is its stress on customer satisfaction. XP empowers developers to respond to changing customer and business requirements, even late in the systems development life cycle, and XP emphasizes teamwork. Managers, customers, and developers are all part of a team dedicated to delivering quality software. XP implements a simple, yet effective way to enable groupware-style development. Kent Beck, the father of XP, proposes conversation as the paradigm and suggests using index cards as a means to create dialog between business and technology. XP is a lot like a jigsaw puzzle; there are many small pieces. Individually the pieces make no sense, but when they are combined (again and again) an organization can gain visibility into the entire new system.

## RATIONAL UNIFIED PROCESS (RUP) METHODOLOGY

The *rational unified process (RUP) methodology,* owned by IBM, provides a framework for breaking down the development of software into four gates. Each gate consists of executable iterations of the software in development. A project stays in a gate until the stakeholders are satisfied, and then it either moves to the next gate or is cancelled. The gates include:

- **Gate One: Inception.** This phase includes inception of the business case. This phase ensures all stakeholders have a shared understanding of the system.
- **Gate Two: Elaboration.** This phase provides a rough order of magnitude. Primary questions answered in this phase deal with agreed-upon details of the system including the ability to provide an architecture to support and build the system.
- **Gate Three: Construction.** This phase includes building and developing the product.
- **Gate Four: Transition.** Primary questions answered in this phase address ownership of the system and training of key personnel.

Because RUP is an iterative methodology, the user can reject the product and force the developers to go back to gate one. Approximately 500,000 developers have used RUP in software projects of varying sizes in the 20 years it has been available, according to IBM. RUP helps developers avoid reinventing the wheel and focuses on rapidly adding or removing reusable chunks of processes addressing common problems.

## SCRUM METHODOLOGY

Another agile methodology, **Scrum methodology** uses small teams to produce small pieces of deliverable software using sprints, or 30-day intervals, to achieve an appointed goal. In rugby, a scrum is a team pack and everyone in the pack works together to move the ball down the field. Under this methodology, each day ends or begins with a stand-up meeting to monitor and control the development effort.

Primavera Systems, Inc., a software solutions company was finding it increasingly difficult to use the traditional waterfall methodology for development so it moved to an agile methodology. Scrum's insistence on delivering complete increments of business value in 30-day learning cycles helped the teams learn rapidly. It forced teams to test and integrate experiments and encouraged them to release them into production. Primavera's shift resulted in highly satisfied customers and a highly motivated, energetic development environment. Dick Faris, CTO of Primavera, said, "Agile programming is very different and new. It is a different feel to the way programming happens. Instead of mindlessly cranking out code, the process is one of team dialogue, negotiation around priorities and time and talents. The entire company commits to a 30-day sprint and delivery of finished, tested software. Maybe it is just one specific piece of functionality but it's the real thing, including delivery and client review against needs and requirements. Those needs and requirements, by the way, change. That is the strength we saw in the Scrum process."

## IMPLEMENTING AGILE METHODOLOGIES

Amos Auringer, an executive adviser for the prestigious Gartner Group, said, "Concepts such as agile, RAD, and XP are all various approaches to the same model—idea, production, delivery. These models represent consolidated steps, skipped steps for project size, and compressed steps to achieve the same result—a delivered product. Emerging process engineering models tend to focus on eliminating or reducing steps. The SDLC phases do not change—we just learn how to do our jobs better and more efficiently."

If organizations choose to adopt agile methodologies, it is important to educate those involved. For an agile process to work, it must be simple and quick. The Agile Alliance is a group of software developers whose mission is to improve software development processes; the group's manifesto is displayed in Figure 17.7. Decisions must be made quickly without analysis paralysis. The best way to do this is to involve stakeholders, develop excellent communication processes, and implement strong project management skills. Understanding that communication is the most crucial aspect of a project is the core of collaborative development. Standish Group reports that projects in which users or user groups have a good understanding of their true needs have a better rate of return and lower risk. Strong project management is key to building successful enterprise applications and is covered in detail in the following section.

# Developing Successful Software

Gartner Research estimates that 65 percent of agile projects are successful. This success rate is extraordinary compared to the 10 percent success rate of waterfall projects. The following are the primary principles an organization should follow for successful agile software development.

## SLASH THE BUDGET

Small budgets force developers and users to focus on the essentials. Small budgets also make it easier to kill a failing project. For example, imagine that a project that has already cost $20 million is going down the tubes. With that much invested, it is tempting to invest another $5 million to rescue it rather than take a huge loss. All too often, the system fails and the company ends up with an even bigger loss.

| The Agile Alliance Manifesto |
| --- |
| Early and continuous delivery of valuable software will satisfy the customer. |
| Changing requirements, even late in development, are welcome. |
| Businesspeople and developers must work together daily throughout the project. |
| Projects should be built around motivated individuals. Give them the environment and support they need, and trust them to get the job done. |
| The best architectures, requirements, and designs emerge from self-organizing teams. |
| At regular intervals, the team should reflect on how to become more effective, then tune and adjust its behavior accordingly. |

**FIGURE** 17.7

The Agile Alliance Manifesto

Jim Johnson, chairman of the Standish Group, says he forced the CIO of one Fortune 500 company to set a $100,000 ceiling on all software development projects. There were no exceptions to this business rule without approval from the CIO and CEO. Johnson claims the company's project success rate went from 0 percent to 50 percent.

### IF IT DOESN'T WORK, KILL IT

Bring all key stakeholders together at the beginning of a project and as it progresses bring them together again to evaluate the software. Is it doing what the business wants and, more important, requires? Eliminate any software that is not meeting business expectations. This is called triage, and it's "the perfect place to kill a software project," said Pat Morgan, senior program manager at Compaq's Enterprise Storage Group. He holds monthly triage sessions and says they can be brutal. "At one [meeting], engineering talked about a cool process they were working on to transfer information between GUIs. No one in the room needed it. We killed it right there. In our environment, you can burn a couple of million dollars in a month only to realize what you're doing isn't useful."

### KEEP REQUIREMENTS TO A MINIMUM

Start each project with what the software must absolutely do. Do not start with a list of everything the software should do. Every software project traditionally starts with a requirements document that will often have hundreds or thousands of business requirements. The Standish Group estimates that only 7 percent of the business requirements are needed for any given application. Keeping requirements to a minimum also means that scope creep and feature creep must be closely monitored. *Scope creep* occurs when the scope of the project increases. *Feature creep* occurs when developers add extra features that were not part of the initial requirements. Both scope creep and feature creep are major reasons software development fails.

### TEST AND DELIVER FREQUENTLY

As often as once a week, and not less than once a month, complete a part of the project or a piece of software. The part must be working and it must be bug-free. Then have the customers test and approve it. This is the agile methodology's most radical departure from traditional development. In some traditional software projects, the customers did not see any working parts or pieces for years.

### ASSIGN NON-IT EXECUTIVES TO SOFTWARE PROJECTS

Non-IT executives should coordinate with the technical project manager, test iterations to make sure they are meeting user needs, and act as liaisons between executives and IT. Having the business side involved full-time will bring project ownership and a desire to succeed to all parties involved. SpreeRide, a Salt Lake City market research outfit, used the agile methodology to set up its company's website. The project required several business executives designated full-time. The company believes this is one of the primary reasons that the project was successfully deployed in less than three months.

## Software Problems Are Business Problems

Only 28 percent of projects are developed within budget and delivered on time and as promised, says a report from the Standish Group, a Massachusetts-based consultancy. The primary reasons for project failure are:

- Unclear or missing business requirements.
- Skipping SDLC phases.
- Failure to manage project scope.

- Failure to manage project plan.
- Changing technology.

## UNCLEAR OR MISSING BUSINESS REQUIREMENTS

The most common reason systems fail is because the business requirements are either missing or incorrectly gathered during the analysis phase. The business requirements drive the entire system. If they are not accurate or complete, the system will not be successful.

It is important to discuss the relationship between the SDLC and the cost for the organization to fix errors. An error found during the analysis and design phase is relatively inexpensive to fix. All that is typically required is a change to a Word document. However, exactly the same error found during the testing or implementation phase is going to cost the organization an enormous amount to fix because it has to change the actual system. Figure 17.8 displays how the cost to fix an error grows exponentially the later the error is found in the SDLC.

## SKIPPING SDLC PHASES

The first thing individuals tend to do when a project falls behind schedule is to start skipping phases in the SDLC. For example, if a project is three weeks behind in the development phase, the project manager might decide to cut testing down from six weeks to three weeks. Obviously, it is impossible to perform all the testing in half the time. Failing to test the system will lead to unfound errors, and chances are high that the system will fail. It is critical that an organization perform all phases in the SDLC during every project. Skipping any of the phases is sure to lead to system failure.

## FAILURE TO MANAGE PROJECT SCOPE

As the project progresses, the project manager must track the status of each activity and adjust the project plan if an activity is added or taking longer than expected. Scope creep and feature creep are difficult to manage and can easily cause a project to fall behind schedule.

## FAILURE TO MANAGE PROJECT PLAN

Managing the project plan is one of the biggest challenges during systems development. The project plan is the road map the organization follows during the development of the system. Developing the initial project plan is the easiest part of the

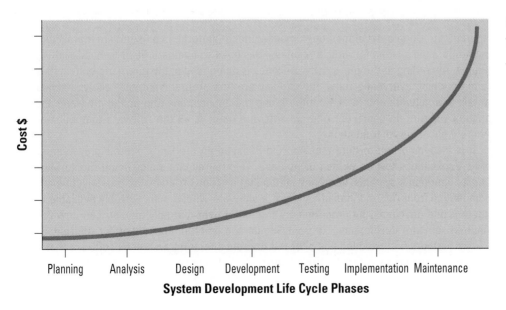

**FIGURE** 17.8

The Cost of Finding Errors

project manager's job. Managing and revising the project plan is the hard part. The project plan is a living document since it changes almost daily on any project. Failing to monitor, revise, and update the project plan can lead to project failure.

## CHANGING TECHNOLOGY

Many real-world projects have hundreds of business requirements, take years to complete, and cost millions of dollars. Gordon Moore, co-founder of Intel Corporation, observed in 1965 that chip density doubles every 18 months. This observation, known as Moore's law, simply means that memory sizes, processor power, and so on, all follow the same pattern and roughly double in capacity every 18 months. As Moore's law states, technology changes at an incredibly fast pace; therefore, it is possible to have to revise an entire project plan in the middle of a project as a result of a change in technology. Technology changes so fast that it is almost impossible to deliver an information system without feeling the pain of changing technology.

### OPENING CASE STUDY QUESTIONS

1. Identify the benefits associated with successful software development.
2. Which of the seven phases of the systems development life cycle is the most critical to the development of an e-espionage application?
3. Which of the seven phases of the systems development life cycle is the least critical to the development of an e-espionage application?
4. If you were consulting to the government on building an e-espionage application, which development methodology would you recommend and why?

## Chapter Seventeen Case:  Software Developing Androids

Android, the Google-developed open mobile phone platform, is a "software stack" development operating system for mobile phones—designed to compete head-to-head with Apple's iPhone. According to Google, a software stack is comprised of the operating system (the platform on which everything runs), the middleware (the programming that allows applications to talk to a network and to one another), and the applications (the actual programs that the phones will run). In short, the Android software stack is all the software that will make an Android phone an Android phone.

It is also important to note that Android is based on the Linux operating system, and all of its applications will be written using Java. This represents a significant risk to Microsoft and its operations systems. Microsoft states that it is unworried by the prospect of increased competition from Android, based on Linux, a software whose code is freely available via the Internet and developed by programmers the world over. Virtually anyone can download an Android software development kit from Google and write an application for Android. Google and its partners first unveiled plans for the Android operating system as software that would run mobile phones, or Android-enabled handsets, but soon, customers will be seeing Android in a number of other electronic devices. Just ask Mark Hamblin, designer of the original touchscreen for the Apple iPhone, who is now the CEO of Touch Revolution and is tinkering with Android so it can work in a slew of gadgets other than wireless phones including:

- A remote control and a touchscreen land-line home phone that will be powered by Android.
- Touchscreen menus for restaurants.
- Android-based medical devices.
- A 15-inch kitchen computer where family members can leave messages for one another.

### Additional Android Applications

Seeing Android applications developed by the thousands would be excellent news for Google and chipmakers such as Qualcomm and Texas Instruments that have invested in its development and would welcome the chance to sell semiconductors in new markets. But Android ubiquity could cause headaches for Microsoft, which would rather see its own software on a wider range of electronic devices. Currently, there are a handful of electronics manufacturers developing Android-based mobile Internet devices (MIDs).

### Designed to Run on Any Device

Android applications may have a unique first-mover advantage as they show up in devices such as netbooks or digital photo frames where Microsoft has yet to establish a beachhead. Manufacturers that work with Texas Instruments have already built Android into video and audio players and picture frames. Rival semiconductor manufacturer Qualcomm is helping vendors ready more than 20 Android-based products, including video players and small tablet PCs.

Google has not announced plans to market Android for use in nonphone gadgets. While Google did not discuss nonwireless devices when they first started talking about Android, they designed Android to run on any device—from a smart phone to a server—as they had the foresight to design it with bigger screens and chips in mind. Unlike many cell-phone and PC-based operating systems, Android can run on devices powered by a variety of semiconductors with minimal modifications needed.

### Competition from Linux

With flexibility comes economy. Manufacturers can keep costs low by being able to choose from a wider range of chips. Android software is also free to use, while Microsoft charges licensing fees. And just in case consumers fret that they will not be able to use their favorite Microsoft applications on an Android device, a company called DataViz will soon unveil software that it says will let people open, edit, and send Word, Excel, and Microsoft PowerPoint files. The software will also allow synching between Android and Outlook email.

As potent as it may be, Android faces competition from Microsoft and Linux. One of Android's creators, Intel recently introduced its own Linux software, Moblin, for use with MIDs and netbooks running its Atom processors. It will be interesting to watch the future of Android.

### Questions

1. List and describe the seven phases in the systems development life cycle and determine which phase you think is most important to an individual developing an application for Android.
2. Identify the primary difference between the different software development methodologies. Which methodology would you recommend an individual developing an application for Android use and why?
3. What are the common reasons why software projects fail and how can an Android developer mitigate these risks?
4. If you could develop software for Android what would it be and what business purpose would it serve? How could you ensure the successful development of the software?

# 18 | Managing Organizational Projects

**18.1.** Explain the triple constraint and its importance in project management.

**18.2.** Describe the fundamentals of project management.

## Project Management

No one would think of building an office complex by turning loose 100 different construction teams to build 100 different rooms with no single blueprint or agreed-upon vision of the completed structure. Yet this is precisely the situation in which many large organizations find themselves when managing information technology projects. Organizations routinely overschedule their resources (human and otherwise), develop redundant projects, and damage profitability by investing in non-strategic efforts that do not contribute to the organization's bottom line. Project management offers a strategic framework for coordinating the numerous activities associated with organizational projects. Business leaders face a rapidly moving and unforgiving global marketplace that will force them to use every possible tool to sustain competitiveness—*project management* is one of those tools.

## Managing Software Development Projects

Analysts predict investment in IT projects worldwide through 2010 will be over $1 trillion. This is a staggering amount, and even more staggering is that nearly 70 percent of it will be merely washed down the drain as a result of failed projects! In addition to lost earnings, companies from Nestlé to Nike have experienced additional consequences of failed projects—a damaged brand, lost goodwill, the dissolution of partnerships, lost investment opportunities, and the effects of low morale.

According to the Standish Group, just 29 percent of IT projects were completed on time, within budget, and with features and functions originally specified by the customer to deliver business value. The grim reality of failed projects faces many businesses today.

With so many skilled and knowledgeable professionals at the helm of projects, how can this happen? Every day, organizations adopt projects that do not align with mission-critical initiatives; they overcommit financial and human capital; they sign off on low-value projects that consume valuable and scarce resources; and they agree to support projects that are poorly defined from requirements to planning.

IT projects typically fail because, in most instances, they are complex, made even more so by poor planning and unrealistic expectations; they are rushed due to increasingly demanding market pressure; and their scope becomes too unmanageable. Because this is today's reality, it is important to apply solid project management techniques and tools to increase the success rate of organizational projects.

## THE TRIPLE CONSTRAINT

A project's vision needs to be clear, concise, and comprehensible, but it also has to be the same to all stakeholders. It is imperative that everyone be on the same page. From a business perspective, everyone has to be aligned with the direction of the overall business and the project's overall objectives. It is key for members of an organization who desire to make meaningful contributions to understand the company's investment and selection strategy for projects and how it determines and prioritizes the project pipeline. Projects consume vast amounts of resources. It is imperative to understand how the organization allocates its scarce and valuable resources in order to get the big picture.

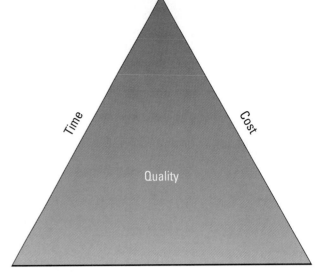

**FIGURE** 18.1

Project Management Interdependent Variables

Figure 18.1 displays the relationships among the three primary variables in any project—time, cost, and scope. These three variables are interdependent. All projects are limited in some way by these three constraints. The Project Management Institute calls the framework for evaluating these competing demands *the triple constraint.*

The relationships among these variables are such that if any one of the three factors changes at least one other factor is likely to be affected. For example, moving up a project's finish date could result in either increasing costs to hire more staff or decreasing the scope to eliminate features or functions. Increasing a project's scope to include additional customer requests could result in extending the project's time to completion or increasing the project's cost—or both—in order to accommodate the new scope changes. Project quality is affected by the project manager's ability to balance these competing demands. High-quality projects deliver the agreed upon product or service on time and on budget.

Project management is the science of making intelligent trade-offs among time, cost, and scope. All three of the factors combined to determine a project's quality. Benjamin Franklin's timeless advice—by failing to prepare, you prepare to fail—applies to many of today's software development projects. A recent survey concluded that the failure rate of IT projects is much higher in organizations that do not exercise disciplined project management. Figure 18.2 displays the top six

**FIGURE** 18.2

Why IT Projects Fall Behind Schedule or Fail

reasons IT projects fail, according to *Information Week*'s survey of 150 IT managers. A successful project is typically on time, within budget, meets the business's requirements, and fulfills the customer's needs. The Hackett Group, an Atlanta-based consultancy, analyzed its client database, which includes 2,000 companies, including 81 Fortune 100 companies, and discovered:

- Three in 10 major IT projects fail.
- Twenty-one percent of the companies state that they cannot adjust rapidly to market changes.
- One in four validates a business case for IT projects after completion.

## Project Management Fundamentals

The Project Management Institute (PMI) defines a ***project*** as a temporary endeavor undertaken to create a unique product, service, or result. ***Project management*** is the application of knowledge, skills, tools, and techniques to project activities to meet project requirements. Projects are short-term efforts such as removing old servers, developing a custom ecommerce site, or merging databases. Figure 18.3 provides an overview of PMI and its fundamental project management terms all managers should know and understand.

Before its merger with Hewlett-Packard, Compaq decided to analyze and prioritize its system development projects. Knowing that the CIO wanted to be able to view every project, project management leaders quickly identified and removed nonstrategic projects. At the end of the review process, the company cancelled 39 projects, saving the organization $15 million. Most Fortune 100 companies are receiving bottom-line benefits similar to Compaq's from implementing a project management solution.

Most business managers are not project managers; however, it is inevitable that all managers will be part of a project team. Therefore, it is important to understand how a business manages its projects and how the culture supports the effort. The art and science of project management must coordinate numerous activities as displayed in Figure 18.4.

**FIGURE** 18.3

Project Management Institute (PMI)

The ***Project Management Institute (PMI)*** develops procedures and concepts necessary to support the profession of project management (www.pmi.org). It has three areas of focus:

1. The distinguishing characteristics of a practicing professional (ethics).
2. The content and structure of the profession's body of knowledge (standards).
3. Recognition of professional attainment (accreditation).

***Project deliverables*** are any measurable, tangible, verifiable outcome, result, or item that is produced to complete a project or part of a project. Examples of project deliverables include design documents, testing scripts, and requirements documents.

***Project milestones*** represent key dates when a certain group of activities must be performed. For example, completing the planning phase might be a project milestone. If a project milestone is missed, then chances are the project is experiencing problems.

***Project manager*** is an individual who is an expert in project planning and management, defines and develops the project plan, and tracks the plan to ensure the project is completed on time and on budget. The project manager is the person responsible for executing the entire project plan.

***Project management office (PMO)*** is an internal department that oversees all organizational projects. This group must formalize and professionalize project management expertise and leadership. One of the primary initiatives of the PMO is to educate the organization on techniques and procedures necessary to run successful projects.

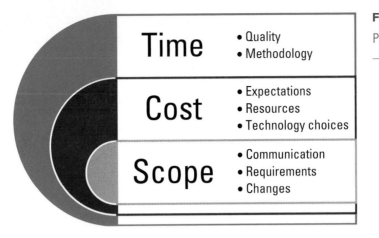

**FIGURE** 18.4

Project Management Roles

| Time | • Quality<br>• Methodology |
| Cost | • Expectations<br>• Resources<br>• Technology choices |
| Scope | • Communication<br>• Requirements<br>• Changes |

# Successful Project Management Strategies

Recreational Equipment, Inc. (REI) needs to consistently develop quality products and decrease the time to deliver them to market. To do that, REI needs to efficiently manage product development processes, projects, and information. The REI Gear and Apparel division takes an integrated project management approach to designing, managing, and tracking its product development projects, while collaborating and managing its workflow. REI's strategy entails combining Microsoft.NET technology, the Microsoft Office Enterprise Project Management (EPM) Solution, and software based on Microsoft Office Visio to create an integrated business solution it can use to model as-is business processes, experiment with what-if scenarios, and then convert the optimized processes into detailed project plans.

Project managers can further develop these plans, assign resources divisionwide, manage projects online, and collaborate globally. REI predicts this integrated solution will help it improve its efficiency, consistency, and scalability so it can deliver its products to market more quickly. Figure 18.5 displays the top five successful project management strategies outlined in *CIO* magazine.

**FIGURE** 18.5

Top Five Successful Project Management Strategies

**Top Five Successful Project Management Strategies**

1. **Define project success criteria.** At the beginning of the project, make sure the stakeholders share a common understanding of how they will determine whether the project is successful. Too often, meeting a predetermined schedule is the only apparent success factor, but there are certainly others. Some examples are increasing market share, reaching a specified sales volume or revenue, achieving specific customer satisfaction measures, retiring a high-maintenance legacy system, and achieving a particular transaction processing volume and correctness.

2. **Develop a solid project plan.** The hard part of developing a plan is the thinking, negotiating, balancing, and communication project managers will have to do to develop a solid and realistic plan. The time they spend analyzing what it will take to solve the business problem will reduce the number of changes later in the project.

3. **Divide and conquer.** Break all large tasks into multiple small tasks to provide more accurate estimates, reveal hidden work activities, and allow for more accurate, fine-grained status tracking.

4. **Plan for change.** Things never go precisely as planned on a project; therefore, the budget and schedule should include some contingency buffers at the end of major phases to accommodate change.

5. **Manage project risk.** Failure to identify and control risks will allow the risks to control the project. Be sure to spend significant time during project planning to brainstorm possible risk factors, evaluate their potential threat, and determine the best way to mitigate or prevent them.

1. What are the three interdependent variables shaping project management? Why are these variables important to an e-espionage software development project?

2. Explain how the government can use the top five successful project management strategies to ensure its project remains on schedule and under budget.

## Chapter Eighteen Case: Business Subject Matter Experts—The Project Manager You Need to Know About

One of the best kept secrets of successful software development projects is to deploy a non-IT business subject matter expert (SME) to the project team to answer questions, solve problems, and troubleshoot—according to Gene Marks of *BusinessWeek* magazine. The SME is relied on to take ownership of the project and ensure everything is executed correctly. The Gartner Group interviewed more than 1,300 IT professionals from large and small companies and found that an alarming 40 percent of their software projects did not produce the intended results.

Overseeing a new software system is incredibly difficult and one of the reasons why project managers are in high demand and can make upwards of $150,000 per project. The ultimate success of a new business system rests on having the right project team whose leader understands the fundamentals of project management and the details of how the business operates. The SME could be a current sales manager, customer service expert, or operations executive. Having an SME on an IT project can make the difference between a great return on investment and a chewing-out from the CEO. Clients have spent thousands of dollars, or millions of dollars, on software projects only to be left with a messy, unreliable mess. Clients have replaced their existing systems with something that promised to do more, but did not. Arguments have been vicious and grown men cry. And in almost all cases it was because there was no SME on the project team.

### The SME Owns the Software

What does an SME or "Super User" do? An SME takes ownership of the software because no matter what business system is purchased—customer relationship management, supply chain management, financial, help desk, etc.—it is all dependent on a single database. And if the data are inaccurate, someone is responsible. That person is the SME. Not that it is the SME's fault if the data are wrong. It is just the SME's responsibility to make it all right. The SME determines the procedures and processes for entering and reviewing data and is the one held accountable. It is a primary part of the SME's job description along with training new employees how to use the system, checking up on users, validating accuracy, and resolving issues. The SME knows the advanced features of the software and knows how to set up automated tasks, work flows, and alerts.

The SME is the single point of contact and has great responsibility for the success of the system. Numerous questions of all sorts are asked to the SME who is an expert at troubleshooting. The best and most valued SME is a businessperson who understands the business and understands software and databases.

## The Risk of No SME

What does an SME or Super User cost? It is not cheap. During a software implementation, an SME may need to spend a few days a week getting up to speed. Once the system is up and running, the SME could be spending another half to full day per week supporting users and performing other tasks. Some firms even have more than one SME so there is a backup. Whether a firm hires SMEs or just reallocates them internally, it is going to be an expense. If the project has not budgeted for this, then the project is underbudgeted.

Project experience clearly demonstrates that if an SME is not part of the budget, then the project will fail spectacularly. People will veer off in their own directions. Untrained users will complain. Data fields will be left blank. Reports will not run correctly. And the minute something goes wrong everyone will start pointing 10 fingers in 20 directions.

Do not wait for a software vendor to ask the business to put an SME on the project team. Many software companies do not care and typically promise customers that all their hopes and dreams will be fulfilled with the push of a button. Consultants and resellers do not always care either. After all, the more work the SME takes on the less revenue the consultant receives. And someone's got to pay their $495-per-hour rate, right?

## Questions

1. How can having an SME on your project alleviate scope creep?

2. How can having an SME on your project impact time constraints?

3. How can having an SME on your project impact costs?

4. Argue for or against the following statement: "There is no need to have an SME on the project management team."

# 19

# Outsourcing in the 21st Century

**19.1.** Describe the advantages and disadvantages of insourcing, outsourcing, and offshore outsourcing.

**19.2.** Describe why outsourcing is a critical business decision.

## Outsourcing Projects

In the high-speed global business environment, an organization needs to maximize its profits, enlarge its market share, and restrain its ever-increasing costs. Businesses need to make every effort to rethink and adopt new processes, especially the prospective resources regarding insourcing and outsourcing. Two basic options are available to organizations wishing to develop and maintain their information systems—insourcing or outsourcing.

*Insourcing* (*in-house development*) is a common approach using the professional expertise within an organization to develop and maintain the organization's information technology systems. Insourcing has been instrumental in creating a viable supply of IT professionals and in creating a better quality workforce combining both technical and business skills.

*Outsourcing* is an arrangement by which one organization provides a service or services for another organization that chooses not to perform them in-house. In some cases, the entire information technology department is outsourced, including planning and business analysis as well as the installation, management, and servicing of the network and workstations. Outsourcing can range from a large contract under which an organization such as IBM manages IT services for a company such as Xerox to the practice of hiring contractors and temporary office workers on an individual basis. Figure 19.1 compares the functions companies have outsourced, and Figure 19.2 displays the primary reasons companies outsource.

**FIGURE** 19.1

Common Departments Outsourced by Organizations

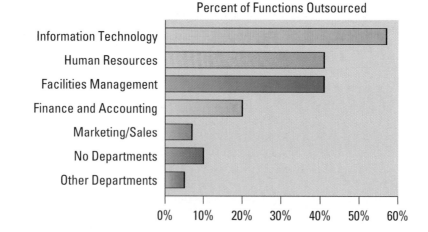

Percent of Functions Outsourced

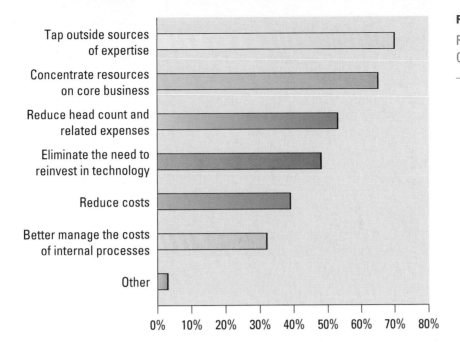

**FIGURE** 19.2

Reasons Companies
Outsource

British Petroleum (BP) began looking at IT outsourcing as a way to radically reduce costs and gain more flexible and higher-quality IT resources that directly improve the overall business. Over the past decade, all companies within the global BP Group have incorporated outsourcing initiatives in their business plans. BP's information technology costs were reduced by 40 percent globally over the first three years of the outsourcing engagement and have continued at a 10 percent reduction year after year, leading to hundreds of millions of dollars in savings to BP.

Information technology outsourcing enables organizations to keep up with market and technology advances—with less strain on human and financial resources and more assurance that the IT infrastructure will keep pace with evolving business priorities (see Figure 19.3). Planning, deploying, and managing IT environments is both a tactical and a strategic challenge that must take into account a company's organizational, industrial, and technological concerns. The three different forms of outsourcing options a project must consider are:

**FIGURE** 19.3

Outsourcing Models and
Cost Savings

1. **Onshore outsourcing**—engaging another company within the same country for services.

2. **Nearshore outsourcing**—contracting an outsourcing arrangement with a company in a nearby country. Often this country will share a border with the native country.

3. **Offshore outsourcing**—using organizations from developing countries to write code and develop systems. In offshore outsourcing the country is geographically far away.

Since the mid-1990s, major U.S. companies have been sending significant portions of their software development work offshore—primarily to vendors in India, but also to vendors in China, Eastern Europe (including Russia), Ireland, Israel, and the Philippines. The big selling point for offshore outsourcing is inexpensive good work. A programmer who earns as much as $63,000 per year in the United States is paid as little as $5,000 per year overseas (see Figure 19.4). Companies can easily realize cost savings of 30 to 50 percent through offshore outsourcing and still get the same, if not better, quality of service.

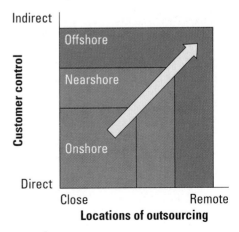

| Country | Salary Range Per Year |
|---|---|
| China | $5,000–$9,000 |
| India | 6,000–10,000 |
| Philippines | 6,500–11,000 |
| Russia | 7,000–13,000 |
| Ireland | 21,000–28,000 |
| Canada | 25,000–50,000 |
| United States | 60,000–90,000 |

**FIGURE** 19.4

Typical Salary Ranges for Computer Programmers

Developed and developing countries throughout Europe and Asia offer some IT outsourcing services, but most are hampered to some degree by language, telecommunications infrastructure, or regulatory barriers. The first and largest offshore marketplace is India, whose English-speaking and technologically advanced population has built its IT services business into a $4 billion industry. Infosys, NIIT, Satyam, TCS, and Wipro are among the biggest Indian outsourcing service providers, each with a significant presence in the United States.

Ever since Eastman Kodak announced it was outsourcing its information systems function to IBM, large organizations have found it acceptable to transfer their IT assets, leases, and staff to outsourcers. In view of the changes in sourcing, the key question now is not "Should we outsource IT?" but rather "Where and how can we take advantage of the rapidly developing market of IT services providers?" Some of the influential drivers affecting the growth of the outsourcing market include:

- **Core competencies.** Many companies have recently begun to consider outsourcing as a means to fuel revenue growth rather than just a cost-cutting measure. Outsourcing enables an organization to maintain an up-to-date technology infrastructure while freeing it to focus on revenue growth goals by reinvesting cash and human capital in areas offering the greatest return on investment.

- **Financial savings.** It is typically cheaper to hire workers in China and India than similar workers in the United States. Technology is advancing at such an accelerated rate that companies often lack the resources, workforce, or expertise to keep up. It is close to impossible for an IT department to maintain a "best-of-breed" status, especially for small and medium-sized enterprises where cost is a critical factor.

- **Rapid growth.** A company's sustainability depends on both speed to market and ability to react quickly to changes in market conditions. By taking advantage of outsourcing, an organization is able to acquire best-practices process expertise. This facilitates the design, building, training, and deployment of business processes or functions.

- **Industry changes.** High levels of reorganization across industries have increased demand for outsourcing to better focus on core competencies. The significant increase in merger and acquisition activity created a sudden need to integrate multiple core and noncore business functions into one business, while the deregulation of the utilities and telecom industries created a need to ensure compliance with government rules and regulations. Companies in either situation turned to outsourcing so they could better focus on industry changes at hand.

- **The Internet.** The pervasive nature of the Internet as an effective sales channel has allowed clients to become more comfortable with outsourcing. Barriers to entry, such as lack of capital, are dramatically reduced in the world of ebusiness due to the Internet. New competitors enter the market daily.

- **Globalization.** As markets open worldwide, competition heats up. Companies may engage outsourcing service providers to deliver international services.

Best Buy Co. Inc. is the number one U.S. specialty retailer for consumer electronics, personal computers, entertainment software, and appliances. Best Buy needed to find a strategic IT partner that could help the company leverage its IT functions to meet its business objectives. Best Buy also wanted to integrate its disparate enterprise systems and minimize its operating expenses. Best Buy outsourced these functions to Accenture, a global management consulting, technology services, and outsourcing company. The comprehensive outsourcing relationship that drove Best Buy's transformation produced spectacular results that were measurable in every key area of its business, such as a 20 percent increase in key category revenue that translated into a $25 million profit improvement.

According to PricewaterhouseCoopers' survey of CEOs from 452 of the fastest growing U.S. companies, "Businesses that outsource are growing faster, larger, and more profitably than those that do not. In addition, most of those involved in outsourcing say they are saving money and are highly satisfied with their outsourcing service providers." Figure 19.5 lists common areas for outsourcing opportunities across industries.

## OUTSOURCING BENEFITS

The many benefits associated with outsourcing include:

- Increased quality and efficiency of a process, service, or function.
- Reduced operating expenses.
- Resources focused on core profit-generating competencies.
- Reduced exposure to risks involved with large capital investments.
- Access to outsourcing service provider's economies of scale.
- Access to outsourcing services provider's expertise and best-in-class practices.
- Access to advanced technologies.
- Increased flexibility with the ability to respond quickly to changing market demands.
- No costly outlay of capital funds.
- Reduced head count and associated overhead expense.
- Reduced frustration and expense related to hiring and retaining employees in an exceptionally tight job market.
- Reduced time to market for products or services.

## OUTSOURCING CHALLENGES

Outsourcing comes with several challenges. These arguments are valid and should be considered when a company is thinking about outsourcing. Many challenges can be avoided with proper research. The challenges include:

- **Contract length.** Most of the outsourced IT contracts are for a relatively long time period (several years). This is because of the high cost of transferring assets

**FIGURE** 19.5

Outsourcing Opportunities

| Industry | Outsourcing Opportunities |
|---|---|
| Banking and finance | Check and electronic payment processing, credit report issuance, delinquency management, securities, and trades processing |
| Insurance | Claims reporting and investigation, policy administration, check processing, risk assessment |
| Telecommunications | Invoice and bill production, transaction processing |
| Health care | Electronic data interchange, database management, accounting |
| Transportation | Ticket and order processing |
| Government | Loan processing, Medicaid processing |
| Retail | Electronic payment processing |

and employees as well as maintaining technological investment. The long contract causes three particular issues:

1. Difficulties in getting out of a contract if the outsourcing service provider turns out to be unsuitable.

2. Problems in foreseeing what the business will need over the next 5 or 10 years (typical contract lengths), hence creating difficulties in establishing an appropriate contract.

3. Problems in reforming an internal IT department after the contract period is finished.

- **Competitive edge.** Effective and innovative use of IT can give an organization a competitive edge over its rivals. A competitive business advantage provided by an internal IT department that understands the organization and is committed to its goals can be lost in an outsourced arrangement. In an outsourced arrangement, IT staff are striving to achieve the goals and objectives of the outsourcing service provider, which may conflict with those of the organization.

- **Confidentiality.** In some organizations, the information stored in the computer systems is central to the enterprise's success or survival, such as information about pricing policies, product mixing formulas, or sales analysis. Some companies decide against outsourcing for fear of placing confidential information in the hands of the provider, particularly if the outsourcing service provider offers services to companies competing in the same marketplace. Although the organization usually dismisses this threat, claiming it is covered by confidentiality clauses in a contract, the organization must assess the potential risk and costs of a confidentiality breach in determining the net benefits of an outsourcing agreement.

- **Scope definition.** Most IT projects suffer from problems associated with defining the scope of the system. The same problem afflicts outsourcing arrangements. Many difficulties result from contractual misunderstandings between the organization and the outsourcing service provider. In such circumstances, the organization believes that the service required is within the contract scope while the service provider is sure it is outside the scope and so is subject to extra fees.

## OPENING CASE STUDY QUESTIONS

1. What are the benefits and risks associated with outsourcing?

2. What are the ethical issues associated with outsourcing government applications?

3. What are the security issues associated with outsourcing government applications?

# Chapter Nineteen Case: UPS in the Computer Repair Business

When people think of UPS they usually think of brown delivery trucks and employees in shorts dropping off and picking up packages. This image is about to change. UPS has now entered the laptop repair business. Toshiba is handing over its entire laptop repair operation to UPS Supply Chain Solutions, the shipper's $2.4 billion logistics outsourcing division. Toshiba's decision to allow a shipping company to fix its laptops might appear odd. However, when you understand that the primary challenge of computer repair is more logistical than technical,

Toshiba's business decision seems brilliant. "Moving a unit around and getting replacement parts consumes most of the time," explained Mark Simons, general manager at Toshiba's digital products division. "The actual service only takes about an hour."

UPS sends broken Toshiba laptops to its facility in Louisville, Kentucky, where UPS engineers diagnose and repair defects. In the past, repairs could take weeks, depending on whether Toshiba needed components from Japan. Since the UPS repair site is adjacent to its air hub, customers should get their machines back, as good as new, in just a matter of days. UPS has been servicing Lexmark and Hewlett-Packard printers since 1996 and has been performing initial inspections on laptops being returned to Toshiba since 1999.

The expanded Toshiba relationship is another step in UPS's strategy to broaden its business beyond package delivery into commerce services. The company works with clients to manage inventory, ordering, and custom processes. It recently introduced a service to dispose of unwanted electrical devices. To take on laptop repair, UPS put 50 technicians through a Toshiba-certified training course.

## Questions

1. Do you think UPS's entrance into the laptop repair business was a good business decision? Why or why not?

2. Explain why Toshiba decided to outsource its computer repair business to UPS.

3. What are some advantages UPS can offer Toshiba in the outsourcing arrangement?

4. Explain the advantages of forming an outsourcing relationship with a parcel delivery company such as UPS.

CHAPTER 20

# Developing a 21st Century Organization

## LEARNING OUTCOMES

**20.1.** List and describe the four 21st century trends that businesses are focusing on and rank them in order of business importance.

**20.2.** Explain how the integration of business and technology is shaping 21st century organizations.

## Developing Organizations

Organizations face changes more extensive and far reaching in their implications than anything since the modern industrial revolution occurred in the early 1900s. Technology is one of the primary forces driving these changes. Organizations that want to survive in the 21st century must recognize the immense power of technology, carry out required organizational changes in the face of it, and learn to operate in an entirely different way. Figure 20.1 displays a few examples of the way technology is changing the business arena.

## 21st Century Organization Trends

On the business side, 21st century organization trends are:

- Uncertainty in terms of future business scenarios and economic outlooks.
- Emphasis on strategic analysis for cost reduction and productivity enhancements.
- Focus on improved business resiliency via the application of enhanced security.

On the technology side, there has been a focus on improved business management of IT in order to extract the most value from existing resources and create alignment between business and IT priorities. Today's organizations focus on defending and safeguarding their existing market positions in addition to targeting new market growth. The four primary information technology areas where organizations are focusing are:

- IT infrastructures
- Security
- Ebusiness
- Integration

### INCREASED FOCUS ON IT INFRASTRUCTURE

A significant trend for the 21st century is to increase the focus on *IT infrastructure*—the hardware, software, and telecommunications equipment that, when combined,

FIGURE 20.1

Examples of How
Technology Is Changing
Business

| Industry | Business Changes Due to Technology |
|---|---|
| Travel | Travel site Expedia.com is now the biggest leisure-travel agency, with higher profit margins than even American Express. |
| Entertainment | The music industry has kept Napster and others from operating, but $35 billion annual online downloads are wrecking the traditional music business. The next big entertainment industry to feel the effects of ebusiness will be the $67 billion movie business. |
| Electronics | Using the Internet to link suppliers and customers, Dell dictates industry profits. Its operating margins have risen, even as it takes prices to levels where rivals cannot make money. |
| Financial services | Nearly every public efinance company remaining makes money, with online mortgage service Lending Tree growing 70 percent a year. Processing online mortgage applications is now 40 percent cheaper for customers. |
| Retail | eBay is on track to become one of the nation's top 15 retailers, and Amazon.com will join the top 40. Wal-Mart's ebusiness strategy is forcing rivals to make heavy investments in technology. |
| Automobiles | The cost of producing vehicles is down because of SCM and web-based purchasing. Also, eBay has become the leading U.S. used-car dealer, and most major car sites are profitable. |
| Education and training | Cisco saved $133 million by moving training sessions to the Internet, and the University of Phoenix online college classes please investors. |

provide the underlying foundation to support the organization's goals. Organizations in the past underestimated the importance that IT infrastructures have for the many functional areas of an organization.

In the early days of the Internet, the basic infrastructure in terms of protocols and standards was unsophisticated (and still is), but software companies managed to enhance the Internet and offer compelling applications for functional business areas. The original design for the Internet and the web was for simple email, document exchange, and the display of static content, not for sophisticated and dynamic business applications that require access to back-end systems and databases.

Organizations today are looking to Internet-based cross-functional systems such as CRM, SCM, and ERP to help drive their business success. The days of implementing independent functional systems are gone. Creating an effective organization requires a 360-degree view of all operations. For this reason, ownership of the IT infrastructure now becomes the responsibility of the entire organization and not just the individual users or functional department. This is primarily because the IT infrastructure has a dramatic influence on the strategic capabilities of an organization (see Figure 20.2).

## INCREASED FOCUS ON SECURITY

With war and terrorist attacks on many people's minds, security is a hot topic. For businesses, too, security concerns are widespread. Increasingly opening up their networks and applications to customers, partners, and suppliers using an ever more diverse set of computing devices and networks, businesses can benefit from deploying the latest advances in security technologies. These benefits include fewer disruptions to organizational systems, increased productivity of employees, and greater advances in administration, authorization, and authentication techniques. For businesses it is important to have the appropriate levels of authentication, access control, and encryption in place, which help to

FIGURE 20.2

The Position of the
Infrastructure within the
Organization

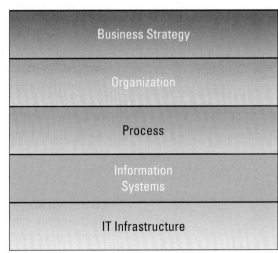

Business Strategy

Organization

Process

Information Systems

IT Infrastructure

**FIGURE** 20.3

Physical Security
Integration and Best
Security Practices

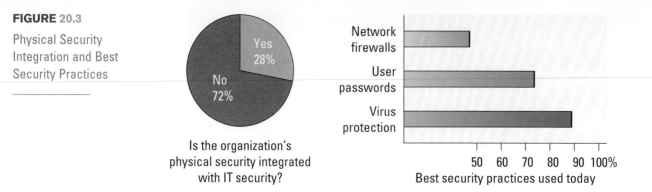

Is the organization's
physical security integrated
with IT security?

Best security practices used today

ensure (1) that only authorized individuals can gain access to the network, (2) that they have access to only those applications for which they are entitled, and (3) that they cannot understand or alter information while in transit. Figure 20.3 displays a recent survey concerning both the level of physical security integration and the current security practices used by most organizations.

Security breaches not only inconvenience business users and their customers and partners, but can also cost millions of dollars in lost revenues or lost market capitalization. The business cost of inadequate security does not stop at inconvenience and loss of revenues or market valuation. It can even force a business out of existence. For example, British Internet service provider CloudNine Communications was the victim of a distributed denial-of-service (DDoS) attack that forced the company to close operations and to eventually transfer over 2,500 customers to a rival organization. While "disruptive technologies" can help a company to gain competitive advantage and market share (and avoid real business disruptions), lack of security can have the opposite effect, causing profitable companies to lose market share or even their entire business within hours or days of an attack.

It is now more important than ever for an organization to have well-rehearsed and frequently updated processes and procedures to insure against a variety of adverse scenarios—Internet email and denial-of-service attacks from worms and viruses, loss of communications, loss of documents, password and information theft, fire, flood, physical attacks on property, and even terrorist attacks.

## INCREASED FOCUS ON EBUSINESS

Mobility and wireless are the new focus in ebusiness, and some upcoming trends are mobile commerce, telematics, electronic tagging, and RFID.

- *Mobile commerce (m-commerce)*—the ability to purchase goods and services through a wireless Internet-enabled device.

- *Telematics*—blending computers and wireless telecommunications technologies with the goal of efficiently conveying information over vast networks to improve business operations. The most notable example of telematics may be the Internet itself, since it depends on a number of computer networks connected globally through telecommunication devices.

- *Electronic tagging*—a technique for identifying and tracking assets and individuals via technologies such as radio frequency identification and smart cards.

- *Radio frequency identification (RFID)*—technologies use active or passive tags in the form of chips or smart labels that can store unique identifiers and relay this information to electronic readers. Within the supply chain, RFID can enable greater efficiencies in business processes such as inventory, logistics, distribution, and asset management. On the mobile commerce side, RFID can enable new forms of ebusiness through mobile phones and smart cards. This can increase loyalty by streamlining purchases for the consumer. For example,

RFID readers are being embedded in store shelving to help retailers, including Marks & Spencer and The Gap, to better manage their assets and inventories and understand customer behavior.

These are all interesting subcategories within mobile business that open up new opportunities for mobility beyond simple employee applications. Electronic tagging and RFID are especially interesting because they extend wireless and mobile technologies not just to humans, but also to a wide range of objects such as consumer and industrial products. These products will gain intelligence via electronic product codes, which are a (potential) replacement for universal product code (UPC) bar codes, and via RFID tags with two-way communication capabilities.

Mobile employees will soon have the ability to leverage technology just as if they were in the office. Improvements in devices, applications, networks, and standards over the past few years have made this far more practical than it was when introduced. The drivers for adoption are finally starting to outweigh the barriers. For example, major vendors such as IBM, Microsoft, Oracle, and Sybase are all playing a larger role and taking a greater interest in mobile business than they had previously. These vendors all have mature, proven offerings for enterprise mobility.

Mobile technology will help extend an organization out to its edges in areas such as sales automation and enterprise operations. Benefits can include improved information accuracy, reduced costs, increased productivity, increased revenues, and improved customer service. Beyond being an additional channel for communications, mobile business will enable an organization to think about the powerful combination of business processes, ebusiness, and wireless communications.

## INCREASED FOCUS ON INTEGRATION

Information technology has penetrated the heart of organizations and will stay there in the future. The IT industry is one of the most dynamic in the global economy. As a sector, it not only creates millions of high-level jobs, but also helps organizations to be more efficient and effective, which in turn stimulates innovation. The integration of business and technology has allowed organizations to increase their share of the global economy, transform the way they conduct business, and become more efficient and effective (see Figure 20.4).

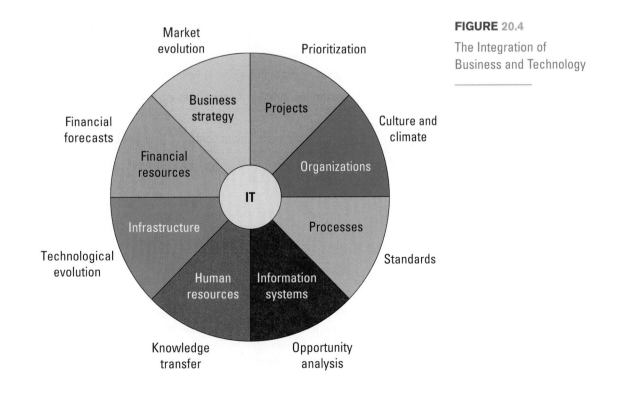

**FIGURE** 20.4

The Integration of Business and Technology

The past few years have produced a confluence of events that has reshaped the global economy. Around the world, free-market competition has flourished and a new globally interdependent financial system has emerged. Reflecting these changes, core business relationships and models are dramatically changing, including shifts from:

- Product-centricity to customer-centricity.
- Mass production to mass customization.
- The value in material things to the value of knowledge and intelligence.

In concert with these trends, a new series of business success factors and challenges has emerged that is helping to determine marketplace winners and losers:

- Organization agility, often supported by a "plug and play" IT infrastructure (with a flexible and adaptable applications architecture).
- A focus on core competencies and processes.
- A redefinition of the value chain.
- Instantaneous business response.
- The ability to scale resources and infrastructure across geographic boundaries.

These developments add up to an environment that is vastly more complex than even five years ago. This in turn has resulted in organizations increasingly embracing new business models. The new environment requires organizations to focus externally on their business processes and integration architectures. The virtually integrated business model will cause a sharp increase in the number of business partners and the closeness of integration between them.

Never before have IT investments played such a critical role in business success. As business strategies continue to evolve, the distinction between "the business" and IT will virtually disappear.

## OPENING CASE STUDY QUESTIONS

1. Why is it critical that the government develop its IT infrastructure using a 21st century strategy?

2. How would the government define security when developing its 21st century strategy?

3. How would the government define its ebusiness infrastructure when developing its 21st century strategy?

4. Why is it important that the government control all integrations into its systems?

## Chapter Twenty Case: Creating a Clearer Picture for Public Broadcasting Service (PBS)

One of the leaders in the transformation of the broadcasting industry is André Mendes, chief technology integration officer, or CTIO, at Public Broadcasting Service (PBS). Mendes oversees the company's technology organization, a 50-person group created by melding PBS's IT and broadcast-engineering departments. The new CTIO position replaces the formerly separate jobs of CIO and CTO at the nonprofit television network.

Mendes encountered a few roadblocks during his first few months as CTIO including resistance from the broadcast engineering staff, his limited knowledge of broadcast engineering, and breaking down barriers between the two departments. Mendes managed through the change with finesse and now refers to it as a "bidirectional learning experience" for him and his staff. "Once you're in a new environment, you start asking a lot of questions," he says. "Every question requires the responder to think about the answer. That helped the process of evaluating why procedures and practices are done a certain way—and identifying possible improvements."

Michael Hunt, PBS's vice president of enterprise applications, states that Mendes broke down many barriers and offered his employees a way to address and respond to change. The united team is currently working on large, sophisticated projects that are improving the efficiency of PBS and its member stations. "Projects are getting bigger and bigger, with more and more collaboration, with a more global picture," says Marilyn Pierce, director of PBS digital assets, who came from the broadcast-engineering side of the company.

"The broadcast environment is becoming an IT environment," states Mendes in reference to the fact that as the worlds of broadcast and traditional information technologies converge, this uncovers new ways to improve quality of service and increase opportunities for innovation through new digitized formats, which replace traditional analog video. The primary drivers of this convergence are advances in digital technologies and the Internet. Though those changes are unique to the television industry, it is not the first—or last—time that welding together different technology organizations has been responsible for advances in technology. For instance, companies pursuing voice-over-IP (VOIP) initiatives are combining their IT and telecommunications groups, and other industries face similar integration challenges as everything from automobiles to appliances becomes increasingly technology dependent.

The integration of broadcast and information technologies is raising the visibility of technology as an organizational infrastructure enabler and a strategic partner for new business models. PBS is launching several projects that are revamping the way the company does business. One project allows producers to send program content digitally rather than on videotapes. In the past, PBS rejected and returned 60 percent of the video content because it did not contain key technical information such as the number of frames in a program to allow for seamless merging of programs. "From a supply chain standpoint, that was highly inefficient," Mendes says.

Another project is saving PBS tens of millions of dollars a year by transporting its programs to TV stations as email files via TCP/IP over satellite. This delivery vehicle greatly improves quality by avoiding weather-related interference that can arise in transmitting programs by streaming signals over satellite. "The change in broadcast is similar to the transformation in the telecom industry as companies moved from switch circuitry to packet circuits," Mendes says. For PBS the business lines are blurring as the industry responds to technology changes, which is making the overall picture much clearer.

## Questions

1. Assess the impact to PBS's business if it failed to focus on IT infrastructures when determining its 21st century business strategy.

2. Assess the impact to PBS's business if it failed to focus on security when determining its 21st century business strategy.

3. Assess the impact to PBS's business if it failed to focus on ebusiness when determining its 21st century business strategy.

4. Assess the impact to PBS's business if it failed to focus on integrations when determining its 21st century business strategy.

An organization must remain competitive in this quick-paced, constantly changing, global business environment. It must implement technology that is adaptive, disruptive, and transformable to meet new and unexpected customer needs. Focusing on the unexpected and understanding disruptive technologies can give an organization a competitive advantage.

Organizations need software that users can transform quickly to meet the requirements of the rapidly changing business environment. Software that effectively meets employee needs will help an organization become more productive and make better decisions. Software that does not meet employee needs may have a damaging effect on productivity. Employee involvement along with using the right implementation methodology in developing software is critical to the success of an organization.

Four areas of focus for organizations heading into the 21st century are IT infrastructure, security, ebusiness (mobility), and integration. Information technology has rapidly expanded from a backroom resource providing competitive advantage (e.g., cost, time, quality) to a front-office resource (e.g., marketing, sales) that is a competitive necessity. The dynamic business and technical environment of the 21st century is driving the need for technology infrastructures and applications architecture that are increasingly flexible, integrated, and maintainable (while always providing functionality, cost effectiveness, timeliness, and security).

## ★ KEY TERMS

Agile methodology, 250
Analysis phase, 248
Business requirement, 248
Design phase, 248
Development phase, 248
Electronic tagging, 272
Extreme programming (XP)
    methodology, 251
Feature creep, 254
Implementation phase, 248
Insourcing (in-house
    development), 264
Iterative development 250
IT infrastructure, 270
Maintenance phase, 248
Methodology 249

Mobile commerce
    (m-commerce), 272
Nearshore outsourcing 265
Offshore outsourcing 265
Onshore outsourcing 265
Outsourcing 264
Planning phase, 248
Project 260
Project deliverable 260
Project management, 260
Project Management Institute
    (PMI) 260
Project management office
    (PMO) 260
Project manager 260
Project milestone 260

Prototype, 251
Radio frequency identification
    (RFID), 272
Rapid application development
    (RAD) (also called
    rapid prototyping)
    methodology, 251
Rational unified process (RUP)
    methodology 252
Scope creep, 254
Scrum methodology 252
Systems development life cycle
    (SDLC), 247
Telematics, 272
Testing phase, 248
Waterfall methodology, 249

## Twitter

Twitter, a privately funded start-up, is a pioneer in the microblogging arena providing a service that allows users to send and receive updates to other users. Twitter customers can keep a network of friends informed of their current status by way of text messaging, instant messaging, email, or the web. Friends, family, and coworkers use Twitter's services to communicate and stay connected through a real-time short messaging service that works over multiple networks and devices. Twitter began as a small project in 2006 and has developed into one of the most popular sites on the Internet. People around the globe use Twitter for various reasons from breaking world news to streamlining business.

## The Business of Twitter

Companies are using Twitter to follow customer dialogs about their brand. Comcast, Dell, General Motors, H&R Block, Kodak, and Whole Foods Market are using Twitter to do everything from building brand awareness to providing customer service. The attention to Twitter reflects the power of new social media tools in letting consumers shape public discussion over brands. "The real control of the brand has moved into the customer's hands, and technology has enabled that," says Lane Becker, president of Get Satisfaction, a website that draws together customers and companies to answer each other's questions and give feedback on products and services.

JetBlue, Comcast, and H&R Block are among the companies that recognize Twitter's potential in providing customer service. A single Twitter message—known informally as a *tweet*—sent in frustration over a product or a service's performance can be read by hundreds or thousands of people. Similarly, positive interaction with a representative of the manufacturer or service provider can help change an influencer's perspective for the better. For companies, tools such as Tweetscan or Twitter's own search tool, formerly known as Summize, make it easy to unearth a company's name mentioned in tweets. Being able to address an issue the moment it appears is a great way to improve customer satisfaction

GM took notice the day a prospective buyer was at a Saturn dealership, ready to make a purchase, but could not find anyone to help him. "He was starting to get upset about it," says Adam Denison, who helps coordinate social media communications at GM. "When we saw it, we immediately let our Saturn colleagues know about it . . . and they could get the ball rolling a little bit better." The person bought a Saturn in the end—though at a different dealership, Denison says.

## Monitoring Customers

Not all customers want Corporate America following their tweets. Jonathan Fields typed a quick tweet to his friends when he spotted William Shatner waiting to board a JetBlue flight at New York's JFK airport. Fields wrote: "JetBlue terminal, William Shatner waiting in pinstripe suit and shades to board flight to Burbank. Why's he flying JetBlue? Free, maybe?" To his surprise he received a reply within 10 seconds, but not from his friends; it was from JetBlue informing Fields that they were following him on Twitter. Fields was at first shocked by the reply, then the JetBlue employee Morgan Johnston quickly explained that the company was not spying on Fields, but uses Twitter as a scanning tool, to find customers who might need information, say, on flight delays or cancellations.

"It has potential for delivering business value, clearly, but at the same time there are some risks to it," says Ray Valdes, research director of web services at consulting firm Gartner. While it is a useful brand-monitoring tool, it "can come across as a little creepy." Christofer Hoff tweeted his displeasure with Southwest when his flight was delayed and his luggage disappeared. The next day he received the following message from Southwest: "Sorry to hear about your flight—weather was terrible in the NE. Hope you give us a 2nd chance to prove that Southwest = Awesomeness." In a blog post about the incident, Hoff wrote that it was "cool and frightening at the same time."

## Twitter Ethics

Of course with all great good comes the potential of great evil and Twitter is no exception. A few individuals purchased unofficial accounts to send messages that were clearly not authorized by the company. For example, Exxon Mobil discovered that a person named Janet was fooling many people by posing as an employee of Exxon Mobil. "Our concern was that people reading the postings would think that this person was speaking on the company's behalf," says Exxon Mobil spokesman Chris Welberry. "We didn't want to do anything heavy-handed about people expressing their views in a social networking environment. We just wanted to make sure that people who are doing that are open and transparent."

After Exxon discovered Janet, the company contacted Twitter. "Twitter does not allow impersonation or domain squatting, which is grabbing a user name and saying you want money," Twitter co-founder Biz Stone says. "But they really do have to be impersonating or infringing on copyright. If somebody's last name happens to be Mobil, the company does not have a strong case there." Janet's account was taken out of commission.

## Twitter Growth

Large organizations are likely to begin integrating microblogging into their existing services to aggregate the various social media outposts. Facebook is already positioning itself to be an aggregator of microblogging sites. The social network's News Feed feature lets people pull in updates from Twitter, Blip.fm, and elsewhere. How valuable could a microblogging service be? Soon after Twitter raised $15 million in funding, it was speculated that the site may be worth as much as $1 billion. Twitter co-founder Biz Stone expects the site's user base to grow 10 times its current size yearly.

## Questions

1. Why do 21st century organizations need to understand the power of micro-blogging?
2. How can a global organization use Twitter to improve operations?
3. How could a project manager use Twitter to help track project progress?

4. How could a global systems development effort use Twitter to improve the development process?

5. What types of strategic information systems could use Twitter to improve the system? Which development methodology would you recommend the company use when integrating Twitter into its current systems?

6. What types of ethical and security issues should a company using Twitter anticipate?

## Women in Technology

Technology is a tough business. Tough for men and sometimes even tougher for women. Women who have succeeded in technology deserve recognition. They are an inspiration for everyone, demonstrating what can be achieved through creativity and hard work. *Fast Company* recently compiled a list of women in technology who are leading the wave of 21st century business. *Fast Company*'s list includes:

■ **Ning: Gina Bianchini, cofounder and CEO**

This custom social-network maker made a splash on the May 2008 cover, and not just because she knew what a viral expansion loop was. With 500,000-plus networks now running on Ning, the company has had its share of developer challenges but remains cashed up and growing.

■ **Flickr: Caterina Fake, cofounder**

Fake not only cofounded photo-sharing behemoth Flickr but also sold it to Yahoo! for a reported $35 million. Now everyone is buzzing about her next project, something called Hunch, which is in stealth mode.

■ **Blurb: Eileen Gittins, CEO**

Gittins's book self-publishing platform is lean and green and has unleashed the insta-author (and book retailer) in everyone from amateur photographers to big brands like Lexus. With one million-plus books created, Blurb is profitable.

■ **Meebo: Sandy Jen and Elaine Wherry, cofounders**

Oft cited as the web's fastest growing IM tool, this third start-up for Jen and Wherry (and fellow cofounder Seth Sternberg) is on a cacophonous track. It lets some 40 million users yap over any IM network and in a variety of settings; new partnerships with Hearst and Universal Music point to an even chattier future.

■ **Pixel Qi: Mary Lou Jepsen, founder and CEO**

As CTO of One Laptop Per Child (OLPC), Jepsen led the design and development of the least expensive and most energy efficient laptop ever made. She founded Pixel Qi in 2008 to commercialize the groundbreaking OLPC screen technology she invented.

■ **Consorte Media: Alicia Morga, CEO**

Using science (not cultural hype) to match brand advertisers with Hispanic-American consumers on the web, Morga's marketing firm had 100 percent growth last year.

- **SpikeSource: Kim Polese, CEO**

  Polese was part of the early Java team at Sun Microsystems and cofounded Marimba. Her new business, which boasts a partnership with Intel, helps companies test the security and quality of open-source software.

- **BabyCenter: Tina Sharkey, president**

  Sharkey's site reaches nearly 80 percent of new moms online in the U.S. and some 6 million visitors a month internationally. With the 2007 acquisition of MayasMom.com, a social-networking site, Sharkey's parental domination is nearly complete.

- **SlideShare: Rashmi Sinha, cofounder and CEO**

  The psychology PhD turned web designer and community expert has created a vibrant social hub around—of all things—the PowerPoint deck. Launched with less than $50,000, SlideShare now has a million registered users, plus a partnership with LinkedIn.

- **Six Apart: Mena Trott, cofounder and president**

  With cofounding husband, Ben, Trott created tools such as Movable Type and TypePad that enabled the blogosphere to bloom. Her firm recently snapped up social network Pownce, too, adding that site's cofounder Leah Culver, another woman we admire, to the team.

- **MyShape: Louise Wannier, CEO**

  Matching technology with fashion, MyShape has created an online bazaar with more than 400,000 members. What else would you expect from a serial entrepreneur with degrees in textile design and business administration?

## Questions

1. Which of the above companies has the most disruptive technology that is capable of making the greatest impact on 21st century business?

2. Choose one of the above companies and create a Porter's Five Forces analysis to highlight potential issues the company might face over the next decade.

3. Choose one of the above companies.

   a. List and describe the seven phases in the systems development life cycle and determine which phase is most important to the company.

   b. Review the primary principles of successful software development and prioritize them in order of importance to the company.

   c. Explain how the company can use project management to ensure success.

   d. Explain the pros and cons of outsourcing for the company.

4. Why is building agile software important for all of the companies?

5. What types of information security issues should the companies be aware of as they enter the 21st century?

6. What types of ethical dilemmas should the companies be aware of as they enter the 21st century?

⭑ **MAKING BUSINESS DECISIONS**

### 1. Selecting a Systems Development Methodology

Exus Incorporated is an international billing outsourcing company. Exus currently has revenues of $5 billion, over 3,500 employees, and operations on every continent. You have recently been hired as the CIO. Your first task is to increase the software development project success rate, which is currently at 20 percent. To ensure that future software development projects are successful, you want to standardize the systems development methodology across the entire enterprise. Currently, each project determines which methodology it uses to develop software.

Create a report detailing three additional system development methodologies that were not covered in this text. Compare each of these methodologies to the traditional waterfall approach. Finally, recommend which methodology you want to implement as your organizational standard. Be sure to highlight any potential roadblocks you might encounter when implementing the new standard methodology.

## 2. Transforming an Organization

Your college has asked you to help develop the curriculum for a new course titled "Building a 21st Century Organization." Use the materials in this text, the Internet, and any other resources to outline the curriculum that you would suggest the course cover. Be sure to include your reasons why the material should be covered and the order in which it should be covered.

## 3. Approving a Project

You are working in the IT development team for Gear International, a privately held sports and recreational equipment manufacturer. To date, you have spent the majority of your career developing applications for your corporate intranet. Your team has an idea to add an application that allows employees to learn about corporate athletic teams, register online, determine team schedules, post team statistics, etc. Your supervisor likes your idea and would like your team to prepare a short presentation with 5 to 10 slides that she can use to convince senior management to approve the project. Be sure to list benefits of the project along with your suggested methodology to help guarantee the project's development success.

## 4. Patrolling by Remote

Today's gadgets offer all-weather, all-knowing, anytime, anyplace. Whether you are trying to keep tabs on your children, your new home theater, or your streaming audio, here are a few wireless tools you can use around your house.

- **Wi-fi camera**—A five-inch-high Wireless Observer lets you take pictures at regular intervals or in response to motion and you can access it anytime through a web browser (www.veo.com).

- **Security sensor**—This detector system alerts you to break-ins and errant pop flies. Its dual sensors record vibration and acoustic disturbances—signs of a shattered window—to help avoid false alarms. (www.getintellisense.com).

- **GPS tracking device**—Total Parental Information Awareness is here. Lock this GPS locator to your kids' wrist and whenever you want to check on them just query Wherify's web page. It pinpoints their location on a street map and displays an aerial photo (www.wherify.com).

- **Wireless speakers**—Sony's versatile 900-MHz speakers connect the RF receiver to your stereo, TV, or PC, and get crystal-clear audio anywhere within 150 feet (www.sonystyle.com).

In a group, create a document discussing how these new wireless technologies could potentially change the business arena and list at least one company for each technology that should view these new products as potential threats.

## 5. Saving Failing Systems

Signatures Inc. specializes in producing personalized products for companies, such as coffee mugs and pens with company logos. The company generates over $40 million in annual revenues and has more than 300 employees. The company is in the middle of a large multimillion-dollar SCM implementation and has just hired your Project Management Outsourcing firm to take over the project management efforts. On your first day, your team is told that the project is failing for the following reasons:

- The project is using the traditional waterfall methodology.
- The SDLC was not followed and the developers decided to skip the testing phase.
- A project plan was developed during the analysis phase, but the old project manager never updated or followed the plan.

In a group determine what your first steps would be to get this project back on track.

## ★ APPLY YOUR KNOWLEDGE

### 1. Connecting Components

Components of a solid enterprise architecture include everything from documentation to business concepts to software and hardware. Deciding which components to implement and how to implement them can be a challenge. New IT components are released daily, and business needs continually change. An enterprise architecture that meets your organization's needs today may not meet those needs tomorrow. Building an enterprise architecture that is scalable, flexible, available, accessible, and reliable is key to your organization's success.

### Project Focus

You are the enterprise architect for a large clothing company called Xedous. You are responsible for developing the initial enterprise architecture. Create a list of questions you will need answered to develop your architecture. Below are examples of a few questions you might ask.

- What are the company's growth expectations?
- Will systems be able to handle additional users?
- How long will information be stored in the systems?
- How much customer history must be stored?
- What are the organization's business hours?
- What are the organization's backup requirements?

### 2. Back on Your Feet

You are working for GetSmart, a document creation company for legal professionals. Due to the highly sensitive nature of the industry, employees must store all work on the network drive and are not allowed to back up the data to a CD, flash drive, or any other type of external storage including home computers. The company has been following this policy for the last three years without any issues. You return to work Monday morning after a long weekend to find that the building was struck by lightning destroying several servers. Unfortunately, the backup strategy failed and all of the data from your department has been lost.

When the head of the company demanded an explanation as to why there were no individual backups, he was shown the company policy he had signed not once but three times. The head of IT along with four of his cronies who had developed this ridiculous policy were fired.

### Project Focus

You have been placed on a committee with several of your peers to revamp the backup and recovery policies and create a new disaster recovery plan. You must create policies and procedures that will preserve the sensitive nature of the documents, while ensuring the company is safe from disasters. Be sure to address a worst-case scenario where the entire building is lost.

## 3. Confusing Coffee

Business requirements are the detailed set of business requests that any new system must meet in order to be successful. A sample business requirement might state, "The system must track all customer sales by product, region, and sales representative." This requirement states what the system must do from the business perspective, giving no details or information on how the system is going to meet this requirement.

### Project Focus

You have been hired to build an employee payroll system for a new coffee shop. Review the following business requirements and highlight any potential issues.

- All employees must have a unique employee ID.
- The system must track employee hours worked based on employee's last name.
- Employees must be scheduled to work a minimum of eight hours per day.
- Employee payroll is calculated by multiplying the employee's hours worked by $7.25.
- Managers must be scheduled to work morning shifts.
- Employees cannot be scheduled to work more than eight hours per day.
- Servers cannot be scheduled to work morning, afternoon, or evening shifts.
- The system must allow managers to change and delete employees from the system.

## 4. Picking Projects

You are a project management contractor attempting to contract work at a large telecommunications company, Hex Incorporated. Your interview with Debbie Fernandez, the senior vice president of IT, went smoothly. The last thing Debbie wants to see from you before she makes her final hiring decision is a prioritized list of the projects below. You are sure to land the job if Debbie is satisfied with your prioritization.

### Project Focus

Create a report for Debbie prioritizing the following projects and be sure to include the business justifications for your prioritization.

- Upgrade accounting system.
- Develop employee vacation tracking system.
- Enhance employee intranet.
- Cleanse and scrub data warehouse information.
- Performance test all hardware to ensure 20 percent growth scalability.
- Implement changes to employee benefits system.

- Develop backup and recovery strategy.
- Implement supply chain management system.
- Upgrade customer relationship management system.
- Build executive information system for CEO.

## 5. Keeping Time

Time Keepers Inc. is a small firm that specializes in project management consulting. You are a senior project manager, and you have recently been assigned to the Tahiti Tanning Lotion account. The Tahiti Tanning Lotion company is currently experiencing a 10 percent success rate (90 percent failure rate) on all internal IT projects. Your first assignment is to analyze one of the current project plans being used to develop a new CRM system (see Figure AYK.1).

### Project Focus

Review the project plan and create a document listing the numerous errors in the plan. Be sure to also provide suggestions on how to fix the errors.

## 6. Growing, Growing, Gone

You are the founder of Black Pearl, a small comic book start-up. The good news is Black Pearl has found tremendous success. You have 34 employees in a creative, yet functional, office in downtown Chicago. The comics you produce are of extremely high quality. The artwork is unmatched and the story lines are compelling, gripping, and addictive, according to your customers. Your comics are quickly becoming a cult classic and Black Pearl customers are extremely loyal. You produce all of the comics and sell them in your store and via the Internet to individuals all over the United States.

**FIGURE AYK.1**

Sample Project Plan

### Project Focus

You had vision when you started Black Pearl. You knew the potential of your business model to revamp the comic industry. You purchased high-end computers and customizable software to support your operations. Now, you are faced with a new dilemma. You have a large international following and you have decided to pursue international opportunities. You would like to open stores in Japan, France, and Brazil during the next year. To determine if this is possible, you need to evaluate your current systems to see if they are flexible and scalable enough to perform business internationally. You know that you are going to run into many international business issues. Create a list of questions you need to answer to determine if your systems are capable of performing international business.

### 7. The Virtualization Opportunity

Virtualization makes good business sense. Organizations recognize the opportunity to use virtualization to break down the silos that keep applications from sharing infrastructure and that contribute to chronic underutilization of IT resources. Virtualization can help an organization simultaneously reduce costs, increase agility, and make IT more responsive to the needs of the business. So for many organizations, the question is not, "Should we virtualize?" Instead, the question is, "How can we transition to a virtualized environment in a predictable, cost-effective manner?"

### Project Focus

You are the CFO for Martello's, a food distribution organization with locations in Chicago, New York, and San Francisco. Your CIO, Jeff Greenwald, has given you a proposal for a budget of $2 million to convert the organization to a virtualized environment. You are unfamiliar with virtualization, how it works, and the long-term goals it will satisfy for the company. You have a meeting with Jeff tomorrow and you want to be able to discuss his proposal. Use the Internet to research virtualization to prepare for your meeting. Once you have a solid understanding of virtualization, create a report detailing your decision to grant or deny Jeff's budget proposal.

---

⁎ **BUSINESS DRIVEN BEST SELLERS**

*Death March: The Complete Software Developer's Guide to Surviving "Mission Impossible" Projects.* **By Edward Yourdon (Prentice Hall, 1997).**

Today, IT projects are expected to achieve the impossible, overcome numerous constraints, and deal with elevated stress levels and imperfect working conditions. In *Death March,* legendary software developer Edward Yourdon comes to the rescue. Yourdan developed the *Death March* project style quadrant as displayed on the top of the next page.

Yourdon takes direct aim at the projects that are "doomed to fail" presenting specific techniques for:

- Managing people and teams.
- Choosing the right processes.
- Making decisions about tools and technologies.
- Getting the flexibility you need to succeed.

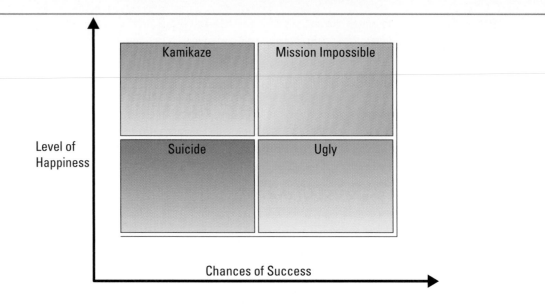

### A Survival Guide for Working with Humans. By Gini Graham Scott (AMACOM, 2004).

To succeed in the workplace, good work relationships must be carefully developed and maintained. Although difficult people, back stabbers, whiners, know-it-alls, and others can make it hard to get through the workweek, many coping mechanisms can be put into place that can improve work relationships and improve productivity and communications. In *A Survival Guide for Working with Humans,* author and consultant Gini Graham Scott offers dozens of practical tools and examples that can help others resolve everyday conflicts and survive their jobs.

*A Survival Guide for Working with Humans* offers an eye-opening approach for coping with the idiosyncrasies and difficulties other people can present in the workplace. By focusing on specific work issues and providing relevant vignettes that describe the work issues involved, as well as a list of instructions to follow in similar circumstances, Scott takes the struggle out of conflicts and replaces it with strategy.

### What Matters Most: How a Small Group of Pioneers Is Teaching Social Responsibility to Big Business, and Why Big Business Is Listening. By Jeffrey Hollender and Stephen Fenichell (Basic Books, 2006).

While many people might assume that corporate social responsibility emerged with the Ben & Jerry's and The Body Shops of this world, the concept of a corporation having more responsibility than just making money for its owners is not new, as Jeffrey Hollender points out in this new book, *What Matters Most.* Hollender quotes Friedman's 1963 book *Capitalism and Freedom,* in which Friedman argued that "there is one and only one social responsibility of business—to use its resources and engage in activities designed to increase its profit so long as it stays within the rules of the game, which is to say, engages in open and free competition without deception or fraud." If corporations start believing that they have any responsibility to society, Friedman continues, the result can only be the end of freedom, for corporations will be ruled by "the iron fist of government bureaucrats."

### Management Challenges for the 21st Century. By Peter F. Drucker (Harpercollins Publishers, 1999).

With the new millennium, much of what we have come to accept as true of business management is about to be challenged. The world is changing at a rapid pace, and only those who understand what those changes mean will be poised to prosper under the new rules. Old paradigms will be replaced by new ones.

This book summarizes which old assumptions are out. You will learn that management is not just business management and that there is no one ideal way to organize an enterprise. Nor, is there one way to manage people. In fact, the manager's role will not be to manage at all. Rather, the manager's job is to lead. National boundaries and even regional markets will no longer define an organization's boundaries.

The book also reveals the trends that will radically alter life and how companies are run. The developed world is experiencing a collapse of its birthrate, and an accompanying increase in the average age of its populations. The result will be political upheaval, a new emphasis on personal investment, and a substantial increase in the length of work life.

# PLUG-IN B

# Business Plug-Ins

The overall goal of the Business Plug-Ins is to enhance the coverage of text topics such as business processes, security, ethics, globalization, supply chain management, and so on. The flexibility of *Business Driven Technology* allows faculty to cover the additional material located in the Business Plug-Ins whenever they choose throughout the course. For example, if you want to cover security and ethics in the beginning of your course you can assign Unit 1, Business Plug-In B6 *Information Security* and Business Plug-In B7 *Ethics* during the first week of classes. If you choose to cover security and ethics during the end of your course you can assign Unit 5, Business Plug-In B6 *Information Security* and Business Plug-In B7 *Ethics* during your final week of classes. The flexibility of the Business Plug-Ins allows faculty to custom develop their course to meet their specific teaching needs. Business Plug-Ins are located in the text and online as downloadable PDFs at www.mhhe.com/bdt4e.

**PLUG-IN B1 >>**

## BUSINESS BASICS   www.mhhe.com/bdt4e

B1 provides a comprehensive overview of business basics and should be assigned to any students who are new to the business environment. Plug-In B1 includes:

- Types of business: sole proprietorship, partnership, corporation
- Internal operations of a corporation: accounting, finance, human resources, sales, marketing, operations/production, and management information systems
- Business fundamentals: sales process, market share, marketing mix, customer segmentation, product life cycle, operations/production, business process reengineering

**PLUG-IN B2 >>**

## BUSINESS PROCESS   www.mhhe.com/bdt4e

B2 dives deeper into the world of business by reviewing business processes and their impacts on organizations. This is a great plug-in to cover early in the course if you plan on spending a significant amount of time covering enterprisewide processes. There are a number of sample business process models diagramming such processes as order entry, online bill payment, ebusiness processes, and process improvement. Plug-In B2 includes:

- Business processes
- Continuous process improvement
- Business process reengineering
- Business process modeling

**<< PLUG-IN B3**

## HARDWARE AND SOFTWARE   www.mhhe.com/bdt4e

B3 covers the two basic categories of information technology; (1) hardware, (2) software. Information technology can be composed of the Internet, a personal computer, a cell phone that can access the web, a personal digital assistant, or presentation software. All of these technologies help to perform specific information processing tasks. Plug-In B3 includes:

- Hardware basics: central processing unit, primary storage, secondary storage, input devices, output devices, communication devices, computer categories
- Software basics: system software, application software

**<< PLUG-IN B4**

## ENTERPRISE ARCHITECTURES   www.mhhe.com/bdt4e

B4 discusses the essentials of how an organization will build, deploy, use, and share its data, processes, and IT assets. To support the volume and complexity of today's user and application requirements, information technology needs to take a fresh approach to enterprise architectures by constructing smarter, more flexible environments that protect it from system failures and crashes. A solid enterprise architecture can decrease costs, increase standardization, promote reuse of IT assets, and speed development of new systems. The end result is that the right enterprise architecture can make IT cheaper, strategic, and more responsive. Plug-In B4 includes:

- Information architecture: backup and recovery, disaster recovery, information security
- Infrastructure architecture: flexibility, scalability, reliability, availability, performance
- Application architecture: web services, open systems

**<< PLUG-IN B5**

## NETWORKS AND TELECOMMUNICATIONS   www.mhhe.com/bdt4e

B5 offers a detailed look at telecommunication systems and networks. Businesses around the world are moving to network infrastructure solutions that allow greater choice in how they go to market; the solutions have a global reach. This plug-in takes a detailed look at key telecommunication and network technologies that are integrating businesses around the world. Plug-In B5 includes:

- Network basics: architecture, peer-to-peer networks, client/server networks
- Topology: bus, star, ring, hybrid, wireless
- Protocols: ethernet, transmission control protocol/Internet protocol
- Media: wire media, wireless media
- Business advantages: voice over IP, networking businesses, increasing the speed of business, securing business networks

- Extended ERP components: business intelligence, customer relationship management, supply chain management, ebusiness
- ERP benefits and risks (costs)
- The Future of ERP: Internet, interface, wireless technology

## EBUSINESS   p. 378

PLUG-IN B11

B11 presents an overview of how business functions are using the Internet to reshape the way they conduct business and explore the complex network of suppliers, distributors, and customers who deal with each other via the Internet. Plug-In B11 includes:

- Accessing Internet information: intranet, extranet, portal, kiosk
- Providing Internet information: Internet service provider, online service provider, application service provider
- Organizational strategies for e-business: marketing, sales, financial services, procurement, customer service
- Measuring ebusiness success: website metrics
- Future trends: egovernment, mcommerce

## GLOBAL TRENDS   www.mhhe.com/bdt4e

PLUG-IN B12

B12 explores the importance for an organization to anticipate and prepare for the future. Having a global view of emerging trends and new technologies as they relate to business can provide an organization with a valuable strategic advantage. Plug-In B12 includes:

- Reasons to watch trends
- Trends shaping our future
- Technologies shaping our future

## STRATEGIC OUTSOURCING   www.mhhe.com/bdt4e

PLUG-IN B13

B13 describes outsourcing as a strategic mechanism that aligns technology initiatives and business goals, manages technology operations in a difficult business environment, and reduces operating costs. Often, companies begin the process by outsourcing nonessential business operations, which may include applications, assets, people, and other resources. As organizations realize the benefits of outsourcing, they extend this approach to other business functions or processes. Plug-In B13 includes:

- The leaders—countries that are leading the outsourcing industry
- The up-and-comers—countries that are beginning to emerge as solid outsourcing options
- The rookies—countries that are just entering the outsourcing industry

## SYSTEMS DEVELOPMENT   p. 400

PLUG-IN B14

B14 reviews the systems development life cycle, which is the foundation for all systems development methodologies, and there are literally hundreds of different activities associated with each phase in the SDLC. Typical activities include determining budgets, gathering system requirements, and writing detailed user documentation. The activities performed during each systems development project will vary. This plug-in takes a detailed look at a few of the more common activities performed during the systems development life cycle, along with common issues facing software development projects. Plug-In B14 includes:

- Phase 1: Planning
- Phase 2: Analysis
- Phase 3: Design
- Phase 4: Development
- Phase 5: Testing
- Phase 6: Implementation
- Phase 7: Maintenance

## PLUG-IN B15 >> PROJECT MANAGEMENT p. 418

B15 takes a deeper look at the project manager's role in developing successful information systems using a variety of project management strategies and tools. Plug-In B15 includes:

- Choosing strategic projects
- Understanding project planning
- Managing projects
- Risk management

## PLUG-IN B16 >> OPERATIONS MANAGEMENT p. 432

B16 covers operations management, which is the management of systems or processes that convert or transform resources (including human resources) into goods and services. Operations management is responsible for managing the core processes used to manufacture goods and produce services. Plug-In B16 includes:

- Operations management's role in business
- Information technology's role in operations management
- Strategic business systems
- Competitive strategy: cost, quality, delivery, flexibility, service
- Operations management and the supply chain

## PLUG-IN B17 >> ORGANIZATIONAL ARCHITECTURE TRENDS p. 448

B17 discusses organizational architecture trends that help keep businesses up-and-running 24x7x365 while continuing to be flexible, scalable, reliable, and available is no easy task. Organizations today must continually watch new architecture trends to ensure they can keep up with new and disruptive technologies. This section discusses four architecture trends that are quickly becoming requirements for all businesses. Plug-In B17 includes:

- Service-oriented architectures
- Virtualization
- Grid computing
- Cloud computing

## BUSINESS INTELLIGENCE   p. 466

<< PLUG-IN B18

B18 uncovers why many organizations today find it next to impossible to understand their own strengths and weaknesses, let alone their enemies', because the enormous volume of organizational data is inaccessible to all but the IT department. Organization data include far more than simple fields in a database; it also includes voice mail, customer phone calls, text messages, video clips, along with numerous new forms of data. Business intelligence (BI) refers to applications and technologies that are used to gather, provide access to, and analyze data and information to support decision-making efforts. Plug-In B18 includes:

- The problem: data rich, information poor
- The solution: business intelligence
- Operational, tactical, and strategic BI
- BI's operational value
- Data mining cluster analysis: association detection, statistical analysis
- Business benefits of BI: quantifiable benefits, indirectly quantifiable benefits, unpredictable benefits, intangible benefits

## GLOBAL INFORMATION SYSTEMS   p. 486

<< PLUG-IN B19

B19 covers globalization and working in an international global economy, which are integral parts of business today. Fortune 500 companies to mom-and-pop shops are now competing globally, and international developments affect all forms of business. Whether they are in Berlin or Bombay, Kuala Lumpur or Kansas City, San Francisco or Seoul, organizations around the globe are developing new business models to operate competitively in a digital economy. These models are structured, yet agile; global, yet local; and they concentrate on maximizing the risk-adjusted return from both knowledge and technology assets. Plug-In B19 includes:

- Globalization
- Global IT business strategies
- Global enterprise architectures
- Global information issues
- Global systems development

## INNOVATION, SOCIAL ENTREPRENEURSHIP, SOCIAL NETWORKING, AND VIRTUAL WORLDS   p. 504

<< PLUG-IN B20

B20 looks at organizations that want to survive in the 21st century and how they must recognize the technological changes and challenges, carry out required organizational changes in the face of it, and learn to operate in an entirely different way. Today's organizations focus on defending and safeguarding their existing market positions in addition to targeting new market growth. Plug-In B20 includes:

- Innovation: finding new
- Social entrepreneurship: going green
- Social networks: who's who
- Virtual worlds: it's a whole new world

B21 examines how mobile computing allows people to use IT without being tied to a single location. However, a relatively small number of enterprises (less than 25 percent) have a specific mobile strategy in place. Most struggle with individual mobile projects or try to link mobility to a broader IT strategy. Companies must focus on building a mobile strategy that addresses the peculiarities inherent in mobile computing. Understanding the different types of mobile technologies available will help executives determine how to best equip their workforce. Plug-In B21 includes:

- Using cellular technologies in business
- Using satellite technologies in business
- Using wireless technologies in business

# Technology Plug-Ins

The overall goal of the Technology Plug-Ins is to provide additional information not covered in the text such as personal productivity using information technology, problem solving using Excel, and decision making using Access. These plug-ins also offer an all-in-one text to faculty, avoiding their having to purchase an extra book to support Microsoft Office. These plug-ins offer integration with the core chapters and provide critical knowledge using essential business applications, such as Microsoft Excel, Microsoft Access, and Microsoft Project with hands-on tutorials for comprehension and mastery. Plug-Ins T1 to T12 are located on this textbook's website at www.mhhe.com/bdt4e.

**PLUG-IN T1 >>**  **PERSONAL PRODUCTIVITY USING IT**   www.mhhe.com/bdt4e

This plug-in covers a number of things to do to keep a personal computer running effectively and efficiently. The 12 topics covered in this plug-in are:

- Creating strong passwords.
- Performing good file management.
- Implementing effective backup and recovery strategies.
- Using Zip files.
- Writing professional emails.
- Stopping spam.
- Preventing phishing.
- Detecting spyware.
- Threads to instant messaging.
- Increasing PC performance.
- Using anti-virus software.
- Installing a personal firewall.

## BASIC SKILLS USING EXCEL   www.mhhe.com/bdt4e

**<< PLUG-IN** T2

This plug-in introduces the basics of using Microsoft Excel, a spreadsheet program for data analysis, along with a few fancy features. The six topics covered in this plug-in are:

- Workbooks and worksheets.
- Working with cells and cell data.
- Printing worksheets.
- Formatting worksheets.
- Formulas.
- Working with charts and graphics.

## PROBLEM SOLVING USING EXCEL   www.mhhe.com/bdt4e

**<< PLUG-IN** T3

This plug-in provides a comprehensive tutorial on how to use a variety of Microsoft Excel functions and features for problem solving. The five areas covered in this plug-in are:

- Lists
- Conditional Formatting
- AutoFilter
- Subtotals
- PivotTables

## DECISION MAKING USING EXCEL   www.mhhe.com/bdt4e

**<< PLUG-IN** T4

This plug-in examines a few of the advanced business analysis tools used in Microsoft Excel that have the capability to identify patterns, trends, and rules, and create "what-if" models. The four topics covered in this plug-in are:

- IF
- Goal Seek
- Solver
- Scenario Manager

## DESIGNING DATABASE APPLICATIONS   www.mhhe.com/bdt4e

**<< PLUG-IN** T5

This plug-in provides specific details on how to design relational database applications. One of the most efficient and powerful information management computer-based applications is the relational database. The four topics covered in this plug-in are:

- Entities and data relationships.
- Documenting logical data relationships.
- The relational data model.
- Normalization.

## BASIC SKILLS USING ACCESS   www.mhhe.com/bdt4e

**<< PLUG-IN** T6

This plug-in focuses on creating a Microsoft Access database file. One of the most efficient information management computer-based applications is Microsoft Access.

Access provides a powerful set of tools for creating and maintaining a relational database. The two topics covered in this plug-in are:

- Create a new database file.
- Create and modify tables.

**PLUG-IN T7 >>** **PROBLEM SOLVING USING ACCESS**   www.mhhe.com/bdt4e

This plug-in provides a comprehensive tutorial on how to query a database in Microsoft Access. Queries are essential for problem solving, allowing a user to sort information, summarize data (display totals, averages, counts, and so on), display the results of calculations on data, and choose exactly which fields are shown. The three topics in this plug-in are:

- Create simple queries using the simple query wizard.
- Create advanced queries using calculated fields.
- Format results displayed in calculated fields.

**PLUG-IN T8 >>** **DECISION MAKING USING ACCESS**   www.mhhe.com/bdt4e

This plug-in provides a comprehensive tutorial on entering data in a well-designed form and creating functional reports using Microsoft Access. A form is essential to use for data entry and a report is an effective way to present data in a printed format. The two topics in this plug-in are:

- Creating, modifying, and running forms.
- Creating, modifying, and running reports.

**PLUG-IN T9 >>** **DESIGNING WEB PAGES**   www.mhhe.com/bdt4e

This plug-in provides a comprehensive assessment into the functional aspects of web design. Websites are beginning to look more alike and to employ the same metaphors and conventions. The web has now become an everyday thing whose design should not make users think. The six topics in this plug-in are:

- The World Wide Web.
- Designing for the unknown(s).
- The process of web design.
- HTML basics.
- Web fonts.
- Web graphics.

**PLUG-IN T10 >>** **CREATING WEB PAGES USING HTML**   www.mhhe.com/bdt4e

This plug-in provides an overview of creating web pages using the HTML language. HTML is a system of codes that you use to create interactive web pages. It provides a means to describe the structure of text-based information in a document—by denoting certain text as headings, paragraphs, lists, and so on. The seven topics in this plug-in are:

- An introduction to HTML.
- HTML tools.
- Creating, saving, and viewing HTML documents.
- Applying style tags and attributes.
- Using fancy formatting.
- Creating hyperlinks.
- Displaying graphics.

## CREATING WEB PAGES USING DREAMWEAVER www.mhhe.com/bdt4e

>> PLUG-IN T11

This plug-in provides a tour of using Dreamweaver to create web pages. Dreamweaver allows anyone with limited web page design experience to create, modify, and maintain full-featured, professional-looking pages without having to learn how to code all the functions and features from scratch. The five topics in this plug-in are:

- Navigation in Dreamweaver.
- Adding content.
- Formatting content.
- Using cascading style sheets.
- Creating tables.

## CREATING GANTT CHARTS WITH EXCEL AND MICROSOFT PROJECT www.mhhe.com/bdt4e

>> PLUG-IN T12

This plug-in offers a quick and efficient way to manage projects. Excel and Microsoft Project are great for managing all phases of a project, creating templates, collaborating on planning processes, tracking project progress, and sharing information with all interested parties. The two topics in this plug-in are:

- Creating Gantt Charts with Excel.
- Creating Gantt Charts with Microsoft Project.

# Information Security

1. Describe the relationship between information security policies and an information security plan.

2. Summarize the five steps to creating an information security plan.

3. Provide an example of each of the three primary security areas: (1) authentication and authorization, (2) prevention and resistance, and (3) detection and response.

4. Describe the relationships and differences between hackers and viruses.

## Introduction

The core units introduced *information security,* which is a broad term encompassing the protection of information from accidental or intentional misuse by persons inside or outside an organization. With current advances in technologies and business strategies such as CRM, organizations are able to determine valuable information such as who are the top 20 percent of the customers that produce 80 percent of all revenues. Most organizations view this type of information as valuable intellectual capital, and they are implementing security measures to prevent the information from walking out the door or falling into the wrong hands. This plug-in discusses how an organization can implement information security lines of defense through people first and through technology second.

## The First Line of Defense—People

Adding to the complexity of information security is the fact that organizations must enable employees, customers, and partners to access information electronically to be successful in this electronic world. Doing business electronically automatically creates tremendous information security risks for organizations. Surprisingly, the biggest issue surrounding information security is not a technical issue, but a people issue.

The CSI/FBI Computer Crime and Security Survey reported that 38 percent of respondents indicated security incidents originated within the enterprise. *Insiders* are legitimate users who purposely or accidentally misuse their access to the environment and cause some kind of business-affecting incident. Most information security breaches result from people misusing an organization's information either advertently or inadvertently. For example, many individuals freely give up their passwords or write them on sticky notes next to their computers, leaving the door wide open to intruders.

The director of information security at a large health care company discovered how easy it was to create an information security breach when she hired outside auditors to test her company's security awareness. In one instance, auditors found that staff members testing a new system had accidentally exposed the network to outside hackers. In another, auditors were able to obtain the passwords of 16 employees when the auditors posed as support staff; hackers frequently use such "social engineering" to obtain passwords. *Social engineering* is using one's social skills to trick people into revealing access credentials or other information valuable to the attacker. Dumpster diving, or looking through people's trash, is another way social engineering hackers obtain information.

*Information security policies* identify the rules required to maintain information security. An *information security plan* details how an organization will implement the information security policies. Figure B6.1 is an example of the University of Denver's Information Security Plan.

### Interim Information Security Plan

This Information Security Plan ("Plan") describes the University of Denver's safeguards to protect information and data in compliance ("Protected Information") with the Financial Services Modernization Act of 1999, also known as the Gramm Leach Bliley Act, 15 U.S.C. Section 6801. These safeguards are provided to:

- Ensure the security and confidentiality of Protected Information;
- Protect against anticipated threats or hazards to the security or integrity of such information; and
- Protect against unauthorized access to or use of Protected Information that could result in substantial harm or inconvenience to any customer.

This Information Security Plan also provides for mechanisms to:

- Identify and assess the risks that may threaten Protected Information maintained by the University of Denver;
- Develop written policies and procedures to manage and control these risks;
- Implement and review the plan; and
- Adjust the plan to reflect changes in technology, the sensitivity of covered data and information and internal or external threats to information security.

**Identification and Assessment of Risks to Customer Information**

The University of Denver recognizes that it has both internal and external risks. These risks include, but are not limited to:

- Unauthorized access of Protected Information by someone other than the owner of the covered data and information
- Compromised system security as a result of system access by an unauthorized person
- Interception of data during transmission
- Loss of data integrity
- Physical loss of data in a disaster
- Errors introduced into the system
- Corruption of data or systems
- Unauthorized access of covered data and information by employees
- Unauthorized requests for covered data and information
- Unauthorized access through hardcopy files or reports
- Unauthorized transfer of covered data and information through third parties

The University of Denver recognizes that this may not be a complete list of the risks associated with the protection of Protected Information. Since technology growth is not static, new risks are created regularly. Accordingly, the Information Technology Department and the Office of Student Affairs will actively participate with and seek advice from an advisory committee made up of university representatives for identification of new risks. The University of Denver believes current safeguards used by the Information Technology Department are reasonable and, in light of current risk assessments, are sufficient to provide security and confidentiality to Protected Information maintained by the University.

*(Continued)*

**Interim Information Security Plan**

**Information Security Plan Coordinators**

The University CIO and the Vice President for Student Affairs, in consultation with an advisory committee, have been appointed as the coordinators of this Plan. They are responsible for assessing the risks associated with unauthorized transfers of covered data and information and implementing procedures to minimize those risks to the University of Denver.

**Design and Implementation of Safeguards Program**

**Employee Management and Training**

During employee orientation, each new employee in departments that handle Protected Information will receive proper training on the importance of confidentiality of Protected Information.

**Physical Security**

The University of Denver has addressed the physical security of Protected Information by limiting access to only those employees who have a business reason to know such information.

**Information Systems**

The University of Denver has policies governing the use of electronic resources and firewall and wireless policies. The University of Denver will take reasonable and appropriate steps consistent with current technological developments to make sure that all Protected Information is secure and to safeguard the integrity of records in storage and transmission. The University of Denver will develop a plan to ensure that all electronic Protected Information is encrypted in transit.

**Selection of Appropriate Service Providers**

Due to the specialized expertise needed to design, implement, and service new technologies, vendors may be needed to provide resources that the University of Denver determines not to provide on its own. In the process of choosing a service provider that will maintain or regularly access Protected Information, the evaluation process shall include the ability of the service provider to safeguard Protected Information. Contracts with service providers may include the following provisions:

- A stipulation that the Protected Information will be held in strict confidence and accessed only for the explicit business purpose of the contract;
- An assurance from the contract partner that the partner will protect the Protected Information it receives.

**Continuing Evaluation and Adjustment**

This Information Security Plan will be subject to periodic review and adjustment, especially when due to the constantly changing technology and evolving risks. The Coordinators, in consultation with the Office of General Counsel, will review the standards set forth in this policy and recommend updates and revisions as necessary. It may be necessary to adjust the plan to reflect changes in technology, the sensitivity of student/customer data and internal or external threats to information security.

**FIGURE B6.1**
*(Continued)*

The first line of defense an organization should follow is to create an information security plan detailing the various information security policies. A detailed information security plan can alleviate people-based information security issues. Businesses consider desktop users to be the biggest security risk to their networks, despite increased concern over outsourced labor and remote users. Figures from a recent Sophos network security survey indicated that businesses still see office-bound employees as those most likely to expose their networks to IT threats. Such users were considered the greatest threat to security by 44 percent of respondents. Mobile employees are considered to be a greater security threat by 31 percent of respondents. Other users considered to be a threat to network security include contractors and outsourced labor, at 14 percent, and guests, at 11 percent. Sophos's head of technology, Paul Ducklin, said, "This is a representation of how common telecommuting and remote working has become," to the extent that half of those in the office are also remote workers. "The obvious thing we can draw from the results is that administrators haven't become complacent about desktop security," Ducklin said. He also pointed out that while some organizations employ a "stricter regimen for outside than inside," the physical risks to equipment associated with mobile users—such as the loss of or damage to a laptop—are unavoidable. Figure B6.2 displays the five steps for creating an information security plan. Figure B6.3 provides the top 10 questions from Ernst & Young that managers should ask to ensure their information is secure.

| Five Steps for Creating an Information Security Plan | |
|---|---|
| 1. **Develop the information security policies** | Identify who is responsible and accountable for designing and implementing the organization's information security policies. Simple, yet highly effective types of information security policies include requiring users to log off of their systems before leaving for lunches or meetings, never sharing passwords with anyone, and changing personal passwords every 60 days. The chief security officer (CSO) will typically be responsible for designing these information security policies. |
| 2. **Communicate the information security policies** | Train all employees on the policies and establish clear expectations for following the policies. For example, let all employees know that they will receive a formal reprimand for leaving a computer unsecured. |
| 3. **Identify critical information assets and risks** | Require the use of user IDs, passwords, and antivirus software on all systems. Ensure any systems that contain links to external networks have the appropriate technical protections such as firewalls or intrusion detection software. A *firewall* is hardware and/or software that guards a private network by analyzing the information leaving and entering the network. *Intrusion detection software (IDS)* searches out patterns in information and network traffic to indicate attacks and quickly responds to prevent any harm. |
| 4. **Test and reevaluate risks** | Continually perform security reviews, audits, background checks, and security assessments. |
| 5. **Obtain stakeholder support** | Gain the approval and support of the information security polices from the board of directors and all stakeholders. |

**FIGURE** B6.2

Creating an Information Security Plan

# The Second Line of Defense—Technology

Arkansas State University (ASU) recently completed a major network upgrade that brought gigabit-speed network capacity to every dorm room and office on its campus. The university was concerned that the new network would be a tempting playground for hackers. To reduce its fear the university decided to install intrusion detection software (IDS) from Cisco Systems to stay on top of security and potential network abuses. Whenever the IDS spots a potential security threat, such as a virus or a hacker, it alerts the central management system. The system automatically

**FIGURE** B6.3

Top 10 Questions Managers Should Ask Regarding Information Security

| Top 10 Questions Managers Should Ask Regarding Information Security |
|---|
| 1. Does the board of directors recognize information security is a board-level issue that cannot be left to the IT department alone? |
| 2. Is there clear accountability for information security in the organization? |
| 3. Do the board members articulate an agreed-upon set of threats and critical assets? How often do they review and update these? |
| 4. How much is spent on information security and what is it being spent on? |
| 5. What is the impact on the organization of a serious security incident? |
| 6. Does the organization view information security as an enabler? (For example, by implementing effective security, could the organization increase business over the Internet?) |
| 7. What is the risk to the business of getting a reputation for low information security? |
| 8. What steps have been taken to ensure that third parties will not compromise the security of the organization? |
| 9. How does the organization obtain independent assurance that information security is managed effectively? |
| 10. How does the organization measure the effectiveness of its information security activities? |

pages the IT staff, who deal with the attack by shutting off access to the system, identifying the hacker's location, and calling campus security.

Once an organization has protected its intellectual capital by arming its people with a detailed information security plan, it can begin to focus its efforts on deploying the right types of information security technologies such as the IDS installed at Arkansas State.

Organizations can deploy numerous technologies to prevent information security breaches. When determining which types of technologies to invest in, it helps to understand the three primary information security areas:

1. Authentication and authorization.
2. Prevention and resistance.
3. Detection and response.

## AUTHENTICATION AND AUTHORIZATION

*Authentication* is a method for confirming users' identities. Once a system determines the authentication of a user, it can then determine the access privileges (or authorization) for that user. *Authorization* is the process of giving someone permission to do or have something. In multiple-user computer systems, user access or authorization determines such things as file access, hours of access, and amount of allocated storage space. Authentication and authorization techniques are broken down into three categories, and the most secure type involves a combination of all three:

1. Something the user knows such as a user ID and password.
2. Something the user has such as a smart card or token.
3. Something that is part of the user such as a fingerprint or voice signature.

### Something the User Knows such as a User ID and Password

The first type of authentication, using something the user knows, is the most common way to identify individual users and typically consists of a unique user ID and password. However, this is actually one of the most *ineffective* ways for determining authentication because passwords are not secure. All it typically takes to crack a password is enough time. More than 50 percent of help-desk calls are password related, which can cost an organization significant money, and passwords are vulnerable to being coaxed out of somebody by a social engineer.

*Identity theft* is the forging of someone's identity for the purpose of fraud. The fraud is often financial fraud, to apply for and use credit cards or to apply for a loan in the victim's name. By 2003, online banking was not yet ubiquitous but everyone could see that, eventually, it would be. "Everyone" includes Internet criminals, who by then had already built software capable of surreptitiously grabbing personal information from online forms, like the ones used for online banking. The first of these so-called form-grabbing viruses was called Berbew and was wildly effective. Lance James, a researcher with Secure Science Corp., believes it operated undetected for as long as nine months and grabbed as much as 113GB of data—millions of personal credentials. Like all exploits, Berbew was eventually detected and contained, but, as is customary with viruses, strands of Berbew's form-grabbing code were stitched into new viruses that had adapted to defenses. The process is not unlike horticulturalists' grafting pieces of one plant onto another in order to create hardier mums. Figure B6.4 displays several examples of identity theft.

Phishing is a common way to steal identities online. *Phishing* is a technique to gain personal information for the purpose of identity theft, usually by means of fraudulent email. One way to accomplish phishing is to send out email messages that look as though they came from legitimate businesses such as AOL, MSN, or Amazon. The messages appear to be genuine with official-looking formats and logos.

| Identity Theft Examples |
| --- |
| An 82-year-old woman in Fort Worth, Texas, discovered that her identity had been stolen when the woman using her name was involved in a four-car collision. For 18 months, she kept getting notices of lawsuits and overdue medical bills that were really meant for someone else. It took seven years for her to get her financial good name restored after the identity thief charged over $100,000 on her 12 fraudulently acquired credit cards. |
| A 42-year-old retired Army captain in Rocky Hill, Connecticut, found that an identity thief had spent $260,000 buying goods and services that included two trucks, a Harley-Davidson motorcycle, and a time-share vacation home in South Carolina. The victim discovered his problem only when his retirement pay was garnished to pay the outstanding bills. |
| In New York, members of a pickpocket ring forged the driver's licenses of their victims within hours of snatching the women's purses. Stealing a purse typically results in around $200, if not less. But stealing the person's identity can net on average between $4,000 and $10,000. |
| A crime gang took out $8 million worth of second mortgages on victims' homes. It turned out the source of all the instances of identity theft came from a car dealership. |
| The largest identity-theft scam to date in U.S. history was broken up by police in 2002 when they discovered that three men had downloaded credit reports using stolen passwords and sold them to criminals on the street for $60 each. Many millions of dollars were stolen from people in all 50 states. |

These emails typically ask for verification of important information like passwords and account numbers. The reason given is often that this personal information is required for accounting or auditing purposes. Since the emails look authentic, up to one in five recipients respond with the information, and subsequently become victim of identity theft and other fraud.

### Something the User Has such as a Smart Card or Token

The second type of authentication, using something that the user has, offers a much more effective way to identify individuals than a user ID and password. Tokens and smart cards are two of the primary forms of this type of authentication. **Tokens** are small electronic devices that change user passwords automatically. The user enters his/her user ID and token displayed password to gain access to the network. A **smart card** is a device that is around the same size as a credit card, containing embedded technologies that can store information and small amounts of software to perform some limited processing. Smart cards can act as identification instruments, a form of digital cash, or a data storage device with the ability to store an entire medical record.

### Something That Is Part of the User such as a Fingerprint or Voice Signature

The third kind of authentication, using something that is part of the user, is by far the best and most effective way to manage authentication. **Biometrics** (narrowly defined) is the identification of a user based on a physical characteristic, such as a fingerprint, iris, face, voice, or handwriting. Unfortunately, biometric authentication can be costly and intrusive. For example, iris scans are expensive and considered intrusive by most people. Fingerprint authentication is less intrusive and inexpensive but is also not 100 percent accurate. Biometrics are being used to help clear airport security in about four minutes. The Clear Card is a preregistered form of ID that lets travelers bypass airport security lines. The card works by storing iris and fingerprint biometrics of inside a microchip on the card. At the airport, the user swipes the card at a security kiosk and the computer matches the biometrics on the card with the customer's fingerprint or iris. If they match, the user is ready for takeoff. The card is available for $100 along with a $28 fee for a Transportation Security Administration background check.

## PREVENTION AND RESISTANCE

Prevention and resistance technologies stop intruders from accessing intellectual capital. A division of Sony Inc., Sony Pictures Entertainment (SPE), defends itself from attacks by using an intrusion detection system to detect new attacks as they occur. SPE develops and distributes a wide variety of products including movies, television, videos, and DVDs. A compromise to SPE security could result in costing the company valuable intellectual capital as well as millions of dollars and months of time. The company needed an advanced threat management solution that would take fewer resources to maintain and require limited resources to track and respond to suspicious network activity. The company installed an advanced intrusion detection system allowing it to monitor all of its network activity including any potential security breaches.

The cost of downtime or network operation failures can be devastating to any business. For example, eBay experienced a 22-hour outage that caused the company's market cap to plunge an incredible $5.7 billion. Downtime costs for businesses can vary from $100 to $1 million per hour. An organization must prepare for and anticipate these types of outages resulting most commonly from hackers and viruses. Technologies available to help prevent and build resistance to attacks include (1) content filtering, (2) encryption, and (3) firewalls.

### Content Filtering

*Content filtering* occurs when organizations use software that filters content to prevent the transmission of unauthorized information. Organizations can use content filtering technologies to filter email and prevent emails containing sensitive information from transmitting, whether the transmission was malicious or accidental. It can also filter emails and prevent any suspicious files from transmitting such as potential virus-infected files. Email content filtering can also filter for *spam,* a form of unsolicited email. Organizational losses from spam were estimated to be about $198 billion in 2007 (see Figure B6.5).

Sean Lane's purchase was supposed to be a surprise for his wife. Then it appeared as a news headline, "Sean Lane Bought 14k White Gold 1/5 ct Diamond Eternity Flower Ring from overstock.com," on the social networking website Facebook. Without Lane's knowledge, the headline was visible to everyone in his online network, including 500 classmates from Columbia University and 220 other friends, co-workers, and acquaintances. And his wife. The wraps came off his Christmas gift thanks to an advertising feature called Beacon, which shares news of Facebook members' online purchases with their friends. The idea, according to the company, is to allow merchants to effectively turn millions of Facebook users into a word-of-mouth promotion service. Lane called it "Christmas ruined," and more than 50,000 other users signed a petition calling on Facebook to stop broadcasting people's transactions without their consent.

### Encryption

*Encryption* scrambles information into an alternative form that requires a key or password to decrypt the information. If there is an information security breach and the information was encrypted, the person stealing the information will be unable to read it. Encryption can switch the order of characters, replace characters with other characters, insert or remove characters, or use a mathematical formula to convert the information into some sort of code. Companies that transmit sensitive customer information over the Internet, such as credit card numbers, frequently use encryption.

**FIGURE B6.5**

Corporate Losses Caused by Spam Worldwide (2003 and 2007 in billions)

Some encryption technologies use multiple keys like public key encryption. **Public key encryption (PKE)** is an encryption system that uses two keys: a public key that everyone can have and a private key for only the recipient (see Figure B6.6). When implementing security using multiple keys, the organization provides the public key to all of its customers (end consumers and other businesses). The customers use the public key to encrypt their information and send it along the Internet. When it arrives at its destination, the organization would use the private key to unscramble the encrypted information.

### Firewalls

One of the most common defenses for preventing a security breach is a firewall. A **firewall** is hardware and/or software that guards a private network by analyzing the information leaving and entering the network. Firewalls examine each message that wants entrance to the network. Unless the message has the correct markings, the firewall prevents it from entering the network. Firewalls can even detect computers communicating with the Internet without approval. As Figure B6.7 illustrates, organizations typically place a firewall between a server and the Internet.

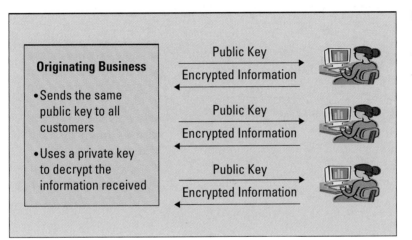

**FIGURE** B6.6

Public Key Encryption
(PKE) System

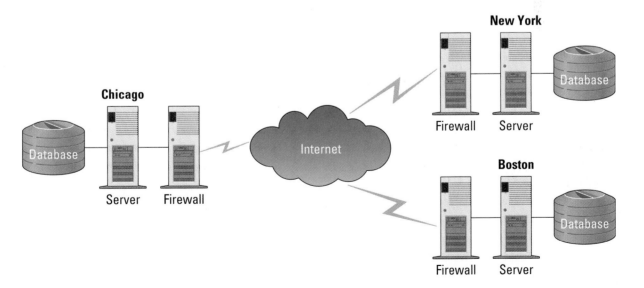

**FIGURE** B6.7

Sample Firewall Architecture Connecting Systems Located in Chicago, New York, and Boston

## DETECTION AND RESPONSE

The final area where organizations can allocate resources is in detection and response technologies. If prevention and resistance strategies fail and there is a security breach, an organization can use detection and response technologies to mitigate the damage. The most common type of defense within detection and response technologies is antivirus software.

A single worm can cause massive damage. The "Blaster worm" infected over 50,000 computers worldwide. Jeffrey Lee Parson, 18, was arrested by U.S. cyber investigators for unleashing the damaging worm on the Internet. The worm replicated itself repeatedly, eating up computer capacity, but did not damage information or programs. The worm generated so much traffic that it brought entire networks down.

The FBI used the latest technologies and code analysis to find the source of the worm. Prosecutors said Microsoft suffered financial losses that significantly exceeded $5,000, the statutory threshold in most hacker cases. Parson, charged with intentionally causing or attempting to cause damage to a computer, was sentenced to 18 months in prison, three years of supervised release, and 100 hours of community service. "What you've done is a terrible thing. Aside from injuring people and their computers, you shook the foundation of technology," U.S. District Judge Marsha Pechman told Parson.

"With this arrest, we want to deliver a message to cyber-hackers here and around the world," said U.S. Attorney John McKay in Seattle. "Let there be no mistake about it, cyber-hacking is a crime. We will investigate, arrest, and prosecute cyber-hackers."

Typically, people equate viruses (the malicious software) with hackers (the people). While not all types of hackers create viruses, many do. Figure B6.8 provides an overview of the most common types of hackers and viruses.

Some of the most damaging forms of security threats to ebusiness sites include malicious code, hoaxes, spoofing, and sniffers (see Figure B6.9).

**FIGURE B6.8**

Hackers and Viruses

---

*Hackers*—people very knowledgeable about computers who use their knowledge to invade other people's computers.

- *White-hat hackers*—work at the request of the system owners to find system vulnerabilities and plug the holes.
- *Black-hat hackers*—break into other people's computer systems and may just look around or may steal and destroy information.
- *Hactivists*—have philosophical and political reasons for breaking into systems and will often deface the website as a protest.
- *Script kiddies* or *script bunnies*—find hacking code on the Internet and click-and-point their way into systems to cause damage or spread viruses.
- *Cracker*—a hacker with criminal intent.
- *Cyberterrorists*—seek to cause harm to people or to destroy critical systems or information and use the Internet as a weapon of mass destruction.

*Viruses*—software written with malicious intent to cause annoyance or damage.

- *Worm*—a type of virus that spreads itself, not only from file to file, but also from computer to computer. The primary difference between a virus and a worm is that a virus must attach to something, such as an executable file, in order to spread. Worms do not need to attach to anything to spread and can tunnel themselves into computers.
- *Denial-of-service attack (DoS)*—floods a website with so many requests for service that it slows down or crashes the site.
- *Distributed denial-of-service attack (DDoS)*—attacks from multiple computers that flood a website with so many requests for service that it slows down or crashes. A common type is the Ping of Death, in which thousands of computers try to access a website at the same time, overloading it and shutting it down.
- *Trojan-horse virus*—hides inside other software, usually as an attachment or a downloadable file.
- *Backdoor programs*—viruses that open a way into the network for future attacks.
- *Polymorphic viruses and worms*—change their form as they propagate.

| Security Threats to Ebusiness |
|---|
| **Elevation of privilege** is a process by which a user misleads a system into granting unauthorized rights, usually for the purpose of compromising or destroying the system. For example, an attacker might log on to a network by using a guest account, and then exploit a weakness in the software that lets the attacker change the guest privileges to administrative privileges. |
| **Hoaxes** attack computer systems by transmitting a virus hoax, with a real virus attached. By masking the attack in a seemingly legitimate message, unsuspecting users more readily distribute the message and send the attack on to their co-workers and friends, infecting many users along the way. |
| **Malicious code** includes a variety of threats such as viruses, worms, and Trojan horses. |
| **Spoofing** is the forging of the return address on an email so that the email message appears to come from someone other than the actual sender. This is not a virus but rather a way by which virus authors conceal their identities as they send out viruses. |
| **Spyware** is software that comes hidden in free downloadable software and tracks online movements, mines the information stored on a computer, or uses a computer's CPU and storage for some task the user knows nothing about. According to the National Cyber Security Alliance, 91 percent of the study had spyware on their computers that can cause extremely slow performance, excessive pop-up ads, or hijacked home pages. |
| A **sniffer** is a program or device that can monitor data traveling over a network. Sniffers can show all the data being transmitted over a network, including passwords and sensitive information. Sniffers tend to be a favorite weapon in the hacker's arsenal. |
| **Packet tampering** consists of altering the contents of packets as they travel over the Internet or altering data on computer disks after penetrating a network. For example, an attacker might place a tap on a network line to intercept packets as they leave the computer. The attacker could eavesdrop or alter the information as it leaves the network. |

**FIGURE B6.9**

Security Threats to
Ebusiness

Implementing information security lines of defense through people first and through technology second is the best way for an organization to protect its vital intellectual capital. The first line of defense is securing intellectual capital by creating an information security plan detailing the various information security policies. The second line of defense is investing in technology to help secure information through authentication and authorization, prevention and resistance, and detection and response.

⁕ **KEY TERMS**

Authentication, 304
Authorization, 304
Backdoor program, 308
Biometrics, 305
Black-hat hacker, 308
Content filtering, 306
Cracker, 308
Cyberterrorist, 308
Denial-of-service attack (DoS), 308
Distributed denial-of-service attack (DDoS), 308
Encryption, 306
Elevation of privilege, 309
Firewall, 307

Hacker, 308
Hactivist, 308
Hoaxes, 309
Identify theft, 304
Information security, 300
Information security plan, 301
Information security policy, 301
Insider, 300
Intrusion detection software (IDS), 303
Malicious code, 309
Packet tampering, 309
Phishing, 304
Polymorphic virus and worm, 308

Public key encryption (PKE), 307
Script kiddies or script bunnies, 308
Smart card, 305
Sniffer, 309
Social engineering, 301
Spam, 306
Spoofing, 309
Spyware, 309
Token, 305
Trojan-horse virus, 308
Virus, 308
White-hat hacker, 308
Worm, 308

⁕ **CLOSING CASE ONE**

### Thinking Like the Enemy

David and Barry Kaufman, the founders of the Intense School, recently added several security courses, including the five-day "Professional Hacking Boot Camp" and "Social Engineering in Two Days."

Information technology departments must know how to protect organizational information. Therefore, organizations must teach their IT personnel how to protect their systems, especially in light of the many new government regulations, such as the Health Insurance Portability and Accountability Act (HIPAA), that demand secure systems. The concept of sending IT professionals to a hacking school seems counterintuitive; it is somewhat similar to sending accountants to an Embezzling 101 course. The Intense School does not strive to breed the next generation of hackers, however, but to teach its students how to be "ethical" hackers: to use their skills to build better locks, and to understand the minds of those who would attempt to crack them.

The main philosophy of the security courses at the Intense School is simply "To know thy enemy." In fact, one of the teachers at the Intense School is none other than Kevin Mitnick, the famous hacker who was imprisoned from 1995 to 2000. Teaching security from the hacker's perspective, as Mitnick does, is more difficult than teaching hacking itself: A hacker just needs to know one way into a system, David Kaufman notes, but a security professional needs to know *all* of the system's vulnerabilities. The two courses analyze those vulnerabilities from different perspectives.

The hacking course, which costs $3,500, teaches ways to protect against the mischief typically associated with hackers: worming through computer systems through vulnerabilities that are susceptible to technical, or computer-based, attacks. Mitnick's $1,950 social engineering course, by contrast, teaches the more frightening art of worming through the vulnerabilities of the people using and maintaining systems—getting passwords and access through duplicity, not technology. People that take this class, or read Mitnick's book, *The Art of Deception,* never again think of passwords or the trash bin the same way.

So how does the Intense School teach hacking? With sessions on dumpster diving (the unsavory practice of looking for passwords and other bits of information on discarded papers), with field trips to case target systems, and with practice runs at the company's in-house "target range," a network of computers set up to thwart and educate students.

One feature of the Intense School that raises a few questions is that the school does not check on morals at the door: Anyone paying the tuition can attend the school. Given the potential danger that an unchecked graduate of a hacking school could represent, it is surprising that the FBI does not collect the names of the graduates. But perhaps it gets them anyhow—several governmental agencies have sent students to the school.

## Questions

1. How could an organization benefit from attending one of the courses offered at the Intense School?

2. What are the two primary lines of security defense and how can organizational employees use the information taught by the Intense School when drafting an information security plan?

3. Determine the differences between the two primary courses offered at the Intense School, "Professional Hacking Boot Camp" and "Social Engineering in Two Days." Which course is more important for organizational employees to attend?

4. If your employer sent you to take a course at the Intense School, which one would you choose and why?

5. What are the ethical dilemmas involved with having such a course offered by a private company?

## ★ CLOSING CASE TWO

### Hacker Hunters

Hacker hunters are the new breed of crime-fighter. They employ the same methodology used to fight organized crime in the 1980s—informants and the cyberworld equivalent of wiretaps. Daniel Larking, a 20-year veteran who runs the FBI's Internet Crime Complaint Center, taps online service providers to help track down criminal hackers. Leads supplied by the FBI and eBay helped Romanian police round up 11 members of a gang that set up fake eBay accounts and auctioned off cell phones, laptops, and cameras they never intended to deliver.

On October 26, 2004, the FBI unleashed Operation Firewall, targeting the ShadowCrew, a gang whose members were schooled in identity theft, bank account pillage, and selling illegal goods on the Internet. ShadowCrew's 4,000 gang members lived in a dozen countries and across the United States. For months, agents had been watching their every move through a clandestine gateway into their website, shadowcrew.com. One member turned informant called a group meeting, ensuring the members would be at home on their computers during a certain time. At 9 p.m. the Secret Service issued orders to move in on the gang. The move was synchronized around the globe to prevent gang members from warning each other via instant messages. Twenty-eight gang members in eight states and six countries were arrested, most still at their computers. Authorities seized dozens of computers and found 1.7 million credit card numbers and more than 18 million email accounts.

## ShadowCrew's Operations

The alleged ringleaders of ShadowCrew included Andres Mantovani, 23, a part-time community college student in Arizona, and David Appleyard, 45, a former New Jersey mortgage broker. Mantovani and Appleyard allegedly were administrators in charge of running the website and recruiting members. The site created a marketplace for over 4,000 gang members who bought and sold hot information and merchandise. The website was open for business 24 hours a day, but since most of the members held jobs, the busiest time was from 10 p.m. to 2 a.m. on Sundays. Hundreds of gang members would meet online to trade credit card information, passports, and even equipment to make fake identity documents. Platinum credit cards cost more than gold ones and discounts were offered for package deals. One member known as "Scarface" sold 115,695 stolen credit card numbers in a single trade. Overall, the gang made more than $4 million in credit card purchases over two years. ShadowCrew was equivalent to an eBay for the underworld. The site even posted crime tips on how to use stolen credit cards and fake IDs at big retailers.

The gang stole credit card numbers and other valuable information through clever tricks. One of the favorites was sending millions of phishing emails—messages that appeared to be from legitimate companies such as Yahoo!—designed to steal passwords and credit card numbers. The gang also hacked into corporate databases to steal account data. According to sources familiar with the investigation, the gang cracked the networks of 12 unidentified companies that were not even aware their systems had been breached.

## Police Operations

Brian Nagel, an assistant director at the Secret Service, coordinated the effort to track the ShadowCrew. Allies included Britain's National High-Tech Crimes unit, the Royal Canadian Mounted Police, and the Bulgarian Interior Ministry. Authorities turned one of the high-ranking members of the gang into a snitch and had the man help the Secret Service set up a new electronic doorway for ShadowCrew members to enter their website. The snitch spread the word that the new gateway was a more secure way to the website. It was the first-ever tap of a private computer network. "We became shadowcrew.com," Nagel said.

## Questions

1. What types of technology could big retailers use to prevent identity thieves from purchasing merchandise?
2. What can organizations do to protect themselves from hackers looking to steal account data?
3. Authorities frequently tap online service providers to track down hackers. Do you think it is ethical for authorities to tap an online service provider and read people's email? Why or why not?
4. Do you think it was ethical for authorities to use one of the high-ranking officials to trap other gang members? Why or why not?
5. In a team, research the Internet and find the best ways to protect yourself from identity theft.

## ★ MAKING BUSINESS DECISIONS

### 1. Firewall Decisions

You are the CEO of Inverness Investments, a medium-sized venture capital firm that specializes in investing in high-tech companies. The company receives over 30,000 email messages per year. On average, there are two viruses and three successful hackings against the company each year, which result in losses to the company of about $250,000. Currently, the company has antivirus software installed but does not have any firewalls.

Your CIO is suggesting implementing 10 firewalls for a total cost of $80,000. The estimated life of each firewall is about three years. The chances of hackers breaking into the system with the firewalls installed are about 3 percent. Annual maintenance costs on the firewalls is estimated around $15,000. Create an argument for or against supporting your CIO's recommendation to purchase the firewalls.

## 2. Drafting an Information Security Plan

Making The Grade is a nonprofit organization that helps students learn how to achieve better grades in school. The organization has 40 offices in 25 states and over 2,000 employees. The company is currently building a website to offer its services online. You have recently been hired by the CIO as the director of information security. Your first assignment is to develop a document discussing the importance of creating information security policies and an information security plan. Be sure to include the following:

- The importance of educating employees on information security.
- A few samples of employee information security policies.
- Other major areas the information security plan should address.
- Signs the company should look for to determine if the new site is being hacked.
- The major types of attacks the company should expect to experience.

## 3. Discussing the Three Areas of Security

Great Granola Inc. is a small business operating out of northern California. The company specializes in selling unique homemade granola, and its primary sales vehicle is through its website. The company is growing exponentially and expects its revenues to triple this year to $12 million. The company also expects to hire 60 additional employees to support its growing number of customers. Joan Martin, the CEO, is aware that if her competitors discover the recipe for her granola, or who her primary customers are, it could easily ruin her business. Joan has hired you to draft a document discussing the different areas of information security, along with your recommendations for providing a secure ebusiness environment.

## 4. College Security

Computer and online security is a growing concern for businesses of all sizes. Computer security issues range from viruses to automated Internet attacks to outright theft, the result of which is lost information and lost time. Security issues pop up in news articles daily, and most business owners understand the need to secure their businesses. Your college is no different from any other business when it comes to information security. Draft a document identifying the questions you should ask your college's CIO to ensure information security across your campus.

# PLUG-IN B7

## Ethics

1. Summarize the guidelines for creating an information privacy policy.
2. Identify the differences between an ethical computer use policy and an acceptable use policy.
3. Describe the relationship between an email privacy policy and an Internet use policy.
4. Explain the effects of spam on an organization.
5. Summarize the different monitoring technologies and explain the importance of an employee monitoring policy.

## Introduction

The core units introduced **ethics,** which are the principles and standards that guide our behavior toward other people. Technology has created many new ethical dilemmas in our electronic society. The following are a few important concepts and terms related to ethical issues stemming from advances in technology:

- **Intellectual property**—intangible creative work that is embodied in physical form.
- **Copyright**—the legal protection afforded an expression of an idea, such as a song, video game, and some types of proprietary documents.
- **Fair use doctrine**—in certain situations, it is legal to use copyrighted material.
- **Pirated software**—the unauthorized use, duplication, distribution, or sale of copyrighted software.
- **Counterfeit software**—software that is manufactured to look like the real thing and sold as such.

The core units also introduced **privacy,** which is the right to be left alone when you want to be, to have control over your own personal possessions, and not to be observed without your consent. Privacy is related to **confidentiality,** which is the assurance that messages and information are available only to those who are authorized to view them. This plug-in takes a detailed look at **ePolicies**—policies and procedures that address the ethical use of computers and Internet usage in the business environment. These ePolicies typically address information privacy and confidentiality issues and include the following:

- Ethical computer use policy.
- Information privacy policy.
- Acceptable use policy.
- Email privacy policy.
- Internet use policy.
- Anti-spam policy.

# Ethics

*Information ethics* concerns the ethical and moral issues arising from the development and use of information technologies, as well as the creation, collection, duplication, distribution, and processing of information itself (with or without the aid of computer technologies). Individuals determine how to use information and how information affects them. How individuals behave toward each other and how they handle information and technology are largely influenced by their ethics. Ethical dilemmas usually arise not in simple, clear-cut situations but out of a clash between competing goals, responsibilities, and loyalties. Inevitably, the decision process may have more than one socially acceptable "correct" decision. Figure B7.1 contains examples of ethically questionable or unacceptable uses of information technology.

People make arguments for or against—justify or condemn—the behaviors in Figure B7.1. Unfortunately, there are few hard and fast rules for always determining what is and is not ethical. Knowing the law will not always help because what is legal might not always be ethical, and what might be ethical is not always legal. For example, Joe Reidenberg received an offer for cell phone service from AT&T Wireless. The offer revealed that AT&T Wireless had used Equifax, a credit reporting agency, to identify Joe Reidenberg as a potential customer. Overall, this strategy seemed like good business. Equifax could generate additional revenue by selling information it already owned and AT&T Wireless could identify target markets, thereby increasing response rates to its marketing campaigns. Unfortunately, by law, credit information cannot be used to sell anything. The Fair Credit Reporting Act (FCRA) forbids repurposing credit information except when the information is used for "a firm offer of credit or insurance." In other words, the only product that can be sold based on credit information is credit. A spokesman for Equifax stated that "as long as AT&T Wireless (or any company for that matter) is offering the cell

| Examples of Questionable Information Technology Use |
| --- |
| Individuals copy, use, and distribute software. |
| Employees search organizational databases for sensitive corporate and personal information. |
| Organizations collect, buy, and use information without checking the validity or accuracy of the information. |
| Individuals create and spread viruses that cause trouble for those using and maintaining IT systems. |
| Individuals hack into computer systems to steal proprietary information. |
| Employees destroy or steal proprietary organization information such as schematics, sketches, customer lists, and reports. |

**FIGURE B7.1**

Ethically Questionable or Unacceptable Information Technology Use

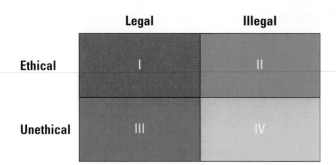

|  | **Legal** | **Illegal** |
|---|---|---|
| **Ethical** | I | II |
| **Unethical** | III | IV |

**FIGURE B7.2**

Acting Ethically and Legally Are Not Always the Same

phone service on a credit basis, such as allowing the use of the service before the consumer has to pay, it is in compliance with the FCRA." But is it ethical?

This is a good example of the ethical dilemmas facing many organizations today; because technology is so new and pervasive in unexpected ways, the ethics surrounding information have not been all worked out. Figure B7.2 displays the four quadrants of ethical and legal behavior. The ideal goal for organizations is to make decisions within quadrant I that are both legal and ethical.

## INFORMATION HAS NO ETHICS

Jerry Rode, CIO of Saab Cars USA, realized he had a public relations fiasco on his hands when he received an email from an irate customer. Saab had hired four Internet marketing companies to distribute electronic information about Saab's new models to its customers. Saab specified that the marketing campaign be *opt-in,* implying that it would contact only the people who had agreed to receive promotions and marketing material via email. Unfortunately, one of the marketing companies apparently had a different definition of opt-in and was emailing all customers regardless of their opt-in decision.

Rode fired the errant marketing company and immediately developed a formal policy for the use of customer information. "The customer doesn't see ad agencies and contracted marketing firms. They see Saab USA spamming them," Rode said. "Finger-pointing after the fact won't make your customers feel better."

Information has no ethics. Information does not care how it is used. It will not stop itself from spamming customers, sharing itself if it is sensitive or personal, or revealing details to third parties. Information cannot delete or preserve itself. Therefore, it falls on the shoulders of those who lord over the information to develop ethical guidelines on how to manage it. Figure B7.3 provides an overview of some of the important laws that individuals must follow when they are attempting to manage and protect information.

**FIGURE B7.3**

Established Information-Related Laws

| Established Information-Related Laws | |
|---|---|
| **Privacy Act—1974** | Restricts what information the federal government can collect; allows people to access and correct information on themselves; requires procedures to protect the security of personal information; and forbids the disclosure of name-linked information without permission. |
| **Family Education Rights and Privacy Act—1974** | Regulates access to personal education records by government agencies and other third parties and ensures the right of students to see their own records. |
| **Cable Communications Act—1984** | Requires written or electronic consent from viewers before cable TV providers can release viewing choices or other personally identifiable information. |
| **Electronic Communications Privacy Act—1986** | Allows the reading of communications by a firm and says that employees have no right to privacy when using the companies' computers. |
| **Computer Fraud and Abuse Act—1986** | Prohibits unauthorized access to computers used for financial institutions, the U.S. government, or interstate and international trade. |

*(Continued)*

| Established Information-Related Laws | |
| --- | --- |
| **The Bork Bill (officially known as the Video Privacy Protection Act)—1988** | Prohibits the use of video rental information on customers for any purpose other than that of marketing goods and services directly to the customer. |
| **Communications Assistance for Law Enforcement Act—1994** | Requires that telecommunications equipment be designed so that authorized government agents are able to intercept all wired and wireless communications being sent or received by any subscriber. The act also requires that subscriber call-identifying information be transmitted to a government when and if required. |
| **Freedom of Information Act—1967, 1975, 1994, and 1998** | Allows any person to examine government records unless it would cause an invasion of privacy. It was amended in 1974 to apply to the FBI, and again in 1994 to allow citizens to monitor government activities and information gathering, and once again in 1998 to allow access to government information on the Internet. |
| **Health Insurance Portability and Accountability Act (HIPAA)—1996** | Requires that the health care industry formulate and implement regulations to keep patient information confidential. |
| **Identity Theft and Assumption Deterrence Act—1998** | Strengthened the criminal laws governing identity theft making it a federal crime to use or transfer identification belonging to another. It also established a central federal service for victims. |
| **USA Patriot Act—2001 and 2003** | Allows law enforcement to get access to almost any information, including library records, video rentals, bookstore purchases, and business records when investigating any act of terrorist or clandestine intelligence activities. In 2003, Patriot II broadened the original law. |
| **Homeland Security Act—2002** | Provided new authority to government agencies to mine data on individuals and groups including emails and website visits; put limits on the information available under the Freedom of Information Act; and gave new powers to government agencies to declare national health emergencies. |
| **Sarbanes-Oxley Act—2002** | Sought to protect investors by improving the accuracy and reliability of corporate disclosures and requires companies to (1) implement extensive and detailed policies to prevent illegal activity within the company, and (2) to respond in a timely manner to investigate illegal activity. |
| **Fair and Accurate Credit Transactions Act—2003** | Included provisions for the prevention of identity theft including consumers' right to get a credit report free each year, requiring merchants to leave all but the last five digits of a credit card number off a receipt, and requiring lenders and credit agencies to take action even before a victim knows a crime has occurred when they notice any circumstances that might indicate identity theft. |
| **CAN-Spam Act—2003** | Sought to regulate interstate commerce by imposing limitations and penalties on businesses sending unsolicited email to consumers. The law forbids deceptive subject lines, headers, return addresses, etc., as well as the harvesting of email addresses from websites. It requires businesses that send spam to maintain a do-not-spam list and to include a postal mailing address in the message. |

# Developing Information Management Policies

Treating sensitive corporate information as a valuable resource is good management. Building a corporate culture based on ethical principles that employees can understand and implement is responsible management. In an effort to provide guidelines for ethical information management, *CIO* magazine (along with over 100 CIOs) developed six principles for ethical information management displayed in Figure B7.4.

To follow *CIO*'s six principles for ethical information management, a corporation should develop written policies establishing employee guidelines, personnel procedures, and organizational rules. These policies set employee expectations about the organization's practices and standards and protect the organization from misuse of computer systems and IT resources. If an organization's employees use computers at work, the organization should, at a minimum, implement ePolicies. Such *ePolicies* are policies and procedures that address the ethical use of computers and Internet usage in the business environment. They typically embody the following:

- Ethical computer use policy.
- Information privacy policy.
- Acceptable use policy.
- Email privacy policy.
- Internet use policy.
- Anti-spam policy.

## ETHICAL COMPUTER USE POLICY

In a case that illustrates the perils of online betting, a leading Internet poker site reported that a hacker exploited a security flaw to gain an insurmountable edge in high-stakes, no-limit Texas hold-'em tournaments—the ability to see his opponents' hole cards. The cheater, whose illegitimate winnings were estimated at between $400,000 and $700,000 by one victim, was an employee of AbsolutePoker.com, who hacked the system to show that it could be done. Regardless of what business a company operates it seems it must protect itself from unethical employee behavior.

One of the essential steps in creating an ethical corporate culture is establishing an ethical computer use policy. An *ethical computer use policy* contains general principles to guide computer user behavior. For example, the ethical computer use policy might explicitly state that users should refrain from playing computer games during working hours. This policy ensures that the users know how to

**FIGURE B7.4**

*CIO* Magazine's Six Principles for Ethical Information Management

| Six Principles for Ethical Information Management |
|---|
| 1. Information is a valuable corporate asset like cash, facilities, or any other corporate asset and should be managed as such. |
| 2. The CIO is steward of corporate information and is responsible for managing it over its life cycle—from its generation to its appropriate destruction. |
| 3. The CIO is responsible for controlling access to and use of information, as determined by governmental regulation and corporate policy. |
| 4. The CIO is responsible for preventing the inappropriate destruction of information. |
| 5. The CIO is responsible for bringing technological knowledge to the development of information management practices and policies. |
| 6. The CIO should partner with executive peers to develop and execute the organization's information management policies. |

the system as openly or as privately as it wishes. That means that if the organization wants to read everyone's email, it can do so. If it chooses not to read any, that is allowable too. Hence, it is up to the organization to decide how much, if any, email it is going to read. Then, when it decides, it must inform the users, so that they can consent to this level of intrusion. In other words, an *email privacy policy* details the extent to which email messages may be read by others.

Organizations are urged to have some kind of email privacy policy and to publish it no matter what the degree of intrusion. Figure B7.8 displays a few of the key stipulations generally contained in an email privacy policy.

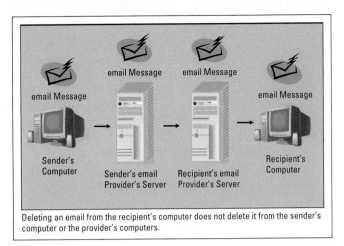

Deleting an email from the recipient's computer does not delete it from the sender's computer or the provider's computers.

**FIGURE B7.7**

Email Is Stored on Multiple Computers

## INTERNET USE POLICY

Similar to email, the Internet has some unique aspects that make it a good candidate for its own policy. These include the large amounts of computing resources that Internet users can expend, thus making it essential that such use be legitimate. In addition, the Internet contains numerous materials that some might feel are offensive and, hence, some regulation might be required in this area. An *Internet use policy* contains general principles to guide the proper use of the Internet. Figure B7.9 displays a few important stipulations that might be included in an Internet use policy.

| Email Privacy Policy Stipulations |
| --- |
| 1. The policy should be complementary to the ethical computer use policy. |
| 2. It defines who legitimate email users are. |
| 3. It explains the backup procedure so users will know that at some point, even if a message is deleted from their computer, it will still be on the backup tapes. |
| 4. It describes the legitimate grounds for reading someone's email and the process required before such action can be taken. |
| 5. It informs that the organization has no control of email once it is transmitted outside the organization. |
| 6. It explains what will happen if the user severs his or her connection with the organization. |
| 7. It asks employees to be careful when making organizational files and documents available to others. |

**FIGURE B7.8**

Email Privacy Policy Stipulations

| Internet Use Policy Stipulations |
| --- |
| 1. The policy should describe available Internet services because not all Internet sites allow users to access all services. |
| 2. The policy should define the organization's position on the purpose of Internet access and what restrictions, if any, are placed on that access. |
| 3. The policy should complement the ethical computer use policy. |
| 4. The policy should describe user responsibility for citing sources, properly handling offensive material, and protecting the organization's good name. |
| 5. The policy should clearly state the ramifications if the policy is violated. |

**FIGURE B7.9**

Internet Use Policy Stipulations

## ANTI-SPAM POLICY

Chief technology officer (CTO) of the law firm Fenwick and West, Matt Kesner reduced incoming spam by 99 percent and found himself a corporate hero. Before the spam reduction, the law firm's partners (whose time is worth $350 to $600 an hour) found themselves spending hours each day sifting through 300 to 500 spam messages. The spam blocking engineered by Kesner traps between 5,000 and 7,000 messages a day.

**Spam** is unsolicited email. An **anti-spam policy** simply states that email users will not send unsolicited emails (or spam). Spam plagues all levels of employees within an organization from receptionists to CEOs. Estimates indicate that spam accounts for 40 percent to 60 percent of most organizations' email traffic. Ferris Research says spam costs U.S. businesses over $15 billion per year and Nucleus Research stated that companies forfeit $874 per employee annually in lost productivity from spam alone. Spam clogs email systems and siphons IT resources away from legitimate business projects.

It is difficult to write anti-spam policies, laws, or software because there is no such thing as a universal litmus test for spam. One person's spam is another person's newsletter. End users have to be involved in deciding what spam is because what is unwanted can vary widely not just from one company to the next, but from one person to the next. What looks like spam to the rest of the world could be essential business communications for certain employees.

John Zarb, CIO of Libbey, a manufacturer of glassware, china, and flatware, tested Guenivere (a virus and subject-line filter) and SpamAssassin (an open source spam filter). He had to shut them off after 10 days because they were rejecting important legitimate emails. As Zarb quickly discovered, once an organization starts filtering email, it runs the risk of blocking legitimate emails because they look like spam. Avoiding an unacceptable level of "false positives" requires a delicate balancing act. The IT team tweaked the spam filters and today the filters block about 70 percent of Libbey's spam. Zarb says the "false positive" rate is far lower but not zero. Figure B7.10 presents a few methods an organization can follow to prevent spam.

## Ethics in the Workplace

Concern is growing among employees that infractions of corporate policies—even accidental ones—will be a cause for disciplinary action. The Whitehouse.gov Internet site displays the U.S. president's official website and updates on bill signings and new policies. Whitehouse.com, however, leads to a trashy site that capitalizes on its famous name. A simple mistype from .gov to .com could potentially cost someone her or his job if the company has a termination policy for viewing illicit websites. Monitoring employees is one of the largest issues facing CIOs when they are developing information management policies.

**FIGURE** B7.10

Spam Prevention Tips

| Spam Prevention Tips |
| --- |
| ■ **Disguise email addresses posted in a public electronic place.** When posting an email address in a public place, disguise the address through simple means such as replacing "jsmith@domain.com" with "jsmith at domain dot com." This prevents spam from recognizing the email address. |
| ■ **Opt-out of member directories that may place an email address online.** Choose not to participate in any activities that place email addresses online. If an email address is placed online be sure it is disguised in some way. |
| ■ **Use a filter.** Many ISPs and free email services now provide spam filtering. While filters are not perfect, they can cut down tremendously on the amount of spam a user receives. |

The question of whether to monitor what employees do on company time with corporate resources has been largely decided by legal precedents that are already holding businesses financially responsible for their employees' actions. Increasingly, employee monitoring is not a choice; it is a risk-management obligation. Michael Soden, CEO of the Bank of Ireland, decided that it was necessary to issue a companywide policy making it grounds for termination to surf an illicit website with company equipment. Soden then hired Hewlett-Packard to run the corporate IT department. A Hewlett-Packard employee soon discovered illicit websites on Soden's computer. Soden resigned.

A recent survey of workplace monitoring and surveillance practices by the American Management Association (AMA) and the ePolicy Institute showed the degree to which companies are turning to monitoring:

- 82 percent of the study's 1,627 respondents acknowledged conducting some form of electronic monitoring or physical surveillance.
- 63 percent of the companies stated that they monitor Internet connections.
- 47 percent acknowledged storing and reviewing employee email messages.

## MONITORING TECHNOLOGIES

Many employees use their company's high-speed Internet access to shop, browse, and surf the web. Fifty-nine percent of all web purchases in the United States are made from the workplace, according to ComScore Networks. Vault.com determined that 47 percent of employees spend at least half an hour a day surfing the web.

This research indicates that managers should monitor what their employees are doing with their web access. Most managers do not want their employees conducting personal business during working hours. For these reasons many organizations have increasingly taken the Big Brother approach to web monitoring with software that tracks Internet usage and even allows the boss to read employees' email. Figure B7.11 highlights a few reasons the effects of employee monitoring are worse than the lost productivity from employee web surfing.

This is the thinking at SAS Institute, a private software company consistently ranked in the top 10 on many "Best Places to Work" surveys. SAS does not monitor its employees' web usage. The company asks its employees to use company resources responsibly, but does not mind if they occasionally check sports scores or use the web for shopping.

Many management gurus advocate that organizations whose corporate cultures are based on trust are more successful than those whose corporate cultures are based on distrust. Before an organization implements monitoring technology it should ask itself, "What does this say about how the organization feels about its employees?" If the organization really does not trust its employees, then perhaps it should find new ones. If an organization does trust its employees, then it might

| Employee Monitoring Effects |
|---|
| 1. Employee absenteeism is on the rise, almost doubling in 2004 to 21 percent. The lesson here might be that more employees are missing work to take care of personal business. Perhaps losing a few minutes here or there—or even a couple of hours—is cheaper than losing entire days. |
| 2. Studies indicate that electronic monitoring results in lower job satisfaction, in part because people begin to believe the quantity of their work is more important than the quality. |
| 3. Electronic monitoring also induces what psychologists call "psychological reactance": the tendency to rebel against constraints. If you tell your employees they cannot shop, they cannot use corporate networks for personal business, and they cannot make personal phone calls, then their desire to do all these things will likely increase. |

**FIGURE** B7.11

Employee Monitoring Effects

| Common Monitoring Technologies | |
|---|---|
| **Key logger, or key trapper, software** | A program that, when installed on a computer, records every keystroke and mouse click. |
| **Hardware key logger** | A hardware device that captures keystrokes on their journey from the keyboard to the motherboard. |
| **Cookie** | A small file deposited on a hard drive by a website containing information about customers and their web activities. Cookies allow websites to record the comings and goings of customers, usually without their knowledge or consent. |
| **Adware** | Software that generates ads that install themselves on a computer when a person downloads some other program from the Internet. |
| **Spyware (sneakware or stealthware)** | Software that comes hidden in free downloadable software and tracks online movements, mines the information stored on a computer, or uses a computer's CPU and storage for some task the user knows nothing about. |
| **Web log** | Consists of one line of information for every visitor to a website and is usually stored on a web server. |
| **Clickstream** | Records information about a customer during a web surfing session such as what websites were visited, how long the visit was, what ads were viewed, and what was purchased. |

want to treat them accordingly. An organization that follows its employees' every keystroke is unwittingly undermining the relationships with its employees.

*Information technology monitoring* is tracking people's activities by such measures as number of keystrokes, error rate, and number of transactions processed. Figure B7.12 displays different types of monitoring technologies currently available.

Monitoring employee behavior should not just extend to the employee, but to how employees monitor each other. A 14-year-old Canadian boy named Ghyslain Raza innocently swung a golfball retriever around in a quiet corner of his high school, pretending he was *The Phantom Menace*'s Darth Maul. Raza videotaped the event and accidently left the tape at school, where it was found several months later. Not long after, Raza became an Internet sensation, known today as the "Star Wars kid," with fans modifying his video to add light-saber effects and music. The embarrassing footage has since become one of the Internet's most popular, having been spoofed on TV shows ranging from *American Dad* to *The Colbert Report* to *Arrested Development*. Raza eventually sued the individuals who posted the video online and the case was settled.

### Employee Monitoring Policies

Women sometimes engage in private discussions in the ladies' room, but imagine how they would feel if the conversation was broadcast on CNN during a presidential speech? Newsreader Kyra Phillips accidentally left her microphone on while in the restroom and broadcast the news that her sister-in-law was a "control freak," among several other pronouncements. Phillips later laughed it off and even provided a *Late Show* "Top 10" list of excuses for why it happened. Sample: "How was I supposed to know we had a reporter embedded in the bathroom?" Although this reporter was able to laugh off the incident, an organization must ensure its employees are comfortable with any monitoring it is undertaking, including monitoring the restroom.

The best path for an organization planning to engage in employee monitoring is open communication surrounding the issue. A recent survey discovered that communication about monitoring issues is weak for most organizations. One in five companies did not even have an acceptable use policy and one in four companies did not have an Internet use policy.

Companies that did have policies usually tucked them into the rarely probed recesses of the employee handbook, and then the policies tended to be of the vague and legal jargon variety: "XYZ company reserves the right to monitor or review any information stored or transmitted on its equipment." Reserving the right to monitor is materially different from clearly stating that the company does monitor, listing what is tracked, describing what is looked for, and detailing the consequences for violations.

An organization must formulate the right monitoring policies and put them into practice. *Employee monitoring policies* explicitly state how, when, and where the company monitors its employees. CSOs that are explicit about what the company does in the way of monitoring and the reasons for it, along with actively educating their employees about what unacceptable behavior looks like, will find that employees not only acclimate quite quickly to a policy, but also reduce the CSO's burden by policing themselves. Figure B7.13 displays several common stipulations an organization can follow when creating an employee monitoring policy.

| Employee Monitoring Policy Stipulations |
|---|
| 1. Be as specific as possible. |
| 2. Always enforce the policy. |
| 3. Enforce the policy in the same way for everyone. |
| 4. Expressly communicate that the company reserves the right to monitor all employees. |
| 5. Specifically state when monitoring will be performed. |
| 6. Specifically state what will be monitored (email, IM, Internet, network activity, etc.). |
| 7. Describe the types of information that will be collected. |
| 8. State the consequences for violating the policy. |
| 9. State all provisions that allow for updates to the policy. |
| 10. Specify the scope and manner of monitoring for any information system. |
| 11. When appropriate, obtain a written receipt acknowledging that each party has received, read, and understood the monitoring policies. |

**FIGURE B7.13**

Employee Monitoring Policy Stipulations

Advances in technology have made ethics a concern for many organizations. Consider how easy it is for an employee to email large amounts of confidential information, change electronic communications, or destroy massive amounts of important company information all within seconds. Electronic information about customers, partners, and employees has become one of corporate America's most valuable assets. However, the line between the proper and improper use of this asset is at best blurry. Should an employer be able to search employee files without employee consent? Should a company be able to sell customer information without informing the customer of its intent? What is a responsible approach to document deletion?

The law provides guidelines in many of these areas, but how a company chooses to act within the confines of the law is up to the judgment of its officers. Since CIOs are responsible for the technology that collects, maintains, and destroys corporate information, they sit smack in the middle of this potential ethical quagmire.

One way an organization can begin dealing with ethical issues is to create a corporate culture that encourages ethical considerations and discourages dubious information dealings. Not only is an ethical culture an excellent idea overall, but it also acts as a precaution, helping prevent customer problems from escalating into front-page news stories. The establishment of and adherence to well-defined rules and policies will help organizations create an ethical corporate culture. These policies include:

- Ethical computer use policy.
- Information privacy policy.
- Acceptable use policy.
- Email privacy policy.
- Internet use policy.
- Anti-spam policy.
- Employee monitoring policy.

## Sarbanes-Oxley: Where Information Technology, Finance, and Ethics Meet

The Sarbanes-Oxley Act (SOX) of 2002 was enacted in response to the high-profile Enron and WorldCom financial scandals to protect shareholders and the general public from accounting errors and fraudulent practices by organizations. One primary component of the Sarbanes-Oxley Act is the definition of which records are to be stored and for how long. For this reason, the legislation not only affects financial departments, but also IT departments whose job it is to store electronic records. The Sarbanes-Oxley Act states that all business records, including electronic records and electronic messages, must be saved for "not less than five years." The consequences for noncompliance are fines, imprisonment, or both. The following are the three rules of Sarbanes-Oxley that affect the management of electronic records.

1. The first rule deals with destruction, alteration, or falsification of records and states that persons who knowingly alter, destroy, mutilate, conceal, or falsify documents shall be fined or imprisoned for not more than 20 years or both.

2. The second rule defines the retention period for records storage. Best practices indicate that corporations securely store all business records using the same guidelines set for public accountants, which state that organizations shall maintain all audit or review work-papers for a period of five years from the end of the fiscal period in which the audit or review was concluded.

3. The third rule specifies all business records and communications that need to be stored, including electronic communications. IT departments are facing the challenge of creating and maintaining a corporate records archive in a cost-effective fashion that satisfies the requirements put forth by the legislation.

Essentially, any public organization that uses IT as part of its financial business processes will find that it must put in place IT controls in order to be compliant with the Sarbanes-Oxley Act. The following are a few practices you can follow to begin to ensure organizational compliance with the Sarbanes-Oxley Act.

- Overhaul or upgrade your financial systems in order to meet regulatory requirements for more accurate, detailed, and speedy filings.

- Examine the control processes within your IT department and apply best practices to comply with the act's goals. For example, segregation of duties within the systems development staff is a widely recognized best practice that helps prevent errors and outright fraud. The people who code program changes should be different from the people who test them, and a separate team should be responsible for changes in production environments.

- Homegrown financial systems are fraught with potential information-integrity issues. Although leading ERP systems offer audit-trail functionality, customizations of these systems often bypass those controls. You must work with internal and external auditors to ensure that customizations are not overriding controls.

- Work with your CIO, CEO, CFO, and corporate attorneys to create a document-retention-and-destruction policy that addresses what types of electronic documents should be saved, and for how long.

Ultimately, Sarbanes-Oxley compliance will require a great deal of work among all of your departments. Compliance starts with running IT as a business and strengthening IT internal controls.

## Questions

1. Define the relationship between ethics and the Sarbanes-Oxley Act.
2. Why is records management an area of concern for the entire organization?
3. What are two policies an organization can implement to achieve Sarbanes-Oxley compliance? Be sure to elaborate on how these policies can achieve compliance.
4. Identify the biggest roadblock for organizations that are attempting to achieve Sarbanes-Oxley compliance.
5. What types of information systems might facilitate SOX compliance?
6. How will electronic monitoring affect the morale and performance of employees in the workplace?
7. What do you think an unethical accountant or manager at Enron thought were the rewards and responsibilities associated with his or her job?

---

### ★ CLOSING CASE TWO

### Invading Your Privacy

Can your employer invade your privacy through monitoring technologies? Numerous lawsuits have been filed by employees who believed their employer was wrong to invade their privacy with monitoring technologies. Below are a few cases highlighting lawsuits over employee privacy and employer rights to monitor.

### Smyth versus Pillsbury Company

An employee was terminated for sending inappropriate and unprofessional messages over the company's email system. The company had repeatedly assured its employees that email was confidential, that it would not be intercepted, and that it would not be used as a basis for discipline or discharge. Michael Smyth retrieved, from his home computer, email sent from his supervisor over Pillsbury's email system. Smyth allegedly responded with several comments concerning the sales management staff, including a threat to "kill the backstabbing bastards" and a reference to an upcoming holiday party as "the Jim Jones Kool-aid affair." Pillsbury intercepted the email and terminated Smyth, who then sued the company for wrongful discharge and invasion of privacy.

The court dismissed the case in 1996, finding that Smyth did not have a reasonable expectation of privacy in the contents of his email messages, despite Pillsbury's assurances, because the messages had been voluntarily communicated over the company's computer system to a second person. The court went on to find that, even if some reasonable expectation of privacy existed, that expectation was outweighed by Pillsbury's legitimate interest in preventing inappropriate or unprofessional communications over its email system.

### Bourke versus Nissan Motor Corporation

While training new employees on the email system, a message sent by Bonita Bourke was randomly selected and reviewed by the company. The message turned out to be a personal email of a sexual nature. Once Bourke's email was discovered, the company decided to review the emails of the rest of Bourke's workgroup. As a result of this investigation, several other personal emails were discovered. Nissan gave the employees who had sent the personal messages written warnings for violating the company's email policy.

The disciplined employees sued Nissan for invasion of privacy. The employees argued that although they signed a form acknowledging the company's policy that company-owned hardware and software was restricted for company business use only, their expectation of privacy was reasonable because the company gave the plaintiffs passwords to access the computer system and told them to guard their passwords. However, a California court in 1993 held that this was not an objectively reasonable expectation of privacy because the plaintiffs knew that email messages "were read from time to time by individuals other than the intended recipient."

## McLaren versus Microsoft Corporation

The Texas Court of Appeals in 1999 dismissed an employee's claim that his employer's review and dissemination of email stored in the employee's workplace personal computer constituted an invasion of privacy. The employee argued that he had a reasonable expectation of privacy because the email was kept in a personal computer folder protected by a password. The court found this argument unconvincing because the email was transmitted over his employer's network.

However, according to a news account of one case, a court held that an employer's use of a supervisor's password to review an employee's email may have violated a Massachusetts state statute against interference with privacy. In that case, Burk Technology allowed employees to use the company's email system to send personal messages, but prohibited "excessive chatting." To use the email system, each employee used a password. The employer never informed employees that their messages would or could be monitored by supervisors or the company president. The president of the company reviewed the emails of two employees who had referred to him by various nicknames and discussed his extramarital affair. The two employees were fired by the company president, who claimed the terminations were for their excessive email use and not because of the messages' content. The court denied the company's attempt to dismiss the suit and allowed the matter to be set for trial on the merits. The court focused on the fact that the employees were never informed that their email could be monitored.

This case illustrates the importance of informing employees that their use of company equipment to send email and to surf the Internet is subject to monitoring to prevent subsequent confusion, and a possible future defense, on the part of employees.

## Questions

1. Pick one of the above cases and create an argument on behalf of the employee.
2. Pick one of the above cases and create an argument against the employee.
3. Pick one of the above cases and create an argument on behalf of the employer's use of monitoring technologies.
4. Pick one of the above cases and create an argument against the employer's use of monitoring technologies.

---

## ★ MAKING BUSINESS DECISIONS

### 1. Information Privacy

A study by the Annenberg Public Policy Center at the University of Pennsylvania shows that 95 percent of people who use the Internet at home think they should have a legal right to know everything about the information that websites collect from them. Research also shows that 57 percent of home Internet users incorrectly believe that when a website has an information privacy policy it will not share personal information with other websites or companies. In fact, the research found that after showing the users how companies track, extract, and share website information to make money, 85 percent found the methods unacceptable, even for a highly valued site. Write a short paper arguing for or against an organization's right to use and distribute personal information gathered from its website.

## 2. Acting Ethically

Describe how you would react to the following scenarios:

- A senior marketing manager informs you that one of her employees is looking for another job and she wants you to give her access to look through her email.

- A vice president of sales informs you that he has made a deal to provide customer information to a strategic partner and he wants you to burn all of the customer information onto a CD.

- You start monitoring one of your employees' email and discover that he is having an affair with one of the other employees in the office.

- You install a video surveillance system in your office and discover that employees are taking office supplies home with them.

## 3. Spying on EMail

Technology advances now allow individuals to monitor computers that they do not even have physical access to. New types of software can capture an individual's incoming and outgoing email and then immediately forward that email to another person. For example, if you are at work and your child is home from school and she receives an email from John at 3:00 p.m., at 3:01 p.m. you will receive a copy of that email sent to your email address. A few minutes later, if she replies to John's email, within seconds you will again receive a copy of what she sent to John. Describe two scenarios (other than the above) for the use of this type of software: (1) where the use would be ethical, (2) where the use would be unethical.

## 4. Stealing Software

The issue of pirated software is one that the software industry fights on a daily basis. The major centers of software piracy are in places like Russia and China where salaries and disposable income are comparatively low. People in developing and economically depressed countries will fall behind the industrialized world technologically if they cannot afford access to new generations of software. Considering this, is it reasonable to blame someone for using pirated software when it could potentially cost him or her two months' salary to purchase a legal copy? Create an argument for or against the following statement: "Individuals who are economically less fortunate should be allowed access to software free of charge in order to ensure that they are provided with an equal technological advantage."

# Supply Chain Management

1. List and describe the four drivers of supply chain management.
2. Explain supply chain management strategies focused on efficiency.
3. Explain supply chain management strategies focused on effectiveness.
4. Summarize the future of supply chain management.

## Introduction

The core units introduced the supply chain and supply chain management. A ***supply chain*** consists of all parties involved, directly or indirectly, in the procurement of a product or raw material. ***Supply chain management (SCM)*** involves the management of information flows between and among stages in a supply chain to maximize total supply chain effectiveness and profitability.

This plug-in takes a detailed look at how an organization can create a supply chain strategy focusing on *efficiency* and *effectiveness*. ***Efficiency IT metrics*** measure the performance of the IT system including throughput, speed, and availability. ***Effectiveness IT metrics*** measure the impact IT has on business processes and activities including customer satisfaction, conversion rates, and sell-through increases. Once an organization determines its supply chain strategy it can begin to estimate the impact that its supply chain will have on its business and ultimately the performance of the organization. The payoff for a successful supply chain strategy can be tremendous. A study by Peter J. Metz, executive director of the MIT Center for ebusiness, found that companies have achieved impressive bottom-line results from managing their supply chains—on average a 50 percent reduction in inventory and a 40 percent increase in timely deliveries.

## Supply Chain Drivers

An organization's goals and strategic objectives should determine its overall supply chain management strategy. The SCM strategy in turn determines how the supply chain will perform with respect to efficiency and effectiveness. The four primary drivers of supply chain management are:

1. Facilities
2. Inventory
3. Transportation
4. Information

An organization can use these four drivers in varying measure to push it toward either a supply chain strategy focusing on efficiency or a supply chain strategy focusing on effectiveness. The organization must decide on the trade-off it desires between efficiency and effectiveness for each driver. The selected combined impact of the various drivers then determines the efficiency and effectiveness of the entire supply chain. Figure B8.1 provides an overview of the four supply chain drivers in terms of their effect on overall efficiency and effectiveness.

## FACILITIES DRIVER

A facility processes or transforms inventory into another product or it stores the inventory before shipping it to the next facility. Toyota is an example of a company that stresses effectiveness in its facilities. Toyota's goal is to open a facility in every major market where it does business. These local facilities protect the company from currency fluctuations and trade barriers and thus are more effective for Toyota's customers. An organization should consider three primary components when determining its facilities strategy:

1. Location
2. Capacity
3. Operational design

### Location

An organization must determine where it will locate its facilities, an important decision that constitutes a large part of its supply chain strategy. The two primary options when determining facilities location are: (1) centralize the location to gain economies of scale, which increases efficiency or (2) decentralize the locations to be closer to the customers, which increases effectiveness.

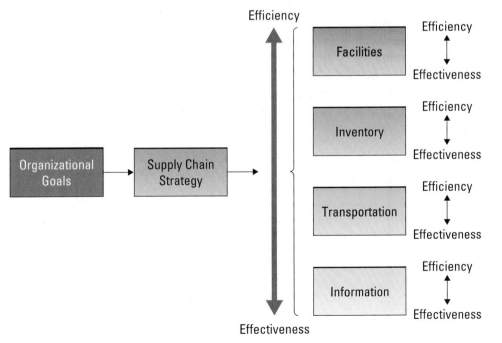

**FIGURE B8.1**

Analyzing the Design of a Supply Chain in Terms of Efficiency and Effectiveness

*The combination of efficiency and effectiveness for all four supply chain drivers determines total supply chain efficiency or effectiveness.*

A company can gain economies of scale when it centralizes its facilities. However, this cost reduction decreases the company's effectiveness, since many of its customers may be located far away from the facility. The opposite is also true; having a number of different facilities located closer to customers reduces efficiency because of the increased costs associated with the additional facilities. Many other factors will influence location decisions including facility costs, employee expense, exchange rates, tax effects, and so on.

UPS uses package flow SCM systems at each of its locations. The custom-built software combines operations research and mapping technology to optimize the way boxes are loaded and delivered. The goal is to use the package flow software to cut the distance that delivery trucks travel by more than 100 million miles each year. The project will also help UPS streamline the profitability of each of its facility locations.

## Capacity

Demand planning SCM software can help an organization determine capacity. An organization must determine the performance capacity level for each of its facilities. If it decides a facility will have a large amount of excess capacity, which provides the flexibility to respond to wide swings in demand, then it is choosing an effectiveness strategy. Excess capacity, however, costs money and can therefore decrease efficiency.

## Operational Design

An organization must determine if it wants a product focus or a functional focus for its facilities operational design. If it chooses a product focus design, it is anticipating that the facility will produce only a certain type of product. All operations, including fabrication and assembly, will focus on developing a single type of product. This strategy allows the facility to become highly efficient in producing a single product.

If it chooses a functional design, the facility will perform a specific function (e.g., fabrication only or assembly only) on many different products. This strategy allows the facility to become more effective since it can use a single process on many different types of products (see Figure B8.2).

**FIGURE** B8.2

The Facilities Driver's Effect on Efficiency and Effectiveness

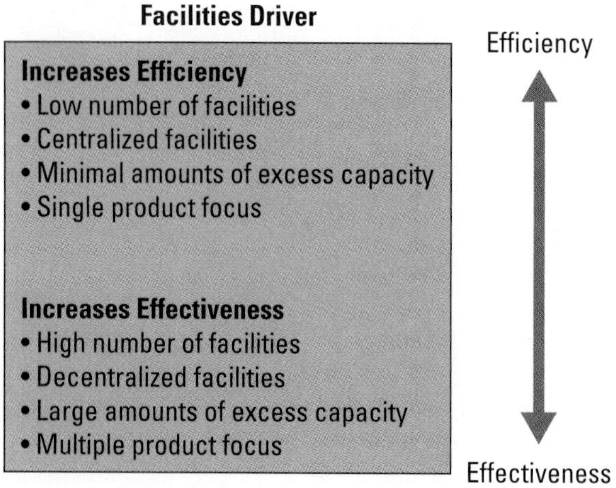

**Facilities Driver**

**Increases Efficiency**
- Low number of facilities
- Centralized facilities
- Minimal amounts of excess capacity
- Single product focus

**Increases Effectiveness**
- High number of facilities
- Decentralized facilities
- Large amounts of excess capacity
- Multiple product focus

Efficiency

Effectiveness

## INVENTORY DRIVER

For most of business history, inventory has been a form of security. A warehouse bulging with components, or a distribution center packed with finished products, meant that even when a customer forecast went wildly awry, there would still be enough supply on hand to meet demand. Ever since the 1980s, when General Motors began adopting Toyota's pioneering methods in lean manufacturing, fast companies have delayered, reengineered, and scrubbed the waste from their assembly lines and supply chains by slashing lead time and stripping inventory and spare capacity from their operations.

Dillard's department store's competitive strategy is to appeal to higher-end customers who are willing to pay a premium to obtain products immediately. Dillard's carries large amounts of inventory to ensure products are always available for its customers. In return, its customers are willing to pay extra for the products.

Companies require inventory to offset any discrepancies between supply and demand, but inventory is a major cost in any supply chain. Inventory's impact on a company's effectiveness versus efficiency can be enormous. Effectiveness results from more inventory, and efficiency results from less inventory. If a company's strategy requires a high level of customer effectiveness, then the company will locate large amounts of inventory in many facilities close to its customers, such as Dillard's strategy demands. If a company's strategy requires a high level of efficiency, the strategy of a low-cost producer, for instance, then the company will maintain low levels of inventory in a single strategic location.

*Inventory management and control software* provides control and visibility to the status of individual items maintained in inventory. The software maintains inventory record accuracy, generates material requirements for all purchased items, and analyzes inventory performance. Inventory management and control software provides the supply chain with information from a variety of sources including:

- Current inventory and order status.
- Cost accounting.
- Sales forecasts and customer orders.
- Manufacturing capacity.
- New product introductions.

Inventory management and control software provides an organization with information when making decisions in regard to two primary inventory strategies:

1. Cycle inventory
2. Safety inventory

### Cycle Inventory

*Cycle inventory* is the average amount of inventory held to satisfy customer demands between inventory deliveries. A company can follow either of two approaches regarding cycle inventory. The first approach is to hold a large amount of cycle inventory and receive inventory deliveries only once a month. The second approach is to hold a small amount of inventory and receive orders weekly or even daily. The trade-off is the cost comparison between holding larger lots of inventory for an effective supply chain and ordering products frequently for an efficient supply chain.

### Safety Inventory

*Safety inventory* is extra inventory held in the event demand exceeds supply. For example, a toy store might hold safety inventory for the Christmas season. The risk a company faces when making a decision in favor of safety inventory is that in addition to the cost of holding it, if it holds too much, some of its products may go unsold and it may have to discount them—after the Christmas season, in the toy store example. However, if it holds too little inventory it may lose sales and risk losing customers. The company must decide if it wants to risk the expense of carrying too much inventory or to risk losing sales and customers (see Figure B8.3).

### TRANSPORTATION DRIVER

Organizations use IT-enabled supply chain management systems that use quantitative analysis, decision support systems, and intelligent systems for configuring shipping plans. FedEx's entire business strategy focuses on its customers' need for highly effective transportation

**FIGURE** B8.3

The Inventory Driver's Effect on Efficiency and Effectiveness

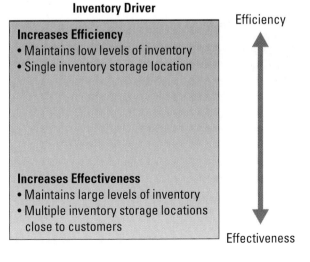

Inventory Driver

**Increases Efficiency**
- Maintains low levels of inventory
- Single inventory storage location

**Increases Effectiveness**
- Maintains large levels of inventory
- Multiple inventory storage locations close to customers

Efficiency

Effectiveness

methods. Any company that uses FedEx to transport a package is focusing primarily on a safe and timely delivery and not on the cost of delivery. Many businesses even locate their facilities near FedEx hubs so that they can quickly transport inventory overnight to their customers.

An organization can use many different methods of transportation to move its inventories between the different stages in the supply chain. Like the other supply chain drivers, transportation cost has a large impact either way on effectiveness and efficiency. If an organization focuses on a highly effective supply chain, then it can use transportation to increase the price of its products by using faster, more costly transportation methods. If the focus is a highly efficient supply chain, the organization can use transportation to decrease the price of its products by using slower, less costly transportation methods. There are two primary facets of transportation an organization should consider when determining its strategy:

1. Method of transportation
2. Transportation route

## Method of Transportation

An organization must decide how it wants to move its inventory through the supply chain. There are six basic methods of transportation it can choose from: truck, rail, ship, air, pipeline, and electronic. The primary differences between these methods are the speed of delivery and price of delivery. An organization might choose an expensive method of transportation to ensure speedy delivery if it is focusing on a highly effective supply chain. On the other hand, it might choose an inexpensive method of transportation if it is focusing on a highly efficient supply chain.

Some organizations will use a *global inventory management system* that provides the ability to locate, track, and predict the movement of every component or material anywhere upstream or downstream in the supply chain. So regardless of the chosen method of transportation, the organization can find its inventory anywhere in the supply chain.

## Transportation Route

An organization will also need to choose the transportation route for its products. Two supply chain software modules can aid in this decision. *Transportation planning software* tracks and analyzes the movement of materials and products to ensure the delivery of materials and finished goods at the right time, the right place, and the lowest cost. *Distribution management software* coordinates the process of transporting materials from a manufacturer to distribution centers to the final customer.

Transportation route directly affects the speed and cost of delivery. For example, an organization might decide to use an effectiveness route and ship its products directly to its customers, or it might decide to use an efficiency route and ship its products to a distributor that ships the products to customers (see Figure B8.4).

## INFORMATION DRIVER

Information is a driver whose importance has grown as companies use it to become both more efficient and more effective. An organization must decide what information is most valuable in efficiently reducing costs or

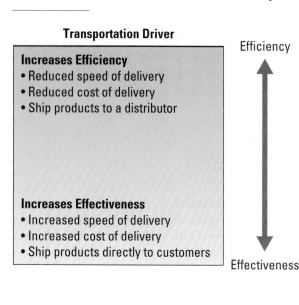

**Transportation Driver**

**Increases Efficiency**
- Reduced speed of delivery
- Reduced cost of delivery
- Ship products to a distributor

**Increases Effectiveness**
- Increased speed of delivery
- Increased cost of delivery
- Ship products directly to customers

Efficiency

Effectiveness

in improving effectiveness. This decision will vary depending on a company's strategy and the design and organization of the supply chain. Two things to consider about information in the supply chain include:

1. Information sharing.
2. Push versus pull information strategy.

### Information Sharing

An organization must determine what information it wants to share with its partners throughout the stages of the supply chain. Information sharing is a difficult decision since most organizations do not want their partners to gain insight into strategic or competitive information. However, they do need to share information so they can coordinate supply chain activities such as providing suppliers with inventory order levels to meet production forecasts. Building trusting relationships is one way to begin to understand how much information supply chain partners require.

If an organization chooses an efficiency focus for information sharing then it will freely share lots of information to increase the speed and decrease the costs of supply chain processing. If an organization chooses an effectiveness focus for information sharing, then it will share only selected information with certain individuals, which will decrease the speed and increase the costs of supply chain processing.

### Push vs. Pull Information Strategy

In a *push technology* environment, organizations send information. In a *pull technology* environment, organizations receive or request information. An organization must decide how it is going to share information with its partners. It might decide that it wants to push information out to partners by taking on the responsibility of sending information to them. On the other hand, it might decide that it wants its partners to take on the responsibility of getting information by having them directly access the information from the systems and pull the information they require.

Again, an organization must determine how much it trusts its partners when deciding on a push versus pull information sharing strategy. Using a push information sharing strategy is more effective because the organization has control over exactly what information is shared and when the information is shared. However, a push strategy is less efficient because there are costs associated with sending information such as computer equipment, applications, time, resources, and so forth.

Using a pull information sharing strategy is more efficient since the organization does not have to undertake the costs associated with sending information. However, the pull strategy is less effective since the organization has no control over when the information is pulled. For example, if the company needs inventory there is no guarantee that the suppliers will pick up the information. Hence, an organization could find itself in trouble if its partners forget to obtain the information and fail to deliver the required products (see Figure B8.5).

## Applying a Supply Chain Design

Figure B8.6 displays Wal-Mart's supply chain management design and how it correlates to its competitive strategy to be a reliable, low-cost retailer for a wide variety of mass consumption goods. Wal-Mart's supply chain emphasizes efficiency, but also maintains an adequate level of effectiveness.

**FIGURE** B8.5

The Information Driver's Effect on Efficiency and Effectiveness

**Information Driver**

**Increases Efficiency**
- Openly shares information with all individuals
- Pull information strategy

**Increases Effectiveness**
- Selectively shares certain information with certain individuals
- Push information strategy

Efficiency ↕ Effectiveness

Wal-Mart uses its four primary supply chain drivers to drive supply chain efficiency.

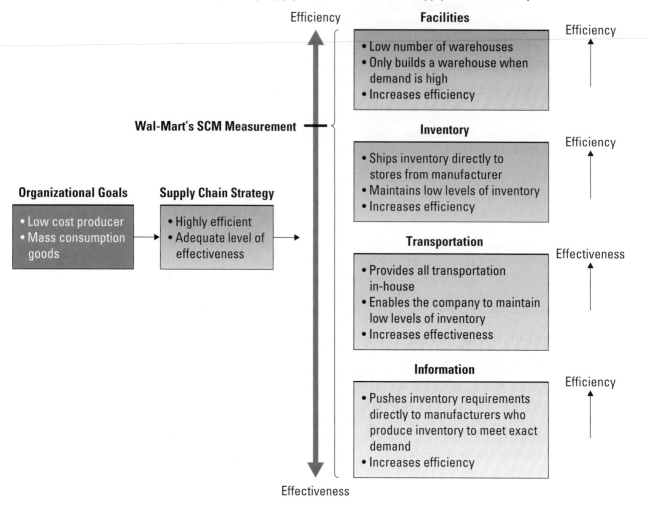

**FIGURE** B8.6

Wal-Mart's Supply Chain
Management Drivers

■ **Facilities focus—efficiency:** Wal-Mart maintains few warehouses and will build a new warehouse only when demand is high enough to justify one.

■ **Inventory focus—efficiency:** Wal-Mart ships directly to its stores from the manufacturer. This significantly lowers inventory levels because stores maintain inventory, not stores and warehouses.

■ **Transportation focus—effectiveness:** Wal-Mart maintains its own fleet of trucks. The benefits in terms of overall supply chain efficiency justify the expense of maintaining its own trucks because effective transportation allows Wal-Mart to keep low levels of inventory.

■ **Information focus—efficiency:** Wal-Mart invests heavily in technology and the flow of information throughout its entire supply chain. Wal-Mart pushes inventory information all the way back up the supply chain to its suppliers who then manufacture only enough inventories to meet demand. The cost to build the information flows between its supply chain partners has been tremendous. However, the result of this investment is a highly successful and efficient supply chain.

# Future Trends

A television commercial shows a man in a uniform quietly moving through a family home. The man replaces the empty cereal box with a full one just before a hungry child opens the cabinet; he then opens a new sack of dog food as the hungry bulldog eyes him warily, and finally hands a full bottle of shampoo to the man in the shower who had just run out. The next wave in supply chain management will be home-based supply chain fulfillment.

Walgreens is differentiating itself from other national chains by marketing itself as the family's just-in-time supplier. Consumers today are becoming incredibly comfortable with the idea of going online to purchase products when they want, how they want, and at the price they want. Walgreens is developing custom websites for each household that allow families to order electronically and then at their convenience go to the store to pick up their goods at a special self-service counter or the drive-through window. Walgreens is making a promise that goes beyond low prices and customer service and extends right into the home.

The functionality in supply chain management systems is becoming more and more sophisticated as supply chain management matures. Now and in the future, the next stages of SCM will incorporate more functions such as marketing, customer service, and product development. This will be achieved through more advanced communication, adoption of more user-friendly decision support systems, and availability of shared information to all participants in the supply chain. SCM is an ongoing development as technology makes it possible to acquire information ever more accurately and frequently from all over the world, and introduces new tools to aid in the analytical processes that deal with the supply chain's growing complexity.

According to Forrester Research, Inc., U.S. firms will spend $35 billion over the next five years to improve business processes that monitor, manage, and optimize their extended supply chains. Figure B8.7 displays the fastest growing SCM components because they have the greatest potential impact on an organization's bottom line.

## RADIO FREQUENCY IDENTIFICATION (RFID)

*Radio frequency identification (RFID)* technologies use active or passive tags in the form of chips or smart labels that can store unique identifiers and relay this information to electronic readers. At Starbucks, good service is nearly as important

| Growing SCM Components | |
|---|---|
| **Supply chain event management (SCEM)** | Enables an organization to react more quickly to resolve supply chain issues. SCEM software increases real-time information sharing among supply chain partners and decreases their response time to unplanned events. SCEM demand will skyrocket as more and more organizations begin to discover the benefits of real-time supply chain monitoring. |
| **Selling chain management** | Applies technology to the activities in the order life cycle from inquiry to sale. |
| **Collaborative engineering** | Allows an organization to reduce the cost and time required during the design process of a product. |
| **Collaborative demand planning** | Helps organizations reduce their investment in inventory, while improving customer satisfaction through product availability. |

**FIGURE B8.7**

Growing SCM Components

as good coffee to customer loyalty. But when a delivery person comes knocking on the back door to drop off muffins, it means employees may need to leave their countertop posts, jeopardizing customer service. To help solve the problem, Starbucks is considering using radio frequency identification technology as part of a proposed plan to let its 40,000 suppliers drop off pastries, milk, coffee beans, and other supplies at night, after stores have closed. This solution solves one problem while causing another: How does Starbucks ensure that delivery people do not walk out with as much stuff as they drop off?

To solve the problem, the company will distribute to its suppliers cards with RFID chips that give delivery people access to stores at night, while recording who is coming and going. RFID tags contain a microchip and an antenna and typically work by transmitting a serial number via radio waves to an electronic reader, which confirms the identity of a person or object bearing the tag.

RFID technology is finally coming into its own. Wal-Mart, the nation's largest retailer, asked suppliers to attach RFID tags to product shipment pallets by the end of 2005 to automate tracking. However, drawbacks to RFID technology, including its high cost and concerns about consumer privacy, must be overcome before it finds widespread use. Figure B8.8 displays the three components of RFID, and Figure B8.9 shows how tracking with RFID tags is expected to work in the supply chain.

As many as 10,000 radio frequency identification tags are taking to the skies, affixed to everything from airline seats to brakes, as part of the Airbus A380, a 550-seat jet. The tags contain serial numbers, codes, and maintenance history that should make it easier to track, fix, and replace parts. Not to be outdone, Boeing is using tags on many of the parts in its upcoming 7E7 Dreamliner. These initiatives are not the first use of RFID in the airline industry, but they represent aggressive plans to further leverage the real-time and detail capabilities of RFID. Boeing and Airbus are equipping all tools and toolboxes with RFID tags.

**FIGURE B8.8**

Three RFID Components

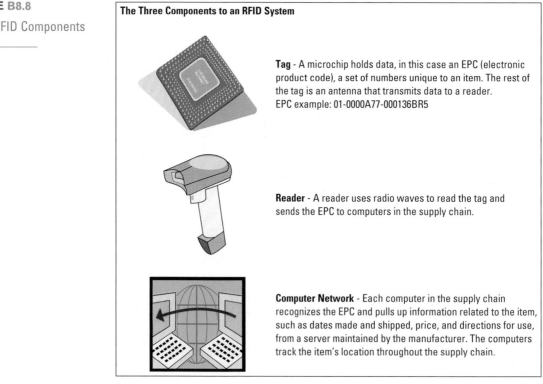

**The Three Components to an RFID System**

**Tag** - A microchip holds data, in this case an EPC (electronic product code), a set of numbers unique to an item. The rest of the tag is an antenna that transmits data to a reader.
EPC example: 01-0000A77-000136BR5

**Reader** - A reader uses radio waves to read the tag and sends the EPC to computers in the supply chain.

**Computer Network** - Each computer in the supply chain recognizes the EPC and pulls up information related to the item, such as dates made and shipped, price, and directions for use, from a server maintained by the manufacturer. The computers track the item's location throughout the supply chain.

## RFID in the Retail Supply Chain

RFID tags are added to every product and shipping box. At every step of an item's journey, a reader scans one of the tags and updates the information on the server.

### The Manufacturer
A reader scans the tags as items leave the factory.

### The Distribution Center
Readers in the unloading area scan the tags on arriving boxes and update inventory, avoiding the need to open packages.

### The Store
Tags are scanned upon arrival to update inventory. At the racks, readers scan tags as shirts are stocked. At the checkout counter, a cashier can scan individual items with a handheld reader. As items leave the store, inventory is updated. Manufacturers and retailers can observe sales patterns in real time and make swift decisions about production, ordering, and pricing.

### The Home
The consumer can have the tag disabled at the store for privacy or place readers in closets to keep track of clothes. With customers' approval, stores can follow purchasing patterns and notify them of sales.

## Integrating RFID and Software

Integrating RFID with enterprise software is expected to change the way companies manage maintenance, combat theft, and even augment Sarbanes-Oxley Act IT initiatives. Oracle and SAP have begun adding RFID capability to their enterprise application suites. Oracle's RFID and Sensor-Based Services analyze and respond to data from RFID so the information can be integrated with Oracle's applications.

RFID tags are evolving, too, and the advances will provide more granular information to enterprise software. Today's tags can store an electronic product code. In time, tags could hold more information, making them portable mini-databases. The possibilities of RFID are endless. Delta Air Lines recently completed a pilot project that used baggage tags incorporating RFID chips instead of the standard bar codes. With RFID readers installed at counters and key sorting locations, not a single duffel was misplaced.

The fundamental decisions an organization needs to make regarding its supply chain strategy concern:

- **Facilities**—An organization must decide between the cost of the number, location, and type of facilities (efficiency) and the level of effectiveness that these facilities provide.

- **Inventory**—An organization can increase inventory levels to make its supply chain more effective for its customers. This choice, however, comes at a cost as added inventory significantly decreases efficiency.

- **Transportation**—An organization can choose between the cost of transporting inventory (efficiency) and the speed of transporting inventory (effectiveness). Transportation choices also influence other drivers such as inventory levels and facility locations.

- **Information**—A focus on information can help improve both supply chain effectiveness and efficiency. The information driver also improves the performance of other drivers.

★ KEY TERMS

Collaborative demand
  planning, 339
Collaborative
  engineering, 339
Cycle inventory, 335
Distributions management
  software, 336
Effectiveness IT metric, 332
Efficiency IT metric, 332

Global inventory management
  system, 336
Inventory management and
  control software, 335
Pull technology, 337
Push technology, 337
Radio frequency identification
  (RFID), 339
Safety inventory, 335

Selling chain management, 332
Supply chain, 332
Supply chain event
  management (SCEM), 339
Supply chain management
  (SCM), 332
Transportation planning
  software, 336

★ CLOSING CASE ONE

### Listerine's Journey

When you use Listerine antiseptic mouthwash, you are experiencing the last step in a complex supply chain spanning several continents and requiring months of coordination by countless businesses and individuals. The resources involved in getting a single bottle of Listerine to a consumer are unbelievable. As raw material is transformed to finished product, what will be Listerine travels around the globe and through multiple supply chains and information systems.

### The Journey Begins

A farmer in Australia is harvesting a crop of eucalyptus for eucalyptol, the oil found in its leathery leaves. The farmer sells the crop to an Australian processing company, which spends about four weeks extracting the eucalyptol from the eucalyptus.

Meanwhile, in New Jersey, Warner-Lambert (WL) partners with a distributor to buy the oil from the Australian company and transport it to WL's Listerine manufacturing and distribution facility in Lititz, Pennsylvania. The load will arrive at Lititz about three months after the harvest.

At the same time, in Saudi Arabia, a government-owned operation is drilling deep under the desert for the natural gas that will yield the synthetic alcohol that gives Listerine its 43-proof punch. Union Carbide Corp. ships the gas via tanker to a refinery in Texas, which purifies it and converts it into ethanol. The ethanol is loaded onto another tanker, then transported from Texas through the Gulf of Mexico to New Jersey, where it is transferred to storage tanks and transported via truck or rail to WL's plant. A single shipment of ethanol takes about six to eight weeks to get from Saudi Arabia to Lititz.

SPI Polyols Inc., a manufacturer of ingredients for the confectionery, pharmaceutical, and oral-care industries, buys corn syrup from farmers in the Midwest. SPI converts the corn syrup into sorbitol solution, which sweetens and adds bulk to the Cool Mint Listerine. The syrup is shipped to SPI's New Castle, Delaware, facility for processing and then delivered on a tank wagon to Lititz. The whole process, from the time the corn is harvested to when it is converted into sorbitol, takes about a month.

By now the ethanol, eucalyptol, and sorbitol have all arrived at WL's plant in Lititz, where employees test them, along with the menthol, citric acid, and other ingredients that make up Listerine, for quality assurance before authorizing storage in tanks. To mix the ingredients, flow meters turn on valves at each tank and measure out the right proportions, according to the Cool Mint formula developed by WL R&D in 1990. (The original amber mouthwash was developed in 1879.)

Next, the Listerine flows through a pipe to fillers along the packaging line. The fillers dispense the product into bottles delivered continuously from a nearby plastics company for just-in-time manufacturing. The bottles are capped, labeled, and fitted with tamper-resistant safety bands, then placed in shipping boxes that each hold one dozen 500-milliliter bottles. During this process, machines automatically check for skewed labels, missing safety bands, and other problems. The entire production cycle, from the delivery via pipe of the Listerine liquid to the point where bottles are boxed and ready to go, takes a matter of minutes. The line can produce about 300 bottles per minute—a far cry from the 80 to 100 bottles that the line produced per minute before 1994.

Each box travels on a conveyor belt to the palletizer, which organizes and shrink-wraps the boxes into 100-case pallets. Stickers with identifying bar codes are affixed to the pallets. Drivers forklift the pallets to the distribution center, located in the same Lititz facility, from which the boxes are shipped around the world.

Finally, the journey is completed when a customer purchases a bottle of Listerine at a local drugstore or grocery store. In a few days, the store will place an order for a replacement bottle of Listerine. And so begins the cycle again.

## Questions

1. Summarize SCM and describe Warner-Lambert's supply chain strategy. Diagram the SCM components.
2. Detail Warner-Lambert's facilities strategy.
3. Detail Warner-Lambert's inventory strategy.
4. Detail Warner-Lambert's transportation strategy.
5. Detail Warner-Lambert's information strategy.
6. What would happen to Warner-Lambert's business if a natural disaster in Saudi Arabia depleted its natural gas resources?

### Katrina Shakes Supply Chains

How do corporations cope with the realities of risk, uncertainty, and crisis? Many businesses prepared well for Hurricane Katrina, responded quickly, and did so because Katrina was exactly the kind of event for which well-run corporations ready themselves. Corporations donated more than $500 million for relief for the hurricane that hit New Orleans in 2005 and were the first to provide help to Katrina victims.

### Home Depot

As the residents of shattered Gulf Coast towns began returning home or crawling from the wreckage in the days after Hurricane Katrina hit, many found their way to the big concrete box with the battered orange sign. Home Depot stores were among the first to reopen in the storm's wake, offering rebuilding supplies plus the even more precious commodities of electricity and normalcy.

Home Depot had started mobilizing four days before Katrina slammed into the coast. Two days before landfall, maintenance teams battened down stores in the hurricane's projected path, while it moved electrical generators and hundreds of extra workers into place. A day after the storm, all but 10 of the company's 33 stores in Katrina's impact zone were open. Within a week, only four of its nine stores in metropolitan New Orleans were closed. "We always take tremendous pride in being able to be among the first responders," Home Depot CEO Bob Nardelli said.

### Wal-Mart

Jessica Lewis could not believe her eyes. Her entire community of Waveland, Mississippi, a Gulf Coast resort town of 7,000, had been laid waste by the storm, and Lewis, co-manager of the local Wal-Mart, was assessing the damage to her store. The fortresslike big box on Highway 90 still stood, but Katrina's floodwaters had surged through the entrance, knocking over freezers full of frozen pizza, shelves of back-to-school items, and racks of clothing. Trudging through nearly two feet of water in the fading light, Lewis wondered how they would ever clean up the mess.

That quickly became the least of Lewis's worries. As the sun set on Waveland, a nightmarish scene unfolded on Highway 90. She saw neighbors wandering around with bloody feet because they had fled their homes with no shoes. Some wore only underwear. "It broke my heart to see them like this," Lewis recalled. "These were my kids' teachers. Some of them were my teachers. They were the parents of the kids on my kids' sports teams. They were my neighbors. They were my customers."

Lewis felt there was only one thing to do. She had her stepbrother clear a path through the mess in the store with a bulldozer. Then she salvaged everything she could and handed it out in the parking lot. She gave socks and underwear to shivering Waveland police officers who had climbed into trees to escape the rising water. She handed out shoes to her barefoot neighbors and diapers for their babies. She gave people bottled water to drink and sausages, stored high in the warehouse, which had not been touched by the flood. She even broke into the pharmacy and got insulin and drugs for AIDS patients. "This is the right thing to do," she recalled thinking. "I hope my bosses aren't going to have a problem with that."

The hurricane was a pivotal moment for Wal-Mart, one that it nearly fumbled. The company dispatched armored cars to the region before the storm hit to remove cash from stores, but it left behind guns that ended up in the hands of looters. As the extent of the devastation became clear, however, Wal-Mart did a remarkable about-face. At the urging of CEO Lee Scott, its truckers hauled $3 million of supplies to the ravaged zone, arriving days before the Federal Emergency Management Agency in many cases. The company also contributed $17 million in cash to relief efforts. Wal-Mart also demonstrated how efficient it could be. Katrina shut down 126 Wal-Mart facilities in the Gulf Coast area, and within weeks all but 13 of the facilities were up and running again. The company located 97 percent of the employees displaced by the storm and offered them jobs at any Wal-Mart operation in the country.

## FedEx

Watching TV in Memphis, Mike Mitchell did not get it. Day after day, the FedEx Express senior technical adviser heard reporters describe how desperately New Orleans rescuers needed communications. Nobody seemed able to fix the problem. Finally, on the Thursday after Katrina hit, Mitchell spied a way to help: an aerial shot of a 54-story building near the convention center showed the intact base for a FedEx radio antenna, part of a system he had visited in 2004 on a maintenance check. That led him to hope that part of the installation had survived. He thought if they could get a generator to the roof and radios to the rescuers, they would have a way of talking to one another. Mitchell shot an email to his boss the next day. It made its way up the ranks. FedEx called FEMA. FEMA called the 82nd Airborne Division. They all liked the idea.

Five days later Mitchell arrived in New Orleans with 125 walkie-talkies, a few changes of clothes, and a sleeping bag. He did not know how he would get to the top of the building or exactly what he would find there. However, he was determined to make the radios work. "I didn't want to let all those people down," he said. There turned out to be just enough fuel in the building's emergency generator for a couple of elevator rides to the top. An Army helicopter dropped in a half-ton of gear, including a nine-foot antenna to replace the one Katrina had sheared off. With help from eight soldiers, Mitchell fixed it. "Radio check," he called into a walkie-talkie after they had finished. "Lima Charlie," a soldier shot back. (Translation: loud and clear.) Thanks to FedEx, members of the 82nd and other rescuers finally had a reliable radio network.

Impressive as Mitchell's radio rescue was, such dramas are almost routine for FedEx. "That's the nature of our business," said Dave Bronczek, who heads FedEx's Express division. "We're used to dealing with crisis." Every day of the year, FedEx must cope with some sort of local disruption. In 2005, the company had to activate contingency plans on 37 tropical storms. Add to that such events as an air-traffic-controller strike in France and a blackout in Los Angeles, and it is no wonder that FedEx gets so much practice in flexibility. FedEx conducts disaster drills several times a year—for everything from big earthquakes to bioterrorism to a monster typhoon hitting the company's hub in the Philippines. Eight disaster kits, each containing two tons of such supplies as fuel and communications gear, stand ready in Memphis in case a facility is in need of repair. Each night, five empty FedEx flights roam the skies, standing by to replace a broken-down plane or assist with an unexpected surge in volume.

All this makes FedEx a national resource during a crisis like Katrina. Before the storm hit, FedEx positioned 30,000 bags of ice, 30,000 gallons of water, and 85 home generators outside Baton Rouge and Tallahassee so that it could move in quickly after the storm to relieve employees. In addition, FedEx dispatched in advance four 4,000-pound facility repair kits. FedEx also made preparations on behalf of the Red Cross, which keeps shipping containers filled with bandages, blankets, batteries, and such at FedEx hubs to be dispatched around the globe at a moment's notice. Before Katrina, FedEx staged 60 tons of Red Cross provisions (it has since delivered another 440 tons of relief supplies, mostly at no charge).

Like Hurricane Andrew before her, Katrina has taught FedEx a thing or two about disaster preparation. Lesson one: Arrange for temporary housing in advance for employees who might be displaced. Lesson two: Do not count on cell phones. The local networks were down for days after the storm; the company is increasing the number of satellite phones it deploys.

## Questions

1. How did Home Depot manage its supply chain to be one of the first stores to reopen after Katrina?

2. How could Wal-Mart have revamped its transportation driver to handle Katrina more efficiently?

3. Why is it critical to FedEx's success to be able to handle all types of global disasters? Highlight FedEx's use of the information driver.

4. How can the government learn from big business in dealing with disasters such as Katrina?

5. What can companies do in terms of facilities, inventory, transportation, and information to prepare themselves for disasters such as Katrina?

## ★ MAKING BUSINESS DECISIONS

### 1. Focusing on Facilities

Focus is a large distributor of films and is owned and operated by Lauren O'Connell. The company has been in business for over 50 years and distributes motion pictures to theaters all over the United States and Canada. Focus is in the middle of a supply chain overhaul and is currently deciding its supply chain strategy. Lauren has asked you to create a report discussing the company's options for its facilities including location, capacity, and operational design. The report should include two primary focuses: one on efficiency and one on effectiveness.

### 2. Investing in Inventory

Poppa's Toy Store Inc. has more than 150 stores in 38 states. The chain has been owned and operated for the last 30 years by CEO Taylor Coombe. Taylor has been reading reports on supply chain management and is particularly interested in updating the company's current supply chain. It is the beginning of April and Taylor wants a new SCM system up and running before the Christmas season starts in November. Taylor is particularly interested in demand planning and forecasting for the entire company's inventory during its busiest season—Christmas. Taylor has asked you to create a report discussing the company's options for its inventory management strategy including cycle and safety inventory. The report should include two primary focuses: one on efficiency and one on effectiveness.

### 3. Targeting Transportation

Extra Express Co. is an overnight freight and parcel delivery business that operates on a global level and has annual revenues in excess of $400 million. You have just been hired as the company's director of transportation. The CEO, Jeff Brewer, has asked you to put together a report detailing how the company can gain efficiencies by streamlining its transportation methods and routes.

### 4. Increasing Information

Galina's is a high-end auction house located in New York City. Galina's specializes in selling jewelry, art, and antique furniture primarily from estate sales. The owner, Galina Bucrya, would like to begin offering certain items for auction over the Internet. Galina is unfamiliar with the Internet and not quite sure how to pursue her new business strategy. You are working for Information Inc., a small business consulting company that specializes in ebusiness strategies. Galina has hired you to help her create her supply chain ebusiness strategy. Compile a report describing supply chain management, the potential benefits her company can receive from an SCM strategy, your recommendation for an efficient or effective SCM strategy, and your views on the future of SCM.

## 5. Increasing Revenues with SCM

Cold Cream is one of the premier beauty supply stores in the metro New York area. People come from all over to sample the store's unique creams, lotions, makeup, and perfumes. The company receives its products from manufacturers around the globe. The company would like to implement an SCM system to help it better understand its customers and their purchasing habits. Create a report summarizing SCM systems and explain how an SCM system can directly influence Cold Cream's revenues.

# Customer Relationship Management

## Introduction

The core units introduced **customer relationship management (CRM),** which involves managing all aspects of a customer's relationship with an organization to increase customer loyalty and retention and an organization's profitability. The two primary components of a CRM strategy are operational CRM and analytical CRM. **Operational CRM** supports traditional transactional processing for day-to-day front-office operations or systems that deal directly with the customers. **Analytical CRM** supports back-office operations and strategic analysis and includes all systems that do not deal directly with the customers. The primary difference between operational CRM and analytical CRM is the degree of direct interaction between the organization and its customers. Figure B9.1 provides an overview of operational CRM and analytical CRM.

## Using IT to Drive Operational CRM

Figure B9.2 displays the different technologies marketing, sales, and customer service departments can use to perform operational CRM.

### MARKETING AND OPERATIONAL CRM

Companies are no longer trying to sell one product to as many customers as possible; instead, they are trying to sell one customer as many products as possible.

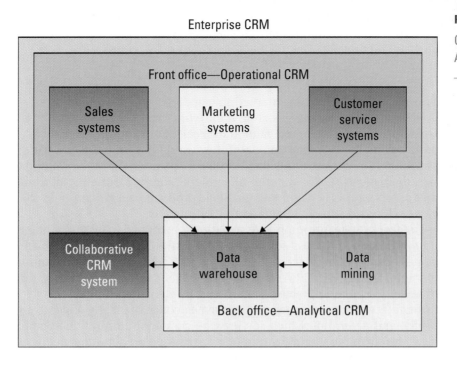

Enterprise CRM

Front office—Operational CRM

Sales systems

Marketing systems

Customer service systems

Collaborative CRM system

Data warehouse

Data mining

Back office—Analytical CRM

Marketing departments are able to transform to this new way of doing business by using CRM technologies that allow them to gather and analyze customer information to deploy successful marketing campaigns. In fact, a marketing campaign's success is directly proportional to the organization's ability to gather and analyze the right information. The three primary operational CRM technologies a marketing department can implement to increase customer satisfaction are:

1. List generator.
2. Campaign management.
3. Cross-selling and up-selling.

### List Generator

*List generators* compile customer information from a variety of sources and segment the information for different marketing campaigns. Information sources include website visits, website questionnaires, online and off-line surveys, fliers, toll-free numbers, current customer lists, and so on. After compiling the customer list, an organization can use criteria to filter and sort the list for potential customers. Filter and sort criteria can include such things as household income, education level, and age. List generators provide the marketing department with a solid understanding of the type of customer it needs to target for marketing campaigns.

### Campaign Management

*Campaign management systems* guide users through marketing campaigns performing such tasks as campaign definition, planning, scheduling, segmentation, and

| Operational CRM Technologies | | |
|---|---|---|
| **Marketing** | **Sales** | **Customer Service** |
| 1. List generator | 1. Sales management | 1. Contact center |
| 2. Campaign management | 2. Contact management | 2. Web-based self-service |
| 3. Cross-selling and up-selling | 3. Opportunity management | 3. Call scripting |

success analysis. These advanced systems can even calculate quantifiable results for return on investment (ROI) for each campaign and track the results in order to analyze and understand how the company can fine-tune future campaigns.

### Cross-Selling and Up-Selling

Two key sales strategies a marketing campaign can deploy are cross-selling and up-selling. *Cross-selling* is selling *additional* products or services to a customer. *Up-selling* is *increasing* the value of the sale. For example, McDonald's performs cross-selling by asking customers if they would like an apple pie with their meal. McDonald's performs up-selling by asking customers if they would like to super-size their meals. CRM systems offer marketing departments all kinds of information about their customers and their products, which can help them identify cross-selling and up-selling marketing campaigns.

California State Automobile Association (CSAA) had to take advantage of its ability to promote and cross-sell CSAA automotive, insurance, and travel services to beat its competition. Accomplishing this task was easy once the company implemented E.piphany's CRM system. The system integrated information from all of CSAA's separate databases, making it immediately available to all employees through a web-based browser. Employees could quickly glance at a customer's profile and determine which services the customer currently had and which services the customer might want to purchase based on her or his needs as projected by the software.

## SALES AND OPERATIONAL CRM

Siebel, one of the largest providers of CRM software, had 33,000 subscribers in January 2005. Salesforce.com, provider of on-demand web-based customer relationship management software, added 40,000 subscribers during the first three months of 2005, more than all of Siebel's subscribers. Salesforce.com's total number of subscribers is over 300,000. Merrill Lynch, one of the biggest customers in the sales force market, signed on for 5,000 subscriptions for its global private client division, making the brokerage firm Salesforce.com's largest customers. Salesforce.com's Customforce includes tools for adding data analysis capabilities, spreadsheet-style mathematical formulas, business processes, and forecasting models.

The sales department was the first to begin developing CRM systems. Sales departments had two primary reasons to track customer sales information electronically. First, sales representatives were struggling with the overwhelming amount of customer account information they were required to maintain and track. Second, companies were struggling with the issue that much of their vital customer and sales information remained in the heads of their sales representatives. One of the first CRM components built to help address these issues was the sales force automation component. *Sales force automation (SFA)* is a system that automatically tracks all of the steps in the sales process. SFA products focus on increasing customer satisfaction, building customer relationships, and improving product sales by tracking all sales information.

Serving several million guests each year, Vail Resorts Inc. maintains dozens of systems across all seven of its properties. These systems perform numerous tasks including recording lift ticket, lodging, restaurant, conference, retail, and ski rental sales. Since a significant percentage of the company's revenue results from repeat guests, building stronger, more profitable relationships with its loyal customers is Vail Resorts first priority.

To improve its customer service and marketing campaign success, Vail deployed the Ascential CRM system, which integrated the customer information from its many disparate systems. The CRM system is providing Vail Resorts with a detailed level of customer insight, which helps the company personalize its guest offerings and promotions. By using a CRM system that integrates information from across all of its resorts and business lines, the company can determine what, where, and how its guests behave across all of its properties. For example, the company can now offer discounts on lift ticket and ski rentals for customers staying in its resorts.

The three primary operational CRM technologies a sales department can implement to increase customer satisfaction are:

1. Sales management
2. Contact management
3. Opportunity management

### Sales Management CRM Systems

Figure B9.3 depicts the typical sales process, which begins with an opportunity and ends with billing the customer for the sale. Leads and potential customers are the lifeblood of all sales organizations, whether the products they are peddling are computers, clothing, or cars. How the leads are handled can make the difference between revenue growth or decline. *Sales management CRM systems* automate each phase of the sales process, helping individual sales representatives coordinate and organize all of their accounts. Features include calendars to help plan customer meetings, alarm reminders signaling important tasks, customizable multimedia presentations, and document generation. These systems even have the ability to provide an analysis of the sales cycle and calculate how each individual sales representative is performing during the sales process.

### Contact Management CRM Systems

A *contact management CRM system* maintains customer contact information and identifies prospective customers for future sales. Contact management systems include such features as maintaining organizational charts, detailed customer notes, and supplemental sale information. For example, a contact management system can take an incoming telephone number and display the caller's name along with notes detailing previous conversations. This allows the sales representative

**FIGURE** B9.3

Overview of the Sales Process

Sales Process

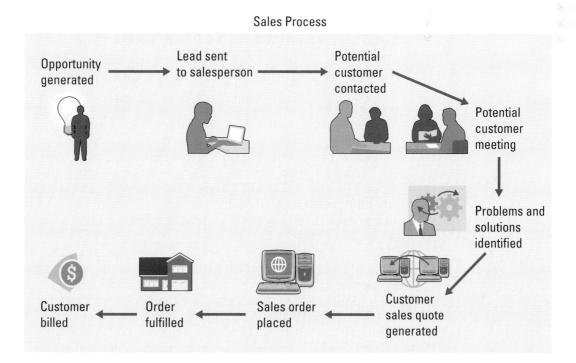

to answer the telephone and say, "Hi, Sue, how is your new laptop working? How was your vacation to Florida?" without receiving any reminders of such details first from the customer. The customer feels valued since the sales associate knows her name and even remembers details of their last conversation!

The $16 billion 3M is a leader in the health care, safety, electronics, telecommunications, office, and consumer markets. The company began to focus on streamlining and unifying its sales processes with the primary goals of better customer segmentation and more reliable lead generation and qualification. To achieve these goals the company implemented a CRM system and soon found itself receiving the following benefits:

- Cutting the time it takes to familiarize sales professionals with new territories by 33 percent.
- Increasing management's visibility of the sales process.
- Decreasing the time it takes to qualify leads and assign sales opportunities by 40 percent.

One of the more successful campaigns driven by the CRM system allowed 3M to quickly deliver direct mail to targeted government agencies and emergency services in response to the anthrax attacks in 2002. All inquiries to the mail campaign were automatically assigned to a sales representative who followed up with a quote. In little more than a week, the company had received orders for 35,000 respirator masks.

### Opportunity Management CRM Systems

*Opportunity management CRM systems* target sales opportunities by finding new customers or companies for future sales. Opportunity management systems determine potential customers and competitors and define selling efforts including budgets and schedules. Advanced opportunity management systems can even calculate the probability of a sale, which can save sales representatives significant time and money when attempting to find new customers. The primary difference between contact management and opportunity management is that contact management deals with existing customers and opportunity management deals with prospective customers. Figure B9.4 displays six CRM pointers a sales representative can use to increase prospective customers.

## CUSTOMER SERVICE AND OPERATIONAL CRM

Andy Taylor became president of Enterprise, his father's $76 million rental-car company, in 1980. Today, it is the largest in North America, with $7 billion in revenue. How has he kept customer service a priority? By quantifying it. Enterprise surveys 1.7 million customers a year. If a branch's satisfaction scores are low, employees, even vice presidents, cannot be promoted. The result is self-propagating. Seeking better scores, managers make better hires. And because Enterprise promotes almost solely from within, nearly every executive—including Taylor, who started out washing cars—has a frontline understanding of what it takes to keep customers happy. "The company would never have gotten that 100-fold growth without Andy's knack for putting systems and processes in place so you can deliver consistent service," said Sandy Rogers, senior vice president of corporate strategy.

Sales and marketing are the primary departments that interact directly with customers before a sale. Most companies recognize the importance of building strong relationships during the marketing and sales efforts; however, many fail to realize the importance of continuing to build these relationships after the sale is complete. It is actually more important to build postsale relationships if the company wants to ensure customer loyalty and satisfaction. The best way to implement postsale CRM strategies is through the customer service department.

| CRM Pointers for Gaining Prospective Customers | |
| --- | --- |
| **1. Get their attention** | If you have a good prospect, chances are that he or she receives dozens of offers from similar companies. Be sure your first contact is professional and gets your customer's attention. |
| **2. Value their time** | When you ask for a meeting, you are asking for the most valuable thing a busy person has—time. Many companies have had great success by offering high-value gifts in exchange for a meeting with a representative. Just be careful because some organizations frown on expensive gifts. Instead, offer these prospective customers a report that can help them perform their jobs more effectively. |
| **3. Overdeliver** | If your letter offered a free DVD in exchange for a meeting, bring a box of microwave popcorn along with the movie. Little gestures like these tell customers that you not only keep your word, but also can be counted on to overdeliver. |
| **4. Contact frequently** | Find new and creative ways to contact your prospective customers frequently. Starting a newsletter and sending out a series of industry updates are excellent ways to keep in contact and provide value. |
| **5. Generate a trustworthy mailing list** | If you are buying a mailing list from a third party be sure that the contacts are genuine prospects, especially if you are offering an expensive gift. Be sure that the people you are meeting have the power to authorize a sale. |
| **6. Follow up** | One of the most powerful prospecting tools is a simple thank-you note. Letting people know that their time was appreciated may even lead to additional referrals. |

**FIGURE** B9.4

CRM Pointers for Gaining Prospective Customers

One of the primary reasons a company loses customers is bad customer service experiences. Providing outstanding customer service is a difficult task, and many CRM technologies are available to assist organizations with this important activity. For example, by rolling out Lotus Instant Messaging to its customers, Avnet Computer Marketing has established an efficient, direct route to push valuable information and updates out to its customers. The company uses Lotus Instant Messaging to provide real-time answers to customer questions by listing its support specialists' status by different colors on its website: green if they are available, red if they are not, or blue if they are out of the office. The customer simply clicks on a name to begin instant messaging or a chat session to get quick answers to questions.

Before access to Lotus Instant Messaging, customers had to wait in "1-800" call queues or for email responses for answers. The new system has increased customer satisfaction along with tremendous savings from fewer long-distance phone charges. Avnet also estimates that Lotus Instant Messaging saves each of its 650 employees 5 to 10 minutes a day.

The three primary operational CRM technologies a customer service department can implement to increase customer satisfaction are:

1. Contact center.
2. Web-based self-service.
3. Call scripting.

### Contact Center

Knowledge-management software, which helps call centers put consistent answers at customer-service representatives' fingertips, is often long on promise and short on delivery. The problem? Representatives have to take time out from answering calls to input things they've learned, putting the "knowledge" in knowledge management.

Brad Cleveland, who heads the Incoming Calls Management Institute, said, "Software is just a tool. It doesn't do any good unless people across the organization are using it to its potential." Sharp Electronics is making it happen. Sharp's frontline representatives built the system from scratch. And as Sharp rolled out its network over the past four years, representatives' compensation and promotions were tied directly to the system's use. As a result, the customer call experience at Sharp has improved dramatically: The proportion of problems resolved by a single call has soared from 76 percent to 94 percent since 2000.

A *contact center* (or *call center*) is where customer service representatives (CSRs) answer customer inquiries and respond to problems through a number of different customer touchpoints. A contact center is one of the best assets a customer-driven organization can have because maintaining a high level of customer support is critical to obtaining and retaining customers. Numerous systems are available to help an organization automate its contact centers. Figure B9.5 displays a few of the features available in contact center systems.

Contact centers also track customer call history along with problem resolutions—information critical for providing a comprehensive customer view to the CSR. CSRs who can quickly comprehend and understand all of a customer's products and issues provide tremendous value to the customer and the organization. Nothing makes frustrated customers happier than not having to explain their problems to yet another CSR.

New emotion-detection software called Perform, created by Nice Systems, is designed to help companies improve customer service by identifying callers who are upset. When an elderly man distressed over high medical premiums hung up during his phone call to the Wisconsin Physician Services Insurance Corp.'s call center, an IT system detected the customer's exasperation and automatically emailed a supervisor. The supervisor listened to a digital recording of the conversation, called the customer, and suggested ways to lower the premium. The system uses algorithms to determine a baseline of emotion during the first 5 to 10 seconds of a call; any deviation from the baseline triggers an alert.

### Web-Based Self-Service

*Web-based self-service systems* allow customers to use the web to find answers to their questions or solutions to their problems. FedEx uses web-based self-service systems to allow customers to track their own packages without having to talk to a CSR. FedEx customers can simply log on to FedEx's website and enter their tracking number. The website quickly displays the exact location of the package and the estimated delivery time.

Another great feature of web-based self-service is click-to-talk buttons. *Click-to-talk* buttons allow customers to click on a button and talk with a CSR via the Internet. Powerful customer-driven features like these add tremendous value to any organization by providing customers with real-time information without having to contact company representatives.

### Call Scripting

Being a CSR is not an easy task, especially when the CSR is dealing with detailed technical products or services. *Call scripting systems* access organizational databases that track similar issues or questions and automatically generate the details

FIGURE B9.5

Common Features Included in Contact Centers

| Common Features Included in Contact Centers | |
|---|---|
| *Automatic call distribution* | A phone switch routes inbound calls to available agents. |
| *Interactive voice response (IVR)* | Directs customers to use touch-tone phones or keywords to navigate or provide information. |
| *Predictive dialing* | Automatically dials outbound calls and when someone answers, the call is forwarded to an available agent. |

for the CSR who can then relay them to the customer. The system can even provide a list of questions that the CSR can ask the customer to determine the potential problem and resolution. This feature helps CSRs answer difficult questions quickly while also presenting a uniform image so two different customers do not receive two different answers.

Documedics is a health care consulting company that provides reimbursement information about pharmaceutical products to patients and health care professionals. The company currently supports inquiries for 12 pharmaceutical companies and receives over 30,000 customer calls per month. Originally, the company had a data file for each patient and for each pharmaceutical company. This inefficient process resulted in the potential for a single patient to have up to 12 different information files if the patient was a client of all 12 pharmaceutical companies. To answer customer questions, a CSR had to download each customer file causing tremendous inefficiencies and confusion.

The company implemented a CRM system with a call scripting feature to alleviate the problem by providing its CSRs with a comprehensive view of every customer, regardless of the pharmaceutical company. The company anticipated 20 percent annual growth primarily because of the successful implementation of its new system.

## Analytical CRM

Maturing analytical CRM and behavioral modeling technologies are helping numerous organizations move beyond legacy benefits like enhanced customer service and retention to systems that can truly improve business profitability. Unlike operational CRM that automates call centers and sales forces with the aim of enhancing customer transactions, analytical CRM solutions are designed to dig deep into a company's historical customer information and expose patterns of behavior on which a company can capitalize. Analytical CRM is primarily used to enhance and support decision making and works by identifying patterns in customer information collected from the various operational CRM systems.

For many organizations, the power of analytical CRM solutions provides tremendous managerial opportunities. Depending on the specific solution, analytical CRM tools can slice-and-dice customer information to create made-to-order views of customer value, spending, product affinities, percentile profiles, and segmentations. Modeling tools can identify opportunities for cross-selling, up-selling, and expanding customer relationships.

**Personalization** occurs when a website can know enough about a person's likes and dislikes that it can fashion offers that are more likely to appeal to that person. Many organizations are now utilizing CRM to create customer rules and templates that marketers can use to personalize customer messages.

The information produced by analytical CRM solutions can help companies make decisions about how to handle customers based on the value of each and every one. Analytical CRM can reveal information about which customers are worth investing in, which should be serviced at an average level, and which should not be invested in at all.

Data gained from customers can also reveal information about employees. When Wachovia Bank surveys customers—25,000 every month—for feedback on their service experience, it asks about individual employees and uses those answers in one-on-one staff coaching. A recent 20-minute coaching session at a Manhattan branch made clear how this feedback—each customer surveyed rates 33 employee behaviors—can improve service. The branch manager urged an employee to focus on sincerity rather than on mere friendliness, to "sharpen her antenna" so she would listen to customers more intuitively, and to slow down rather than hurry up.

| Analytical CRM Information Examples | |
|---|---|
| 1. **Give customers more of what they want** | Analytical CRM can help an organization go beyond the typical "Dear Mr. Smith" salutation. An organization can use its analytical CRM information to make its communications more personable. For example, if it knows a customer's shoe size and preferred brand it can notify the customer that there is a pair of size 12 shoes set aside to try on the next time the customer visits the store. |
| 2. **Find new customers similar to the best customers** | Analytical CRM might determine that an organization does a lot of business with women 35 to 45 years old who drive SUVs and live within 30 miles of a certain location. The company can then find a mailing list that highlights this type of customer for potential new sales. |
| 3. **Find out what the organization does best** | Analytical CRM can determine what an organization does better than its competitors. For example, if a restaurant caters more breakfasts to midsized companies than its competition does, it can purchase a specialized mailing list of midsized companies in the area and send them a mailing that features the breakfast catering specials. |
| 4. **Beat competitors to the punch** | Analytical CRM can determine sales trends allowing an organization to offer the best customers deals before the competition has a chance to. For example, a clothing store might determine its best customers for outdoor apparel and send them an offer to attend a private sale right before the competition runs its outdoor apparel sale. |
| 5. **Reactivate inactive customers** | Analytical CRM can highlight customers who have not done any business with the organization in a while. The organization can then send them a personalized letter along with a discount coupon. It will remind them of the company and may help spark a renewed relationship. |
| 6. **Let customers know they matter** | Analytical CRM can determine what customers want and need, so an organization can contact them with this information. Anything from a private sale to a reminder that the car is due for a tune-up is excellent customer service. |

**FIGURE** B9.6

Analytical CRM
Information Examples

That focus on careful, sincere, intuitive service has paid off: Wachovia has held the top score among banks in the American Customer Satisfaction Index since 2001.

Analytical CRM relies heavily on data warehousing technologies and business intelligence to glean insights into customer behavior. These systems quickly aggregate, analyze, and disseminate customer information throughout an organization. Figure B9.6 displays a few examples of the kind of information insights analytical CRM can help an organization gain.

UPS's data-intensive environment is supported by the largest IBM DB2 database in the world, consisting of 236 terabytes of data related to its analytical CRM tool. The shipping company's goal is to create one-to-one customer relationships, and it is using Quantum View tools that allow it to let customers tailor views of such things as shipment history and receive notices when a package arrives or is delayed. UPS has built more than 500 customer relationship management applications that run off of its data warehouse.

Sears, Roebuck and Company is the third-largest U.S. retailer. Over the past two decades, Sears has experienced a well-publicized encroachment by discount mass merchandisers. Even though Sears does not know exactly "who" its customers are (by name and address) since many customers use cash or non-Sears credit cards, it can still benefit from analytical CRM technologies. Sears uses these technologies to determine what its generic customers prefer to buy and when they buy it, which enables the company to predict what they will buy. Using analytical CRM, Sears can view each day's sales by region, district, store, product line, and individual item. Sears can now monitor the precise impact of advertising, weather, and other factors on sales of specific items. For the first time, Sears can even group together, or "cluster," widely divergent types of items. For example, merchandisers can track sales of a store display marked "Gifts under $25" that might include sweatshirts, screwdrivers, and other unrelated items. The advertising department can then follow the sales of "Gifts under $25" to determine which products to place in its newspaper advertisements.

# Current Trends: SRM, PRM, and ERM

Organizations are discovering a wave of other key business areas where it is beneficial to take advantage of building strong relationships. These emerging areas include supplier relationship management (SRM), partner relationship management (PRM), and employee relationship management (ERM).

## SUPPLIER RELATIONSHIP MANAGEMENT

***Supplier relationship management (SRM)*** focuses on keeping suppliers satisfied by evaluating and categorizing suppliers for different projects, which optimizes supplier selection. SRM applications help companies analyze vendors based on a number of key variables including strategy, business goals, prices, and markets. The company can then determine the best supplier to collaborate with and can work on developing strong relationships with that supplier. The partners can then work together to streamline processes, outsource services, and provide products that they could not provide individually.

With the merger of the Bank of Halifax and Bank of Scotland, the new company, HBOS, implemented an SRM system to supply consistent information to its suppliers. The system integrates procurement information from the separate Bank of Halifax and Bank of Scotland operational systems, generating a single repository of management information for consistent reporting and analysis. Other benefits HBOS derived from the SRM solution include:

- A single consolidated view of all suppliers.
- Consistent, detailed management information allowing multiple views for every executive.
- Elimination of duplicate suppliers.

## PARTNER RELATIONSHIP MANAGEMENT

Organizations have begun to realize the importance of building relationships with partners, dealers, and resellers. ***Partner relationship management (PRM)*** focuses on keeping vendors satisfied by managing alliance partner and reseller relationships that provide customers with the optimal sales channel. PRM's business strategy is to select and manage partners to optimize their long-term value to an organization. In effect, it means picking the right partners, working with them to help them be successful in dealing with mutual customers, and ensuring that partners and the ultimate end customers are satisfied and successful. Many of the features of a PRM application include real-time product information on availability, marketing materials, contracts, order details, and pricing, inventory, and shipping information.

PRM is one of the smaller segments of CRM that has superb potential. PRM has grown to more than a $1 billion industry. This is a direct reflection of the growing interdependency of organizations in the new economy. The primary benefits of PRM include:

- Expanded market coverage.
- Offerings of specialized products and services.
- Broadened range of offerings and a more complete solution.

## EMPLOYEE RELATIONSHIP MANAGEMENT

Jim Sinegal runs Costco, one of the largest wholesale club chains, but there are two things he does not discount: employee benefits and customer service. Average hourly wages trounce those of rival Sam's Club, and 86 percent of workers have health insurance (versus a reported 47 percent at Sam's). Sinegal is not just being nice. Happy employees, he believes, make for happier customers. Low prices (he caps per-item profits at 14 percent) and a generous return policy certainly help. Although Wall Street has long been arguing for smaller benefits, a stingier return policy, and bigger profits, Sinegal sides with customers and staff. "We're trying to run Costco in a fashion that is not just going to satisfy our shareholders this year or this month," he said, "but next year and on into the future."

*Employee relationship management (ERM)* provides employees with a subset of CRM applications available through a web browser. Many of the ERM applications assist the employee in dealing with customers by providing detailed information on company products, services, and customer orders.

At Rackspace, a San Antonio-based web-hosting company, customer focus borders on the obsessive. Joey Parsons, 24, won the Straightjacket Award, the most coveted employee distinction at Rackspace. The award recognizes the employee who best lives up to the Rackspace motto of delivering "fanatical support," a dedication to customers that is so intense it borders on the loony. Rackspace motivates its staff by treating each team as a separate business, which is responsible for its own profits and losses and has its own ERM website. Each month, employees can earn bonuses of up to 20 percent of their monthly base salaries depending on the performance of their units by both financial and customer-centric measurements such as customer turnover, customer expansion, and customer referrals. Daily reports are available through the team's ERM website.

## Future Trends

CRM revenue forecast for 2008 is $11.5 billion. In the future, CRM applications will continue to change from employee-only tools to tools used by suppliers, partners, and even customers. Providing a consistent view of customers and delivering timely and accurate customer information to all departments across an organization will continue to be the major goal of CRM initiatives.

As technology advances (intranet, Internet, extranet, wireless), CRM will remain a major strategic focus for companies, particularly in industries whose product is difficult to differentiate. Some companies approach this problem by moving to a low-cost producer strategy. CRM will be an alternative way to pursue a differentiation strategy with a nondifferentiable product.

CRM applications will continue to adapt wireless capabilities supporting mobile sales and mobile customers. Sales professionals will be able to access email, order details, corporate information, inventory status, and opportunity information all from a PDA in their car or on a plane. Real-time interaction with human CSRs over the Internet will continue to increase.

CRM suites will also incorporate PRM and SRM modules as enterprises seek to take advantage of these initiatives. Automating interactions with distributors, resellers, and suppliers will enhance the corporation's ability to deliver a quality experience to its customers.

A s organizations migrate from the traditional product-focused organization toward customer-driven organizations, they are recognizing their customers as experts, not just revenue generators. Organizations are quickly realizing that without customers they simply would not exist and it is critical they do everything they can to ensure their customers' satisfaction. In an age when product differentiation is difficult, CRM is one of the most valuable assets a company can acquire.

Sales, marketing, and customer service departments can implement many different types of CRM technologies that can assist in the difficult tasks of customer identification, segmentation, and prediction (see Figure B9.7).

Analytical CRM relies on data warehousing and business intelligence to find insights into customer information in order to build stronger relationships. Organizations are also discovering a wave of other key business areas where it is beneficial to take advantage of building strong relationships including supplier relationship management (SRM), partner relationship management (PRM), and employee relationship management (ERM). The sooner a company embraces CRM the better off it will be and the harder it will be for competitors to steal loyal and devoted customers.

| Operational CRM Technologies | | |
|---|---|---|
| **Marketing** | **Sales** | **Customer Service** |
| 1. List generator | 1. Sales management | 1. Contact center |
| 2. Campaign management | 2. Contact management | 2. Web-based self-service |
| 3. Cross-selling and up-selling | 3. Opportunity management | 3. Call scripting |

**FIGURE** B9.7

Operational CRM Technologies for Sales, Marketing, and Customer Service Departments

Analytical CRM, 348
Automatic call distribution, 354
Call scripting system, 354
Campaign management
    system, 349
Click-to-talk, 354
Contact center (call center), 354
Contact management CRM
    system, 351
Cross-selling, 350
Customer relationship
    management (CRM), 348

Employee relationship
    management (ERM), 358
Interactive voice response
    (IVR), 354
List generator, 349
Operational CRM, 348
Opportunity management CRM
    system, 352
Partner relationship
    management (PRM), 357
Personalization, 355
Predictive dialing, 354

Sales force automation
    (SFA), 350
Sales management CRM
    system, 351
Supplier relationship
    management (SRM), 357
Up-selling, 350
Web-based self-service
    system, 354

### Fighting Cancer with Information

"The mission of the American Cancer Society (ACS) is to cure cancer and relieve the pain and suffering caused by this insidious disease," states Zachary Patterson, chief information officer, ACS.

The ACS is a nationwide voluntary health organization dedicated to eliminating cancer as a major health problem by supporting research, education, advocacy, and volunteer service. Headquartered in Atlanta, Georgia, with 17 divisions and more than 3,400 local offices throughout the United States, the ACS represents the largest source of private nonprofit cancer research funds in the United States.

To support its mission, the ACS must perform exceptionally well in three key areas. First, it must be able to provide its constituents—more than 2 million volunteers, patients, and donors—with the best information available regarding the prevention, detection, and treatment of cancer. Second, ACS must be able to demonstrate that it acts responsibly with the funds entrusted to it by the public. "Among other things, that means being able to provide exceptional service when someone calls our call center with a question about mammography screening or our latest antismoking campaign," says Terry Music, national vice president for Information Delivery at the ACS. Third, ACS must be able to continually secure donations of time and money from its constituent base. Its success in this area is directly related to providing excellent information and service, as well as having an integrated view of its relationship with constituents. "To succeed, we need to understand the full extent of each constituent's relationship with us so we can determine where there might be opportunities to expand that relationship," says Music.

The ACS was experiencing many challenges with its current information. "Our call center agents did not know, for example, if a caller was both a donor and a volunteer, or if a caller was volunteering for the society in multiple ways," he says. "This splintered view made it challenging for American Cancer Society representatives to deliver personalized service and make informed recommendations regarding other opportunities within the society that might interest a caller."

The ACS chose to implement a customer relationship management solution to solve its information issues. Critical to the CRM system's success was consolidating information from various databases across the organization to provide a single view of constituents and all information required to serve them. After an evaluation process that included participation from individuals across the organization, the ACS chose Siebel Systems as its CRM solution provider. The society wanted to work with a company that could address both its immediate needs with a best-in-class ebusiness solution and its future requirements.

The Siebel Call Center is specifically designed for the next generation of contact centers, enabling organizations to provide world-class customer service, generate increased revenue, and create a closed-loop information flow seamlessly over multichannel sales, marketing, and customer service operations. Siebel Call Center empowers agents at every level by providing up-to-the-minute information and in-depth customer and product knowledge. This approach enables quick and accurate problem resolution and generates greater relationship opportunities. The ACS has received numerous benefits from the system including:

1. Increased constituent satisfaction and loyalty by supporting personalized interactions between constituents and cancer information specialists.

2. Improved productivity of cancer information specialists by consolidating all information required to serve constituents into a single view.

3. Increased donations of time and money by helping call center agents identify callers who are likely to be interested in expanding their relationship with the ACS.

## Questions

1. How could the ACS's marketing department use operational CRM to strengthen its relationships with its customers?

2. How could the ACS's customer service department use operational CRM to strengthen its relationships with its customers?

3. Review all of the operational CRM technologies and determine which one would add the greatest value to ACS's business.

4. Describe the benefits ACS could gain from using analytical CRM.

5. Summarize SRM and describe how ACS could use it to increase efficiency in its business.

---

## ✱ CLOSING CASE TWO

### Calling All Canadians

With multiple communication channels available and so many CRM failures, many companies are concluding that the best method for providing customer service is good old-fashioned customer service provided by a live person. At the same time companies consider outsourcing their customer service departments to other countries in order to save money, many worry about foreign accents as well as time-zone issues related to offshore outsourcing.

Canada has become one of the primary targets for outsourcing customer service centers by U.S. companies. Not only are accent and time-zone issues nonexistent, but companies also receive a favorable exchange rate. The Bank of Canada estimates that over the past five years, the currency exchange rate between the United States and Canada favors Americans by 44 percent. For every dollar an American business spends in Canada, it receives over a dollar and a half in goods and services.

Additional factors that make Canada even more attractive include a high Canadian unemployment rate estimated at 7.5 percent in 2003, while the U.S. unemployment rate was 5.9 percent. Canadians also have high education rates with 63 percent of Canadians over the age of 15 being high school graduates. The country's predominantly rural population and strong work ethic along with a declining industrial base have made call center outsourcing an attractive solution for Canada, too.

Canada has been a leader in the call center industry for over a decade. Since the early 1990s, "the Canadian call center industry has grown at an annual rate of 20 percent," according to Steve Demmings, president of Site Selection Canada of Winnipeg, Manitoba. Site Selection Canada promotes and assists site selection for American and Canadian firms. Demmings estimates there are 14,000 call centers in Canada with six or more agents employing 500,000 people, contributing about $36 billion (Canadian) in annual salaries.

In 1994, two Canadian provinces—Manitoba and New Brunswick—made a concerted effort to develop a local call center industry, recognizing the area's high unemployment with little native industry, says Demmings. The other provinces soon followed. Then the call center industry "made a big move" to bring educational institutions on board. "Many colleges have set up call center training programs," Demmings reports. The result has been an established industry with a highly skilled labor pool. "American companies come up here to go shopping, and we need to have the tableware on the table," states Demmings.

What is important to outsourcing buyers is that many Canadian call center customer service representatives have made it their career. Consequently, there is a much lower turnover rate for call centers than in the United States. Demmings reports the CSR turnover rate in the Province of Ontario was 18.3 percent last year. Compare that to the United States, where call center staffing can be a problem. Christopher Fletcher, vice president and research director of

CRM for the Aberdeen Group, states, "It is tough to find people to staff a call center. Turnover ranges from 25 percent to 50 percent annually or above. The skill sets of the people you have available are often equivalent to McDonald's."

## Questions

1. What are the two different types of CRM and how can they be used to help an organization gain a competitive advantage?

2. Explain how a contact center (or call center) can help an organization achieve its CRM goals.

3. Describe three ways an organization can perform CRM functions over the Internet.

4. How will outsourcing contact centers (call centers) to Canada change as future CRM technologies replace current CRM technologies?

5. Do you believe that call centers in the future will be replaced by robot technology? Why or why not.

---

## ★ MAKING BUSINESS DECISIONS

### 1. Driving Up Profits with Successful Campaigns (or Driving Down?)

The Butterfly Café is a local hot spot located in downtown San Francisco that offers specialty coffee, teas, and organic fruits and vegetables. The café holds a number of events to attract customers such as live music venues, poetry readings, book clubs, charity events, and local artists' nights. A listing of all participants attending each event is tracked in the café's database. The café uses the information for marketing compaigns and offers customers who attend multiple events additional discounts. A maketing database company, InTheKnow.com, has offered to pay the Butterfly Café a substantial amount of money for access to its customer database, which it will then sell to other local businesses. The owner of the Butterfly Café, Mary Conzachi, has come to you for advice. Mary is not sure if her customers would appreciate her selling their personal information and how it might affect her business. However, the amount of money InTheKnow.com is offering is enough to finance her much needed new patio for the back of the café. InTheKnow.com has promised Mary that the sale will be completely confidential. What should Mary do?

### 2. Searching for Employee Loyalty

You are the CEO of Razz, a start-up web-based search company, which is planning to compete directly with Google. The company had an exceptional first year and is currently receiving over 500,000 hits a day from customers all over the world. You have hired 250 people in the last four months, doubling the size of your organization. With so many new employees starting so quickly you are concerned about how your company's culture will evolve and whether your employees are receiving enough attention. You are already familiar with customer relationship management and how CRM systems can help an organization create strong customer relationships. However, you are unfamiliar with employee relationship management and you are wondering what ERM systems might be able to offer your employees and your company. Research the web, create a report detailing features and functions of ERM systems, and determine what value will be added to your organization if you decide to implement an ERM solution.

### 3. Increasing Revenues with CRM

Cold Cream is one of the premier beauty supply stores in the metro New York area. People come from all over to sample the store's unique creams, lotions, makeup, and perfumes. The store is four stories high with each department located on a separate floor. The company would like to implement a CRM system to help it better understand its customers and their purchasing habits. Create a report summarizing CRM systems and detail how such a system can directly influence Cold Cream's revenues.

### 4. Employee Relationship Management

All new employees at the Shinaberry Inn & Spa wear bathing suits during orientation to experience the spa's exfoliating showers and hot mineral baths. At the Shinaberry San Francisco, new employees get the same penthouse champagne toast the hotel uses to woo meeting planners. And at many properties, employees arriving for their first day have their cars parked by the valet or get vouchers for a free night's stay. This innovative orientation program, which lets employees experience what guests experience, began two years ago after focus groups pointed to empathy as a service differentiator. As a result, the company added empathy to the attributes for which it screens and a training program that involves listening to recorded guest phone calls. Even its discounted employee travel program gives employees yet another way to understand the guest experience. Design an ERM system that would help Shinaberry further its employee-centered culture. The ERM system must take into account all employee needs.

### 5. Supporting Customers

Creative.com is an ebusiness that sells craft materials and supplies over the Internet. You have just started as the vice president of customer service, and you have a team of 45 customer service representatives. Currently, the only form of customer service is the 1-800 number, and the company is receiving a tremendous number of calls regarding products, orders, and shipping information. The average wait time for a customer to speak to a customer service representative is 35 minutes. Orders are being canceled and Creative.com is losing business due to its lack of customer service. Create a strategy to revamp the customer service center at Creative.com and get the company back on track.

# Enterprise Resource Planning

1. Compare core enterprise resource planning components and extended enterprise resource planning components.

2. Describe the three primary components found in core enterprise resource planning systems.

3. Describe the four primary components found in extended enterprise resource planning systems.

4. Explain the benefits and risks associated with enterprise resource planning systems.

5. Assess the future of enterprise resource planning systems.

## Introduction

***Enterprise resource planning (ERP)*** integrates all departments and functions throughout an organization into a single IT system (or integrated set of IT systems) so that employees can make decisions by viewing enterprisewide information on all business operations.

SAP, the leading ERP vendor, boasts 20,000 installations and 10 million users worldwide. These figures represent only 30 percent of the overall ERP market. Figure B10.1 highlights a few reasons ERP solutions have proven to be such a powerful force.

ERP as a business concept resounds as a powerful internal information management nirvana: Everyone involved in sourcing, producing, and delivering the company's product works with the same information, which eliminates redundancies, reduces wasted time, and removes misinformation.

## Core and Extended ERP Components

Turner Industries grew from $300 million in sales to $800 million in sales in less than 10 years thanks to the implementation of an ERP system. Ranked number 369 on the Forbes 500 list of privately held companies, Turner Industries is a leading industrial services firm. Turner Industries develops and deploys advanced software

| Reasons ERP Systems Are Powerful Organizational Tools |
| --- |
| ERP is a logical solution to the mess of incompatible applications that had sprung up in most businesses. |
| ERP addresses the need for global information sharing and reporting. |
| ERP is used to avoid the pain and expense of fixing legacy systems. |

applications designed to maximize the productivity of its 25,000 employees and construction equipment valued at more than $100 million.

The company considers the biggest challenges in the industrial services industry to be completing projects on time, within budget, while fulfilling customers' expectations. To meet these challenges the company invested in an ERP system and named the project Interplan. Interplan won Constructech's Vision award for software innovation in the heavy construction industry. Interplan runs all of Turner's construction, turnaround, shutdown, and maintenance projects and is so adept at estimating and planning jobs that Turner Industries typically achieves higher profit margins on projects that use Interplan. As the ERP solution makes the company more profitable, the company can pass on the cost savings to its customers, giving the company an incredible competitive advantage.

Figure B10.2 provides an example of an ERP system with its core and extended components. ***Core ERP components*** are the traditional components included in most ERP systems and they primarily focus on internal operations. ***Extended ERP components*** are the extra components that meet the organizational needs not covered by the core components and primarily focus on external operations.

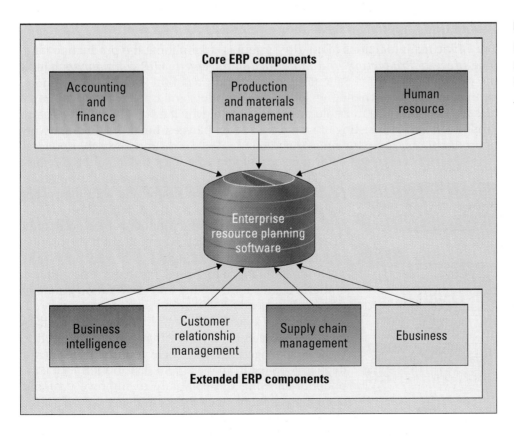

**FIGURE** B10.2

Core ERP Components and Extended ERP Components

## CORE ERP COMPONENTS

The three most common *core* ERP components focusing on internal operations are:

1. Accounting and finance.
2. Production and materials management.
3. Human resources.

### Accounting and Finance ERP Components

Deeley Harley-Davidson Canada (DHDC), the exclusive Canadian distributor of Harley-Davidson motorcycles, has improved inventory, turnaround time, margins, and customer satisfaction—all with the implementation of a financial ERP system. The system has opened up the power of information to the company and is helping it make strategic decisions when it still has the time to change things. The ERP system provides the company with ways to manage inventory, turnaround time, and warehouse space more effectively.

*Accounting and finance ERP components* manage accounting data and financial processes within the enterprise with functions such as general ledger, accounts payable, accounts receivable, budgeting, and asset management. One of the most useful features included in an ERP accounting/finance component is its credit-management feature. Most organizations manage their relationships with customers by setting credit limits, or a limit on how much a customer can owe at any one time. The company then monitors the credit limit whenever the customer places a new order or sends in a payment. ERP financial systems help to correlate customer orders with customer account balances determining credit availability. Another great feature is the ability to perform product profitability analysis. ERP financial components are the backbone behind product profitability analysis and allow companies to perform all types of advanced profitability modeling techniques.

### Production and Materials Management ERP Components

One of the main functions of an ERP system is streamlining the production planning process. *Production and materials management ERP components* handle the various aspects of production planning and execution such as demand forecasting, production scheduling, job cost accounting, and quality control. Companies typically produce multiple products, each of which has many different parts. Production lines, consisting of machines and employees, build the different types of products. The company must then define sales forecasting for each product to determine production schedules and materials purchasing. Figure B10.3 displays the typical ERP production planning process. The process begins with forecasting sales in order to plan operations. A detailed production schedule is developed if the product is produced and a materials requirement plan is completed if the product is purchased.

Grupo Farmanova Intermed, located in Costa Rica, is a pharmaceutical marketing and distribution company that markets nearly 2,500 products to approximately 500 customers in Central and South America. The company identified a need for software that could unify product logistics management in a single country. It decided to deploy PeopleSoft financial and distribution ERP components allowing the company to improve customer data management, increase confidence among internal and external users, and coordinate the logistics of inventory. With the software the company enhanced its capabilities for handling, distributing, and marketing its pharmaceuticals.

**FIGURE** B10.3

The Production Planning Process

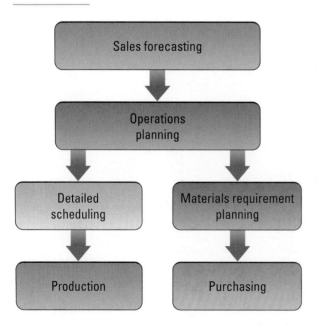

## Human Resources ERP Components

*Human resources ERP components* track employee information including payroll, benefits, compensation, and performance assessment, and assure compliance with the legal requirements of multiple jurisdictions and tax authorities. Human resources components even offer features that allow the organization to perform detailed analysis on its employees to determine such things as the identification of individuals who are likely to leave the company unless additional compensation or benefits are provided. These components can also identify which employees are using which resources, such as online training and long-distance telephone services. They can also help determine whether the most talented people are working for those business units with the highest priority—or where they would have the greatest impact on profit.

## EXTENDED ERP COMPONENTS

*Extended ERP components* are the extra components that meet the organizational needs not covered by the core components and primarily focus on external operations. Many of the numerous extended ERP components are Internet enabled and require interaction with customers, suppliers, and business partners outside the organization. The four most common extended ERP components are:

1. Business intelligence.
2. Customer relationship management.
3. Supply chain management.
4. Ebusiness.

### Business Intelligence Components

ERP systems offer powerful tools that measure and control organizational operations. Many organizations have found that these valuable tools can be enhanced to provide even greater value through the addition of powerful business intelligence systems. *Business intelligence* describes information that people use to support their decision-making efforts. The business intelligence components of ERP systems typically collect information used throughout the organization (including data used in many other ERP components), organize it, and apply analytical tools to assist managers with decisions. Data warehouses are one of the most popular extensions to ERP systems, with over two-thirds of U.S. manufacturers adopting or planning such systems.

### Customer Relationship Management Components

ERP vendors are expanding their functionality to provide services formerly supplied by customer relationship management (CRM) vendors such as Siebel. *Customer relationship management (CRM)* involves managing all aspects of a customer's relationship with an organization to increase customer loyalty and retention and an organization's profitability. CRM components provide an integrated view of customer data and interactions allowing organizations to work more effectively with customers and be more responsive to their needs. CRM components typically include contact centers, sales force automation, and marketing functions. These improve the customer experience while identifying a company's most (and least) valuable customers for better allocation of resources.

### Supply Chain Management Components

ERP vendors are expanding their functionality to provide services formerly supplied by supply chain management vendors such as i2 Technologies and Manugistics. *Supply chain management (SCM)* involves the management of information flows between and among stages in a supply chain to maximize total supply chain effectiveness and profitability. SCM components help an organization plan, schedule, control, and optimize the supply chain from its acquisition of raw materials to the receipt of finished goods by customers.

### Ebusiness Components

The original focus of ERP systems was the internal organization. In other words, ERP systems are not fundamentally ready for the external world of ebusiness. The newest and most exciting extended ERP components are the ebusiness components. *Ebusiness* means conducting business on the Internet, not only buying and selling, but also serving customers and collaborating with business partners. Two of the primary features of ebusiness components are elogistics and eprocurement. *Elogistics* manages the transportation and storage of goods. *Eprocurement* is the business-to-business (B2B) purchase and sale of supplies and services over the Internet.

Ebusiness and ERP complement each other by allowing companies to establish a web presence and fulfill orders expeditiously. A common mistake made by many businesses is deploying a web presence before the integration of back-office systems or an ERP system. For example, one large toy manufacturer announced less than a week before Christmas that it would be unable to fulfill any of its web orders. The company had all the toys in the warehouse, but it could not organize the basic order processing function to get the toys delivered to the consumers on time.

Customers and suppliers are now demanding access to ERP information including order status, inventory levels, and invoice reconciliation. Plus, the customers and partners want all this information in a simplified format available through a website. This is a difficult task to accomplish because most ERP systems are full of technical jargon, which is why employee training is one of the hidden costs associated with ERP implementations. Removing the jargon to accommodate untrained customers and partners is one of the more difficult tasks when web-enabling an ERP system. To accommodate the growing needs of the ebusiness world, ERP vendors need to build two new channels of access into the ERP system information—one channel for customers (B2C) and one channel for businesses, suppliers, and partners (B2B).

## ERP Benefits and Risks (Cost)

There is no guarantee of success for an ERP system. ERPs focus on how a corporation operates internally, and optimizing these operations takes significant time and energy. According to Meta Group, it takes the average company 8 to 18 months to see any benefits from an ERP system. The good news is that the average savings from new ERP systems are $1.6 million per year. Figure B10.4 displays a list of the five most common benefits an organization can expect to achieve from a successful ERP implementation.

Along with understanding the benefits an organization can gain from an ERP system, it is just as important to understand the primary risk associated with an ERP implementation—cost. ERP systems do not come cheap. Meta Group studied the total cost of ownership (TCO) for an ERP system. The study included hardware, software, professional services, and internal staff costs. Sixty-three companies were surveyed ranging in size from small to large over a variety of industries. The average TCO was $15 million (highest $300 million and lowest $400,000). The price tag for an ERP system can easily start in the multiple millions of dollars and implementation can take an average of 23 months. Figure B10.5 displays a few of the costs associated with an ERP system.

| Common ERP Benefits |
| --- |
| 1. **Integrate financial information:** To understand an organization's overall performance, managers must have a single financial view. |
| 2. **Integrate customer order information:** With all customer order information in a single system it is easier to coordinate manufacturing, inventory, and shipping to send a common message to customers regarding order status. |
| 3. **Standardize and speed up manufacturing processes:** ERP systems provide standard methods for manufacturing companies to use when automating steps in the manufacturing process. Standardizing manufacturing processes across an organization saves time, increases production, and reduces head count. |
| 4. **Reduce inventory:** With improved visibility in the order fulfillment process, an organization can reduce inventories and streamline deliveries to its customers. |
| 5. **Standardize human resource information:** ERPs provide a unified method for tracking employees' time, as well as communicating HR benefits and services. |

## The Future of ERP

ERP places new demands not only on support and delivery information technology, but also on the way business processes have to be designed, implemented, monitored, and maintained. For example, several persons in different locations and with different hardware and software resources may simultaneously initiate a purchase process for the same product but with different selection criteria. Reliability, efficiency, and scalability are among the features that have to be embedded in ebusiness processes in ERP systems. Despite the rapid growth in the number of ERP installations, conducting ERP operations is still challenging.

Understanding the many different types of core and extended ERP components can help an organization determine which components will add the most value. The two biggest vendors in the ERP market are Oracle, which purchased PeopleSoft in 2005, and SAP. Figure B10.6 is an overview of a few of the components offered by each ERP vendor.

In the future, the line between ERP, SCM, and CRM will continue to blur as ERP vendors broaden the functionality of their product suites and redefine the packaging of their products. ERP vendors with comprehensive but modular components

| Associated ERP Risks (Cost) |
| --- |
| **Software cost:** Purchasing the software. |
| **Consulting fees:** Hiring external experts to help implement the system correctly. |
| **Process rework:** Redefining processes in order to ensure the company is using the most efficient and effective processes. |
| **Customization:** If the software package does not meet all of the company's needs, customizing the software may be required. |
| **Integration and testing:** Ensuring all software products, including disparate systems not part of the ERP system, are working together or are integrated. Testing the ERP system includes testing all integrations. |
| **Training:** Training all new users. |
| **Data warehouse integration and data conversion:** Moving data from an old system into the new ERP system. |

| PeopleSoft (Purchased by Oracle) | |
|---|---|
| **Component** | **Description** |
| Application Integration | Integrate PeopleSoft and non-PeopleSoft applications at all levels with Portal Solutions, AppConnect, and Data Warehousing and Analytic Solutions. |
| Customer Relationship Management | Get immediate, seamless integration among customer, financial, supply chain, and employee management systems. |
| Enterprise Performance Management | Enable customers, suppliers, and employees to connect to set goals, develop plans, and measure progress with our integrated, scalable applications. |
| Financial Management | Get the power to compete in the business world with a comprehensive suite of pure Internet financial applications. |
| Human Capital Management (including Human Resources Management Solutions) | Manage and mobilize a unified, global workforce, and align workforce contribution with business objectives. |
| Service Automation | Optimize project investments, reduce project delivery costs, and maximize resources to increase utilization and value to the organization. |
| Supplier Relationship Management | Manage all aspects of supplier relationships including indirect and direct goods, as well as services procurement. |
| Supply Chain Management | Take advantage of solutions that promote business-to-business interaction throughout the supply chain, from customer to supplier. |

| Oracle | |
|---|---|
| **Component** | **Description** |
| Oracle Financials | Financial applications manage the flow of cash and assets into, out of, and within the enterprise: tracking thousands of transactions, setting fiscal goals for various departments, and allowing managers to project future financial health as they record today's profits. |
| Oracle Human Resources Management | Oracle Human Resources Management System (HRMS) empowers businesses with the tools to find, extract, and analyze data related to human capital. This intelligence readies a company to rapidly deploy the best resources for maximum employee productivity, satisfaction, and retention. |
| Oracle Intelligence | Oracle Daily Business Intelligence accesses and shares unified information and analysis across the enterprise with a single definition of customers, suppliers, employees, and products. |
| Oracle Learning Management | Oracle Learning Management (Oracle iLearning, Oracle Training Management, and Oracle Human Resources Management System) provides a complete infrastructure that lets organizations manage, deliver, and track training, in both online and classroom environments. |
| Oracle Supply Chain Management | Oracle Supply Chain Management lets organizations gain global visibility, automate internal processes, and readily collaborate with suppliers, customers, and partners. |
| Oracle Manufacturing | Oracle Manufacturing optimizes production capacity beginning with raw materials through final products. |
| Oracle Order Management | Oracle's support of the complete fulfillment process from order to cash. |
| Oracle Marketing | Oracle Marketing drives profit by intelligently marketing to the most profitable customers. By leveraging a single repository of customer information, marketing professionals can better target and personalize their campaigns, and refine them in real time with powerful analytical tools. |
| Oracle Projects | To consistently deliver on time and on budget, an organization must fine-tune execution, align global organization with projects, and assign the right resources to the most important initiatives at the right time. |
| Oracle Sales | Oracle Sales allows an organization to learn more about its entire business to identify and target profitable opportunities. |

*(Continued)*

| SAP | |
|---|---|
| **Component** | **Description** |
| mySAP™ Customer Relationship Management | The fully integrated CRM solution that facilitates world-class service across all customer touchpoints. |
| mySAP™ Financials | The leading solution for operational, analytical, and collaborative financial management. |
| mySAP™ Human Resources (mySAP HR) | The HR resource that helps more than 7,800 organizations worldwide maximize their return on human capital. |
| mySAP™ Marketplace | An online marketplace solution that allows a company to buy, sell, and conduct business around the clock and around the world. |
| mySAP™ Product Lifecycle Management | The collaborative solution that helps designers, engineers, and suppliers achieve new levels of innovation. |
| mySAP™ Supplier Relationship Management | Covers the full supply cycle—from strategic sourcing for lower costs to faster process cycles. |
| mySAP™ Supply Chain Management | Gives an organization the power to dramatically improve its planning, responsiveness, and execution to suppliers, customers, and partners. |

**FIGURE** B10.6

*(Continued)*

will dominate the next high-growth phase of the enterprise applications market. Since core functionality is virtually the same for all vendors, a vendor's success will primarily depend upon how quickly it incorporates other kinds of functionality such as the Internet, interface, and wireless technology.

## INTERNET

The adoption of the Internet is one of the single most important forces reshaping the architecture and functionality of ERP systems and is responsible for the most important new developments in ERP. The Internet serves as a basis for extending ERP's traditional vision of integrating data and processes across an organization's functional departments to include sharing data and processes among multiple enterprises.

## INTERFACE

Most ERP suites offer a customizable browser that allows each employee to configure his or her own view of the system. A manager can also customize each employee's view of the system. This feature allows managers to control access to highly sensitive information such as payroll and performance appraisals. The same customizable browser will be used in the future to allow customers and partners to see only select ERP information via the Internet.

## WIRELESS TECHNOLOGY

Wireless technologies provide a means for users with handheld devices, such as PDAs and web-enabled telephones, to connect to and interact with ERP systems. Most large ERP vendors will acquire smaller companies that specialize in wireless access. If they fail to do so, they will need to develop their own expertise in this area to build wireless access packages.

Wireless technologies will enable users to carry out the same transactions from their mobile devices as they used to do from any fixed device. Being able to buy and sell goods and services over mobile devices is an important step toward achieving the anywhere-anytime paradigm. In the future, location and time will no longer constrain organizations from completing their operations.

Core ERP components are the traditional components included in most ERP systems and they primarily focus on internal operations:

- Accounting and finance components.
- Production and materials management components.
- Human resources components.

Extended ERP components are the extra components that meet the organizational needs not covered by the core components and primarily focus on external operations:

- Business intelligence.
- Customer relationship management.
- Supply chain management.
- Ebusiness.

ERP vendors with comprehensive but modular components will dominate the next high-growth phase of the enterprise applications market. Since core functionality is virtually the same for all vendors, a vendor's success will primarily depend upon how quickly it incorporates other kinds of functionality such as the Internet, interfaces, and wireless technologies.

## ✳ KEY TERMS

Accounting and finance ERP component, 366
Business intelligence, 367
Core ERP component, 365
Customer relationship management (CRM), 367

Ebusiness, 368
Elogistics, 368
Enterprise resource planning (ERP), 364
Eprocurement, 368
Extended ERP component, 365, 367

Human resources ERP component, 367
Production and materials management ERP component, 366
Supply chain management (SCM), 367

## ✳ CLOSING CASE ONE

### PepsiAmericas' Enterprises

Headquartered in Rolling Meadows, Illinois, PepsiAmericas generates $2.97 billion in revenues yearly. The supplier of PepsiCo products has over 15,000 employees and 365,000 customers. The challenge facing PepsiAmericas was the integration of its enterprise systems. The company chose to implement a PeopleSoft ERP solution to enable it to deliver top-line growth and superior customer service through improved selling and delivery methods using standard processes along with proven technology.

With the introduction of numerous products, distribution gaps, and lost promotion opportunities, PepsiAmericas realized it needed a new strategy for managing its enterprise. It needed real-time access to enterprise information and seamless integration between its systems. The company especially required real-time customer information for its telemarketing agents to be able to effectively do their jobs. "It's important for a tel-sell (telemarketing) agent to understand if the customer has any issues or needs based on what's going on with the account.

An error in credit status, a balance history, issues they've logged with the company—all of this will have an impact on how they interact with the customer," said John Kreul, director of enterprise applications for PepsiAmericas.

One of the biggest benefits of the PeopleSoft ERP solution was that it provided complete integration between PepsiAmericas' front-office and back-office systems. This integration allowed tel-sell agents to gain a clear picture of customers and their relationship with the company. "We can more readily see additional sales opportunities. For example, if the customer ordered certain products in the past and there's a promotion going on for a similar product, the agents can offer that to the customer," Kreul said.

PepsiAmericas also implemented PeopleSoft's supply chain management component to automate its inventory accounting. Before implementing PeopleSoft SCM, portions of the company's monthly inventory accounting were done manually and took two weeks to conduct. "Now product inventory accounting is done at period end automatically. It provides us much greater control of the data and has shaven one to two days off our close," said Dave Van Volkenburg, manager of IT applications. Transferring products from one division to another was also a problem with the old system. Differences in product quantities shipped and received would create bottlenecks and result in days spent going back and forth between divisions to determine the accurate amount of products transferred. The SCM component changed all that. "Now our divisions have to send and receive product transfers within the system—so there's much tighter control on the activity, and the data is more accurate," Van Volkenburg said.

The following are the overall benefits PepsiAmericas received from its PeopleSoft ERP solution:

- Convert disparate sales systems to a single, integrated Internet application solution.
- Integrate computer telephony for tel-sell/pre-sell methodology.
- Deliver a 360-degree view of entire customer base.
- Improve customer distribution and profit potential.
- Simplify the issue resolution process.
- Provide more accurate and timely deliveries of products.
- Reduce product inventory close time by one to two days.

## Questions

1. How have core ERP components helped PepsiAmericas improve its business?
2. How have extended ERP components helped PepsiAmericas improve its business?
3. Explain how future ERP systems will help PepsiAmericas increase revenues.
4. Assess the impact on PepsiAmericas' business if it failed to implement the CRM component of its ERP system.
5. Review the different components in Figure B10.6. Which component would you recommend PepsiAmericas implement if it decided to purchase an additional component?
6. Compare PepsiAmericas' experience with other ERP cases you can find in most business articles.

### Campus ERP

When Stefanie Fillers returned to college she needed to log in to the school's new online registration system to make certain that the courses she was taking would allow her to graduate. She also wanted to waive her participation in her college's health insurance plan. When the system crashed the day before classes began, Fillers, a senior, was annoyed. But at least she knew where her classes were—unlike most first-year students.

Several colleges around the country have experienced problems with nonfunctioning web portals that prevented students from finding out where their classes were. At one college, financial aid was denied to 3,000 students by a buggy new ERP system, even though they had already received loan commitments. The college provided short-term loans for the cash-strapped students while the IT department and financial aid administrators scrambled to fix the complex system.

Disastrous ERP implementations have given more than a few colleges black eyes. These recent campus meltdowns illustrate how the growing reliance on expensive ERP systems has created nightmare scenarios for some colleges. In every case, the new systems were designed to centralize business processes in what historically has been a hodgepodge of discrete legacy systems. College administrators are drawn to ERP systems offering integrated views of finance, HR, student records, financial aid, and more.

ERP implementations are difficult, even in very top-down corporate environments. Getting them to work in colleges, which are essentially a conglomeration of decentralized fiefdoms, has been nearly impossible. Staff members in the largely autonomous departments do not like the one-size-fits-all strategy of an ERP implementation. Plus, these nonprofit organizations generally lack the talent and financial resources to create and manage a robust enterprise system. Representatives from Oracle, which dominates the higher education market for ERP, say that a large part of the problem results from the inexperience of college IT departments and their tendency to rush implementations and inadequately test the new systems.

## Standardizing at Stanford

Stanford University bought into the late 1990s enterprise software pitch and never slowed down its implementation engine. "In hindsight, we tried to do too much in too little time," said Randy Livingston, Stanford's vice president of business affairs and CFO.

Starting in 2001, Stanford implemented student administration systems, PeopleSoft HR, Oracle financials, and several other ancillary applications. Years later, users still complain that they have lower productivity with the new systems than with the previous ones, which were supported by a highly customized mainframe. Users also have had difficulty accessing critical information on a timely basis. Livingston said many transactions, such as initiating a purchase requisition or requesting a reimbursement, now take longer for users than with the prior legacy system.

Stanford has also not realized any of the projected savings the vendors promised. "We are finding that the new ERP applications cost considerably more to support than our legacy applications," Livingston said. He does not know how much it will cost to get the enterprise systems working at acceptable user levels.

Stanford's IT department is still trying to get campuswide buy-in for the enterprise applications, which have necessitated new ways of doing business, which leads to nonuse of the new systems and costly customizations to keep all users satisfied. For example, Stanford's law school operates on a semester schedule, while the other six schools operate on a trimester schedule. "This means that every aspect of the student administration system needs to be configured differently for the law school," Livingston said. Within the schools, some faculty members are paid a 12-month salary; other schools pay by 9 months, 10 months, or 11 months. "The standard HR payroll system is not designed to handle all these unusual pay schedules," Livingston said.

To resolve the issues, Livingston has reorganized the IT department, which he hopes will be better able to manage the enterprise projects going forward. He also created a separate administrative systems group that reports directly to him, with responsibility for development, integration, and support of the major ERP systems.

The hurdles Stanford and other colleges face with ERP systems are largely cultural ones. For instance, lean staffs and tight budgets at most university campuses usually lead to a lack of proper training and systems testing. At Stanford, plenty of training was offered, but many users did not take it, Livingston said. He has set up new training programs, including a group of trainers who sit side by side with users to help them learn how to do complex tasks; periodic user group meetings; website and email lists that offer more help; and expert users embedded in the various departments who aid their colleagues.

Stanford's IT was still struggling with integrating the enterprise systems when the newly launched PeopleSoft web portal (called Axess) crashed in 2004. Axess could not handle the load of all the returning students trying to log in to the untested web-based system at the same time, Livingston said. Stanford was able to fix those problems relatively quickly, but the struggle with the enterprise projects continued. The university's departments remain "highly suspicious and resistant" of his efforts to standardize and centralize business processes, Livingston said.

## Questions

1. How could core ERP components help improve business operations at your college?
2. How could extended ERP components help improve business operations at your college?
3. How can integrating SCM, CRM, and ERP help improve business operations at your college?
4. Review the different components in Figure B10.6. Which components would you recommend your college implement if it decided to purchase three components?

## ★ MAKING BUSINESS DECISIONS

### 1. CRM, SCM, and ERP Vendors

Health Caring Inc. recently purchased 12 hospitals in the Denver, Colorado, area. Three of the 12 hospitals currently use SAP products for their CRM and SCM systems. The other nine hospitals use systems from a variety of vendors including Oracle, IBM, and Microsoft. With so many separate systems it is currently impossible to track patients, nurses, doctors, inventory, food services, etc. Health Caring Inc. wants to be able to leverage economies of scale by using its buying clout to drive down prices of such things as inventory and food service, along with creating an environment for flexible staffing in the hospitals for its nurses and doctors. The company's mission is to become known as the "Hospital That Cares." Treating its patients with understanding, care, and high quality service is vitally important to the company's success.

You are the newly appointed CIO and the board of directors is expecting you to develop a plan for moving Health Caring Inc. into the future. The plan should include details of the issues the company is likely to experience with so many disparate systems, along with your recommendation and reasons for implementing an ERP solution.

### 2. Building an ERP Solution—Cirris Minerals

You are working for Cirris Minerals, a multibillion-dollar mining company, which operates over 3,000 mines in 25 countries. The company is currently looking at implementing an ERP system to help streamline its operations and manage its 150,000 employees. You are leading the team that has to make the decision as to whether the company should buy or build an ERP solution. For the most part, your company's system requirements are similar to other companies in your industry. Compile a list of questions you would require answers to in order to make your buy versus build decision.

### 3. Building an ERP Solution—Cirris Minerals *(continued)*

You (in the decision above) have recommended that Cirris Minerals implement an Oracle ERP solution. The CEO is on board with your recommendation. However, she wants you to use a phased approach to implementation. This means you must implement the new system in phases until it is evident that the new system performs correctly. The company will implement the remaining phases as soon as the first phase is completed successfully. You must now recommend which components the company should implement first. From the table below, choose the first two components that Cirris Minerals should implement. Be sure to include the justifications for the implementation of these components.

| Oracle | |
|---|---|
| **Component** | **Description** |
| Application Integration | Integrate Oracle and non-Oracle applications at all levels with Portal Solutions, AppConnect, and Data Warehousing and Analytic Solutions. |
| Customer Relationship Management | Get immediate, seamless integration among customer, financial, supply chain, and employee management systems. |
| Enterprise Performance Management | Enable customers, suppliers, and employees to connect to set goals, develop plans, and measure progress with our integrated, scalable applications. |
| Financial Management | Get the power to compete in the business world with a comprehensive suite of pure Internet financial applications. |
| Human Capital Management (including Human Resources Management Solutions) | Manage and mobilize a unified, global workforce, and align workforce contribution with business objectives. |
| Service Automation | Optimize project investments, reduce project delivery costs, and maximize resources to increase utilization and value to your organization. |
| Supplier Relationship Management | Manage all aspects of supplier relationships including indirect and direct goods, as well as services procurement. |
| Supply Chain Management | Take advantage of solutions that promote business-to-business interaction throughout the supply chain, from customer to supplier. |

### 4. Most Popular ERP Component

Mackenzie Coombe is currently thinking about implementing an ERP solution in her online music company, The Burford Beat. The company is generating over $12 million in revenues and is growing by 150 percent a year. Create a one-page document explaining the advantages and disadvantages of ERP systems, why ERP systems include CRM and SCM components, and why the most popular ERP component in today's marketplace is the accounting and finance core component.

### 5. Value-Added ERP

Pirate's Pizza is a large pizza chain that operates 700 franchises in 15 states. The company is contemplating implementing a new ERP system, which is expected to cost $7 million and take 18 months to implement. Once the system is completed, it is expected to generate $12 million a year in decreased costs and increased revenues. You are working in the finance department for the company and your boss has asked you to compile a report detailing the different financial metrics you can use to assess the business value of the new ERP system. Once your report is completed, the company will make a decision about purchasing the ERP system.

## 6. Increasing Revenues with ERP

Cold Cream is one of the premier beauty supply stores in the metro New York area. People come from all over to sample the store's unique creams, lotions, makeup, and perfumes. The company receives its products from manufacturers around the globe. The company would like to implement an ERP system to help it better understand its customers and their purchasing habits. Create a report summarizing ERP systems and explain how an ERP system can directly influence Cold Cream's revenues.

# Ebusiness

1. Describe the four common tools an organization can use to access Internet information.
2. Compare ISPs, OSPs, and ASPs. Be sure to include an overview of common services offered by each.
3. Describe how marketing, sales, financial services, and customer service departments can use ebusiness to increase revenues or reduce costs.
4. Explain why an organization would use metrics to determine a website's success.
5. Identify the different types of egovernment business models.
6. Define mcommerce and explain how an egovernment could use it to increase its efficiency and effectiveness.

## Introduction

As organizations, governments, and academia embrace the Internet to conduct business, new approaches in the way they reach their target customers have resulted in numerous ebusiness opportunities. A ***pure play (virtual) business*** is a business that operates on the Internet only without a physical store, such as Expedia.com and Amazon.com. New technologies, competition, and cost savings along with the global nature of the Internet have significantly transformed traditional businesses into ebusinesses. The core units introduced the concepts of ebusiness as well as ebusiness models. This plug-in will build on the units' discussion, providing specific details on the functions of ebusiness as well as current and future trends.

## Accessing Internet Information

Many restaurant and franchise experts believe that Cold Stone Creamery's franchisee intranet is what keeps the company on the fast track. Franchisee owners communicate with other owners through Creamery Talk, the company's intranet-based chat room. Since it launched, Creamery Talk has turned into a franchisee's black book, with tips on everything from storefront design to equipment repair. When one owner's freezer broke recently, a post to the chat room turned up an easy fix involving a $21 motor fan.

Four common tools for accessing Internet information include:

- Intranet
- Extranet
- Portal
- Kiosk

## INTRANET

An *intranet* is an internalized portion of the Internet, protected from outside access, that allows an organization to provide access to information and application software to only its employees. An intranet is an invaluable tool for presenting organizational information as it provides a central location where employees can find information. It can host all kinds of company-related information such as benefits, schedules, strategic directions, and employee directories. At many companies, each department has its own web page on the intranet for departmental information sharing. An intranet is not necessarily open to the external Internet and enables organizations to make internal resources available using familiar Internet clients, such as web browsers, newsreaders, and email.

Intranet publishing is the ultimate in electronic publishing. Companies realize significant returns on investment (ROI) simply by publishing information, such as employee manuals or telephone directories, on intranets rather than printed media.

Citigroup's Global Corporate and Investment Banking division uses an intranet to provide its entire IT department with access to all IT projects including information on project owners, delivery dates, key resources, budget information, and project metrics. Providing this information via an intranet, or one convenient location, has enabled Citigroup to gain a 15 percent improvement in IT project delivery.

## EXTRANET

An *extranet* is an intranet that is available to strategic allies (such as customers, suppliers, and partners). Many companies are building extranets as they begin to realize the benefit of offering individuals outside the organization access to intranet-based information and application software such as order processing. Having a common area where employees, partners, vendors, and customers access information can be a major competitive advantage for an organization.

Wal-Mart created an extranet for its suppliers, which can view detailed product information at all Wal-Mart locations. Suppliers log on to Wal-Mart's extranet and view metrics on products such as current inventory, orders, forecasts, and marketing campaigns. This helps Wal-Mart's suppliers maintain their supply chains and ensure Wal-Mart never runs out of products.

## PORTAL

*Portal* is a very generic term for what is in essence a technology that provides access to information. A *portal* is a website that offers a broad array of resources and services, such as email, online discussion groups, search engines, and online shopping malls. There are general portals and specialized or niche portals. Leading general portals include Yahoo!, Netscape, Microsoft, and America Online. Examples of niche portals include Garden.com (for gardeners), Fool.com (for investors), and SearchNetworking.com (for network administrators).

Pratt & Whitney, one of the largest aircraft-engine manufacturers in the world, has saved millions of dollars with its field service portal initiative. Pratt & Whitney's sales and service field offices are geographically scattered around the globe and were connected via expensive dedicated lines. The company saved $2.6 million annually by replacing the dedicated lines with high-speed Internet access to its field service portal. Field staff can find information they need in a fraction of the time it took before. The company estimates this change will save another $8 million per year in "process and opportunity" savings.

## KIOSK

A *kiosk* is a publicly accessible computer system that has been set up to allow interactive information browsing. In a kiosk, the computer's operating system has been hidden from view, and the program runs in a full-screen mode, which provides a few simple tools for navigation.

Jason Suker walked into the Mazda showroom in Bountiful, Utah, and quickly found what he was looking for in a car dealership—a web kiosk, one of six stationed around the showroom. Using the web kiosk, he could track down the latest pricing information from sites like Kelley Blue Book and Edmunds.com. Suker, eyeing a four-year-old limited-edition Miata in mint condition, quickly pulled up the average retail price on Kelley Blue Book. At $16,000, it was $500 more than the dealer's price. Then, on eBay, Suker checked bids for similar models and found they were going for far less. With a sales representative looking over his shoulder to confirm his findings, the skeptical Suker made a lowball offer and expected the worst: endless haggling over price. However, the sales representative, after commending Suker for his research talent, eventually compromised and offered up the Miata for $13,300.

It was an even better deal for Bountiful Mazda. By using a kiosk to help Suker find the bargain price he wanted, the dealership moved a used car (with a higher profit margin than a new model) and opened the door to the unexpected up-sell with a $1,300, 36,000-mile service warranty.

# Providing Internet Information

British Airways, the $11.9 billion airline, outsourced the automation of its FAQ (frequently asked questions) web pages. The airline needed to automatically develop, manage, and post different sets of FAQs for British Airway's loyalty program customers, allowing the company to offer special promotions based on the customer's loyalty program status (gold, silver, bronze). The company outsourced the project to application service provider RightNow Technologies. The new system is helping British Airways create the right marketing programs for the appropriate customer tier.

There are three common forms of service providers including:

1. Internet service provider (ISP).
2. Online service provider (OSP).
3. Application service provider (ASP).

## INTERNET SERVICE PROVIDER

An *Internet service provider (ISP)* is a company that provides individuals and other companies access to the Internet along with additional related services, such as website building. An ISP has the equipment and the telecommunication line access required to have a point of presence on the Internet for different geographic areas. Larger ISPs have their own high-speed leased lines so they are less dependent on telecommunication providers and can deliver better service to their customers. Among the largest national and regional ISPs are AT&T WorldNet, IBM Global Network, MCI, Netcom, UUNet, and PSINet.

Navigating the different options for an ISP can be daunting and confusing. There are more than 7,000 ISPs in the United States; some are large with household names, and others are literally one-person operations. Although Internet access is

| Common ISP Services |
|---|
| ■ **Web hosting**. Housing, serving, and maintaining files for one or more websites is a widespread offering. |
| ■ **Hard-disk storage space**. Smaller sites may need only 300 to 500 MB (megabytes) of website storage space, whereas other ebusiness sites may need at least 10 GB (gigabytes) of space or their own dedicated web server. |
| ■ **Availability**. To run an ebusiness, a site must be accessible to customers 24×7. ISPs maximize the availability of the sites they host using techniques such as load balancing and clustering many servers to reach 100 percent availability. |
| ■ **Support**. A big part of turning to an ISP is that there is limited worry about keeping the web server running. Most ISPs offer 24×7 customer service. |

**FIGURE B11.1**

Common ISP Services

viewed as a commodity service, in reality features and performance can differ tremendously among ISPs. Figure B11.1 highlights common ISP features.

Another member of the ISP family is the **_wireless Internet service provider (WISP),_** an ISP that allows subscribers to connect to a server at designated hotspots or access points using a wireless connection. This type of ISP offers access to the Internet and the web from anywhere within the zone of coverage provided by an antenna. This is usually a region with a radius of one mile. Figure B11.2 displays a brief overview of how this technology works.

One example of a WISP is T-Mobile International, a company that provides access to wireless laptop users in more than 2,000 locations including airports, airline clubs, Starbucks coffeehouses, and Borders Books. A wireless service called T-Mobile HotSpot allows customers to access the Internet and T-Mobile's corporate intranet via a wireless network from convenient locations away from their home or office. T-Mobile International is the first mobile communications company to extend service on both sides of the Atlantic, offering customers the advantage of using their wireless services when traveling worldwide.

## ONLINE SERVICE PROVIDER

An **_online service provider (OSP)_** offers an extensive array of unique services such as its own version of a web browser. The term *online service provider* helps to distinguish ISPs that offer Internet access and their own online content, such as America

**FIGURE B11.2**

Wireless Access Diagram

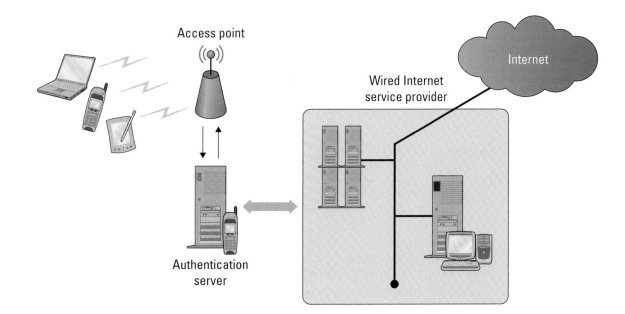

Online (AOL), from ISPs that simply connect users directly with the Internet, such as EarthLink. Connecting to the Internet through an OSP is an alternative to connecting through one of the national ISPs, such as AT&T or MCI, or a regional or local ISP.

### APPLICATION SERVICE PROVIDER

An *application service provider (ASP)* is a company that offers an organization access over the Internet to systems and related services that would otherwise have to be located in personal or organizational computers. Employing the services of an ASP is essentially outsourcing part of a company's business logic. Hiring an ASP to manage a company's software allows the company to hand over the operation, maintenance, and upgrade responsibilities for a system to the ASP.

One of the most important agreements between the customer and the ASP is the service level agreement. *Service level agreements (SLAs)* define the specific responsibilities of the service provider and set the customer expectations. SLAs include such items as availability, accessibility, performance, maintenance, backup/recovery, upgrades, equipment ownership, software ownership, security, and confidentiality. For example, an SLA might state that the ASP must have the software available and accessible from 7:00 a.m. to 7:00 p.m. Monday through Friday. It might also state that if the system is down for more than 60 minutes, there will be no charge for that day. Most industry analysts agree that the ASP market is growing rapidly. International Data Corporation (IDC) estimates the worldwide ASP market will grow from around $25 billion by 2008 to $40 billion by 2011. Figure B11.3 displays the top ISPs, OSPs, and ASPs.

## Organizational Strategies for Ebusiness

To be successful in ebusiness, an organization must master the art of electronic relationships. Traditional means of customer acquisition such as advertising, promotions, and public relations are just as important with a website. Primary business areas taking advantage of ebusiness include:

- Marketing/sales
- Financial services
- Procurement
- Customer service
- Intermediaries

### MARKETING/SALES

Direct selling was the earliest type of ebusiness and has proven to be a stepping-stone to more complex commerce operations. Successes such as eBay, Barnes and Noble, Dell Inc., and Travelocity have sparked the growth of this segment, proving customer acceptance of ebusiness direct selling. Marketing and sales departments are initiating some of the most exciting ebusiness innovations (see Figure B11.4).

Cincinnati's WCPO-TV once was a ratings blip and is now the number three ABC affiliate in the nation. WCPO-TV credits its success largely to digital billboards that promote different programming depending on the time of day. The billboards are updated directly from a website. The station quickly noticed that when current events for the early-evening news were plugged during the afternoon, ratings spiked.

The digital billboards let several companies share one space and can change messages directly from the company's computer. In the morning, a department store can advertise a sale, and in the afternoon, a restaurant can advertise its specials. Eventually customers will be able to buy billboard sign time in hour or minute increments. Current costs to share a digital billboard are $40,000 a month, compared with $10,000 for one standard billboard.

Agency leaders maintain that technology is one of the keys to making the USPS more competitive, as they have started a heavy campaign to combat declining revenues using a series of web technology projects. One of the most significant projects for the USPS is a web front-end for PostalOne, a system that seeks to eliminate the administrative paperwork for bulk mail, which accounts for 70 percent of total mail volume and 50 percent of the agency's $65 billion in revenue. More than 770,000 businesses use the USPS to send bulk mail.

PostalOne is one of the main customer-facing portions of the USPS's plan to build the Information Platform, which comprises the core IT systems that receive, process, transport, and deliver the mail. A tremendous amount of paperwork is associated with verifying a mailing to receive a discounted postage rate and creating related documentation. Business customers will install a USPS application that will reside on their server and manage the online paperwork, validate and encrypt files, and handle communications with PostalOne servers.

The Information Platform will include a web interface to the agency's Processing Operations Information System (POIS), which collects, tracks, and ultimately delivers performance data on the agency's more than 350 processing and distribution facilities. These efforts follow several ebusiness projects:

- **NetPost Mailing Online** lets small businesses transmit documents, correspondence, newsletters, and other first-class, standard, and nonprofit mail over the web to the USPS. Electronic files are transmitted to printing contractors, which print the documents, insert them into addressed envelopes, sort the mail pieces, and then add postage. The finished pieces are taken to a local post office for processing and delivery. Customers get the automated first-class rate, which is a few cents less per piece than the first-class rate.

- **Post Electronic Courier Service, or PosteCS,** a secure messaging product, allows mailers to send documents by email or over the web to recipients via a secure communication session. PosteCS has an electronic postmark, an electronic time and date stamp developed by USPS, embedded for proof of delivery. PosteCS is used mainly to transfer large files, such as financial statements. Cost is based on the security option chosen and file size.

- **NetPost.Certified,** a secure messaging product, was developed to help federal agencies comply with the Government Paperwork Elimination Act. NetPost.Certified is used, for example, by the Social Security Administration to receive notification from prisons when inmates are no longer eligible for benefits. NetPost.Certified includes an electronic postmark. The service costs 50 cents per transaction.

- **EBillPay** lets customers receive, view, and pay their bills via the agency's website. The Postal Service partners with CheckFree, which offers its service on the USPS site and performs back-end processing. Some enhancements to this service are being developed, including an embedded electronic postmark, person-to-person payments, and the ability to receive and pay bills via email. The ability to offer businesses and consumers online bill payment options is vital for the Postal Service, which estimates that $17 billion in annual revenue is at risk from first-class mail going through electronic alternatives for bill payment and presentment.

Despite its problems, the USPS has been resilient over the years, in large part because of its enormous resources. It is the nation's second largest employer behind Wal-Mart, and its revenue would rank it eighth in the Fortune 500.

## Questions

1. Do you think the steps by the USPS are far-reaching enough to ensure its relevance in ebusiness?

2. What other strategic alliances, akin to its partnership with CheckFree, can the USPS develop to stay competitive?

3. Why would the USPS compete in a market that private companies already serve well?

4. How can the USPS use portals to help grow its business?

5. How can the USPS use ebusiness sales and marketing techniques such as blogs, podcasts, and SEO to improve its business?

6. How can the USPS use ASPs to improve its business?

### Made-to-Order Businesses

In the past, customers had two choices for purchasing products: (1) purchase a mass-produced product like a pair of jeans or a candy bar, or (2) commission a custom-made item that was perfect but cost a lot more. Mass customization is a new trend in the retail business. Mass customization hits that sweet spot between harnessing the cost efficiencies of mass production and offering so many different options that customers feel the product has been designed just for them. Today, strategic information systems help many companies implement mass customization business strategies.

### Lands' End

Lands' End built a decision support system that could pinpoint a person's body size by taking just a few of their measurements and running a series of algorithms. The process begins when the customer answers questions on Lands' End's website about everything from waist size to inseam. Lands' End saves the data in its customer relationship management system, which is used for reorders, promotions, and marketing campaigns. When a customer places an order, the order is sent to San Francisco where supply chain management software determines which one of five contracted manufacturers should receive the order. The chosen manufacturer then cuts and sews the material and ships the finished garment directly to the customer.

Over 40 percent of Lands' End shoppers prefer a customized garment to the standard-sized equivalent, even though each customized garment costs at least $20 more and takes four weeks to deliver. Customized clothes account for a growing percentage of Lands' End's $511 million online business. Reorder rates for Lands' End custom-clothing buyers are 34 percent higher than for buyers of its standard-sized clothing.

### Nike

The original business model for Nike iD concentrated on connecting with consumers and creating customer loyalty. Nike iD's website allows customers to build their own running shoes. The process begins when customers choose from one of seven styles and a multitude of color combinations. Think dark-pink bottoms, red mesh, bright yellowing lining, purple laces, blue swoosh, and a eucalyptus green accent. Customers can even place eight-character personalized messages on the side of the shoe. The cost averages about $30 more than buying the regular shoes in a store.

Once Nike receives the custom order, its supply chain management system sends it to one of 15 plants depending on production availability. Customers receive their shoes within four weeks. The program has experienced triple-digit annual growth for two years.

### Stamps.com

Stamps.com, which provides online stamp purchases, made an agreement with the U.S. Postal Service to sell customized stamps. Customers could put pictures of their choice on an actual U.S. postage stamp. Pictures ranged from dogs to fiancées. The response was phenomenal: Within seven weeks, Stamps.com processed and sold more than 2 million PhotoStamps at $1 each (37 cents for a regular stamp). Unfortunately, pranksters managed to slip controversial photos through the system, and the U.S. Postal Service temporarily canceled the agreement.

Making mass customization a goal changes the way businesses think about their customers. Using supply chain management and customer relationship management to implement mass customization can have a direct impact on a business's bottom line.

## Questions

1. What role does ebusiness play in a mass customization business strategy?
2. How can Lands' End use additional sales and marketing ebusiness techniques to improve its business?
3. How can Nike use ebusiness financial services to improve its business?
4. How can Stamps.com use ASPs and electronic bill payment to improve its business?
5. Choose one of the examples above and analyze its ebusiness approach. Would you invest $20,000 in the company?
6. Choose one of the examples above and explain how the company is attempting to gain a competitive advantage with mass customization and personalization. How could this company use podcasts, blogs, and SEO to improve its business?

## ★ MAKING BUSINESS DECISIONS

### 1. Analyzing Websites

Stars Inc. is a large clothing corporation that specializes in reselling clothes worn by celebrities. The company's four websites generate 75 percent of its sales. The remaining 25 percent of sales occur directly through the company's warehouse. You have recently been hired as the director of sales. The only information you can find on the success of the four websites follows:

| Website | Classic | Contemporary | New Age | Traditional |
|---|---|---|---|---|
| Traffic analysis | 5,000 hits/day | 200 hits/day | 10,000 hits/day | 1,000 hits/day |
| Stickiness (average) | 20 min. | 1 hr. | 20 min. | 50 min. |
| Number of abandoned shopping carts | 400/day | 0/day | 5,000/day | 200/day |
| Number of unique visitors | 2,000/day | 100/day | 8,000/day | 200/day |
| Number of identified visitors | 3,000/day | 100/day | 2,000/day | 800/day |
| Average revenue per sale | $1,000 | $1,000 | $50 | $1,300 |

You decide that maintaining four separate websites is expensive and adds little business value. You want to propose consolidating to one website. Create a report detailing the business value gained by consolidating to a single website, along with your recommendation for consolidation. Be sure to include your website profitability analysis.

### 2. A Portal into Saab

Saab Cars USA, a marketing and distribution arm for the Swedish automaker, knew it had to improve communication with dealerships. Specifically, Saab wanted to ensure that dealers could communicate more reliably and easily access all the business systems and tools they needed. That meant upgrading the current system so dealers could tap into several of the company's legacy systems without having to install any Saab-specific hardware or software onsite. In addition, the refined system had to be reliable and inexpensive to maintain, easily support future upgrades, work within existing network and hardware designs, and integrate with existing systems. The portal was designed to make it easy for dealers across the United States to instantly access remote inventory, order parts, conduct online training sessions or research, and submit warranty claims. Identify the specific technological services Saab is looking to integrate into its new portal.

### 3. Online Auction Sites

You are working for a new Internet start-up company, eMart.com, an online marketplace for the sale of goods and services. The company offers a wide variety of features and services that enable online members to buy and sell their goods and services quickly and conveniently. Its mission is to provide a global trading platform where anyone can trade practically anything. Suggest some ways that eMart.com can gain business efficiencies in its marketing, sales, customer service, financial service, and purchasing departments. Be sure to include intranets, extranets, portals, ASPs, and OSPs.

### 4. Brewing Marketplace

Founded in 2003, the Foothills Brewing Company, foothillsbrew.com, is a pure play Internet brewing master. In its first year, the brewery sold 1,500 barrels of beer online. Its lagers and ales are brewed in small batches, handcrafted by a team of dedicated workers with high ideals of quality. Identify the advantages and disadvantages foothillsbrew.com will experience if it continues to operate as a pure play in the midst of a highly competitive marketplace.

### 5. Ebusiness Metrics

The Razor is a revolutionary mountain bike with full-suspension and shock-adjustable forks that is being marketed via the Internet. The Razor needs an ebusiness solution that will easily enable internal staff to deliver fresh and relevant product information through its website. To support its large audience, it also needs the ability to present information in multiple languages and serve more than 1 million page-views per month to global visitors. Identify the many different website metrics Razor should be evaluating to ensure its ebusiness solution is as efficient and effective as possible.

# Systems Development

1. Summarize the activities associated with the planning phase in the SDLC.
2. Summarize the activities associated with the analysis phase in the SDLC.
3. Summarize the activities associated with the design phase in the SDLC.
4. Summarize the activities associated with the development phase in the SDLC.
5. Summarize the activities associated with the testing phase in the SDLC.
6. Summarize the activities associated with the implementation phase in the SDLC.
7. Summarize the activities associated with the maintenance phase in the SDLC.

## Introduction

Today, systems are so large and complex that teams of architects, analysts, developers, testers, and users must work together to create the millions of lines of custom-written code that drive enterprises. For this reason, developers have created a number of different system development methodologies including waterfall, prototyping, rapid application development (RAD), extreme programming, agile, and others. All these methodologies are based on the *systems development life cycle (SDLC),* which is the overall process for developing information systems from planning and analysis through implementation and maintenance (see Figure B14.1).

The systems development life cycle is the foundation for all systems development methodologies, and there are literally hundreds of different activities associated with each phase in the SDLC. Typical activities include determining budgets, gathering system requirements, and writing detailed user documentation. The activities performed during each systems development project will vary. This plug-in takes a detailed look at a few of the more common activities performed during the systems development life cycle, along with common issues facing software development projects (see Figure B14.2).

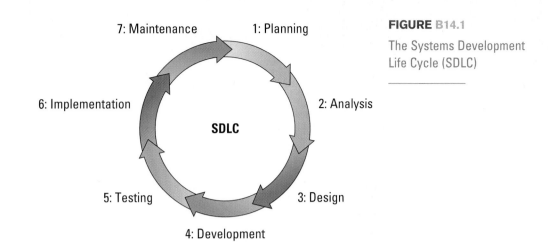

| SDLC Phase | Activities |
|---|---|
| **1.** Planning | ■ Identify and select the system for development<br>■ Assess project feasibility<br>■ Develop the project plan |
| **2.** Analysis | ■ Gather business requirements<br>■ Create process diagrams<br>■ Perform a buy versus build analysis |
| **3.** Design | ■ Design the IT infrastructure<br>■ Design system models |
| **4.** Development | ■ Develop the IT infrastructure<br>■ Develop the database and programs |
| **5.** Testing | ■ Write the test conditions<br>■ Perform the system testing |
| **6.** Implementation | ■ Determine implementation method<br>■ Provide training for the system users<br>■ Write detailed user documentation |
| **7.** Maintenance | ■ Build a help desk to support the system users<br>■ Perform system maintenance<br>■ Provide an environment to support system changes |

**FIGURE** B14.2

Common Activities
Performed During
Systems Development

# Systems Development Life Cycle

### PHASE 1: PLANNING

The ***planning phase*** involves establishing a high-level plan of the intended project
and determining project goals. The three primary activities involved in the planning phase are:

1. Identify and select the system for development.
2. Assess project feasibility.
3. Develop the project plan.

| Evaluation Criteria | Description |
|---|---|
| Value chain analysis | The value chain determines the extent to which the new system will add value to the organization. Systems with greater value are given priority over systems with less value. |
| Strategic alignment | Projects that are in line with the organization's strategic goals and objectives are given priority over projects not in line with the organization's strategic goals and objectives. |
| Cost-benefit analysis | A cost-benefit analysis determines which projects offer the organization the greatest benefits with the least amount of cost. |
| Resource availability | Determine the amount and type of resources required to complete the project and determine if the organization has these resources available. |
| Project size, duration, and difficulty | Determine the number of individuals, amount of time, and technical difficulty of the project. |

### Identify and Select the System for Development

Systems are successful only when they solve the right problem or take advantage of the right opportunity. Systems development focuses on either solving a problem or taking advantage of an opportunity. Determining which systems are required to support the strategic goals of an organization is one of the primary activities performed during the planning phase. Typically, employees generate proposals to build new information systems when they are having a difficult time performing their jobs. Unfortunately, most organizations have limited resources and cannot afford to develop all proposed information systems. Therefore, they look to critical success factors to help determine which systems to build.

A *critical success factor (CSF)* is a factor that is critical to an organization's success. To determine which system to develop, an organization tracks all the proposed systems and prioritizes them by business impact or critical success factors. This allows the business to prioritize which problems require immediate attention and which problems can wait. Figure B14.3 displays possible evaluation criteria for determining which projects to develop.

### Assess Project Feasibility

A *feasibility study* determines if the proposed solution is feasible and achievable from a financial, technical, and organizational standpoint. Typically, an organization will define several alternative solutions that it can pursue to solve a given problem. A feasibility study is used to determine if the proposed solution is achievable, given the organization's resources and constraints in regard to technology, economics, organizational factors, and legal and ethical considerations. Figure B14.4 displays the many different types of feasibility studies an organization can perform.

### Develop the Project Plan

Developing a project plan is one of the final activities performed during the planning phase and it is one of the hardest and most important activities. The project plan is the guiding force behind on-time delivery of a complete and successful system. It logs and tracks every single activity performed during the project. If an activity is missed, or takes longer than expected to complete, the project plan must be updated to reflect these changes. Updating of the project plan must be performed in every subsequent phase during the systems development effort.

| Types of Feasibility Studies | |
|---|---|
| **Economic feasibility study** (often called a **cost-benefit analysis**) | Identifies the financial benefits and costs associated with the systems development project. |
| **Legal and contractual feasibility study** | Examines all potential legal and contractual ramifications of the proposed system. |
| **Operational feasibility study** | Examines the likelihood that the project will attain its desired objectives. |
| **Schedule feasibility study** | Assesses the likelihood that all potential time frames and completion dates will be met. |
| **Technical feasibility study** | Determines the organization's ability to build and integrate the proposed system. |

**FIGURE** B14.4

Types of Feasibility Studies

## PHASE 2: ANALYSIS

The *analysis phase* involves analyzing end-user business requirements and refining project goals into defined functions and operations of the intended system. The three primary activities involved in the analysis phase are:

1. Gather business requirements.
2. Create process diagrams.
3. Perform a buy versus build analysis.

### Gather Business Requirements

*Business requirements* are the detailed set of business requests that the system must meet to be successful. At this point, there is little or no concern with any implementation or reference to technical details. For example, the types of technology used to build the system, such as an Oracle database or the Java programming language, are not yet defined. The only focus is on gathering the true business requirements for the system. A sample business requirement might state, "The system must track all customer sales by product, region, and sales representative." This requirement states what the system must do from the business perspective, giving no details or information on how the system is going to meet this requirement.

Gathering business requirements is basically conducting an investigation in which users identify all the organization's business needs and take measurements of these needs. Figure B14.5 displays a number of ways to gather business requirements.

The *requirements definition document* contains the final set of business requirements, prioritized in order of business importance. The system users review the requirements definition document and determine if they will sign off on the business requirements. *Sign-off* is the system users' actual signatures indicating they approve all of the business requirements. One of the first major milestones on the project plan is usually the users' sign-off on business requirements.

A large data storage company implemented a project called Python whose purpose was to control all the company's information systems. Seven years, tens of millions of dollars, and 35 programmers later Python was canceled. At the end of the project, Python had over 1,800 business requirements of which 900 came from engineering and were written in order to make the other 900 customer requirements work. By the time the project was canceled, it was unclear what the primary goals, objectives, and needs of the project were. Management should have realized Python's issues when the project's requirements phase dragged on, bulged, and took years to complete. The sheer number of requirements should have raised a red flag.

| Methods for Gathering Business Requirements |
| --- |
| Perform a *joint application development (JAD)* session where employees meet, sometimes for several days, to define or review the business requirements for the system. |
| Interview individuals to determine current operations and current issues. |
| Compile questionnaires to survey employees to discover issues. |
| Make observations to determine how current operations are performed. |
| Review business documents to discover reports, policies, and how information is used throughout the organization. |

## Create Process Diagrams

Once a business analyst takes a detailed look at how an organization performs its work and its processes, the analyst can recommend ways to improve these processes to make them more efficient and effective. *Process modeling* involves graphically representing the processes that capture, manipulate, store, and distribute information between a system and its environment. One of the most common diagrams used in process modeling is the data flow diagram. A *data flow diagram (DFD)* illustrates the movement of information between external entities and the processes and data stores within the system (see Figure B14.6). Process models and data flow diagrams establish the specifications of the system. *Computer-aided software engineering (CASE)* tools are software suites that automate systems analysis, design, and development. Process models and data flow diagrams can provide the basis for the automatic generation of the system if they are developed using a CASE tool.

**FIGURE** B14.6

Sample Data Flow
Diagram

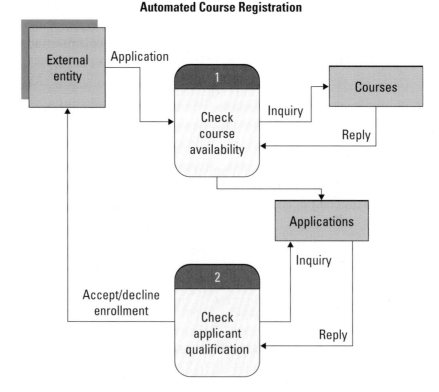

**Automated Course Registration**

## Perform a Buy versus Build Analysis

An organization faces two primary choices when deciding to develop an information system: (1) it can *buy* the information system from a vendor or (2) it can *build* the system itself. ***Commercial off-the-shelf (COTS)*** software is a software package or solution that is purchased to support one or more business functions and information systems. Most customer relationship management, supply chain management, and enterprise resource planning solutions are COTS. Typically, a cost-benefit analysis forms the basis of the buy versus build decision. Organizations must consider the questions displayed in Figure B14.7 during the buy versus build decision.

Three key factors an organization should also consider when contemplating the buy versus build decision are: (1) time to market, (2) corporate resources, and (3) core competencies. Weighing the complex relationship between each of these three variables will help an organization make the right choice (see Figure B14.8).

When making the all-important buy versus build decision consider when the product must be available, how many resources are available, and how the organization's core competencies affect the product. If these questions can be definitely answered either yes or no, then the answer to the buy versus build question is easy. However, most organizations cannot answer these questions with a solid yes or no. Most organizations need to make a trade-off between the lower cost of buying a system and the need for a system that meets all of their requirements. Finding a system to buy that meets all an organization's unique business requirements is next to impossible.

| Buy versus Build Decision Questions |
|---|
| Do any currently available products fit the organization's needs? |
| Are unavailable features important enough to warrant the expense of in-house development? |
| Can the organization customize or modify an existing COTS to fit its needs? |
| Is there a justification to purchase or develop based on the cost of acquisition? |

**FIGURE B14.7**

Buy versus Build Decision Questions

| Three Key Factors in Buy versus Build Decisions | |
|---|---|
| 1. **Time to market** | If time to market is a priority, then purchasing a good base technology and potentially building on to it will likely yield results faster than starting from scratch. |
| 2. **Availability of corporate resources** | The buy versus build decision is a bit more complex to make when considering the availability of corporate resources. Typically, the costs to an organization to buy systems such as SCM, CRM, and ERP are extremely high. These costs can be so high—in the multiple millions of dollars—that acquiring these technologies might make the entire concept economically unfeasible. Building these systems, however, can also be extremely expensive, take indefinite amounts of time, and constrain resources. |
| 3. **Corporate core competencies** | The more an organization wants to build a technical core competency, the less likely it will want to buy. |

**FIGURE B14.8**

Key Factors in Buy versus Build Decisions

## PHASE 3: DESIGN

The ***design phase*** involves describing the desired features and operations of the system including screen layouts, business rules, process diagrams, pseudo code, and other documentation. The two primary activities involved in the design phase are:

1. Design the IT infrastructure.
2. Design system models.

### Design the IT Infrastructure

The system must be supported by a solid IT infrastructure or chances are the system will crash, malfunction, or not perform as expected. The IT infrastructure must meet the organization's needs in terms of time, cost, technical feasibility, and flexibility. Most systems run on a computer network with each employee having a client and the application running on a server. During this phase, the IT specialists recommend what types of clients and servers to buy including memory and storage requirements, along with software recommendations. An organization typically explores several different IT infrastructures that must meet current as well as future system needs. For example, databases must be large enough to hold the current volume of customers plus all new customers that the organization expects to gain over the next several years (see Figure B14.9).

### Design System Models

***Modeling*** is the activity of drawing a graphical representation of a design. An organization should model everything it builds including reports, programs, and

**FIGURE** B14.9

Sample IT Infrastructure

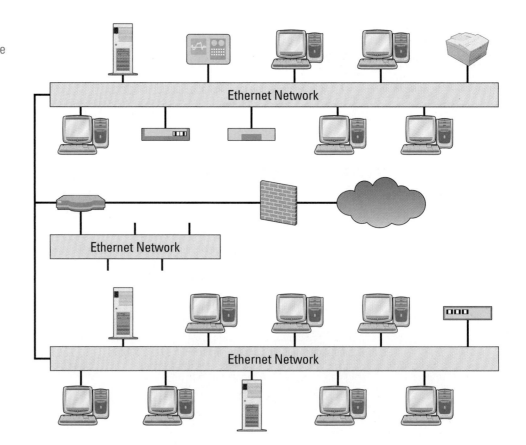

databases. Many different types of modeling activities are performed during the design phase, including:

■ The **graphical user interface (GUI)** is the interface to an information system. **GUI screen design** is the ability to model the information system screens for an entire system using icons, buttons, menus, and submenus.

■ **Data models** represent a formal way to express data relationships to a database management system (DBMS).

■ **Entity relationship diagram (ERD)** is a technique for documenting the relationships between entities in a database environment (see Figure B14.10).

**FIGURE** B14.10

Sample Entity Relationship Diagram

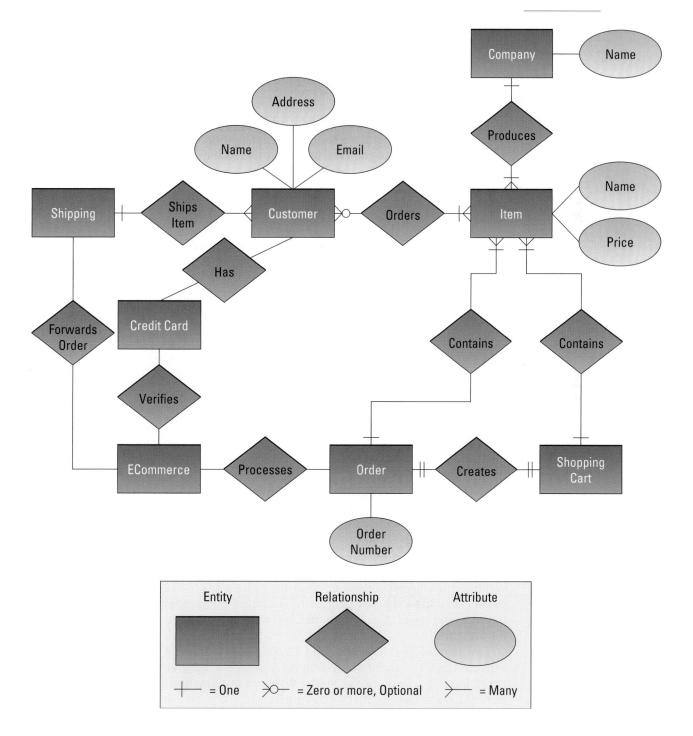

## PHASE 4: DEVELOPMENT

The ***development phase*** involves taking all of the detailed design documents from the design phase and transforming them into the actual system. The two primary activities involved in the development phase are:

1. Develop the IT infrastructure.
2. Develop the database and programs.

### Develop the IT Infrastructure

The platform upon which the system will operate must be built before building the actual system. In the design phase, an organization creates a blueprint of the proposed IT infrastructure displaying the design of the software, hardware, and telecommunication equipment. In the development phase, the organization purchases and implements the required equipment to support the IT infrastructure.

Most new systems require new hardware and software. It may be as simple as adding memory to a client or as complex as setting up a wide area network across several states.

### Develop the Database and Programs

Once the IT infrastructure is built, the organization can begin to create the database and write the programs required for the system. IT specialists perform these functions and it may take months or even years to design and create all the needed elements to complete the system.

## PHASE 5: TESTING

According to a report issued by the National Institute of Standards and Technology (NIST), defective software costs the U.S. economy an estimated $87.5 billion each year. Of that total, software users incurred 64 percent of the costs and software developers 36 percent. NIST suggests that improvements in testing could reduce this cost by about a third, or $30 billion, but that unfortunately testing improvements would not eliminate all software errors.

The ***testing phase*** involves bringing all the project pieces together into a special testing environment to test for errors, bugs, and interoperability, in order to verify that the system meets all the business requirements defined in the analysis phase. The two primary activities involved in the testing phase are:

1. Write the test conditions.
2. Perform the system testing.

### Write the Test Conditions

Testing is critical. An organization must have excellent test conditions to perform an exhaustive test. ***Test conditions*** are the detailed steps the system must perform along with the expected results of each step. Figure B14.11 displays several test conditions for testing user log-on functionality in a system. The tester will execute each test condition and compare the expected results with the actual results in order to verify that the system functions correctly. Notice in Figure B14.11 how each test condition is extremely detailed and states the expected results that should occur when executing each test condition. Each time the actual result is different from the expected result, a "bug" is generated and the system goes back to development for a bug fix.

Test condition 6 in Figure B14.11 displays a different actual result than the expected result because the system failed to allow the user to log on. After this test condition fails, it is obvious that the system is not functioning correctly and it must be sent back to development for a bug fix.

| Test Condition Number | Date Tested | Tested | Test Condition | Expected Result | Actual Result | Pass/ Fail |
|---|---|---|---|---|---|---|
| 1 | 1/1/09 | Emily Hickman | Click on System Start Button | Main Menu appears | Same as expected result | Pass |
| 2 | 1/1/09 | Emily Hickman | Click on Log-on Button in Main Menu | Log-on Screen appears asking for User name and Password | Same as expected result | Pass |
| 3 | 1/1/09 | Emily Hickman | Type Emily Hickman in the User Name Field | Emily Hickman appears in the User Name Field | Same as expected result | Pass |
| 4 | 1/1/09 | Emily Hickman | Type Zahara123 in the password field | XXXXXXXXX appears in the password field | Same as expected result | Pass |
| 5 | 1/1/09 | Emily Hickman | Click on O.K. button | User log-on request is sent to database and user name and password are verified | Same as expected result | Pass |
| 6 | 1/1/09 | Emily Hickman | Click on Start | User name and password are accepted and the system main menu appears | Screen appeared stating log-on failed and user name and password were incorrect | Fail |

**FIGURE** B14.11

Sample Test Conditions

A typical system development effort has hundreds or thousands of test conditions. Every single test condition must be executed to verify that the system performs as expected. Writing all the test conditions and performing the actual testing of the software takes a tremendous amount of time and energy. Testing is critical to the successful development of any system.

## Perform the System Testing

System developers must perform many different types of testing to ensure that the system works as expected. Figure B14.12 displays a few of the more common types of tests performed during this phase.

## PHASE 6: IMPLEMENTATION

The *implementation phase* involves placing the system into production so users can begin to perform actual business operations with the system. The three primary activities involved in the implementation phase are:

1. Write detailed user documentation.
2. Determine implementation method.
3. Provide training for the system users.

## Write Detailed User Documentation

System users require *user documentation* that highlights how to use the system. This is the type of documentation that is typically provided along with the new system. System users find it extremely frustrating to have a new system without documentation.

| Types of Tests Performed During the Testing Phase | |
|---|---|
| Application (or system) testing | Verifies that all units of code work together and the total system satisfies all of its functional and operational requirements. |
| Backup and recovery testing | Tests the ability of an application to be restarted after failure. |
| Documentation testing | Verifies that the instruction guides are helpful and accurate. |
| Integration testing | Exposes faults in the integration of software components or software units. |
| Regression testing | Determines if a functional improvement or repair to the system has affected the other functional aspects of the software. |
| Unit testing | Tests each unit of code as soon as the unit is complete to expose faults in the unit regardless of its interaction with other units. |
| User acceptance testing (UAT) | Determines whether a system satisfies its acceptance criteria, enabling the customer to decide whether or not to accept a system. |

### Determine Implementation Method

An organization must choose the right implementation method to ensure a successful system implementation. Figure B14.13 highlights the four primary implementation methods an organization can choose from.

### Provide Training for the System Users

An organization must provide training for the system users. The two most popular types of training are online training and workshop training. **Online training** runs over the Internet or off a CD-ROM. System users perform the training at any time, on their own computers, at their own pace. This type of training is convenient for system users because they can set their own schedule for the training. **Workshop training** is set in a classroom-type environment and led by an instructor. Workshop training is recommended for difficult systems where the system users require one-on-one time with an individual instructor.

| Primary Implementation Methods | |
|---|---|
| 1. Parallel implementation | Using both the old and new systems until it is evident that the new system performs correctly. |
| 2. Phased implementation | Implementing the new system in phases (e.g., accounts receivables then accounts payable) until it is evident that the new system performs correctly and then implementing the remaining phases of the new system. |
| 3. Pilot implementation | Having only a small group of people use the new system until it is evident that the new system performs correctly and then adding the remaining people to the new system. |
| 4. Plunge implementation | Discarding the old system completely and immediately using the new system. |

## PHASE 7: MAINTENANCE

The **maintenance phase** involves performing changes, corrections, additions, and upgrades to ensure the system continues to meet the business goals. Once a system is in place, it must change as the organization changes. The three primary activities involved in the maintenance phase are:

1. Build a help desk to support the system users.
2. Perform system maintenance.
3. Provide an environment to support system changes.

### Build a Help Desk to Support the System Users

A **help desk** is a group of people who respond to internal system user questions. Typically, internal system users have a phone number for the help desk they call whenever they have issues or questions about the system. Staffing a help desk that answers internal user questions is an excellent way to provide comprehensive support for new systems.

### Perform System Maintenance

**Maintenance** is fixing or enhancing an information system. Many different types of maintenance must be performed on the system to ensure it continues to operate as expected. These include:

- **Adaptive maintenance**—making changes to increase system functionality to meet new business requirements.
- **Corrective maintenance**—making changes to repair system defects.
- **Perfective maintenance**—making changes to enhance the system and improve such things as processing performance and usability.
- **Preventive maintenance**—making changes to reduce the chance of future system failures.

### Provide an Environment to Support System Changes

As changes arise in the business environment, an organization must react to those changes by assessing the impact on the system. It might well be that the system needs to adjust to meet the ever-changing needs of the business environment. If so, an organization must modify its systems to support the business environment.

A **change management system** includes a collection of procedures to document a change request and define the steps necessary to consider the change based on the expected impact of the change. Most change management systems require that a change request form be initiated by one or more project stakeholders (users, customers, analysts, developers). Ideally, these change requests are reviewed by a **change control board (CCB)** responsible for approving or rejecting all change requests. The CCB's composition typically includes a representative for each business area that has a stake in the project. The CCB's decision to accept or reject each change is based on an impact analysis of the change. For example, if one department wants to implement a change to the software that will increase both deployment time and cost, then the other business owners need to agree that the change is valid and that it warrants the extended time frame and increased budget.

The systems development life cycle (SDLC) is the foundation for all systems development methodologies. Understanding the phases and activities involved in the systems development life cycle is critical when developing information systems regardless of which methodology is being used. The SDLC contains the following phases:

1. The *planning phase* involves establishing a high-level plan of the intended project and determining project goals.

2. The *analysis phase* involves analyzing end-user business requirements and refining project goals into defined functions and operations of the intended system.

3. The *design phase* involves describing the desired features and operations of the system including screen layouts, business rules, process diagrams, pseudo code, and other documentation.

4. The *development phase* involves taking all the detailed design documents from the design phase and transforming them into the actual system.

5. The *testing phase* involves bringing all the project pieces together into a special testing environment to test for errors, bugs, and interoperability, in order to verify that the system meets all the business requirements defined in the analysis phase.

6. The *implementation phase* involves placing the system into production so users can begin to perform actual business operations with the system.

7. The *maintenance phase* involves performing changes, corrections, additions, and upgrades to ensure the system continues to meet the business goals.

★ **KEY TERMS**

### Disaster at Denver International Airport

One good way to learn how to develop successful systems is to review past failures. One of the most infamous system failures is Denver International Airport's (DIA) baggage system. When the automated baggage system design for DIA was introduced, it was hailed as the savior of modern airport design. The design relied on a network of 300 computers to route bags and 4,000 telecars to carry luggage across 21 miles of track. Laser scanners were to read bar-coded luggage tags, while advanced scanners tracked the movement of toboggan-like baggage carts.

When DIA finally opened its doors for reporters to witness its revolutionary baggage handling system the scene was rather unpleasant. Bags were chewed up, lost, and misrouted in what has since become a legendary systems nightmare.

One of the biggest mistakes made in the baggage handling system fiasco was that not enough time was allowed to properly develop the system. In the beginning of the project, DIA assumed it was the responsibility of individual airlines to find their own way of moving the baggage from the plane to the baggage claim area. The automated baggage system was not involved in the initial planning of the DIA project. By the time the developers of DIA decided to create an integrated baggage system, the time frame for designing and implementing such a complex and huge system was not possible.

Another common mistake that occurred during the project was that the airlines kept changing their business requirements. This caused numerous issues including the implementation of power supplies that were not properly updated for the revised system design, which caused overloaded motors and mechanical failures. Besides the power supplies design problem, the optical sensors did not read the bar codes correctly, causing issues with baggage routing.

Finally, BAE, the company that designed and implemented the automated baggage system for DIA, had never created a baggage system of this size before. BAE had created a similar system in an airport in Munich, Germany, where the scope was much smaller. Essentially, the baggage system had an inadequate IT infrastructure since it was designed for a much smaller system.

DIA simply could not open without a functional baggage system so the city had no choice but to delay the opening date for over 16 months, costing taxpayers roughly $1 million per day, which totaled around $500 million.

### Questions

1. One of the problems with DIA's baggage system was inadequate testing. Describe the different types of tests DIA could have used to help ensure its baggage system's success.

2. Evaluate the different implementation approaches. Which one would have most significantly increased the chances of the project's success?

3. Explain the cost of finding errors. How could more time spent in the analysis and design phase have saved Colorado taxpayers hundreds of millions of dollars?

4. Why could BAE not take an existing IT infrastructure and simply increase its scale and expect it to work?

### Reducing Ambiguity in Business Requirements

The number one reason projects fail is bad business requirements. Business requirements are considered "bad" because of ambiguity or insufficient involvement of end users during analysis and design.

A requirement is unambiguous if it has the same interpretation for all parties. Different interpretations by different participants will usually result in unmet expectations. Here is an example of an ambiguous requirement and an example of an unambiguous requirement:

- **Ambiguous requirement:** The financial report must show profits in local and U.S. currencies.
- **Unambiguous requirement:** The financial report must show profits in local and U.S. currencies using the exchange rate printed in *The Wall Street Journal* for the last business day of the period being reported.

Ambiguity is impossible to prevent completely because it is introduced into requirements in natural ways. For example:

- Requirements can contain technical implications that are obvious to the IT developers but not to the customers.
- Requirements can contain business implications that are obvious to the customer but not to the IT developers.
- Requirements may contain everyday words whose meanings are "obvious" to everyone, yet different for everyone.
- Requirements are reflections of detailed explanations that may have included multiple events, multiple perspectives, verbal rephrasing, emotion, iterative refinement, selective emphasis, and body language—none of which are captured in the written statements.

### Tips for Reviewing Business Requirements

When reviewing business requirements always look for the following words to help dramatically reduce ambiguity:

- **"And"** and **"or"** have well-defined meanings and ought to be completely unambiguous, yet they are often understood only informally and interpreted inconsistently. For example, consider the statement "The alarm must ring if button T is pressed and if button F is pressed." This statement may be intended to mean that to ring the alarm, both buttons must be pressed or it may be intended to mean that either one can be pressed. A statement like this should never appear in a requirement because the potential for misinterpretation is too great. A preferable approach is to be very explicit, for example, "The alarm must ring if both buttons T and F are pressed simultaneously. The alarm should not ring in any other circumstance."
- **"Always"** might really mean "most of the time," in which case it should be made more explicit. For example, the statement "We always run reports A and B together" could be challenged with "In other words, there is never any circumstance where you would run A without B and B without A?" If you build a system with an "always" requirement, then you are actually building the system to never run report A without report B. If a user suddenly wants report B without report A, you will need to make significant system changes.
- **"Never"** might mean "rarely," in which case it should be made more explicit. For example, the statement "We never run reports A and B in the same month" could be challenged with, "So that means that if I see that A has been run, I can be absolutely certain that

no one will want to run B." Again, if you build a system that supports a "never" requirement then the system users can never perform that requirement. For example, the system would never allow a user to run reports A and B in the same month, no matter what the circumstances.

- **Boundary conditions** are statements about the line between true and false and do and do not. These statements may or may not be meant to include end points. For example, "We want to use method X when there are up to 10 pages, but method Y otherwise." If you were building this system, would you include page 10 in method X or in method Y? The answer to this question will vary causing an ambiguous business requirement.

## Questions

1. Why are ambiguous business requirements the leading cause of system development failures?

2. Why do the words *and* and *or* tend to lead to ambiguous requirements?

3. Research the web and determine other reasons for "bad" business requirements.

4. What is wrong with the following business requirement: "The system must support employee birthdays since every employee always has a birthday every year."

---

## ★ MAKING BUSINESS DECISIONS

### 1. Understanding Project Failure

You are the director of project management for Stello, a global manufacturer of high-end writing instruments. The company sells to primarily high-end customers, and the average price for one of its fine writing instruments is about $350. You are currently implementing a new customer relationship management system and you want to do everything you can to ensure a successful systems development effort. Create a document summarizing the five primary reasons this project could fail, along with your strategy to eliminate the possibility of system development failure on your project.

### 2. Missing Phases in the Systems Development Life Cycle

Hello Inc. is a large concierge service for executives operating in Chicago, San Francisco, and New York. The company performs all kinds of services from dog walking to airport transportation. Your manager, Dan Martello, wants to skip the testing phase during the company's financial ERP implementation. Dan feels that since the system came from a vendor it should work correctly. To meet the project's looming deadline he wants to skip the testing phase. Draft a memo explaining to Dan the importance of following the SDLC and the ramifications to the business if the financial system is not tested.

### 3. Saving Failing Systems

Crik Candle Company manufactures low-end candles for restaurants. The company generates over $40 million in annual revenues and has over 300 employees. You are in the middle of a large multimillion-dollar supply chain management implementation. Your project manager has just come to you with the information that the project might fail for the following reasons:

- Several business requirements were incorrect and the scope has to be doubled.
- Three developers recently quit.
- The deadline has been moved up a month.

Develop a list of options that your company can follow to ensure the project remains on schedule and within budget.

## 4. Refusing to Sign Off

You are the primary client on a large extranet development project. After carefully reviewing the requirements definition document, you are positive that there are missing, ambiguous, inaccurate, and unclear requirements. The project manager is pressuring you for your sign-off since he has already received sign-off from five of your co-workers. If you fail to sign off on the requirements, you are going to put the entire project at risk since the time frame is nonnegotiable. What would you do? Why?

## 5. Feasibility Studies

John Lancert is the new managing operations director for a large construction company, LMC. John is currently looking for an associate who can help him prioritize the 60 proposed company projects. You are interested in working with John and have decided to apply for the job. John has asked you to compile a report detailing why project prioritization is critical for LMC, along with the different types of feasibility studies you would recommend that LMC use when determining which projects to pursue.

# PLUG-IN
# B15

# Project Management

## Introduction

The core units introduced project management. A **project** is a temporary endeavor undertaken to create a unique product or service. According to the Project Management Institute, **project management** is the application of knowledge, skills, tools, and techniques to project activities in order to meet or exceed stakeholder needs and expectations from a project. A **project manager** is an individual who is an expert in project planning and management, defines and develops the project plan, and tracks the plan to ensure the project is completed on time and on budget. The project manager is the person responsible for executing the entire project plan. Figure B15.1 displays the numerous roles project managers must perform. This plug-in takes a deeper look at the project manager's role in developing successful information systems using a variety of project management strategies and tools including:

1. Choosing strategic projects.
2. Understanding project planning.
3. Managing projects.
4. Risk management.

## Choosing Strategic Projects

One of the most difficult decisions organizations make is determining the projects in which to invest time, energy, and resources. An organization must identify what it wants to do and how it is going to do it. The "what" part of this question focuses

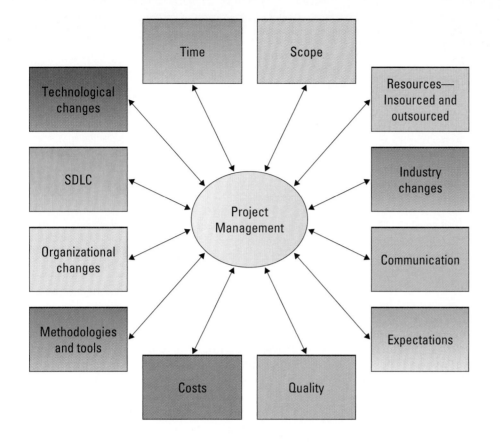

on issues such as justification for the project, definition of the project, and expected results of the project. The "how" part of the question deals with issues such as project approach, project schedule, and analysis of project risks. Determining which projects to focus corporate efforts on is as necessary to projects as each project is to an organization.

Organizations also need to choose and prioritize projects in such a way that they can make responsible decisions as to which projects to eliminate. Jim Johnson, chairman of the Standish Group, has identified project management as the process that can make the difference in project success. According to Johnson, "Companies need a process for taking a regular look at their projects and deciding, again and again, if the investment is going to pay off. As it stands now, for most companies, projects can take on a life of their own." Figure B15.2 displays the three common techniques an organization can use to select projects.

*Project stakeholders* are individuals and organizations actively involved in the project or whose interests might be affected as a result of project execution or project completion. Stakeholders are not necessarily involved in the completion of project deliverables. For example, a chief financial officer (CFO) probably will not help test a new billing system, but she surely will be expecting the successful completion of the project.

Stakeholders, such as the CFO, also can exert influence over the project's objectives and outcomes. It is important for all stakeholders to understand the business objective of the project—once again, it is about getting the big picture. Stakeholders measure projects based on such factors as customer satisfaction, increased revenue, or decreased cost.

The project management team must identify stakeholders, determine their requirements and expectations, and, to the extent possible, manage their influence in relationship to the requirements to ensure a successful project. While all stakeholders are important, one stands out as having the most impact on the success or

| Techniques for Choosing Strategic Projects |
|---|
| 1. **Focus on organizational goals**—Managers are finding tremendous value in choosing projects that align with the organization's goals. Projects that address organizational goals tend to have a higher success rate since they are important to the entire organization. |
| 2. **Categorize projects**—There are various categories that an organization can group projects into to determine a project's priority. One type of categorization includes problem, opportunity, and directives. Problems are undesirable situations that prevent an organization from achieving its goals. Opportunities are chances to improve the organization. Directives are new requirements imposed by management, government, or some other external influence. It is often easier to obtain approval for projects that address problems or directives because the organization must respond to these categories to avoid financial losses. |
| 3. **Perform a financial analysis**—A number of different financial analysis techniques can be performed to help determine a project's priority. A few of these include net present value, return on investment, and payback analysis. These financial analysis techniques help determine the organization's financial expectations for the project. |

failure of a project. That person is the executive sponsor. PMI defines the ***executive sponsor*** as the person or group who provides the financial resources for the project. However, research has shown that the leadership strength of the executive sponsor has more to do with the success or failure of a project than any other critical success factor. In fact, the executive sponsor should be accountable to the project team for much more than the financial backing. The executive sponsor communicates up the chain on behalf of the project; he or she supports the project manager by championing the project to others sharing the vision and benefit of the successfully completed project; and the executive sponsor demonstrates the commitment and accountability necessary to survive a project! If a team has a hands-off sponsor who merely reviews invoices and inquires as to the status of a project, then that project surely is in trouble from the start.

Another part of the equation is influence. If the executive sponsor has influence, he or she can use that influence to gain and direct essential resources needed to accomplish the project. A highly connected executive sponsor could mean the difference between success and failure. The executive sponsor should be committed to use this influence to ensure the health of the project. Executive management support influences the process and progress of a project. No matter what the case, the lack of executive support and input can place a project at a severe disadvantage.

# Understanding Project Planning

Once an organization has selected strategic projects and identified its project manager it is time to build the critical component—the project plan. Building a project plan involves two key components:

- Project charter
- Project plan

## PROJECT CHARTER

Many project professionals believe that a solid project is initiated with documentation that includes a project charter, a scope statement, and the project management plan. A ***project charter*** is a document issued by the project initiator or sponsor that formally authorizes the existence of a project and provides the project manager with the authority to apply organizational resources to project activities. In short, this means someone has stepped up to pay for and support the project. A project charter typically includes several elements.

**FIGURE** B15.3

SMART Criteria for Successful Objective Creation

- **Project scope** defines the work that must be completed to deliver a product with the specified features and functions. A project scope statement describes the business need, justification, requirements, and current boundaries for the project. The business need can be characterized by the problem the results of the project will satisfy. This is important in linking the project with the organization's overall business goals. The project scope statement includes constraints, assumptions, and requirements—all components necessary for developing accurate cost estimates.

- **Project objectives** are quantifiable criteria that must be met for the project to be considered a success.

- **Project constraints** are specific factors that can limit options. They include: budget, delivery dates, available skilled resources, and organizational policies.

- **Project assumptions** are factors that are considered to be true, real, or certain without proof or demonstration. Examples include hours in a workweek or time of year the work will be performed.

The project objectives are one of the most important areas to define because they are essentially the major elements of the project. When an organization achieves the project objectives, it has accomplished the major goals of the project and the project scope is satisfied. Project objectives must include metrics so that the project's success can be measured. The metrics can include cost, schedule, and quality metrics along with a number of other metrics. Figure B15.3 displays the SMART criteria—useful reminders on how to ensure that the project has created understandable and measurable objectives.

## PROJECT PLAN

The **project plan** is a formal, approved document that manages and controls project execution. Figure B15.4 displays the characteristics of a well-defined project plan. The project plan should include a description of the project scope, a list of activities, a schedule, time estimates, cost estimates, risk factors, resources, assignments, and responsibilities. In addition to these basic components, most project professionals also include contingency plans, review and communications strategies, and a **kill switch**—a trigger that enables a project manager to close the project prior to completion.

A good project plan should include estimates for revenue and strategic necessities. It also should include measurement and reporting methods and details as to how top leadership will engage in the project. A good plan informs stakeholders of the benefits of the project and justifies the investment, commitment, and risk of the project as it relates to the overall mission of the organization.

**FIGURE** B15.4

Project Plan Characteristics

| Characteristics of a Well-Defined Project Plan |
| --- |
| Easy to understand |
| Easy to read |
| Communicated to all key participants (key stakeholders) |
| Appropriate to the project's size, complexity, and criticality |
| Prepared by the team, rather than by the individual project manager |

An organization must build in continuous self-assessment, which allows earlier termination decisions on failing projects, with the associated cost savings. This frees capital and personnel for dedication to projects that are worth pursuing. The elimination of a project should be viewed as successful resource management, not as an admission of failure.

The most important part of the plan is communication. The project manager must communicate the plan to every member of the project team and to any key stakeholders and executives. The project plan must also include any project assumptions and be detailed enough to guide the execution of the project. A key to achieving project success is earning consensus and buy-in from all key stakeholders. By including key stakeholders in project plan development, the project manager allows them to have ownership of the plan. This often translates to greater commitment, which in turn results in enhanced motivation and productivity. The two primary diagrams most frequently used in project planning are PERT and Gantt charts.

### PERT Chart

A **_PERT (Program Evaluation and Review Technique) chart_** is a graphical network model that depicts a project's tasks and the relationships between those tasks. A **_dependency_** is a logical relationship that exists between the project tasks, or between a project task and a milestone. PERT charts define dependency between project tasks before those tasks are scheduled (see Figure B15.5). The boxes in Figure B15.5 represent project tasks, and the project manager can adjust the contents of the boxes to display various project attributes such as schedule and actual start and finish times. The arrows indicate that one task is dependent on the start or completion of another task. The **_critical path_** is a path from the start to the finish that passes through all the tasks that are critical to completing the project in the shortest amount of time. PERT charts frequently display a project's critical path.

**FIGURE** B15.5

PERT Chart Expert, a PERT Chart Example

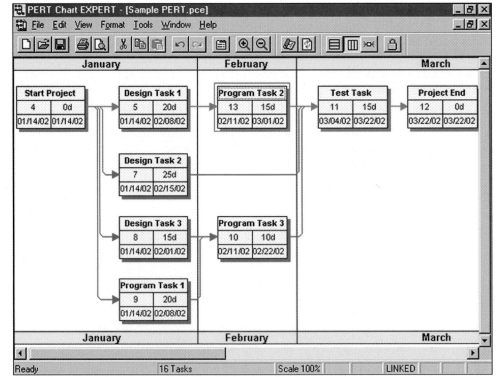

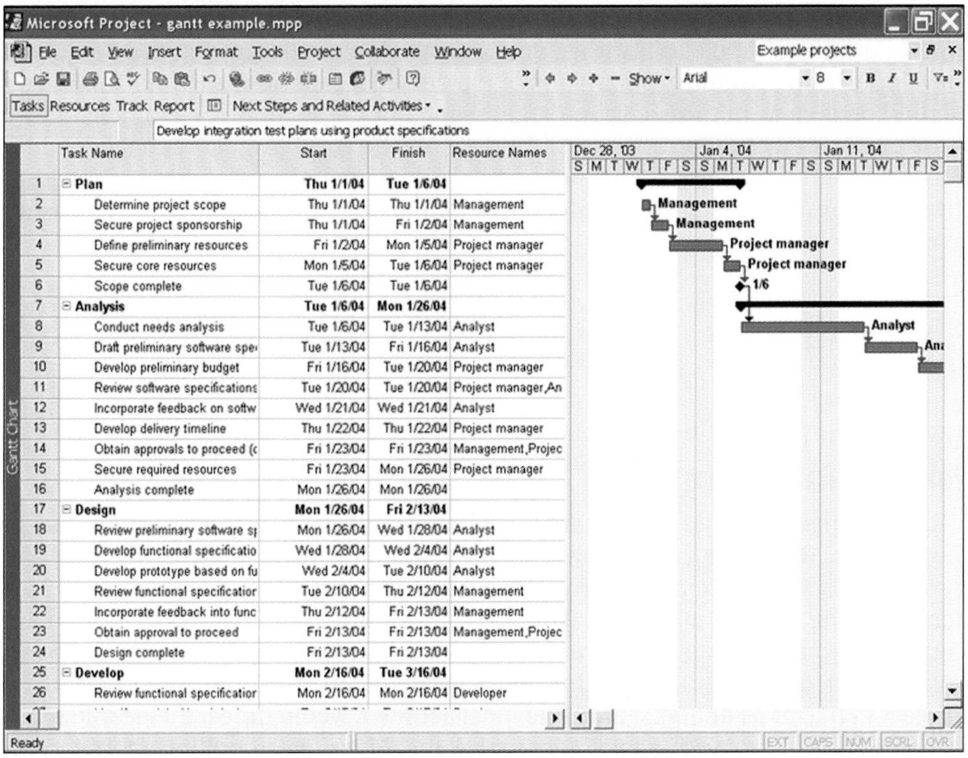

FIGURE B15.6

Microsoft Project, a Gantt Chart Example

## Gantt Chart

A **Gantt chart** is a simple bar chart that depicts project tasks against a calendar. In a Gantt chart, tasks are listed vertically and the project's time frame is listed horizontally. A Gantt chart works well for representing the project schedule. It also shows actual progress of tasks against the planned duration. Figure B15.6 displays a software development project using a Gantt chart.

# Managing Projects

Standish Group research clearly shows that projects are likely to be less challenged and more successful with a competent and skilled project manager on board. Again, a **project manager** is an individual who is an expert in project planning and management, defines and develops the project plan, and tracks the plan to ensure the project is completed on time and on budget. A project manager can, of course, bring enormous benefits to an organization such as reduced project expense, high company morale, and quicker time to market. A competent project manager sets the correct expectations early in the project with achievable milestones. Managing a project includes:

- Identifying requirements.
- Establishing clear and achievable objectives.
- Balancing the competing demands of quality, scope, time, and cost.
- Adapting the specifications, plans, and approach to the different concerns and expectations of the various stakeholders.

In addition to managing these objectives, a successful project manager possesses a variety of hard and soft skills. Standish Group research also shows that successful project managers have basic business operational knowledge and good business skills. When a project manager has a good grasp of the business operations, he or she can improve critical communication among the designers, developers, user community, and top leadership. An experienced project manager should be able to minimize scope and create a better estimate. He or she knows how to say no without creating controversy. And a good project manager should have learned that a happy stakeholder is one who is underpromised and overdelivered! A project manager must focus on managing four primary areas to ensure success:

1. People
2. Communications
3. Change
4. Risk

## MANAGING PEOPLE

Managing people is one of the hardest and most critical efforts a project manager undertakes. Resolving conflicts within the team and balancing the needs of the project with the personal and professional needs of the team are two of the challenges facing project managers. More and more project managers are the main (and sometimes sole) interface with the client during the project. As such, communication, negotiation, marketing, and salesmanship are just as important to the project manager as financial and analytical acumen. Many times, the people management side of project management makes the difference in pulling off a successful project.

## MANAGING COMMUNICATIONS

While many companies develop unique project management frameworks based on familiar project management standards, all of them agree that communication is the key to excellent project management. This is quite easy to state, but not so easy to accomplish! It is extremely helpful if a project manager plans what and how he or she will communicate as a formal part of the project management plan. Most often a document, it is referred to as a communications plan. A project manager distributes timely, accurate, and meaningful information regarding project objectives that involve time, cost, scope, and quality, and the status of each. The project manager also shares small wins as the project progresses, informs others of needed corrections, makes requests known for additional resources, and keeps all stakeholders informed of the project schedule.

### Receiving Feedback

Another important aspect of a project management communications plan is to provide a method for continually obtaining and monitoring feedback from and for all stakeholders. This is not to say that a project manager needs to spend countless hours answering every email and responding to every question posed. Rather, the manager should develop a method for asking for specific feedback as part of the plan and responding to it in a timely, organized manner. Team members remain closest to the project and should be encouraged to share open and honest feedback. It is the project manager's role and responsibility to foster an environment of trust so that members feel safe to contribute their knowledge and ideas—even if it means relaying bad news or offering an opposing viewpoint.

## MANAGING CHANGE

Change, whether it comes in the form of a crisis, a market shift, or a technological development, is challenging for all organizations. Successful organizations and successful people learn to anticipate and react appropriately to change. Snap-on, a maker of tools and equipment for specialists such as car mechanics, is successful at managing change. The company recently increased profits by 12 percent while sales were down 6.7 percent. Dennis Leitner, vice president of IT, runs the IT group on a day-to-day basis and leads the implementation of all major software development initiatives. Each software development initiative is managed by both the business and IT. In fact, business resources are on the IT group's payroll, and they spend as much as 80 percent of their time learning what a business unit is doing and how IT can help make it happen. Leitner's role focuses primarily on strategic planning, change management, and setting up metrics to track performance.

Dynamic organizational change is inevitable, and an organization must effectively manage change as it evolves. With the numerous challenges and complexities that organizations face in today's rapidly changing environment, effective change management thus becomes a critical core competency. *Change management* is a set of techniques that aid in evolution, composition, and policy management of the design and implementation of a system. Figure B15.7 displays a few of the more common reasons change occurs.

A *change management system* includes a collection of procedures to document a change request and define the steps necessary to consider the change based on the expected impact of the change. Most change management systems require that a change request form be initiated by one or more project stakeholders (systems owners, users, customers, analysts, developers). Ideally, these change requests are considered by a *change control board (CCB)* that is responsible for approving or rejecting all change requests. The CCB's composition typically includes a representative from each business area that has a stake in the project. The CCB's decision to accept or reject each change is based on an impact analysis of the change. For example, if one department wants to implement a change to the software that will increase both deployment time and cost, then the other business owners need to agree that the change is valid and that it warrants the extended time frame and increased budget.

Change is an opportunity, not a threat. Realizing that change is the norm rather than the exception will help an organization stay ahead. Becoming a change leader and accepting the inevitability of change can help ensure that an organization can survive and even thrive in times of change. Figure B15.8 displays the three important guidelines change leaders can follow to make change effective both inside and outside their organizations.

| Common Reasons Change Occurs |
|---|
| 1. An omission in defining initial scope |
| 2. A misunderstanding of the initial scope |
| 3. An external event such as government regulations that create new requirements |
| 4. Organizational changes, such as mergers, acquisitions, and partnerships, that create new business problems and opportunities |
| 5. Availability of better technology |
| 6. Shifts in planned technology that force unexpected and significant changes to the business organization, culture, and/or processes |
| 7. The users or management simply wanting the system to do more than they originally requested or agreed to |
| 8. Management reducing the funding for the project or imposing an earlier deadline |

**FIGURE B15.7**

Common Reasons Change Occurs

| Three Important Guidelines for Effectively Dealing with Change Management |
|---|
| 1. **Institute change management polices**—Create clearly defined policies and procedures that must be followed each time a request for change is received. |
| 2. **Anticipate change**—View change as an opportunity and embrace it. |
| 3. **Seek change**—Every 6 to 12 months look for changes that may be windows of opportunity. Review successes and failures to determine if there are any opportunities for innovation. |

## MANAGING RISK

Altria Group, Inc., the tobacco and food-products conglomerate, has a well-defined process for choosing projects based on project risk. The company gathers project information such as cash flow, return on investment, interfaces, and regulatory-compliance issues and creates a risk-based score of each project. The company then plots them on a grid with risk on the horizontal axis and value on the vertical axis. Managers then choose projects based on an optimal balance of risk and return.

*Project risk* is an uncertain event or condition that, if it occurs, has a positive or negative effect on a project objective(s). *Risk management* is the process of proactive and ongoing identification, analysis, and response to risk factors. The best place to address project risk is during the project plan creation. Elements of risk management are outlined in Figure B15.9.

Risks vary throughout a project and in general are more significant at the later phases of a project. Risk factors that may not be immediately obvious and are often the root causes of IT project success or failure are displayed in Figure B15.10.

| Elements of Risk Management |
|---|
| **Risk identification**—Determining which risks might affect the project and documenting their characteristics |
| **Qualitative risk analysis**—Performing a qualitative analysis of risks and conditions to prioritize their effects on project objectives |
| **Quantitative risk analysis**—Measuring the probability and consequences of risks as well as estimating their implications for the project objectives |
| **Risk response planning**—Developing procedures and techniques to enhance opportunities and reduce threats to the project's objectives |

| Common Project Risk Factors |
|---|
| Changing business circumstances that undermine expected benefits |
| Reluctance to report negative information or to "blow the whistle" on a project |
| Significant change management issues including resistance to change |
| The rush to get a project done quickly, often compromising the end result and desired outcome |
| Executives who are strongly wedded to a project and unwilling to admit that it may have been a mistake |
| A common tendency in IT projects to overengineer technology solutions, stemming from a belief in the superiority of technical solutions over simpler, people-based solutions |
| Building the project plan in conjunction with the budget or to validate some basic assumptions about the project's fiscal requirements and business base payback calculations |

## MITIGATING RISK

An organization must devise strategies to reduce or mitigate risk. A wide range of strategies can be applied, with each risk category necessitating different mitigation strategies. When considering risk mitigation, the importance of choice, opportunities, and inexactitude should be kept clearly in mind. Organizations should take several actions at the enterprise level to improve risk management capabilities; these are displayed in Figure B15.11.

Audit and tax firm KPMG LLP and software maker SeeCommerce unveiled a service, called SeeRisk, to help companies assess supply chain management risk. SeeRisk helps a company establish common metrics and measure performance against them by identifying operational problems and risks. The SeeRisk system is integrated with operational and transactional systems along with external vendor systems. The goal of the system is to improve revenue as well as reduce costs by increasing visibility of inventory, and by knowing what is on the shelf and what is downstream in production. SeeRisk can calculate the implications that defective components would have on revenue, operating costs, what it would cost to start production over, and ultimately the effect on corporate profitability.

| Actions to Improve Risk Management Capabilities |
| --- |
| **Promote project leadership skills**—Hire individuals with strong project management and project leadership skills as well as business management skills. These individuals can be extremely helpful in advisory and steering committee roles as well as coaching roles. |
| **Learn from previous experience**—Over many years of collective experiences, organizations have encountered hundreds of large IT projects. Document and revisit development methodologies, software tools, and software development best practices in order to share this vital information across the organization. |
| **Share knowledge**—Working in team or group environments tends to yield the most successful projects since individuals can share their unique learning experiences. |
| **Create a project management culture**—Orient people from day one on the importance of project management, change management, and risk management. Be sure to measure and reward project management skills and promote individuals based on successful projects. |

**FIGURE B15.11**

Actions to Improve Risk Management Capabilities

L arge IT projects require significant investment of time and resources. Successful software development projects have proven challenging and often elusive, wasting many resources and jeopardizing the goodwill of stakeholders, including customers and employees. Bringing strong, effective project, change, and risk management disciplines to large IT projects is essential to successful organizations. The days when a project manager could just concentrate on bringing a project in on time, on budget, and with agreed-upon deliverables are fading.

★ KEY TERMS

Change control board (CCB), 425
Change management, 425
Change management
   system, 425
Critical path, 422
Dependency, 422
Executive sponsor, 420
Gantt chart, 423

Kill switch, 421
PERT (Program Evaluation
   and Review Technique)
   chart, 422
Project, 418
Project assumptions, 421
Project charter, 420
Project constraints, 421

Project management, 418
Project manager, 418, 423
Project objective, 421
Project plan, 421
Project risk, 426
Project scope, 421
Project stakeholders, 419
Risk management, 426

★ CLOSING CASE ONE

### Staying on Track—Toronto Transit

Schedules are at the heart of Toronto Transit Commission's (TTC) celebrated transit system, which services over 1 million customers daily. More than 50 large engineering and construction projects are under way to expand, upgrade, and maintain Toronto's transit systems and structures. One such project is the Sheppard project, which consists of constructing the new six-kilometer line north of the city. Sheppard is estimated to take more than five years to complete, with a total cost of $875 million.

TTC's challenge is to keep its 50 individual projects, most of which fall within the $2 million to $100 million price range and span an average of five years, on schedule and under budget. Staying on top of so many multifaceted, multiyear, and often interdependent projects adds additional complexity for the commission. TTC uses Primavera Project Planner (P3) to create a single master schedule for all of its engineering and construction projects.

TTC's 50 individual projects average 100 to 150 activities each, with some projects encompassing as many as 500 to 600 activities. "Seeing the big picture is important, not only for the 300 people who work in the Engineering and Construction branch of the TTC, but for the entire 9,000-person organization," said Vince Carroll, head scheduler for the Engineering and Construction branch. "Engineering managers need to see how other projects may impact their own. Materials and procurement managers need to track project progress. Senior managers need to be able to communicate with city government to secure funding. Marketing and public relations people need the latest information to set public expectations. And most important of all," said Carroll, "the operations group needs to stay informed of what is happening so that they can adjust the schedules that run the trains."

Carroll and his team of 25 people create, update, and publish a master schedule that summarizes the individual status of each project, shows the logical links between projects, and provides an integrated overview of all projects. The master schedule helps the team effectively and regularly communicate the status of all projects currently under way throughout the Toronto Transit system.

The master schedule organizes projects according to their location in the capital budget. For example, projects can be organized according to those that have been allotted funding for expansion, state of good repair, legislative reasons, or environmental reasons. Each project is organized by its logical flow—from planning, analysis, and design, through the maintenance phase. The final report shows positive and negative balances for each project and a single overview of the status of all the engineering and construction projects. Carroll and his team use PERT charts to create time-scaled logic diagrams and then convert this information to bar charts for presentation purposes in the master schedule. TTC is currently linking its master schedule directly to its payroll system, enabling it to track the number of hours actually worked versus hours planned.

## Questions

1. Describe Gantt charts and explain how TTC could use one to communicate project status.
2. Describe PERT charts and explain how TTC could use one to communicate project status.
3. How could TTC use its master schedule to gain efficiencies in its supply chain?
4. How could TTC use its master schedule to identify change management and risk management issues?

---

### ✱ CLOSING CASE TWO

### Change at Toyota

At Toyota Motor Sales USA's headquarters in Torrance, California, a circular patch of manicured earth separates the IS building and corporate headquarters. A brook winds its way through lush flowers and pine trees, and a terraced path connects the two buildings. For many years, this was about the only thing the two groups shared with each other.

For the business executives at Toyota Motor Sales (TMS) peering across the courtyard at the Data building, the deep black windows were a symbol of IS's opacity. These executives felt that IS was unresponsive, and they had little clue where the money was going. "One of the complaints was that we spent a lot of money on IT projects, and the business was frequently disappointed with the results," recalled Bob Daly, group vice president of Toyota Customer Services. Daly says badly handled projects, such as a delayed PeopleSoft ERP implementation and a protracted parts inventory initiative, led to finger-pointing between the two factions.

Meanwhile, behind the darkened windows of the Data building, CIO Barbra Cooper's IS staff was buried under the weight of six enterprisewide projects. Called the Big Six, they included a new extranet for Toyota dealers and the PeopleSoft ERP rollout, as well as four new systems for order management, parts forecasting, advanced warranty and financial document management. Feeling besieged, the IS group made the mistake of not explaining to the business side all the things it was doing and how much it all cost. It was a classic case of mismanaged expectations and fractured alignment.

By late 2002, Cooper realized that if she wanted to win back the respect of the business managers—and remain in her post—she would have to make some radical changes. A conversation with Toyota Motor Sales CEO, in which he questioned the sharp incline of IS's spending curve, stopped her in her tracks. In her 30 years in IT, Cooper had developed something of a reputation for coming in to clean up other CIOs' messes. Now, she had to take a long look in the mirror and fix herself.

### Cooper's Path to Success

Cooper could no longer ignore the rumblings from across the courtyard that had worked their way into the rank-and-file business staff. To them, IS had become an unresponsive, bureaucratic machine.

Cooper started soliciting informal feedback from a wide range of businesspeople. What she discovered was an accumulation of "very painful projects for both IT and the business," she said. "Clearly there was not enough communication and education on our part."

In late 2002, Cooper hired an outside consultancy to interview TMS's top 20 executives. She wanted their honest opinions of how IS was doing. The results did not provide all the answers to the ailments, but she certainly saw the trouble spots. "Parts of the survey results were stinging," Cooper said. "But you can't be a CIO and not face that."

Cooper spent many introspective weeks in 2003 formulating her vision for a new IT department. What she developed was a strategy for a decentralized and transparent IS organization that focused all of its energy on the major business segments. In the summer of 2003, she presented her vision to her senior IS staffers. Some of the managers were excited by the prospect of change; others were less so.

The first thing Cooper did was set up the Toyota Value Action Program, a team of eight staffers responsible for translating her vision into actionable items for the department and her direct reports. Using the survey results and Cooper's direction, the team winnowed the list to 18 initiatives, including increasing employee training and development, gaining cost savings, making process improvements, overcoming IS inefficiencies, and implementing a metrics program. Each initiative got a project owner and a team. Cooper insisted that each initiative have a mechanism to check its success. The most significant initiative called for improved alignment with the business side. At the heart of this new effort would be a revamped Office of the CIO structure—with new roles, reporting lines, and responsibilities.

As part of the rehaul, Cooper took top-flight personnel out of the Data building and embedded them as divisional information officers, or DIOs, in all of the business units. These DIOs are accountable for IT strategy, development, and services, and they sit on the management committees headed by top business executives. The DIOs' goal is to forge relationships with tier-one executives and executives at the vice president level.

The DIOs were not alone. Business operation managers and relationship managers from IS sat alongside the business folks. "I still believe in managing IT centrally, but it was incumbent on us to physically distribute IT into the businesses," Cooper said. "They could provide more local attention while keeping the enterprise vision alive."

Cooper upended the structure of Toyota's IS department in six months in a bid to weave IT functions more closely into the daily business operations. The process was painful: She changed IS employees' jobs, exposed all of IS's shortcomings, and forced her staff into the business offices. However, just over a year into the new plan, IS and the businesses were standing shoulder-to-shoulder when planning and implementing IT projects. And Cooper was still CIO of Toyota Motor Sales.

## A Little Kicking and Screaming

Change can be scary for anyone, especially during an upheaval of an entire 400-person IS department. Cooper changed the jobs of 50 percent of her staffers within six months, yet no one left or was let go. Some took on new responsibilities; others took on expanded or new roles. Cooper said some mid- and upper-level staffers were initially uncomfortable with their new roles, but she spent a lot of time fostering a new attitude about the change. "I dragged them into the conversations kicking and screaming," Cooper said. "But I said to them, 'Unless you think of what it means to change on this level, you will never make it happen.' " The key, Cooper said, is that all IS staffers were brought into the development of the new organization early.

## Questions

1. What would be the impact on Toyota's business if it failed to implement a project management solution and managed its projects using a myriad of spreadsheets and Word documents?

2. Why would Toyota find it important to focus on implementing good project management techniques?

3. Why are project management, change management, and risk management critical to a global company such as Toyota?

4. Describe the ramifications to Toyota's business if it failed to anticipate change.

## ★ MAKING BUSINESS DECISIONS

### 1. Explaining Project Management

Prime Time Inc. is a large consulting company that specializes in outsourcing people with project management capabilities and skills. You are in the middle of an interview for a job with Prime Time. The manager performing the interview asks you to explain why managing a project plan is critical to a project's success. The manager also wants you to explain scope creep and feature creep and your tactics for managing them on a project. Finally, the manager wants you to elaborate on your strategies for delivering successful projects and reducing risks.

### 2. Applying Project Management Techniques

You have been hired by a medium-sized airline company, Sun Best. Sun Best currently flies over 300 routes in the East. The company is experiencing tremendous issues coordinating its 3,500 pilots, 7,000 flight attendants, and 2,000 daily flights. Determine how Sun Best could use a Gantt chart to help it coordinate its pilots, flight attendants, and daily flights. Using Excel, create a sample Gantt chart highlighting the different types of activities and resources Sun Best could track with the tool.

### 3. Prioritizing Projects

Nick Zele is the new managing operations director for a large construction company, CMA. Nick is looking for a project manager who can help him manage the 60 ongoing company projects. You are interested in working with Nick and have decided to apply for the job. Nick has asked you to compile a report detailing why project prioritization is critical for CMA, along with the different types of prioritization techniques you would recommend CMA use when determining which projects to pursue.

### 4. Managing Expectations

Trader is the name for a large human resource project that is currently being deployed at your organization. Your boss, Pam Myers, has asked you to compile an expectations management matrix for the project. The first thing you need to determine is management's expectations. Compile a list of questions you would ask to help determine management's expectations for the Trader project.

### 5. Mitigating Risk

Alicia Fernandez owns and operates a chain of nine seafood restaurants in the Boston area. Alicia is currently considering purchasing one of her competitors, which would give her an additional six restaurants. Alicia's primary concerns with the purchase are the constantly changing seafood prices and high staff turnover rate in the restaurant industry. Explain to Alicia what risk management is and how she can use it to mitigate the risks for the potential purchase of her competitor.

# Operations Management

1. Define the term operations management.
2. Explain operations management's role in business.
3. Describe the correlation between operations management and information technology.
4. Describe the five characteristics of competitive priorities.

## Introduction

*Production* is the creation of goods and services using the factors of production: land, labor, capital, entrepreneurship, and knowledge. Production has historically been associated with manufacturing, but the nature of business has changed significantly in the last 20 years. The service sector, especially Internet services, has grown dramatically. The United States now has what is called a service economy— that is, one dominated by the service sector.

Organizations that excel in operations management, specifically supply chain management, perform better in almost every financial measure of success, according to a report from Boston-based AMR Research Inc. When supply chain excellence improves operations, companies experience a 5 percent higher profit margin, 15 percent less inventory, 17 percent stronger "perfect order" ratings, and 35 percent shorter cycle times than their competitors. "The basis of competition for winning companies in today's economy is supply chain superiority," said Kevin O'Marah, vice president of research at AMR Research. "These companies understand that value chain performance translates to productivity and market-share leadership. They also understand that supply chain leadership means more than just low costs and efficiency: It requires a superior ability to shape and respond to shifts in demand with innovative products and services."

# Operations Management Fundamentals

Books, DVDs, downloaded MP3s, and dental and medical procedures are all examples of goods and services. **Production management** describes all the activities managers do to help companies create goods. To reflect the change in importance from manufacturing to services, the term *production* often has been replaced by operations to reflect the manufacturing of both goods and services. **Operations management (OM)** is the management of systems or processes that convert or transform resources (including human resources) into goods and services. Operations management is responsible for managing the core processes used to manufacture goods and produce services.

Essentially, the creation of goods or services involves transforming or converting inputs into outputs. Various inputs such as capital, labor, and information are used to create goods or services using one or more transformation processes (e.g., storing, transporting, and cutting). A **transformation process** is often referred to as the technical core, especially in manufacturing organizations, and is the actual conversion of inputs to outputs. To ensure that the desired outputs are obtained, an organization takes measurements at various points in the transformation process (feedback) and then compares them with previously established standards to determine whether corrective action is needed (control). Figure B16.1 depicts the conversion system.

Figure B16.2 displays examples of inputs, transformation processes, and outputs. Although goods and services are listed separately in Figure B16.1 it is important to note that goods and services often occur jointly. For example, having the oil changed in a car is a service, but the oil that is delivered is a good. Similarly, house painting is a service, but the paint is a good. The goods–service combination is a continuum. It ranges from primarily goods with little service to primarily service with few goods (see Figure B16.3). There are relatively few pure goods or pure services; therefore, organizations typically sell product packages, which are a combination of goods and services. This makes managing operations more interesting, and also more challenging.

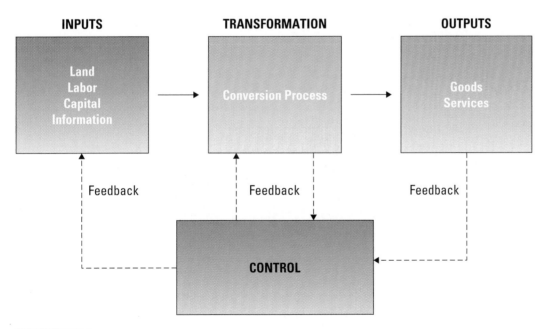

**FIGURE** B16.1

Operations Involves the Conversion of Inputs into Outputs

| Inputs | Transformation | Outputs |
|---|---|---|
| Restaurant inputs include hungry customers, food, wait staff | Well-prepared food, well served: agreeable environment | Satisfied customers |
| Hospital inputs include patients, medical supplies, doctors, nurses | Health care | Healthy individuals |
| Automobile inputs include sheet steel, engine parts, tires | Fabrication and assembly of cars | High-quality cars |
| College inputs include high school graduates, books, professors, classrooms | Imparting knowledge and skills | Educated individuals |
| Distribution center inputs include stock keeping units, storage bins, workers | Storage and redistribution | Fast delivery of available products |

**FIGURE** B16.3

The Goods–Service
Continuum: Most Products
Are a Bundle of Goods
and Services

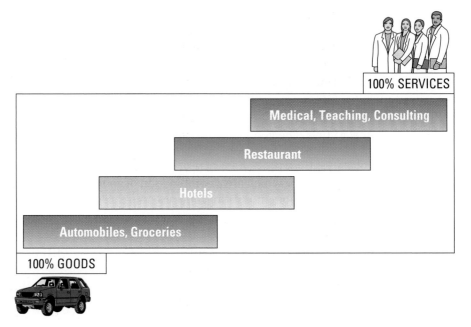

*Value-added* is the term used to describe the difference between the cost of inputs and the value of price of outputs. OM is critical to an organization because of its ability to increase value-added during the transformation process. In nonprofit organizations, the value of outputs (highway construction, police, and fire protection) is their value to society; the greater the value-added, the greater the effectiveness of the operations. In for-profit organizations, the value of outputs is measured by the prices that customers are willing to pay for those goods or services. Firms use the money generated by value-added for research and development, investment in new facilities and equipment, worker salaries, and profits. Consequently, the greater the value-added, the greater the amount of funds available for these important activities.

## OM in Business

The scope of OM ranges across the organization and includes many interrelated activities, such as forecasting, capacity planning, scheduling, managing inventories, assuring quality, motivating employees, deciding where to locate facilities, and more.

Reviewing the activities performed in an airline company makes it easy to understand how a service organization's OM team adds value. The company consists of the airplanes, airport facilities, and maintenance facilities, and typical OM activities include:

- **Forecasting:** Estimating seat demand for flights, weather and landing conditions, and estimates for growth or reduction in air travel are all included in forecasting.
- **Capacity planning:** This is the key essential metric for the airline to maintain cash flow and increase revenues. Underestimating or overestimating flights will hurt profits.
- **Scheduling:** The airline operates on tight schedules that must be maintained including flights, pilots, flight attendants, ground crews, baggage handlers, and routine maintenance.
- **Managing inventory:** Inventory of such items as foods, beverages, first-aid equipment, in-flight magazines, pillows, blankets, and life jackets is essential for the airline.
- **Assuring quality:** Quality is indispensable in an airline where safety is the highest priority. Today's travelers expect high-quality customer service during ticketing, check-in, curb service, and unexpected issues where the emphasis is on efficiency and courtesy.
- **Motivating and training employees:** Airline employees must be highly trained and continually motivated, especially when dealing with frustrated airline travelers.
- **Locating facilities:** Key questions facing airlines include which cities to offer services, where to host maintenance facilities, and where to locate major and minor hubs.

Opposite from an airline is a bike factory, which is typically an assembly operation: buying components such as frames, tires, wheels, gears, and other items from suppliers, and then assembling bicycles. A bike factory also does some of the fabrication work itself, forming frames and making the gears and chains. Obviously, an airline company and a bike factory are completely different types of operations. One is primarily a service operation, the other a producer of goods. Nonetheless, these two operations have much in common. The same as the airline, the bike factory must schedule production, deal with components, order parts and materials, schedule and train employees, ensure quality standards are met, and above all satisfy customers. In both organizations, the success of the business depends on short- and long-term planning and the ability of its executives and managers to make informed decisions.

# IT's Role in OM

Managers can use IT to heavily influence OM decisions including productivity, costs, flexibility, quality, and customer satisfaction. One of the greatest benefits of IT on OM is in making operational decisions because operations management exerts considerable influence over the degree to which the goals and objectives of the organization are realized. Most OM decisions involve many possible alternatives that can have varying impacts on revenues and expenses. OM information systems are critical for managers to be able to make well-informed decisions.

*Decision support systems* and *executive information systems* can help an organization perform what-if analysis, sensitivity analysis, drill-down, and consolidation. Numerous managerial and strategic key decisions are based on OM information systems that affect the entire organization, including:

- **What:** What resources will be needed, and in what amounts?
- **When:** When will each resource be needed? When should the work be scheduled? When should materials and other supplies be ordered? When is corrective action needed?

- **Where:** Where will the work be performed?
- **How:** How will the product or service be designed? How will the work be done (organization, methods, equipment)? How will resources be allocated?
- **Who:** Who will perform the work?

## OM STRATEGIC BUSINESS SYSTEMS

UPS uses package flow information systems at each of its locations. The custom-built systems combine operations strategy and mapping technology to optimize the way boxes are loaded and delivered. The goal is to use the package flow software to cut the distance that delivery trucks travel by more than 100 million miles each year. The project will also help UPS streamline the profitability of each of its facility locations.

Operations strategy is concerned with the development of a long-term plan for determining how to best utilize the major resources of the firm so that there is a high degree of compatibility between these resources and the firm's long-term corporate strategy. Operations strategy addresses very broad questions about how these major resources should be configured to achieve the desired corporate objectives. Some of the major long-term issues addressed in operations strategy include:

- How big to make the facilities?
- Where to locate the facilities?
- When to build additional facilities?
- What type of process(es) to install to make the products?

Each of these issues can be addressed by OM decision support systems. In developing an operations strategy, management needs to consider many factors. These include (*a*) the level of technology that is or will be available, (*b*) the required skill levels of the workers, and (*c*) the degree of vertical integration, in terms of the extent to which outside suppliers are used.

Today, many organizations, especially larger conglomerates, operate in terms of ***strategic business units (SBUs),*** which consist of several stand-alone businesses. When companies become really large, they are best thought of as being composed of a number of businesses (or SBUs). As displayed in Figure B16.4, operations strategy supports the long-range strategy developed at the SBU level.

**FIGURE** B16.4

Hierarchy of Operational Planning

| Type of Planning | Time Frame | Issues | Decisions | Systems |
|---|---|---|---|---|
| Strategic Planning | Long range | Plant size, location, type of processes | How will we make the products? Where do we locate the facility or facilities? How much capacity do we require? When should we add additional capacity? | Materials requirement planning (MRP) systems |
| Tactical Planning | Intermediate range | Workforce size, material requirements | How many workers do we need? When do we need them? Should we work overtime or put on a section shift? When should we have material delivered? Should we have a finished goods inventory? | Global inventory management systems |
| Operational Planning and Control (OP&C) | Short range | Daily scheduling of employees, jobs, and equipment, process management, inventory management | What jobs do we work on today or this week? To whom do we assign what tasks? What jobs have priority? | Inventory management and control systems, transportation planning systems, distribution management systems |

Decisions at the SBU level focus on being effective, that is, "on doing the right things." These decisions are sometimes referred to as **strategic planning,** which focuses on long range planning such as plant size, location, and type of process to be used. The primary system used for strategic planning is a materials requirement planning system. **Materials requirement planning (MRP) systems** use sales forecasts to make sure that needed parts and materials are available at the right time and place in a specific company. The latest version of MRP is enterprise resource planning.

Strategic decisions impact intermediate-range decisions, often referred to as tactical planning, which focuses on being efficient, that is, "doing things right." **Tactical planning** focuses on producing goods and services as efficiently as possible within the strategic plan. Here the emphasis is on producing quality products, including when material should be delivered, when products should be made to best meet demand, and what size the workforce should be. One of the primary systems used in tactical planning includes global inventory management. **Global inventory management systems** provide the ability to locate, track, and predict the movement of every component or material anywhere upstream or downstream in the production process. This allows an organization to locate and analyze its inventory anywhere in its production process.

Finally, **operational planning and control (OP&C)** deals with the day-to-day procedures for performing work, including scheduling, inventory, and process management. **Inventory management and control systems** provide control and visibility to the status of individual items maintained in inventory. The software maintains inventory record accuracy, generates material requirements for all purchased items, and analyzes inventory performance. Inventory management and control software provides organizations with the information from a variety of sources including:

- Current inventory and order status.
- Cost accounting.
- Sales forecasts and customer orders.
- Manufacturing capacity.
- New-product introductions.

Two additional OP&C systems include transportation planning and distribution management. **Transportation planning systems** track and analyze the movement of materials and products to ensure the delivery of materials and finished goods at the right time, the right place, and the lowest cost. **Distribution management systems** coordinate the process of transporting materials from a manufacturer to distribution centers to the final customers. Transportation routes directly affect the speed and cost of delivery. An organization will use these systems to help it decide if it wants to use an effectiveness route and ship its products directly to its customers or use an efficiency route and ship its products to a distributor that ships the products to customers.

## Competitive OM Strategy

The key to developing a competitive OM strategy lies in understanding how to create value-added goods and services for customers. Specifically, value is added through the competitive priority or priorities that are selected to support a given strategy. Five key competitive priorities translate directly into characteristics that are used to describe various processes by which a company can add value to its OM decisions including:

1. Cost
2. Quality

3. Delivery
4. Flexibility
5. Service

## COST

Every industry has low-cost providers. However, being the low-cost producer does not always guarantee profitability and success. Products sold strictly on the basis of cost are typically commodity-like products including such goods as flour, petroleum, and sugar. In other words, customers cannot distinguish the products made by one firm from those of another. As a result, customers use cost as the primary determinant in making a purchasing decision.

Low-cost market segments are frequently very large, and many companies are lured by the potential for significant profits, which are associated with large unit volumes of product. As a consequence, the competition in this segment is exceedingly fierce—and so is the failure rate. After all, there can be only one lowest-cost producer, and that firm usually establishes the selling price in the market.

## QUALITY

Quality can be divided into two categories—product quality and process quality. Product quality levels vary as to the particular market that it aims to serve. For example, a generic bike is of significantly different quality than the bike of a world-class cyclist. Higher quality products command higher prices in the marketplace. Organizations must establish the "proper level" of product quality by focusing on the exact requirements of their customers. Overdesigned products with too much quality will be viewed as being prohibitively expensive. Underdesigned products, on the other hand, will lose customers to products that cost a little more but are perceived by the customers as offering greater value.

Process quality is critical in every market segment. Regardless of whether the product is a generic bike or a bike for an international cyclist, customers want products without defects. Thus, the primary goal of process quality is to produce error-free products. The investment in improving quality pays off in stronger customer relationships and higher revenues. Many organizations use modern quality control standards, including:

- **Six sigma quality:** The goal is to detect potential problems to prevent their occurrence and achieve no more than 3.4 defects per million opportunities. That is important to companies like Bank of America, which makes 4 million transactions a day.

- **Malcolm Baldrige National Quality Awards:** In 1987 in the United States, a standard was set for overall company quality with the introduction of the Malcolm Baldrige National Quality Awards, named in honor of the late U.S. secretary of commerce. Companies can apply for these awards in each of the following areas: manufacturing, services, small businesses, education, and health care. To qualify, an organization has to show quality in seven key areas: leadership, strategic planning, customer and market focus, information and analysis, human resources focus, process management, and business results.

- **ISO 900:** The common name given to quality management and assurance standards comes from the *International Organization for Standardization (ISO),* a nongovernmental organization established in 1947 to promote the development of world standards to facilitate the international exchange of goods and services. ISO is a worldwide federation of national standards bodies from more than 140 countries. ISO 900 standards require a company to determine customer needs, including regulatory and legal requirements. The company must also make communication arrangements to handle issues such as complaints. Other standards involve process control, product testing, storage, and delivery.

■ **ISO 14000:** This collection of the best practices for managing an organization's impact on the environment does not prescribe specific performance levels, but establishes environmental management systems. The requirements for certification include having an environmental policy, setting specific improvement targets, conducting audits of environmental programs, and maintaining top management review of processes. Certification in ISO 14000 displays that a firm has a world-class management system in both quality and environmental standards.

■ **CMMI:** Capability Maturity Model Integration is a framework of best practices. The current version, CMMI-DEV, describes best practices in managing, measuring, and monitoring software development processes. CMMI does not describe the processes themselves; it describes the characteristics of good processes, thus providing guidelines for companies developing or honing their own sets of processes.

## DELIVERY

Another key factor in purchasing decisions is delivery speed. The ability of a firm to provide consistent and fast delivery allows it to charge a premium price for its products. George Stalk, Jr., of the Boston Consulting Group, has demonstrated that both profits and market share are directly linked to the speed with which a company can deliver its products relative to its competition. In addition to fast delivery, the reliability of the delivery is also important. In other words, products should be delivered to customers with minimum variance in delivery times.

## FLEXIBILITY

Flexibility, from a strategic perspective, refers to the ability of a company to offer a wide variety of products to its customers. Flexibility is also a measure of how fast a company can convert its process(es) from making an old line of products to producing a new product line. Product variety is often perceived by the customers to be a dimension of quality.

The flexibility of the manufacturing process at John Deere's Harvester Works in Moline, Illinois, allows the firm to respond to the unpredictability of the agricultural industry's equipment needs. By manufacturing such small-volume products as seed planters in "modules," or factories within a factory, Deere can offer farmers a choice of 84 different planter models with such a wide variety of options that farmers can have planters virtually customized to meet their individual needs. Its manufacturing process thus allows Deere to compete on both speed and flexibility.

Currently, there appears to be a trend toward offering environmentally friendly products that are made through environmentally friendly processes. As consumers become more aware of the fragility of the environment, they are increasingly turning toward products that are safe for the environment. Several flexible manufacturers now advertise environmentally friendly products, energy-efficient products, and recycled products.

## SERVICE

With shortened product life cycles, products tend to migrate toward one common standard. As a consequence, these products are often viewed as commodities in which price is the primary differentiator. For example, the differences in laptops offered among PC manufactures are relatively insignificant so price is the prime selection criterion. For this reason, many companies attempt to place an emphasis on high-quality customer service as a primary differentiator. Customer service can add tremendous value to an ordinary product.

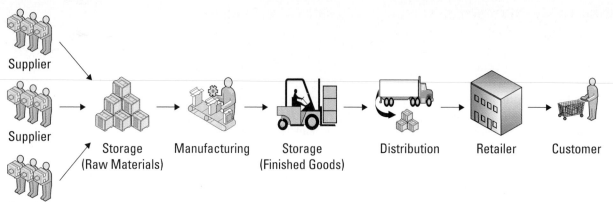

**FIGURE** B16.5

A Typical Manufacturing
Supply Chain

Businesses are always looking toward the future to find the next competitive advantage that will distinguish their products in the marketplace. To obtain an advantage in such a competitive environment, firms must provide "value-added" goods and services, and the primary area where they can capitalize on all five competitive priorities is in the supply chain.

## OM and the Supply Chain

A *supply chain* consists of all parties involved, directly or indirectly, in the procurement of a product or raw material. *Supply chain management (SCM)* involves the management of information flows between and among stages in a supply chain to maximize total supply chain effectiveness and profitability. SCM software can enable an organization to generate efficiencies within these steps by automating and improving the information flows throughout and among the different supply chain components. Figures B15.5 and B16.6 display the typical supply chains for goods and services.

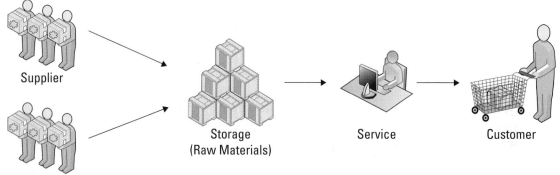

**FIGURE** B16.6

A Typical Service Supply Chain

This plug-in introduced the concept of operations management showcasing how information technology can be used to improve fundamental business processes. Operations management exists across a variety of sectors and industries. Various examples were given showcasing information technology's ability to help organizations improve their interactions with suppliers, manufacturers, distributors, warehouses, and customers.

As a business student, you should understand this pivotal role that information technology plays in facilitating operations management and in supporting the basic infrastructure and coordination needed for core business operations to function.

✳ KEY TERMS

Distribution management
  system, 437
Global inventory management
  system, 437
International Organization for
  Standardization (ISO), 438
Inventory management and
  control system, 437
Materials requirement planning
  (MRP) systems, 437

Operational planning and
  control (OP&C), 437
Operations management
  (OM), 433
Production, 432
Production management, 433
Strategic business unit
  (SBU), 436
Strategic planning, 437
Supply chain, 440

Supply chain management
  (SCM), 440
Tactical planning, 437
Transformation process, 433
Transportation planning
  system, 437
Value-added, 434

✳ CLOSING CASE ONE

### How Levi's Got Its Jeans into Wal-Mart

People around the world recognize Levi's as an American icon, the cool jeans worn by movie stars James Dean and Marilyn Monroe. However, the company failed to keep up with the fast-changing tastes of American teenagers. In particular, it missed the trend to baggy jeans that caught hold in the mid-1990s. Sales plummeted from $7.1 billion in 1996 to $4.1 billion in 2003, and Levi's U.S. market share dropped from 18.7 percent in 1997 to 12 percent in 2003, a huge decline of almost one-third in both dollars and market share.

### Analyzing and Responding to What Happened

Competition hit Levi Strauss on both the high and low ends. Fashion-conscious buyers were drawn to high-priced brands like Blue Cult, Juicy, and Seven, which had more fashion cachet than Levi's. On the low end, parents were buying Wrangler and Lee jeans for their kids because on average they cost about $10 less than Levi's Red Tab brand. Wrangler and Lee were also the brands they found at discount retailers such as Wal-Mart, Target, and T. J. Maxx. David Bergen, Levi's chief information officer (CIO), described the company as "getting squeezed," and "caught in the jaws of death."

Levi Strauss's new CEO, Philip A. Marineau, came to the company from PepsiCo in 1999, a year after he helped PepsiCo surpass Coca-Cola in sales for the first time. Marineau recruited Bergen in 2000 from Carstation.com. Marineau quickly realized that turning Levi

Strauss around would entail manufacturing, marketing, and distributing jeans that customers demanded, particularly customers at the low end where the mass market was located.

Bergen was eager to join Marineau's team because of his background in clothing, retailing, and manufacturing with companies such as The Gap and Esprit de Corps in the 1980s. He knew that Marineau's plan to anticipate customer wants would require up-to-date IT applications such as data warehousing, data mining, and customer relationship management (CRM) systems. He also knew that selling to mass market retailers would require upgrades to the supply chain management (SCM) systems, and he understood that globalization would necessitate standardized enterprise resource planning (ERP) systems. Overall, it was a challenge any ambitious CIO would covet. After all, designing and installing IT systems that drive and achieve key business initiatives is what it is all about.

### Joining Wal-Mart

Wal-Mart was a pioneer in supply chain management systems, having learned early on that driving costs out of the supply chain would let it offer products to customers at the lowest possible prices, while at the same time assuring that products the customers demanded were always on store shelves. Becoming one of Wal-Mart's 30,000 suppliers is not easy. Wal-Mart insists that its suppliers do business using up-to-date IT systems to manage the supply chain—not just the supply chain between Wal-Mart and its suppliers, but the supply chains between the suppliers and their suppliers as well. Wal-Mart has strict supply chain management system requirements that its business partners must meet.

Wal-Mart's requirements presented Levi Strauss with a serious hurdle to overcome because its supply chain management systems were in bad shape. Levi Strauss executives did not even have access to key information required to track where products were moving in the supply chain. For example, they did not know how many pairs of jeans were in the factory awaiting shipment, how many were somewhere en route, or how many had just been unloaded at a customer's warehouse. According to Greg Hammann, Levi's U.S. chief customer officer, "Our supply chain could not deliver the services Wal-Mart expected."

Bergen created a cross-functional team of key managers from IT, finance, and sales to transform Levi Strauss's systems to meet Wal-Mart's requirements. Their recommendations included network upgrades, modifications to ordering and logistics applications, and data warehouse improvements, among others. Although Bergen realized that about half the changes required to current IT systems to accommodate the state-of-the-art demands of Wal-Mart would be a waste of resources since these systems were being replaced by a new SAP enterprise software system over the next five years, Levi Strauss could not wait for the SAP installation if it wanted Wal-Mart's business now, so it decided to move forward with the changes to the current systems.

The successful transformation of its supply chain management system allowed the company to collaborate with Wal-Mart. The company introduced its new signature line at Wal-Mart, which sells for around $23 and has fewer details in the finish than Levi's other lines, no trademark pocket stitching or red tab, for example. Wal-Mart wants big-name brands to lure more affluent customers into its stores, while still maintaining the low price points all Wal-Mart customers have come to expect. Wal-Mart Senior Vice President Lois Mikita noted that Wal-Mart "continues to tailor its selection to meet the needs of customers from a cross section of income levels and lifestyles." She also stated she is impressed with the level of detail Levi Strauss has put into its systems transformation efforts to "make the execution of this new launch 100 percent."

### Achieving Business Success Through IT

Bergen's changes were a success and the percentage of products delivered on time quickly rose from 65 percent to 95 percent primarily because of the updated supply chain management system. Levi's total sales were also up in the third and fourth quarters of 2003, for the first time since 1996. NPD Group's Fashionworld is a research group that tracks apparel and footwear market trends. In 2003, Levi's appeared on NPD Fashionworld's top 10 list of brands preferred by young women, ending an absence of several years. Marshall Cohen, a senior industry analyst at NPD Fashionworld, noted that Levi's "hadn't been close to that for a while. Teens hadn't gravitated toward Levi's in years. That was incredible. A lot of that has to do with having the right style in the right place at the right time." The improved systems, Cohen noted, also helped the company get the right sizes to the right stores.

Another highly successful IT system implemented by Levi Strauss is a digital dashboard that executives can display on their PC screens. The dashboard lets an executive see the status of a product as it moves from the factory floor to distribution centers to retail stores. For example, the dashboard can display how Levi's 501 jeans are selling at an individual Kohl's store compared to forecasted sales. "When I first got here I didn't see anything," Hammann said. "Now I can drill down to the product level."

The digital dashboard alerts executives to trends that under the previous systems would have taken weeks to detect. For example, in 2003 Levi Strauss started to ship Dockers Stain Defender pants. Expected sales for the pants were around 2 million pairs. The digital dashboard quickly notified key executives that the trousers were selling around 2.5 million pairs. This information enabled them to adjust production upward in time to ship more pants, meet the increased demand, and avoid lost sales. Levi Strauss also uses the systems to control supply during key seasonal sales periods such as back-to-school and Christmas.

"If I look overconfident, I'm not," Bergen said. "I'm very nervous about this change. When we trip, we have to stand up real quick and get back on the horse, as they say." As if to reinforce Bergen's point, Gib Carey, a supply chain analyst at Bain, noted, "The place where companies do fail is when they aren't bringing anything new to Wal-Mart. Wal-Mart is constantly looking at 'How can I get the same product I am selling today at a lower price somewhere else?' "

## Questions

1. How did Levi Strauss achieve business success through the use of supply chain management?

2. What might have happened to Levi Strauss if its top executives had not supported investments in SCM?

3. David Bergen, Levi's CIO, put together a cross-functional team of key managers from IT, finance, and sales to transform Levi's systems to meet Wal-Mart's requirements. Analyze the relationships between these three business areas and OM. How can OM help support these three critical business areas?

4. Describe the five basic SCM components in reference to Wal-Mart's business model.

5. Explain the future trends of SCM and provide an example of how Levi Strauss could use these technologies to streamline its business operations.

6. Identify any security and ethical issues that might occur for a company doing business with Wal-Mart.

---

## ★ CLOSING CASE TWO

### The Digital Hospital

For years, health care has missed the huge benefits that information technology has bestowed upon the rest of the economy. During the 1990s, productivity in health care services declined, according to estimates from Economy.com Inc. That is a huge underachievement in a decade of strong gains from the overall economy. This is beginning to change as hospitals, along with insurers and the government, are stepping up their IT investments. Hospitals are finally discarding their clumsy, sluggish first-generation networks and are beginning to install laptops, software, and Internet technologies.

### Hackensack University Medical Center's IT Projects

- Patients can use 37-inch plasma TVs in their rooms to surf the Internet for information about their medical conditions. They can also take interactive classes about their condition and find out how to take care of themselves after discharge.

- From virtually anywhere in the world, physicians can make their hospital rounds with the help of a life-size robot, Mr. Rounder. Using laptops with joysticks and web links, doctors drive the robot around the hospital to confer by remote video with patients and other doctors. When a blizzard prevented Dr. Garth Ballantynes from reaching the hospital, he used Mr. Rounder to make his rounds from his home 82 miles away.

- Pocket-sized PCs that hook wirelessly into the hospital's network allow doctors the freedom to place pharmacy orders and pull up medical records from anywhere in the hospital.

- Nurses use wireless laptops to record patients' vitals signs, symptoms, and medications. Doctors can sign into the same central system from the laptops to order prescriptions and lab tests and read their patient's progress.

- The hospital's internal website stores all of its medical images. Doctors can view crystal-clear digital versions of their patients' X-rays, MRIs, and CT scans from any computer in or out of the hospital.

- A giant robot named Robbie, equipped with arms, reads prescriptions entered into the hospital's computer system and then grabs medications stored on pegs on the wall. The pills are then dropped into containers that are marked for each patient.

Hackensack University Medical Center in Hackensack, New Jersey, is one of the nation's most aggressive technology adopters, investing $72 million in IT projects since 1998. The IT investments are paying off for the hospital with patient mortality rates decreasing—down 16 percent in four years—and quality of care and productivity increasing. The most important piece of Hackensack's digital initiatives is the networked software that acts as the hospital's central nervous system. Using wireless laptops, nurses log in to the system to record patient information and progress. Doctors tap into the network via wireless devices to order prescriptions and lab tests. Everything is linked, from the automated pharmacy to the X-ray lab, eliminating the need for faxes, phone calls, and other administrative hassles. Figure B16.7 displays the hospital's IT systems development projects.

Health care spending accounts for 15 percent of the U.S. economy, or $1.7 trillion. It is so gargantuan that any efficiency gains will affect the overall economy. Dr. David Brailer, President George W. Bush's point man on health IT initiatives, predicts that IT investments will lead to $140 billion a year in cost savings by 2014. More important than saving money is saving lives. Poor information kills some 7,000 Americans each year just by missing drug-interaction problems, according to the National Academy of Sciences Institute of Medicine. Hospital errors result in 100,000 deaths annually. Early evidence indicates that proper technology can reduce this amount. Hospitals using electronic prescription systems have seen 80 percent fewer prescription errors.

### Questions

1. How would operations management be a critical component to a hospital?

2. How would a hospital use each of the three OM planning strategies to improve its operations?

3. How might a hospital use each of the five competitive priorities to increase value to its goods and services?

## 1. Operational Mowing

Mary Lou has worked for the same Fortune 500 company for almost 15 years. Although the company had gone through some tough times, things were starting to turn around. Customer orders were up, and quality and productivity had improved dramatically from what they had been only a few years earlier due to a companywide quality improvement program. So it came as a real shock to Mary Lou and about 400 of her co-workers when they were suddenly terminated following the new CEO's decision to downsize the company.

After recovering from the initial shock, Mary Lou tried to find employment elsewhere. Despite her efforts, after eight months of searching she was no closer to finding a job than the day she started. Her funds were being depleted and she was getting more discouraged. There was one bright spot, though: She was able to bring in a little money by mowing lawns for her neighbors. She got involved quite by chance when she heard one neighbor remark that now that his children were on their own, nobody was around to cut the grass. Almost jokingly, Mary Lou asked him how much he'd be willing to pay. Soon Mary Lou was mowing the lawns of 10 neighbors. Other neighbors wanted her to work on their lawns, but she did not feel that she could spare any more time from her job search.

However, as the rejection letters began to pile up, Mary Lou knew she had to make a decision if she would go into business for herself or continue her job search.

By the end of her first year in business, Mary Lou was easily earning a good living. She began performing other services such as fertilizing lawns, weeding gardens, trimming shrubs, and installing sprinkler systems. Business was so good that Mary Lou hired several employees to assist her and believed she could further expand her business. As Mary Lou begins to plan her expansion, she needs your assistance in answering the following questions:

1. In what ways are Mary Lou's customers most likely to judge the quality of her lawn care services?

2. Mary Lou is the operations manager of her business. Among her responsibilities are forecasting, inventory management, scheduling, quality assurance, and maintenance.

   1. What kinds of things would likely require forecasts?
   2. What inventory items does Mary Lou probably have? Name one inventory decision she has to make periodically.
   3. What scheduling must she do? What things might occur to disrupt schedules and cause Mary Lou to reschedule?
   4. How important is quality assurance to Mary Lou's business?

3. What are some of the trade-offs that Mary Lou probably considered relative to:

   1. Working for a company instead of for herself?
   2. Expanding the business?
   3. Launching a website?

4. The town is considering an ordinance that would prohibit grass clippings at the curb for pickup because local landfills cannot handle the volume. What options might Mary Lou consider if the ordinance is passed?

5. Mary Lou decided to offer her employees a bonus of $250 for ideas on how to improve the business, and they provided several good ideas. One idea that she initially rejected

now appears to hold great promise. The employee who proposed the idea has left the company and is currently working for a competitor. Should Mary Lou send the employee a check for the idea?

## 2. Total Recall

In mid-2000, the Firestone Tire Company issued a recall of some of its tires—those mounted on certain sport-utility vehicles (SUV) of the Ford Motor Company. This was done in response to reports that tire treads on some SUVs separated in use, causing accidents, some of which involved fatal injuries as vehicles rolled over.

At first, Firestone denied there was a problem with its tires, but it issued the recall under pressure from consumer groups and various government agencies. All of the tires in question were produced at the same tire plant, and there were calls to shut down that facility. Firestone suggested that Ford incorrectly matched the wrong tires with its SUVs. There were also suggestions that the shock absorbers of the SUVs were rubbing against the tires, causing or aggravating the problem.

Both Ford and Firestone denied that this had been an ongoing problem. However, there was a public outcry when it was learned that Firestone had previously issued recalls of these tires in South America, and the companies had settled at least one lawsuit involving an accident caused by tread separation several years earlier.

This case raises a number of issues, some related to possible causes and others to ethics. Discuss each of these factors and their actual or potential relevance to what happened:

1. Product
2. Quality control
3. Ethics

# B17

## Organizational Architecture Trends

1. Describe the business value in deploying a service oriented architecture.
2. Explain the need for interoperability and loose coupling in building today's IT systems.
3. Identify the logical functions used in a virtualized environment.
4. Explain the business benefits of grid computing.

## Architecture Trends

To keep business systems up-and-running 24 × 7 × 365 while continuing to be flexible, scalable, reliable, and available is no easy task. Organizations today must continually watch new architecture trends to ensure they can keep up with new and disruptive technologies. This plug-in discusses three architecture trends that are quickly becoming requirements for all businesses:

- Service Oriented Architecture
- Virtualization
- Grid Computing

## Service Oriented Architecture

***Service oriented architecture (SOA)*** is a business-driven IT architectural approach that supports integrating a business as linked, repeatable tasks or services. SOA helps today's businesses innovate by ensuring that IT systems can adapt quickly, easily, and economically to support rapidly changing business needs. It helps businesses increase the flexibility of their processes, strengthen their underlying IT architecture, and reuse their existing IT investments by creating connections among disparate applications and information sources.

SOA is not a concrete architecture: It is something that leads to a concrete architecture (as illustrated in Figure B17.1). It might be described as a style, paradigm, concept, perspective, philosophy, or representation. That is, SOA is not a

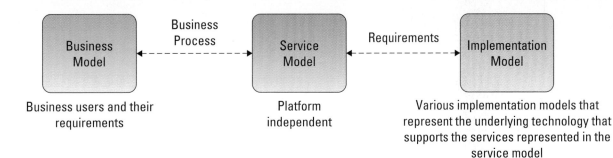

concrete tool or framework to be purchased. It is an approach, a way of thinking, a value system that leads to certain concrete decisions when designing a concrete architecture.

Crutchfield, in Charlottesville, Virginia, sells electronics through three channels: the web, a call center, and two retail shops. With a service oriented architecture, a single application now handles the initial order processing from all three sales channels, with fraud checking and the workflow encapsulated using a series of messages. Although simple to build, Crutchfield's SOA is rigorous, averaging 3,800 daily orders that book on average $1.1 million daily in revenues.

## SOA BUSINESS BENEFITS

The reality in IT enterprises is that architectures are heterogeneous across operating systems, applications, system software, and application infrastructure. Some existing applications are used to run current business processes, so starting from scratch to build a new architecture is not an option. Enterprises should quickly respond to business changes with agility; leverage existing investments in applications and application infrastructure to address newer business requirements; and support new channels of interactions with customers, partners, and suppliers. SOA with its loosely coupled nature allows enterprises to plug in new services or upgrade existing services in a granular fashion. This enables businesses to address the new business requirements, provides the option to make the services consumable across different channels, and exposes the existing enterprise and legacy applications as services, thereby safeguarding existing IT infrastructure investments (see Figure B17.2). The key technical concepts of SOA are:

- **Service**—a business task
- **Interoperability**—the capability of two or more computer systems to share data and resources, even though they are made by different manufacturers
- **Loose coupling**—the capability of services to be joined together on demand to create composite services, or disassembled just as easily into their functional components

## SERVICE

Service oriented architecture begins with a service—an SOA *service* being simply a business task, such as checking a potential customer's credit rating when opening a new account. It is important to stress that this is part of a business process. As mentioned in the previous section, services are "like" software products; however, when describing SOA, do not think about software or IT. Think about what a company does on a day-to-day basis, and break up those business processes into repeatable business tasks or components.

SOA provides the technology underpinnings for working with services that are not just software or hardware, but rather business tasks. It is a pattern for developing a more flexible kind of software application that can promote loose coupling

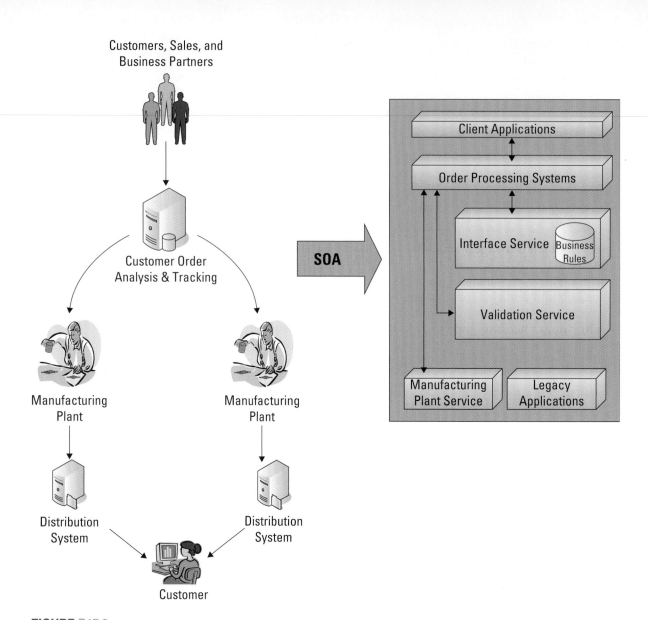

**FIGURE** B17.2

SOA Integration

among software components while reusing existing investments in technology in new, more valuable ways across the organization. SOA is based on standards that enable interoperability, business agility, and innovation to generate more business value for those who use these principles.

SOA helps companies become more agile by aligning business needs and the IT capabilities that support these needs. Business drives requirements for IT; SOA enables the IT environment to effectively and efficiently respond to these requirements. SOA is about helping companies apply reusability and flexibility that can lower cost (of development, integration, maintenance), increase revenue, and obtain sustainable competitive advantage through technology.

It is very important to note that SOA is an evolution. Although its results are revolutionary, it builds on many technologies used in the marketplace, such as web services, transactional technologies, information-driven principles, loose coupling, components, and object-oriented design. The beauty of SOA is that these technologies exist together in SOA through standards, well-defined interfaces, and organizational commitments to reuse key services instead of reinventing the wheel. SOA is not just about technology, but about how technology and business link themselves for a common goal of business flexibility.

Businesses have become increasingly complex over the past couple of decades. Factors such as mergers, regulations, global competition, outsourcing, and partnering have resulted in a massive increase in the number of applications any given company might use. These applications were implemented with little knowledge of the other applications with which they would be required to share information in the future. As a result, many companies are trying to maintain IT systems that coexist but are not integrated.

SOA can help provide solutions to companies that face a variety of business issues; Figure B17.3 lists some of those.

## INTEROPERABILITY

As defined above, *interoperability* is the capability of two or more computer systems to share data and resources, even though they are made by different manufacturers. Businesses today use a variety of systems that have resulted in a heterogeneous environment. This heterogeneity has inundated businesses with the lack of interoperability. However, since SOA is based on open standards, businesses can create solutions that draw upon functionality from these existing, previously isolated systems that are portable and/or interoperable, regardless of the environment in which they exist.

A *web service* is an open standards way of supporting interoperability. Web services are application programming interfaces (API) that can be accessed over a network, such as the Internet, and executed on a remote system hosting the requested services. SOA is a style of architecture that enables the creation

| Business Issues | SOA Solutions |
|---|---|
| ■ Agents unable to see policy coverage information remotely<br>■ Calls/faxes used to get information from other divisions<br>■ Clinical patient information stored on paper<br>■ Complex access to supplier design drawings | Integrate information to make it more accessible to employees. |
| ■ High cost of handling customer calls<br>■ Reconciliation of invoice deductions and rebates<br>■ Hours on hold to determine patient insurance eligibility<br>■ High turnover leading to excessive hiring and training costs | Understand how business processes interact to better manage administrative costs. |
| ■ Decreasing customer loyalty due to incorrect invoices<br>■ Customers placed on hold to check order status<br>■ Inability to quickly update policy endorsements<br>■ Poor service levels | Improve customer retention and deliver new products and services through reuse of current investments. |
| ■ Time wasted reconciling separate databases<br>■ Manual processes such as handling trade allocations<br>■ Inability to detect quality flaws early in cycle<br>■ High percentage of scrap and rework | Improve people productivity with better business integration and connectivity. |

**FIGURE** B17.3

Business Issues and SOA Solutions

of applications that are built by combining loosely coupled and interoperable services. These services interoperate based on a formal definition that is independent of the underlying platform and programming language. In SOA, since the basic unit of communication is a message rather than an operation, web services are usually loosely coupled. Although SOA can exist without web services, the best-practice implementation of SOA for flexibility always involves web services.

Technically, web services are based on ***Extensible Markup Language (XML),*** a markup language for documents containing structured information. The technical specifics of XML's capabilities go beyond the scope of this book, but for our purposes, they support things such as ebusiness transactions, mathematical equations, and a thousand other kinds of structured information. XML is a common data representation that can be used as the medium of exchange between programs that are written in different programming languages and execute different kinds of machine instructions. In simple terms, think about XML as the official translator for structured information. Structured information is both the content (word, picture, and so on) and the role it plays. XML is the basis for all web service technologies and the key to interoperability; every web service specification is based on XML.

## LOOSE COUPLING

Part of the value of SOA is that it is built on the premise of loose coupling of services. ***Loose coupling*** is the capability of services to be joined on demand to create composite services or disassembled just as easily into their functional components.

Loose coupling is a way of ensuring that the technical details such as language, platform, and so on are decoupled from the service. For example, look at currency conversion. Today all banks have multiple currency converters, all with different rate refreshes at different times. By creating a common service "conversion of currency" that is loosely coupled to all banking functions that require conversion, the rates, times, and samplings can be averaged to ensure floating the treasury in the most effective manner possible. Another example is common customer identification. Most businesses lack a common customer ID and, therefore, have no way to determine who the customers are and what they buy for what reason. Creating a common customer ID that is independent of applications and databases allows loosely coupling the service "Customer ID" to data and applications without the application or database ever knowing who it is or where it is.

The difference between traditional, tightly bound interactions and loosely coupled services is that, before the transaction occurs, the functional pieces (services) operating within the SOA are dormant and disconnected. When the business process initiates, these services momentarily interact with each other. They do so for just long enough to execute their piece of the overall process, and then they go back to their dormant state, with no long-standing connection to the other services with which they just interacted. The next time the same service is called, it could be as part of a different business process with different calling and destination services.

A great way to understand this is through the analogy of the telephone system. At the dawn of widespread phone usage, operators had to physically plug in a wire to create a semipermanent connection between two parties. Callers were "tightly bound" to each other. Today you pick up your cell phone and put it to your ear, and there's no dial tone—it's disconnected. You enter a number, push "Talk," and only then does the process initiate, establishing a loosely coupled connection just long enough for your conversation. Then when the conversation is over, your cell phone goes back to dormant mode until a new connection is made with another party. As a result, supporting a million cell phone subscribers does not require that the cell phone service provider support a million live connections; it requires supporting only the number of simultaneous conversations at any given time. It allows for a much more flexible and dynamic exchange.

# Virtualization

*Virtualization* is a framework of dividing the resources of a computer into multiple execution environments. It is a way of increasing physical resources to maximize the investment in hardware. Generally, this process is done with virtualization software, running on the one physical unit that emulates multiple pieces of hardware.

In a virtualized environment, the logical functions of computing, storage, and network elements are separated from their physical functions. Functions from these resources can then be manually or automatically allocated to meet the changing needs and priorities of a business. These concepts can be applied broadly across the enterprise, from data-center resources to PCs and printers.

Through virtualization, people, processes, and technology work together more efficiently to meet increased service levels. Since capacity can be allocated dynamically, chronic over-provisioning is eliminated and an entire IT architecture is simplified (see Figure B17.4).

Even something as simple as partitioning a hard drive is considered virtualization because you take one drive and partition it to create two separate hard drives. Devices, applications, and users are able to interact with the virtual machine as if it were a real single logical resource.

## WHAT ARE VIRTUAL MACHINES?

*System virtualization* (often referred to as "server virtualization" or "desktop virtualization," depending on the role of the virtualized system) is the ability to present the resources of a single computer as if it is a collection of separate computers ("virtual machines"), each with its own virtual CPUs, network interfaces, storage, and operating system.

Virtual machine technology was first implemented on mainframes in the 1960s to allow the expensive systems to be partitioned into separate domains and used

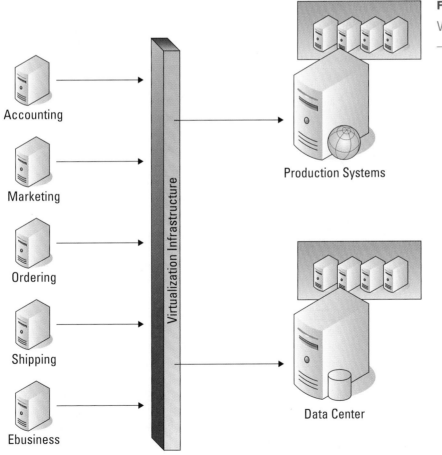

**FIGURE B17.4**

Virtualization Architecture

more efficiently by more users and applications. As standard PC servers became more powerful in the past decade, virtualization has been brought to the desktop and notebook processors to provide the same benefits.

Virtual machines appear both to the user within the system and the world outside as separate computers, each with its own network identity, user authorization and authentication capabilities, operating system version and configuration, applications, and data. The hardware is consistent across all virtual machines: While the number or size of them may differ, devices are used that allow virtual machines to be portable, independent of the actual hardware type on the underlying systems.

Figure B17.5 shows an overview of what a system virtualization framework looks like.

## VIRTUALIZATION BUSINESS BENEFITS

Virtualization is by no means a new technology. As previously mentioned, mainframe computers have offered the ability to host multiple operating systems for over 30 years. However, several trends have moved virtualization into the spotlight, such as hardware being underutilized, data centers running out of space, energy costs increasing, and system administration costs mounting. The U.S. Environmental Protection Agency recently proclaimed that data centers consumed 61 billion kilowatt-hours of electricity. That is roughly 1.6 percent of total U.S. electricity consumption and is worth about $4.5 billion. Assuming current trends continue, by 2011 the national energy consumption by data centers is expected to nearly double, making energy efficiency a top priority.

The first major virtualization trend highlights hardware being underutilized. In the April 1965 issue of *Electronics* magazine, Gordon Moore first offered his observation about processor computing power, which has come to be known as Moore's law. In describing the increasing power of computing power, Moore stated: "The complexity for minimum component costs has increased at a rate of roughly a factor of two per year." What he means is that each year (actually, most people estimate the time frame at around 18 months), for a given size processor, twice as many individual components can be squeezed onto a similarly sized piece of silicon. Put another way, every new generation of chip delivers twice as much processing power as the previous generation—at the same price.

**FIGURE** B17.5

System Virtualization

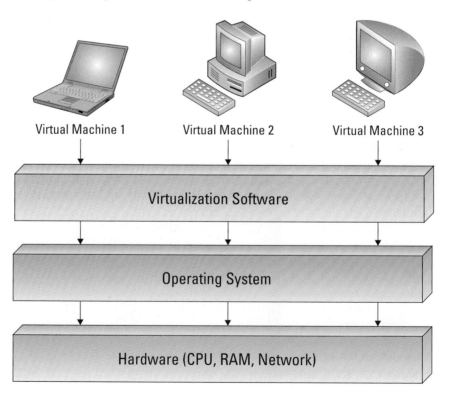

Moore's law demonstrates increasing returns—the amount of improvement itself grows over time because there's an exponential increase in capacity for every generation of processor improvement. That exponential increase is responsible for the mind-boggling improvements in computing—and the increasing need for virtualization.

Today, many data centers have machines running at only 10 to 15 percent of total processing capacity, which translates to 85 to 90 percent of the machine's power being unused. In a way, Moore's law is no longer relevant to most companies because they are not able to take advantage of the increased power available to them.

Moore's law not only enables virtualization, but also effectively makes it mandatory. Otherwise, increasing amounts of computing power will go to waste each year.

A second virtualization trend concentrates on data centers running out of space. The business world has undergone an enormous transformation over the past 20 years. In 1985, the vast majority of business processes were paper based. Computerized systems were confined to so-called backroom automation: payroll, accounting, and the like. That has all changed, thanks to the steady march of Moore's law. Business process after business process has been captured in software and automated, moving from paper to computers.

The rise of the Internet has exponentially increased this transformation. Companies want to communicate with customers and partners in real time, using the worldwide connectivity of the Internet. Naturally, this has accelerated the move to computerized business processes.

Boeing's latest airliner, the 787 Dreamliner, is being designed and built in a radically new way. Boeing and each of its suppliers use computer-aided design (CAD) software to design their respective parts of the plane. All communication about the project uses the CAD designs as the basis for discussion. Use of CAD software enables testing to be done in computer models rather than the traditional method of building physical prototypes, thereby speeding completion of the plane by a year or more.

The Dreamliner project generates enormous amounts of data. Just one piece of the project—a data warehouse containing project plans—runs to 19 terabytes of data. The net effect of all this and similar projects at other companies is that huge numbers of servers have been put into use over the past decade, which is causing a real-estate problem—companies are running out of space in their data centers.

Virtualization, by offering the ability to host multiple guest systems on a single physical server, helps organizations to reclaim data center territory, thereby avoiding the expense of building out more data center space. This is an enormous benefit of virtualization because data centers cost in the tens of millions of dollars to construct.

Rapidly escalating energy costs are also furthering the trend toward virtualization. The cost of running computers, coupled with the fact that many of the machines filling up data centers are running at low utilization rates, means that virtualization's ability to reduce the total number of physical servers can significantly reduce the overall cost of energy for companies. Data center power is such an issue that energy companies are putting virtualization programs into place to address it.

These trends reveal why virtualization is a technology whose time has come. The exponential power growth of computers, the substitution of automated processes for manual work, the increasing cost to power the multitude of computers, and the high personnel cost to manage that multitude all cry out for a less expensive way to run data centers. In fact, a newer, more efficient method of running data centers is critical because, given the trends mentioned above, the traditional methods of delivering computing are becoming cost prohibitive.

Virtualization enables data center managers to make far better use of computer resources than in nonvirtualized environments, and it enables an enterprise to maximize its investment in hardware. Underutilized hardware platforms and server sprawl—today's norm—can become things of the past. By virtualizing a large deployment of older systems on a few highly scalable, highly reliable, enterprise-class servers, businesses can substantially reduce costs related to hardware purchases, provisioning, and maintenance.

## ADDITIONAL VIRTUALIZATION BENEFITS

Virtualization offers more than server consolidation benefits as described in the previous section. Rapid application deployment, dynamic load balancing, and streamlined disaster recovery top the list of additional benefits. Virtualization technologies can reduce application test and deployment time from days or weeks to a matter of hours by enabling users to test and qualify software in isolation but also in the same environment as the production workload.

Virtualization, in all its forms, is a highly disruptive yet clearly beneficial technology. Enterprises are deploying virtualization for a number of real and significant benefits. The strongest driver—business continuity—is surprising, but many of the other drivers, such as flexibility and agility, server consolidation, and reduced administration costs, are fully expected.

Other advantages of virtualization include a variety of security benefits (stemming from centralized computing environments); improved service-level management (i.e., the ability to manage resource allocation against service levels for specific applications and business users); the ability to more easily run legacy systems; greater flexibility in locating staff; and reduced hardware and software costs.

In its 620-acre facility in Lafayette, Indiana, Subaru of Indiana produces cars and SUVs for its parent company, Fuji Heavy Industries, and Camry vehicles for Toyota. It has the capacity to produce 21,800 vehicles a month, using the just-in-time method of manufacturing. This method requires a streamlined production line, with highly accurate and reliable inventory controls. A lack of any one component can stop the assembly line and trigger problems up and down the supply chain.

The facility suffered from several problems. Some of its applications had reliability issues, but the IT staff faced compatibility issues when it tried to use newer servers as standbys for older models. However, expanding the number of servers would necessitate a major upgrade of the data center's power needs and the associated cooling system. To reduce complexity and increase capacity and reliability, the IT staff installed a virtualization architecture to increase flexibility and system reliability, as well as reduce downtime, system administration workload, power consumption, and the overall number of physical servers by more than two-thirds.

# Grid Computing

When you turn on the light, the power grid delivers exactly what you need, instantly. Computers and networks can now work that way using grid computing. *Grid computing* is an aggregation of geographically dispersed computing, storage, and network resources, coordinated to deliver improved performance, higher quality of service, better utilization, and easier access to data.

Grid computing enables the virtualization of distributed computing and data resources such as processing, network bandwidth, and storage capacity to create a single system image, granting users and applications seamless access to vast IT capabilities. Virtualizing these resources yields a scalable, flexible pool of processing and data storage that the enterprise can use to improve efficiency. Moreover, it will help create a sustainable competitive advantage by streamlining product development and allowing focus to be placed on the core business. Over time, grid environments will enable the creation of virtual organizations and advanced web services as partnerships and collaborations become more critical in strengthening each link in the value chain (see Figure B17.6).

## GRID COMPUTING BUSINESS BENEFITS

At its core, grid computing is based on an open set of standards and protocols (e.g., Open Grid Services Architecture) that enable communication across heterogeneous, geographically dispersed environments, as shown in Figure B17.7. With grid computing, organizations can optimize computing and data resources,

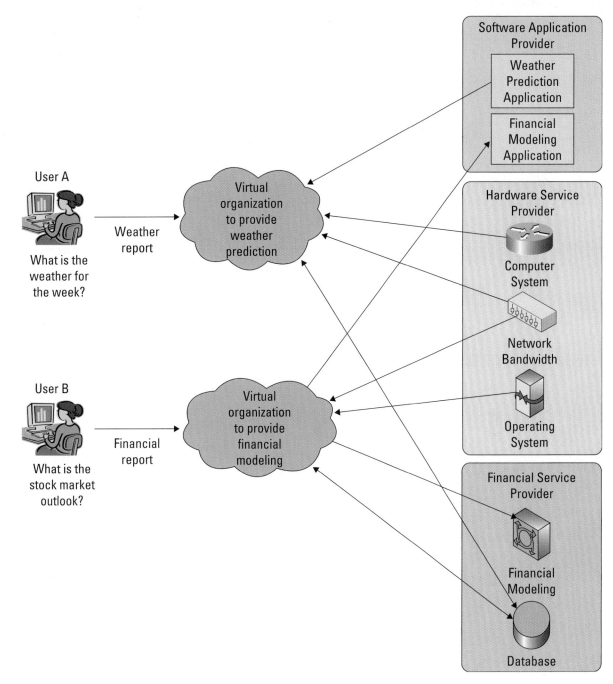

**FIGURE** B17.6

Virtual Organizations
Using Grid Computing

pool them for large-capacity workloads, share them across networks, and enable collaboration.

Google, the secretive, extraordinarily successful global search engine company, is one of the most recognized brands in the world. Yet it selectively discusses its innovative information management architecture—which is based on one of the largest grid computing systems in the world. Google runs on hundreds of thousands of servers—by one estimate, in excess of one million—racked up in thousands of clusters in dozens of data centers around the world. It has data centers in Ireland, Virginia, and California. It recently opened a new center in Atlanta and is currently building two football-field-sized centers in The Dalles, Oregon. By having its servers and data centers distributed geographically, Google delivers faster performance to its worldwide audience.

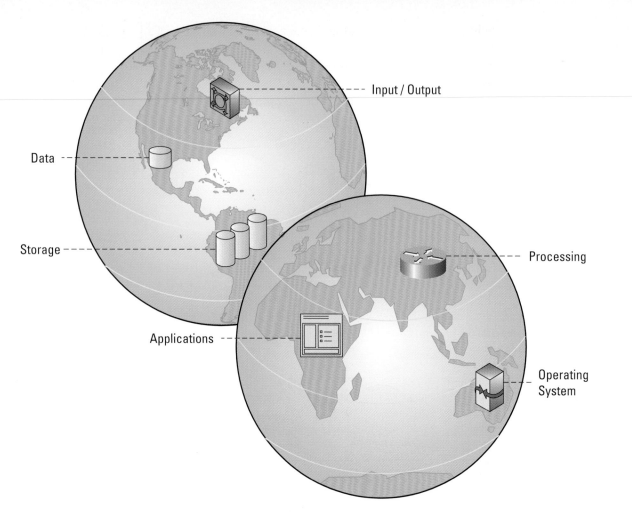

Data

Storage

Applications

Input / Output

Processing

Operating System

**FIGURE** B17.7

Virtualization of Grid Computing

Grid computing goes far beyond sheer computing power. Today's operating environments must be resilient, flexible, and integrated as never before. Organizations around the world are experiencing substantial benefits by implementing grids in critical business processes to achieve both business and technology benefits. These business benefits include:

- Improving productivity and collaboration of virtual organizations and respective computing and data resources.
- Allowing widely dispersed departments and businesses to create virtual organizations to share data and resources.
- Building robust and infinitely flexible and resilient operational architectures.
- Providing instantaneous access to massive computing and data resources.
- Leveraging existing capital investments, which in turn help to ensure optimal utilization and costs of computing capabilities.

Many organizations have started identifying the major business areas for grid computing business applications. Some examples of major business areas include:

- Life sciences, for analyzing and decoding strings of biological and chemical information.
- Financial services, for running long, complex financial models and arriving at more accurate decisions.
- Higher education for enabling advanced, data- and computation-intensive research.

- Engineering services, including automotive and aerospace, for collaborative design and data-intensive testing.

- Government, for enabling seamless collaboration and agility in both civil and military departments and other agencies.

- Collaborative games for replacing the existing single-server online games with more highly parallel, massively multiplayer online games.

With our pervasive need of information anytime and anywhere, the explosive grid computing environments have now proven to be so significant that they are often referred to as being the world's single and most powerful computer solutions.

# Cloud Computing

***Cloud computing*** refers to resources and applications hosted remotely as a shared service over the Internet. The term *cloud computing* comes from (at least partly) the use of a cloud image to represent the Internet or some large networked environment. Like grid computing, cloud computing requires the use of software that can divide and distribute components of a program to thousands of computers. New advances in processors, virtualization technology, disk storage, broadband Internet access, and fast, inexpensive servers have all combined to make cloud computing a compelling solution for almost every business.

Cloud computing allows users and companies to pay for and use the services and storage that they need, when they need them and, as wireless broadband connection options grow, where they need them. Customers can be billed based upon server utilization, processing power used or bandwidth consumed. With more reliable, affordable broadband access, the Internet no longer functions solely as a communications network. The Internet has become a platform for computing. Rather than running software on a local computer or server, Internet users reach to the "cloud" to combine software applications, data storage, and massive computing power.

Google operates several well-known cloud computing services. It offers its users applications such as email, word processing, spreadsheets and storage, and hosts them "in the cloud"—in other words, on its own servers. For example, you can type a document without maintaining any word processing software on your computer.

Other examples of cloud computing include:

- Web-based email services such as Microsoft Hotmail

- Photo storing services such as Google's Picassa

- Spreadsheet applications such as Zoho

- Online computer backup services such as Mozy

- File transfer services such as YouSendIt

- Online medical records storage such as Microsoft's HealthVault

- Applications associated with social networking sites such as Facebook

Cloud computing incorporates software as a service (SaaS), Web 2.0, and other recent, well-known technology trends, in which the common theme is reliance on the Internet for satisfying the computing needs of the users. ***Software as a Service (SaaS)*** is a model of software deployment where an application is licensed for use as a service provided to customers on demand. Delivering software over the Internet, SaaS is increasingly popular for its ability to simplify deployment and reduce customer acquisition costs; it also allows developers to support many customers with a single version of a product. SaaS is also often associated with a "pay as you go" subscription licensing model. One example of SaaS is Salesforce.com, which offers complete sales force automation and CRM functionality for a flat per-user, per-month fee. There is no upfront license fee, and small deployments can be up and running in days or even hours.

The SaaS model can offer numerous benefits over traditional licensed software approaches:

- **Easy to switch providers**—SaaS provides significantly more power and control to the corporate buyer than traditional software license models. SaaS applications are sold on a subscription basis for a monthly recurring fee. Unsatisfied clients can cancel their subscriptions and transfer to a different application provider without the purchasing and licensing costs that would be assumed in a licensed software model.

- **Pay only for what you use**—Often, IT organizations will overestimate the actual software utilization by the end-user community. For example, an IT organization may forecast an active end-user community for a particular application to grow to 10,000 employees within a year. However, customization and implementation delays may result in only 500 employees actually using the software a year later. With SaaS, corporate buyers only pay for the active users of the system—not the forecasted user community.

- **Lower total cost of ownership**—One of the historical complaints about licensed software models has been the unknown cost to deploy and operate. With SaaS the total cost to operate the application is fixed. SaaS providers typically will bundle all of the necessary hardware, software and support services such as implementation, training, help desk, troubleshooting, upgrades, security, and business continuity into a single fee. As a result, the overall total cost of ownership is known in advance.

- **Time-to-market**—The SaaS provider takes responsibility for the provisioning of hardware, software, and network infrastructure at the data center. Additionally, SaaS applications typically have limited customization of features and the user interface. As a result, there are no delays resulting from the need for internal IT organizations to perform development, enhancement or deployment of the application.

- **Easier upgrades**—SaaS providers manage the upgrade process. New releases and feature enhancements are deployed centrally to the hosted applications. There are no client applications on end-user desktops to be upgraded. SaaS providers typically deliver two to four major upgrades per year and several minor updates that the user gets automatically. Users of SaaS-based applications can always be certain that they are using the latest version of the software supplied by the provider.

- **Improved security**—SaaS providers are in the business of providing uninterrupted reliable services. Providers understand that data must be backed up religiously, and information security is of fanatic priority. Skilled resources, network redundancies, stand-by power, up-to-date security and intrusion detection are mandatory infrastructure required to provide an enterprise class service. This level of infrastructural investment is usually overkill for a single organization or team.

SaaS has the potential to totally change the way in which companies run their IT infrastructures. It allows relatively small companies to use feature-rich applications that are traditionally used only by the larger organizations because of the acquisition cost and the level of IT support required to run the applications efficiently. SaaS brings down these barriers and allows many more companies to streamline and simplify their IT infrastructures, improve application deployment in geographically dispersed locations, and realize significant cost savings.

Organizations pay special attention to computing basics since these form the underlying foundation that supports a firm's information systems. A solid underlying infrastructure is a necessity for ensuring the security, reliability, quality, and responsiveness of a firm's information systems. These systems are the tools that companies utilize and heavily rely upon to run their businesses and compete in today's competitive environment. As a business student, it is important that you understand the components and activities underpinning an organization's computing infrastructure so that you may be attuned to what is involved and be able to take steps to ensure this infrastructure is kept up-to-date and running as smoothly as possible.

## ★ KEY TERMS

Cloud computing, 459
Extensible Markup Language
   (XML) 452
Grid computing 456
Interoperability 449, 451

Loose coupling, 449, 452
Service oriented architecture
   (SOA) 448
Service 449
Software as a service (SaaS) 459

System virtualization 453
Virtualization 453
Web service 451

## ★ CLOSING CASE ONE

### The U.S. Open Supports SOA

The U.S. Open is a tennis event sponsored by the United States Tennis Association (USTA), a not-for-profit organization with more than 665,000 members. It devotes 100 percent of its proceeds to the advancement of tennis. At last count, more than 5 million viewers checked out the U.S. Open online.

The USTA created an integrated scoring system for the U.S. Open. This scoring system helps collect data from all tennis courts and then stores and distributes the information to USOpen.org, the official website of the U.S. Open. The ability to immediately and simultaneously distribute scoring information, supporting more than 156 million scoring updates, illustrates how the USTA leverages SOA to support its business goals. SOA helped the USTA use its existing computing systems to become more responsive and more closely aligned with the needs of its customers and partners.

For example, umpires officiating at each of the U.S. Open matches hold a device they use to keep score. These devices feed into a database that holds the collective tournament scores. From there, the constantly changing scoring information is fed to numerous servers that can be accessed through the U.S. Open website. When visitors go to USOpen.org and click the "Live Scores" link, they see the scoreboards for all 18 courts that are updated before the visitors' eyes. This is then used to present visitors with instantly updated scoring information that is presented on the site's On Demand Scoreboards and the "matches in progress" pages.

Scores and statistics can also be instantly viewed on the website and compared with past U.S. Open events and similar competitions. Additionally, SOA is helping support the integration of information and statistics related to the tournament, such as individual scores and how they compare with current and past performance of the players and competitors.

Linking all of the tournament's information and delivering scores in real time requires a sophisticated information technology infrastructure that can be easily accessed and understood by USTA subscribers, many of whom are not IT professionals. The USTA is at the beginning stages of an SOA, and the USOpen.org website will be able to accommodate a growing audience of tennis fans worldwide.

The U.S. Open is the world's largest annually attended sporting event, and USOpen.org is among the top five most-trafficked sports event websites. The site has seen a 62 percent year-over-year traffic increase, with 5 million unique users, 27 million visits, and 79,000 concurrent real-time scoreboards. Since SOAs are scalable and flexible, they can easily meet the demands of the constantly changing USOpen.org website and the anticipated heavy site traffic produced by 27 million visits—with each visitor spending nearly an hour and a half per visit.

## Questions

1. Review the five characteristics of infrastructure architecture and rank them in order of their potential impact on the USOpen.org.

2. What are the USTA security concerns regarding interoperability between the tournament database and its website?

3. How could the USTA benefit from virtualization?

4. Identify the value of integrating the tournament information with the USTA website, USOpen .org.

5. Why would a sudden surge in server utilization during the middle of the U.S. Open spell disaster for the USTA?

6. Why is loose coupling a critical business component to the USTA architecture?

---

**✴ CLOSING CASE TWO**

### eBay's Grid

eBay Inc. is using grid computing to deliver online auction services to millions of users. The biggest technology issue facing eBay is managing its shared grid infrastructure, which currently spreads across more than 15,000 servers. Instead of managing individual servers, eBay wants its systems administrators to manage aggregations of servers, a process that would be eased considerably with grid standards.

With 222 million registered users at the last count, 610 million listings each quarter, and 6 million new items added every day, it takes a lot of computing power to keep eBay operating as fast and reliably as users have come to expect. However, eBay experienced a major outage in 1999 that resulted in a total loss of service. The architecture of the system made it vulnerable: Bid information was maintained in a single massive database that was both a point of contention and a single point of failure. The business logic for all except one application was also centralized.

Following the disastrous outage of 1999, eBay launched an overhaul of its IT infrastructure, rebuilding its data centers around a grid-type architecture. The first task was to eliminate the single point of failure in the huge system. Then eBay needed to reconstruct the application to ensure that it had fault isolation and that processes and tasks of like size and cost weren't congesting and competing with each other. Basically, eBay had to disaggregate the monolithic system and ensure scale and fault tolerance.

The auction site abandoned its one huge back-end system and four or five very large search databases. Search used to update in 6 to 12 hours from the time in which someone would place a bid or an item for sale. Today, updates are usually less than 90 seconds. At present, eBay has 200 back-end databases, all of them in the 6- to 12-processor range. Not all those are necessary to run the site; many are for disaster recovery and for data replication.

The extra redundancy built into the system allows eBay to run $24 \times 7 \times 365$; it is never brought down for scheduled maintenance as was required with the old implementation. The operating results have been exceptional: Although system usage went up by about an order of magnitude, downtime went down from about 15 days per year to just a few hours.

eBay also ensures that security is built into every piece of its infrastructure and architecture. To date, it has never been hacked. In addition, eBay believes this infrastructure will allow it to scale nearly indefinitely.

## Questions

1. Review the five characteristics of infrastructure architecture and rank them in order of their potential impact on eBay's business.
2. What are the business benefits that eBay enjoys thanks to grid computing?
3. What precautions would eBay take to ensure 100 percent security?
4. How can eBay take advantage of implementing SOA?
5. Explain how eBay uses fault tolerance.
6. Describe the potential value of eBay using virtualization.
7. What ethical and security concerns should eBay be aware of to ensure its business operates properly?

## ✱ MAKING BUSINESS DECISIONS

### 1. The *New York Times* Is in the Clouds

Cloud-based opportunities come in all business sizes—large, midsize, and small. Consider a big enterprise like the *New York Times*. Recently the *Times* was looking for a way to make its archives—150 years of daily newspaper editions—available online. Digitizing so much material was only half the challenge; the storage requirements were vast. The *Times* archives included 11 million articles; when digitized, they would consume 1.5 terabytes of disk space. The paper tried to manage the process internally, but it proved unrealistic. So it turned to Amazon's Web Services, the online retail giant's cloud offering. Using Amazon's Simple Storage Service (S3), the *Times* launched a web application called Times-Machine. The launch took days instead of months, and it cost hundreds of dollars instead of thousands. Users can read PDFs of newspapers from the mid-19th century, zooming in on articles, photos, and even advertising.

You are working for a competitor to the *New York Times*. Your boss has asked you to research cloud computing. Specifically he has asked you to find out what advantages the *New York Times* enjoys due to cloud computing. What are the down sides to using cloud computing?

### 2. Salesforce.com and SaaS

Instead of inventing a new software category, companies like Salesforce.com, NetSuite, and RightNow Technologies are reinventing the way customers buy software. They're all making basic corporate software to manage finances or a sales team, run a business or run a call center—not new stuff, and in many cases, with fewer features than existing products.

But the innovation is in the business model. These companies deliver software over the Internet—a web service where companies pay as they go with monthly fees. That means less costly integration, no hiring an in-house administrator, and no big up-front contracts.

It's a considerably cheaper and easier approach that gives these software-as-a-service companies an entrée into the last wide-open sector of software customers—small and midsize companies.

Salesforce.com attributes its success to the many benefits of its on-demand model of software distribution. The on-demand model eliminates the need for large up-front capital investments in systems and lengthy implementations on corporate computers. Salesforce .com implementations take 0–3 months. There is no hardware for subscribers to purchase, scale, and maintain, no operating systems, database servers, or application servers to install, no consultants and staff, and no expensive licensing and maintenance fees. The system is accessible via a standard web browser, and Salesforce.com continually updates its software behind the scenes. There are tools for customizing some features of the software to support a company's unique business processes. Salesforce.com's solutions offer better scalability than those provided by large enterprise software vendors because they eliminate the cost and complexity of managing multiple layers of hardware and software.

You have just started your own online business and need a reliable CRM system. Investigate the advantages of using the software-as-a-service model. What kinds of businesses could benefit from switching to Salesforce.com and why?

### 3. Thomson Reuters SOA

When an event happens that might affect your business, you want to know about it fast. This event may be political, financial, environmental, or about your toughest competitor. Whatever it is and wherever it takes place, you want the information to be accurate, and you want the information delivered in real time—or as close to real time as you can get it.

One of the largest global companies with a mission of making sure that you receive the news you're looking for is Thomson Reuters. This $12.4-billion company was formed in April 2008 when Thomson Corporation (one of the largest providers of digital financial, medical, and legal data and content) acquired Reuters Group PLC (one of Thomson's top competitors in the delivery of financial information). With media professionals like journalists and photographers numbering in the thousands, this company delivers news and financial data to businesses and news media all over the world. However, information and content delivery represents only a portion of the complex set of information analysis and management offerings provided by Thomson Reuters.

The Thomson One Framework, the flagship product line for Thomson Reuters, is composed of individual business services the company refers to as Thomlets. Each business service (such as market quotes, news, market polls, and charting services) is available in three alternative frameworks—web-based, installed at the customer site, and mobile. Many different Thomlets are available, and the company often customizes services to the specific needs of particular clients. Each business unit has control of the Thomlets that are designed for its clients; however, there are many opportunities for the same or similar products to apply across different business units. For example, the investment management business unit might want to include a component—a Thomlet—that belongs to the investment banking portfolio of services. The investment management unit wants to have the new solution available on the market immediately.

Create a report that outlines the business value that SOA provides Thomson Reuters or another business that interests you. Make sure that you address the business problems SOA solves.

1. Explain the problem associated with business intelligence. Describe the solution to this business problem.
2. Describe the three common forms of data-mining analysis.
3. Compare tactical, operational, and strategic BI.
4. Explain the organizationwide benefits of BI.
5. Describe the four categories of BI business benefits.

## Business Intelligence

*Business intelligence (BI)* refers to applications and technologies that are used to gather, provide access to, and analyze data and information to support decision-making efforts. An early reference to business intelligence occurs in Sun Tzu's book *The Art of War*. Sun Tzu claims that to succeed in war, one should have full knowledge of one's own strengths and weaknesses and full knowledge of the enemy's strengths and weaknesses. Lack of either one might result in defeat. A certain school of thought draws parallels between the challenges in business and those of war, specifically:

- Collecting information.
- Discerning patterns and meaning in the information.
- Responding to the resultant information.

Many organizations today find it next to impossible to understand their own strengths and weaknesses, let alone their enemies', because the enormous volume of organizational data is inaccessible to all but the IT department. Organization data includes far more than simple fields in a database; it also includes voice mail, customer phone calls, text messages, video clips, along with numerous new forms of data.

### THE PROBLEM: DATA RICH, INFORMATION POOR

As businesses increase their reliance on enterprise systems such as CRM, they are rapidly accumulating vast amounts of data. Every interaction between departments or with the outside world, historical information on past transactions, as well as external market information, is entered into information systems for future use and access. Research from IDC expects businesses to face a data explosion over the next few years as the number of digital images, email in-boxes, and broadband connections doubles by 2010. The amount of data being generated is doubling every year, and some think it will soon begin to double every month. Data is a strategic asset for a business, and if the asset is not used, the business is wasting resources.

An ideal business scenario would be as follows: An account manager, on her way to a client visit, looks up past proposals, as well as the client's ordering, payment, delivery, support, and marketing history. At a glance, she can tell that the client's ordering volumes have dropped lately. A few queries later she understands that the client has a support issue with a given product. The account manager calls her support department and learns that the defective part will be replaced within 24 hours. In addition, the marketing records show that the client recently attended a user conference and expressed interest in the new product line. With this information, the account manager is fully prepared for a constructive sales call. She understands all aspects of her client's relationship with her firm, understands the client's issues, and can confidently address new sales opportunities.

In most organizations, it would take the account manager, in the example above, hours or days to get answers to questions about her client. With all the data available, it is surprising how difficult it is for managers to get a clear picture of fundamental business information, such as inventory levels, orders in the pipeline, or client history. Many organizations contain disparate silos of information. Client orders and payment records are kept in the accounting system; installation and support information is stored in the customer service database; contact management software tracks the proposals and sales call history; and marketing contact history is kept by marketing. Rarely do these systems speak the same language, and there is no simple way for a nontechnical user to get answers quickly.

As a result, information has to be requested from different departments or IT, who must dedicate staff to pull together various reports. Responses can take weeks, by which time the information may be outdated. It has been said that organizations are data rich and information poor. The challenge is to transform data into useful information. With this information, employees gain knowledge that can be leveraged to increase company profitability.

## THE SOLUTION: BUSINESS INTELLIGENCE

In every organization, employees make hundreds of decisions each day. They can range from whether to give a customer a discount, to whether to start producing a part, whether to launch another direct-mail campaign, whether to order additional materials, and so on. These decisions are sometimes based on facts, but mostly based on experience, accumulated knowledge, and rule of thumb.

That poses a problem because experience, knowledge, and rule of thumb can take years to develop. Some employees never acquire them. Those who do may still fall prey to decision traps or biases in judgment. Improving the quality of business decisions has a direct impact on costs and revenue. For instance, giving a customer a discount may or may not help the bottom line, depending on the profitability of the client over the duration of the relationship. To improve the quality of business decisions, managers can provide existing staff with BI systems and tools that can assist them in making better, more informed decisions. The result creates an agile intelligent enterprise. A few examples of using BI to make informed business decisions include:

- **Retail and sales:** Predicting sales; determining correct inventory levels and distribution schedules among outlets; and loss prevention.
- **Banking:** Forecasting levels of bad loans and fraudulent credit card use, credit card spending by new customers, and which kinds of customers will best respond to (and qualify for) new loan offers.

- **Operations management:** Predicting machinery failures; finding key factors that control optimization of manufacturing capacity.

- **Brokerage and securities trading:** Predicting when bond prices will change; forecasting the range of stock fluctuations for particular issues and the overall market; determining when to buy or sell stocks.

- **Insurance:** Forecasting claim amounts and medical coverage costs; classifying the most important elements that affect medical coverage; predicting which customers will buy new insurance policies.

- **Hardware and software:** Predicting disk-drive failures; forecasting how long it will take to create new chips; predicting potential security violations.

- **Law enforcement:** Tracking crime patterns, locations, and criminal behavior; identifying attributes to assist in solving criminal cases.

- **Government and defense:** Forecasting the cost of moving military equipment; testing strategies for potential military engagements; predicting resource consumption.

- **Airlines:** Capturing data on where customers are flying and the ultimate destination of passengers who change carriers in hub cities; thus, airlines can identify popular locations that they do not service and can check the feasibility of adding routes to capture lost business.

- **Health care:** Correlating demographics of patients with critical illnesses; developing better insights on symptoms and their causes and how to provide proper treatments.

- **Broadcasting:** Predicting what is best to air during prime time and how to maximize returns by interjecting advertisements.

- **Marketing:** Classifying customer demographics that can be used to predict which customers will respond to a mailing or buy a particular product.

The solution of implementing business intelligence systems and tools allows business users to receive data for analysis. (See Figure B18.1.)

Shell Services International's BI solution gave the company access to information about revenues between fuel and nonfuel business. Seeing that 20 percent of products were delivering 80 percent of sales, Shell significantly improved margin and turnover. It also negotiated better deals with suppliers and improved product master file management, which helped reduce working capital.

Figure B18.2 displays how organizations using BI can find the root causes to problems and provide solutions simply by asking "Why?" The process is initiated by analyzing a global report, say of sales per quarter. Every answer is followed by a new question, and users can drill deep down into a report to get to fundamental

**FIGURE** B18.1

BI Data Analysis

| Reliable | The data have been documented as the certified or approved data for the enterprise. The business users are confident that the data are the best possible and that they suit the decision-making purposes. |
|---|---|
| Consistent | The processes that deliver the data to the business community are well documented; there are no surprises such as missing or inaccurate data in the mix, analytics that will not run, response times that are unpredictable. |
| Understandable | The data have been defined in business terms; calculations and algorithms are easily accessed for comprehension. These are documented in a data dictionary or metadata repository that is easy to access and understand. |
| Easily manipulated | It is no longer required to have a PhD in statistics to get sophisticated analytics delivered to users' fingertips. And it is just as easy to change the question or set different parameters to twist and turn the data in ways unimaginable just a few years ago. |

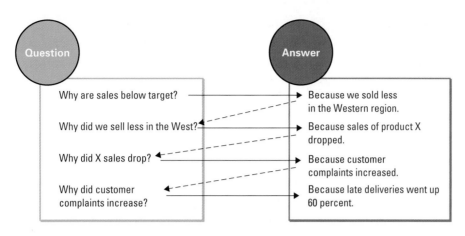

**FIGURE** B18.2

How BI Can Answer Tough Customer Questions

causes. Once they have a clear understanding of root causes, they can take highly effective action.

Finding the answers to tough business questions by using data that is reliable, consistent, understandable, and easily manipulated allows a business to gain valuable insight into such things as:

- **Where the business has been.** Historical perspective is always important in determining trends and patterns of behavior.

- **Where it is now.** Current situations are critical to either modify if not acceptable or encourage if they are trending in the right direction.

- **And where it will be in the near future.** Being able to predict with surety the direction of the company is critical to sound planning and to creating sound business strategies.

# Operational, Tactical, and Strategic BI

Claudia Imhoff, president of Intelligent Solutions, believes it is useful to divide the spectrum of data mining analysis and business intelligence into three categories: operational, tactical, and strategic. Two trends are displayed when viewing the spectrum from operational through tactical to strategic. First, the analysis becomes increasingly complex and ad hoc. That is, it is less repetitive, less predictable, and it requires varying amounts and types of data. Second, both the risks and rewards of the analysis increase. That is, the often time-consuming, more strategic queries produce value less frequently but, when they do, the value can be extraordinary. Figure B18.3 illustrates the differences between operational, tactical, and strategic BI.

These three forms are not performed in isolation from each other. It is important to understand that they must work with each other, feeding results from strategic to

|  | **Operational BI** | **Tactical BI** | **Strategic BI** |
|---|---|---|---|
| Business focus | Manage daily operations, integrate BI with operational systems | Conduct short-term analysis to achieve strategic goals | Achieve long-term organizational goals |
| Primary users | Managers, analysts, operational users | Executives, managers | Executives, managers |
| Time frame | Intraday | Day(s) to weeks to months | Months to years |
| Data | Real-time metrics | Historical metrics | Historical metrics |

**FIGURE** B18.3

Operational, Tactical, Strategic BI

tactical to promote better operational decision making. Figure B18.4 demonstrates this synergy. In this example, strategic BI is used in the planning stages of a marketing campaign. The results of these analytics form the basis for the beginnings of a new campaign, targeting specific customers or demographics, for example. The daily analyses of the campaign are used by the more tactical form of BI to change the course of the campaign if its results are not tracking where expected.

For example, perhaps a different marketing message is needed, or the inventory levels are not sufficient to maintain the current sales pace so the scope of marketing might be changed. These results are then fed into the operational BI for immediate actions—offering a different product, optimizing the sale price of the product, or changing the daily message sent to selected customer segments.

For this synergy to work, the three forms of BI must be tightly integrated with each other. Minimal time should be lost transporting the results from one technological environment to another. Seamlessness in terms of data and process flow is a must. TruServ, the parent company of True Value Hardware has used BI software to improve efficiency of its distribution operations and reap a $50 million reduction in inventory costs. The marketing department uses BI to track sales promotion results such as which promotions were most popular by store or by region. Now that TruServ is building promotion histories in its databases, it can ensure all stores are fully stocked with adequate inventory. TruServ was able to achieve a positive return on investment in about five to six months.

## BI'S OPERATIONAL VALUE

A leading risk insurance company allows customers to access account information over the Internet. Previously, the company sent paper reports and diskettes to all of its customers. Any errors in the reports would take one to two months to correct because customers would first have to receive the report, catch the mistake, and then notify the company of the error. Now customers spot the errors in real time and notify the insurance company directly through an extranet, usually within a couple of days.

Richard Hackathorn of Bolder Technologies developed an interesting graph to demonstrate the value of operational BI. Figure B18.5 shows the three latencies that impact the speed of decision making. These are data, analysis, and decision latencies.

- **Data latency** is the time duration to make data ready for analysis (i.e., the time for extracting, transforming, and cleansing the data) and loading the data into the database. All this can take time depending on the state of the operational data to begin with.
- **Analysis latency** is the time from which data are made available to the time when analysis is complete. Its length depends on the time it takes a business

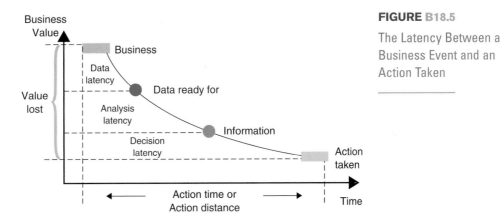

to do analysis. Usually, we think of this as the time it takes a human to do the analysis, but this can be decreased by the use of automated analytics that have thresholds. When the thresholds are exceeded, alerts or alarms can be issued to appropriate personnel, or they can cause exception processes to be initiated with no human intervention needed.

■ **Decision latency** is the time it takes a human to comprehend the analytic result and determine an appropriate action. This form of latency is very difficult to reduce. The ability to remove the decision-making process from the human and automate it will greatly reduce the overall decision latency. Many forward-thinking companies are doing just that. For example, rather than send a high-value customer a letter informing him of a bounced check (which takes days to get to the customer), an automated system can simply send an immediate email or voice message informing the customer of the problem.

The key is to shorten these latencies so that the time frame for opportunistic influences on customers, suppliers, and others is faster, more interactive, and better positioned. As mentioned above, the best time to influence customers is not after they have left the store or the website. It is while they are still in the store or still wandering around the website.

For example, a customer who is searching a website for travel deals is far more likely to be influenced by appropriate messaging actions then and there. Actions taken immediately, while customers are still in the site, might include:

■ Offering customers an appropriate coupon for the trip they showed interest in while searching for cheap airfares.

■ Giving customers information about their current purchase such as the suggestion that visas are needed.

■ Congratulating them on reaching a certain frequent-buyer level and giving them 10 percent off an item.

A website represents another great opportunity to influence a customer, if the interactions are appropriate and timely. For example:

■ A banner could announce the next best product to offer right after the customer puts an item in her basket.

■ The customer could receive an offer for a product he just removed from his shopping basket.

■ Appropriate instructions for the use of a product could come up on the customer's screen; perhaps warning a parent that the product should not be used by children under three.

# Data Mining

At the center of any strategic, tactical, or operational BI effort is data mining. Ruf Strategic Solutions helps organizations employ statistical approaches within a large data warehouse to identify customer segments that display common traits. Marketers can then target these segments with specially designed products and promotions. *Data mining* is the process of analyzing data to extract information not offered by the raw data alone. Data mining can also begin at a summary information level (coarse granularity) and progress through increasing levels of detail (drilling down), or the reverse (drilling up). Data mining is the primary tool used to uncover business intelligence in vast amounts of data.

To perform data mining, users need data-mining tools. *Data-mining tools* use a variety of techniques to find patterns and relationships in large volumes of information and infer rules from them that predict future behavior and guide decision making. Data mining uses specialized technologies and functionalities such as query tools, reporting tools, multidimensional analysis tools, statistical tools, and intelligent agents. Data mining approaches decision making with basically a few different activities in mind including:

- *Classification*—assign records to one of a predefined set of classes.
- *Estimation*—determine values for an unknown continuous variable behavior or estimated future value.
- *Affinity grouping*—determine which things go together.
- *Clustering*—segment a heterogeneous population of records into a number of more homogeneous subgroups.

Sega of America, one of the largest publishers of video games, uses data mining and statistical tools to distribute its advertising budget of more than $50 million a year. Using data mining, product line specialists and marketing strategists "drill" into trends of each retail store chain. Their goal is to find buying trends that help them determine which advertising strategies are working best and how to reallocate advertising resources by media, territory, and time.

Data-mining tools apply algorithms to information sets to uncover inherent trends and patterns in the information, which analysts use to develop new business strategies. Analysts use the output from data-mining tools to build models that, when exposed to new information sets, perform a variety of information analysis functions. The analysts provide business solutions by putting together the analytical techniques and the business problem at hand, which often reveals important new correlations, patterns, and trends. The more common forms of data-mining analysis capabilities include:

- Cluster analysis
- Association detection
- Statistical analysis.

## CLUSTER ANALYSIS

*Cluster analysis* is a technique used to divide an information set into mutually exclusive groups such that the members of each group are as close together as possible to one another and the different groups are as far apart as possible. Cluster analysis is frequently used to segment customer information for customer relationship management systems to help organizations identify customers with similar behavioral traits, such as clusters of best customers or onetime customers. Cluster analysis also has the ability to uncover naturally occurring patterns in information (see Figure B18.6).

Data-mining tools that "understand" human language are finding unexpected applications in medicine. IBM and the Mayo Clinic unearthed hidden patterns in

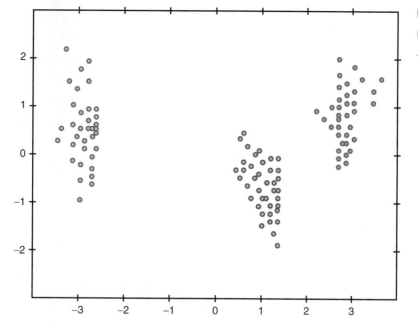

medical records, discovering that infant leukemia has three distinct clusters, each of which probably benefits from tailored treatments. Caroline A. Kovac, general manager of IBM Life Sciences, expects that mining the records of cancer patients for clustering patterns will turn up clues pointing the way to "tremendous strides in curing cancer."

A great example of cluster analysis occurs when attempting to segment customers based on zip codes. Understanding the demographics, lifestyle behaviors, and buying patterns of the most profitable segments of the population at the zip code level is key to a successful target marketing strategy. Targeting only those who have a high propensity to purchase products and services will help a high-end business cut its sales and marketing costs tremendously. Understanding each customer segment by zip code allows a business to determine the importance of each segment.

## ASSOCIATION DETECTION

Whirlpool Corporation, a $4.3 billion home and commercial appliance manufacturer, employs hundreds of R&D engineers, data analysts, quality assurance specialists, and customer service personnel who all work together to ensure that each generation of appliances is better than the previous generation. Whirlpool is an example of an organization that is gaining business intelligence with association detection data-mining tools.

*Association detection* reveals the degree to which variables are related and the nature and frequency of these relationships in the information. Whirlpool's warranty analysis tool, for instance, uses statistical analysis to automatically detect potential issues, provide quick and easy access to reports, and perform multidimensional analysis on all warranty information. This association detection data-mining tool enables Whirlpool's managers to take proactive measures to control product defects even before most of its customers are aware of the defect. The tool also allows Whirlpool personnel to devote more time to value-added tasks such as ensuring high quality on all products rather than waiting for or manually analyzing monthly reports.

Many people refer to association detection algorithms as *association rule generators* because they create rules to determine the likelihood of events occurring together at a particular time or following each other in a logical progression. Percentages usually reflect the patterns of these events; for example, "55 percent of the time, events A and B occurred together," or "80 percent of the time that items A and B occurred together, they were followed by item C within three days."

One of the most common forms of association detection analysis is market basket analysis. **Market basket analysis** analyzes such items as websites and checkout scanner information to detect customers' buying behavior and predict future behavior by identifying affinities among customers' choices of products and services (see Figure B18.7). Market basket analysis is frequently used to develop marketing campaigns for cross-selling products and services (especially in banking, insurance, and finance) and for inventory control, shelf-product placement, and other retail and marketing applications.

## STATISTICAL ANALYSIS

**Statistical analysis** performs such functions as information correlations, distributions, calculations, and variance analysis. Data-mining tools offer knowledge workers a wide range of powerful statistical capabilities so they can quickly build a variety of statistical models, examine the models' assumptions and validity, and compare and contrast the various models to determine the best one for a particular business issue.

Kraft is the producer of instantly recognizable food brands such as Oreo, Ritz, DiGiorno, and Kool-Aid. The company implemented two data-mining applications to assure consistent flavor, color, aroma, texture, and appearance for all of its food lines. One application analyzed product consistency and the other analyzed process variation reduction (PVR).

The product consistency tool, SENECA (Sensory and Experimental Collection Application), gathers and analyzes information by assigning precise definitions and numerical scales to such qualities as chewy, sweet, crunchy, and creamy. SENECA then builds models, histories, forecasts, and trends based on consumer testing and evaluates potential product improvements and changes.

The PVR tool ensures consistent flavor, color, aroma, texture, and appearance for every Kraft product since even small changes in the baking process can result in huge disparities in taste. Evaluating every manufacturing procedure, from recipe instructions to cookie dough shapes and sizes, the PVR tool has the potential to generate significant cost savings for each product. Using these types of data-mining techniques for quality control and cluster analysis makes sure that the billions of Kraft products that reach consumers annually will continue to taste great with every bite.

**FIGURE** B18.7

Market Basket Analysis

Forecasting is a common form of statistical analysis. Formally defined, ***forecasts*** are predictions made on the basis of time-series information. ***Time-series information*** is time-stamped information collected at a particular frequency. Examples of time-series information include web visits per hour, sales per month, and calls per day. Forecasting data-mining tools allow users to manipulate the time series for forecasting activities.

When discovering trends and seasonal variations in transactional information, use a time-series forecast to change the transactional information by units of time, such as transforming weekly information into monthly or seasonal information or hourly information into daily information. Companies base production, investment, and staffing decisions on a host of economic and market indicators in this manner. Forecasting models allow organizations to consider all sorts of variables when making decisions.

Nestlé Italiana is part of the multinational giant Nestlé Group and currently dominates Italy's food industry. The company improved sales forecasting by 25 percent with its data-mining forecasting solution that enables the company's managers to make objective decisions based on facts instead of subjective decisions based on intuition. Determining sales forecasts for seasonal confectionery products is a crucial and challenging task. During Easter, Nestlé Italiana has only four weeks to market, deliver, and sell its seasonal products. The Christmas time frame is a little longer, lasting from six to eight weeks, while other holidays such as Valentine's Day and Mother's Day have shorter time frames of about one week.

The company's data-mining solution gathers, organizes, and analyzes massive volumes of information to produce powerful models that identify trends and predict confectionery sales. The business intelligence created is based on five years of historical information and identifies what is important and what is not important. Nestlé Italiana's sophisticated data-mining tool predicted Mother's Day sales forecasts that were 90 percent accurate. The company has benefited from a 40 percent reduction in inventory and a 50 percent reduction in order changes, all due to its forecasting tool. Determining sales forecasts for seasonal confectionery products is now an area in which Nestlé Italiana excels.

Today, vendors such as Business Objects, Cognos, and SAS offer complete data-mining decision-making solutions. Moving forward, these companies plan to add more predictive analytical capabilities to their products. Their goal is to give companies more "what-if" scenario capabilities based on internal and external information.

# Business Benefits of BI

Rapid innovations in systems and data-mining tools are putting operational, tactical, and strategic BI at the fingertips of executives, managers, and even customers. With the successful implementation of BI systems an organization can expect to receive the following:

- **Single Point of Access to Information for All Users.** With a BI solution, organizations can unlock information held within their databases by giving authorized users a single point of access to data. Wherever the data reside, whether stored in operational systems, data warehouses, data marts and/or enterprise applications, users can prepare reports and drill deep down into the information to understand what drives their business, without technical knowledge of the underlying data structures. The most successful BI applications allow users to do this with an easy-to-understand, nontechnical, graphical user interface.

- **BI across Organizational Departments.** There are many different uses for BI and one of its greatest benefits is that it can be used at every step in the value chain.

All departments across an organization from sales to operations to customer service can benefit from the value of BI.

Volkswagen AG uses BI to track, understand, and manage data in every department—from finance, production, and development, to research, sales and marketing, and purchasing. Users at all levels of the organization access supplier and customer reports relating to online requests and negotiations, vehicle launches, and vehicle capacity management and tracking.

- **Up-to-the-Minute Information for Everyone.** The key to unlocking information is to give users the tools to quickly and easily find immediate answers to their questions. Some users will be satisfied with standard reports that are updated on a regular basis, such as current inventory reports, sales per channel, or customer status reports. However, the answers these reports yield can lead to new questions. Some users will want dynamic access to information. The information that a user finds in a report will trigger more questions, and these questions will not be answered in a prepackaged report.

While users may spend 80 percent of their time accessing standard or personalized reports, for 20 percent of their tasks, they need to obtain additional information not available in the original report. To address this need and to avoid frustration (and related report backlog for the IT team), a BI system should let users autonomously make ad hoc requests for information from corporate data sources.

For merchants of MasterCard International, access to BI offers the opportunity to monitor their businesses more closely on a day-to-day basis. Advertising agencies are able to use information from an extranet when developing campaigns for merchants. On the authorization side, a call center can pull up cardholder authorization transactions to cut down on fraud. MasterCard expects that in the long term and as business partners increasingly demand access to system data, the system will support more than 20,000 external users.

## CATEGORIES OF BI BENEFITS

Management is no longer prepared to sink large sums of money into IT projects simply because they are the latest and greatest technology. Information technology has come of age, and it is expected to make a significant contribution to the bottom line.

When looking at how BI affects the bottom line, an organization should analyze not only the organizationwide business benefits, but also the various benefits it can expect to receive from a BI deployment. A practical way of breaking down these numerous benefits is to separate them into four main categories:

1. Quantifiable benefits.
2. Indirectly quantifiable benefits.
3. Unpredictable benefits.
4. Intangible benefits.

### Quantifiable Benefits

Quantifiable benefits include working time saved in producing reports, selling information to suppliers, and so on. A few examples include:

- Moët et Chandon, the famous champagne producer, reduced its IT costs from approximately 30 cents per bottle to 15 cents per bottle.
- A leading risk insurance company provides customers with self-service access to their information in the insurance company's database and no longer sends

paper reports. This one benefit alone saves the organization $400,000 a year in printing and shipping costs. The total three-year ROI for this BI deployment was 249 percent.

- Ingram Micro, a wholesale provider of high-tech goods and technology solutions providers, is working to create a new BI extranet to deliver advanced information to the company's suppliers and business partners. Says Ingram Micro CIO Guy Abramo, "Today it's incumbent on us to provide our partners with sell-through information so they can see what happened once their PCs hit distribution. That's critical for them to do inventory planning and manufacturing planning— helping them to understand what products are selling to what segments of the marketplace."

## Indirectly Quantifiable Benefits

Indirectly quantifiable benefits can be evaluated through indirect evidence— improved customer service means new business from the same customer, and differentiated service brings new customers. A few examples include:

- A customer of Owens & Minor cited extranet access to the data warehouse as the primary reason for giving the medical supplies distributor an additional $44 million in business.

- "When salespeople went out to visit TaylorMade's customers at golf pro shops and sporting goods retail chains, they didn't have up-to-date inventory reports. The sales reps would take orders for clubs, accessories, and clothing without confidence that the goods were available for delivery as promised," Tom Collard, information systems director with TaylorMade, said. "The technology has helped TaylorMade not only reduce costs by eliminating the reporting backlog . . . it has eliminated a lot of wasted effort that resulted from booking orders that it couldn't fill."

## Unpredictable Benefits

Unpredictable benefits are the result of discoveries made by creative users; a few examples include:

- Volkswagen's finance BI system allowed an interesting discovery that later resulted in significant new revenue. The customers of a particular model of the Audi product line had completely different behaviors than customers of other cars. Based on their socioeconomic profiles, they were thought to want long lease terms and fairly large up-front payments. Instead, the information revealed that Audi customers actually wanted shorter leases and to finance a large part of the purchase through the lease. Based on that insight, the company immediately introduced a new program combining shorter length of lease, larger upfront payments, and aggressive leasing rates, especially for that car model. The interest in the new program was immediate, resulting in over $2 million in new revenue.

- Peter Blundell, former knowledge strategy manager for British Airways, and various company executives had a suspicion that the carrier was suffering from a high degree of ticket fraud. To address this problem, Blundell and his team rolled out business intelligence. "Once we analyzed the data, we found that this ticket fraud was not an issue at all. What we had supposed was fraud was in fact either data quality issues or process problems," Blundell said. "What it did was give us so many unexpected opportunities in terms of understanding our business." Blundell estimated that the BI deployment has resulted in around $100 million in cost savings and new revenues for the airline.

## Intangible Benefits

Intangible benefits include improved communication throughout the enterprise, improved job satisfaction of empowered users, and improved knowledge sharing. A few examples include:

- The corporate human resources department at ABN AMRO Bank uses BI to gain insight into its workforce by analyzing information on such items as gender, age, tenure, and compensation. Thanks to this sharing of intellectual capital, the HR department is in a better position to demonstrate its performance and contribution to the business successes of the corporation as a whole.

- Ben & Jerry's uses BI to track, understand, and manage information on the thousands of consumer responses it receives on its products and promotional activities. Through daily customer feedback analysis, Ben & Jerry's is able to identify trends and modify its marketing campaigns and its products to suit consumer demand.

Most corporations today are inundated with data—from their own internal operational systems, their vendors, suppliers, and customers and from other external sources such as credit bureaus or industry sales data. The problem with understanding where your company is going is not in the amount of data coming into it. The problem is that this tidal wave of data is not in a form that can easily be digested, comprehended, or even accessed. Ask simple questions like who are your best customers or what are your most profitable products and you will most likely get as many answers as there are employees. Not a comforting position to have in today's era of economic stress.

This is where business intelligence or BI comes in. The goal of BI is to provide the enterprise with a repository of "trusted" data—data that can be used in a multitude of applications to answer the questions about customers, products, supply and demand chains, production inefficiencies, financial trends, fraud, and even employees. It can be used to flag anomalies via alerts, provide visualization and statistical models, and understand the cause and effects of decisions upon the enterprise. Just about every aspect of an enterprise's business can benefit from the insights garnered from BI.

You, as a business student, must understand how technology can help you make intelligent decisions. But at the end of the day, how you interact with a customer face-to-face is the real test of your ability to foster and promote healthy customer relations.

### ✳ KEY TERMS

Affinity grouping 472
Analysis latency 470
Association detection 473
Business intelligence (BI), 466
Classification 472
Cluster analysis 472

Clustering 472
Data latency 470
Data mining 472
Data-mining tools 472
Decision latency 471
Estimation 472

Forecasts 475
Market basket analysis 474
Statistical analysis 474
Time-series information 475

### ✳ CLOSING CASE ONE

#### Intelligent Business: Is It an Oxymoron?

In a pilot program by the State of New York, suburban Rockland County announced that it had uncovered $13 million in improper Medicaid claims made over a 21-month period. Because the problems were discovered before the reimbursements were made, Rockland saved itself the headaches it would have faced if it had paid out the money first and asked questions later.

The credit goes not to a crew of hardworking sleuths but to search and analysis software created by IBM that automatically sorted through thousands of forms, plucked out key bits of information, and sized them up against Medicaid rules. Government officials believe that if the program were to be applied statewide, it could deliver $3.8 billion in savings per year. "This may change the Medicaid industry in New York," said Rockland County Supervisor C. Scott Vanderhoef.

This is just one example of a change in the way corporations and governments find and use information. Data are becoming much easier to access and vastly more useful.

### Better Understanding

Organizations have huge amounts of data that pass through their computer systems as they place orders, record sales, and otherwise transact business. Much of this information is stored for future use and analysis. But advances in software and hardware make it easier for companies to analyze data in real time—when the data are first whizzing through their computers—and make them available to all kinds of employees.

Technological innovations also make it possible to analyze unstructured data, such as Rockland County's Medicaid claims, that do not easily fit into the tables of a traditional database. The result of all these changes: It is now possible for companies to understand what is happening in their businesses in a detailed way and quickly take actions based on that knowledge.

These improvements have come largely as a result of advances in business intelligence software. This software—a $3 billion segment growing at about 7 percent a year—gathers information in data warehouses where it can easily be reviewed, analyzes the data, and presents reports to decision makers. In the past, the reports had to be painstakingly assembled by tech-savvy business analysts and were typically made available only to top-tier people.

### Personal Google

Information easily available to anybody in an organization is a phenomenon industry folks have dubbed "pervasive business intelligence." Companies are moving from a place where only the more technical people had access to information to more of a self-service situation. People can get information themselves, said Christina McKeon, global business intelligence strategist for software maker SAS Institute, based in Cary, North Carolina.

SAS and other BI software makers are reaching out to the masses in a variety of ways. Several of them have hooked up with search leader Google to give businesspeople easier access to those data warehouses via the familiar Google search bar. They have redesigned their business intelligence web portals so people who do Google searches get not only documents that include their keywords, but also others that are thematically related.

For instance, if a business-unit leader searches for first-quarter financial results, he might also get reports on the 10 largest customers in the quarter and the customers who deliver the most profits. "The data warehouse is starting to go mainstream," said analyst Mark Beyer of tech market researcher Gartner.

### Directing Traffic

Business intelligence is also being added to other standard run-the-business applications, such as order fulfillment, logistics, inventory management, and the like. Consider a busy warehouse with a limited number of loading docks. Trucking companies do not want their rigs to wait in line for hours, so some of them charge fees for waiting time at the warehouse.

To avoid those costs, companies can build business intelligence into their logistics planning systems that lets them know when trucks are stacking up and directs supervisors in the warehouse to load the trucks that charge waiting fees before those that do not. The supervisors get this information via their PCs or handhelds on the warehouse floor. People are receiving the benefit of business intelligence without knowing it, said Randy Lea, vice president for product and services marketing at Teradata, a division of NCR, a leader in data warehousing software.

This kind of real-time, behind-the-curtains intelligence is even becoming available to end customers. Travelocity, one of the leading travel websites, has long used business intelligence software to help it analyze buying trends and segment customer types so new services can be tailored for them. Now it has rigged its vast data warehouse directly to its consumer website so it can gather and analyze information about what is going on as it is happening.

### Computer Intuition

Travelocity links the profile of individual customers who are on the site to a monitor of their current activity and to information about available airplane flights, rental cars, and vacation packages. If a customer begins asking about flights to Orlando over the fourth of July weekend, Travelocity's system will understand that the customer is probably planning a family vacation and will place advertisements that are relevant to that kind of trip and even pitch special travel promotions. "If we want to, we could give every customer a custom offer," said Mark Hooper, Travelocity's vice president for product development.

What is next in easy-to-use business intelligence? Gartner has a concept it calls "Biggle"—the intersection of BI and Google. The idea is that the data warehousing software will be so sophisticated that it understands when different people use different words to describe the same concepts or products. It creates an index of related information—á là Google—and dishes relevant results out in response to queries.

In computer science, they refer to this capability as non-obvious relationship awareness. "Nobody's doing this yet," said Gartner's Beyer. Judging from the speed of recent advances in business intelligence, though, it may not be long before companies add the term "Biggling" to their tech lexicon.

## Questions

1. What is the problem of gathering business intelligence from a traditional company? How can BI solve this problem?
2. Choose one of the three common forms of data-mining analysis and explain how Travelocity could use it to gain BI.
3. How will tactical, operational, and strategic BI be different when applied to personal Google?
4. How is IBM's search and analysis software an example of BI?
5. What does the term *pervasive business intelligence* mean?
6. How could any business benefit from technology such as personal Google?
7. How could a company use BI to improve its supply chain?
8. Highlight any security and ethical issues associated with Biggle.

---

★ CLOSING CASE TWO

### The Brain behind the Big, Bad Burger and Other Tales of Business Intelligence

Jay Leno, the *New York Times,* and health nutrition advocacy groups have commented on the newest Hardee's fast-food item "The Monster Thickburger," which consists of:

- Two charbroiled 100 percent Angus beef patties, each weighing in at a third of a pound (150 grams)
- Three slices of processed cheese
- Four crispy strips of bacon
- Dollop of mayonnaise
- Toasted butter sesame seed bun

The Monster Thickburger sounds like a hungry person's dream and the dieter's worst nightmare. Yes, this delicious sounding burger nirvana contains 1,420 calories (5945 kilojoules) and an artery-clogging 107 grams of fat. Even though the Monster Thickburger is one of the most fattening burgers on the market—not to mention that most people add a coke and fries to their order—it is selling like crazy, according to Jeff Chasney, CIO and executive vice president of strategic planning at CKE Restaurants, the company that owns and operates Hardee's.

With the national diet obsession and health-related warnings concerning obesity, most fast-food companies probably would never have even put the Monster Thickburger on the menu. CKE confidently introduced the Monster Thickburger nationwide convinced that the product would sell based on intelligence the company obtained from its business intelligence (BI) system. CKE's BI system—known ironically inside the company as CPR (CKE Performance Reporting)—monitored the performance of burger sales in numerous test markets to determine the monster burger's increase to sales and ensure it was not simply cannibalizing other burger sales. CKE monitored several variables including menu mixes, production costs, Thickburger sales, overall burger sales, profit increases, and Thickburger's contribution to the stores' bottom-line. Using its BI system CKE quickly determine that the production costs of the Thickburger were minimal compared to the increase in sales. Armed with burger intelligence CKE confidently paid $7 million in advertising and successfully released the burger nationwide. In its first quarter sales of the burger exceeded CKE's expectations and the company knew the $7 million it paid in advertising was a smart investment.

Hardee's, Wendy's, Ruby Tuesday, T.G.I. Friday's and others are heavy users of BI software. Many of the big chains have been using BI for the past 10 years, according to Chris Hartmann, managing director of technology strategies at HVS International, a restaurant and hospitality consultancy. The restaurants use operational BI to determine everything from which menu items to add and remove to which locations to close. They use tactical BI for renegotiating contracts and identifying opportunities to improve inefficient processes. BI is an essential tool for operational-driven restaurants and if implemented correctly they can highlight operational efficiency and effectiveness such as:

- Carlson Restaurants Worldwide (T.G.I. Friday's, Pick Up Stix) saved $200,000 by renegotiating contracts with food suppliers based on discrepancies between contract prices and the prices suppliers were actually charging restaurants. Carlson's BI system, which at the time was from Cognos, had identified these discrepancies.

- Ruby Tuesday's profits and revenue have grown by at least 20 percent each year as a result of the improvements the chain has made to its menu and operations based on insights provided by its BI infrastructure, which consists of a data warehouse, analytical tools from Cognos and Hyperion, and reporting tools from Microsoft.

- CPR helped CKE, which was on the brink of bankruptcy, increase sales at restaurants open more than a year, narrow its overall losses and even turn a profit in 2003. A home-grown proprietary system, CPR consists of a Microsoft SQL server database and uses Microsoft development tools to parse and display analytical information.

- In June 2003, Wendy's decided to accept credit cards in its restaurants based on information it got from its BI systems. Because of that decision, Wendy's restaurants have boosted sales; customers who use a credit card spend an average of 35 percent more per order than those who use cash, according to Wendy's executive vice president and CIO John Deane.

Other industries could learn a great deal about BI by analyzing such strategic use of BI. "Most BI implementations fall below the midpoint on the scale of success," says Ted Friedman, an analyst with Gartner. It appears that the restaurant industry has avoided the three common barriers to BI success by cleansing voluminous amounts of irrelevant data, ensuring high-data quality, and decreasing user resistance.

## Questions

1. What does business intelligence really mean to a business? How did CPR save millions for CKE?
2. What are the negative impacts of CKE's business intelligence?
3. Explain the three forms of data-mining analysis and explain how CKE can use it to gain BI.
4. How can CKE use tactical, operational, and strategic BI?
5. What types of ethical and security issues could CKE face from CPR?

### 1. Gaining Business Intelligence from Strategic Initiatives

You are a new employee in the customer service department at Premier One, a large pet food distributor. The company, founded by several veterinarians, has been in business for three years and focuses on providing nutritious pet food at a low cost. The company currently has 90 employees and operates in seven states. Sales over the past three years have tripled, and the manual systems currently in place are no longer sufficient to run the business. Your first task is to meet with your new team and create a presentation for the president and chief executive officer describing tactical, operational, and strategic business intelligence. The presentation should highlight the main benefits Premier One can receive from business intelligence along with any additional added business value that can be gained from the systems.

### 2. Second Life BI

The virtual world of Second Life could become the first point of contact between companies and customers and could transform the whole customer experience. Since it began hosting the likes of Adidas, Dell, Reuters, and Toyota, Second Life has become technology's equivalent of India or China—everyone needs an office and a strategy involving it to keep their shareholders happy. But beyond opening a shiny new building in the virtual world, what can such companies do with their virtual real estate?

Like many other big brands, PA Consulting has its own offices in Second Life and has learned that simply having an office to answer customer queries is not enough. Real people, albeit behind avatars, must be staffing the offices—in the same way having a website is not enough if there is not a call center to back it up when a would-be customer wants to speak to a human being. The consultants believe call centers could one day ask customers to follow up a phone call with them by moving the query into a virtual world.

Unlike many corporate areas in the virtual world, the National Basketball Association incorporates capabilities designed to keep fans coming back, including real-time 3-D diagrams of games as they are being played.

You are the executive director of BI at StormPeak, an advanced AI company that develops robots. You are in charge of overseeing the first virtual site being built in Second Life. Create a BI strategy for gathering information in a virtual world. Here are a few questions to get you started:

- How will gathering BI for a business be different in a virtual world?
- How can BI help a business become more efficient in a virtual world?
- How will supporting BI in Second Life differ from supporting BI in a traditional company?
- What BI security issues might you encounter in Second Life?
- What BI ethical issues might you encounter in Second Life?

### 3. Searching for BI

Imagine being able to Google customer phone requests for information, sort through the recorded files of customer complaint calls, or decipher the exact moment when an interaction between a customer and store employee went awry. Being able to query voice records using the same methods as querying textual ones would open up boundless areas of business opportunity. Web surfers can already search audio files and audio/video feeds, but now enterprise can use this technology to help employees search voice mails or recorded calls for keywords and phrases, and, in the end, to decode important customer concerns.

You have recently started your own marketing firm. You have built a BI tool that allows customers to query all of their unique data stores. Now all you need is to prepare your marketing materials to send to potential customers. Create a marketing pitch that you will deliver to customers detailing the business opportunities they could uncover if they purchase your product. Your marketing pitch can be a one-page document, a catchy tune, a video, or a PowerPoint presentation.

### 4. Mining Physician Data

NPR recently released a story discussing how large pharmaceutical companies are mining physician data. Thousands of pharmaceutical drug company sales representatives visit doctors and try to entice them to prescribe their company's newest drugs. The pharmaceutical companies buy prescription information from pharmacies all over the country describing which drugs are prescribed by which doctors. There is no patient information in the data. The sales representatives receive this BI from their companies and can tailor their sales pitch based on what that particular doctor has been prescribing to patients. Many doctors do not even realize that the sales representatives have this information and know exactly what drugs each individual doctor prescribes. The drug companies love mining data, but critics contend it is an invasion of privacy and drives up the cost of health care. Maine has just become the third state to pass a measure limiting access to the data.

You are working for your state government and your boss has asked you to create an argument for or against pharmaceutical data mining of physician data in your state. A few questions to get you started:

Do you agree that mining physician data should be illegal? Why or why not?

As a patient how do you feel about pharmaceutical companies mining your doctor's data?

As an employee of one of the pharmaceutical companies how do you feel about mining physician data?

### 5. The Value of Plastic

Accepting credit cards at Wendy's restaurants was a big decision facing corporate executives in early 2003. There was no doubt that customers would appreciate the convenience of plastic, but could this option hurt overall sales? Wendy's executives decided that the best way to determine the value of plastic was to test it at several stores. The BI system was set to monitor how a credit card purchase affects sales, service speed, and cash sales. The intelligence gained from the system told executives that plastic sales were typically 35 percent higher than cash sales. Case sales typically include a value meal—great for the customer but less profitable for the store. Plastic customers showed a trend of purchasing a la carte items generating a higher bill. Armed with BI Wendy's introduced credit card readers nationally in June 2003.

You are the vice president of BI for McDonald's restaurants. The board of directors would like you to generate a report discussing the details of how you can use BI to analyze sales trends of menu items for all of its restaurants, including international locations. Identify several different variables you would monitor to determine menu item sales trends.

# Global Information Systems

1. Explain the cultural, political, and geoeconomic challenges facing global businesses.
2. Describe the four global IT business drivers that should be included in all IT strategies.
3. Describe governance and compliance and the associated frameworks an organization can implement.
4. Identify why an organization would need to understand global enterprise architectures when expanding operations abroad.
5. Explain the many different global information issues an organization might encounter as it conducts business abroad.
6. Identify global system development issues organizations should understand before building a global system.

## Introduction

Whether they are in Berlin or Bombay, Kuala Lumpur or Kansas City, San Francisco or Seoul, organizations around the globe are developing new business models to operate competitively in a digital economy. These models are structured, yet agile; global, yet local; and they concentrate on maximizing the risk-adjusted return from both knowledge and technology assets.

Globalization and working in an international global economy are integral parts of business today. Fortune 500 companies to mom-and-pop shops are now competing globally, and international developments affect all forms of business.

## Globalization

According to Thomas Friedman, the world is flat! Businesses are strategizing and operating on a global playing field. Traditional forms of business are simply not good enough in a global environment. Recall the way the Internet is changing

| Industry | Business Changes Due to Technology |
|---|---|
| Travel | Travel site Expedia.com is now the biggest leisure-travel agency, with higher profit margins than even American Express. Thirteen percent of traditional travel agencies closed in 2002 because of their inability to compete with online travel. |
| Entertainment | The music industry has kept Napster and others from operating, but $35 billion annual online downloads are wrecking the traditional music business. U.S. music unit sales are down 20 percent since 2000. The next big entertainment industry to feel the effects of ebusiness will be the $67 billion movie business. |
| Electronics | Using the Internet to link suppliers and customers, Dell dictates industry profits. Its operating margins rose from 7.3 percent in 2002 to 8 percent in 2003, even as it took prices to levels where rivals couldn't make money. |
| Financial services | Nearly every public efinance company remaining makes money, with online mortgage service LendingTree growing 70 percent a year. Processing online mortgage applications is now 40 percent cheaper for customers. |
| Retail | Less than 5 percent of retail sales occur online, but eBay was on track in 2003 to become one of the nation's top 15 retailers, and Amazon.com will join the top 40. Wal-Mart's ebusiness strategy is forcing rivals to make heavy investments in technology. |
| Automobiles | The cost of producing vehicles is down because of SCM and web-based purchasing. Also, eBay has become the leading U.S. used-car dealer, and most major car sites are profitable. |
| Education and training | Cisco saved $133 million in 2002 by moving training sessions to the Internet, and the University of Phoenix online college classes please investors. |

**FIGURE B19.1**

Examples of How the Internet Is Changing Business

business by reviewing Figure B19.1. To succeed in a global business environment, cultural, political, and geoeconomic (geographic and economic) business challenges must be confronted.

## CULTURAL BUSINESS CHALLENGES

Cultural business challenges include differences in languages, cultural interests, religions, customs, social attitudes, and political philosophies. Global businesses must be sensitive to such cultural differences. McDonald's, a truly global brand, has created several minority-specific websites in the United States: McEncanta for Hispanics, 365Black for African-Americans, and i-am-asian for Asians. But these minority groups are not homogenous. Consider Asians: There are East Asian, Southeast Asian, Asian Indian, and, within each of these, divisions of national, regional, and linguistic nature. No company has the budget to create a separate website for every subsegment, but to assume that all Asian Americans fit into a single room—even a virtual room—risks a serious backlash. A company should ask a few key questions when creating a global website:

- Will the site require new navigational logic to accommodate cultural preferences?
- Will content be translated? If so, into how many languages?
- Will multilingual efforts be included in the main site or will it be a separate site, perhaps with a country-specific domain?
- Which country will the server be located in to support local user needs?
- What legal ramifications might occur by having the website targeted at a particular country, such as laws on competitive behaviors, treatment of children, or privacy?

## POLITICAL BUSINESS CHALLENGES

Political business challenges include the numerous rules and regulations surrounding data transfers across national boundaries, especially personal information, tax implications, hardware and software importing and exporting, and trade agreements. The protection of personal information is a real concern for all countries. For example, evidence from a national survey about citizen satisfaction with the Canadian government online services speaks to the importance of paying attention to privacy concerns. This highly publicized survey, known as Citizens First, was administered by the Institute for Citizen-Centered Service (ICCS) and the Institute for Public Administration in Canada (IPCA). Results from the survey indicate that although other factors help promote citizen satisfaction with the Internet, such as ease of finding information, sufficient information, site navigation, and visual appeal, the key driver that directly impacts whether citizens will conduct online transactions is their concerns over information security and privacy.

For security, there are high levels of concerns over information storage, transmission, and access and identity verification. For privacy and the protection of personal information, there are even stronger concerns about consolidation of information, unauthorized access, and sharing without permission.

## GLOBAL GEOECONOMIC BUSINESS CHALLENGES

*Geoeconomic* refers to the effects of geography on the economic realities of international business activities. Even with the Internet, telecommunications, and air travel, the sheer physical distances covering the globe make it difficult to operate multinational business. Flying IT specialists into remote sites is costly, communicating in real-time across the globe's 24 time zones is challenging, and finding quality telecommunication services in every country is difficult. Skilled labor supplies, cost of living, and labor costs also differ among the various countries. When developing global business strategies, all of these geoeconomic challenges must be addressed.

Understanding the cultural, political, and geoeconomic business challenges is a good start to understanding global business, but the problems facing managers run far deeper. The remainder of this plug-in focuses on business management issues that are central to all global business. Business managers must understand four primary areas—global IT business strategies, global enterprise architectures, global information issues, and global systems development—when running multinational companies (see Figure B19.2).

**FIGURE** B19.2

Global IT Business Management Areas

## Global IT Business Strategies

Global IT business strategies must include detailed information on the application of information technology across the organization. IT systems depend on global business drivers such as the nature of the industry, competitive factors, and environmental forces. For example, airlines and hotels have global customers who travel extensively and expect the same service regardless of location. Organizations require global IT systems that can provide fast, convenient service to all international employees who are servicing these customers. When a high-end hotel customer checks into a hotel in Asia she expects to receive the same high-end service as when she is checking into a hotel in Chicago or London. Figure B19.3 displays the global IT business drivers that should be included in all IT strategies.

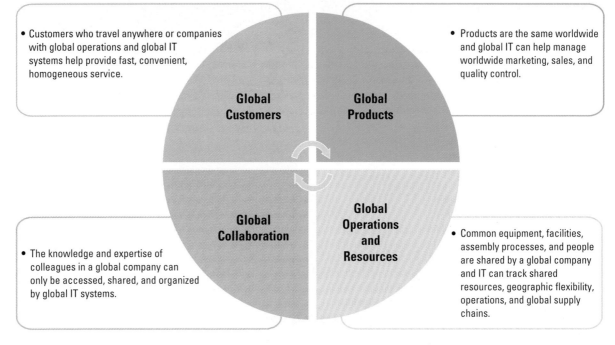

- Customers who travel anywhere or companies with global operations and global IT systems help provide fast, convenient, homogeneous service.

**Global Customers**

**Global Products**

- Products are the same worldwide and global IT can help manage worldwide marketing, sales, and quality control.

**Global Collaboration**

**Global Operations and Resources**

- The knowledge and expertise of colleagues in a global company can only be accessed, shared, and organized by global IT systems.

- Common equipment, facilities, assembly processes, and people are shared by a global company and IT can track shared resources, geographic flexibility, operations, and global supply chains.

**FIGURE** B19.3

Global IT Business Drivers

Many global IT systems, such as finance, accounting, and operations management, have been in operation for years. Most multinational companies have global financial budgeting and cash management. As global operations expand and global competition heats up, pressure increases for companies to install global ebusiness applications for customers, suppliers, and employees. Examples include portals and websites geared toward customer service and supply chain management. In the past, such systems relied almost exclusively on privately constructed or government-owned telecommunications networks. But the explosive business use of the Internet, intranets, and extranets for electronic commerce has made such applications more feasible for global companies.

## GOVERNANCE AND COMPLIANCE

One fast-growing key area for all global business strategies is governance and compliance. *Governance* is a method or system of government for management or control. *Compliance* is the act of conforming, acquiescing, or yielding. A few years ago the ideas of governance and compliance were relatively obscure. Today, the concept of formal IT governance and compliance is a must for virtually every company, both domestic and global. Key drivers for governance and compliance include financial and technological regulations as well as pressure from shareholders and customers.

Organizations today are subject to many regulations governing data retention, confidential information, financial accountability, and recovery from disasters. By implementing IT governance, organizations have the internal controls they need to meet the core guidelines of many of these regulations, such as the Sarbanes-Oxley Act of 2002.

IT governance essentially places structure around how organizations align IT strategy with business strategy, ensuring that companies stay on track to achieve their strategies and goals, and implementing good ways to measure IT's performance. Governance makes sure that all stakeholders' interests are considered and that processes provide measurable results. IT governance should answer key questions including how the IT department is functioning overall, what key metrics management requires, and what return the business is getting from its IT investment. Figure B19.4 displays the five key areas of focus according to the IT Governance Institute.

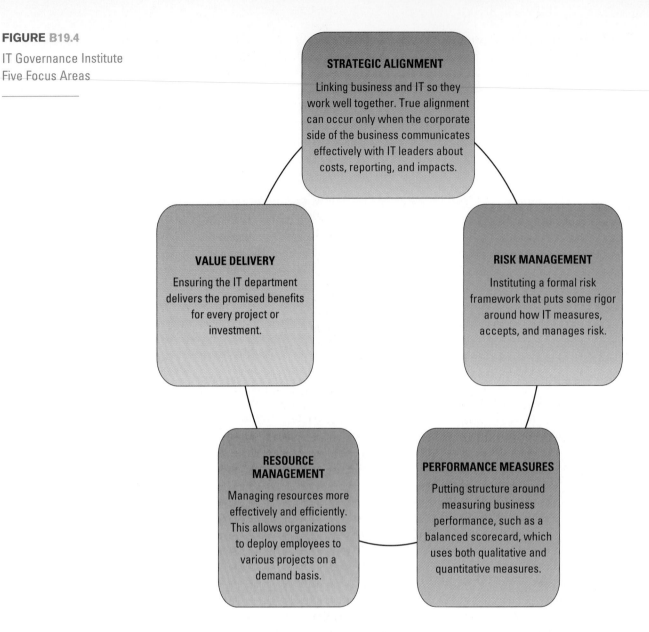

**STRATEGIC ALIGNMENT**

Linking business and IT so they work well together. True alignment can occur only when the corporate side of the business communicates effectively with IT leaders about costs, reporting, and impacts.

**VALUE DELIVERY**

Ensuring the IT department delivers the promised benefits for every project or investment.

**RISK MANAGEMENT**

Instituting a formal risk framework that puts some rigor around how IT measures, accepts, and manages risk.

**RESOURCE MANAGEMENT**

Managing resources more effectively and efficiently. This allows organizations to deploy employees to various projects on a demand basis.

**PERFORMANCE MEASURES**

Putting structure around measuring business performance, such as a balanced scorecard, which uses both qualitative and quantitative measures.

Organizations can follow a few different IT governance frameworks, including:

- **CoBIT:** *Information Systems Audit and Control Association (ISACA)* is a set of guidelines and supporting tools for IT governance that is accepted worldwide and generally used by auditors and companies as a way to integrate technology to implement controls and meet specific business objectives.

- **ITIL:** The *Information Technology Infrastructure Library (ITIL)* is a framework provided by the government of the United Kingdom and offers eight sets of management procedures: (1) service delivery, (2) service support, (3) service management, (4) Information and Communication Technology (ICT) infrastructure management, (5) software asset management, (6) business perspective, (7) security management, and (8) application management. ITIL is a good fit for organizations concerned about operations.

- **COSO:** The framework developed by the *Committee of Sponsoring Organizations (COSO)* is key for evaluating internal controls such as human resources, logistics, information technology, risk, legal, marketing and sales, operations, financial functions, procurement, and reporting. This is a more business-general framework that is less IT-specific.

- **CMMI:** Created by a group from government, industry, and Carnegie Mellon's Software Engineering Institute, the **Capability Maturity Model Integration method (CMMI)** is a process improvement approach that contains 22 process areas. It is divided into appraisal, evaluation, and structure. CMMI is particularly well-suited to organizations that need help with application development, life cycle issues, and improving the delivery of products throughout the life cycle.

# Global Enterprise Architectures

An **enterprise architecture** includes the plans for how an organization will build, deploy, use, and share its data, processes, and IT assets. An organization must manage its global enterprise architecture to support its global business operations. Management of a global enterprise architecture is not only technically complex, but also has major political and cultural implications. For example, hardware choices are difficult in some countries because of high prices, high tariffs, import restrictions, long lead times for government approvals, lack of local service or replacement parts, and lack of documentation tailored to local conditions. Software choices also present issues; for example, European data standards differ from American or Asian standards, even when purchased from the same vendor. Some software vendors also refuse to offer service and support in countries that disregard software licensing and copyright agreements.

The Internet and the World Wide Web are critical to international business. This interconnected matrix of computers, information, and networks that reaches tens of millions of users in hundreds of countries is a business environment free of traditional boundaries and limits. Linking to online global businesses offers companies unprecedented potential for expanding markets, reducing costs, and improving profit margins at a price that is typically a small percentage of the corporate communications budget. The Internet provides an interactive channel for direct communication and data exchange with customers, suppliers, distributors, manufacturers, product developers, financial backers, information providers—in fact, with all parties involved in an international organization.

The Paris-based organization Reporters Without Borders notes that 45 countries restrict their citizens' access to the Internet. "At its most fundamental, the struggle between Internet censorship and openness at the national level revolves around three main means: controlling the conduits, filtering the flows, and punishing the purveyors. In countries such as Burma, Libya, North Korea, Syria, and the countries of Central Asia and the Caucasus, Internet access is either banned or subject to tight limitations through government-controlled ISPs. These countries face a lose-lose struggle against the information age. By denying or limiting Internet access, they stymie a major engine of economic growth. But by easing access, they expose their citizenry to ideas potentially destabilizing to the status quo. Either way, many people will get access to the electronic information they want. In Syria, for example, people go to Lebanon for the weekend to retrieve their email," said Virgini Locussol, Reporters Without Borders desk officer for the Middle East and North Africa.

Figure B19.5 displays the top 10 international telecommunication issues as reported by the IT executives at 300 Fortune 500 multinational companies. Political issues dominate the listing over technology issues, clearly emphasizing their importance in the management of global enterprise architectures.

Estimating the operational expenses associated with international IT operations is another global challenge. Companies with global business operations usually establish or contract with systems integrators for additional IT facilities for their subsidiaries in other countries. These IT facilities must meet local and regional computing needs, and even help balance global computing workloads through communications satellite links. However, offshore IT facilities can pose major problems in headquarters' support, hardware and software acquisition, maintenance, and

**Network**
- Improving the operational efficiency of networks
- Dealing with different networks
- Controlling data communication security

**Regulatory Issues**
- Dealing with transborder data flow restrictions
- Managing international telecommunication regulations
- Handling international politics

**Technology and Country-Oriented Issues**
- Managing network infrastructure across countries
- Managing international integration of technologies
- Reconciling national differences
- Dealing with international tariff structures

security. This is why many global companies prefer to outsource these facilities to application service providers or systems integrators such as IBM or Accenture to manage overseas operations. Managing global enterprise architectures, including Internet, intranet, extranet, and other telecommunication networks, is a key global IT challenge for the 21st century.

## Global Information Issues

While many consumer gadgets and software applications can benefit a company—for instance, by helping employees get their jobs done more efficiently—the security implications are legion, said Ken Silva, chief security officer at VeriSign, which specializes in network security software. "When we bolt those things onto corporate networks, we open up holes in the environment." Drugmaker Pfizer found this out the hard way. An employee's spouse loaded file-sharing software onto a Pfizer laptop at home, creating a security hole that appears to have compromised the names and Social Security numbers of 17,000 current and former Pfizer employees, according to a letter Pfizer sent to state attorneys general. Pfizer's investigation showed that 15,700 of those employees actually had their data accessed and copied.

Rather than fight the trend, some companies are experimenting with giving employees more choice regarding the technology they use—so long as they accept more responsibility for it. In 2005, BP began a pilot project that gives employees about $1,000 to spend on productivity-enhancing tools in addition to standard-issue equipment, according to a report from the Leading Edge Forum. But before they can participate, employees must pass a test of their computer literacy skills.

The company takes other steps to give employees free rein while mitigating risk. BP cordons off its network by letting employees link to the Internet via consumer connections, from outside the firewall, in the case of its 18,000 laptops. At the same time it beefs up security on those machines. This lets employees safely experiment with software such as Amazon's on-demand computing and storage services.

***Deperimeterization*** occurs when an organization moves employees outside its firewall, a growing movement to change the way corporations address technology security. In a business world where many employees are off-site or on the road, or where businesses increasingly must collaborate with partners and customers, some say it's not practical to rely on a hardened perimeter of firewalls. Instead, proponents of deperimeterization say companies should focus on beefing up security in end-user devices and organization's critical information assets.

## INFORMATION PRIVACY

For many years, global data access issues have been the subject of political controversy and technology barriers in global business environments. These issues have become more prevalent with the growth of the Internet and the expansion of ebusinesses. *Transborder data flows (TDF)* occur when business data flows across international boundaries over the telecommunications networks of global information systems. Many countries view TDF as violating their national sovereignty because transborder data flows avoid customs duties and regulations for the import or export of goods and services. Others view transborder data flows as violating their laws to protect the local IT industry from competition or their labor regulations from protecting local jobs. In many cases, the data flow issues that seem particularly politically sensitive are those that affect the movement out of a country of personal data in ebusiness and human resource applications.

Many countries, especially those in the European Union (EU), may view transborder data flows as a violation of their privacy legislation since, in many cases, data about individuals are being moved out of the country without stringent privacy safeguards. Figure B19.6 highlights the key provisions of a data privacy agreement between the United States and the European Union. The agreement exempts U.S. companies engaging in international ebusiness from EU data privacy sanctions if they join a self-regulatory program that provides EU consumers with basic information about, and control over, how their personal data are used. Thus, the agreement is said to provide a "safe harbor" for such companies from the requirements of the EU's Data Privacy Directive, which bans the transfer of personal information on EU citizens to countries that do not have adequate data privacy protection.

*Information privacy* concerns the legal right or general expectation of individuals, groups, or institutions to determine for themselves when and to what extent information about them is communicated to others. In essence, information privacy is about how personal information is collected and shared. To facilitate information privacy, many countries have established legislation to protect the collection and sharing of personal information. However, this legislation varies greatly around the globe.

**FIGURE B19.6**

U.S.–EU Data Privacy Requirements

## EUROPE

On one end of the spectrum lie European nations with their strong information privacy laws. Most notably, all member countries of the European Union adhere to a directive on the protection of personal data. A directive is a legislative act of the European Union that requires member states to achieve a particular result without dictating the means of how to achieve that result.

The directive on the protection of personal data grants European Union members the following rights:

- The right to know the source of personal data processing and the purposes of such processing.

- The right to access and/or rectify inaccuracies in one's own personal data.

- The right to disallow the use of personal data.

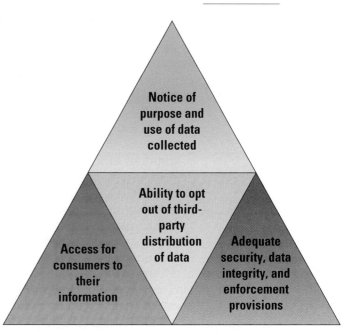

These rights are based on key principles pertaining to the collection or storage of personal data. The directive defines personal data to cover both facts and opinions about an individual. Any organization processing personal data of a person living in the European Union must comply with these key principles as outlined in the directive; these state that the data must be:

- Fairly and lawfully processed.
- Processed for limited purposes.
- Adequate, relevant, and not excessive.
- Accurate.
- Not kept longer than necessary.
- Processed in accordance with the data subject's rights.
- Not transferred to countries without adequate protection.

This last right restricts the flow of personal information outside the European Union by permitting its transfer to only countries that provide an "adequate" level of privacy protection—adequate in the sense that these other countries have to offer a level of privacy protection equivalent to that of the European Union. When first implemented, this part of the directive caused some concerns since countries outside the EU had much weaker privacy protection laws. Organizations in the United States were greatly concerned because they were at a legal risk if the personal data of EU citizens were transferred to computer servers in the United States—a likely scenario in today's global world of ebusiness. This led to extensive negotiations. The result was the establishment of a "safe harbor" program in the United States. This program provides a framework for U.S. organizations to show evidence of compliance with the EU directive. In this way, American companies can self-declare their compliance with the key principles of the directive and do business with EU nations without worrying about EU citizens suing them.

## THE UNITED STATES

On the other end of the spectrum lies the United States. Information privacy is not highly legislated nor regulated. There is no all-encompassing law that regulates the use of personal data or information. In many cases, access to public information is considered culturally acceptable, such as obtaining credit reports for employment or housing purposes. The reason for this may be historical. In the United States, the first amendment protects free speech, and in many instances the protection of privacy might conflict with this amendment.

There are some exceptions. Though very few states recognize an individual's right to privacy, California's constitution protects an inalienable right to privacy. The California legislature has enacted several pieces of legislation aimed at protecting citizen information privacy. For example, California's Online Privacy Protection Act, established in 2003, requires commercial websites or online services that collect personal information of California residents to clearly post a privacy policy on the website or online service and to comply with this policy. Other nationwide exceptions include the Children's Online Privacy Protection Act (COPPA) and the Health Insurance Portability and Accountability Act (HIPAA).

COPPA is a federal law established in 1998 that applies to the collection of personal information from American children who are under 13 years of age. The act outlines what a website should include in its privacy policy, how to seek consent from a parent or guardian, and the responsibilities a website operator has to protect children's online safety and privacy. This law applies to any website that is perceived to be targeting American children. For example, if a toy company established in Canada wanted to sell toys in the United States, the company's website should have to comply with the collection and use of information as outlined in COPPA. To show compliance requires a substantial amount of paperwork. As a result, many websites disallow underage users to join online communities and websites. Not complying with COPPA can be costly. In September 2006, the website Xanga, an online community, was fined $1 million for violating COPPA legislation.

HIPAA was enacted by the U.S. Congress in 1996. Provisions in HIPPA establish national standards for the electronic data interchange of health care-related transactions between health care providers, insurance plans, and employers. Embedded in these standards are rules for the handling and protection of personal health care information.

### CANADA

Canada's privacy laws follow very closely to the European model. Canada as a nation is quite concerned about protecting the personal information of its citizens. Its primary privacy law is the Personal Information Protection and Electronic Document Act (PIPEDA). The purpose of PIPEDA is to provide Canadians with a right of privacy with respect to how their personal information is collected, used, or disclosed by an organization. This is most important today, especially in the private sector, when information technology increasingly facilitates the collection and free flow of information.

Its precursor was the Privacy Act established in 1983 that restricted the handling of personal information within federal government departments and agencies only. This information concerned such things as pension and employment insurance files, medical records, tax records, and military records.

PIPEDA took effect in January 2001 and, like the Privacy Act, applied only to federally regulated organizations. By January 2004, PIPEDA's reach extended beyond government borders and applied to all other types of organizations, including commercial businesses. By doing so, Canada's PIPEDA law brought Canada into compliance with the European Union's directive on the protection of personal data. Hence, since January 2004, Canada no longer needed to implement safe harbor provisions for organizations wishing to collect and store personal information on European Union citizens.

# Global Systems Development

It is extremely difficult to develop a domestic information system, but the added complexity of developing a global information system quadruples the effort. Global information systems must support a diverse base of customers, users, products, languages, currencies, laws, and so on. Developing efficient, effective, and responsive information systems for multiple countries, differing cultures, and global ebusinesses is an enormous challenge for any organization. Managers should expect conflicts over local versus global system requirements and difficulties agreeing on common system features. For the project to succeed, the development environment should promote involvement and ownership by all local system users.

One of the most important global information systems development issues is the global standardization of data definitions. Common data definitions are necessary for sharing information among the parts of an international business. Difference in language, culture, and technology platforms can make global data standardization quite difficult. For example, what Americans call a "sale" may be called "an order booked" in the United Kingdom, an "order scheduled" in Germany, and an "order produced" in France. These are all referring to the exact same business event, but could cause problems if global employees have different versions of the data definition. Businesses are moving ahead to standardize data definitions and business processes. Many organizations are implementing corporate wikis where all global employees can post and maintain common business definitions.

Organizations can use several strategies to solve some of the problems that arise in global information systems development. First is transforming and customizing an information system used by the home office into a global application. This ensures the system uses the established business processes and supports the primary needs of the end users. Second, is setting up a multinational development team with key people from several subsidiaries to ensure that the system design meets the needs of all local sites as well as corporate headquarters. Third, an organization could use centers of excellence where an entire system might be assigned for development to a particular subsidiary based on its expertise in the business or technical dimensions needed for successful development. A final approach that has rapidly become a major development option is to outsource the development work to global or offshore development countries that have the required skills and experience to build global information systems. All of these approaches require development team collaboration and managerial oversight to meet the global needs of the business.

Whether you aspire to be an entrepreneur, manager, or other type of business leader, it is increasingly important to think globally in planning your career. As this plug-in points out, global markets offer many opportunities yet are laced with significant challenges and complexities including cultural, political, and geoeconomic issues, such as:

- Global business strategies.
- Global enterprise architectures.
- Global information issues.
- Global systems development.

Capability Maturity Model
   Integration method
   (CMMI) 491
Committee of Sponsoring
   Organizations (COSO) 490
Compliance 489
Deperimeterization 492

Enterprise architecture 491
Geoeconomic 488
Governance 489
Information privacy 493
Information Systems Audit
   and Control Association
   (ISACA) 490

Information Technology
   Infrastructure Library
   (ITIL) 490
Transborder data flows
   (TDF) 493

### Tata's Nano $2,500 Car

The announcement by Tata Motors of its newest car, the Nano, priced at $2,500, was revealing on many levels. The announcement generated extensive coverage and commentary, but just about everyone missed the Nano's real significance, which goes far beyond the car itself.

At about $2,500 retail, the Nano is the most inexpensive car in the world. Its closest competitor, the Maruti 800, made in India by Maruti Udyog, sells for roughly twice as much. To put this in perspective, the price of the entire Nano car is roughly equivalent to the price of a DVD player option in a luxury Western car. The low price point has left other auto companies scrambling to catch up.

### Thinking Outside the Patent Box

How could Tata Motors make a car so inexpensively? It started by looking at everything from scratch, applying what some analysts have described as "Gandhian engineering" principles— deep frugality with a willingness to challenge conventional wisdom. A lot of features that Western consumers take for granted—air conditioning, power brakes, radios, etc.—are missing from the entry-level model.

More fundamentally, the engineers worked to do more with less. The car is smaller in overall dimensions than the Maruti, but it offers about 20 percent more seating capacity as a result of design choices such as putting the wheels at the extreme edges of the car. The Nano is also much lighter than comparable models as a result of efforts to reduce the amount of steel in the car (including the use of an aluminum engine) and the use of lightweight steel where possible.

The car currently meets all Indian emission, pollution, and safety standards, though it only attains a maximum speed of about 65 mph. The fuel efficiency is attractive—50 miles to the gallon.

Hearing all this, many Western executives doubt that this new car represents real innovation. Too often, when they think of innovation, they focus on product innovation using breakthrough technologies; often, specifically, on patents. Tata Motors has filed for 34 patents associated with the design of the Nano, which contrasts with the roughly 280 patents awarded to General Motors (GM) every year. Admittedly that figure tallies all of GM's research efforts, but if innovation is measured only in terms of patents, no wonder the Nano is not of much interest to Western executives. Measuring progress solely by patent creation misses a key dimension of innovation: Some of the most valuable innovations take existing, patented components and remix them in ways that more effectively serve the needs of large numbers of customers.

## A Modular Design Revolution

But even this broader perspective fails to capture other significant dimensions of innovation. In fact, Tata Motors itself did not draw a lot of attention to what is perhaps the most innovative aspect of the Nano: its modular design. The Nano is constructed of components that can be built and shipped separately to be assembled in a variety of locations. In effect, the Nano is being sold in kits that are distributed, assembled, and serviced by local entrepreneurs. As Ratan Tata, chairman of the Tata group of companies, observed in an interview with *The Times* of London: "A bunch of entrepreneurs could establish an assembly operation and Tata Motors would train their people, would oversee their quality assurance and they would become satellite assembly operations for us. So we would create entrepreneurs across the country that would produce the car. We would produce the mass items and ship it to them as kits. That is my idea of dispersing wealth. The service person would be like an insurance agent who would be trained, have a cell phone and scooter and would be assigned to a set of customers."

In fact, Tata envisions going even further, providing the tools for local mechanics to assemble the car in existing auto shops or even in new garages created to cater to remote rural customers. With the exception of Manjeet Kripalani, *BusinessWeek*'s India bureau chief, few have focused on this breakthrough element of the Nano innovation.

This is part of a broader pattern of innovation emerging in India in a variety of markets, ranging from diesel engines and agricultural products to financial services. While most of the companies pursuing this type of innovation are Indian, the U.S. engineering firm Cummins (CMI) demonstrates that Western companies can also harness this approach and apply it effectively. In 2000 Cummins designed innovative "gensets" (generation sets) to enter the lower end of the power generator market in India. These modular sets were explicitly designed to lower distribution costs and make it easy for distributors and customers to tailor the product for highly variable customer environments. Using this approach, Cummins captured a leading position in the Indian market and now actively exports these new products to Africa, Latin America, and the Middle East.

## Lessons Executives Should Learn

What are the broader lessons that Western executives should learn from this innovation story? Emerging markets are a fertile ground for innovation. The challenge of reaching dispersed, low-income consumers in emerging markets often spurs significant innovation. Western executives should be careful about compartmentalizing the impact of these innovations on the edge of the global economy. These innovations will become the basis for "attacker" strategies that can be used to challenge incumbents in more developed economies. What is initially on the edge soon comes to the core.

- Find ways to help customers and others on the edge to tinker with your products. Modular and open product designs help engage large numbers of motivated users in tailoring and pushing the performance boundaries of your products, leading to significant insight into unmet customer needs and creative approaches to addressing those needs.

- Pay attention to institutional innovation. Western executives often become too narrowly focused on product or process innovation. Far higher returns may come from investing in institutional innovation—redefining the roles and relationships that bring together independent entities to deliver more value to the market. Tata is innovating in all three dimensions simultaneously.

- Rethink distribution models. In our relentless quest for operating efficiency, we have gone for more standardization and fewer business partners in our efforts to reach customers. As customers gain more power, they will demand more tailoring and value-added service to meet their needs. Companies that innovate on this dimension are likely to be richly rewarded.

## Questions

1. How can cultural and political issues affect Tata Motor's Nano car?
2. How would governance and compliance affect Tata Motors?
3. Identify the different global system development issues Tata Motors might encounter as it deploys its Nano.

## ✳ CLOSING CASE TWO

### Global Governance

Tarun Khanna, a Harvard professor, states that Indian companies exhibit corporate governance superior to their Chinese rivals. Khanna has just released a new book, *Billions of Entrepreneurs: How China and India Are Reshaping Their Future and Yours.* However, Khanna believes that Chinese organizations might not require world-class governance to emerge as fierce competitors. Here are edited excerpts from a recent conversation between Khanna and *BusinessWeek's* William J. Holstein:

**Much as their societies and political systems are different, are Indian and Chinese companies complete opposites when it comes to corporate governance?**
Absolutely. Indian companies are so much better governed. India is sort of a noisier version of the U.S. system, which is that you have to be accountable to shareholders and all the other stakeholders. The principles are the same, but the information acquisition is a little bit more problematic in India compared to the U.S. It's not so easy to figure out everything you need to. But there's a very vibrant, credible business media. No opinion is forbidden to be expressed. Information is noisy and unbiased—no one is willfully distorting the truth.

China is the opposite—it is noise-free but biased. You get a clean story but the story is not always right. There are views that cannot be expressed.

**Which country has more independent boards of directors?**
In India, there is a spectrum of companies, such as Infosys, which on some dimensions is better governed than companies in the West in terms of how quickly it discloses things and how quickly it complies with Nasdaq norms. At the other end of the spectrum you have companies that are still the fiefdoms of families, many of which are badly governed. But even those companies are accountable to the market. Market pressures will force them to clean up their act to some extent. The equity markets function so well that it's hard to believe you could be a continuous violator of norms of good governance and still have access to the equity markets.

In China, none of that matters because the financial markets still do not work in the sense that we think of them working in the U.S. In China, all stock prices move together. They move up on a given day or they move down. There is no company-specific information embodied in the stock price. You cannot possibly decide that a company is good or bad because the market isn't working in that sense. What you see is aggregate enthusiasm, or lack thereof, for China Inc. The market is not putting pressure on managers to behave in ways that approximate corporate governance in the West.

**Are companies in India and China making progress in developing talent in the same way that Western multinationals do?**

They are both making progress. But Indian companies are significantly further along, partly because India never had a Cultural Revolution as China did, which wiped out much of the business class. It had a residue of corporations already in existence. Some companies are 100 or 150 years old and they have an established way of doing things.

**Where are the Chinese when it comes to managing multiculturally?**

Utterly zero. It is hard to blame them because there is a language barrier also. A lot of the internal tensions were about language and cultural barriers, and questions like, Can a Frenchman report to a Chinese? And what if the French guy makes more than the Chinese guy?

**How do companies of the two countries compare when it comes to corruption?**

Here, I am not positive on India at all. Transparency International puts out these indices, and India and China are both close to the bottom of that list. China does a little bit better than India. In China, there is corruption, but it is constructive corruption. You, as a bureaucrat, get to be corrupt but only after you generate some value for society. You get a piece of it.

In India, there is corruption but it is not constructive. You are not fostering new bridges or highways. It is just shuffling stuff back and forth. I do not think we have cracked that in India at all. I am very sorry about that.

**In the final analysis, does it matter that Indian companies, on the whole, have an edge over the Chinese in reaching international standards of governance? The Chinese have huge capital at their disposal because of their $1.5 trillion in foreign exchange reserves. Could not they still be fearsome competitors?**

I think that is right. Corporate governance matters because you want to reassure the providers of inputs—whether it is time and talent, or ideas, or capital—that their rights will be respected and they will get a return on it. But if you are already sitting on hundreds of billions of dollars of capital, and you do not need to reassure anybody else because you already have your capital, why have good corporate governance?

The reason the Chinese feel less pressured to do something about it is not because they do not know how to do it—far from it, they have the best technical help from Hong Kong and other places. It is because they make a reasoned judgment that it is not worth their while.

## Questions

1. Explain governance and compliance and why they are important to any company looking to perform global business.

2. How can an organization use governance and compliance to help protect itself from global security breaches?

3. If you were choosing between outsourcing to India or China, based on this case, which country would you choose and why?

4. What types of ethical dilemmas might an organization face when dealing with IT governance in India or China?

---

### ★ MAKING BUSINESS DECISIONS

#### 1. Transforming an Organization

Your college has asked you to help develop the curriculum for a new course titled "Building a 21st Century Organization." Use the materials in this text, the Internet, and any other resources to outline the curriculum that you would suggest the course cover. Be sure to include your reasons why the material should be covered and the order in which it should be covered.

## 2. Connecting Components

Components of a solid enterprise architecture include everything from documentation to business concepts to software and hardware. Deciding which components to implement and how to implement them can be a challenge. New IT components are released daily, and business needs continually change. An enterprise architecture that meets your organization's needs today may not meet those needs tomorrow. Building an enterprise architecture that is scalable, flexible, available, accessible, and reliable is key to your organization's success.

You are the enterprise architect for a large clothing company called Xedous. You are responsible for developing the initial enterprise architecture. Create a list of questions you will need answered to develop your architecture. Below is an example of a few questions you might ask.

- What are the company's growth expectations?
- Will systems be able to handle additional users?
- How long will information be stored in the systems?
- How much customer history must be stored?
- What are the organization's business hours?
- What are the organization's backup requirements?

## 3. IT Gets Its Say

CIOs need to speak the language of business to sell IT's strategic benefits. It is no secret that the most successful companies today are the ones that deliver the right products and services faster, more efficiently, more securely, and more cost-effectively than their competitors, and the key to that is a practical implementation of enterprise technology to improve business performance. IT executives and managers therefore must speak the language of business to articulate how technology can solve business problems.

CIOs of tomorrow will focus on a number of changing dynamics: enabling the business to grow versus just optimizing performance, saying yes instead of no; allowing open innovation rather than closed, traditional R&D practices; creating a culture of strategic growth and innovation; and empowering the customer to make decisions that drive a heightened value proposition for both the customer and supplier. You have been charged with creating a slogan for your company that explains the correlation of business and IT. A few examples include:

- IT should no longer be viewed as just an enabler of somebody else's business strategy.
- The distinction between technology and business is antediluvian – it's gone.

Create a slogan that you can use to explain to your employees the importance of business and IT.

## 4. Mom-and-Pop Multinationals

Global outsourcing is no longer just for big corporations as small businesses jump into the multisourcing game. Increasingly, Main Street businesses from car dealers to advertising agencies are finding it easier to farm out software development, accounting, support services, and design work to distant lands. For example, Randy and Nicola Wilburn run a micro-multinational organization right from their home. The Wilburns run real estate, consulting, design, and baby food companies from their home by taking outsourcing to the extreme. Professionals from around the globe are at their service. For $300, an Indian artist designed the cute logo of an infant peering over the words "Baby Fresh Organic Baby Foods" and Nicola's letterhead. A London freelancer wrote promotional materials. Randy has hired "virtual assistants" in Jerusalem to transcribe voice mail, update his website, and design PowerPoint graphics. Retired brokers in Virginia and Michigan handle real estate paperwork.

Elance, an online-services marketplace, boasts 48,500 small businesses as clients—up 70 percent in the past year—posting 18,000 new projects a month. Other online-services marketplaces such as Guru.com, Brickwork India, DoMyStuff.com, and RentACoder also report fast growth. You have decided to jump in the micro-multinational game and start your own online-services marketplace. Research the following as you compile your start-up business plan.

1. To compete in this market what types of services would you offer?
2. What types of cultural, political, and geoeconomic challenges would your business experience?
3. How would governance and compliance fit into your business strategy?
4. What types of global information issues might your company experience?
5. What types of customers would you want to attract and what vehicle would you use to find your customers?
6. What types of global systems development issues would your company experience?
7. What types of information security and ethical dilemmas should you anticipate?

# Innovation, Social Entrepreneurship, Social Networking, and Virtual Worlds

## 21st Century Organization Trends

Many people have no idea how they would get any work done on business trips if they did not have a laptop. They simply cannot remember how they lived without their BlackBerry. Their cell phones might as well be surgically attached to their ear, it is so crucial to their job. It is hard to conceive of getting through the day without Google, or, if the person is under 40, text messaging or Facebook to stay in touch with an extended network of colleagues. In just a decade or less, technology has done a number on the way we work.

And in the next decade, the relentless march of computer power and Internet connection speeds will bring more profound changes to work than anything seen so far. Consider just a few of the breakthroughs technology visionaries think will occur in coming years. Picture Apple's slick iPhone shrunk to the size of a credit card. Then imagine it can connect not only to contacts on the latest social network, but also to billions of pea-sized wireless sensors attached to buildings, streets, retail products, and clothes—all simultaneously sending data over the Internet. This will allow tracking and managing more than static information; users will be able to track events in the physical world, from production on a factory floor to colleagues' whereabouts to how customers are using products. All that information will be much easier to view and analyze, using hand and arm gestures to control commands and viewing results with special glasses that make it seem as if the user is gazing at a life-size screen. Just imagine producing detailed prototypes of product or design ideas via a 3D printer that creates plastic models from computerized specs as easily as a paper printer spews out reports today.

Organizations are facing technological changes and challenges more extensive and far reaching in their implications than anything since the modern industrial revolution occurred in the early 1900s. Organizations that want to survive in the 21st century must recognize these technological changes and challenges, carry out required organizational changes in the face of this new world, and learn to operate in an entirely different way. Today's organizations have focused on defending and safeguarding their existing market positions in addition to targeting new market growth. The primary changes and challenges organizations are and will be focusing on in the 21st century include:

- Innovation: finding new.
- Social entrepreneurship: going green.
- Social networks: who's who.
- Virtual worlds: it's a whole new world.

## Innovation: Finding New

In the past, a company primarily focused on operational excellence, but now innovation is driving the wheels of IT. ***Innovation*** is the introduction of new equipment or methods. The current impetus to innovate comes from the need to cut costs, while still creating a competitive advantage. Fundamental shifts in technology will make it possible for businesses to realize IT's promise of technology-enabled innovation, responsiveness, and speed.

Surfers from around the world converged on Maverick's at Pillar Point, just a few miles from San Francisco, to challenge each other on the big waves that have made this a legendary surfing destination. The sixth Maverick's Surf Contest had been announced only 48 hours earlier to ensure optimal wave conditions for the contestants. Surfers from as far away as Australia, Brazil, and South Africa scrambled to make their way to this invitation-only competition. It was magical to watch these athletes challenge 20-foot waves with an ease and grace that made it all seem so natural.

While all attention was on the athletes riding their surfboards, however, a different story was being told beneath the surface, one that contains important lessons for business executives. Making the surfers' artistry possible, the technology and techniques used to master big-wave surfing have evolved over decades, driven by dedicated, perhaps even obsessed, groups of athletes and craftsmen. Executives can gain significant insight into the innovation process by looking at this sport and following the six best practices of innovation (see Figure B20.1).

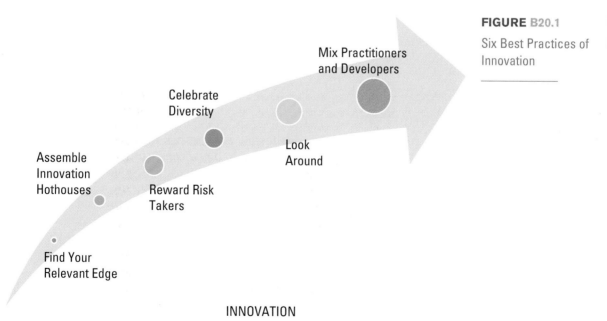

**FIGURE** B20.1

Six Best Practices of Innovation

INNOVATION

## FIND YOUR RELEVANT EDGE

First, to push performance levels, organizations must find the relevant edge. In the case of big-wave surfers, there has been an ever-expanding search for the breaks that would produce bigger and rougher waves to test new board designs and surfing practices.

Following the lead of surfers, business executives need to find relevant edges that will test and push their current performance. For example, companies making diesel engines and power generators should be actively engaged in finding ways to more effectively serve lower-income customers in remote rural areas of emerging economies. These demanding customers could prompt significant innovation in both product design and distribution processes in an effort to deliver greater value at lower cost. The innovations resulting from these efforts on the edge could lead to significant improvements in product lines.

## ASSEMBLE INNOVATION HOTHOUSES

Second, attract motivated groups of people to these edges to work together around challenging performance issues. In the late 1950s, Waimea Bay, on the north shore of Oahu, became the test bed for athletes seeking to push the boundaries of big-wave surfing. In the isolation of the north shore, dedicated surfers spent 8 to 10 hours each day, every day, challenging themselves and each other on the big waves. The real advances in surfing technology and practices occurred at the breaks where surfers gathered and formed deep relationships over extended periods. They learned rapidly from each other and pushed each other to go to the next level.

Large companies have become very adept at establishing remote outposts in places like Beijing, Hyderabad, Haifa, and St. Petersburg to attract local talent and push forward challenging research and development projects. Often, though, these outposts either become disconnected from their parent companies or fail to establish deep links with other leading-edge participants in the area. The key challenge is to connect these company-owned facilities more effectively with their local environments as well as with each other through challenging and sustained innovation initiatives that build long-term, trust-based relationships. Performance improvement generally comes first in the form of tacit knowledge that is difficult to express and communicate more broadly. People have to be there to gain access to this tacit knowledge.

## REWARD RISK TAKERS

Third, recognize that the people who are likely to be attracted to the edge are big risk takers. This is a key reason the edge becomes such a fertile ground for innovation. It attracts people who are not afraid to take risks and to learn from their experiences. They relentlessly seek new challenges. Executives need to be thoughtful about how to attract these people, provide them with environments to support risk taking, and reward them for both successes and failures.

## CELEBRATE DIVERSITY

Fourth, recognize that the edge fosters not just risk taking, but very different cultures that are also edgy. The advances in big-wave surfing did not come from the casual surfers but from those who developed an entire lifestyle and culture, fostered by intense and even obsessive concentration on pushing the envelope. Executives need to find ways to protect and honor these edgy cultures, whether they are inhabited by tattooed web designers or the next generation of employees who learned how to innovate as members of guilds in World of Warcraft.

## LOOK AROUND

Fifth, find ways to appropriate insights from adjacent disciplines and even more remote areas of activity. Early advances in surfing technology came from the aerospace industry because some of the employees in this industry were also avid surfers. Some of surfer Laird Hamilton's greatest insights came from his experiences as an expert windsurfer and his colleagues' experiences with snowboarding. By attracting diverse backgrounds and experiences to the edge, executives can foster creative breakthroughs.

## MIX PRACTITIONERS AND DEVELOPERS

Sixth, bring users and developers of technology close together. It is no accident that the most innovative surfers also tend to be expert shapers of surfboards. These folks not only design surfboards but also shape the materials into the finished product and then take them out to life-threatening breaks to test and refine them. They are relentless tinkerers, integrating experience, intuition, and craft to come up with creative new boards. Technology and practice are intimately linked. Very little performance improvement comes directly out of the technology itself. It is only when seasoned practitioners engage with the technology, especially in close-knit communities, and evolve their practices to better use it, that the real performance breakthroughs occur.

# Social Entrepreneurship: Going Green

**Social responsibility** implies that an entity whether it is a government, corporation, organization, or individual has a responsibility to society. **Corporate policy** is a dimension of social responsibility that refers to the position a firm takes on social and political issues. **Corporate responsibility** is a dimension of social responsibility that includes everything from hiring minority workers to making safe products. **Sustainable, or "green," IT** describes the manufacture, management, use, and disposal of information technology in a way that minimizes damage to the environment, which is a critical part of a corporation's responsibility. As a result, the term has many different meanings, depending on whether you are a manufacturer, manager, or user of technology. This section covers energy consumption, recycling IT equipment, and greener IT.

## ENERGY CONSUMPTION

As a threat to operations and the bottom line, corporate computing's fast-growing power consumption is forcing companies to adopt green energy practices. Engineers at Hewlett-Packard made a startling realization about the servers running the company's computing systems. Surging power consumption, along with rising energy costs, will soon make it more expensive to keep a server going for a year than to acquire one in the first place. Left unchecked, costs like these interfere with HP's goal of cutting energy consumption 15 percent by 2010.

When HP began constructing a new 50,000-square-foot building to house high-powered computers, it sought advice from Pacific Gas & Electric. By following the California power company's recommendations, HP will save $1 million a year in power costs for that data center alone, PG&E says.

Like HP, companies across the globe are adding equipment to keep up with surging computing needs—and then are forced to make substantial changes to curtail the leap in costs associated with running the big buildings, or data centers, housing all that gear. "Data centers use 50 times the energy per square foot than an office [does]," said Mark Bramfitt, principal program manager at PG&E. Figure B20.2 displays the breakdown of power usage in the typical data center.

Industry experts say the power consumption of data centers is doubling every five years or so, making them one of the fastest-growing drags on energy in the United States. Figure B20.3 displays data center energy bills.

# Breakdown of Power Usage in The Typical Data Center

Percentage

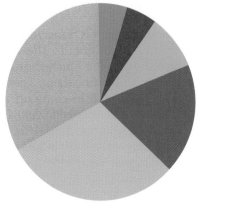

- Lighting, Humidifier
- Power Distribution Units
- Air Conditioners
- UPS
- IT Equipment
- Chiller

## The Electric Bill

How Does Company Track Data Center Usage?

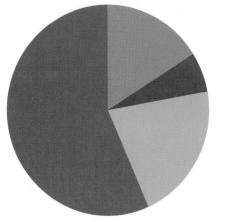

- IT pays bill
- Incentive to keep electric costs low
- IT does not manage bill
- Facilities pays IT bill; IT unaware

With demand for computer power exploding, energy consumption by data centers doubled between 2000 and 2006, and could double again by 2011. So the pressure is on tech companies, utilities, and builders to come up with new ways of cutting energy consumption. Here are some of the ways they are responding.

### Sun Microsystems: Throughput Computing

A decade ago, the chip industry had a single focus: making the digital brains of computers process data ever faster. But Sun Microsystems chip architect Marc Tremblay saw a fatal flaw in that strategy. Faster chips would run hotter, and eventually they would burn out. So he designed what's known as a multicore chip, which has several processors on a single sliver of silicon, each of them running cooler and sucking less energy but collectively getting more work done. He also enabled each processor to perform more than one task at a time. The processors on Sun's Niagara server computers, based on Tremblay's designs, consumed just 70 watts of power, about one-third of a conventional microprocessor.

## Virtualization

It used to be possible to run only one application at a time on a given server. That meant if the application was not needed at any given time, the server just was not being used. Analysts estimate only 10 to 20 percent of the capability of a typical server is used. *Virtualization* is a framework of dividing the resources of a computer into multiple execution environments. Virtualization software allows IT managers to easily load multiple programs on a single machine and move programs from one computer to another on the fly to make maximum use of a cluster of servers. This significantly reduces energy use because fewer servers are needed. Virtualization software has been used for decades on mainframe computers, but it only became popular on PC servers recently.

## Energy Rebate Programs

Pacific Gas & Electric's Mark Bramfitt saw virtualization as a great way to reduce energy use in Northern California's data centers, so he designed an innovative data center energy-saving program. Companies get rebates for reducing the number of servers they use in their data centers. In just one year, Bramfitt received more than 47 applications from data center operators and paid out four rebates. He is also urging other utilities to adopt similar programs. So far, three others have followed suit.

## Smart Cooling

Hewlett-Packard Research Fellow Chandrakant Patel came up with a new approach to data center energy use: Think of the data center as one giant machine. Out of that came HP's Dynamic Smart Cooling technology. Thousands of heat sensors monitor temperatures, and software directs the air-conditioning system to put the big chill on the places that need it most. Projected energy savings: 20 to 45 percent.

## Alternative Energy Sources

Web search giant Google, which operates some of the largest data centers in the world, has committed to using cutting-edge technologies to power and cool its data centers, including wind and solar power. It's already using wind to power a data center in the Netherlands, and there's speculation it may tap wind for a major new facility in Council Bluffs, Iowa.

## Biology Meets Chips

IBM researcher Bruno Michel and his team at IBM Zurich Research Laboratory are applying biological principles to deal with the heat problem in computing. Just as the human vascular system cools our bodies, Michel is designing devices that cool chips using liquid delivered through capillary-like circulation systems. Typically, the processors in server computers are air-cooled; chilled air is blown over metal caps on top of the chips, where tiny fins dissipate heat. One of Michel's inventions is a metal cap that fits over a processor and sprays jets of water out of 50,000 nozzles into microscopic channels etched in the metal. The channels behave like capillaries, circulating the liquid efficiently and cutting the energy required to pump the water.

## Government Involvement

The European Union has imposed limits on carbon emissions. Since 2005, the Emission Trading Scheme has required 12,000 iron, steel, glass, and power plants to buy $CO_2$ permits, which allows them to emit the gas into the atmosphere. If a company exceeds its limit, it can buy unused permits from other companies that have successfully cut their emissions. If they are unable to buy spare permits, however, they are fined for every excess ton of $CO_2$. Because IT contributes to the total carbon emissions in a company, carbon cap and trade or tax laws will impact how technology is managed. The EU and many U.S. states also have laws that require computer equipment, which contains many toxic substances, be recycled.

## RECYCLE IT EQUIPMENT

*Sustainable IT disposal* refers to the safe disposal of IT assets at the end of their life cycle. It ensures that *ewaste,* or old computer equipment, does not end up in a landfill, where the toxic substances it contains can leach into groundwater, among other problems. Many of the major hardware manufacturers offer take-back programs, so IT departments do not have to take responsibility for disposal. Some U.S. states and the European Union have laws requiring that ewaste be recycled. For example, Dell and Sony will take back any of their products for free and Toshiba will take back its laptops. Apple charges a fee, but will waive it if you are purchasing a new product. HP also will charge you, but will give you a credit toward future HP purchases. For a complete list of recycling programs in the United States, visit the Computer TakeBack Campaign website (www.computertakeback.com). According to the Computer TakeBack Campaign, Maine, California, Texas, Oregon, Maryland, Washington, and Minnesota have ewaste laws. Some of these laws apply only to equipment manufacturers; others apply to end users. In 2007, ewaste bills were introduced in 23 states. Companies that mind their energy consumption and dispose of used equipment responsibly now will be better off when regulations are imposed.

Complying with ewaste regulations should become easier for IT managers due to new manufacturing regulations. The EU Directive on the Restriction of the Use of Certain Hazardous Substances in Electrical and Electronic Equipment, which took effect July 1, 2006, restricts the use of six hazardous materials in the manufacture of certain electronics: lead, mercury, cadmium, hexavalent chromium, polybrominated biphenyls, and polybrominated diphenyl ether (the last two are flame retardants used in plastics). Such requirements reduce the toxicity of electronics, and thus, the ewaste they produce.

In 2006, obsolete desktops, laptops, and servers accounted for 18 billion pounds of electronic trash worldwide, but the major companies involved in ewaste recovery (Dell, HP, and IBM) recovered only 356 million pounds—about 2 percent.

Only about one-third of all U.S. companies have an IT asset disposal policy. The rest are either doing nothing or dumping them into municipal landfills. According to National Geographic's *The Green Guide,* 50 to 80 percent of recycled electronics end up in developing nations, where they are disassembled by untrained workers without the proper equipment. This exposes them to toxic substances such as mercury, cadmium, and lead. If the equipment is left in landfills, those same toxins end up in water sources.

## GREENER IT

At Sun Microsystems, OpenWork, the company's telecommuting program, provides employees with shared office space, home equipment, and subsidies for DSL and electricity, according to Dave Douglas, vice president of eco responsibility at Sun. More than 56 percent of Sun's employees are currently in the program. "In the last five years we have cut our office space by one-sixth and have saved over $60 million a year on space and power," Douglas said. Sun also saves an estimated 29,000 tons of $CO_2$ per year due to reduced employee commuting. That is equivalent to taking 5,694 cars off the road for one year, according to the EPA's carbon calculator.

Dow Chemical's process control automation system will shut a plant down if it is not compliant with air and water emissions requirements. Dow also uses a monitoring system to measure the air and water emissions at its plants and is deploying an environmental reporting system to manage reporting of this data to state and federal authorities, said CIO and Chief Sustainability Officer David Kepler.

IT systems can also help save energy by controlling heat and air-conditioning in office buildings. Wireless sensors can be used to measure airflow and room occupancy. If the occupancy sensors (which turn lights on and off when people enter or leave a room) are networked to airflow sensors, the amount of air-conditioning used when people are not in a room can be reduced, said David Kepler. "The basic idea is to collect data on how the facility is using energy and use that information to define patterns that can help change what you are doing and reduce operating costs."

To keep up with its explosive growth, Google is building data centers off the beaten path, in places like Lenoir, North Carolina; Mount Holly, South Carolina; and Council Bluffs, Iowa. A 30-acre facility in The Dalles, Oregon, is the most recent of them to be completed and put into operations. The Dalles, a town of about 12,000, provided the perfect location for Google, with its hydroelectric dam, affordable land, and a 15-year tax incentive. An industrial-strength power grid connects the dam to Google's complex, where massive cooling systems rise above two data center buildings. Google spends approximately $600 million to build a major data center, requiring a staff of 100 to 200 to operate. Figure B20.4 displays the current ways companies are choosing to go green.

## Social Networks: Who's Who

Encover Chief Executive Officer Chip Overstreet was on the hunt for a new vice president for sales. He had homed in on a promising candidate and dispensed with the glowing but unsurprising remarks from references. Now it was time to dig for any dirt. So he logged on to LinkedIn, an online business network. "I did 11 backdoor checks on this guy and found people he had worked with at five of his last six companies," said Overstreet, whose firm sells and manages service contracts for manufacturers. "It was incredibly powerful."

So powerful, in fact, that more than a dozen sites like LinkedIn have cropped up in recent years. They are responding to a growing impulse among web users to build ties, communities, and networks online, fueling the popularity of sites such as News Corp.'s MySpace. As of April, the 10 biggest social-networking sites, including MySpace, reached a combined unique audience of 68.8 million users, drawing in 45 percent of active web users, according to Nielsen/NetRatings.

Corporations and smaller businesses have not embraced online business networks with nearly the same abandon as teens and college students who have flocked to social sites. Yet companies are steadily overcoming reservations and

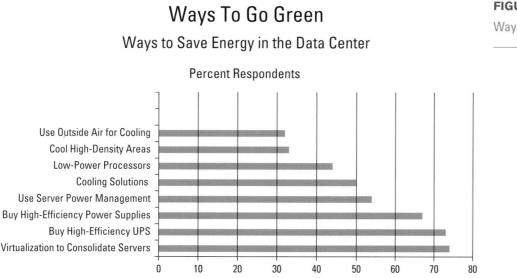

## Ways To Go Green

### Ways to Save Energy in the Data Center

Percent Respondents

FIGURE B20.4

Ways to Go Green

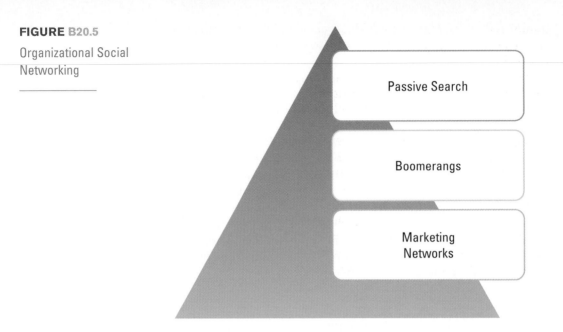

Passive Search

Boomerangs

Marketing
Networks

using the sites and related technology to craft potentially powerful business tools. Figure B20.5 displays the three types of social networking an organization can implement: passive search, boomerangs, and marketing networks.

## PASSIVE SEARCH

Recruiters at Microsoft and Starbucks, for instance, troll online networks such as LinkedIn for potential job candidates. Goldman Sachs and Deloitte run their own online alumni networks for hiring back former workers and strengthening bonds with alumni-cum-possible clients. Boston Consulting Group and law firm Duane Morris deploy enterprise software that tracks employee communications to uncover useful connections in other companies. And companies such as Intuit and Mini USA have created customer networks to build brand loyalty.

Many companies are leery of online networks. Executives do not have time to field the possible influx of requests from acquaintances on business networks. Employees may be dismayed to learn their workplace uses email monitoring software to help sales associates' target pitches. Companies considering building online communities for advertising, branding, or marketing will need to cede some degree of control over content.

None of those concerns are holding back Carmen Hudson, manager of enterprise staffing at Starbucks, who said she swears by LinkedIn. "It's one of the best things for finding mid-level executives," she said.

The holy grail in recruiting is finding so-called passive candidates, people who are happy and productive working for other companies. LinkedIn, with its 6.7 million members, is a virtual Rolodex of these types. Hudson says she has hired three or four people this year as a result of connections through LinkedIn. "We've started asking our hiring managers to sign up on LinkedIn and help introduce us to their contacts," she says. "People have concerns about privacy, but once we explain how we use it and how careful we would be with their contacts, they're usually willing to do it."

## BOOMERANGS

Headhunters and human resources departments are taking note. "LinkedIn is a tremendous tool for recruiters," said Bill Vick, the author of *LinkedIn for Recruiting*. So are sites such as Ryze, Spoke, OpenBc, and Ecademy. Many companies are turning to social networks and related technology to stay in touch with former employees. Consulting firm Deloitte strives to maintain ties with ex-workers and has had a formal alumni-relations program for years. It bolstered those efforts earlier this year, tapping business networking services provider SelectMinds to launch an online alumni network.

Ex-Deloitte employees can go to the site to browse 900 postings for jobs at a range of companies. They can also peruse open positions at Deloitte. The online network is an extension of an offline program that includes networking receptions and seminars.

Deloitte makes no bones about its aim to use the network to lure back some former employees, or so-called boomerangs. "Last year, 20 percent of our experienced hires were boomerangs," said Karen Palvisak, a national leader of alumni relations for Deloitte.

Boomerangs cost less to train than new hires and they tend to hit the ground running. As the labor market tightens, alumni become an increasingly attractive source of talent. Last year, 13 percent of employees who had previously been laid off were rehired by their former employers, according to a survey by Right Management Consultants of more than 14,000 displaced employees at 4,900 organizations.

## MARKETING NETWORKS

Business-oriented networks help executives find employees, and they're increasingly useful in other areas, such as sales and marketing. When Campbell Soup Co. asked independent location booker Marilyn Jenett to select a castle in Europe for a promotion, she put a note on business networking site Ryze, offering a finder's fee to anyone who could suggest the right place.

Jenett got seven responses, including one pointing her to Eastnor Castle. She was so pleased with the location that she booked it again for another event. Jenett said Ryze also helped her develop another small business, a personal mentoring program called Feel Free to Prosper.

Social networks also help forge community with, and among, would-be customers. A group of Mini Cooper owners joined the company for its two-week cross-country car rally. Participants took part in company-sponsored events, such as the official wrap party overlooking the Hudson River and the Manhattan skyline in New Jersey.

But they also planned their own side events along the way with the help of the community forums on the Mini Owner's Lounge site, sponsored by Mini USA. Each month, about 1,500 to 2,000 new owners become active in the community. "Our very best salespeople are Mini owners, and they like to talk about their cars," said Martha Crowley, director of consulting for Beam Interactive, which provides various Internet marketing services for Mini USA.

**FIGURE** B20.6

It's a Whole New World

## Virtual Worlds: It's a Whole New World

Virtual is the theme of Web 2.0. Two primary types of virtual must be considered when looking at the 21st century world. This includes virtual worlds and virtual workforces (see Figure B20.6).

## VIRTUAL WORLDS

In the midst of the sprawling online virtual world Second Life, a new edifice recently surfaced, the digitized headquarters of *Wired* magazine on a one-acre lot. Garish neon-pink sliding doors lead to a conference room shaped like a Shuttle PC where as many as 50 people can sit on chairs that resemble circuit breakers and watch a screen that looks like a graphics card. *Wired,* meanwhile, unveiled its building in Second Life to kick off a package of stories on the game. The company expects to use its new virtual building to let writers chat with one another and to host three or four virtual Q&A events

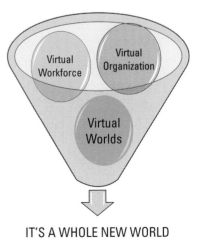

IT'S A WHOLE NEW WORLD

a month with real-world as well as Second Life notables, says Chris Baker, senior associate editor at *Wired* magazine. "It's kind of a toe in the water for us," he said, adding that *Wired* is also actively looking to set up in other virtual worlds as well. "We are still not sure how to make use of this space; this is the test case."

*Wired*'s virtual headquarters are right next to the offices of CNET Networks, which recently unveiled its own five-story office in Second Life. The building is an exact replica of the company's glass-and-brick headquarters in San Francisco, and it is set amid vast lawns overlooking Second Life's blue ocean.

Big media's land grab is well under way in Second Life, the online realm where real people, under the guise of avatars, mill and mingle and, in some cases, make a living. The game's audience, swiftly approaching 1 million, is growing at about 38 percent month over month, according to its creator, Linden Lab. The out-fit added 200,000 to 250,000 new players—many of them the coveted younger early adopters—in one month alone. "Second Life is almost a phenomenon like YouTube, it's reached critical mass," said Baker.

Like so many other companies already setting up shop in Second Life, news organizations and other media outlets do not want to be left behind. As the virtual world grows up, it will get more attractive to companies that want to send a multi-media message. "Everyone's been searching for the killer broadband offering, and this is it," said Justin Bovington, CEO of Rivers Run Red, which helps companies like BBC Radio One create events and design buildings inside Second Life.

Companies as varied as Adidas, Sun Microsystems, and Toyota want to promote their products and ensure their brands are getting exposure amid the consumers, many of them young, who are spending increasingly long stretches not just on the Internet, but also immersed in virtual worlds. In-game advertising revenue in the United States was expected to rise from $186 million in 2005 to $875 million in 2009, according to Yankee Group.

Media companies even face competition from virtual upstarts inside Second Life, including "New World Notes" and "SL Herald." Reuters commissioned its long-time tech reporter, Adam Pasick, to cover Second Life full-time and act as Reuters' Second Life bureau chief. Pasick's avatar sports a green shirt, a grim businesslike expression, and a press badge. One of his first stories reported on a U.S. congres-sional committee's investigation of online virtual economies like Second Life and Vivendi Universal's World of Warcraft and how virtual assets and income received in the games should be taxed.

Another Reuters story is an interview with the virtual president of Second Life's most popular bank, Ginko Financial. The Reuters site also offers a variety of market information, such as the exchange rate between the Linden dollar, a currency used in Second Life, and the U.S. dollar. Another table tracks the number of U.S. dollars ($404,063, at recent count) spent by players on Second Life in the past 24 hours. "Second Life is a really hot economy," said Pasick, who, in the game, goes under the name of Adam Reuters. "It was a natural for Reuters." "Second Life offers numer-ous features and options for businesses, and is a canvas that allows companies to do what they want to do in Second Life," said David Fleck, Linden's vice president of marketing. The following are a few examples of how businesses are using Second Life to compete in the global economy.

### Sun Microsystems

Sun Microsystems held a Second Life press conference with John Gage, chief sci-entist at Sun. The company created an area called Sun Pavilion, where a video blog of all of Sun's activities will be streamed. There were 60 avatars at the press conference—in Second Life terms, that's a full house.

### Warner Bros. Records

Warner Bros. promoted singer Regina Spektor's fourth album, *Begin to Hope,* by building a chic Manhattan loft within Second Life. As Spektor's music played, the loft's lighting and décor changed to roughly illustrate the song lyrics—a new marketing experience that was part video game, part music video.

### American Apparel

American Apparel launched a virtual store in Second Life in July 2006. The hip T-shirt maker is debuting styles before they are launched in the physical world and is offering cross-promotions. Visitors to the virtual store receive 15 percent off real-world purchases.

### Lego

Lego regularly visits university and corporate campuses to host events where new types of robots are built using Lego's popular Mindstorm Robotics Inventions kits. Recently, Lego hosted one such Big Robot on Campus gathering in Second Life, drawing robot makers from different locales to meet in cyberspace.

### Adidas

Adidas is working on selling virtual gym shoes in Second Life. The company hopes to test-market styles before rolling them out in the real world, tracking which color combos or designs prove popular among Second Lifers.

### Toyota

Toyota's marketing plan for its hip, boxy Scion includes an art gallery in Los Angeles (Scion Space) and sponsored screenings of indie films (the Scion Independent Film Series). Now the pop-culture-aware carmaker is also a presence in Second Life, where it offers a virtual version of the Scion xB.

### Dartmouth College

Educational institutions such as Dartmouth College are increasingly becoming a presence in the virtual world. In a Second Life version of Hanover, New Hampshire, where Dartmouth is located, the school's Institute for Security Technology Studies conducts emergency-response exercises in the virtual space.

### Major League Baseball

Major League Baseball held a simulcast of its home-run derby within Second Life, with video streams of the event shown on screens within a digitized baseball stadium. Branching into Second Life made sense to MLB execs; MLB.com has a robust online community in its chat rooms.

### Virtual Hospital

Palomar Pomerado Health opened a new state-of-the-art hospital—in Second Life. The opening of the virtual hospital followed the December 2007 groundbreaking for the health care provider's real-world $773 million, 600-bed Palomar Medical Center west in Escondido, California. With completion of the first phase of the hospital still three years away, PPH created the facility and all of its technology in the Second Life virtual world to show its 900,000 clients in Southern California what is to come. The Second Life hospital shows off operating rooms equipped with robotics technology and functional imaging systems that support medical procedures such as cardiovascular surgery. Using Second Life to receive user feedback is a cost-effective method—much better than just herding people into a room for a focus group.

## VIRTUAL WORKFORCE

Sunday morning and Tuesday afternoon are becoming completely the same, said KLM Chief Information Officer Boet Kreiken. At the same time, employees throughout organizations are becoming much more comfortable with a range of technologies.

In years past, employees might have had only a PC at home. Today they may juggle a network linking several PCs, printers, and backup devices connected to a high-speed Internet connection—in addition to a set-top box, gaming console, high-definition TV, and all manner of other web-based services such as YouTube and News Corp.'s MySpace. The benefits for businesses include lower costs and greater productivity, but figuring out how to communicate with off-site employees is crucial.

Traffic surrounding Microsoft headquarters in Redmond, Washington, has become so congested that Washington State Governor Chris Gregoire nearly missed a 9 a.m. speech at the company's main campus. Roads leading to the software maker simply were not designed to handle the 35,000 commuters who report for work there each day. The gridlock that greeted Gregoire was just the latest reminder that Microsoft needs to tackle its commuter crisis—and quickly.

Microsoft has embarked on a program aimed at getting more employees to work from home and other off-site locales, joining the growing ranks of companies to catch the virtual-workplace wave. About 17 percent of the U.S. workforce in 2009 was expected to get its job done at a home office more than two days per week, said Charlie Grantham, executive producer of consulting firm Work Design Collaborative. That is up from 11 percent in 2004.

Letting employees work from outside the office keeps cars off the road, plus the practice can foster employee retention, boost worker productivity, and slash real estate costs. At IBM, about 42 percent of the company's 330,000 employees work on the road, from home, or at a client location, saving the computer company about $100 million in real estate-related expenses a year. VIPdesk, an employer of at-home customer-service reps, hangs onto 85 percent of its employees each year, compared with the 10 to 20 percent rate for traditional call centers, according to consulting firm IDC. And virtual workers are about 16 percent more productive than office workers, according to Grantham's research.

For all the benefits of freeing workers from the office, drawbacks abound. First, not everyone wants to leave. Some fear they will step off the corporate ladder, while others need a busy environment to stay productive. Some managers are reluctant to scatter direct reports because keeping tabs on a virtual workforce can be harder than managing those close at hand. Some virtual workers can feel lonely, isolated, or deprived of vital training and mentoring. And communication breakdowns can impede innovation, trust, job satisfaction, and performance.

Obstacles like these have prompted IBM, Sun Microsystems, and other companies to seek a host of creative solutions to the problems that virtual work presents. Some turn to a combination of mobile devices, email, instant messaging, and collaboration software to help colleagues stay in touch.

Other companies, including Microsoft, WebEx, and Citrix, also specialize in online conferencing and collaboration software that makes it easier for people in different locations to work together and conduct meetings. At Groove Networks, the company set a policy that if one person was operating virtually in a meeting, then everyone would sit in their offices and the entire meeting would be virtual. "Because there's a big sensory difference in that experience, it made sure that everyone was on a level playing field," she said. Another way to bridge the physical distance is to provide a worker with the tools needed to stay connected to colleagues.

For the virtual worker, a laptop, high-speed Internet access, and a personal digital assistant or mobile phone are required. But some companies go an extra mile to outfit virtual employees. IBM provides a universal messaging service that lets executives give a single phone number to clients and colleagues. The service then forwards calls to wherever that executive might be located, at home, on a cell phone, or in a so-called emobility center, one of the temporary offices set up by IBM in locations around the world. Patrick Boyle, director of health care and life-sciences sales at IBM, spends about half his time traveling, working from taxis, airport lounges, planes, and coffee shops. He is also a frequent user of emobility centers and considers headsets an essential tool of the trade.

Developing a global business perspective will help you reap the potential of global markets. New trends for the 21st century include:

- Innovation: finding new.
- Social entrepreneurship: going green.
- Social networks: who's who.
- Virtual worlds: it's a whole new world.

✱ **KEY TERMS**

| | | |
|---|---|---|
| Corporate policy 507 | Innovation 505 | Sustainable or green IT 507 |
| Corporate responsibility 507 | Social responsibility 507 | Virtualization 509, 510 |
| ewaste 510 | Sustainable IT disposal 510 | |

✱ **CLOSING CASE ONE**

### Collective Innovation

Open innovation has been a hot management phrase for the past five years. So far, though, these collaborations have generally been focused on small-scale research and development or on technology ventures between giant global brands and smaller partners. Think Procter & Gamble's collaborations with universities and suppliers or IBM's embrace of an open-source software language that both saves the company money and provides it with a new revenue stream.

But what if you brought together design heads from some of the world's biggest global brands with the aim of stimulating innovation? That was the premise of the fifth annual Raymond conference in Rotterdam attended by 17 design managers from companies as diverse as Heineken, Philips, Lego, Airbus, and Hewlett-Packard. Designers are accustomed to working with external consultants and customers, but Raymond's aim is different: fostering cooperation between design teams at big global companies in radically different markets.

The conference is the brainchild of two Dutch design companies: Park Advanced Design Management and Eden, an interactive-experience design firm. Tired of attending crowded conferences dominated by endless speeches, they decided to start an invitation-only event where designers from noncompeting companies could freely share ideas with the aim of finding new ways to get more and better products out faster.

"Everyone talks about open innovation, but the design department is the place within a company most open to doing it," said Tim Selders, Raymond co-founder and Park director. Designers, especially those involved in corporate branding and product or service design, are accustomed to working with external partners and customers. "It's about finding new ways for companies to share design processes, resources, and tools," Selders said.

### An Imaginary Global Firm

A recent Raymond conference followed an unusual format that led to some surprising insights and even a few potential commercial collaborations. Holed up together in a room for nearly two days, the attendees were asked to imagine they were part of a new global design company called design-Inc.com, with a team of some 1,200 designers.

Their mission, they were informed in a video presentation by the unseen "Raymond" (think Charlie from *Charlie's Angels*), was to deliver the best, fastest, and most inexpensive design solutions for a broad range of businesses across a variety of industries: medical, retail, toys, sports equipment, and clothing.

To do this, they had to figure out how to motivate staff to keep innovation fresh, which design tools and processes to use, how to benchmark their performance, and how to share knowledge of trends, materials, and technologies among designers. "Although we're all from different backgrounds and industries, we all face similar problems and we all have different ways of solving them," said Loe Limpens, a design manager for Dutch supermarket chain Albert Heijn.

### The Spirit of a Collective Company

The process worked by asking six designers at a time to sit around a fictitious boardroom table to bat around ideas on how the new company would operate. Each board member was asked to contribute to the discussion on the three broad themes. While the participants brought their own experience to the exercise, the idea was to shed their own backgrounds in the spirit of creating a new company that would benefit from their collective expertise.

The experience got designers to break free from their own corporate silos and look at their businesses from another industry's perspective. So Clive Grinyer, director of product design at Orange France Telecom, was able to get designers from fashion retailer Mexx to see the mobile phone as more than just a fashion accessory. Instead of thinking in terms of a designer-branded phone, he said, a mobile phone company such as Orange could provide a fashion brand with access to a customer blog on street fashion, for instance, enabling both companies to get more detailed consumer insight from a target customer group. "These kinds of ideas may not pan out, but it's a great test-bed for innovation," Grinyer said.

On the second day of Raymond, designers created a marketplace, taking turns manning their own stalls, where they listed what they were willing to give another designer and what they would like to receive. Philippe Picaud, head of design at French sports retailer. Decathlon, invited designers from other companies such as Lego and high-end stroller manufacturer Bugaboo to visit his team (comprising 120 designers) in Lille to get a closer look at the company's internal design processes—including sharing some of the key metrics and processes he uses internally to measure design effectiveness. "These tools show design's added value to management, but they also act as an education tool for designers to better understand a company's values and what measurements drive management," Picaud said.

Picaud has used design to help transform Decathlon from a retailer that sold other sporting brands such as Nike and Adidas to a company where 60 percent of sales now come from Decathlon's 15 private-label brands. He'd like to send some of his designers to other companies on short-term exchanges. These, he said, "are a way for my team to get new ideas and develop new ways of dealing with various design problems."

Design-led companies such as Decathlon and Lego boast an impressive track record of innovation. But even they believe opening up their studios to other companies has real potential benefits. Lego's design director, Torsten Bjorn, plans to visit some of the design departments of companies that were at Raymond with the aim of seeing how they integrate different design functions. "We all have different cultures and processes, and sharing our experience can inspire you to think and work in a different way," he said.

### Stretching the Mind of Design

It's a point of view shared by most of the participants. Orange's Grinyer offered to share online branding tools with designers from other industries. "When Orange and France Telecom's broadband provider Wanadoo came together we learned how to control 20 different websites within 20 different countries," he said. In exchange, Grinyer "bought" knowledge of Picaud's design metrics system. "This way I can go back and show management just how valuable my website tools are," he joked.

For others, such as Trevor Withell, director of innovation for Bugaboo, the main benefit of this open innovation exchange was discovering new ways to motivate his design team. "For designers, motivation isn't all about money," he said. He thinks the best way to keep designers motivated and innovation flowing is to open them up to new ideas and experiences. So he planned to send one of his head designers to a totally different type of company, such as a heavy engineering firm, to "really stretch the mind."

While Raymond reinforced the almost unlimited potential of open innovation in design, participants conceded the concept is not without challenges. As James Woudhuysen, professor of forecasting and innovation at De Montfort University in Leicester, England—who acted as an adviser at the event—points out, such ventures take time, money, and management commitment to develop and can lead to disputes about intellectual property. Still, Raymond showed open innovation is possible. "Getting 17 of the world's top corporate design directors in one room around a program of collaboration rather than egoism is already an achievement," Woudhuysen said. "To get, within two days, six agreements for pairs of design directors to embark on common projects is an even bigger success."

## Questions

1. Explain how the six best practices of innovation work at the Raymond conference.
2. How could social networking influence innovation?
3. How could innovation help create new forms of green IT?
4. How could a virtual world help innovation?
5. How could virtual workforces take advantage of innovation to create new products?
6. What ethical issues might a company find when pursing innovation?

---

## ✱ CLOSING CASE TWO

### Confusing Carbon

To help shoppers make green choices, companies are slapping carbon labels on products. But even if the public can interpret the information, will it help reduce greenhouse gas emissions?

Next time you are in a shoe store, pick up a pair of clogs or leather walking shoes from Timberland. Inside, right by the heel, you will find a single number that tells you how "green" the shoe is. This number is explained in a card in the shoe box that provides a 0-to-10 carbon rating. A zero means less than 2.5 kilograms of carbon and other greenhouse gases were emitted when the shoe was produced and shipped. And a 10? That is a whopping 100 kg, roughly equal to the carbon released if you drive a car 240 miles.

There is a simple premise behind the new label. Everyday activities, whether making pancakes or jetting across the sky, are linked to the combustion of fuel, which releases gases that contribute to global warming. Timberland believes climate-conscious shoppers will buy shoes that help them cut their carbon count. And those same customers will feel more loyal to the brand because Timberland respects their wishes. Sixty different Timberland products sport such numbers. They reflect both the "carbon footprint" of the shoes and other factors, such as the quantities of harmful chemicals used to make them. By 2010, Timberland plans to put the labels on all its shoes and clothing, and other companies are set to follow its lead. The goal, said Timberland CEO Jeffrey Swartz, is "to arm consumers with as much information as we can."

But will shoppers really be able to interpret such information? And even if the tags catch on, will they make a difference in reducing greenhouse gases?

Experts are divided on these questions. Climate scholars point out that it is almost impossible to distill into a single number the intricacies of carbon chemistry, manufacturing processes, supply chains—and how they all affect global warming. And the very idea of doing so is controversial. Britain-based Tesco, the world's third-largest retailer, has announced plans to make public how much carbon is released in the production, transport, and consumption of all 70,000 products on its supermarket shelves. The plan immediately drew howls of protests from manufacturers, who thought the burden of measuring emissions would land on their shoulders. Global environmental groups declared labels a distraction from more important corporate efforts to improve energy efficiency. Shoppers, meanwhile, seemed confused by the first such tags that appeared on store shelves, except when they were part of a larger education campaign. "It requires leadership, commitment, and pressure to make something like this happen," said Edgar Blanco, a research associate at the Massachusetts Institute of Technology who has studied carbon labels. "The truth is, no one knows how to educate consumers about this, or how it will work." The skeptics certainly have a point. Yet many shoppers are eager to understand how their own activities affect the environment. In a survey last summer by AccountAbility, a nonprofit that advises corporations and governments on sustainable business practices, nearly half of 2,734 U.S. and British consumers polled said they wanted to know which products caused the least harm.

Pioneers like Tesco understand they are in the midst of a Europewide crackdown on greenhouse gas emissions, and that if they don't act on reducing carbon, they could get slammed with punitive regulations. Since 2005 major carbon emitters such as power plants and oil refineries within the European Union have been forced to curtail greenhouse gases. A climate change bill will make Britain the first country in the world to introduce legally binding $CO_2$ reduction targets. The new law, aimed at lowering Britain's emissions 20 percent by 2010, will extend the cap on carbon to large, nonenergy-intensive businesses such as retailers, hotel chains, and banks. Retailer Marks & Spencer, for one, has an ambitious plan to become carbon-neutral and send zero waste to landfills by 2012.

Carbon labels were a logical outgrowth of the crackdown on greenhouse gases, which is also playing out in Washington and many state capitals. Timberland, for example, is pushing other shoemakers to agree on an industry standard. But companies heading down this path might learn from the challenges encountered by the pioneers.

The highest hurdle is simply obtaining an accurate carbon count on different goods, a laborious process that may initially cost $10,000 or more per item. In most countries, each manufacturer figures out for itself how to gather the data that become the number on the label. Britain is trying to hash out a national standard for measuring the greenhouse gas associated with each product and service, working with the Carbon Trust, a government-funded nonprofit. That should bring down the cost of counting carbon over time.

Even with a standard, counting can involve mind-boggling complexity. Unilever, a top supplier of household products to Tesco, operates 260 factories in 70 countries and works with more than 10,000 subcontractors. With a supply chain like that, even labeling a line of packaged noodles is a chore. Say Unilever decides to shift production of the noodles from Poland to South Wales to save money. Because of fuel consumption and other factors, that change has a big impact on the carbon tally, even though the same recipe is used. Unilever worries that Tesco may ask it to recalculate the carbon footprint for such products each time it moves production, which might be as often as once a week. If asked, "we couldn't do it," said Gavin Neath, Unilever's senior vice president for global corporate responsibility. "Our supply chain is constantly changing."

Tesco admits there are difficulties to work out. Said David North, Tesco's director of government affairs, "We have to bring suppliers with us on this journey. It is early days." Once the labels are in place, companies find, it's hard to tell if consumers get the point. In a survey PepsiCo commissioned from researchers Populus, half of the 1,000 people interviewed said they were more likely to buy a product with a carbon label. But such numbers, while well-intended, may not convey much. "What does it mean to say a bag of chips contains 75 grams of carbon?" asks Steve Howard, CEO of the Climate Group in London. "I have a PhD in environmental physics, and it doesn't mean a thing to me."

There's another complication in labeling products: By focusing consumers' attention on this one issue, the retailer risks undercutting other store programs that are also socially responsible. When Tesco unveiled its carbon program, as an interim step it put little airplane stickers on products that were air-freighted, to alert shoppers that more fuel was burned in transport than for goods shipped by boat or truck. That prompted protests from governments of developing countries, including Uganda and Kenya, which felt Tesco's plans unfairly punished producers there. "The moment consumers looked at this sticker, they would stigmatize those products," said Abraham Barno, agricultural attaché at Kenya's embassy in Britain. Tesco has promised to work with developing countries to promote their products.

Despite the controversy surrounding labeling and the challenges in counting the carbon, defenders say there are big side benefits. In times of $100-per-barrel oil, most companies want to be more energy-efficient, and calculating a carbon footprint is one of the best ways to find where energy is wasted in the production and distribution network.

## Questions

1. How can companies help reduce carbon emissions?
2. How can finding alternative energy sources help reduce IT energy consumption?
3. How can labeling IT equipment green help promote green initiatives?
4. Why do global organizations need to be concerned with green or social entrepreneurship initiatives?
5. What ethical issues are associated with green technology?

## ✱ MAKING BUSINESS DECISIONS

### 1. Buying Green

You have recently been hired by Exclusive Recycling, an IT recycling company. The company is paid to pick up organizational IT equipment and safely dispose of the waste. After working for the company for a few weeks you realize that the company does not dispose of the majority of the equipment, instead it fixes or upgrades the equipment and then sells it on eBay. The firms paying to have their IT equipment recycled are not aware of this practice. Do you believe Exclusive Recycling is acting ethically? Why or why not?

### 2. Running the Glove

Running IT is a collaborative social networking site for runners. It has tremendous success in the United State and has over 10 million members who use the site to pick runs, find running partners, register for marathons, discuss apparel, and so on. Running IT has hired you to help develop global websites in Europe, Asia, and Canada. What advice do you have for Running IT when it comes to expanding globally?

### 3. Building Alternatives

IBM plans to invest $1 billion a year in products and services that will help reduce IT power consumption in data centers. By using new techniques, within the next three years IBM plans to double the computing capacity of its data centers—more than 8 million square feet worldwide—without increasing power consumption. Explain why all organizations should be interested in similar plans.

## 4. Peace of Mind

Virtual Margaret is the nickname for Margaret Hooshmand, an executive assistant at Cisco Systems who works in San Jose, California, even though she's physically located in Richardson, Texas. Margaret uses a so-called telepresence system made by Cisco, which provides real-time videoconferencing on 65-inch high-definition plasma screens. A life-sized screen that shows her working at her desk 1,600 miles away in Texas now sits in her cubicle in San Jose. But she can see and interact with her boss, Senior Vice President Marthin De Beer, and co-workers say it's almost like she's really there. Although these systems cost upwards of $80,000 today, another five to 10 years of chip and Internet connection price improvements could make systems like this common—and further erode the geographical limitations of any job that doesn't absolutely require physical presence.

Virtual Margaret is the first of many uses for Cisco's telepresence system. You have been hired by First Corporation as the Vice president of new business and your boss, Mark Wallburg, has asked you to develop other uses for telepresence systems. Be sure to compile your ideas in a PowerPoint presentation highlighting your ideas, including pictures or diagrams indicating how the system will work and look.

## 5. Virtual Work

Nearly every business that wants to look remotely hip is opening an outlet in Second Life, the online virtual world where people can interact via computer-generated avatars, or graphic representations of themselves. But a few companies are starting to go further, taking real work, not just marketing, into these strange new worlds. For instance, 1-800-Flowers.com opened a "virtual greenhouse" where customers can view flower arrangements and chat with 1-800-Flowers avatars. About a dozen telesalespeople are literally working inside Second Life now. Chief Executive Jim McCann, who helped pioneer the concept of telesales, thinks virtual worlds could change the nature of employment even further, by allowing customers to design their own arrangements more easily. "The line between our customers and our staff continues to blur," he says.

LivingLive is a start-up consulting company specializing in virtual worlds. You are a recent new hire and your boss would like you to spend a few hours familiarizing yourself with virtual worlds and how businesses are competing in this new environment. Search the Internet and find several examples of current companies that are using virtual worlds in new and exciting ways to promote, change, and enhance business.

## 6. Experimenting Virtually

Virtual worlds like Second Life are not just for games. Companies are experimenting with virtual environments for everything from training exercises to meeting spaces for remote workers. But the technology still has pitfalls. For emergency responders working along Interstate 95, accidents are not a game; they are a way of life. So it seemed odd to a group of firefighters, police, and medics, when researchers from the University of Maryland suggested it use a virtual world to collaborate on training for rollovers, multicar pileups, and life-threatening injuries. At first, the emergency responders who make up the I-95 Corridor Coalition didn't take seriously the idea of a virtual world as a training tool, said Michael Pack, director of research with the University of Maryland's Center for Advanced Transportation Technology. "It wasn't until we started to do elaborate demos that the first responders started to realize the true potential," said Pack, who has begun rolling out a virtual world pilot project that could accommodate training for hundreds of emergency workers.

Industry analysts and developers of virtual worlds believe that by immersing users in an interactive environment that allows for social interactions, virtual worlds have the potential to succeed where other collaborative technologies, like teleconferencing, have failed.

Phone-based meetings begin and end abruptly. In a virtual world conversations between employees can continue within the virtual space—just like they do in company hallways after a meeting ends. Explain the value added by using a virtual world for interactive demonstrations and training. What other businesses in the 21st century could use virtual worlds for demonstrations and training?

# B21

# Mobile Technology

1. Identify the advantages and disadvantage of deploying cellular technology.
2. Describe how satellite technology works.
3. Explain how LBS, GPS, and GIS help to create business value.
4. Describe RFID and how it can be used to help make a supply chain more effective.

## Introduction

Mobile computing allows people to use IT without being tied to a single location. However, a relatively small number of enterprises (less than 25 percent) have a specific mobile strategy in place. Most struggle with individual mobile projects or try to link mobility to a broader IT strategy. Companies must focus on building a mobile strategy that addresses the peculiarities inherent in mobile computing. The strategy should leverage a number of uses across a variety of lines of businesses within the company to maximize the ROI (return on investment), standardize on architectures and platforms, and provide the most secure infrastructure available to eliminate (as much as possible) extremely costly data loss and security breaches inherent in mobile business. Understanding the different types of mobile technologies available will help executives determine how to best equip their workforce. These mobile technologies are discussed in this plug-in under the following topic headings:

- Using cellular technologies in business.
- Using satellite technologies in business.
- Using wireless technologies in business.

## Using Cellular Technologies In Business

Continental Airlines passengers in Houston will be able to board flights using just a cell phone or personal-digital assistant instead of a regular boarding pass at Bush Intercontinental Airport. The program could expand to airlines and airports nationwide. Instead of a paper pass, Continental Airlines and the Transportation Security Administration will let passengers show a code the airline has sent to their cell phone or PDA. The two-dimensional bar code, a jumble of squares and rectangles, stores the passenger's name and flight information. A TSA screener will confirm the bar code's authenticity with a handheld scanner. Passengers still need to show photo identification. The electronic boarding pass also works at airport gates. If a passenger's cell phone or mobile device loses power, the passenger can get a paper boarding pass from a kiosk or a Continental agent. Houston-based Continental, the nation's number four airline, has been working on the new feature for years to increase efficiency, eliminate paperwork, and make travel easier.

In less than 20 years, the mobile telephone has gone from being rare, expensive equipment of the business elite to a pervasive, low-cost personal item. Several countries, including the United Kingdom, now have more mobile phones than people. There are over 500 million active mobile phone accounts in China. Luxembourg has the highest mobile phone penetration rate in the world, at 164 percent. The total number of mobile phone subscribers in the world was estimated at 3.3 billion at the end of 2007, thus reaching an equivalent of over half the planet's population. At present, Africa has the largest growth rate of cellular subscribers in the world, its markets expanding nearly twice as fast as Asian markets. The availability of prepaid or pay-as-you-go services, where the subscriber is not committed to a long-term contract, has helped fuel this growth in Africa as well as in other continents.

Cellular telephones (cell phones) work by using radio waves to communicate with radio antennas (or towers) placed within adjacent geographic areas called cells. A telephone message is transmitted to the local cell by the cellular telephone and then is passed from antenna to antenna, or cell to cell, until it reaches the cell of its destination, where it is transmitted to the receiving telephone. As a cellular signal travels from one cell into another, a computer that monitors signals from the cells switches the conversation to a radio channel assigned to the next cell. In a typical analog cell phone system in the United States, the cell phone carrier receives about 800 frequencies to use across the city. The carrier chops up the city into cells. Each cell is typically 10 square miles. Cells are normally thought of as hexagons on a big hexagonal grid, as illustrated in Figure B21.1. Each cell has a base station that consists of a tower and a small building containing the radio equipment.

Older cellular systems are analog, and newer cellular systems are digital. Personal communication services (PCS) are one popular type of digital cellular service.

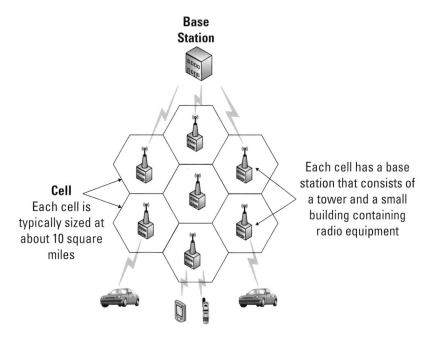

**Base Station**

**Cell**
Each cell is typically sized at about 10 square miles

Each cell has a base station that consists of a tower and a small building containing radio equipment

**FIGURE** B21.1

Cellular Technology Overview

| Generation | Technology | Advantages and Disadvantages |
|---|---|---|
| 1G | AMPS (Advanced Mobile Phone Service) | – Analog voice service only |
| 2G | CDMA (Code Division Multiple Access)<br>TDMA (Time Division Multiple Access)<br>GSM (Global Systems for Mobile Communications<br>PDC (Personal Digital Cellular) | – Digital voice service<br>– 9.6 Kbps to 14.4 Kbps data service<br>– Enhanced calling features (such as caller ID)<br>– No always-on data connection |
| 3G | W-CDMA (Wideband Code Division Multiple Access) | – Superior voice quality<br>– Always-on data connection up to 2 Mbps<br>– Broadband data services (such as streaming audio and video) |
| 4G | W-CDMA (Wideband Code Division Multiple Access)<br>MC-CDMA (Multi Carrier CDMA) | – Wi-fi access networks<br>– Always-on data connection 20–100 Mbps<br>– Converged data and voice over IP |

**FIGURE** B21.2

Cellular Technology
Advantages and
Disadvantages

PCS are entirely digital. They can transmit both voice and data and operate in a higher frequency range (1,900 MHz) than analog cellular telephones (analog cellular service operates in the 800 and 900 MHz bands). These digital cellular systems are capable of sending and receiving short text messages.

PCS are second-generation (2G) mobile communications technology, and analog cellular systems are first generation (1G). Second-generation cellular networks are circuit-switched digital networks that can transmit data at about 10 kilobits per second (Kbps), which is extremely slow. Third-generation (3G) networks use a newer packet-switched technology that is much more efficient (and hence faster) than dedicated circuit-switched networks. Third-generation networks have speeds ranging from 120 to 144 Kbps for mobile users in, for example, a car, and up to 2 gigabits per second (Gbps) for stationary users. These 3G networks are designed for high-speed transmission of multimedia data and voice. The major network operators are providing 3G services, and some groups and companies have already started working on fourth-generation (4G) mobile phone system. The 4G technology will take mobile communication another step up to integrate radio and television transmissions and to consolidate the world's phone standards into one high-speed technology. Figure B21.2 displays many of the cellular technologies along with their advantages and disadvantages.

The Finnish government decided that the fastest way to warn citizens of disasters was the mobile phone network. In Japan, mobile phone companies provide immediate notification of earthquakes and other natural disasters to their customers free of charge. In the event of an emergency, disaster response crews can locate trapped or injured people using the signals from their mobile phones. An interactive menu accessible through the phone's Internet browser notifies the company if the user is safe or in distress. In Finland, rescue services suggest hikers carry mobile phones in case of emergency even when deep in the forests beyond cellular coverage, as the radio signal of a cell phone attempting to connect to a base station can be detected by overflying rescue aircraft with special detection gear. In addition, users in the United States can sign up through their provider for free text messages when an Amber Alert goes out for a missing person in their area.

The latest trends in cell phones reflect a convergence of voice, video, and data communications. By blending information with entertainment, cell phones are center-stage in the evolving trend of mobile infotainment. As an example, the Apple iPhone is a revolutionary mobile phone that allows users to make calls, surf the web (Google and Yahoo! are built right in) over a wi-fi connection, email a photo, and use a widescreen iPod with touch controls to various content—including music, audiobooks, videos, TV shows, and movies. Technically speaking, the iPhone is a smartphone, discussed in the next section.

## PERSONAL DIGITAL ASSISTANTS

Personal digital assistants (PDA) are small, handheld computers capable of entirely digital communications transmission. They have built-in wireless telecommunications capabilities as well as work-organization software. PDAs can display, compose, send, and receive email messages, and some models can provide wireless access to the Internet. Unlike mobile phones, PDAs do not require subscription-based network services. They are stand-alone minicomputers, much like PCs before the Internet.

The first generation of successful PDAs were Palm Pilots. They primarily functioned as electronic organizers with support for address books, calendars, email, notes, and so on. The PDA only occasionally needs to connect to a companion PC for synchronization. For instance, a PDA can be synchronized with a PC address book, calendar, and email inbox via a USB cable. Newer PDA models can also connect to PCs wirelessly via Bluetooth (described in the next section), or connect to the Internet via wireless.

A *smartphone* combines the functions of a cellular phone and a PDA in a single device. It differs from a normal cell phone in that it has an operating system and local storage, so users can add and store information, send and receive email, and install programs to the phone as they could with a PDA. A smartphone gives users the best of both worlds—it has much the same capabilities as a PDA and the communications ability of a mobile phone.

As the old saying goes, "timing is everything." Nowhere is that more true than in the real estate business in Hawaii. Real estate agents continue to look for tools that will give them an edge. Real-time access to their area's multiple listing service (MLS) provides one way for agents to take advantage of timing. MLS offers a database of local properties for sale, with the ability to sort them by a variety of criteria. An agent who accesses a home's listing as soon as it hits the MLS gains a key advantage against the competition because the agent can immediately request a viewing or, at a minimum, simply drive by the location with a client.

Real estate agents are rarely in their offices, so they require technology that not only provides real-time access to their local MLS but also enables them to manage contact information, keep their calendars current, send and receive emails, view documents, calculate basic mortgage numbers and more. The lighter the solution, the better, so that they can leave the laptop behind when necessary. In addition, if they can combine that with cell phone functionality, they need only one device to conduct business.

Many real estate agents in Hawaii are using smartphones as a solution to their needs. Easy to carry and dependable, smartphones give them real-time access to their local MLS, enabling them to learn about properties as soon as they are listed for sale.

## BLUETOOTH

Electronic devices can connect to one another in many different ways. The various pieces and parts of computers, entertainment systems, and telephones, make up a community of electronic devices. These devices communicate with each other using a variety of wires, cables, radio signals, and infrared light beams, and an even greater variety of connectors, plugs, and protocols. Bluetooth technology eliminates the need for wires that tangle everyday lives. *Bluetooth* is a telecommunications industry specification that describes how mobile phones, computers, and personal digital assistants (PDAs) can be easily interconnected using a short-range wireless connection. Bluetooth headsets allow users to cut the cord and make calls even while their cell phones are tucked away in a briefcase. Wireless Bluetooth printing allows

**FIGURE** B21.3

Bluetooth Virtual Keyboard

**Beams of light, which detect the user's movements, make up this virtual keyboard.**

users of a Bluetooth-enabled PDA or laptop to attach to a printer via a Bluetooth adapter connected to the printer's communication port.

Since Bluetooth's development in 1994 by the Swedish telecommunications company Ericsson, more than 1,800 companies worldwide have signed on to build products to the wireless specification and promote the new technology in the marketplace. The engineers at Ericsson codenamed the new wireless technology Bluetooth to honor a 10th century Viking king, Harald Bluetooth, who is credited with uniting Denmark and bringing order to the country.

Bluetooth capability is enabled in a device by means of an embedded Bluetooth chip and supporting software. Although Bluetooth is slower than competing wireless LAN technologies, the Bluetooth chip enables Bluetooth networking to be built into a wide range of devices—even small devices such as cellular phones and PDAs. Bluetooth's maximum range is 30 feet, limiting it to gadget-to-gadget communication.

One challenge to wireless devices is their size. Everyone wants their mobile devices to be small, but many people also curse the tiny, cryptic keyboards that manufacturers squeeze into smart phones and PDAs. The laws of physics have proved a significant barrier to solving this problem, but VKB Inc.'s Bluetooth Virtual Keyboard offers a possible solution (see Figure B21.3). VKB's technology uses a red laser to illuminate a virtual keyboard outline on any surface. Despite its futuristic look, the laser is really just a visual guide to where users put their fingers. A separate illumination and sensor module invisibly tracks when and where each finger touches the surface, translating that into keystrokes or other commands.

## Using Satellite Technologies In Business

A special variation of wireless transmission employs satellite communication to relay signals over very long distances. A communications *satellite* is a big microwave repeater in the sky; it contains one or more transponders that listen to a particular portion of the electromagnetic spectrum, amplifying incoming signals, and retransmitting them back to Earth. A *microwave transmitter* uses the atmosphere (or outer space) as the transmission medium to send the signal to a microwave receiver. The microwave receiver then either relays the signal to another microwave transmitter or translates the signal to some other form, such as digital impulses. Microwave signals follow a straight line and do not bend with the curvature of the Earth; there-

**FIGURE** B21.4

Satellite Microwave Link

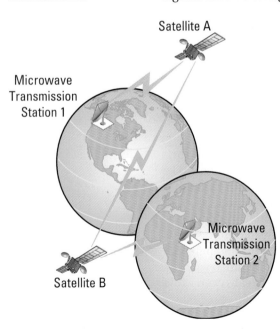

Satellite A

Microwave Transmission Station 1

Microwave Transmission Station 2

Satellite B

fore, long-distance terrestrial transmission systems require that microwave transmission stations be positioned about 37 miles apart, making this form of transmission expensive.

This problem can be solved by bouncing microwave signals off communication satellites, enabling them to serve as relay stations for microwave signals transmitted from terrestrial stations (as illustrated in Figure B21.4). Communication satellites are cost effective for transmitting large quantities of data over very long distances. Satellites are typically used for communication in large, geographically dispersed organizations that would be difficult to tie together through cabling media or terrestrial microwave. Originally, this microwave technology was used almost exclusively for satellite and long-range communication. Recently, however, developments in cellular technology allow complete wireless access to networks, intranets, and the Internet via microwave transmission.

Conventional communication satellites move in stationary orbits approximately 22,000 miles above the Earth. A newer satellite medium, the low-orbit satellite, travels much closer to the Earth and is able to pick up signals from weak transmitters.

Low-orbit satellites also consume less power and cost less to launch than conventional satellites. With such wireless networks, businesspeople almost anywhere in the world will have access to full communication capabilities, including voice communication via satellite phones, videoconferencing, and multimedia-rich Internet access.

General Motors is serious about satellite radio. Previously, GM made XM satellite radio standard on all Cadillacs, and now the subscription radio service will also be available for all new Buick, Hummer, and Saab models as well. The move enlarges XM's customer base while also giving drivers a chance to test the technology for three months free of charge.

The devices used for satellite communication range from handheld units to mobile base stations to fixed satellite dish receivers. The peak data transmission speeds range from 2.4 Kbps to 2 Mbps, depending on the solution being sought. For the everyday mobile professional, satellite communication does not provide a compelling benefit, but for people requiring voice and data access from remote locations or guaranteed coverage in non-remote locations, satellite technology may be worth while. Also, some satellite service providers offer roaming between existing cellular systems and satellite systems.

Satellite-based location will shape the future, creating new applications. Besides emergency call location and navigation in cars and on mobile phones, a range of new services will appear: personal assistance and medical care, localized presence services, finding friends, gaming, localized blogs, and so on. To enable the wide commercial success of each service, several key technological challenges need to be met: accuracy; ubiquity of service, including in dense urban areas and inside buildings; and delivery of information instantaneously.

**Location-based services (LBS)** are wireless mobile content services that provide location-specific information to mobile users moving from location to location. The market for location-based services is tremendous, with a variety of available and future services in a number of market segments: mobile telephony, enterprise, vertical markets, automotive and consumer devices. Figure B21.5 highlights many of the location-based services market segments that are currently pushing this technology.

| Mass Market | |
|---|---|
| Emergency Services | ■ Locate emergency call<br>■ Roadside assistance |
| Navigation Services | ■ Navigation to point of interest (directions, maps)<br>■ Etourism<br>■ Avoidance of traffic jams |
| Tracking Services | ■ Find-a-friend<br>■ Tracking of children<br>■ Elderly |
| Location Advertising | ■ Located video push |
| Gaming | ■ N-Gage (allows multiple gamers to play against each other over Bluetooth or wireless phone network connections) |
| Professional Market | |
| Workforce Organization | ■ Field force management<br>■ Optimization of routes<br>■ Logistics<br>■ Enterprise resource planning |
| Security | ■ Field tracking<br>■ Worker protection |

**FIGURE** B21.5

Location-Based Services Market Segments

Have you ever needed an ATM and not known where to find one? For tourists and businesspeople traveling far from home, that is an all-too-familiar predicament. Each year, 2 million cardholders contact MasterCard via telephone or the website looking for the location of nearby ATMs; some 70 percent of inquiries are received from international travelers venturing outside their home countries.

MasterCard now provides cardholders with a mobile, location-based search and directory service, so they can request the location of the nearest ATM be sent to their mobile phone via SMS (Short Message Service, or text message). The service, which works with all major mobile operators in the United States, is provided by MasterCard to cardholders free of charge (although operator text message rates may apply).

A user that employs location-based services on a regular basis faces a potential privacy problem. Many users consider location information to be highly sensitive and are concerned about a number of privacy issues, including:

- Target marketing: Mobile users' locations can be used to classify customers for focused marketing efforts.
- Embarrassment: One customer's knowledge of another's location may lead to embarrassing situations.
- Harassment: Location information can be used to harass or attack a user.
- Service denial: A health insurance firm might deny a claim if it learned that a user visited a high-risk area.
- Legal restrictions: Some countries regulate the use of personal data.

Unlike other information in cyberspace, location information has the potential to allow an adversary to physically locate a person, and therefore most wireless subscribers have legitimate concerns about their personal safety if such information should fall into the wrong hands. Laws and rules of varying clarity, offering different degrees of protection, have been or are being enacted in the United States, the European Union, and Japan.

### GLOBAL POSITIONING SYSTEM (GPS)

The most popular location-based service used today is the global positioning system. The *global positioning system (GPS)* is a constellation of 24 well-spaced satellites that orbit the Earth and make it possible for people with ground receivers to pinpoint their geographic location. The location accuracy is anywhere from 10 to 100 meters for most equipment. Accuracy can be pinpointed to within one meter with special military-approved equipment. Figure B21.6 illustrates the GPS architecture.

The GPS is owned and operated by the U.S. Department of Defense but is available for general use around the world. In 1993, the Defense Department made this global positioning technology available for commercial use to anyone who has a GPS device. GPS devices have special microprocessors that analyze satellite signals. Sirf Technology specializes in building GPS microprocessors for phones, electronics, and car navigation systems. Since going public in 2004, Sirf Technology has seen revenue climb 60 percent to $117 million with net profits of $30.7 million. With new federal regulation forcing wireless operators to include GPS in their phones and networking equipment, chip demand is exploding. Recently Sirf Technology has developed a golf GPS that helps golfers calculate the distance from the tee to the pin, or to know exactly where they are with relation to features such as hidden bunkers, water hazards, or greens. The United States Golf Association now permits distance-measuring devices for use in tournaments at the discretion of the organizers.

The market for GPS services has grown to more than $5 billion with expectations for demand to double over the next few years. Tracking, navigation, and hardware promise to be multibillion-dollar markets by 2010. UPS has outfitted 75,000 drivers with GPS-enabled handhelds to help them reach destinations more efficiently. The

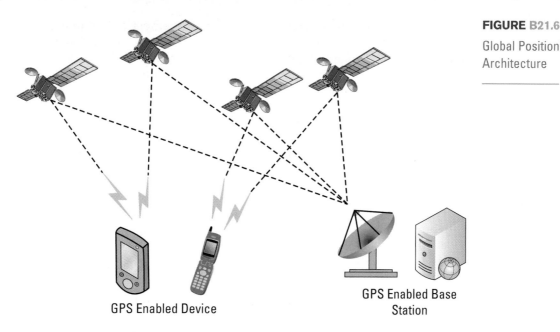

GPS Enabled Device

GPS Enabled Base
Station

handhelds will also trigger email alerts if a company vehicle speeds or ventures into unauthorized areas. Steve Wozniak, Apple co-founder, started a company in 2002 named Wheels of Zeus that combines GPS data with local wireless networking. The technology helps parents keep tabs on their children or can alert IT managers when company-owned computers leave the premises. Zingo, in the United Kingdom, uses GPS-enabled cars and text messaging to help subscribers hail cabs.

A **geographic information system (GIS)** is designed to work with information that can be shown on a map. Companies that deal in transportation use GISs combined with database and GPS technology. Airlines and shipping companies can plot routes with up-to-the-second information on the location of all their transport vehicles. Hospitals can keep track of where personnel are located by using a GIS and sensors that pick up the transmission of badges worn by hospital staff.

Automobiles have GPSs linked to maps that display, in a screen on the dashboard, driving directions and exact location of the vehicle. GM offers the OnStar system, which sends a continuous stream of information to the OnStar center about the car's exact location. The OnStar Vehicle Diagnostics automatically performs hundreds of diagnostic checks on four key operating systems—the engine/transmission, antilock brakes, air bags, and OnStar systems—in GM vehicles. The vehicle is programmed to send the results via email to the owner each month. The unique email report also provides maintenance reminders based on the current odometer reading, remaining engine oil life, and other relevant ownership information.

Some cell phone providers equip their phones with GPS chips that enable users to be located to within a geographical location about the size of a tennis court. This allows emergency services such as 911 to find a cell phone user. Marketers are monitoring cell phone GPS development, hoping to be able to call potential customers when they are walking past their store to let them know of a special sale.

American farmers on the leading edge use GPS satellite navigation to map and analyze fields, telling them where to apply the proper amounts of seeds, fertilizer, and herbicides. In the past farmers managed their business on a per-field basis; now they can micromanage. One Illinois farmer found that parts of his fields did not need any fertilizer after monitoring the soil. Less fertilizer lowers costs and reduces pollution from the runoff of water from the fields. One GPS application is to use geographic fixes from the GPS and a computerized counter to record how much grain is being harvested each second from each meter of the field. Then the farmer downloads this information into a personal computer, which produces a contour map that shows variations of, say, more than 60 bushels an acre. Cross-referencing this information to other variables, such as characteristics of the soil, allows the farmer to analyze why some land is less productive. The farmer combines these data with GPS navigational fixes to precisely apply herbicides or fertilizer only where it is really needed.

A GIS is useful for mobile applications, but it offers benefits that go well beyond what is required in a mobile environment. For example, using a GIS, users can decide what information is and is not relevant to them, and formulate their queries based on their personal criteria. Unlike a paper map, a GIS allows for in-depth analysis and problem solving that can make marketing, sales, and planning much more successful. The following are some common GIS uses:

- **Finding what is nearby.** This is the most common use for mobile users. Given a specific location, the GIS finds sources within a defined radius. This may include entertainment venues, medical facilities, restaurants, or gas stations. Users might also use the GIS to locate vendors that sell a specific item they want. This promotes mcommerce by matching buyers with sellers. The results can be provided using a map of the surrounding area or the destination addresses.

- **Routing information.** This is another common use for mobile users. Once users have an idea of where they want to go, a GIS can provide directions on how to get there. Once again, this can be provided graphically using a map or with step-by-step instructions. For mobile applications, it is often helpful to provide routing information in conjunction with search services.

- **Information alerts.** Users may want to be notified when information that is relevant to them becomes available based on their location. For example, a commuter might want to know if he or she is entering a section of the highway that has traffic congestion, or a shopper might want to be notified if his or her favorite store is having a sale on a certain item.

- **Mapping densities.** For business analysis, knowing population densities can be extremely useful. This allows users to find out where high concentrations of a certain population may be. Densities are typically mapped based on a standard area unit, such as hectares or square miles making it easy to see distributions. Examples of density mapping may include the location of crime incidents for police to determine where additional patrolling is required, or of customers to help determine ideal field delivery routes.

- **Mapping quantities.** People map quantities to find out where the most or least of a feature may be. This information could, for example, be used to determine where to locate a new business or service. For example, if someone is interested in opening a Laundromat, it would be prudent to determine how many others are in the area and what the population base is. This type of mapping can be useful for urban planning and environmental studies; for example, for city planners who are trying to determine where to build more parks.

A GIS can provide information and insight to both mobile users and people at fixed locations. This information uses the location coordinates provided by one of the positioning technologies to give details that are relevant to the user at that specific moment. Many of the location-based services discussed earlier would benefit from the information provided from a GIS.

## Using Wireless Technologies In Business

Denver International Airport (DIA) is betting that travelers will like getting something free, and so far, it looks like a good bet. The airport, one of the busiest in the Unites States, switched its public wi-fi offering from paid to advertising-supported. Within a week, and with no public notice of the change, wi-fi use grew tenfold. About 50 million passengers pass through DIA every year, with as many as 165,000 per day during busy times of the year. Now that wi-fi is free, there are 7,000 to 8,000 connections to the network per day. To link all those free users with the Internet, the airport had to increase its bandwidth and network infrastructure to allow 10 Mbps connections just for the wi-fi users.

***Wireless fidelity (wi-fi)*** is a means of linking computers using infrared or radio signals. Wi-fi, or what is sometimes referred to as wireless LANs, represent only a small proportion of LANs in operation today, but a rapidly growing proportion. Wi-fi technology has obvious advantages for people on the move who need access to the Internet in airports, restaurants, and hotels. Wi-fi is also gaining acceptance as a home or neighborhood network, permitting an assortment of laptop and desktop computers to share a single broadband access point to the Internet. Wireless LANs are also moving into the corporate and commercial world, especially in older buildings and confined spaces where it would be difficult or impossible to establish a wired LAN or where mobility is paramount. Even in newer buildings, wireless LANs are often being employed as overlay networks. In such cases, wi-fi is installed in addition to wired LANs so that employees can easily move their laptops from office to office and can connect to the network in places such as lunchrooms and patios.

After years of discussion and delay, U.S. airlines will start offering in-flight Internet connections, instant messaging, and wireless email, thus turning the airplane cabin into a wi-fi hotspot. Helping lead many of the airlines into the new era is AirCell, which in June 2006 won exclusive air-to-ground wi-fi rights by plunking down $31.3 million for 3 MHz of terrestrial digital wireless spectrum at a Federal Communications Commission auction. The company has already inked deals with American Airlines and Virgin America to install its air-to-ground system equipment, which company founder Jimmy Ray has been fine-tuning for the past decade and a half. The system will take to the air as soon as American Airlines retrofits a few of its transcontinental 767-200s. Virgin America will do the same for its 10-plane fleet, in addition to 31 planes on order from Airbus. Figure B21.7 illustrates how this "wi-fi in the sky" will work.

**FIGURE B21.7**
Wi-fi in the Sky

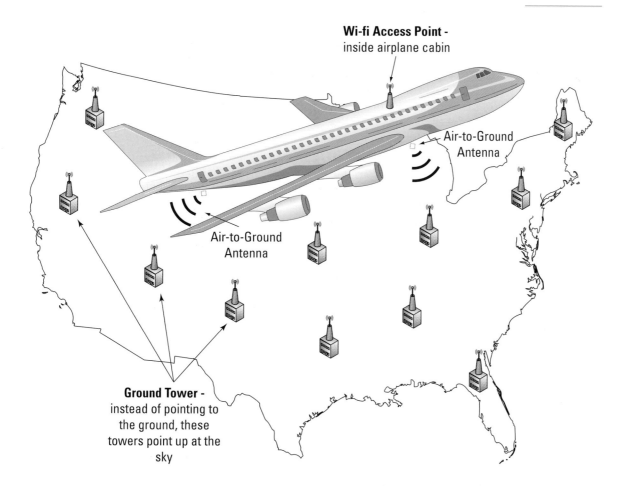

**Wi-fi Access Point -** inside airplane cabin

**Air-to-Ground Antenna**

**Air-to-Ground Antenna**

**Ground Tower -** instead of pointing to the ground, these towers point up at the sky

Recently, McDonald's has promised to outfit 14,000 of its locations with upscale coffee bars accompanied by expanded wi-fi service as the fast-food chain inches closer to offering the wireless technology free of charge. Currently, McDonald's provides wi-fi service to 15,000 of its 30,000 U.S. and international locations. The service is available most often through a credit card purchase or through Internet service provider Wayport.

While wi-fi is hot, security is not. With a laptop in the passenger seat of his SUV and a special antenna on the roof, Mike Outmesguine ventured off to sniff out wireless networks between Los Angeles and San Francisco. While en route, he got a big whiff of insecurity.

While his 800-mile drive confirmed that the number of wireless networks is growing explosively, he also found that only a third used basic encryption, a key security measure. In nearly 40 percent of the networks not a single change had been made to the gear's wide-open default settings.

"They took it out of the box, powered it up, and it worked. And they left it alone," said Outmesguine, who owns a technical services company. He frequently goes out on such drives in search of insecure networks. While Outmesguine says he doesn't try to break in, others aren't so benign. If criminals were to target unsecured wireless routers, they could create an attack that could piggyback across thousands of wi-fi networks in urban areas such as Chicago or New York City. A wi-fi attack could take over 20,000 wireless routers in New York City within a two-week period, with most of the infections occurring within the first day.

## WiMAX

The main problems with broadband access are that it is expensive and it does not reach all areas. The main problem with wi-fi access is that hotspots are very small, so coverage is sparse. An evolving technology that can solve all of these problems is called WiMAX. *WiMAX,* or Worldwide Interoperability for Microwave Access, is a telecommunications technology aimed at providing wireless data over long distances in a variety of ways, from point-to-point links to full mobile cellular type access. WiMAX can cover a stretch of as much as 3,000 square miles depending on the number of users. In New York City, for example, many base stations will be required around the city to meet the heavy demand, while a sparsely populated region will need fewer.

Sprint Nextel along with Google is developing a new mobile Internet portal using WiMAX wireless technology to offer web search and social networking. Sprint's WiMAX for high-speed wireless and its services for detecting location will be combined with Google tools including email, chat, and other applications. Sprint aims to use the emerging WiMAX technology to better compete with rival wireless and wired broadband networks. Sprint planned to test the WiMAX service in Chicago, Baltimore, and Washington by the end of 2008 with a goal of attaining coverage for 100 million people.

WiMAX offers web access speeds that are five times faster than typical wireless networks, though they are still slower than wired broadband. Higher-end notebook computers will have WiMAX technology built starting in late in 2008, though WiMAX cards that plug into a slot in the computer will also be available. Companies such as Nokia, Motorola, and Samsung Electronics are also making mobile devices and infrastructure with WiMAX technology.

WiMAX could potentially erase the suburban and rural blackout areas that currently have no broadband Internet access because phone and cable companies have not yet run the necessary wires to those remote locations.

A WiMAX system consists of two parts:

■ A WiMAX tower. A single WiMAX tower can provide coverage to a very large area—as big as 3,000 square miles.

■ A WiMAX receiver. The receiver and antenna could be built into a laptop the way wi-fi access is today.

A WiMAX tower station can connect directly to the Internet using a high-bandwidth, wired connection (for example, a T3 line). It can also connect to another WiMAX tower using a line-of-sight, microwave link. This connection to a second tower (often referred to as a backhaul) is what allows WiMAX to provide coverage to remote rural areas. Figure B21.8 illustrates the WiMAX architecture.

Wi-fi-style access will be limited to a four-to-six mile radius (25 square miles of coverage, which is similar in range to a cell-phone zone). Through the stronger line-of-sight antennas, the WiMAX transmitting station would send data to WiMAX-enabled computers or routers set up within the transmitter's 30-mile radius. This is what allows WiMAX to achieve its maximum range. Figure B21.9 displays many of the benefits of the WiMAX technology.

## RADIO FREQUENCY IDENTIFICATION (RFID)

***Radio frequency identification (RFID)*** technologies use active or passive tags in the form of chips or smart labels that can store unique identifiers and relay this information to electronic readers. RFID tags, often smaller than a grain of sand, combine tiny chips with an antenna. When a tag is placed on an item, it automatically radios its location to RFID readers on store shelves, checkout counters, loading bay doors, and shopping carts. With RFID tags, inventory is taken automatically and continuously. RFID tags can cut costs by requiring fewer workers for scanning items; they also can provide more current and more accurate information to the entire supply chain. Wal-Mart saves on average $8.4 billion a year by installing RFID in many of its operations. Figure B21.10 illustrates one example of an RFID architecture.

The advent of RFID has allowed everyone from shipping companies to hospitals to reduce costs and overhead by creating visibility into inefficient business processes.

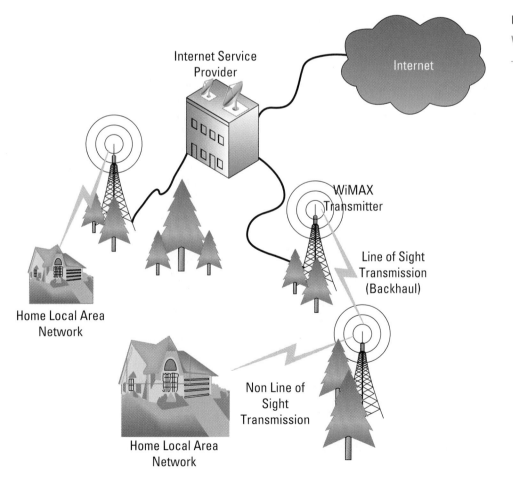

**FIGURE B21.8**

WiMAX Architecture

Internet Service Provider

Internet

WiMAX Transmitter

Line of Sight Transmission (Backhaul)

Home Local Area Network

Non Line of Sight Transmission

Home Local Area Network

| Benefit | Description |
|---------|-------------|
| Long Range | The most significant benefit of WiMAX compared to existing wireless technologies is the range. WiMAX has a communication range of up to 30 miles, enough to blanket an entire city. |
| Low Cost | Base stations will cost less than $20,000 but will still provide customers with T1-class connections. |
| Wireless | By using a WiMAX system, companies/residents no longer have to rip up buildings or streets or lay down expensive cables. |
| High Bandwidth | WiMAX can provide shared data rates of up to 70 Mbps. This is enough bandwidth to support more than 60 businesses at once with T1-type connectivity. It can also support over a thousand homes at 1 Mbps DSL-level connectivity. |
| Service | WiMAX can provide users with two forms of wireless service:<br>1. Non-line of sight operates at 2 to 11 GHz, which at a lower level frequency has the ability to bend around obstacles more easily. A small antenna on a computer connects to the tower and is backward compatible with existing wi-fi technologies.<br>2. Line of sight can go as high as 66 GHz since the signal is stronger and more stable, which leads to greater bandwidth. A fixed dish antenna points straight at the tower or for communication between tower to tower. |

**FIGURE B21.9**

WiMAX Benefits

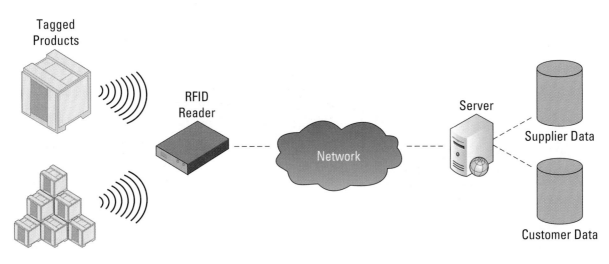

**FIGURE B21.10**

RFID Architecture

Aberdeen's research shows that 38 percent of enterprises using RFID are doing so to improve the cost, safety, and reliability of managing business processes. Organizations are leveraging RFID to improve the productivity of their workforce all while simplifying the implementation and ongoing management costs of their networks.

When Wal-Mart announced its RFID strategy in 2003, it was just one of many retailers that had become enamored of the technology. By placing RFID tags on cases and pallets shipped from manufacturers to Wal-Mart distribution centers, companies would be able to keep close tabs on their shipments. In turn, that would allow Wal-Mart and its suppliers to streamline their supply chains and ultimately ensure shelves were always fully stocked.

RFID tags represented the next big step forward from bar codes, the ubiquitous stripes on the sides of packages that provide basic product and pricing information. The simplest tags, passive RFID tags, require no internal power supply. Incoming radio frequency signals from RFID readers can transmit a minute electrical current, enough to power the integrated circuit in the tag and transmit a response. The key benefit is that the bar code on a case or pallet no longer needs to be swiped to identify the contents; the tag just needs to come within range of a reader—anywhere from a few feet up to 600 feet. In addition, RFID tags can transmit far more information about a product, including price, serial number, and even when and where it was made.

Much of the recent interest surrounding RFID has arisen from mandates and recommendations by government agencies such as the U.S. Department of Defense (DoD) and the Food and Drug Administration (FDA), and from a few private-sector megacorporations.

RFID technologies offer practical benefits to almost anyone who needs to keep track of physical assets. Manufacturers improve supply chain planning and execution by incorporating RFID technologies. Retailers use RFID to control theft, increase efficiency in their supply chains, and improve demand planning. Pharmaceutical manufacturers use RFID systems to combat the counterfeit drug trade and reduce errors in filling prescriptions. Machine shops track their tools with RFID to avoid misplacing tools and to track which tools touched a piece of work. RFID-enabled smart cards help control perimeter access to buildings. In the last couple of years, owing in large part to Wal-Mart and DoD mandates, many major retail chains and consumer goods manufacturers have begun testing pallet- and case-level merchandise tagging to improve management of shipments to customers.

RFID tags differ from conventional bar code tags in a number of ways. These differences create the benefit of adopting the technology, while simultaneously creating the greatest concern over the privacy issues involved. For example, under today's bar code technology, a pack of Wrigley's gum sold in Houston has the same bar code as a pack sold in New York City. With RFID, however, each pack would have a unique ID code that could be tied to the purchaser of that gum when the buyer uses an "item registration system" such as a frequent shopper card or a credit card.

The purchaser could then be tracked if he or she entered that same store again, or perhaps more frightening, entered any other store with RFID reading capability. Unlike a bar code, RFID tags can be read from much greater distances and the reading of such devices is nondirectional. This means that if someone enters a store with a pack of gum in a pocket or purse, the RFID reader can identify that pack of gum, the time and date it was purchased, where it was purchased, and how frequently the consumer comes into the store. If a credit card or a frequent shopper card was used to purchase the gum, the manufacturer and store could also tie that information to the consumer's name, address, and email and then direct targeted advertisements by gum companies as the shopper walks down the aisles, or send mailings through email or regular mail about other products.

As the technology behind RFID advances, the potential for privacy infringement does as well. RFID already has the capability to determine the distance of a tag from the reader location. With such technology already available, it is not difficult to imagine a situation in which retailers could determine the location of individuals within the store, and thus target specific advertisements to that customer based upon past purchases (as in the gum example used above). In effect, that store would be creating a personal log of past purchases, shopping patterns, and ultimately behavioral patterns. While such information gathering would be considered intrusive enough by many consumers' standards, the danger that such information could be sold to other retailers (similar to the way such profiles are currently sold regarding Internet commerce) could create potentially devastating information vulnerabilities. While some RFID critics have pointed out that the technology could lead to some sort of corporate "Big Brother," concern more widespread that allowing RFID to develop without legal restrictions will eliminate the possibility for consumers to refuse to give such information to retailers.

Some steps are being taken to mitigate these privacy issues. For example, a recent proposal would require that all RFID-tagged products be clearly labeled.

This would give consumers the choice to select products without RFID, or at a minimum to recognize that the items they select are being tracked. For those unsatisfied with disclosure, a growing number of products are designed to limit exposure to RFID tagged products. One such product is "Kill Codes," a command that turns off all RFID tags immediately as the consumer comes into contact with them, thus eliminating the effectiveness of the technology. Another countermeasure against RFID privacy invasion is "RSA Blocker Tags," which try to address privacy concerns while maintaining the integrity of the product. Under this technology, the item can be tracked only by that store's authorized reader, meaning customers cannot be tracked outside of the store in which they purchased the item.

With RFID becoming both smarter and smaller, the possibilities for its uses are endless (see Figure B21.11). While RFID poses certain ethical dilemmas for government and commercial operations, it also simplifies life for the common person. As medical benefits are explored further, RFID tags will not only be used for convenience and profit, but also for saving lives.

**FIGURE B21.11**

Unusual Uses of RFID

| RFID Use | Description |
|---|---|
| Preventing toilets from overflowing | You can purchase a "smart" toilet, one that shuts itself off when it is close to overflowing. According to AquaOne, its RFID-enhanced toilets are not only convenient, but they also prevent health risks in public places such as hospitals and nursing homes. |
| Identifying human remains | Hurricane Katrina left behind many unclaimed casualties, despite the tireless searches by countless people. Thanks to the VeriChip, RFID tags are now being used to locate bodies in an effort to reunite loved ones. This helps to identify cadavers during transport, and coroners are now able to collect body parts for burial in their rightful places. |
| Getting into nightclubs | Barcelona's Baja Beach Club is now grafting RFID tags into the arms of patrons who want instant access to the exclusive hangout. The tag also functions as a debit card. |
| Cooking with robots | Robotic pots and pans with RFID chips in the handles make it almost impossible to botch a meal. With these RFID chips, the cookware can be coordinated with a recipe card that has a similar chip. Then, the cookware will set its temperature and duration to the exact specifications the food calls for. |
| Timing athletic events | RFID transponders are being used as timing systems in major sporting events all over the world, including the Boston Marathon and Ironman championships (as described in the opening case). With a chip attached to an athlete's shoe, bicycle, etc., timing can begin and end with the utmost accuracy; the timer stops when the person crosses the finishing mat, which contains an antenna that will be signaled by the RFID chip. The technology is especially handy in very close finishes between competitors. |
| Tracking wheels of cheese | To track cheese through each process and handler until it is sold, RFID tags are being placed just under the edges of the food products. The industry is having problems with theft, loss, and even counterfeit cheese. While the idea of black market cheese may sound ridiculous, consider this—just one wheel of Parmesan cheese can be worth several hundred dollars. |
| Monitoring casinos | Casinos are already heavily monitored, but the unique betting habits of each player can now be logged, thanks to RFID tags inside betting chips. The chips keep track of high rollers and their spending patterns, and they make it even harder for thieves to counterfeit chips or steal them from other players. All of this technology is used to stack more odds in the house's favor. |
| Tracking razor blades | Thanks to low-cost RFID tags, Gillette can now afford to place small transponders in each package of its popular razor products. This is done in an attempt to salvage more razors as they make their way through a very convoluted supply chain. Many of the small products are lost or stolen. While it might sound trivial for the company to worry about losing a razor here and there, the problem is really far worse than that. Gillette's Mach 3 razor, retailing at more than $10 each, is one of the most commonly stolen items in a store. |
| Issuing passports | The U.S. State Department has approved of passports with microchips inside, and the technology is already being tested in trials. While the government maintains that its purpose is to improve communication between law enforcement agencies, others feel there will be more sinister repercussions. |

M obile computing allows people to use IT without being tied to a single location. Mobile IT devices can change the way people do business—new technologies lead to new ways of working and new products and services that can be offered to customers. Mobility can bring new business opportunities, for example, the spin-off businesses surrounding the mobile phone industry.

Organizations are taking advantage of global positioning systems, location-based services, wireless fidelity, and mobile technologies in the information systems applications they are building. It is important to understand which technologies are available and how businesses can leverage these technologies in their daily and long-term strategic operations.

## ✱ KEY TERMS

Bluetooth, 527
Geographic information system (GIS), 531
Global positioning system (GPS), 530

Location-based services (LBS), 529
Microwave transmitter, 528
Radio frequency identification (RFID), 535

Satellite, 528
Smartphone, 527
WiMAX, 534
Wireless fidelity (wi-fi), 533

## ✱ CLOSING CASE ONE

### Loopt

Loopt, a company started by two Stanford graduate students based in Mountain View, California, is a revolutionary "social mapping" service that aims to change the way people use mobile phones to keep in touch with their friends. Loopt uses GPS (and other location technology) to show you where your friends are by automatically updating maps on your mobile handset. The most frequent text message in the world is "Where R U?" Loopt answers that question. Available on Boost Mobile, Sprint Nextel, Verizon, AT&T, MetroPCS, select BlackBerry devices, the iPhone and the T-Mobile G1, Loopt helps friends connect on the fly and navigate their social lives by orienting them to people, places and events. Users can also share location updates, geo-tagged photos and comments with friends in their mobile address book or on online social networks, communities and blogs. Loopt was designed with user privacy at its core and offers a variety of effective and intuitive privacy controls.

A few Loopt products and services are:

- **Loopt's geosocial networking services:** This service shows users where friends are located and what they are doing via maps on their mobile phones.

- **Mobile application:** The Loopt software provides real-time location updating. Users can update location and status and share with friends.

- **Website:** Loopt provides a web portal which is synchronized with the mobile version of the service.

- **Facebook application:** The application was developed for users to share location with friends in the Facebook network.

- **Twitter and Facebook integration:** Status updates with a location link can be sent via Loopt to a user's Twitter status or Facebook status.
- **Loopt for the iPhone:** In addition to the location and status updating, Loopt integrated Yelp! (a social networking website) content into the iPhone version of the service. The iPhone application was also the first to have Twitter integration.

The way that Loopt works is users of Loopt must register their cell phone number, full name, date of birth, and email address. Loopt's privacy notice states that users can control who receives geo-location information via privacy setting.

Loopt has signed a deal with CBS Mobile to provide advertising based on GPS location information. This means that if you're a Loopt user and happen to be browsing a CBS Mobile site, such as CBS Sports, you may see an ad for a restaurant that happens to be right down the street. The ads are delivered on micro browser web pages versus SMS, so they will feel similar to a banner ad on the web, except they will be hyper-targeted. The CBS deal is a sizable media partner; the company currently claims more than 75 million page views across its mobile sites every month.

Currently, Loopt is a mobile social networking tool of sorts for keeping track of the physical location of your friends—useful for planning a spontaneous meetup or, for the more adventurous, meeting new people. The service also recently added the ability to broadcast your location to non-Loopt users by way of IM or text messaging. Advertisers pay a premium for hyper-targeting, and in Loopt's case, not only will they have demographic information based on user profiles, but also know a user's precise location at a given time.

## Questions

1. What business services or functions can benefit from using location-based services?
2. With competitors such as Pelago's Whrrl and Google Latitude, what is Loopt's competitive advantage?
3. With security and privacy major concerns for users thinking of using location-based services, what precautions should they take?

---

### ★ CLOSING CASE TWO

### Clearwire

Some of the biggest names in the technology and media business, including Intel, Google, Sprint, and Comcast, have teamed up to invest $3.2 billion in the start-up Clearwire. The Kirkland, Washington, company founded by entrepreneur Craig McCaw has high hopes of shaking up the wireless industry. The idea is that Clearwire will offer an alternative to the two big incumbent U.S. operators, AT&T and Verizon Wireless, by rolling out a technology called WiMAX to provide superfast Internet service for cell phones, laptops, and other devices. Clearwire offers a robust suite of advanced high-speed Internet services to consumers and businesses. The company is building the first nationwide 4G mobile Internet wireless network, bringing together an unprecedented combination of speed and mobility. Clearwire's network, combined with significant wireless spectrum holdings, provides unmatched network capacity to deliver next-generation broadband access. Clearwire currently provides mobile WiMAX-based service, to be branded Clear™, in Baltimore, Maryland, and Portland, Oregon, and provides pre-WiMAX communications services in 50 markets across the United States and Europe.

Clearwire's network provides customers with average download speeds initially of 2M to 4M bps and peak rates that are considerably faster. In the Portland rollout, mobile, residential and business plans can be purchased by the day or by the month without long-term service contracts. Home Internet service plans start at $20 per month, while mobile Internet plans start at $30 per month, or customers can purchase a day pass for $10.

Portland's WiMAX mobile customers will access the service through a WiMAX-enabled USB modem for laptops that costs $49.99. Customers can purchase the modem from a local retail store or online, and activate service at their convenience, anywhere in Clearwire's coverage area.

For residential service, Clearwire offers customers a wireless high-speed modem. Customers plug the modem into a power outlet anywhere in their home or office and connect the modem to a PC. The residential modem can be leased for $4.99 monthly.

Clearwire hopes its combined wireless spectrum with Sprint will allow the company to achieve greater coverage, cost and operational efficiency, and bandwidth utilization than either company could by operating alone.

The only current competitor to Clearwires's WiMAX is a similar technology called LTE which is part of the third-generation membership project (or 3GPP), backed by such major wireless carriers as AT&T, China Mobile, Verizon Wireless, and Vodafone. LTE uses a 700 MHz spectrum, which AT&T and Verizon Wireless recently acquired parts of through the FCC's spectrum auction. The unique advantage of the low frequency is that it is better suited for passing through office buildings and walls in urban environments. LTE can also cover longer distances than WiMAX in 2.5 GHz, but it is believed that more cell sites will be required to match the capacity of 2.5 GHz. Verizon Wireless and Vodafone currently have an ongoing trial, although AT&T doesn't.

## Questions

1. From a security perspective, what key advantages does WiMAX offer over traditional WiMAX implementations?

2. What types of business applications would benefit from using WiMAX and GPS? Or WiMAX and GIS? WiMAX and RFID?

3. What competitive advantages does WiMAX have over LTE?

## ★ MAKING BUSINESS DECISIONS

### 1. Smart-Fi's Wi-Fi

Smart-Fi is a new start-up company developing devices that will track your position or any items that you own—everywhere you go. Currently Smart-Fi plans a hybrid system that will combine RFID tags, Bluetooth and wi-fi in small keychain-sized devices that communicate with a central hub—perhaps an advanced smartphone. Currently the technology can tag 100 items and has a range of around 325 feet and uses the existing wi-fi infrastructure in buildings to triangulate different tags and hub locations. Smart-Fi's wi-fi network is augmented with special transmitters that improve positional accuracy down to about three feet. The potential for this technology is boundless. Create a list of the many opportunities this type of technology opens up to businesses and consumers.

### 2. Flexible Garments 2.0

You have just been hired to work for a new garment manufacturing company called FG 2.0, or Flexible Garments 2.0, that makes clothing with wearable electronics sewn in. One such product that FG 2.0 is current working on is the Aspen jacket that has a joystick built into the wrist flaps for controlling an iPod for music on the slopes without opening the jacket and letting the cold air in. In addition, there's also the set of T-shirts with dynamic illumination, like the wi-fi T-shirt which shows the strength of a wi-fi signal near the wearer, or the T-equalizer "fun" T-shirt which reacts to external noise and displays a graphic equalizer on the T-shirt front, perfect for music festivals. You have been asked to develop a report on how the future of wearable electronics will be really smart clothing. The current FG 2.0 products are all very neat and convenient, but they're not very smart.

### 3. Mapping the Future of Eco-Systems

Eco-Systems, a tech start-up in Denver, Colorado, has created a geographic information system (GIS) capable of capturing, storing, analyzing, and displaying geographically referenced information, that is, data identified according to location. In addition, the company's GIS includes the procedures, operating personnel, and spatial data that go into the system.

Eco-Systems uses its GIS for development and analysis of map data for informed decision making. The map data the company uses might be represented in several different layers such as waterlines, road systems, soils, hydrology, or 911 addresses. Each layer is linked to a database that contains information about each feature in that layer.

Currently Eco-Systems is looking to use GPS technology along with their GIS application. They need your help in identifying the advantages that GPS will offer them. Create a brief report on your findings as well as who they could market their products to.

### 4. Getting Smart with RedRover, RedRover

RedRover Corporation develops wireless technology solutions that make things smarter. Their unique capability is developing low-cost RFID systems with:

- Highly miniaturized and durable tags
- Portable handheld readers
- Moderate to long-range detection
- Directional communication
- Innovative power management design

There are many potential applications for their technology, including RFID golf balls that help a player locate golf balls quickly which can save time, penalty strokes and the frustration of searching for lost golf balls. Their breakthrough RFID golf balls have been a huge success. RedRover produces a findable golf ball system powered by a radio-frequency microchip that is embedded in the core of the ball. The RedRover golf ball has been benchmarked favorably against leading premium golf balls for both distance and spin and is included on the USGA list of conforming golf balls.

RedRover needs help in identifying new innovative products to add to their current offering. You have been asked to assist with identifying a few unique yet marketable products or services that are based on RFID technology.

| Project Number | Project Name | Project Type | Plug-In | Focus Area | Project Level | Skill Set | Page Number |
|---|---|---|---|---|---|---|---|
| 19 | Too Much Information | Excel | T3 | CRM | Advanced | PivotTable | 555 |
| 20 | Turnover Rates | Excel | T3 | Data Mining | Advanced | PivotTable | 555 |
| 21 | Vital Information | Excel | T3 | Data Mining | Advanced | PivotTable | 556 |
| 22 | Breaking Even | Excel | T4 | Business Analysis | Advanced | Goal Seek | 556 |
| 23 | Profit Scenario | Excel | T4 | Sales Analysis | Advanced | Scenario Manager | 557 |
| 24 | Electronic Résumés | HTML | T9, T10, T11 | Electronic Personal Marketing | Introductory | Structural Tags | 557 |
| 25 | Gathering Feedback | Dreamweaver | T9, T10, T11 | Data Collection | Intermediate | Organization of Information | 557 |
| 26 | Daily Invoice | Access | T5, T6, T7, T8 | Business Analysis | Introductory | Entities, Relationships, and Databases | 558 |
| 27 | Billing Data | Access | T5, T6, T7, T8 | Business Intelligence | Introductory | Entities, Relationships, and Databases | 560 |
| 28 | Inventory Data | Access | T5, T6, T7, T8 | SCM | Intermediate | Entities, Relationships, and Databases | 561 |
| 29 | Call Center | Access | T5, T6, T7, T8 | CRM | Intermediate | Entities, Relationships, and Databases | 562 |
| 30 | Sales Pipeline | Access | T5, T6, T7, T8 | Business Intelligence | Advanced | Entities, Relationships, and Databases | 563 |
| 31 | Second Life—Virtual Networking | N/A | N/A | Collaboration | Introductory | The Digital Economy | 564 |
| 32 | Creating a Podcast | N/A | N/A | Collaboration | Introductory | The Digital Economy | 565 |
| 33 | Google Earth—Geographic Information | N/A | N/A | Geographic Web | Intermediate | The Digital Economy | 566 |
| 34 | Photo Story 3—Show-n-Tell | N/A | N/A | Electronic Personal Marketing | Intermediate | The Digital Workforce | 567 |
| 35 | Sticky Wiki | N/A | N/A | Collaboration | Intermediate | The Digital Workforce | 568 |

**NOTE:** Many of the Excel projects support multiple data files. Therefore the naming convention that you see in the text may not be the same as what you see in a data folder. As an example, in the text we reference data files as AYK1_Data.xlsx; however, you may see a file named AYK1_Data_Version_1.xlsx, or AYK1_Data_Version_2.xlsx.

## Project 1:
## Financial Destiny

You have been introduced to Microsoft Excel and are ready to begin using it to help track your monthly expenses and take charge of your financial destiny. The first step is to create a personal budget so you can see where you are spending money and if you need to decrease your monthly expenses or increase your monthly income.

### Project Focus

Create a template for a monthly budget of your income and expenditures, with some money set aside for savings (or you can use the data file, AYK1_Data.xlsx, we created). Create variations of this budget to show how much you could save if you cut back on certain expenses, found a roommate, or got a part-time job. Compare the costs of a meal plan to costs of groceries. Consider how much interest would be earned if you saved $100 a month, or how much debt paid on student loans or credit card bills. To expand your data set, make a fantasy budget for 10 years from now, when you might own a home, have student loan payments, and have a good salary.

**Data File: AYK1_Data.xlsx**

## Project 2:
## Cash Flow

Gears is a five-year-old company that specializes in bike components. The company is having trouble paying for its monthly supplies and would like to perform a cash flow analysis so it can understand its financial position. Cash flow represents the money an investment produces after subtracting cash expenses from income. The statement of cash flows summarizes sources and uses of cash, indicates whether enough cash is available to carry on routine operations, and offers an analysis of all business transactions, reporting where the firm obtained its cash and how it chose to allocate the cash. The cash flow statement shows where money comes from, how the company is going to spend it, and when the company will require additional cash. Gears would like to project a cash flow statement for the next month.

### Project Focus

Using the data file AYK2_Data.xlsx complete the cash flow statement for Gears using Excel. Be sure to create formulas so the company can simply input numbers in the future to determine cash flow.

**Data File: AYK2_Data.xlsx**

## Project 3:
## Technology Budget

Tally is a start-up website development company located in Seattle, Washington. The company currently has seven employees and is looking to hire six new employees in the next month.

### Project Focus

You are in charge of purchasing for Tally. Your first task is to purchase computers for the new employees. Your budget is $250,000 to buy the best computer systems with a scanner, three color printers, and business software. Use the web to research various products and calculate the costs of different systems using Excel. Use a variety of Excel formulas as you analyze costs and compare prices. Use the data file AYK3_Data.xlsx as a template.

**Data File: AYK3_Data.xlsx**

## Project 4:

### Tracking Donations

Lazarus Consulting is a large computer consulting company in New York. Pete Lazarus, the CEO and founder, is well known for his philanthropic efforts. Pete knows that most of his employees contribute to nonprofit organizations and wants to reward them for their efforts while encouraging others to contribute to charities. Pete began a program that matches 50 percent of each employee donation. The only stipulations are that the charity must be a nonprofit organization and the company will only match up to $2,000 per year per employee.

### Project Focus

Open the data file AYK4_Data.xlsx and determine the following:

- What was the total donation amount per organization?
- What were the average donations per organization?

**Data File: AYK4_Data.xlsx**

## Project 5:

### Convert Currency

You have decided to spend the summer traveling abroad with your friends. Your trip is going to take you to France, England, Italy, Switzerland, Germany, Norway, and Ireland. You want to use Excel to convert currencies as you travel around the world.

### Project Focus

Locate one of the exchange rate calculators on the Internet (www.xe.com or www.x-rates.com). Find the exchange rates for each of the countries listed above and create formulas in Excel to convert $100, $500, and $1,000. Use the data file AYK5_Data.xlsx as a template.

**Data File: AYK5_Data.xls**

## Project 6:

### Cost Comparison

You are thinking about purchasing a new computer since the machine you are using now is four years old, slow, not always reliable, and does not support the latest operating system. Your needs for the new computer are simple: anti-virus software, email, web browsing, word processing, spreadsheet, database, iTunes, and some light-weight graphical tools. Your concern is what the total cost of ownership will be for the next three years. You have to factor in a few added costs beyond just the initial purchase price for the computer itself, such as: added hardware (this could include a new printer, docking station, or scanner), software (purchase of a new operating system), training (you're thinking about pursuing web training to get an internship next term), subsequent software upgrades, and maintenance.

### Project Focus

- It is useful to think about costs over time—both direct as well as indirect costs. Part of the reason this distinction is important is that a decision should rest not on the nominal sum of the purchase, but rather on the present value of the purchase.
- A dollar today is worth more than a dollar one year from now.
- The relevant discount rate (interest rate) is your marginal cost of capital corresponding to a level of risk equal with the purchase.
- Use the data file AYK6_Data.xlsx as a template.

| | A | B | C | D | E | F |
|---|---|---|---|---|---|---|
| 1 | COST OF NEW COMPUTER | | | | | |
| 2 | Discount Rate | 1 | 0.9325 | 0.9109 | 0.7051 | |
| 3 | | Time 0 | Year 1 | Year 2 | Year 3 | Present Value Costs |
| 4 | Computer | | | | | |
| 5 | Software | | | | | |
| 6 | Additional Hardware | | | | | |
| 7 | Training | | | | | |
| 8 | Software upgrades | | | | | |
| 9 | Maintenance | | | | | |
| 10 | | | | | | |
| 11 | Total Costs | | | | | |
| 12 | | | | | | |

**Data File: AYK6_Data.xlsx**

## Project 7:

## Time Management

You have just been hired as a business analyst by a new start-up company called Multi-Media. Multi-Media is an interactive agency that constructs phased and affordable website market-ing, providing its clients with real and measurable solutions that are supported by easy-to-use tools. Since the company is very new to the business arena, it needs help in creating a project management plan for developing its own website. The major tasks for the development team have been identified but you need to create the timeline.

## Project Focus

1. The task names, durations, and any prerequisites are:
   - Analyze and plan—two weeks. Cannot start anything else until done.
   - Create and organize content—four weeks. Can start to develop "look and feel" before this is done.
   - Develop the "look and feel"—four weeks. Start working on graphics and HTML at the same time.
   - Produce graphics and HTML documents—two weeks. Create working prototype after the first week.
   - Create a working prototype—two weeks. Give to test team when complete.
   - Test, test, test—four weeks.
   - Upload to a web server and test again—one week.
   - Maintain.

2. Using Microsoft Excel or Microsoft Project, create a Gantt chart using the information provided above.

## Project 8:

## Maximize Profit

Books, Books, Books is a wholesale distributor of popular books. The business buys over-stocked books and sells them for a discount of more than 50 percent to local area bookstores. The owner of the company, BK Kane, would like to determine the best approach to boxing books so he can make the most profit possible. The local bookstores accept all shipments from Books, Books, Books because of BK's incredibly low prices. BK can order as many over-stocked books as he requires, and this week's options include:

| Title | Weight | Cost | Sale Price |
|-------|--------|------|------------|
| *Harry Potter and the Deathly Hallows,* J. K. Rowling | 5 lb | $9 | $17 |
| *The Children of Húrin,* J. R. R. Tolkien | 4 lb | $8 | $13 |
| *The Time Traveler's Wife,* Audrey Niffenegger | 3.5 lb | $7 | $11 |
| *The Dark River,* John Twelve Hawks | 3 lb | $6 | $ 9 |
| *The Road,* Cormac McCarthy | 2.5 lb | $5 | $ 7 |
| *Slaughterhouse-Five,* Kurt Vonnegut | 1 lb | $4 | $ 5 |

## Project Focus

When packing a single box, BK must adhere to the following:

- 20 books or less.
- Books by three different authors.
- Between four and eight books from each author.
- Weight equal to or less than 50 pounds.

BK has come to you to help him determine which books he should order to maximize his profit based on the above information. Using the data file AYK8_Data.xlsx, determine the optimal book order for a single box of books.

**Data File: AYK8_Data.xlsx**

## Project 9:

### Security Analysis

SecureWorks, Inc., is a small computer security contractor that provides computer security analysis, design, and software implementation for the U.S. government and commercial clients. SecureWorks competes for both private and U.S. government computer security contract work by submitting detailed bids outlining the work the company will perform if awarded the contracts. Because all of the work involves computer security, a highly sensitive area, almost all of SecureWorks tasks require access to classified material or company confidential documents. Consequently, all of the security engineers (simply known as "engineers" within the company) have U.S. government clearances of either Secret or Top Secret. Some have even higher clearances for the 2 percent of SecureWorks work that involves so-called "black box" security work. Most of the employees also hold clearances because they must handle classified documents.

Leslie Mamalis is SecureWorks' human resources (HR) manager. She maintains all employee records and is responsible for semiannual review reports, payroll processing, personnel records, recruiting data, employee training, and pension option information. At the heart of an HR system are personnel records. Personnel record maintenance includes activities such as maintaining employee records, tracking cost center data, recording and maintaining pension information, and absence and sick leave record keeping. While most of this information resides in sophisticated database systems, Leslie maintains a basic employee worksheet for quick calculations and ad hoc report generation. Because SecureWorks is a small company, Leslie can take advantage of Excel's excellent list management capabilities to satisfy many of her personnel information management needs.

## Project Focus

Leslie has asked you to assist with a number of functions (she has provided you with a copy of her "trusted" personnel data file, AYK9_Data.xlsx):

1. Copy the worksheet Data to a new worksheet called Sort. Sort the employee list in ascending order by department, then by last name, then by first name.

2. Copy the worksheet Data to a new worksheet called Autofilter. Using the Autofilter feature, create a custom filter that will display employees whose birth date is greater than or equal to 1/1/1965 and less than or equal to 12/31/1975.

3. Copy the worksheet Data to a new worksheet called Subtotal. Using the subtotal feature create a sum of the salary for each department.

4. Copy the worksheet Data to a new worksheet called Formatting. Using the salary column, change the font color to red if the cell value is greater than or equal to 55000. You must use the conditional formatting feature to complete this step.

**Data File: AYK9_Data.xlsx**

## Project 10:

## Gathering Data

You have just accepted a new job offer from a firm that has offices in San Diego, Los Angeles, and San Francisco. You need to decide which location to move to. Because you have not visited any of these three cities and want to get in a lot of golf time, you determine that the main factor that will affect your decision is weather.

Go to www.weather.com and locate the box in which you can enter the city or ZIP code for which you want information. Enter San Diego, CA, and when the data appears, click the Averages and Records tab. Print this page and repeat this for Los Angeles and San Francisco. You will want to focus on the Monthly Average and Records section on the top of the page.

### Project Focus

1. Create a spreadsheet to summarize the information you find.

2. Record the temperature and rainfall in columns, and group the cities into four groups of rows labeled Average High, Average Low, Mean, and Average Precipitation.

3. Fill in the appropriate data for each city and month.

4. Because rain is your greatest concern, use conditional formatting to display the months with an average precipitation below 2.5 inches in blue and apply boldface.

5. You also want to be in the warmest weather possible while in California. Use conditional formatting to display the months with average high temperatures above 65 degrees in green and apply an italic font face.

6. Looking at the average high temperatures above 65 degrees and average precipitation below two inches, to which city do you think you should relocate? Explain your answer.

## Project 11:

## Scanner System

FunTown is a popular amusement park filled with roller coasters, games, and water features. Boasting 24 roller coasters, 10 of which exceed 200 feet and 70 miles per hour, and five water parks, the park's attendance remains steady throughout the season. Due to the park's popularity, it is not uncommon for entrance lines to exceed one hour on busy days. FunTown would like your help to find a solution to decrease park entrance lines.

### Project Focus

FunTown would like to implement a hand-held scanner system that can allow employees to walk around the front gates and accept credit card purchases and print tickets on the spot. The park anticipates an overall increase in sales of 4 percent per year with online ticketing, with an expense of 6 percent of total sales for the scanning equipment. FunTown has created a data file for you to use, AYK11_Data.xlsx, that compares scanning sales and traditional sales. You will need to create the necessary formulas to calculate all the assumptions including:

- Tickets sold at the booth.
- Tickets sold by the scanner.
- Revenues generated by booth sales.
- Revenues generated by scanner sales.
- Scanner ticket expense.
- Revenue with and without scanner sales.
- Three year row totals.

**Data File: AYK11_Data.xlsx**

## Project 12:
### Competitive Pricing

Bill Schultz is thinking of starting a store that specializes in handmade cowboy boots. Bill is a longtime rancher in the town of Taos, New Mexico. Bill's reputation for honesty and integrity is well-known around town, and he is positive that his new store will be highly successful.

### Project Focus

Before opening his store, Bill is curious about how his profit, revenue, and variable costs will change depending on the amount he charges for his boots. Bill would like you to perform the work required for this analysis and has given you the data file AYK12_Data.xlsx. Here are a few things to consider while you perform your analysis:

- Current competitive prices for custom cowboy boots are between $225 and $275 a pair.
- Variable costs will be either $100 or $150 a pair depending on the types of material Bill chooses to use.
- Fixed costs are $10,000 a month.

**Data File: AYK12_Data.xlsx**

## Project 13:
### Adequate Acquisitions

XMark.com is a major Internet company specializing in organic food. XMark.com is thinking of purchasing GoodGrow, another organic food Internet company. GoodGrow has current revenues of $100 million, with expenses of $150 million. Current projections indicate that GoodGrow's revenues are increasing at 35 percent per year and its expenses are increasing by 10 percent per year. XMark.com understands that projections can be erroneous, however; the company must determine the number of years before GoodGrow will return a profit.

### Project Focus

You need to help XMark.com determine the number of years required to break even, using annual growth rates in revenue between 20 percent and 60 percent and annual expense growth rates between 10 and 30 percent. You have been provided with a template, AYK13_Data.xlsx, to assist with your analysis.

**Data File: AYK13_Data.xlsx**

## Project 14:
### Customer Relations

Schweizer Distribution specializes in distributing fresh produce to local restaurants in the Chicago area. The company currently sells 12 different products through the efforts of three sales representatives to 10 restaurants. The company, like all small businesses, is always interested in finding ways to increase revenues and decrease expenses.

The company's founder, Bob Schweizer, has recently hired you as a new business analyst. You have just graduated from college with a degree in marketing and a specialization in customer relationship management. Bob is eager to hear your thoughts and ideas on how to improve the business and help the company build strong lasting relationships with its customers.

## Project Focus

Bob has provided you with last year's sales information in the data file AYK14_Data.xlsx. Help Bob analyze his distribution company by using a PivotTable to determine the following:

1. Who is Bob's best customer by total sales?
2. Who is Bob's worst customer by total sales?
3. Who is Bob's best customer by total profit?
4. Who is Bob's worst customer by total profit?
5. What is Bob's best-selling product by total sales?
6. What is Bob's worst-selling product by total sales?
7. What is Bob's best-selling product by total profit?
8. What is Bob's worst-selling product by total profit?
9. Who is Bob's best sales representative by total profit?
10. Who is Bob's worst sales representative by total profit?
11. What is the best sales representative's best-selling product (by total profit)?
12. Who is the best sales representative's best customer (by total profit)?
13. What is the best sales representative's worst-selling product (by total profit)?
14. Who is the best sales representative's worst customer (by total profit)?

**Data File: AYK14_Data.xlsx**

## Project 15:

### Shipping Costs

One of the main products of the Fairway Woods Company is custom-made golf clubs. The clubs are manufactured at three plants (Denver, Colorado; Phoenix, Arizona; and Dallas, Texas) and are then shipped by truck to five distribution warehouses in Sacramento, California; Salt Lake City, Utah; Chicago, Illinois; Albuquerque, New Mexico; and New York City, New York. Since shipping costs are a major expense, management has begun an analysis to determine ways to reduce them. For the upcoming golf season, the output from each manufacturing plant and how much each warehouse will require to satisfy its customers have been estimated.

The CIO from Fairway Woods Company has created a data file for you, AYK15_Data.xlsx, of the shipping costs from each manufacturing plant to each warehouse as a baseline analysis. Some business rules and requirements you should be aware of include:

■ The problem presented involves the shipment of goods from three plants to five regional warehouses.

■ Goods can be shipped from any plant to any warehouse, but it costs more to ship goods over long distances than over short distances.

### Project Focus

1. Your goal is to minimize the costs of shipping goods from production plants to warehouses, thereby meeting the demand from each metropolitan area while not exceeding the supply available from each plant. To complete this project it is recommended that you use the Solver function in Excel to assist with the analysis.

2. Specifically you want to focus on:

   ■ Minimizing the total shipping costs.

   ■ Total shipped must be less than or equal to supply at a plant.

   ■ Total shipped to warehouses must be greater than or equal to the warehouse demand.

   ■ Number to ship must be greater than or equal to 0.

   **Data File: AYK15_Data.xlsx**

## Project 16:
## Formatting Grades

Professor Streterstein is a bit absentminded. His instructor's grade book is a mess, and he would like your help cleaning it up and making it easier to use. In Professor Streterstein's course, the maximum possible points a student can earn is 750. The following table displays the grade equivalent to total points for the course.

| Total Points | Calculated Grade |
|--------------|------------------|
| 675 | A |
| 635 | A- |
| 600 | B |
| 560 | B- |
| 535 | C |
| 490 | C- |
| 450 | D |
| 0 | F |

### Project Focus

Help Professor Streterstein rework his grade book. Open the data file AYK16_Data.xlsx and perform the following:

1. Reformat the workbook so it is readable, understandable, and consistent. Replace column labels, format and align the headings, add borders and shading as appropriate.

2. Add a column in the grade book for final grade next to the total points earned column.

3. Use the VLookup Function to automatically assess final grades based on the total points column.

4. Using the If Function, format the workbook so each student's grade shows a pass or fail—P for pass, F for fail—based on the total points.

   **Data File: AYK16_Data.xlsx**

## Project 17:
## Moving Dilemma

Pony Espresso is a small business that sells specialty coffee drinks at office buildings. Each morning and afternoon, trucks arrive at offices' front entrances, and the office employees purchase various beverages such as Java du Jour and Café de Colombia. The business is profitable. Pony Espresso offices, however, are located north of town, where lease rates are less expensive, and the principal sales area is south of town. This means the trucks must drive across town four times each day.

The cost of transportation to and from the sales area plus the power demands of the trucks' coffee brewing equipment are a significant portion of variable costs. Pony Espresso could reduce the amount of driving and, therefore, the variable costs, if it moved the offices closer to the sales area.

Pony Espresso presently has fixed costs of $10,000 per month. The lease of a new office, closer to the sales area, would cost an additional $2,200 per month. This would increase the fixed costs to $12,200 per month.

Although the lease of new offices would increase the fixed costs, a careful estimate of the potential savings in gasoline and vehicle maintenance indicates that Pony Espresso could reduce the variable costs from $0.60 per unit to $0.35 per unit. Total sales are unlikely to increase as a result of the move, but the savings in variable costs should increase the annual profit.

## Project Focus

Consider the information provided to you from the owner in the data file AYK17_Data.xlsx. Especially look at the change in the variability of the profit from month to month. From November through January, when it is much more difficult to lure office workers out into the cold to purchase coffee, Pony Espresso barely breaks even. In fact, in December, the business lost money.

1. Develop the cost analysis on the existing lease information using the monthly sales figures provided to you in the data file.
2. Develop the cost analysis from the new lease information provided above.
3. Calculate the variability that is reflected in the month-to-month standard deviation of earnings for the current cost structure and the projected cost structure.
4. Do not consider any association with downsizing such as overhead—simply focus on the information provided to you.
5. You will need to calculate the EBIT (earnings before interest and taxes).

**Data File: AYK17_Data.xlsx**

## Project 18:

### Operational Efficiencies

Hoover Transportation, Inc., is a large distribution company located in Denver, Colorado. The company is currently seeking to gain operational efficiencies in its supply chain by reducing the number of transportation carriers that it is using to outsource. Operational efficiencies for Hoover Transportation, Inc., suggest that reducing the number of carriers from the Denver distribution center to warehouses in the selected states will lead to reduced costs. Brian Hoover, the CEO of Hoover Transportation, requests that the number of carriers transporting products from its Denver distribution center to wholesalers in Arizona, Arkansas, Iowa, Missouri, Montana, Oklahoma, Oregon, and Washington be reduced from the current five carriers to two carriers.

## Project Focus

Carrier selection should be based on the assumptions that all environmental factors are equal and historical cost trends will continue. Review the historical data from the past several years to determine your recommendation for the top two carriers that Hoover Transportation should continue to use.

1. Analyze the last 24 months of Hoover's Transportation carrier transactions found in the data file AYK18_Data.xlsx.
2. Create a report detailing your recommendation for the top two carriers with which Hoover Transportation should continue to do business. Be sure to use PivotTables and PivotCharts in your report. A few questions to get you started include:
   - Calculate the average cost per carrier.
   - Calculate the total shipping costs per state.

- Calculate the total shipping weights per state.
- Calculate the average shipping costs per pound.
- Calculate the average cost per carrier.

**Data File: AYK18_Data.xlsx**

## Project 19:

### Too Much Information

You have just landed the job of vice president of operations for The Pitt Stop Restaurants, a national chain of full-service, casual-themed restaurants. During your first week on the job, Suzanne Graham, your boss and CEO of the company, has asked you to provide an analysis of how well the company's restaurants are performing. Specifically, she would like to know which units and regions are performing extremely well, which are performing moderately well, and which are underperforming. Her goal is to identify where to spend time and focus efforts to improve the overall health of the company.

### Project Focus

Review the data file AYK19_Data.xlsx and determine how best to analyze and interpret the data. Create a formal presentation of your findings. A few things to consider include:

- Should underperforming restaurants be closed or sold?
- Should high-performing restaurants be expanded to accommodate more seats?
- Should the company spend more or less on advertising?
- In which markets should the advertising budget be adjusted?
- How are The Pitt Stop Restaurants performing compared to the competition?
- How are units of like size performing relative to each other?

**Data File: AYK19_Data.xlsx**

## Project 20:

### Turnover Rates

Employee turnover rates are at an all-time high at Gizmo's Manufacturing plants. The company is experiencing severe worker retention issues, which are leading to productivity and quality control problems. The majority of the company's workers perform a variety of tasks and are paid by the hour. The company currently tests each potential applicant to ensure they have the skills necessary for the intense mental concentration and dexterity required to fill the positions. Since significant costs are associated with employee turnover, Gizmo Manufacturing wants to find a way to predict which applicants have the characteristics of being a short-term versus a long-term employee.

### Project Focus

1. Review the information that Gizmo Manufacturing has collected from two of its different data sources. The first data file, AYK20_Data_A.xlsx, contains information regarding employee wages. The second data file, AYK20_Data_B.xlsx, contains information regarding employee retention.

2. Using Excel analysis functions, determine the employee characteristics that you would recommend Gizmo Manufacturing look for when hiring new personnel. It is highly recommended that you use PivotTables as part of your analysis.

3. Prepare a report based on your findings (which should include several forms of graphical representation) for your recommendations.

**Data Files: AYK20_Data_A.xlsx and AYK20_Data_B.xlsx**

## Project 21:

### Vital Information

Martin Resorts, Inc., owns and operates four Spa and Golf resorts in Colorado. The company has five traditional lines of business: (1) golf sales; (2) golf lessons; (3) restaurants; (4) retail and rentals; and (5) hotels. David Logan, director of marketing technology at Martin Resorts, Inc., and Donald Mayer, the lead strategic analyst for Martin Resorts, are soliciting your input for their CRM strategic initiative.

Martin Resorts' IT infrastructure is pieced together with various systems and applications. Currently, the company has a difficult time with CRM because its systems are not integrated. The company cannot determine vital information such as which customers are golfing and staying at the hotel or which customers are staying at the hotel and not golfing.

For example, the three details that the customer Diego Titus (1) stayed four nights at a Martin Resorts' managed hotel, (2) golfed three days, and (3) took an all-day spa treatment the first day are discrete facts housed in separate systems. Martin Resorts hopes that by using data warehousing technology to integrate its data, the next time Diego reserves lodging for another trip, sales associates may ask him if he would like to book a spa treatment as well, and even if he would like the same masseuse that he had on his prior trip.

Martin Resorts is excited about the possibility of taking advantage of customer segmentation and CRM strategies to help increase its business.

### Project Focus

The company wants to use CRM and data warehouse technologies to improve service and personalization at each customer touch point. Using a data warehousing tool, important customer information can be accessed from all of its systems either daily, weekly, monthly, or once or twice per year. Analyze the sample data in AYK21_Data.xlsx for the following:

1. Currently, the quality of the data within the above disparate systems is low. Develop a report for David and Donald discussing the importance of high quality information and how low quality information can affect Martin Resorts' business.

2. Review the data that David and Donald are working with from the data warehouse in the data file AYK21_Data.xlsx.

   a. Give examples from the data showing the kind of information Martin Resorts might be able to use to gain a better understanding of its customers. Include the types of data quality issues the company can anticipate and the strategies it can use to help avoid such issues.

   b. Determine who are Martin Resorts' best customers, and provide examples of the types of marketing campaigns the company should offer these valuable customers.

   c. Prepare a report that summarizes the benefits Martin Resorts can receive from using business intelligence to mine the data warehouse. Include a financial analysis of the costs and benefits.

   **Data File: AYK21_Data.xlsx**

## Project 22:

### Breaking Even

Mountain Cycle specializes in making custom mountain bikes. The company founder, PJ Steffan, is having a hard time making the business profitable. Knowing that you have great business knowledge and solid financial sense, PJ has come to you for advice.

## Project Focus

PJ would like you to determine how many bikes Mountain Cycle needs to sell per year to break even. Using Goal Seek in Excel solve using the following:

- Fixed cost equals        $65,000.
- Variable cost equals     $1,575.
- Bike price equals        $2,500.

## Project 23:

### Profit Scenario

Murry Lutz owns a small shop, Lutz Motors, that sells and services vintage motorcycles. Murry is curious how his profit will be affected by his sales over the next year.

### Project Focus

Murry would like your help creating best, worst, and most-likely scenarios for his motorcycle sales over the next year. Using Scenario Manager, help Murry analyze the information in the data file AYK23_Data.xlsx.

> **Data File: AYK23_Data.xlsx**

## Project 24:

### Electronic Résumés

Résumés are the currency of the recruitment industry. They are the cornerstone of communication between candidates, recruiters, and employers. Technology is automating elements of the recruitment process, but a complete solution requires proper handling of the actual development of all the pieces and parts that comprise not just a résumé, but also an e-résumé. Electronic résumés, or e-résumés, have moved into the mainstream of today's job market at lightning speed. E-résumés have stepped up the efficiency of job placement to such a point that you could get a call from a recruiter just hours after submitting your e-résumé. With this kind of opportunity, you cannot afford to be left in the dark ages of using only a visual résumé.

### Project Focus

In the text or HTML editor of your choice, write your e-résumé as though you were really putting it online and inviting prospective employers to see it. We recommend typing in all the text and then later adding the HTML tags (rather than trying to type in the tags as you go).

Use the following checklist to make sure you're covering the basics. You do not need to match it exactly; it just shows what can be done.

- Add structural tags.
- Add paragraphs and headings.
- Find an opportunity to include a list.
- Add inline styles.
- Play with the alignment of elements.
- Add appropriate font selection, font size, and color.

## Project 25:

### Gathering Feedback

Gathering feedback from website's visitors can be a valuable way of assessing a site's success, and it can help build a customer or subscriber database. For example, a business could collect the addresses of people who are interested in receiving product samples, email newsletters, or notifications of special offers.

## Project Focus

Adding form elements to a web page is simple: They are created using a set of HTML form tags that define menus, text fields, buttons, and so on. Form elements are generally used to collect information from a web page.

In the text or HTML editor of your choice, create a web form that would collect information for a customer ordering a customized bicycle. Use proper web design and HTML tools to understand the process and function of form elements. Be sure to pay attention to:

- Form layout and design.
- Visual elements, including labels, alignment, font selection, font size, color.
- Required versus nonrequired fields.
- Drop-down boxes, text fields, and radio buttons.

## Project 26:

### Daily Invoice

Foothills Animal Hospital is a full-service small animal veterinary hospital located in Morrison, Colorado, specializing in routine medical care, vaccinations, laboratory testing, and surgery. The hospital has experienced tremendous growth over the past six months due to customer referrals. While Foothills Animal Hospital has typically kept its daily service records in a workbook format, it feels the need to expand its reporting capabilities to develop a relational database as a more functional structure.

Foothills Animal Hospital needs help developing a database, specifically:

- Create a customer table—name, address, phone, and date of entrance.
- Create a pet table—pet name, type of animal, breed, gender, color, neutered/spayed, weight, and comments.
- Create a medications table—medication code, name of medication, and cost of medication.
- Create a visit table—details of treatments performed, medications dispensed, and date of the visit.
- Produce a daily invoice report.

Figure AYK.2 displays a sample daily invoice report that the Foothills Animal Hospital accountants have requested. Foothills Animal Hospital organizes its treatments using the codes displayed in Figure AYK.3. The entities and primary keys for the database have been identified in Figure AYK.4.

The following business rules have been identified:

1. A customer can have many pets but must have at least one.
2. A pet must be assigned to one and only one customer.
3. A pet can have one or more treatments per visit but must have at least one.
4. A pet can have one or more medications but need not have any.

## Project Focus

Your job is to complete the following tasks:

1. Develop and describe the entity-relationship diagram.
2. Use normalization to assure the correctness of the tables (relations).
3. Create the database using a personal DBMS package (preferably Microsoft Access).
4. Use the data in Figure AYK.3 to populate your tables. Feel free to enter your own personal information.
5. Use the DBMS package to create the basic report in Figure AYK.2.

Foothills Animal Hospital
Daily Invoice Report

## Foothills Daily Hospital Report

| Customer Name | Pet Name | Type of Animal | Treatment | Price |
|---|---|---|---|---|
| Amanda Smith | | | | |
| | Indigo | Cat | Eye/Ear Examination | $20.00 |
| Summary for Amanda Smith | | | | $20.00 |
| Anita Zimmerman | | | | |
| | Midnight | Cat | Lab Work - Blood | $50.00 |
| Summary for Anita Zimmerman | | | | $50.00 |
| Barbara Williamson | | | | |
| | Hoppi | Dog | General Exam | $50.00 |
| Summary for Barbara Williamson | | | | $50.00 |
| Betsy Walsh | | | | |
| | Ren | DOG | General Exam | $50.00 |
| | Stimpy | CAT | General Exam | $50.00 |
| | Stimpy | CAT | Tetrinious Shot | $10.00 |
| Summary for Betsy Walsh | | | | $110.00 |
| John Williamson | | | | |
| | Barney | DOG | Flea Spray | $25.00 |
| Summary for John Williamson | | | | $25.00 |
| Mike Phillips | | | | |
| | Micro | CAT | General Exam | $50.00 |
| Summary for Mike Phillips | | | | $50.00 |
| Peter Prentice | | | | |
| | Buck | Dog | Eye/Ear Examination | $20.00 |
| | Buck | Dog | Lab Work - Blood | $50.00 |
| Summary for Peter Prentice | | | | $70.00 |

**FIGURE AYK.3**

Treatment Codes,
Treatments, and Price
Descriptions

| Treatment Code | Treatment | Price |
|---|---|---|
| 0100 | Tetrinious Shot | $10.00 |
| 0201 | Rabonius Shot | $20.00 |
| 0300 | General Exam | $50.00 |
| 0303 | Eye/Ear Examination | $20.00 |
| 0400 | Spay/Neuter | $225.00 |
| 0405 | Reset Dislocation | $165.00 |
| 0406 | Amputation of Limb | $450.00 |
| 0407 | Wrap Affected Area | $15.00 |
| 0408 | Cast Affected Area | $120.00 |
| 1000 | Lab Work—Blood | $50.00 |
| 1003 | Lab Work—Misc | $35.00 |
| 2003 | Flea Spray | $25.00 |
| 9999 | Other Not Listed | $10.00 |

**FIGURE AYK.4**

Entity Names and Primary
Keys Foothills Animal
Hospital

| Entity | Primary Key |
|---|---|
| CUSTOMER | Customer Number |
| PET | Pet Number |
| VISIT | Visit Number |
| VISIT DETAIL | Visit Number and Line Number (a composite key) |
| TREATMENT | Treatment Code |
| MEDICATION | Medication Code |

**ON-THE-LEVEL CONSTRUCTION PROJECT DETAIL**

| PROJECT NAME | ASSIGN DATE | EMPLOYEE LAST NAME | FIRST NAME | JOB DESCRIPTION | ASSIGN HOUR | CHARGE/HOUR |
|---|---|---|---|---|---|---|
| Chatfield | | | | | | |
| | 6/10/2007 | Olenkoski | Glenn | Structure | 2.1 | $35.75 |
| | 6/10/2007 | Ramora | Anne | Plumbing | 2.6 | $98.75 |
| | 6/10/2007 | Sullivan | David | Electrical | 1.2 | $105.00 |
| | 6/11/2007 | Frommer | Matt | Plumbing | 1.4 | $98.75 |
| Summary of Assignment Hours and Charges | | | | | 7.30 | $588.08 |
| Evergreen | | | | | | |
| | 6/10/2007 | Sullivan | David | Electrical | 1.8 | $105.00 |
| | 6/10/2007 | Jones | Anne | Heating and Ventilation | 3.4 | $84.50 |
| | 6/11/2007 | Frommer | Matt | Plumbing | 4.1 | $98.75 |
| | 6/16/2007 | Bavangi | Terry | Plumbing | 4.1 | $98.75 |
| | 6/16/2007 | Newman | John | Electrical | 1.7 | $105.00 |
| Summary of Assignment Hours and Charges | | | | | 15.10 | $1,448.15 |
| Roxborough | | | | | | |
| | 6/10/2007 | Ramora | Anne | Plumbing | 2.6 | $98.75 |
| | 6/10/2007 | Washberg | Jeff | Plumbing | 3.9 | $98.75 |
| | 6/11/2007 | Smithfield | William | Structure | 2.4 | $35.75 |
| | 6/11/2007 | Bavangi | Terry | Plumbing | 2.7 | $98.75 |
| | 6/16/2007 | Joen | Denise | Plumbing | 2.5 | $98.75 |
| | 6/16/2007 | Johnson | Peter | Electrical | 5.2 | $105.00 |
| Summary of Assignment Hours and Charges | | | | | 19.30 | $1,763.78 |

## Project 27:

## Billing Data

On-The-Level Construction Company is a Denver-based construction company that specializes in subcontracting the development of single-family homes. In business since 1998, On-The-Level Construction has maintained a talented pool of certified staff and independent consultants providing the flexibility and combined experience required to meet the needs of its nearly 300 completed projects in the Denver metropolitan area. The field of operation methods that On-The-Level Construction is responsible for includes structural development, heating and cooling, plumbing, and electricity.

The company charges its clients by billing the hours spent on each contract. The hourly billing rate is dependent on the employee's position according to the field of operations (as noted above). Figure AYK.5 shows a basic report that On-The-Level Construction foremen would like to see every week concerning what projects are being assigned, the overall assignment hours, and the charges for the assignment. On-The-Level Construction organizes its internal structure in four different operations—Structure (500), Plumbing (501), Electrical (502), and Heating and Ventilation (503). Each of these operational departments can and should have many subcontractors who specialize in that area. Due to the boom in home sales over the last several years, On-The-Level Construction has decided to implement a relational database model to track project details according to project name, hours assigned, and charges per hour for each job description. Originally, On-The-Level Construction decided to let one of its employees handle the construction of the database. However, that employee has not had the time to completely implement the project. On-The-Level Construction has asked you to take over and complete the development of the database.

The entities and primary keys for the database have been identified in Figure AYK.6.

The following business rules have been identified:

1. A job can have many employees assigned but must have at least one.

2. An employee must be assigned to one and only one job number.

| Entity | Primary Key |
|---|---|
| PROJECT | Project Number |
| EMPLOYEE | Employee Number |
| JOB | Job Number |
| ASSIGNMENT | Assignment Number |

3. An employee can be assigned to work on one or more projects.

4. A project can be assigned to only one employee but need not be assigned to any employee.

## Project Focus

Your job is to complete the following tasks:

1. Develop and describe the entity relationship diagram.

2. Use normalization to assure the correctness of the tables (relations).

3. Create the database using a personal DBMS package (preferably Microsoft Access).

4. Use the DBMS package to create the basic report in Figure AYK.5.

5. You may not be able to develop a report that looks exactly like the one in Figure AYK.5. However, your report should include the same information.

6. Complete personnel information is tracked by another database. For this application, include only the minimum: employee number, last name, and first name.

7. Information concerning all projects, employees, and jobs is not readily available. You should create information for several fictitious projects, employees, and jobs to include in your database.

## Project 28:

### Inventory Data

An independent retailer of mobile entertainment and wireless phones, iToys.com has built its business on offering the widest selection, expert advice, and outstanding customer service. However, iToys.com does not use a formal, consistent inventory tracking system. Periodically, an iToys.com employee visually checks to see what items are in stock. Although iToys.com does try to keep a certain level of each "top seller" in stock, the lack of a formal inventory tracking system has led to the overstocking of some items and understocking of other items. On occasion, a customer will request a hot item, and it is only then that iToys.com realizes that the item is out of stock. If an item is not available, iToys.com risks losing a customer to a competitor.

Lately, iToys.com has become concerned with its inventory management methods. The owner of iToys.com, Dan Connolly, wants to better manage his inventory. The company receives orders by mail, by telephone, or through its website. Regardless of how the orders are received, Dan needs a database to automate the inventory checking and ordering process.

## Project Focus

Dan has provided you with a simplified version of the company's current system (an Excel workbook) for recording inventory and orders in an Excel spreadsheet data file AYK28_Data.xlsx.

1. Develop an ERD diagram before you begin to create the database. You will need to use the information provided here as well as the data given in the Excel workbook.

2. Create the database using a personal DBMS package (preferably Microsoft Access) that will track items (i.e., products), orders, order details, categories, suppliers, and shipping methods.

3. In addition to what is mentioned above, the database needs to track the inventory levels for each product, according to a reorder level and lead time.

4. At this time, Dan does not need information stored about the customer; he simply needs you to focus on the inventory structure.

5. Develop a query that will display the products that need to be ordered from their supplier. To complete this, you will want to compare a reorder level with how many units are in stock.

6. Develop several reports that display:

   a. Each product ordered by its supplier. The report should include the product name, quantity on hand, and reorder level.

   b. Each supplier ordered by shipping method.

   c. Each product that requires more than five days lead time. (Hint: You will want to create a query for this first).

   d. Each product ordered by category.

7. Here are some additional business rules to assist you in completing this task:

   a. An order must have at least one product, but can contain more than one product.

   b. A product can have one or more orders, but need not have any orders.

   c. A product must belong to one and only one category, but a category many contain many different products.

   d. A product can only be stocked by one supplier, but a supplier can provide more than one product.

   e. A supplier will use one type of shipping method, but shipping methods can be used by more than one supplier.

   **Data File: AYK28_Data.xlsx**

## Project 29:

## Call Center

A manufacturing company, Teleworks, has been a market leader in the wireless telephone business for the past 10 years. Other firms have imitated its product with some degree of success, but Teleworks occupies a dominant position in the marketplace because it has a first morer advantage with a quality product.

Recently Teleworks began selling a new, enhanced wireless phone. This new phone does not replace its current product, but offers additional features, greater durability, and better performance for a somewhat higher price. Offering this enhanced phone has established a new revenue stream for the company.

Many sales executives at Teleworks seem to subscribe to the-more-you-have, the-more-you-want theory of managing customer data. That is, they believe they can never accumulate too much information about their customers, and that they can do their jobs more effectively by collecting infinite amounts of customer details. Having a firm grasp on a wide range of customer-focused details—specifically reports summarizing call center information—can be critical in enabling your company to successfully manage a customer relationship management (CRM) solution that creates a positive impact.

To continue to provide excellent customer support, and in anticipation of increased calls due to the release of its new product, Teleworks needs a database that it can use to record, track, and query call center information. Teleworks CIO KED Davisson has hired you to develop this database.

## Project Focus

1. Teleworks has provided you with a data file AYK29_Data.xlsx; its current approach for recording cell center information is a spreadsheet file.

2. Develop an ERD diagram before you begin to create the database.

3. Create the database using a personal DBMS package (preferably Microsoft Access) that will allow data analysts to enter call center data according to the type of issue and the customer, assign each call to a consultant, and prioritize the call.

4. Develop a query that will display all issues that are "open."

5. Develop a screen form to browse all issues.

6. Develop several reports that display:

    a. All closed issues.

    b. Each issue in detail ordered by issue ID.

    c. Each issue in detail ordered by consultant.

    d. Each issue in detail ordered by category.

    e. Each issue in detail ordered by status.

7. Here are some additional business rules to assist you in completing this task:

    a. An issue must have at least one customer.

    b. A customer can have more than one issue.

    c. Each issue must be assigned to one consultant.

    d. Each consultant can be assigned to more than one issue.

    e. An issue can only belong to one category.

    f. An issue must be assigned only one status code.

    g. An issue must be assigned a priority code.

8. Priorities are assigned accordingly:

| Priority Level |
| --- |
| Critical |
| High |
| Moderate |
| Standard |
| Low |

9. Status is recorded as either open or closed.

10. The categories of each issue need to be recorded as:

| Category |
| --- |
| Hardware/Phone |
| Software/Voice mail |
| Internet/Web |

**Data File:** AYK29_Data.xlsx

## Project 30:

## Sales Pipeline

Sales drive any organization. This is true for every for-profit business irrespective of size or industry type. If customers are not buying your goods or services, you run the risk of not having a business. This is when tough decisions have to be made like whether to slash budgets, lay off staff, or seek additional financing.

    Unfortunately, you do not wield ultimate power over your customers' buying habits. While you can attempt to influence buying behavior through strategic marketing, smart businesses remain one step ahead by collecting and analyzing historical and current customer information from a range of internal and external sources to forecast future sales. In other words, managing the sales pipeline is an essential ingredient to business success.

You have recently been hired by RealTime Solutions, a new company that collects information to understand, manage, and predict specific sales cycle (including the supply chain and lead times) in the automobile business. Having an accurate forecast of future sales will allow the company to increase or decrease the production cycle as required and manage personnel levels, inventory, and cash flow.

### Project Focus

Using a personal DBMS package (preferably Microsoft Access) create a sales pipeline database that will:

1. Track opportunities from employees to customers.
   - Opportunities should have a ranking, category, source of opportunity, open date, closed date, description.
2. Create a form for inputting customer, employee, and opportunity data.
3. Create a few reports that display:
   - All open opportunities, including relevant customer and employee information.
   - Closed opportunities, including relevant customer and employee information.
   - All customers.
4. Create your own data to test the integrity of the relationships. Use approximately 10 records per table.

### Project 31:

### Second Life–Virtual Networking

Second Life is a whole new society that exists only in cyberspace. What this shared 3-D space offers is wide open—anything is possible. It will grow and evolve and become what the inhabitants make of it. You are about to enter a new world where you can be or do almost anything. If you can imagine it, you can do it in Second Life.

Right now, Second Life is fresh and new and most inhabitants can do the following:

- Explore.
- Meet others with similar (or new) interests, network, make friends.
- Participate in social events.
- Participate in deadly battles in the Outlands.
- Participate in various contests.
- Create things and places others will want to explore.
- Experiment with scripting.
- Create textures and sounds out-of-world, and upload them.
- Collaborate with others to build something big.
- Start businesses that charge for Second Life products or services.

Opening a virtual office, selling and market-testing digital replicas of products, and asking employees to create 3-D online personas or "avatars" are quickly becoming action items at companies seeking to brand themselves as hip, or simply wanting to reach Second Life users, nearly half of whom are female and whose median age is 32.

This has made the online world a hot advertising outlet for brands ranging from Warner Bros. to Adidas to Microsoft. While advertising's traditional media seem to be losing eyeballs, the population of Second Life is growing at 35 percent per month and its economy at 15 percent per month. Or in terms of annual growth rates, the population is growing at 978 percent and the economy at 270 percent.

In Second Life, the products offered by true-life brands can be customized by the people using them—a growing trend in the real-world marketplace. Second Life is an interactive, social-networking zone where companies hope not only to find customers but also to connect remote employees to one another and recruit new hires.

For a company considering jumping into Second Life now, serious homework is needed. Competition among big brands is heating up. It's no longer enough to be the first in an industry to launch a presence in Second Life. Just as Toyota, and now Nissan and General Motors, conducted market research in the digital world before unveiling its plan to sell virtual cars, savvy corporations and their Second Life developers must carefully analyze the competition and differentiate their products.

### Project Focus

1. Go to www.secondlife.com, and click on the "Join Now" button (membership is free). Fill out the Second Life registration details, including choosing an Avatar and a Second Life name (alias).

2. Log in with the name and password you selected when you signed up.

3. Point to the Downloads menu and select Second Life Client from the drop-down menu.

4. Download Second Life Setup and save it to your hard drive in a place where you can find it easily, then run Second Life Setup.

5. Follow the instructions on the screen.

6. Double-click the Second Life icon on your desktop. You will see the Second Life sign-on screen.

7. Enter your first and last name, and your password. Click on "Connect." Within seconds, you will be in your Second Life.

8. Project Challenge:

   - Create a business for Second Life that involves concepts from this course, such as supply chain management, decision support, or e-marketing. There are as many opportunities for innovation and profit in Second Life as in the real world. Open a nightclub, sell jewelry, become a land speculator; the choice is yours to make. Thousands of residents are making part or all of their real life income from their Second Life Businesses. By way of example, here are just a few in-world business occupations that Residents founded and currently run, and make part or all of their real life living from.

     - Party and wedding planner.
     - Pet manufacturer.
     - Tattoo artist.
     - Nightclub owner.
     - Fashion designer.
     - Game developer.

### Project 32:
### Creating a Podcast

Podcasting is a form of audio broadcasting on the Internet. The reason it became linked with the iPod in name was because people download podcasts (audio shows) to listen to on their iPods. However, you don't have to listen to podcasts only on iPods; you can use your computer with some music software such as Windows built-in Media Player or Winamp, or other portable music players (iPod competitors) such as Creative Zen or iRiver. It really does not matter. As long as you have some way to play music on your computer, you will be able to listen to podcasts.

## Project Focus

1. Download Audacity from audacity.sourceforge.net. It is open source, cross-platform, free and lets you mix multiple audio files. There are Windows, Mac OS 9 or X, and Linux/Unix versions available. You will also have to download the LAME MP3 encoder, which allows Audacity to export MP3 files. You will see the download link for that on the same page as the Audacity download. Once you download the LAME MP3 encoder, place it in the Audacity program folder (C:\Program Files\Audacity\Plug-Ins\). Then, open a .WAV file in Audacity, and select the menu option "File" then choose "Export As MP3." When you do, you will see this message: At this Point, browse to where you placed the "lame_enc.dll" file (such as C:\Program Files\Audacity\Plug-Ins). Click on the "lame_enc.dll" file. Once finished, you can now effectively use the Export As MP3 menu option to create MP3 files.

2. Open Audacity and check the preferences. Make sure your playback and recording device are set. If you are going to record a stereo signal, set the number of channels to record to 2 (Stereo) on the Audio I/O preferences. When picking a device to record from, make sure you have set up all the connections properly, such as plugging a microphone into the Mic Input, and any other device into the Line In of your sound card.

3. Click on the red "Record" button to begin recording. You can also:
   - Click on the blue "Pause" button to pause the recording. Press it again to continue.
   - Click on the yellow "Stop" button to cease recording. The cursor will return to its previous position, before the recording was started.

4. MP3 is the de facto standard format for podcasts. When saving, use the minimum bit rate that provides good results. Here are some suggested settings:
   - 48–56k Mono—sermons, audio books, talk radio.
   - 64k + Stereo—music, music and talk combinations.
   - 128k Stereo—good quality music.

5. Create a two to three minute podcast that you can share with your class about a successful entrepreneurial e-business. Here are a few suggestions:
   - SecondLife.com
   - YouTube.com
   - Zillow.com
   - Linkedin.com
   - Digg.com
   - CraigsList.com
   - Karmaloop.com

6. Before you get the ball rolling on creating a podcast, it is important to figure out what will be said (or not said) during the show. What limits are there when it comes to choosing content? In short, there are almost no limits to what can be included in podcasts. Podcasting allows you to create shows, dramatizations, vignettes, commentaries, documentaries, and any other content imaginable. Indeed, podcasting is limited only by individual podcasters' imaginations. However, you need to script out your content before you start to record.

## Project 33:
## Google Earth–Geographic Information

Google Earth combines the power of Google Search with satellite imagery, maps, terrain, and 3-D buildings to put the world's geographic information at your fingertips. Using Google Earth, you can:

- Fly to your house. Just type in an address, press "Search," and you will zoom right in.
- Search for schools, parks, restaurants, and hotels. Get driving directions.

- Tilt and rotate the view to see 3-D terrain and buildings.
- Save and share your searches and favorites.

Since Google Earth was launched, users have been exploring the world and creating content overlays (otherwise known as KML files) to share their explorations with others. Google Earth is a broadband, 3-D application that not all computers can run. Desktop computers four years and older and notebook computers two years and older might not be able to run Google Earth. Go to earth.google.com/download-earth.html to see specific requirements for each operating system on this page. If your computer has the needed requirements, click on the "Download Google Earth" button. This is a free application.

Once you download and install Google Earth, your computer becomes a window to anywhere on the planet, allowing you to view high-resolution aerial and satellite imagery, elevation terrain, road and street labels, business listings, and more.

Try any of the following:

1. View an image of your home, school, or any place on Earth—click "Fly To." Enter the location in the input box and click the "Search" button. In the search results (Places panel), double-click the location. Google Earth flies you to this location.
2. Go on a tour of the world—in the Places panel, check the Sightseeing folder, and click the "Play Tour" button.
3. Get driving directions from one place to another and fly (follow) the route.
4. View other cool locations and features created by other Google Earth users—in the Layers panel, check Community Showcase. Interesting places and other features appear in the 3-D viewer. Double-click these points of interest to view and explore.
5. View 3-D terrain of a place—this is more fun with hilly or mountainous terrain, such as the Grand Canyon. Go to a location (see number 1 above). When the view shows the location, use the tilt slider to tilt the terrain.

### Project Focus

1. Google Earth Enterprise Solutions are also available for on-site deployment of custom Google Earth databases within an enterprise. List a few ways an enterprise could take advantage of this application.
2. Since Google Earth has been released as a free application, numerous people have expressed concerns over the availability of such data for either individual privacy or the possibility of terrorists using the satellite photos. Do you agree or disagree? Explain your position.

### Project 34:

### Photo Story 3–Show-n-Tell

Microsoft Photo Story 3 for Windows helps create exciting video stories from pictures. For example, you could create a video story that features narrated photographs from a family vacation or a video story that includes pictures and sounds of an athletic race or game.

In a few simple steps, you can import and edit your pictures, add titles, record narration, add background music, and save your story using the optimal quality settings (profile) for the way your story will be played.

Download Photo Story 3 from www.microsoft.com/windowsxp/using/digitalphotography/photostory/default.mspx. Review the requirements section to make sure your computer is able to run this application. Click the "Continue" button in the Validation Required section to begin the short validation process. Once validated, you will be sent to a page with specific instructions for obtaining the download.

When you run Photo Story 3, with the view to making a new project, the first option is to select "Begin a new story." After clicking this option your first task is to "import" pictures. You can import pictures from your computer, a network folder, or a website. For each story, you can import up to 300 pictures, which can be files with .bmp, .dib, .eps, .gif, .jhif, .jpe, .jpeg, .jpg, .pcd, .pcx, .png, .psd, .rle, .tga, and .tif file name extensions.

Your pictures appear in the filmstrip at the bottom of the page. If you import more pictures, Microsoft Photo Story 3 adds them at the end of the filmstrip.

By clicking on a series of buttons or options, you can remove black borders, add titles to your picture, add narration and custom motion, and add background music to your story.

### Project Focus

1. Develop a 30-second professional commercial. This is a short description of who you are, what job you are looking for, and the skills that make you suited for the job.

2. Building a quality 30-second commercial can be tougher than it sounds. The goal is to be able to contact a stranger and let him or her know who you are, what your skills are, and why you are approaching the person.

3. Create a list of words describing your skills and interests. Begin broadly and then narrow your list to skills related to your current job search.

4. Compile your script and present it to the class.

### Project 35:

### Sticky Wiki

Wiki (Hawaiian for "quick") is software that allows users to freely create and edit web page content using any web browser. The most common Wiki is Wikipedia. Wikis offer a powerful yet flexible collaborative communication tool for developing websites. The best part of a wiki is that it grows and evolves by the collaborative community adding content—the owner of the wiki does not have to add all of the content as is typical in a standard web page.

There are many sites which offer free wiki software such as Socialtext, a group-editable website. As one of the first wiki companies, Socialtext wikis are designed for anyone that wants to accelerate team communications, better enable knowledge sharing, foster collaboration, and build online communities. Socialtext also offers WikiWidgets, which make it easy for non-technical business users to create rich, dynamic wiki content. Today, over 3,000 organizations use Socialtext, including Symantec, Nokia, IKEA, Conde Nast, Ziff-Davis, Kodak, University of Southern California, Boston College, and numerous others.

### Project Focus

Create your own wiki. Wikis can address a variety of needs from student involvement, fraternities and sororities, group activities, sport team updates, local band highlights, etc. Choose a free wiki software vendor and create a wiki for any of the following:

- Student organization
- Fraternity or sorority
- Academic organization
- Favorite author or book
- Favorite band or musician
- Favorite sports team
- Favorite movie
- Basically, anything you are involved in or excited about and want to create a site to collaborate with other

## Wiki Software Sites

- www.socialtext.com—easy-to-use, business-grade wikis proven by Fortune 500 companies
- www.wetpaint.com—a free easy-to-use wiki building site
- www.CentralDesktop.com—Easy-to-use, a wiki for non-techies
- www.xwiki.com—Open source and free hosting with professional services

If you have different wiki software you prefer to use please feel free to use it to create your wiki.

## A

**acceptable use policy (AUP)** A policy that a user must agree to follow in order to be provided access to a network or to the Internet.

**accounting** Analyzes the transactional information of the business so the owners and investors can make sound economic decisions.

**accounting and finance ERP component** Manages accounting data and financial processes within the enterprise with functions such as general ledger, accounts payable, accounts receivable, budgeting, and asset management.

**accounting department** Provides quantitative information about the finances of the business including recording, measuring, and describing financial information.

**adware** Software that generates ads that install themselves on a computer when a person downloads some other program from the Internet.

**affinity grouping** Determine which things go together.

**agile methodology** Aims for customer satisfaction through early and continuous delivery of useful software components developed by an iterative process with a design point that uses the bare minimum requirements.

**analysis latency** The time from which data are made available to the time when analysis is complete.

**analysis phase** Analyzing end-user business requirements and refining project goals into defined functions and operations of the intended system.

**analytical CRM** Supports back-office operations and strategic analysis and includes all systems that do not deal directly with the customers.

**analytical information** Encompasses all organizational information, and its primary purpose is to support the performing of managerial analysis tasks.

**anti-spam policy** States that email users will not send unsolicited emails (or spam).

**application architecture** Determines how applications integrate and relate to each other.

**application programming interface (API)** A set of routines, protocols, and tools for building software applications.

**application service provider (ASP)** A company that offers an organization access over the Internet to systems and related services that would otherwise have to be located in personal or organizational computers.

**application software** Used for specific information processing needs, including payroll, customer relationship management, project management, training, and many others.

**arithmetic/logic unit (ALU)** Performs all arithmetic operations (for example, addition and subtraction) and all logic operations (such as sorting and comparing numbers).

**artificial intelligence (AI)** Simulates human intelligence such as the ability to reason and learn.

**As-Is process model** Represents the current state of the operation that has been mapped, without any specific improvements or changes to existing processes.

**asset** Anything owned that has value or earning power.

**associates program (affiliate program)** Businesses can generate commissions or royalties from an Internet site.

**association detection** Reveals the degree to which variables are related and the nature and frequency of these relationships in the information.

**attribute** Characteristics or properties of an entity class.

**authentication** A method for confirming users' identities.

**authorization** The process of giving someone permission to do or have something.

**automatic call distribution** A phone switch routes inbound calls to available agents.

**autonomic computing** A self-managing computing model named after, and patterned on, the human body's autonomic nervous system.

**availability** Addresses when systems can be accessed by employees, customers, and partners.

## B

**backdoor program** Viruses that open a way into the network for future attacks.

**backup** An exact copy of a system's information.

**backward integration** Takes information entered into a given system and sends it automatically to all upstream systems and processes.

**balance sheet** Gives an accounting picture of property owned by a company and of claims against the property on a specific date.

**balanced scorecard** A management system that enables organizations to clarify their vision and strategy and translate them into action.

**bandwidth** The difference between the highest and the lowest frequencies that can be transmitted on a single medium; a measure of the medium's capacity.

**benchmark** Baseline values the system seeks to attain.

**benchmarking** The process of continuously measuring system results, comparing those results to optimal system performance (benchmark values), and identifying steps and procedures to improve system performance.

**binary digit (bit)**   The smallest unit of information that a computer can process.

**biometric**   The identification of a user based on a physical characteristic, such as a fingerprint, iris, face, voice, or handwriting.

**black-hat hacker**   Breaks into other people's computer systems and may just look around or steal and destroy information.

**blog**   Website in which items are posted on a regular basis and displayed in reverse chronological order.

**Bluetooth**   An omnidirectional wireless technology that provides limited-range voice and data transmission over the unlicensed 2.4-GHz frequency band, allowing connections with a wide variety of fixed and portable devices that normally would have to be cabled together.

**bookkeeping**   The actual recording of the business's transactions, without any analysis of the information.

**break-even point**   The point at which revenues equal costs.

**brick-and-mortar business**   A business that operates in a physical store without an Internet presence.

**broadband**   High-speed Internet connections transmitting data at speeds greater than 200 kilobytes per second (Kbps), compared to the 56 Kbps maximum speed offered by traditional dial-up connections.

**bullwhip effect**   Occurs when distorted product demand information passes from one entity to the next throughout the supply chain.

**business continuity planning (BCP)**   A plan for how an organization will recover and restore partially or completely interrupted critical function(s) within a predetermined time after a disaster or extended disruption.

**business-critical integrity constraint**   Enforces business rules vital to an organization's success and often requires more insight and knowledge than relational integrity constraints.

**business facing process**   Invisible to the external customer but essential to the effective management of the business and includes goal setting, day-to-day planning, performance feedback, rewards, and resource allocation.

**business intelligence**   Refers to applications and technologies that are used to gather, provide access to, and analyze data and information to support decision-making efforts.

**business process**   A standardized set of activities that accomplish a specific task, such as processing a customer's order.

**business process management (BPM)**   Integrates all of an organization's business processes to make individual processes more efficient.

**business process management tool**   Used to create an application that is helpful in designing business process models and also helpful in simulating, optimizing, monitoring, and maintaining various processes that occur within an organization.

**business process model**   A graphic description of a process, showing the sequence of process tasks, which is developed for a specific purpose and from a selected viewpoint.

**business process modeling** (or **mapping**)   The activity of creating a detailed flow chart or process map of a work process showing its inputs, tasks, and activities, in a structured sequence.

**business process reengineering (BPR)**   The analysis and redesign of workflow within and between enterprises.

**business requirement**   The detailed set of business requests that the system must meet in order to be successful.

**business-to-business (B2B)**   Applies to businesses buying from and selling to each other over the Internet.

**business-to-consumer (B2C)**   Applies to any business that sells its products or services to consumers over the Internet.

**business wiki**   Collaborative web pages that allow users to edit documents, share ideas, or monitor the status of a project.

**buyer power**   Is assessed by analyzing the ability of buyers to directly impact the price they are willing to pay for an item.

**byte**   Group of eight bits represents one natural language character.

## C

**cache memory**   A small unit of ultra-fast memory that is used to store recently accessed or frequently accessed data so that the CPU does not have to retrieve this data from slower memory circuits such as RAM.

**call scripting system**   Accesses organizational databases that track similar issues or questions and automatically generate the details for the CSR who can then relay them to the customer.

**campaign management system**   Guides users through marketing campaigns performing such tasks as campaign definition, planning, scheduling, segmentation, and success analysis.

**capability maturity model integration method (CMMI)**   A process improvement approach that contains 22 process areas.

**capacity planning**   Determines the future IT infrastructure requirements for new equipment and additional network capacity.

**capital**   Represents money whose purpose is to make more money, for example, the money used to buy a rental property or a business.

**central processing unit (CPU)** (or **microprocessor**)   The actual hardware that interprets and executes the program (software) instructions and coordinates how all the other hardware devices work together.

**change control board (CCB)**   Responsible for approving or rejecting all change requests.

**change management**   A set of techniques that aid in evolution, composition, and policy management of the design and implementation of a system.

**change management system**   Includes a collection of procedures to document a change request and define the steps necessary to consider the change based on the expected impact of the change.

**chief information officer (CIO)**   Responsible for (1) overseeing all uses of information technology and (2) ensuring the strategic alignment of IT with business goals and objectives.

**chief knowledge officer (CKO)**   Responsible for collecting, maintaining, and distributing the organization's knowledge.

**chief privacy officer (CPO)**   Responsible for ensuring the ethical and legal use of information within an organization.

**chief security officer (CSO)**   Responsible for ensuring the security of IT systems and developing strategies and IT safeguards against attacks from hackers and viruses.

**chief technology officer (CTO)**   Responsible for ensuring the throughput, speed, accuracy, availability, and reliability of an organization's information technology.

**classification**   Assigns records to one of a predefined set of classes.

**click-and-mortar business**   A business that operates in a physical store and on the Internet.

**clickstream**   Records information about a customer during a web surfing session such as what websites were visited, how long the visit was, what ads were viewed, and what was purchased.

**clickstream data**   Exact pattern of a consumer's navigation through a site.

**click-through**   A count of the number of people who visit one site and click on an advertisement that takes them to the site of the advertiser.

**click-to-talk**   Buttons allow customers to click on a button and talk with a CSR via the Internet.

**client**   Computer that is designed to request information from a server.

**client/server network**   A model for applications in which the bulk of the back-end processing, such as performing a physical search of a database, takes place on a server, while the front-end processing, which involves communicating with the users, is handled by the clients.

**cloud computing**   Refers to resources and applications hosted remotely as a shared service over the Internet.

**cluster analysis**   A technique used to divide an information set into mutually exclusive groups such that the members of each group are as close together as possible to one another and the different groups are as far apart as possible.

**clustering**   Segmenting a heterogeneous population of records into a number of more homogeneous subgroups.

**coaxial cable**   Cable that can carry a wide range of frequencies with low signal loss.

**cold site**   A separate facility that does not have any computer equipment, but is a place where employees can move after a disaster.

**collaboration system**   An IT-based set of tools that supports the work of teams by facilitating the sharing and flow of information.

**collaborative demand planning**   Helps organizations reduce their investment in inventory, while improving customer satisfaction through product availability.

**collaborative engineering**   Allows an organization to reduce the cost and time required during the design process of a product.

**commercial off-the-shelf (COTS)**   A software package or solution that is purchased to support one or more business functions and information systems.

**Committee of Sponsoring Organizations (COSO)**   Key for evaluating internal controls such as human resources, logistics, information technology, risk, legal, marketing and sales, operations, financial functions, procurement, and reporting.

**communication device**   Equipment used to send information and receive it from one location to another.

**competitive advantage**   A product or service that an organization's customers place a greater value on than similar offerings from a competitor.

**complex instruction set computer (CISC) chip**   Type of CPU that can recognize as many as 100 or more instructions, enough to carry out most computations directly.

**compliance**   The act of conforming, acquiescing, or yielding.

**computer**   Electronic device operating under the control of instructions stored in its own memory that can accept, manipulate, and store data.

**computer-aided software engineering (CASE)**   Software suites that automate systems analysis, design, and development.

**computer simulation**   Complex systems, such as the U.S. economy, can be modeled by means of mathematical equations and different scenarios can be run against the model to determine "what if" analysis.

**confidentiality**   The assurance that messages and information are available only to those who are authorized to view them.

**consolidation**   Involves the aggregation of information and features simple roll-ups to complex groupings of interrelated information.

**consumer-to-business (C2B)**   Applies to any consumer that sells a product or service to a business over the Internet.

**consumer-to-consumer (C2C)**   Applies to sites primarily offering goods and services to assist consumers interacting with each other over the Internet.

**contact center (call center)**   Customer service representatives (CSRs) answer customer inquiries and respond to problems through a number of different customer touch points.

**contact management CRM system**   Maintains customer contact information and identifies prospective customers for future sales.

**content filtering**   Occurs when organizations use software that filters content to prevent the transmission of unauthorized information.

**content management system**   Provides tools to manage the creation, storage, editing, and publication of information in a collaborative environment.

**content provider**   Companies that use the Internet to distribute copyrighted content, including news, music, games, books, movies, and many other types of information.

**continuous process improvement model**   Attempts to understand and measure the current process, and make performance improvements accordingly.

**control unit**   Interprets software instructions and literally tells the other hardware devices what to do, based on the software instructions.

**cookie**   A small file deposited on a hard drive by a website containing information about customers and their web activities.

**copyright**   The legal protection afforded an expression of an idea, such as a song, video game, and some types of proprietary documents.

**core competency**   An organization's key strength or business function that it does better than any of its competitors.

**core competency strategy**   When an organization chooses to focus specifically on what it does best (its core competency) and forms partnerships and alliances with other specialist organizations to handle nonstrategic business processes.

**core ERP component**   Traditional components included in most ERP systems and they primarily focus on internal operations.

**corporate policy** A dimension of social responsibility that refers to the position a firm takes on social and political issues.

**corporate responsibility** A dimension of social responsibility that includes everything from hiring minority workers to making safe products.

**corporation** (also called **organization, enterprise,** or **business**) An artificially created legal entity that exists separate and apart from those individuals who created it and carry on its operations.

**counterfeit software** Software that is manufactured to look like the real thing and sold as such.

**cracker** A hacker with criminal intent.

**critical path** A path from the start to the finish that passes through all the tasks that are critical to completing the project in the shortest amount of time.

**critical success factor (CSF)** A factor that is critical to an organization's success.

**CRM analysis technologies** Help organizations segment their customers into categories such as best and worst customers.

**CRM predicting technologies** Help organizations make predictions regarding customer behavior such as which customers are at risk of leaving.

**CRM reporting technologies** Help organizations identify their customers across other applications.

**cross-selling** Selling additional products or services to a customer.

**cube** The common term for the representation of multidimensional information.

**customer facing process** Results in a product or service that is received by an organization's external customer.

**customer metric** Assesses the management of customer relationships by the organization.

**customer relationship management (CRM)** Involves managing all aspects of a customer's relationship with an organization to increase customer loyalty and retention and an organization's profitability.

**cyberterrorist** Seeks to cause harm to people or to destroy critical systems or information and use the Internet as a weapon of mass destruction.

**cycle inventory** The average amount of inventory held to satisfy customer demands between inventory deliveries.

## D

**data** Raw facts that describe the characteristics of an event.

**database** Maintains information about various types of objects (inventory), events (transactions), people (employees), and places (warehouses).

**database-based workflow system** Stores documents in a central location and automatically asks the team members to access the document when it is their turn to edit the document.

**database management system (DBMS)** Software through which users and application programs interact with a database.

**data-driven website** An interactive website kept constantly updated and relevant to the needs of its customers through the use of a database.

**data flow diagram (DFD)** Illustrates the movement of information between external entities and the processes and data stores within the system.

**data latency** The time duration to make data ready for analysis (i.e., the time for extracting, transforming, and cleansing the data) and loading the data into the database.

**data mart** Contains a subset of data warehouse information.

**data mining** The process of analyzing data to extract information not offered by the raw data alone.

**data-mining tool** Uses a variety of techniques to find patterns and relationships in large volumes of information and infer rules from them that predict future behavior and guide decision making.

**data model** A formal way to express data relationships to a database management system (DBMS).

**data warehouse** A logical collection of information—gathered from many different operational databases—that supports business analysis activities and decision-making tasks.

**decision latency** The time it takes a human to comprehend the analytic result and determine an appropriate action.

**decision support system (DSS)** Models information to support managers and business professionals during the decision-making process.

**demand planning software** Generates demand forecasts using statistical tools and forecasting techniques.

**denial-of-service attack (DoS)** Floods a website with so many requests for service that it slows down or crashes the site.

**dependency** A logical relationship that exists between the project tasks, or between a project task and a milestone.

**deperimeterization** Occurs when an organization moves employees outside its firewall, a growing movement to change the way corporations address technology security.

**design phase** Involves describing the desired features and operations of the system including screen layouts, business rules, process diagrams, pseudo code, and other documentation.

**development phase** Involves taking all of the detailed design documents from the design phase and transforming them into the actual system.

**digital asset management system (DAM)** Though similar to document management, DAM generally works with binary rather than text files, such as multimedia file types.

**digital Darwinism** Organizations that cannot adapt to the new demands placed on them for surviving in the information age are doomed to extinction.

**digital dashboard** Integrates information from multiple components and tailors the information to individual preferences.

**digital divide** When those with access to technology have great advantages over those without access to technology.

**digital ink** (or **electronic ink**) Technology that digitally represents handwriting in its natural form.

**digital paper** (or **electronic paper**) Any paper that is optimized for any type of digital printing.

**digital wallet** Both software and information—the software provides security for the transaction and the information includes payment and delivery information (for example, the credit card number and expiration date).

**disaster recovery cost curve**   Charts (1) the cost to the organization of the unavailability of information and technology and (2) the cost to the organization of recovering from a disaster over time.

**disaster recovery plan**   A detailed process for recovering information or an IT system in the event of a catastrophic disaster such as a fire or flood.

**disruptive technology**   A new way of doing things that initially does not meet the needs of existing customers.

**distributed denial-of-service attack (DDoS)**   Attacks from multiple computers that flood a website with so many requests for service that it slows down or crashes.

**distribution management software**   Coordinates the process of transporting materials from a manufacturer to distribution centers to the final customer.

**dividend**   A distribution of earnings to shareholders.

**document management system (DMS)**   Supports the electronic capturing, storage, distribution, archival, and accessing of documents.

**drill-down**   Enables users to get details, and details of details, of information.

# E

**ebusiness**   The conducting of business on the Internet, not only buying and selling, but also serving customers and collaborating with business partners.

**ebusiness model**   An approach to conducting electronic business on the Internet.

**ecommerce**   The buying and selling of goods and services over the Internet.

**effectiveness IT metric**   Measures the impact IT has on business processes and activities including customer satisfaction, conversion rates, and sell-through increases.

**efficiency IT metric**   Measures the performance of the IT system itself including throughput, speed, and availability.

**egovernment**   Involves the use of strategies and technologies to transform government(s) by improving the delivery of services and enhancing the quality of interaction between the citizen-consumer within all branches of government.

**electronic bill presentment and payment (EBPP)**   System that sends bills over the Internet and provides an easy-to-use mechanism (such as clicking on a button) to pay the bill.

**electronic catalog**   Presents customers with information about goods and services offered for sale, bid, or auction on the Internet.

**electronic check**   Mechanism for sending a payment from a checking or savings account.

**electronic data interchange (EDI)**   A standard format for exchanging business data.

**electronic marketplace (emarketplace)**   Interactive business communities providing a central market space where multiple buyers and suppliers can engage in ebusiness activities.

**electronic tagging**   A technique for identifying and tracking assets and individuals via technologies such as radio frequency identification and smart cards.

**elevation of privilege**   Process by which a user misleads a system into granting unauthorized rights, usually for the purpose of compromising or destroying the system.

**elogistics**   Manages the transportation and storage of goods.

**email privacy policy**   Details the extent to which email messages may be read by others.

**emall**   Consists of a number of eshops; it serves as a gateway through which a visitor can access other eshops.

**employee monitoring policy**   States how, when, and where the company monitors its employees.

**employee relationship management (ERM)**   Provides employees with a subset of CRM applications available through a web browser.

**encryption**   Scrambles information into an alternative form that requires a key or password to decrypt the information.

**enterprise application integration (EAI) middleware**   Represents a new approach to middleware by packaging together commonly used functionality, such as providing prebuilt links to popular enterprise applications, which reduces the time necessary to develop solutions that integrate applications from multiple vendors.

**enterprise architect (EA)**   Person grounded in technology, fluent in business, a patient diplomat, and provides the important bridge between IT and the business.

**enterprise architecture**   Includes the plans for how an organization will build, deploy, use, and share its data, processes, and IT assets.

**enterprise resource planning (ERP)**   Integrates all departments and functions throughout an organization into a single IT system (or integrated set of IT systems) so that employees can make decisions by viewing enterprisewide information on all business operations.

**entity**   In the relational database model, a person, place, thing, transaction, or event about which information is stored.

**entity-relationship diagram (ERD)**   A technique for documenting the relationships between entities in a database environment.

**entry barrier**   A product or service feature that customers have come to expect from organizations in a particular industry and must be offered by an entering organization to compete and survive.

**environmental scanning**   The acquisition and analysis of events and trends in the environment external to an organization.

**ePolicies**   Policies and procedures that address the ethical use of computers and Internet usage in the business environment.

**eprocurement**   The B2B purchase and sale of supplies and services over the Internet.

**eshop (estore or etailer)**   A version of a retail store where customers can shop at any hour of the day without leaving their home or office.

**estimation**   Determine values for an unknown continuous variable behavior or estimated future value.

**ethernet**   A physical and data layer technology for LAN networking.

**ethical computer use policy**   Contains general principles to guide computer user behavior.

**ethics**   Principles and standards that guide our behavior toward other people.

**ewaste**   Old computer equipment, does not end up in a landfill, where the toxic substances it contains can leach into groundwater, among other problems.

**executive information system (EIS)**   A specialized DSS that supports senior level executives within the organization.

**executive sponsor**   The person or group who provides the financial resources for the project.

**expense**   Refers to the costs incurred in operating and maintaining a business.

**expert system**   Computerized advisory programs that imitate the reasoning processes of experts in solving difficult problems.

**explicit knowledge**   Consists of anything that can be documented, archived, and codified, often with the help of IT.

**extended ERP component**   The extra components that meet the organizational needs not covered by the core components and primarily focus on external operations.

**extensible markup language (XML)**   A markup language for documents containing structured information.

**extraction, transformation, and loading (ETL)**   A process that extracts information from internal and external databases, transforms the information using a common set of enterprise definitions, and loads the information into a data warehouse.

**extranet**   An intranet that is available to strategic allies (such as customers, suppliers, and partners).

**extreme programming (XP) methodology**   Breaks a project into tiny phases, and developers cannot continue on to the next phase until the first phase is complete.

## F

**failover**   Backup operational mode in which the function of a computer component (such as a processor, server, network, or database) is assumed by secondary system components when the primary component becomes unavailable through either failure or scheduled down time.

**fair use doctrine**   In certain situations, it is legal to use copyrighted material.

**fault tolerance**   A computer system designed so that in the event a component fails, a backup component or procedure can immediately take its place with no loss of service.

**feasibility study**   Determines if the proposed solution is feasible and achievable from a financial, technical, and organizational standpoint.

**feature creep**   Occurs when developers add extra features that were not part of the initial requirements.

**fiber optic (optical fiber)**   The technology associated with the transmission of information as light impulses along a glass wire or fiber.

**finance**   Deals with the strategic financial issues associated with increasing the value of the business while observing applicable laws and social responsibilities.

**financial accounting**   Involves preparing financial reports that provide information about the business's performance to external parties such as investors, creditors, and tax authorities.

**financial cybermediary**   Internet-based company that facilitates payments over the Internet.

**financial EDI (financial electronic data interchange)**   Standard electronic process for B2B market purchase payments.

**financial quarter**   A three-month period (four quarters per year).

**financial statement**   Written records of the financial status of the business that allow interested parties to evaluate the profitability and solvency of the business.

**firewall**   Hardware and/or software that guards a private network by analyzing the information leaving and entering the network.

**first-mover advantage**   An organization can significantly impact its market share by being first to market with a competitive advantage.

**Five Forces model**   Helps determine the relative attractiveness of an industry.

**flash memory**   A special type of rewriteable read-only memory (ROM) that is compact and portable.

**for profit corporations**   Primarily focus on making money and all profits and losses are shared by the business owners.

**forecast**   Predictions made on the basis of time-series information.

**foreign key**   A primary key of one table that appears as an attribute in another table and acts to provide a logical relationship between the two tables.

**forward integration**   Takes information entered into a given system and sends it automatically to all downstream systems and processes.

**fuzzy logic**   A mathematical method of handling imprecise or subjective information.

## G

**Gantt chart**   A simple bar chart that depicts project tasks against a calendar.

**genetic algorithm**   An artificial intelligence system that mimics the evolutionary, survival-of-the-fittest process to generate increasingly better solutions to a problem.

**geoeconomic**   Refers to the effects of geography on the economic realities of international business activities.

**geographic information system (GIS)**   Designed to work with information that can be shown on a map.

**gigabyte (GB)**   Roughly 1 billion bytes.

**gigahertz (GHz)**   The number of billions of CPU cycles per second.

**global inventory management system**   Provides the ability to locate, track, and predict the movement of every component or material anywhere upstream or downstream in the supply chain.

**global positioning system (GPS)**   A device that determines current latitude, longitude, speed, and direction of movement.

**goal-seeking analysis**   Finds the inputs necessary to achieve a goal such as a desired level of output.

**governance**   Method or system of government for management or control.

**graphical user interface (GUI)**   The interface to an information system.

**grid computing**   An aggregation of geographically dispersed computing, storage, and network resources, coordinated to deliver improved performance, higher quality of service, better utilization, and easier access to data.

**groupware** Software that supports team interaction and dynamics including calendaring, scheduling, and videoconferencing.

**GUI screen design** The ability to model the information system screens for an entire system using icons, buttons, menus, and submenus.

## H

**hacker** People very knowledgeable about computers who use their knowledge to invade other people's computers.

**hactivist** Person with philosophical and political reasons for breaking into systems who will often deface website as a protest.

**hard drive** Secondary storage medium that uses several rigid disks coated with a magnetically sensitive material and housed together with the recording heads in a hermetically sealed mechanism.

**hardware** Consists of the physical devices associated with a computer system.

**hardware key logger** A hardware device that captures keystrokes on their journey from the keyboard to the motherboard.

**help desk** A group of people who respond to internal system user questions.

**hierarchical database model** Information is organized into a tree-like structure that allows repeating information using parent/child relationships, in such a way that it cannot have too many relationships.

**high availability** Refers to a system or component that is continuously operational for a desirably long length of time.

**historical analysis** Historical events are studied to anticipate the outcome of current developments.

**hoaxes** Attack computer systems by transmitting a virus hoax, with a real virus attached.

**hot site** A separate and fully equipped facility where the company can move immediately after a disaster and resume business.

**human resource ERP component** Tracks employee information including payroll, benefits, compensation, and performance assessment, and assures compliance with the legal requirements of multiple jurisdictions and tax authorities.

**human resources (HR)** Includes the policies, plans, and procedures for the effective management of employees (human resources).

**hypertext transfer protocol (HTTP)** The Internet standard that supports the exchange of information on the WWW.

## I

**identity theft** The forging of someone's identity for the purpose of fraud.

**implementation phase** Involves placing the system into production so users can begin to perform actual business operations with the system.

**income statement** (also referred to as **earnings report, operating statement,** and **profit-and-loss (P&L) statement**) Reports operating results (revenues minus expenses) for a given time period ending at a specified date.

**information** Data converted into a meaningful and useful context.

**information accuracy** Extent to which a system generates the correct results when executing the same transaction numerous times.

**information architecture** Identifies where and how important information, like customer records, is maintained and secured.

**information cleansing or scrubbing** A process that weeds out and fixes or discards inconsistent, incorrect, or incomplete information.

**information granularity** Refers to the extent of detail within the information (fine and detailed or "coarse" and abstract information).

**information integrity** A measure of the quality of information.

**information partnership** Occurs when two or more organizations cooperate by integrating their IT systems, thereby providing customers with the best of what each can offer.

**information privacy** Concerns the legal right or general expectation of individuals, groups, or institutions to determine for themselves when and to what extent information about them is communicated to others.

**information privacy policy** Contains general principles regarding information privacy.

**information reach** Refers to the number of people a business can communicate with, on a global basis.

**information richness** Refers to the depth and breadth of information transferred between customers and businesses.

**information security** A broad term encompassing the protection of information from accidental or intentional misuse by persons inside or outside an organization.

**information security plan** Details how an organization will implement the information security policies.

**information security policy** Identifies the rules required to maintain information security.

**Information Systems Audit and Control Association (ISACA)** A set of guidelines and supporting tools for IT governance that is accepted worldwide and generally used by auditors and companies as a way to integrate technology to implement controls and meet specific business objectives.

**information technology (IT)** The field concerned with the use of technology in managing and processing information.

**Information Technology Infrastructure Library (ITIL)** A framework provided by the government of the United Kingdom that offers eight sets of management procedures.

**information technology monitoring** Tracking people's activities by such measures as number of keystrokes, error rate, and number of transactions processed.

**infrastructure architecture** Includes the hardware, software, and telecommunications equipment that, when combined, provide the underlying foundation to support the organization's goals.

**innovation** The introduction of new equipment or methods.

**input device** Equipment used to capture information and commands.

**insider** Legitimate users who purposely or accidentally misuse their access to the environment and cause some kind of business-affecting incident.

**insourcing (in-house development)** A common approach using the professional expertise within an organization to develop and maintain the organization's information technology systems.

**instant messaging (IM or IMing)**   A type of communications service that enables someone to create a kind of private chat room with another individual in order to communicate in real-time over the Internet.

**integration**   Allows separate systems to communicate directly with each other.

**integrity constraint**   The rules that help ensure the quality of information.

**intellectual property**   Intangible creative work that is embodied in physical form.

**intelligent agent**   A special-purpose knowledge-based information system that accomplishes specific tasks on behalf of its users.

**intelligent system**   Various commercial applications of artificial intelligence.

**interactive voice response (IVR)**   Directs customers to use touch-tone phones or keywords to navigate or provide information.

**interactivity**   Measures the visitor interactions with the target ad.

**intermediary**   Agent, software, or business that brings buyers and sellers together to provide a trading infrastructure to enhance ebusiness.

**International Organization for Standardization (ISO)**   A nongovernmental organization established in 1947 to promote the development of world standards to facilitate the international exchange of goods and services.

**Internet**   A global public network of computer networks that pass information from one to another using common computer protocols.

**Internet service provider (ISP)**   A company that provides individuals and other companies access to the Internet along with additional related services, such as website building.

**Internet use policy**   Contains general principles to guide the proper use of the Internet.

**interoperability**   Capability of two or more computer systems to share data and resources, even though they are made by different manufacturers.

**intranet**   An internalized portion of the Internet, protected from outside access, that allows an organization to provide access to information and application software to only its employees.

**intrusion detection software (IDS)**   Searches out patterns in information and network traffic to indicate attacks and quickly responds to prevent any harm.

**inventory management and control software**   Provides control and visibility to the status of individual items maintained in inventory.

**iterative development**   Consists of a series of tiny projects.

**IT infrastructure**   Includes the hardware, software, and telecommunications equipment that, when combined, provide the underlying foundation to support the organization's goals.

## J

**joint application development (JAD)**   A session where employees meet, sometimes for several days, to define or review the business requirements for the system.

## K

**key logger, or key trapper, software**   A program that, when installed on a computer, records every keystroke and mouse click.

**key performance indicator (KPI)**   Measures that are tied to business drivers.

**kill switch**   A trigger that enables a project manager to close the project prior to completion.

**kiosk**   Publicly accessible computer system that has been set up to allow interactive information browsing.

**knowledge management (KM)**   Involves capturing, classifying, evaluating, retrieving, and sharing information assets in a way that provides context for effective decisions and actions.

**knowledge management system (KMS)**   Supports the capturing, organization, and dissemination of knowledge (i.e., know-how) throughout an organization.

## L

**liability**   An obligation to make financial payments.

**limited liability**   Means that the shareholders are not personally liable for the losses incurred by the corporation.

**limited liability corporation (LLC)**   A hybrid entity that has the legal protections of a corporation and the ability to be taxed (one time) as a partnership.

**limited partnership**   Much like a general partnership except for one important fundamental difference; the law protects the limited partner from being responsible for all of the partnership's losses.

**list generator**   Compiles customer information from a variety of sources and segments the information for different marketing campaigns.

**local area network (LAN)**   Computer network that uses cables or radio signals to link two or more computers within a geographically limited area, generally one building or a group of buildings.

**location-based services (LBS)**   Wireless mobile content services that provide location-specific information to mobile users moving from location to location.

**logical view**   Focuses on how users logically access information to meet their particular business needs.

**logistics**   The set of processes that plans for and controls the efficient and effective transportation and storage of supplies from suppliers to customers.

**loose coupling**   The capability of services to be joined together on demand to create composite services, or disassembled just as easily into their functional components.

**loss**   Occurs when businesses sell products or services for less than they cost to produce.

**loyalty program**   Rewards customers based on the amount of business they do with a particular organization.

## M

**magnetic medium**   Secondary storage medium that uses magnetic techniques to store and retrieve data on disks or tapes coated with magnetically sensitive materials.

**magnetic tape**   Older secondary storage medium that uses a strip of thin plastic coated with a magnetically sensitive recording medium.

**mail bomb**   Sends a massive amount of email to a specific person or system resulting in filling up the recipient's disk space, which, in some cases, may be too much for the server to handle and may cause the server to stop functioning.

**maintenance**   The fixing or enhancing of an information system.

**maintenance phase**   Involves performing changes, corrections, additions, and upgrades to ensure the system continues to meet the business goals.

**maintenance, repair, and operations (MRO) materials** (also called **indirect materials**)   Materials necessary for running an organization but that do not relate to the company's primary business activities.

**malicious code**   Includes a variety of threats such as viruses, worms, and Trojan horses.

**management information systems (MIS)**   A general name for the business function and academic discipline covering the application of people, technologies, and procedures—collectively called information systems—to solve business problems.

**managerial accounting**   Involves analyzing business operations for internal decision making and does not have to follow any rules issued by standard-setting bodies such as GAAP.

**market basket analysis**   Analyzes such items as websites and checkout scanner information to detect customers' buying behavior and predict future behavior by identifying affinities among customers' choices of products and services.

**marketing**   The process associated with promoting the sale of goods or services.

**marketing communication**   Seeks to build product or service awareness and to educate potential consumers on the product or service.

**marketing mix**   Includes the variables that marketing managers can control in order to best satisfy customers in the target market.

**market maker**   Intermediaries that aggregate three services for market participants: (1) a place to trade, (2) rules to govern trading, and (3) an infrastructure to support trading.

**market segmentation**   The division of a market into similar groups of customers.

**market share**   Calculated by dividing the firm's sales by the total market sales for the entire industry.

**mashup editor**   WYSIWYGs (What You See Is What You Get) for mashups that provide a visual interface to build a mashup, often allowing the user to drag and drop data points into a web application.

**mass customization**   Ability of an organization to give its customers the opportunity to tailor its products or services to the customers' specifications.

**materials requirement planning (MRP) system**   Sales forecasts to make sure that needed parts and materials are available at the right time and place in a specific company.

**megabyte (MB** or **M** or **Meg)**   Roughly 1 million bytes.

**megahertz (MHz)**   The number of millions of CPU cycles per second.

**memory card**   Contains high-capacity storage that holds data such as captured images, music, or text files.

**memory stick**   Provides nonvolatile memory for a range of portable devices including computers, digital cameras, MP3 players, and PDAs.

**messaging-based workflow system**   Sends work assignments through an email system.

**methodology**   A set of policies, procedures, standards, processes, practices, tools, techniques, and tasks that people apply to technical and management challenges.

**metropolitan area network (MAN)**   A computer network that provides connectivity in a geographic area or region larger than that covered by a local area network, but smaller than the area covered by a wide area network.

**microwave transmitter**   Commonly used to transmit network signals over great distances.

**middleware**   Different types of software that sit in the middle of and provide connectivity between two or more software applications.

**mobile commerce,** or **mcommerce**   The ability to purchase goods and services through a wireless Internet-enabled device.

**model**   A simplified representation or abstraction of reality.

**modeling**   The activity of drawing a graphical representation of a design.

**monopsony**   A market in which there are many suppliers and only one buyer.

**multisourcing**   A combination of professional services, mission-critical support, remote management, and hosting services that are offered to customers in any combination needed.

**multitasking**   Allows more than one piece of software to be used at a time.

# N

**nearshore outsourcing**   Contracting an outsourcing agreement with a company in a nearby country.

**net income**   The amount of money remaining after paying taxes.

**network**   A communications, data exchange, and resource-sharing system created by linking two or more computers and establishing standards, or protocols, so that they can work together.

**network database model**   A flexible way of representing objects and their relationships.

**network operating system (NOS)**   The operating system that runs a network, steering information between computers and managing security and users.

**network topology**   Refers to the geometric arrangement of the actual physical organization of the computers (and other network devices) in a network.

**network transmission media**   Various types of media used to carry the signal between computers.

**neural network (an artificial neural network)**   A category of AI that attempts to emulate the way the human brain works.

**nonrepudiation**   A contractual stipulation to ensure that ebusiness participants do not deny (repudiate) their online actions.

**not for profit (or nonprofit) corporation**   Usually exists to accomplish some charitable, humanitarian, or educational purpose, and the profits and losses are not shared by the business owners.

## O

**offshore outsourcing**   Using organizations from developing countries to write code and develop systems.

**online ad**   Box running across a web page that is often used to contain advertisements.

**online analytical processing (OLAP)**   The manipulation of information to create business intelligence in support of strategic decision making.

**online broker**   Intermediaries between buyers and sellers of goods and services.

**online service provider (OSP)**   Offers an extensive array of unique services such as its own version of a web browser.

**online training**   Runs over the Internet or off a CD-ROM.

**online transaction processing (OLTP)**   The capturing of transaction and event information using technology to (1) process the information according to defined business rules, (2) store the information, and (3) update existing information to reflect the new information.

**onshore outsourcing**   The process of engaging another company within the same country for services.

**open system**   A broad term that describes nonproprietary IT hardware and software made available by the standards and procedures by which their products work, making it easier to integrate them.

**operating system software**   Controls the application software and manages how the hardware devices work together.

**operational CRM**   Supports traditional transactional processing for day-to-day front-office operations or systems that deal directly with the customers.

**operational planning and control (OP&C)**   Deals with the day-to-day procedures for performing work, including scheduling, inventory, and process management.

**operations management**   The management of systems or processes that convert or transform resources (including human resources) into goods and services.

**opportunity management CRM system**   Targets sales opportunities by finding new customers or companies for future sales.

**opt-in**   Indicates that a company will contact only the people who have agreed to receive promotions and marketing material via email.

**output device**   Equipment used to see, hear, or otherwise accept the results of information processing requests.

**outsourcing**   An arrangement by which one organization provides a service or services for another organization that chooses not to perform them in-house.

**owner's equity**   The portion of a company belonging to the owners.

## P

**packet-switching**   Occurs when the sending computer divides a message into a number of efficiently sized units called packets, each of which contains the address of the destination computer.

**packet tampering**   Altering the contents of packets as they travel over the Internet or altering data on computer disks after penetrating a network.

**partner relationship management (PRM)**   Focuses on keeping vendors satisfied by managing alliance partner and reseller relationships that provide customers with the optimal sales channel.

**partnership**   Similar to sole proprietorships, except that this legal structure allows for more than one owner.

**partnership agreement**   A legal agreement between two or more business partners that outlines core business issues.

**peer-to-peer (P2P) network**   Any network without a central file server and in which all computers in the network have access to the public files located on all other workstations.

**performance**   Measures how quickly a system performs a certain process or transaction.

**personalization**   Occurs when a website can know enough about a person's likes and dislikes that it can fashion offers that are more likely to appeal to that person.

**PERT (Program Evaluation and Review Technique) chart**   A graphical network model that depicts a project's tasks and the relationships between those tasks.

**phishing**   Technique to gain personal information for the purpose of identity theft, usually by means of fraudulent email.

**physical view**   The physical storage of information on a storage device such as a hard disk.

**pirated software**   The unauthorized use, duplication, distribution, or sale of copyrighted software.

**planning phase**   Involves establishing a high-level plan of the intended project and determining project goals.

**podcasting**   Distribution of audio or video files, such as radio programs or music videos, over the Internet to play on mobile devices and personal computers.

**polymorphic virus and worm**   Change their form as they propagate.

**pop-under ad**   Form of a pop-up ad that users do not see until they close the current web browser screen.

**pop-up ad**   Small web page containing an advertisement that appears on the web page outside the current website loaded in the web browser.

**portal**   A website that offers a broad array of resources and services, such as email, online discussion groups, search engines, and online shopping malls.

**predictive dialing**   Automatically dials outbound calls and when someone answers, the call is forwarded to an available agent.

**primary key**   A field (or group of fields) that uniquely identifies a given entity in a table.

**primary storage**   Computer's main memory, which consists of the random access memory (RAM), cache memory, and read-only memory (ROM) that is directly accessible to the CPU.

**privacy**   The right to be left alone when you want to be, to have control over your own personal possessions, and not to be observed without your consent.

**process modeling**   Involves graphically representing the processes that capture, manipulate, store, and distribute information between a system and its environment.

**product life cycle**   Includes the four phases a product progresses through during its life cycle including introduction, growth, maturity, and decline.

**production**   The creation of goods and services using the factors of production: land, labor, capital, entrepreneurship, and knowledge.

**production and materials management ERP component** Handles the various aspects of production planning and execution such as demand forecasting, production scheduling, job cost accounting, and quality control.

**production management** Describes all the activities managers do to help companies create goods.

**profit** Occurs when businesses sell products or services for more than they cost to produce.

**project** A temporary endeavor undertaken to create a unique product or service.

**project assumption** Factor that is considered to be true, real, or certain without proof or demonstration.

**project charter** A document issued by the project initiator or sponsor that formally authorizes the existence of a project and provides the project manager with the authority to apply organizational resources to project activities.

**project constraint** Specific factor that can limit options.

**project deliverable** Any measurable, tangible, verifiable outcome, result, or item that is produced to complete a project or part of a project.

**project management** The application of knowledge, skills, tools, and techniques to project activities in order to meet or exceed stakeholder needs and expectations from a project.

**project management institute** Develops procedures and concepts necessary to support the profession of project management.

**project management office** An internal department that oversees all organizational projects.

**project management software** Supports the long-term and day-to-day management and execution of the steps in a project.

**project manager** An individual who is an expert in project planning and management, defines and develops the project plan, and tracks the plan to ensure all key project milestones are completed on time.

**project milestone** Represents key dates when a certain group of activities must be performed.

**project objective** Quantifiable criteria that must be met for the project to be considered a success.

**project plan** A formal, approved document that manages and controls project execution.

**project risk** An uncertain event or condition that, if it occurs, has a positive or negative effect on a project objective(s).

**project scope** Defines the work that must be completed to deliver a product with the specified features and functions.

**project stakeholders** Individuals and organizations actively involved in the project or whose interests might be affected as a result of project execution or project completion.

**protocol** A standard that specifies the format of data as well as the rules to be followed during transmission.

**prototype** A smaller-scale representation or working model of the user's requirements or a proposed design for an information system.

**public key encryption (PKE)** Encryption system that uses two keys: a public key that everyone can have and a private key for only the recipient.

**pull technology** Organizations receive or request information.

**pure-play (virtual) business** A business that operates on the Internet only without a physical store.

**push technology** Organizations send information.

# R

**radio frequency identification (RFID)** Technologies using active or passive tags in the form of chips or smart labels that can store unique identifiers and relay this information to electronic readers.

**RadioPaper** A dynamic high-resolution electronic display that combines a paper-like reading experience with the ability to access information anytime, anywhere.

**random access memory (RAM)** The computer's primary working memory, in which program instructions and data are stored so that they can be accessed directly by the CPU via the processor's high-speed external data bus.

**rapid application development (RAD) (also called rapid prototyping) methodology** Emphasizes extensive user involvement in the rapid and evolutionary construction of working prototypes of a system to accelerate the systems development process.

**rational unified process (RUP) methodology** Provides a framework for breaking down the development of software into four gates.

**read-only memory (ROM)** The portion of a computer's primary storage that does not lose its contents when one switches off the power.

**real simple syndication (RSS)** Family of web feed formats used for web syndication of programs and content.

**real-time information** Immediate, up-to-date information.

**real-time system** Provides real-time information in response to query requests.

**recovery** The ability to get a system up and running in the event of a system crash or failure and includes restoring the information backup.

**reduced instruction set computer (RISC) chip** Limits the number of instructions the CPU can execute to increase processing speed.

**redundancy** The duplication of information or storing the same information in multiple places.

**reintermediation** Using the Internet to reassemble buyers, sellers, and other partners in a traditional supply chain in new ways.

**relational database model** A type of database that stores information in the form of logically related two-dimensional tables.

**relational integrity constraint** The rules that enforce basic and fundamental information-based constraints.

**reliability** Ensures all systems are functioning correctly and providing accurate information.

**report generator** Allows users to define formats for reports along with what information they want to see in the report.

**requirements definition document** Contains the final set of business requirements, prioritized in order of business importance.

**response time** The time it takes to respond to user interactions such as a mouse click.

**revenue** Refers to the amount earned resulting from the delivery or manufacture of a product or from the rendering of a service.

**RFID tag**   Contains a microchip and an antenna, and typically works by transmitting a serial number via radio waves to an electronic reader, which confirms the identity of a person or object bearing the tag.

**risk management**   The process of proactive and ongoing identification, analysis, and response to risk factors.

**rivalry among existing competitors**   High when competition is fierce in a market and low when competition is more complacent.

**router**   An intelligent connecting device that examines each packet of data it receives and then decides which way to send it onward toward its destination.

# S

**safety inventory**   Includes extra inventory held in the event demand exceeds supply.

**sales**   The function of selling a good or service that focuses on increasing customer sales, which increases company revenues.

**sales force automation (SFA)**   A system that automatically tracks all of the steps in the sales process.

**sales management CRM system**   Automates each phase of the sales process, helping individual sales representatives coordinate and organize all of their accounts.

**satellite**   A big microwave repeater in the sky; it contains one or more transponders that listen to a particular portion of the electromagnetic spectrum, amplifying incoming signals, and retransmitting them back to Earth.

**scalability**   Refers to how well a system can adapt to increased demands.

**scope creep**   Occurs when the scope of the project increases.

**script kiddies** or **script bunnies**   Find hacking code on the Internet and click-and-point their way into systems to cause damage or spread viruses.

**SCRUM methodology**   Uses small teams to produce small pieces of deliverable software using sprints, or 30-day intervals, to achieve an appointed goal.

**search engine optimization (SEO)**   Set of methods aimed at improving the ranking of a website in search engine listings.

**secondary storage**   Consists of equipment designed to store large volumes of data for long-term storage.

**secure electronic transaction (SET)**   Transmission security method that ensures transactions are secure and legitimate.

**secure socket layer (SSL)**   (1) Creates a secure and private connection between a client and server computer, (2) encrypts the information, and (3) sends the information over the Internet.

**selling chain management**   Applies technology to the activities in the order life cycle from inquiry to sale.

**semantic web**   An evolving extension of the World Wide Web in which web content can be expressed not only in natural language, but also in a format that can be read and used by software agents, thus permitting them to find, share, and integrate information more easily.

**sensitivity analysis**   The study of the impact that changes in one (or more) parts of the model have on other parts of the model.

**server**   Computer that is dedicated to providing information in response to external requests.

**service**   A business task.

**service level agreement (SLA)**   Defines the specific responsibilities of the service provider and sets the customer expectations.

**service-oriented architecture (SOA)**   A collection of services that communicate with each other, for example, passing data from one service to another or coordinating an activity between one or more services.

**shareholder**   Another term for business owners.

**shopping bot**   Software that will search several retailer websites and provide a comparison of each retailer's offerings including price and availability.

**sign-off**   The system users' actual signatures indicating they approve all of the business requirements.

**slice-and-dice**   The ability to look at information from different perspectives.

**smart card**   A device that is around the same size as a credit card, containing embedded technologies that can store information and small amounts of software to perform some limited processing.

**smartphone**   Combines the functions of a cellular phone and a PDA in a single device.

**sniffer**   A program or device that can monitor data traveling over a network.

**social engineering**   Using one's social skills to trick people into revealing access credentials or other information valuable to the attacker.

**social responsibility**   Implies that an entity whether it is a government, corporation, organization, or individual has a responsibility to society.

**software**   The set of instructions that the hardware executes to carry out specific tasks.

**Software as a Service (SaaS)**   A model of software deployment where an application is licensed for use as a service provided to customers on demand.

**sole proprietorship**   A business form in which a single person is the sole owner and is personally responsible for all the profits and losses of the business.

**solvency**   Represents the ability of the business to pay its bills and service its debt.

**source document**   Describes the basic transaction data such as its date, purpose, and amount and includes cash receipts, canceled checks, invoices, customer refunds, employee time sheet, etc.

**spam**   Unsolicited email.

**spamdexing**   Uses a variety of deceptive techniques in an attempt to manipulate search engine rankings, whereas legitimate search engine optimization focuses on building better sites and using honest methods of promotion.

**spoofing**   The forging of the return address on an email so that the email message appears to come from someone other than the actual sender.

**spyware**   Software that comes hidden in free downloadable software and tracks online movements, mines the information stored on a computer, or uses a computer's CPU and storage for some task the user knows nothing about.

**statement of cash flow** Summarizes sources and uses of cash, indicates whether enough cash is available to carry on routine operations, and offers an analysis of all business transactions, reporting where the firm obtained its cash and how it chose to allocate the cash.

**statement of owner's equity** (also called the **statement of retained earnings** or **equity statement**) Tracks and communicates changes in the shareholder's earnings.

**strategic business units (SBUs)** Consists of several stand-alone businesses.

**strategic planning** Focuses on long-range planning such as plant size, location, and type of process to be used.

**structured collaboration (or process collaboration)** Involves shared participation in business processes, such as workflow, in which knowledge is hard coded as rules.

**supplier power** High when one supplier has concentrated power over an industry.

**supplier relationship management (SRM)** Focuses on keeping suppliers satisfied by evaluating and categorizing suppliers for different projects, which optimizes supplier selection.

**supply chain** Consists of all parties involved, directly or indirectly, in the procurement of a product or raw material.

**supply chain event management (SCEM)** Enables an organization to react more quickly to resolve supply chain issues.

**supply chain execution (SCE) software** Automates the different steps and stages of the supply chain.

**supply chain management (SCM)** Involves the management of information flows between and among stages in a supply chain to maximize total supply chain effectiveness and profitability.

**supply chain planning (SCP) software** Uses advanced mathematical algorithms to improve the flow and efficiency of the supply chain while reducing inventory.

**supply chain visibility** The ability to view all areas up and down the supply chain.

**sustainable, or "green," IT** Describes the manufacture, management, use, and disposal of information technology in a way that minimizes damage to the environment, which is a critical part of a corporation's responsibility.

**sustainable IT disposal** Refers to the safe disposal of IT assets at the end of their life cycle.

**sustaining technology** Produces an improved product customers are eager to buy, such as a faster car or larger hard drive.

**switching cost** The costs that can make customers reluctant to switch to another product or service.

**system availability** Number of hours a system is available for users.

**systems development life cycle (SDLC)** The overall process for developing information systems from planning and analysis through implementation and maintenance.

**system software** Controls how the various technology tools work together along with the application software.

**system virtualization** The ability to present the resources of a single computer as if it is a collection of separate computers ("virtual machines"), each with its own virtual CPUs, network interfaces, storage, and operating system.

# T

**tacit knowledge** The knowledge contained in people's heads.

**tactical planning** Focuses on producing goods and services as efficiently as possible within the strategic plan.

**telecommunication system** Enables the transmission of data over public or private networks.

**teleliving** Using information devices and the Internet to conduct all aspects of life seamlessly.

**telematic** Blending computers and wireless telecommunications technologies with the goal of efficiently conveying information over vast networks to improve business operations.

**terabyte (TB)** Roughly 1 trillion bytes.

**test condition** The detailed steps the system must perform along with the expected results of each step.

**testing phase** Involves bringing all the project pieces together into a special testing environment to test for errors, bugs, and interoperability and verify that the system meets all of the business requirements defined in the analysis phase.

**threat of new entrants** High when it is easy for new competitors to enter a market and low when there are significant entry barriers to entering a market.

**threat of substitute products or services** High when there are many alternatives to a product or service and low when there are few alternatives from which to choose.

**throughput** The amount of information that can travel through a system at any point in time.

**time-series information** Time-stamped information collected at a particular frequency.

**To-Be process model** Shows the results of applying change improvement opportunities to the current (As-Is) process model.

**token** Small electronic devices that change user passwords automatically.

**transaction** Exchange or transfer of goods, services, or funds involving two or more people.

**transaction processing system (TPS)** The basic business system that serves the operational level (analysts) in an organization.

**transaction speed** Amount of time a system takes to perform a transaction.

**transborder data flows (TDF)** When business data flows across international boundaries over the telecommunications networks of global information systems.

**transactional information** Encompasses all of the information contained within a single business process or unit of work, and its primary purpose is to support the performing of daily operational tasks.

**transformation process** The technical core, especially in manufacturing organizations; the actual conversion of inputs to outputs.

**Transmission Control Protocol/Internet Protocol (TCP/IP)** Provides the technical foundation for the public Internet as well as for large numbers of private networks.

**transportation planning software** Tracks and analyzes the movement of materials and products to ensure the delivery of materials and finished goods at the right time, the right place, and the lowest cost.

**trend analysis** A trend is examined to identify its nature, causes, speed of development, and potential impacts.

**trend monitoring** Trends viewed as particularly important in a specific community, industry, or sector are carefully monitored, watched, and reported to key decision makers.

**trend projection** When numerical data are available, a trend can be plotted to display changes through time and into the future.

**Trojan-horse virus** Hides inside other software, usually as an attachment or a downloadable file.

**twisted-pair wiring** A type of cable composed of four (or more) copper wires twisted around each other within a plastic sheath.

## U

**unstructured collaboration (or information collaboration)** Includes document exchange, shared whiteboards, discussion forums, and email.

**up-selling** Increasing the value of a sale.

**user documentation** Highlights how to use the system.

**utility software** Provides additional functionality to the operating system.

## V

**value-added** The term used to describe the difference between the cost of inputs and the value of price of outputs.

**value-added network (VAN)** A private network, provided by a third party, for exchanging information through a high-capacity connection.

**value chain** Views an organization as a series of processes, each of which adds value to the product or service for each customer.

**videoconference** A set of interactive telecommunication technologies that allow two or more locations to interact via two-way video and audio transmissions simultaneously.

**viral marketing** Technique that induces websites or users to pass on a marketing message to other websites or users, creating exponential growth in the message's visibility and effect.

**virtual assistant** A small program stored on a PC or portable device that monitors emails, faxes, messages, and phone calls.

**virtualization** Protected memory space created by the CPU allowing the computer to create virtual machines.

**virtual private network (VPN)** A way to use the public telecommunication infrastructure (e.g., Internet) to provide secure access to an organization's network.

**virus** Software written with malicious intent to cause annoyance or damage.

**voice over IP (VoIP)** Uses TCP/IP technology to transmit voice calls over long-distance telephone lines.

**volatility** Refers to RAM's complete loss of stored information if power is interrupted.

## W

**waterfall methodology** A sequential, activity-based process in which each phase in the SDLC is performed sequentially from planning through implementation and maintenance.

**Web 2.0** A set of economic, social, and technology trends that collectively form the basis for the next generation of the Internet—a more mature, distinctive medium characterized by user participation, openness, and network effects.

**web-based self-service system** Allows customers to use the web to find answers to their questions or solutions to their problems.

**web conference** Blends audio, video, and document-sharing technologies to create virtual meeting rooms where people "gather" at a password-protected website.

**web content management system (WCM)** Adds an additional layer to document and digital asset management that enables publishing content both to intranets and to public websites.

**web log** Consists of one line of information for every visitor to a website and is usually stored on a web server.

**web mashup** A website or web application that uses content from more than one source to create a completely new service.

**web service** Contains a repertoire of web-based data and procedural resources that use shared protocols and standards permitting different applications to share data and services.

**web traffic** Includes a host of benchmarks such as the number of page views, the number of unique visitors, and the average time spent viewing a web page.

**what-if analysis** Checks the impact of a change in an assumption on the proposed solution.

**white-hat hacker** Works at the request of the system owners to find system vulnerabilities and plug the holes.

**wide area network (WAN)** Computer network that provides data communication services for business in geographically dispersed areas (such as across a country or around the world).

**wiki** Web-based tools that make it easy for users to add, remove, and change online content.

**WiMAX** The Worldwide Interoperability for Microwave Access is a telecommunications technology aimed at providing wireless data over long distances in a variety of ways, from point-to-point links to full mobile cellular type access.

**wireless fidelity (wi-fi)** A means of linking computers using infrared or radio signals.

**wireless Internet service provider (WISP)** An ISP that allows subscribers to connect to a server at designated hotspots or access points using a wireless connection.

**wire media** Transmission material manufactured so that signals will be confined to a narrow path and will behave predictably.

**wireless media** Natural parts of the Earth's environment that can be used as physical paths to carry electrical signals.

**workflow** Defines all the steps or business rules, from beginning to end, required for a business process.

**workflow management system** Facilitates the automation and management of business processes and controls the movement of work through the business process.

**workshop training** Set in a classroom-type environment and led by an instructor.

**World Wide Web (WWW)** A global hypertext system that uses the Internet as its transport mechanism.

**worm** A type of virus that spreads itself, not only from file to file, but also from computer to computer.

## Unit One

*2005 CSI/FBI Computer Crime and Security Survey,* www.usdoj.gov/criminal/cybercrime/FBI2005.pdf, accessed February 2005.

Adam Horowitz and the editors of *Business 2.0, The Dumbest Moments in Business History: Useless Products, Ruinous Deals, Clueless Bosses, and Other Signs of Unintelligent Life in the Workplace* (New York: Portfolio, 2004).

"Apple Profit Surges 95 Percent on iPod Sales," Yahoo! News, news.yahoo.com/s/afp/20060118/bs_afp/uscompanyearningsit_060118225009, accessed January 18, 2005.

"Apple's IPod Success Isn't Sweet Music for Record Company Sales," Bloomberg.com, quote.bloomberg.com/apps/news?pid=nifea&& sid=aHP5Ko1pozM0, accessed November 2, 2005.

Audra Ang , "China Court Upholds 5 Sentences in Milk Scandal," *BusinessWeek Online,* March 26, 2009, http://www.businessweek.com/ap/financialnews/D975PBH00.htm.

Barbara Ettorre, "Reengineering Tales from the Front," *Management Review,* January 1995, p. 13.

Ben Worthen, "ABC: An Introduction to SCM," www.cio.com/article/40940/ABC_An_Introduction_to_Supply_Chain_Management, accessed May 30, 2007.

Bittorrent, http://www.bittorrent.com/, accessed June 15, 2004.

Booze, Allen, Hamilton, *Information Sharing* (New York: HarperCollins, 2006).

Larry Bossidy and Ram Charan, *Execution* (New York: Random House, 2002).

Bruce Caldwell, "Missteps, Miscues-Business Reengineering Failures," *InformationWeek,* June 20, 1994, p. 50.

*Business Dictionary,* www.glossarist.com/glossaries/business/, accessed December 15, 2003.

Chi-Chu Tschang , "Contaminated Milk Sours China's Dairy Business," *BusinessWeek Online,* September 26, 2008, http://www.businessweek.com/globalbiz/content/sep2008/gb20080926_543133.htm.

Christopher Koch, "The ABC's of Supply Chain Management," www.cio.com, accessed October 12, 2003.

Cisco Press, www.ciscopress.com/index.asp?rl=1, accessed October 2003.

"CRM Enterprise," *CIO Magazine,* www.cio.com.au/index.php/secid;2, accessed May 28, 2007.

"Customer Success Stories—Charles Schwab," www.siebel.com, accessed November 12, 2003.

"Customer Success Stories—Saab," www.siebel.com, accessed November 12, 2005.

Dave Lindorff, "General Electric and Real Time," www.cioinsight.com/article2/0,3959,686147,00.asp, accessed October 2003.

Dexter Roberts, "Starbucks Caffeinates Its China Growth Plan," *BusinessWeek Online,* October 25, 2006, http://www.businessweek.com/globalbiz/content/oct2006/gb20061025_712453.htm.

*eBay Financial News,* Earnings and Dividend Release, January 15, 2002.

"Enron, Who's Accountable?" www.time.com/time/business/article/0,8599,193520,00.html, accessed June 7, 2005.

*ERP White Paper,* www.bitpipe.com/rlist/term/ERP.html, accessed July 3, 2007.

Exact Software, "ERP-II," www.exact.com, accessed April 17, 2007.

"Mastering Management," *Financial Times,* www.ft.com/pp/mfm, accessed December 15, 2003.

Thomas Friedman, www.thomaslfriedman.com, accessed September 14, 2005.

Gabriel Kahn and Cris Prystay, "'Charge It,' Your Cellphone Tells Your Bank," *The Wall Street Journal,* August 13, 2003.

*Glossary of Business Terms,* www.powerhomebiz.com/Glossary/glossary-A.htm, accessed December 15, 2003.

*Glossary of Business Terms,* www.smallbiz.nsw.gov.au/smallbusiness/, accessed December 15, 2003.

*Glossary of Financial Terms,* www.nytimes.com/library/financial/glossary/bfglosa.htm, accessed December 15, 2003.

Google Analytics, www.google.com/analytics, accessed July 13, 2007.

Health Information Management, www.gartner.com, accessed November 16, 2003.

Integrated Solutions, "The ABCs of CRM," www.integratedsolutionsmag.com, accessed November 12, 2003.

"Integrating Information at Children's Hospital," KMWorld, www.kmworld.com/Articles/ReadArticle.aspx?ArticleID=10253, accessed June 1, 2005.

IT Centrix, "Optimizing the Business Value of Information Technology," http://www.unisys.com/products/mainframes/insights/insights__compendium, accessed December 10, 2004.

"IT Master of the Senate," *CIO Magazine Online,* www.cio.com/archive/050104/tl_govt.html, accessed May 1, 2004.

Jay Yarow , "MLB's Real Competitive Advantage," *BusinessWeek Online,* August 29, 2008, http://www.businessweek.com/technology/content/aug2008/tc20080828_061722.htm.

John Heilmann, "What's Friendster Selling?" *Business 2.0,* March 2004, p. 46.

Jon Surmacz, "By the Numbers," *CIO Magazine,* www.cio.com, accessed October 2004.

Joshua Ramo, "Jeffrey Bezos," www.time.com/time/poy2000/archive/1999.html, accessed June 8, 2004.

*Kaiser's Diabetic Initiative,* www.businessweek.com, accessed November 15, 2003.

Robert Kaplan and David Norton, *The BSC: Translating Strategy into Action* (New York: Vintage Books, 1998).

Ken Blanchard, "Effectiveness vs. Efficiency," Wachovia Small Business, www.wachovia.com, accessed October 2003.

Kim Girard, "How Levi's Got Its Jeans into Wal-Mart," *CIO Magazine,* July 15, 2003.

Mark Eppler, *The Wright Way: 7 Problem-Solving Principles from the Wright Brothers That Can Make Your Business Soar,* Amacon (2003).

Maureen Weicher, "Business Process Reengineering: Analysis and Recommendation," www.netlib.com, accessed February 12, 2005.

Michael E. Porter, *Competitive Strategy: Techniques for Analyzing Industries and Competitors.* Free Press (1998)

Michael Hammer and James Champy, *Reengineering the Corporation* (New York: Harper Collins, 2003).

Michael Schrage, "Build the Business Case," *CIO Magazine Online,* www.cio.com, accessed November 17, 2003.

Michael Watkins, *The First 90 Days* (Boston: Harvard Business School Press, 2003).

news.com.com/NikeiPod+raises+RFID+privacy+concerns/ 2100-1029_3-6143606.html, accessed June 7, 2007.

*Nicomachean Ethics: Aristotle,* with an introduction by Hye-Kyung Kim, translated by F.H. Peters in Oxford, 1893 (Barnes & Noble, 2004).

*Oracle Customer Study,* "Trek Standardizes Worldwide Operations for Boost in Decision-Making Power Business Driver: Standardization for Cost and Process Efficiency," www.oracle .com/customers/snapshots/trek, accessed October 11, 2003,

Paul Ormerod, *Why Most Things Fail: Evolution, Extinction, and Economics* (Hoboken, NJ: John Wiley & Sons, 2005).

Peter Burrows, "How Apple Could Mess Up Again," *BusinessWeek Online,* yahoo.businessweek.com/technology/content/jan2006/ tc20060109_432937.htm, accessed January 9, 2006.

Privacy.org, www.privacy.org/, accessed July 3, 2004.

"Q&A with Michael Porter," *BusinessWeek Online,* August 21, 2006, http://www.businessweek.com/magazine/content/06_34/ b3998460.htm.

Saul Berman, "Strategic Direction: Don't Reengineer without It; Scanning the Horizon for Turbulence," *Planning Review,* November 1994, p. 18.

Scott Berianato, "Take the Pledge," *CIO Magazine Online,* www.cio.com, accessed November 17, 2003.

Sharon Gaudin, "Smokers Open the Door for Hackers," www.informationweek.com/news/articleID=9875367, accessed August 23, 2007.

"Shop Amazon.com with Your Voice," www.amazon.com/exec/ obidos/subst/misc/anywhere/anywhere.html/ref=gw_hp_ ls_1_2/002-7628940-9665649, accessed June 8, 2004.

Supply Chain Metrics.com, www.supplychainmetric.com/, accessed June 12, 2007.

The Balanced Scorecard Institute, www.balancedscorecard.org/, accessed May 15, 2007.

"The Business World According to Peter Drucker," www.peter-drucker.com, accessed May 25, 2007.

*The New Real Minority Report,* www.dailygalaxy.com/my_ weblog/2007/08/project-hostile.html, accessed June 13, 2003.

Thomas H. Davenport, "Will Participative Makeovers of Business Processes Succeed Where Reengineering Failed?" *Planning Review,* January 1995, p. 24.

"Top 10 Bad Business Decisions," www.business20.com, accessed April 16, 2007.

"Trek Standardizes Worldwide Operations on J. D. Edwards," www.jdedwards.com, accessed November 15, 2003.

United Nations Division for Public Economics and Public Administration, www.un.com, accessed November 10, 2003.

"What Concerns CIOs the Most?" www.cio.com, accessed November 17, 2003.

www.apple.com/iphone, accessed June 7, 2007.

www.boozallen.com/publications/article/659327, accessed November, 10, 2003.

www.hipaa.org, accessed June 14, 2007.

www.norcrossgroup.com/casestudies.html, accessed October 2004.

## Unit Two

"Alaska Fish and Game Yields a Bounty of High-Quality Information to Manage Natural Resources," www.oracle.com, accessed September 20, 2003.

Alice LaPante, "Big Things Come in Smaller Packages," *ComputerWorld,* June 24, 1996, pp. DW/6–7.

Barbara DePompa Reimers, "Too Much of a Good Thing," *ComputerWorld,* www.computerworld.com, April 14, 2003.

Bill Gates, *Business @ The Speed of Thought* (Grand Central Publishing, 1999).

Chicago Police Department, gis.chicagopolice.org/, accessed June 23, 2004.

*Customer Success Stories,* www.cognos.com, accessed January 2005.

"Cyber Bomb—Search Tampering," *BusinessWeek,* March 1, 2004.

Daniel Pink, "The Book Stops Here," *Wired,* March 2005, pp.125–39.

"Tapping the World's Brainpower with Wiki," *BusinessWeek,* October 11, 2004, p. 132.

"Data Mining: What General Managers Need to Know," *Harvard Management Update,* October 1999.

"Dr Pepper/Seven Up, Inc.," www.cognos.com, accessed September 10, 2003.

"Ford's Vision," donate.pewclimate.org/docUploads/Ford.pdf, accessed June 18, 2003.

Gary Loveman, "Diamonds in the Data Mine," *Harvard Business Review,* May 2003, p. 109.

*Glossary of Business Terms,* www.powerhomebiz.com/Glossary/ glossary-A.htm, accessed December 15, 2003.

*Glossary of Business Terms,* www.smallbiz.nsw.gov.au/ smallbusiness/, accessed December 15, 2003.

*Glossary of Financial Terms,* www.nytimes.com/library/financial/ glossary/bfglosa.htm, accessed December 15, 2003.

"Google Knows Where You Are," *BusinessWeek,* February 2, 2004.

"Google Reveals High-Profile Users of Data Search Machine," *Reuters News Service,* August 13, 2003.

Julia Kiling, "OLAP Gains Fans among Data-Hungry Firms," *ComputerWorld,* January 8, 2001, p. 54.

Julie Schlosser, "Looking for Intelligence in Ice Cream," *Fortune,* March 17, 2003.

Kathleen Melymuka, "Premier 100: Turning the Tables at Applebee's," *ComputerWorld,* www.computerworld.com, accessed February 24, 2003.

Kim Nash, "Casinos Hit Jackpot with Customer Data," www.cnn.com, accessed October 14, 2003.

Leslie Goff, "Summertime Heats Up IT at Ben & Jerry's," *Computer World,* July 2001.

"Massachusetts Laws about Identity Theft," www.lawlib.state .ma.us/identity.html, accessed June 10, 2007.

Meridith Levinson, "Harrah's Knows What You Did Last Night," May 2001. http://www.cio.com.au/article/44514/harrah_knows_what_did_last_night

"Harrah's Entertainment Wins TDWI's 2000 DW Award," www.hpcwire.com, accessed October 10, 2003.

Michael S. Malone, "IPO Fever," *Wired,* March 2004.

Mitch Betts, "Unexpected Insights," *ComputerWorld,* April 14, 2003, www.computerworld.com, accessed September 4, 2003.

MSI Business Solutions, "Case Study: Westpac Financial Services," www.MSI.com, accessed August 4, 2003.

NCR, "Harrah's Entertainment, Inc.," www.ncr.com, accessed October 12, 2003.

"Cognos and Harrah's Entertainment Win Prestigious Data Warehousing Award," www.cognos.com, accessed October 14, 2003.

Nikhil Hutheesing, "Surfing with Sega," *Forbes,* November 4, 2002, p. 58.

Oracle Database, www.oracle.com/database/index.html, accessed May 17, 2007.

Robert Hoff, "Something Wiki This Way Comes," *BusinessWeek Online,* accessed June 7, 2004.

Serena Gordon, "Database Helps Assess Your Breast Cancer Risk", *BusinessWeek Online,* January 25, 2009, http://www.businessweek.com/lifestyle/content/healthday/618891.html.

Stephen Baker, "What Data Crunchers Did for Obama," January 23, 2009, *BusinessWeek Online,* http://www.businessweek.com/print/technology/content/jan2009/tc20090123_026100.htm.

"Sun Tzu on the Art of War," www.chinapage.com/sunzi-e.html, accessed September 15, 2007.

Sydney Finkelstein, *Why Smart Executives Fail.* Portfolio Hardcover, (2003)

Tommy Peterson, "Data Cleansing," *ComputerWorld,* www.computerworld.com, accessed February 10, 2003.

Webopedia.com, www.webopedia.comTERM/d/database.html, accessed May 15, 2007.

"Why Data Quality," www.trilliumsoft.com, accessed October 3, 2003.

www.chron.com, accessed September 3, 2003.

www.google.com, accessed September 13, 2003.

www.sitepoint.com/article/publishing-mysql-data-web, accessed May 16, 2007.

www.wikipedia.com, accessed November 2005.

www.wikipedia.org, accessed May, 22, 2007.

## Unit Three

"1,000 Executives Best Skillset," *The Wall Street Journal,* July 15, 2003.

"1800 flowers.com," *Business 2.0,* February 2004.

"50 People Who Matter Now," money.cnn.com/magazines/business2/peoplewhomatter/, *Business 2.0,* accessed July 16, 2007.

Alison Overholt, "Smart Strategies: Putting Ideas to Work," *Fast Company,* April 2004, p. 63.

Andrew Binstock, "Virtual Enterprise Comes of Age," *InformationWeek,* November 6, 2004.

Michael A. Arbib (Ed.), *The Handbook of Brain Theory and Neural Networks* The MIT Press(1995).

Barclays, "Giving Voice to Customer-Centricity," crm.insightexec.com, accessed July 15, 2007

Beth Bacheldor, "Steady Supply," *InformationWeek,* November 24, 2003, www.informationweek.com, accessed June 6, 2003.

L. Biacino and G. Gerla, "Fuzzy logic, Continuity and Effectiveness," *Archive for Mathematical Logic* (2002).

Bill Breen, "Living in Dell Time," *Fast Company,* November 2004, p. 86.

"Boston Coach Aligns Service with Customer Demand in Real Time," www-1.ibm.com/services/us/index.wss, accessed November 4, 2003.

Bruce Caldwell, "Harley-Davidson Revs Up IT Horsepower," Internetweek.com, December 7, 2000.

"Bullwhips and Beer: Why Supply Chain Management Is So Difficult," forio.com/resources/bullwhips-and-beer/, accessed June 10, 2003.

cio.de/news/cio_worldnews/809030/index7.html, accessed May 4, 2005.

"Computerworld 100 Best Places to Work in IT 2003," *Computerworld,* June 9, 2003, pp. 36-48.

"Creating a Value Network," *Wired,* September 2003, p. S13.

"Customer First Awards," *Fast Company,* May, 2005.

"Customer Success—Brother," www.sap.com, accessed January 12, 2004.

"Customer Success—Cisco," www.sap.com, accessed April 5, 2003.

"Customer Success—PNC Retail Bank," www.siebel.com, accessed May 5, 2003.

"Customer Success—UPS," www.sap.com, accessed April 5, 2003.

"Customer Trust: Reviving Loyalty in a Challenging Economy," *Pivotal Webcast,* September 19, 2002.

"Darpa Grand Challenge," www.darpa.mil/grandchallenge/, accessed September 1, 2005.

"Del Monte Organic RFID," *BusinessWeek,* March 15, 2007.

Emanuel Rosen, *The Anatomy of Buzz* (New York: DoubleDay, 2000).

ERP Success, www.sap.com, accessed April 5, 2003, and March 15, 2007.

Exact Software, "ERP-II: Making ERP Deliver On Its Promise to the Enterprise," jobfunctions.bnet.com/whitepaper.aspx?docid=144338, accessed July 25, 2007.

"Finding the Best Buy," www.oracle.com, accessed April 4, 2003.

"Finding Value in the Real-Time Enterprise," *Business 2.0,* November 2003, pp. S1-S5.

"Forecasting Chocolate," www.sas.com, accessed October 3, 2003.

Fred Hapgood, "Smart Decisions," *CIO Magazine,* www.cio.com, August 15, 2001.

Frederick F. Reichheld, *Loyalty Rules* (Bain and Company, 2001).

*Glossary of Business Terms,* www.powerhomebiz.com/Glossary/glossary-A.htm, accessed December 15, 2003.

*Glossary of Business Terms,* www.smallbiz.nsw.gov.au/smallbusiness/, accessed December 15, 2003.

*Glossary of Financial Terms,* www.nytimes.com/library/financial/glossary/bfglosa.htm, accessed December 15, 2003.

Hagerty, "How Best to Measure Our Supply Chain."

James Harkin, "Get a (Second) Life," *Financial Times Online,* November 17, 2006, accessed June 15, 2007.

"Harley-Davidson Announces Go-Live: Continues to Expand Use of Manugistics Supplier Relationship Management Solutions," www.manugistics.com, May 7, 2002.

"How Creamy? How Crunchy?" www.sas.com, accessed October 3, 2003.

"Case Study: IBM Helps Shell Canada Fuel New Productivity with PeopleSoft EnterpriseOne," August 8, 2005, validated February 5, 2007, www-306 .ibm.com/software/success/cssdb.nsf.

"Industry Facts and Statistics," Insurance Information Institute, www.iii.org, accessed December 2005.

Internet Retailer, www.internetretailer.com, accessed February 17, 2005.

Jim Collins, *Built to Last* (Collins Business Essentials, 1994).

Jim Collins, *Good to Great* (Collins Business Essentials, 2001).

John Hagerty, "How Best to Measure Our Supply Chain," www. AMRresearch.com, March 3, 2005.

Keving Kelleher, "BudNet: 66,207,896 Bottles of Beer on the Wall," *Business 2.0,* February 2004.

Christopher Koch, "How Verizon Flies by Wire," *CIO Magazine,* November 1, 2004, and "Sleepless in Manhattan," CIO.com.

Leroy Zimdars, "Supply Chain Innovation at Harley-Davidson: An Interview with Leroy Zimdars," April 15, 2000. http://www.ascet .com/authors.asp?a_id=168

"Linden Lab to Open Source Second Life Software," Linden Lab, January 8, 2007, www.secondlife.org, accessed May 22, 2007.

"Maytag—Washing Away Maintenance," www.sas.com, accessed October 3, 2003.

Mitch Betts, "Kinks in the Chain," *ComputerWorld,* December 17, 2005.

Neil McManus, "Robots at Your Service," *Wired,* January 2003, p. O59.

Neil Raden, "Data, Data Everywhere," DSSResources.com, February 16, 2003.

"Neural Network Examples and Definitions," ece-www.colorado .edu/~ecen4831/lectures/NNdemo.html, accessed June 24, 2007.

"New York Knicks—Success," www.jdedwards.com, accessed January 15, 2004.

"Put Better, Faster Decision-Making in Your Sights," www.teradata.com, accessed July 7, 2003.

"REI Pegs Growth on Effective Multi-channel Strategy," *Internet Retailer,* www.internetretailer.com, accessed February 17, 2005,

Roger Villareal, "Docent Enterprise Increases Technician and Dealer Knowledge and Skills to Maximize Sales Results and Customer Service," www.docent.com, August 13, 2002.

S. Begley, "Software au Natural," *Newsweek,* May 8, 2005.

Santa Fe Institute, www.dis.anl.gov/abms/, accessed June 24, 2007.

Secondlife.com, accessed May 28, 2007.

secondlife.com/community/land-islands.php.

Irene Sege, "Leading a Double Life," *The Boston Globe Online,* October 25, 2006, accessed June 22, 2007.

"Smart Tools," *BusinessWeek,* March 24, 2003.

"Technology Terms," www.techterms.com/, accessed May 3, 2003.

"The 'New' *New York Times,*" *Business 2.0,* January 2004.

"The Corporate Portal Market 2005," BEA White Paper, www.bea .com, January 2005.

"The e-Biz Surprise," *BusinessWeek,* May 12, 2003, pp. 60–65.

"The Visionary Elite," *Business 2.0,* December 2003, pp. S1–S5.

"Verizon Executives," newscenter.verizon.com/leadership/ shaygan-kheradpir.html, accessed may 17, 2003.

Vinod Gupta, "Databases: Where the Customers Are," *BusinessWeek Online,* May 12, 2004, http://www.businessweek. com/smallbiz/content/may2004/sb20040512_9369.htm.

Walid Mougayar, "Old Dogs Learn New Tricks," *Business 2.0,* October 2000, www.Business2.com, accessed June 14, 2003.

Webopedia, www.webopedia.com, accessed May 14, 2003.

Whatis.com, whatis.techtarget.com, accessed May 4, 2003.

www.bae.com, accessed May 24, 2007.

www.dell.com, accessed September, 15, 2003.

www.investor.harley-davidson.com, accessed October 10, 2003.

www.netflix.com, accessed May 23, 2007.

www.secondlife.com, accessed May 25, 2007.

www.usps.com, accessed June 17, 2004.

www.wal-mart.com, accessed May 26, 2007.

## Unit Four

"10 Tips for Wireless Home Security," compnetworking.about.com/ od/wirelesssecurity/tp/wifisecurity.htm, accessed September 15, 2006.

"Amazon Finds Profits in Outsourcing," *CIO Magazine,* October 15, 2002, www.cio.com/archive/101502/tl_ec.html, accessed November 14, 2003.

"A Site Stickier than a Barroom Floor," *Business 2.0,* June 2005, p. 741.

Adam Lashinsky, "Kodak's Developing Situation," *Fortune,* January 20, 2003, p. 176.

Adam Lashinsky, "The Disrupters," *Fortune,* August 11, 2003, pp. 62–65.

Anne Zelenka , "The Hype Machine, Best Mashup of Mashup Camp 3," gigaom.com/2007/01/18/the-hype-machine-bestmashup-of-mashup-camp-3/, accessed June 14, 2007.

"CenterCup Releases PDA Caddy to Leverage Legalized Golf GPS," www.golfgearreview.com/article-display/1665.html, accessed February 3, 2008.

Charles Waltner, "Florida Hospital Cuts Cord, Goes Wireless," newsroom.cisco.com, accessed February 1, 2008.

Chris Silva, Benjamin Gray, "Key Wireless Trends That Will Shape Enterprise Mobility in 2008," www.forrester.com, accessed February 12, 2008.

Cisco Press, www.ciscopress.com, accessed March 23, 2005.

"City of Logan, Utah," www.techrepublic.com, accessed February 2, 2008.

Clayton Christensen, *The Innovator's Dilemma* (Boston: Harvard Business School, 1997).

Coco Masters, "Bringing Wi-Fi to the Skies," www.time.com/time/ specials/2007/article/0,28804,1665220_1665225,00.html, accessed February 20, 2008.

Dan Nystedt, "Mobile Phones Grow Even More Popular," *PC World,* April 2006.

Deepak Pareek, "WiMAX: Taking Wireless to the MAX," *CRC Press,* 2006, pp. 150–51.

"D-FW Defense Contractors Show Mixed Fortunes since September 11," www.bizjournals.com/dallas/stories/2002/09/09/ focus2.htm, accessed June 8, 2004.

"Evolution of Wireless Networks," www.cisco.com, accessed September 15, 2007.

"GPS Innovation Gives Weather Bots a New Ride," www.cio.com/ article/108500/GPS, accessed September 15, 2007.

Gunjan Bagla, "Bringing IT to Rural India One Village at a Time," *CIO Magazine,* March 1, 2005.

Heather Harreld, "Lemon Aid," *CIO Magazine,* July 1, 2000.

"How Do Cellular Devices Work," www.cell-phone101.info/ devices.php, accessed February 9, 2008.

Internet Pioneers, www.ibiblio.org/pioneers/andreesen.html, accessed June 2004.

Internet World Statistics, www.internetworldstats.com, accessed January 2007.

Jim Rapoza, "First Movers That Flopped," etech.eweek.com/slideshow/index.php?directory _ first_movers, accessed June 26, 2007.

"Keeping Weeds in Check with Less Herbicide," www.ars.usda.gov/is/AR/archive/aug06/weeds0806.htm, accessed February 11, 2008.

Kevin Shult, "UPS vs. FedEx: Battle of the Brands," www.bloggingstocks.com/2007/04/09/ups-vs-fedex-battle-ofthe-brands/, accessed February 10, 2008.

Knowledge Management Research Center, *CIO Magazine,* www.cio.com/research/knowledge, December 2005.

Megan Santosus, "In The Know," *CIO Magazine,* January 2006.

Michael Dortch, "Winning RFID Strategies for 2008," *Benchmark Report,* December 31, 2007.

mobilementalism.com, accessed February 2, 2008.

Mohsen Attaran, "RFID: An Enabler of Supply Chain Operations," *Supply Chain Management: An International Journal* 12 (2007), pp. 249–57.

"Navigating the Mobility Wave," www.busmanagement.com, accessed February 2, 2008.

onstar.com, accessed February 10, 2008.

"RFID Privacy and You," www.theyaretrackingyou.com/rfid-privacy-and-you.html, accessed February 12, 2008.

"RFID Roundup," www.rfidgazette.org, accessed February 10, 2008.

"Security-Free Wireless Networks," www.wired.com, accessed February 11, 2008.

"Sprint Plans Launch of Commercial WiMAX Service in Q2 2008," www.intomobile.com, accessed February 10, 2008.

Steve Konicki, "Collaboration Is Cornerstone of $19B Defense Contract," www.business2.com/content/magazine/indepth/2000/07/11/17966, accessed June 8, 2004.

"Technology Terms," www.techterms.com/, accessed May 3, 2003.

"The 21st Century Meeting," February 27, 2007, www.businessweek.com/magazine/content/07_09/b4023059.htm, accessed June 2, 2007.

Thomas Claburn, "Law Professor Predicts Wikipedia's Demise," www.informationweek.com/showArticle.jhtml;jsessionid _ 2ZYHJY4LGVHBOQSNDLRSKHSCJUNN2JVN?articleID _ 196601766&queryText _ wikipedia, accessed June 8,2007.

"Toyota's One-Stop Information Shop," www.istart.co.nz/index/HM20/PC0/PV21873/EX236/CS25653, accessed June 8, 2004.

V. C. Gungor, F. C. Lambert, "A Survey on Communication Networks for Electric System Automation, Computer Networks," *The International Journal of Computer and Telecommunications Networking,* May 15, 2006, pp. 877–97.

"Video Conference," en.wikipedia.org/wiki/Video_conference, accessed June 1, 2007.

W. David Gardner, "McDonald's Targets Starbucks with Free Wi-Fi, Upscale Coffee Bars," *InformationWeek,* January 7, 2008.

Webmashup.com, www.webmashup.com/Insert New 25, accessed June 14, 2007.

*Webopedia,* www.webopedia.com, accessed May 14, 2003.

Whitfield Diffie, "Sun's Diffie AT&T Cyber Security Conference," accessed September 2, 2007. http://research.sun.com/people/diffie/accessed July 15, 2007

wimax.com, accessed February 9, 2008.

Whatis.com, whatis.techtarget.com, accessed May 4, 2003.

ww.emarketer.com, accessed January 2006.

www.amazon.com/Into-Leadership-Lessons-Westward-Expedition/dp/0814408168, accessed February 9, 2008.

www.drpepper.com, accessed February 1, 2008.

www.ebags.com, accessed June 21, 2007.

www.gis.rgs.org/10.html, accessed February 7, 2008.

www.ironman.com, accessed January 14, 2008.

www.lockheedmartin.com, accessed April 23, 2003.

www.mbia.com, accessed February 3, 2008.

www.powerofmobility.com, accessed February 9, 2008.

www.wired.com, accessed November 15, 2003.

## Unit Five

"A New View," *Business 2.0,* November 10, 2003, pp. S1–S5.

Adam Lashinsky, "The Disrupters," *Fortune,* August 11, 2003, pp. 62–65.

"Agile Alliance Manifesto," www.agile.com, accessed November 1, 2003.

Art Jahnke, "Kodak Stays in the Digital Picture," www.cnn.com/TECH/computing/9908/06/kodak.ent.idg/, accessed June 8, 2004.

"Building Events," www.microsoft.com, accessed November 15, 2003.

"Building Software That Works," www.compaq.com, accessed November 14, 2003.

Charles Pelton, "How to Solve the IT Labor Shortage Problem," www.informationweek.com/author/eyeonit15.htm, accessed June 8, 2004.

Christopher Null, "How Netflix Is Fixing Hollywood," *Business 2.0,* July 2003, pp. 31–33.

"Customer Success Story—PHH," www.informatica.com, accessed December 12, 2003.

"Customer Success—Horizon," www.businessengine.com, accessed October 15, 2003.

"Defective Software Costs," National Institute of Standards and Technology (NIST), June 2002.

Edward Yourdon, *Death March: The Complete Software Developer's Guide to Surviving "Mission Impossible" Projects* (Upper Saddle River, NJ: Pearson Education, 1997).

"Future Three Partners with Ideal Technology Solutions, U.S. for Total Automotive Network Exchange (ANX) Capability," www.itsusnow.com/news_future3.htm, accessed June 8, 2004.

Gene Marks, "The Super User for Your Software Project," *BusinessWeek Online,* June 11, 2008, http://www.businessweek.com/print/technology/content/jun2008/tc20080610_363466.htm

Geoffrey James, "The Next Delivery? Computer Repair," CNNMoney.com, July 1, 2004.

Gini Graham Scott, *A Survival Guide for Working with Humans* (New York: AMACOM, 2004).

*Glossary of Business Terms,* www.powerhomebiz.com/Glossary/glossary-A.htm, accessed December 15, 2003

*Glossary of Business Terms,* www.smallbiz.nsw.gov.au/smallbusiness/, accessed December 15, 2003

*Glossary of Financial Terms,* www.nytimes.com/library/financial/glossary/bfglosa.htm, accessed December 15, 2003

"How Secure Is Digital Hospital," *Wired,* March 28, 2001.

Jaikumar Vijayan, "Companies Expected to Boost Offshore Outsourcing," www.computerworld.com/managementtopics/outsourcing/story/0,10801,78583,00.html, accessed June 8, 2004.

Jeffrey Hollender and Stephen Fenichell, *What Matters Most: The Future of Corporate Social Responsibility.* Basic Books (2006)

John Blau, "German Researchers Move Forward on Plastic RFID," *Computer World,* January 13, 2005.

Julia Scheeres, "Three R's: Reading, Writing, and RFID," *Wired,* October 14, 2003.

Kevin Kelleher, "The Wired 40," *Wired,* www.wired.com, accessed March 3, 2004.

Lynne Johnson, Ellen McGirt, and Sherri Smith, "The Most Influential Women in Technology", www.fastcompany.com, January 14, 2009, http://www.fastcompany.com/magazine/132/the-most-influential-women-in-technology.html.

"Merrill Lynch and Thomson Financial to Develop Wealth Management Workstation," www.advisorpage.com/modules.php?name=News&file=print&sid=666, accessed June 8, 2004.

Michael Kanellos, "IDC: PC Market on the Comeback Trail," news.com.com/2100-1001-976295. html?part=dtx&tag=ntop, accessed June 8, 2004.

Olga Kharif , "Android: One Multitasking Operating System," *BusinessWeek Online,* February 5, 2009, http://www.businessweek.com/print/technology/content/feb2009/tc2009024_366125.htm.

Peter F. Drucker Foundation, *The Leader of the Future: Visions, Practices, and Strategies for a New Era.* Jossey-Bass, (August 19, 1997)

Peter F. Drucker, *Management Challenges for the 21st Century.* Collins Business, (April 21, 1999)

"Sneaker Net," *CIO Magazine,* www.cio.com/archive/webbusiness/080199_nike.html, accessed June 8, 2004.

"Software Costs," *CIO Magazine,* www.cio.com, accessed December 5, 2003.

"Software Metrics," *CIO Magazine,* www.cio.com, accessed December 2, 2003.

Stephanie Overby, "In or Out?" *CIO Magazine,* www.cio.com/archive/081503/sourcing.html, accessed June 8, 2004.

"Technology Terms," www.techterms.com/, accessed May 3, 2003.

"The Web Smart 50," *BusinessWeek Online,* www.businessweek.com, accessed March 3, 2004.

Timothy Mullaney and Arlene Weintraub, "The Digital Hospital," *BusinessWeek,* March 28, 2005.

Tom Schultz, "PBS: A Clearer Picture," *Business 2.0,* January 2003.

"Top Reasons Why IT Projects Fail," *InformationWeek,* www.infoweek.com, accessed November 5, 2003.

Webopedia, www.webopedia.com, accessed May 14, 2003.

Whatis.com, whatis.techtarget.com, accessed May 4, 2003.

www.agile.com, accessed November 10, 2003.

www.businessweek.com, accessed November 1, 2005.

www.gartner.com, accessed November 3, 2003.

www.wired.com, accessed October 15, 2003.

## Plug-In B1

Adrian Danescu, "Save $55,000," *CIO Magazine,* December 15, 2004, p. 70.

Alison Overholdt, "The Housewife Who Got Up Off the Couch," *Fast Company,* September 2004, p. 94.

*Business Dictionary,* www.glossarist.com/glossaries/business/, accessed December 15, 2003

"Can the Nordstroms Find the Right Style?" *BusinessWeek,* July 30, 2001.

"Mastering Management," *Financial Times,* www.ft.com/pp/mfm, accessed December 15, 2003.

"From the Bottom Up," *Fast Company,* June 2004, p. 54.

Geoff Keighley, "Will Sony's PSP Become the iPod of Gaming Devices?" *Business 2.0,* May 2004, p. 29.

*Glossary of Business Terms,* www.powerhomebiz.com/Glossary/glossary-A.htm, accessed December 15, 2003.

*Glossary of Business Terms,* www.smallbiz.nsw.gov.au/smallbusiness/, accessed December 15, 2003.

*Glossary of Financial Terms,* www.nytimes.com/library/financial/glossary/bfglosa.htm, accessed December 15, 2003.

"Harley-Davidson: Ride Your Heritage," *Fast Company,* August 2004, p. 44.

"Ford on Top," *Fast Company,* June 2004, p. 54.

"Innovative Managers," *BusinessWeek,* April 24, 2005.

Julie Schlosser, "Toys 'R'Us Braces for a Holiday Battle," *Money,* December 22, 2003.

Michael Hammer, *Beyond Reengineering: How the Process-Centered Organization Is Changing Our Work and Our Lives* (New York: HarperCollins Publishers, 1997).

"Progressive Insurance," *BusinessWeek,* March 13, 2004.

"Toy Wars," www.pbs.org, accessed December 23, 2003.

## Plug-In B2

Bjorn Andersen, *Business Process Improvement Toolbox* (Milwaukee, WI: ASQ Quality Press, 1999).

"BPR Online," www.prosci.com/mod1.htm, accessed October 10, 2005.

"Business Process Reengineering Six Sigma," www .isixsigma.com/me/bpr/, accessed October 10, 2005.

"Customer Success Stories: Adidas," www.global360.com/collateral/Adidas_Case_History.pdf, accessed October 10, 2005.

*Government Business Process Reengineering (BPR) Readiness Assessment Guide,* General Services Administration (GSA), 1996.

H. James Harrington, *Business Process Improvement Workbook: Documentation, Analysis, Design, and Management of Business Process Improvement* (New York: McGraw-Hill, 1997).

H. James Harrington, *Business Process Improvement: The Breakthrough Strategy for Total Quality, Productivity, and Competitiveness* (New York: McGraw-Hill, 1991).

Michael Hammer and James Champy, "Reengineering the Corporation: A Manifest for Business Revolution," 1993. HarperBusiness (January 1, 1994)

Michael Hammer, *Beyond Reengineering: How the Process-Centered Organization Is Changing Our Work and Our Lives* (New York: HarperCollins, 1996).

Richard Chang, "Process Reengineering in Action: A Practical Guide to Achieving Breakthrough Results (Quality Improvement Series)," 1996.

"Savvion Helps 3Com Optimize Product Promotion Processes," www.savvion.com/customers/marketing_promotions.php, accessed October 10, 2005.

SmartDraw.com, www.smartdraw.com/, accessed October 11, 2005.

"What Is BPR?" searchcio.techtarget.com/sDefinition/0,,sid182_gci536451,00.html, accessed October 10, 2005.

## Plug-In B3

Aaron Ricadela, "Seismic Shift," *InformationWeek,* March 14, 2005.

Denise Brehm, "Sloan Students Pedal Exercise," www.mit.edu, accessed May 5, 2003.

"Electronic Breaking Points," www.pcworld.com, accessed August 2005.

Hector Ruiz, "Advanced Micro Devices," *BusinessWeek*, January 10, 2005.

Margaret Locher, "Hands That Speak," *CIO Magazine*, June 1, 2005.

Meridith Levinson, "Circuit City Rewires," *CIO Magazine*, July 1, 2005.

"The Linux Counter," counter.li.org, accessed October 2005.

Tom Davenport, "Playing Catch-Up," *CIO Magazine*, May 1, 2001.

www.mit.com, accessed October 2005.

www.needapresent.com, accessed October 2005.

www.powergridfitness.com, accessed October 2005.

## Plug-In B4

"Agile Enterprise," www.agiledata.org/essays/enterpriseArchitecture.html, accessed May 14, 2003.

"Can American Keep Flying?" *CIO Magazine*, www.cio.com, February 15, 2003.

Christine McGeever, "FBI Database Problem Halts Gun Checks," www.computerworld.com, accessed May 22, 2000.

Christopher Koch, "A New Blueprint for the Enterprise," *CIO Magazine*, March 1, 2005.

"Distribution of Software Updates of Thousands of Franchise Locations Was Slow and Unpredictable," www.fountain.com, accessed October 10, 2003.

Erick Schonfeld, "Linux Takes Flight," *Business 2.0*, January 2003, pp. 103–5.

Institute for Enterprise Architecture, www.enterprise-architecture.info/, May 2, 2003.

John Fontana, "Lydian Revs up with Web Services," *Network World*, March 10, 2004.

"Looking at the New," *InformationWeek*, May 2005.

Martin Garvey, "Manage Passwords," *InformationWeek*, May 20, 2005.

Martin Garvey, "Security Action Plans," *InformationWeek*, May 30, 2005.

Otis Port, "Will the Feud Choke the Life Out of Linux?" *BusinessWeek*, July 7, 2003, p. 81.

"Technology Terms," www.techterms.com/, accessed May 3, 2003.

Tim Wilson, "Server Consolidation Delivers," *InformationWeek*, May 30, 2005.

Webopedia, www.webopedia.com, accessed May 14, 2003.

"What Every Executive Needs to Know," www.akamai.com, accessed September 10, 2003.

Whatis.com, swhatis.techtarget.com, accessed May 4, 2003.

www.abercrombie&fitch.com, accessed November 2005.

www.gartner.com, accessed November 2005.

www.websidestory.com, accessed November 2005.

## Plug-In B5

Enrique De Argaez, "What You Should Know about Internet Broadband Access," www.internetworldstats.com/articles/art096.htm, accessed January 29, 2008.

Eva Chen, "Shop Talk," *CIO Magazine*, October 15, 2004.

Networking.com, www.networking.com, accessed May 15, 2003.

"Overcoming Software Development Problems," www.samspublishing.com, October 7, 2002, accessed November 16, 2003.

"Rip Curl Turns to Skype for Global Communications," www.voipinbusiness.co.uk/rip_curl_turns_to_skype_for_gl.asp July 07, 2006, accessed January 21, 2008.

"Technology Terms," www.techterms.com/, accessed May 3, 2003.

"The Security Revolution," *CIO Magazine*, www.cio.com, accessed June 6, 2003.

"VoIP Business Solutions," www.vocalocity.com, accessed January 21, 2008.

Webopedia, www.webopedia.com, accessed May 14, 2003.

Whatis.com, whatis.techtarget.com, accessed May 4, 2003.

www.rei.com, accessed February 23, 2008.

www.skype.com, accessed February 15, 2008.

## Plug-In B6

"2002 CSI/FBI Computer Crime and Security Survey," www.gocsi.com, accessed November 23, 2003.

"Hacker Hunters," *BusinessWeek*, May 30, 2005.

"Losses from Identity Theft to Total $221 Billion Worldwide," *CIO Magazine*, www.cio.com, May, 2005.

Mark Leon, "Keys to the Kingdom," www.computerworld.com, April 14, 2003, accessed August 8, 2003.

Scott Berinato and Sarah Scalet, "The ABCs of Information Security," *CIO Magazine*, www.cio.com, accessed July 7, 2003.

"Sony Fights Intrusion with 'Crystal Ball'," *CIO Magazine*, www.cio.com, accessed August 9, 2003.

"Spam Losses to Grow to $198 Billion," *CIO Magazine*, www.cio.com, accessed August 9, 2003.

"Teen Arrested in Internet 'Blaster' Attack," www.cnn.com, August 29, 2003.

"The Security Revolution," *CIO Magazine*, www.cio.com, accessed June 6, 2003.

www.ey.com, accessed November 25, 2003.

## Plug-In B7

Alice Dragon, "Be a Spam Slayer," *CIO Magazine*, November 1, 2003, www.cio.com, accessed March 9, 2004.

AMA Research, "Workplace Monitoring and Surveillance," www.amanet.org, April 2003, accessed March 1, 2004.

AnchorDeskStaff, "How to Spy on Your Employees and Why You May Not Want To," www.reviews-zdnet.com, August 21, 2003, accessed March 5, 2004.

"Computer Security Policy," www.computer-security-policies.com/, accessed March 24, 2007.

"FedLaw Computers and Information Technology," www.thecre.com/fedlaw/legal8.htm, accessed March 21, 2004

Information Security Policy World, www.information-security-policies-and-standards.com/, accessed March 23, 2004

Paul Roberts, "Report: Spam Costs $874 per Employee per Year," www.computerworld.com, July 2, 2003, accessed March 9, 2004.

Sarbanes-Oxley Act, www.workingvalues.com, accessed March 3, 2004.

Scott Berinato, "Take the Pledge—The CIO's Code of Ethical Data Management," *CIO Magazine*, July 1, 2002, www.cio.com, accessed March 7, 2004.

"Technology Terms," www.techterms.com/, accessed May 3, 2003.

Webopedia, www.webopedia.com, accessed May 14, 2003.

Whatis.com, whatis.techtarget.com, accessed May 4, 2003.

www.vault.com, accessed January 2006.

## Plug-In B8

Bob Evans, "Business Technology: Sweet Home," *InformationWeek*, February 7, 2005.

Frank Quinn, "The Payoff Potential in Supply Chain Management," www.ascet.com, accessed June 15, 2003.

Jennifer Bresnahan, "The Incredible Journey," *CIO Enterprise,* August 15, 1998, www.cio.com, accessed March 12, 2004.

Justin Fox, "A Meditation on Risk," *Fortune,* October 3, 2005.

"Logistics and Supply Chain," logistics.about.com, accessed June 2, 2003.

Navi Radjou, "Manufacturing Sector IT Spending Profile for 2004," September 12, 2003, www.forrester.com, accessed March 15, 2004.

Parija Bhatnagar, "Wal-Mart Closes 123 Stores from Storm," www.cnnmoney.com, accessed August 2005.

William Copacino, "How to Become a Supply Chain Master," *Supply Chain Management Review,* September 1, 2001, www.manufacturing.net, accessed June 12, 2003.

Supply Chain Council, www.supply-chain.org/cs/root/home, accessed June 22, 2003.

"Technology Terms," www.techterms.com/, accessed May 3, 2003.

Walid Mougayar, "Old Dogs Learn New Tricks," *Business 2.0,* October 2000, www.Business2.com, accessed June 14, 2003.

Webopedia, www.webopedia.com, accessed May 14, 2003.

Whatis.com, whatis.techtarget.com, accessed May 4, 2003.

### Plug-In B9

"3M Accelerates Revenue Growth Using Siebel eBusiness Applications," July 30, 2002, www.siebel.com, accessed July 10, 2003.

"Avnet Brings IM to Corporate America with Lotus Instant Messaging," websphereadvisor.com/doc/12196, accessed July 11, 2003.

"Barclays, Giving Voice to Customer-Centricity," crm.insightexec .com, accessed July 15, 2003.

Bob Evans, "Business Technology: Sweet Home," *InformationWeek,* February 7, 2005.

"California State Automobile Association Case Study," www.epiphany.com/customers/detail_csaa.html, accessed July 4, 2003.

"Customer Success," www.costco.com, accessed June 2005.

"Customer Success," www.rackspace.com, accessed June 2005.

"Customer Success—UPS," www.sap.com, accessed April 5, 2003.

"Documedics," www.siebel.com, accessed July 10, 2003.

"Partnering in the Fight against Cancer," www.siebel.com, accessed July 16, 2003.

"Sears: Redefining Business," *BusinessWeek,* www.businessweek.com, accessed April 15, 2003.

Supply Chain Planet, June 2003, newsweaver.co.uk/supplychainplanet/e_article000153342.cfm, accessed July 12, 2003.

"The Expanding Territory of Outsourcing," www.outsourcing.com, accessed August 15, 2003.

"Vail Resorts Implements FrontRange HEAT," *CRM Today,* October 16, 2003, www.crm2day.com/news/crm/EpyykllFyAqEUbqOhW.php, accessed December 2, 2003.

www.FedEx.com, accessed July 13, 2003.

www.nicesystems.com, accessed June 2005.

www.salesforce.com, accessed June 2005.

### Plug-In B10

"Customer Success Stories," www.jdedwards.com, accessed October 15, 2003.

"Customer Success Story—Grupo Farmanova Intermed," www.jdedwards.com, accessed October 15, 2003.

"Customer Success Story—PepsiAmerica," www.peoplesoft.com, accessed October 22, 2003.

"Customer Success Story—Turner Industries," www.jdedwards.com, accessed October 15, 2003.

"Harley-Davidson on the Path to Success," www.peoplesoft.com/media/success, accessed October 12, 2003.

Michael Doane, "A Blueprint for ERP Implementation Readiness," www.metagroup.com, accessed October 17, 2003.

Thomas Wailgum, "Big Mess on Campus," *CIO Magazine,* May 1, 2005.

### Plug-In B11

Amy Johnson, "A New Supply Chain Forged," *ComputerWorld,* September 30, 2002.

ColdStone Creamery Talk, www.creamerytalk.com/press/in_the_news_2005.html, accessed September 23, 2004.

Frank Quinn, "The Payoff Potential in Supply Chain Management," www.ascet.com, accessed June 15, 2003.

"Info on 3.9M Citigroup," *Money,* June 6, 2005.

Jack Welch, "What's Right about Wal-Mart," *CIO Magazine,* www.cio.com, accessed May 2005.

Joshua Ramo, "Jeffrey Bezos," www.time.com/time/poy2000/archive/1999.html, accessed June 8, 2004.

Laura Rohde, "British Airways Takes Off with Cisco," *Network World,* May 11, 2005.

"Let's Remake a Deal," *Business 2.0,* March 2004.

"Manage Your Mailing Experience Electronically, All in One Place," United States Postal Service, www.usps.com, accessed July 2005.

Penelope Patsuris, "Marketing Messages Made to Order," *Forbes,* August 2003.

Pratt & Whitney, *BusinessWeek,* June 2004.

Rachel Metz, "Changing at the Push of a Button," *Wired,* September 27, 2004.

"Watch Your Spending," *BusinessWeek,* May 23, 2004.

www.hotel-gatti.com, accessed June 2003.

www.idc.com, accessed June 2005.

www.ingenio.com, accessed July 2005.

www.oecd.org, accessed June 2005.

www.t-mobile.com, accessed June 2005.

www.vanguard.com, accessed June 2005.

www.yankeegroup.com, accessed May 2005.

### Plug-In B12

Denise Dubie, "Tivoli Users Discuss Automation," *Network World,* April 14, 2003.

Marvin Cetron and Owen Davies, "50 Trends Shaping the Future," *2003 World Future Society Special Report,* April 2004.

Penelope Patsuris, "Marketing Messages Made to Order," *Forbes,* August 2003.

"Progressive Receives Applied Systems' 2003 Interface Best Practices Award," www.worksite.net/091203tech.htm, accessed June 18, 2004.

Stacy Crowley, "IBM, HP, MS Discuss Autonomic Computing Strategies," *Infoworld,* May 19, 2004.

"The Art of Foresight," *The Futurist,* May-June 2004, pp. 31–35.

William Halal, "The Top 10 Emerging Technologies," *The Futurist Special Report,* July 2004.

## Plug-In B13

"BP: WebLearn," www.accenture.com/xd/xd.asp?it=enweb&xd=industries%5Cresources%5Cenergy%5Ccase%5Cener_bpweblearn.xml, accessed June 8, 2004.

"Call Center and CRM Statistics," www.cconvergence.com/shared/printableArticle. jhtml?articleID=7617915, accessed June 8, 2004.

"Coors Brewing Company," www.eds.com/case_studies/case_coors.shtml, accessed June 8, 2004.

Deni Connor, "IT Outlook Declines Due to Outsourcing, Offshoring," www.nwfusion.com/careers/2004/0531manside.html, accessed June 8, 2004.

IBM/Lotus Domino Server Hosting Service, www.macro.com.hk/solution_Outsourcing.htm, accessed June 8, 2004.

Stan Gibson, "Global Services Plays Pivotal Role," www.eweek.com/article2/0,1759,808984,00.asp, accessed June 8, 2004.

Todd Datz, "Outsourcing World Tour," *CIO Magazine,* July 15, 2004, pp. 42–48.

www.forrester.com, accessed June 8, 2004.

## Plug-In B14

"Baggage Handling System Errors," www.flavors.com, accessed November 16, 2003.

Gary McGraw, "Making Essential Software Work," *Software Quality Management,* April 2003, www.sqmmagazine.com, accessed November 14, 2003.

Overcoming Software Development Problems," October 7, 2002, www.samspublishing.com, accessed November 16, 2003.

"Python Project Failure," www.systemsdev.com, accessed November 14, 2003.

www.microsoft.com, accessed November 16, 2003.

www.standishgroup.com, accessed November 14, 2003.

## Plug-In B15

"Staying on Track at the Toronto Transit Commission," www.primavera.com, accessed December 16, 2003.

"Supply and Demand Chain," www.isourceonline.com, accessed December 14, 2003.

"Taking on Change," *CIO Magazine,* June 2005.

"The Project Manager in the IT Industry," www.si2.com, accessed December 15, 2003.

www.altria.com, accessed December 15, 2003.

www.calpine.com, accessed December 14, 2003.

www.change-management.org, accessed December 12, 2003.

www.microsoft.com, accessed December 13, 2003.

www.snapon.com, accessed December 13, 2003.

www.standishgroup.com, accessed December 12, 2003.

## Plug-In B16

Aasron Bernstein, "Backlash: Behind the Anxiety of Globalization," *BusinessWeek,* April 24, 2006, pp. 36–42.

Terry Hill, *Manufacturing Strategy: Text and Cases,* 3rd ed. (New York: McGraw-Hill, 2000).

Andrew Binstock, "Virtual Enterprise Comes of Age," *InformationWeek,* November 6, 2004.

Bill Breen, "Living in Dell Time," *Fast Company,* November 2004, p. 86.

Christopher A. Bartlett and Sumantra Ghoshal, "Going Global: Lessons from Late Movers," *Harvard Business Review,* March–April 2000, pp. 132–34.

"Creating a Value Network," *Wired,* September 2003, p. S13.

Frank Quinn, "The Payoff Potential in Supply Chain Management," www.ascet.com, accessed June 15, 2003.

Fred Hapgood, "Smart Decisions," *CIO Magazine,* www.cio.com, accessed August 15, 2001.

Geoffrey Colvin, "Managing in the Info Era," *Fortune,* March 6, 2007, pp. F6–F9.

James Fitzsimmons and Mona Fitzsimmons, *Service Management,* 4th ed. (New York: McGraw-Hill Irwin, 2004).

James P. Womack, Daniel Jones, and Daniel Roos, *The Machine That Changed the World* (New York, Harper Perennial, 1991).

Jennifer Bresnahan, "The Incredible Journey," *CIO Enterprise Magazine,* August 15, 1998, www.cio.com, accessed March 12, 2004.

Jim Collins, *Built to Last* (Collins Business Essentials, 2004).

Jim Collins, *Good to Great* (Collins Business Essentials, 2001).

John Hagerty, "How Best to Measure Our Supply Chain," www.amrresearch.com, accessed March 3, 2005.

Kevin Kelleher, "BudNet: 66,207,896 Bottles of Beer on the Wall," *Business 2.0,* February 2004.

Kim Girard, "How Levi's Got Its Jeans into Wal-Mart," *CIO Magazine,* July 15, 2003.

Mitch Betts, "Kinks in the Chain," *Computerworld,* December 17, 2005.

Norman E. Bowie (Ed.), *The Blackwell Guide to Business Ethics* (Malden, MA: Blackwell, 2002).

William Copacino, "How to Become a Supply Chain Master," *Supply Chain Management Review,* September 1, 2001, www.manufacturing.net, accessed June 12, 2003.

Sharon Shinn, "What about the Widgets?" *BizEd,* November–December 2004, pp. 30–35.

Stuart Crainer, *The Management Century* (New York: Jossey-Bass, 2000).

"Success Story," www.perdue.com, accessed September 2003.

"The e-Biz Surprise," *BusinessWeek,* May 12, 2003, pp. 60–65.

Walid Mougayar, "Old Dogs Learn New Tricks," Business 2.0, October 2000, www.Business2.com, accessed June 14, 2003.

William J. Hopp and Mark Spearman, *Factory Physics: Foundations of Manufacturing Management,* 2nd ed. (Burr Ridge, IL: Irwin, 2001).

## Plug-In B17

"Achieving a Single Customer View," www.sun.com, accessed January 12, 2008.

Alan Joch, "Grid Gets Down to Business," *Network World,* December 27, 2004.

Dirk Slama, Robert Paluch, "Key Concepts of Service-Oriented Architecture," www.csc.com/cscworld/012006/web/web002.html, accessed on January 4, 2008.

"EPA Report to Congress on Server and Data Center Energy Efficiency," www.energystar.gov/ia/partners/prod_development/downloads/EPA_Report_Exec_Summary_Final.pdf, accessed January 23, 2008.

Geoffrey Thomas, "Seeing Is Believing," *Air Transport World,* June 2007, p. 54.

"Google Groans under Data Strain," www.byteandswitch.com/document.asp?doc_id _ 85804, accessed January 30, 2008.

Grant Gross, "Grids Help eBay Do Big Business," www.infoworld.com/article/06/09/12/HNebaygarids_1.html?GRID%20COMPUTING, accessed January 23, 2008.

Julie Bort, "SOA Made Fast and Easy," *Network World,* October 22, 2007.

Julie Bort, "Subaru Takes a Virtual Drive," *Network World,* September 25, 2006.

Mark Morley, "Business Benefits of SaaS," www.gxs.com/insights/strategy_execution/0708_SaaS_02_MarkMorley.htm, accessed February 14, 2009.

Paul Krill, "Impending Death of Moore's Law Calls for Software Development Changes," *InfoWorld,* May 24, 2005.

Tim Wilson, "Don't Stop the Presses!" www.networkcomputing.com, accessed January 28, 2008.

"VMware—History of Virtualization," www.virtualizationworks.com/Virtualization-History.asp, accessed January 23, 2008.

www.usopen.org, accessed January 28, 2008.

## Plug-In B18

Emanuel Rosen, *The Anatomy of Buzz* (New York:DoubleDay, 2000).

"Enterprise Business Intelligence," May 2006. Used with Permission: Dr. Claudia Imhoff, Intelligent Solutions, Inc.

Frederick F. Reichheld, *Loyalty Rules* (Bain and Company, 2001).

Meridith Levinson, "The Brain Behind the Big Bad Burger and Other Tales of Business Intelligence", www.cio.com, May 15, 2007, http://www.cio.com/article/109454/The_Brain_Behind_the_Big_Bad_Burger_and_Other_Tales_of_Business_Intelligence.

Second Life, www.secondlife.org, accessed March 2008.

Steve Hamm, "Business Intelligence Gets Smarter," *BusinessWeek,* May 15, 2006.

Jill Dyche, "The Business Case for Data Warehousing," 2005. Used with permission.

"The Critical Shift to Flexible Business Intelligence." Used with Permission: Dr. Claudia Imhoff, Intelligent Solutions, Inc.

"What Every Marketer Wants—And Needs—From Technology." Used with Permission: Dr. Claudia Imhoff, Intelligent Solutions, Inc.

## Plug-In B19

Brian Grow, Keith Epstein, and Chi-Chu Tschang, "E-Spionage," *BusinessWeek,* April 10, 2008.

"Innovation," *BusinessWeek,* http://www.businessweek.com/innovate/, accessed February 15, 2008.

David Bornstein, *How to Change the World.* Oxford University Press, USA; Updated edition (September 17, 2007)

Harold Sirkin, "Tata's Nano: An Ingenious Coup," *BusinessWeek,* February 14, 2008.

Heather Green and Kerry Capell, "Carbon Confusion," *BusinessWeek,* March 6, 2008.

Jeffrey Hollender and Stephen Fenichell, *What Matters Most: The Future of Corporate Social Responsibility.* Basic Books (January 2, 2006)

Kerry Capell, "Building Expertise through Collective Innovation," *BusinessWeek,* March 5, 2008.

Peter F. Drucker Foundation, *The Leader of the Future: Visions, Practices, and Strategies for a New Era.*

Peter F. Drucker, *Management Challenges for the 21st Century.* Collins Business; (June 26, 2001)

William J. Holstein , "Corporate Governance in China and India," *BusinessWeek Online,* March 6, 2008, http://www.businessweek.com/managing/content/mar2008/ca2008036_282896.htm.

## Plug-In B20

Brian Grow, Keith Epstein, and Chi-Chu Tschang, "E-Spionage," *BusinessWeek,* April 10, 2008.

"Innovation," *BusinessWeek,* http://www.businessweek.com/innovate/, accessed February 15, 2008.

David Bornstein, *How to Change the World.* Oxford University Press, USA; Updated edition (September 17, 2007)

Harold Sirkin, "Tata's Nano: An Ingenious Coup," *BusinessWeek,* February 14, 2008.

Heather Green and Kerry Capell, "Carbon Confusion," *BusinessWeek,* March 6, 2008.

Jeffrey Hollender and Stephen Fenichell, *What Matters Most: The Future of Corporate Social Responsibility.* Basic Books (January 2, 2006)

Kerry Capell, "Building Expertise through Collective Innovation," *BusinessWeek,* March 5, 2008.

Peter F. Drucker Foundation, *The Leader of the Future: Visions, Practices, and Strategies for a New Era.*

Peter F. Drucker, *Management Challenges for the 21st Century.* Collins Business; (June 26, 2001)

William J. Holstein , "Corporate Governance in China and India," *BusinessWeek Online,* March 6, 2008, http://www.businessweek.com/managing/content/mar2008/ca2008036_282896.htm.

## Plug-In B21

"CenterCup Releases PDA Caddy to Leverage Legalized Golf GPS," www.golfgearreview.com/article-display/1665.html, accessed February 3, 2008.

clearwire.com, accessed January 27, 2009.

Coco Masters, "Bringing Wi-Fi to the Skies," www.time.com/time/specials/2007/article/0,28804,1665220_1665225,00.html, accessed February 20, 2008.

Dan Nystedt, "Mobile Phones Grow Even More Popular," *PC World,* April 2006.

Deepak Pareek, "WiMAX: Taking Wireless to the MAX," CRC Press, 2006, pp. 150–51.

"How Do Cellular Devices Work," www.cell-phone101.info/devices.php, accessed February 9, 2008.

"Keeping Weeds in Check with Less Herbicide," www.ars.usda.gov/is/AR/archive/aug06/weeds0806.htm, accessed February 11, 2008.

loopt.com, accessed January 29, 2009.

Michael Dortch, "Winning RFID Strategies for 2008," *Benchmark Report,* December 31, 2007.

mobilementalism.com, accessed February 2, 2008.

Mohsen Attaran, "RFID: an Enabler of Supply Chain Operations," *Supply Chain Management: An International Journal* 12 (2007), pp. 249–57.

onstar.com, accessed February 10, 2008.

"RFID Privacy and You," www.theyaretrackingyou.com/rfid-privacy-and-you.html, accessed February 12, 2008.

"RFID Roundup," www.rfidgazette.org, accessed February 10, 2008.

"Security-Free Wireless Networks," www.wired.com, accessed February 11, 2008.

"Sprint Plans Launch of Commercial WiMAX Service in Q2 2008," www.intomobile.com, accessed February 10, 2008.

V. C. Gungor, F. C. Lambert, "A Survey on Communication Networks for Electric System Automation, Computer Networks," *The International Journal of Computer and Telecommunications Networking,* May 15, 2006, pp. 877–897.

W. David Gardner, "McDonald's Targets Starbucks with Free Wi-Fi, Upscale Coffee Bars," *InformationWeek,* January 7, 2008.

wimax.com, accessed February 9, 2008.

www.gis.rgs.org/10.html, accessed February 7, 2008.

www.mbia.com, accessed February 3, 2008.

P 1.1A, page 3, ©McGraw-Hill Companies/Jill Braaten, photographer.

P 1.1B, page 3, The McGraw-Hill Companies, Inc./Lars A. Niki, photographer.

P 1.1C, page 3, The McGraw-Hill Companies, Inc./Christopher Kerrigan, photographer.

Figure 1.1, page 8, Paige Baltzan.

Figure 1.2, page 9, www.cio.com, accessed August 2005.

Figure 2.4a, page 21, Photo courtesy of Hyundai Motor America.

Figure 2.4b, page 21, Photo courtesy of Audi.

Figure 2.4c, page 21, Copyright © 2004 Kia Motors America, Inc. All Rights Reserved.

Figure 2.6, page 22, Porter, Michael E., Competitive Strategy: Techniques for Analyzing Industries and Competitors, The Free Press, 1998.

Figure 3.4, page 30, Caldwell, Bruce, "Missteps, Miscues—Business Reengineering Failures," Information Week, June 20, 1994, p. 50.

Figure 3.10, page 33, ERP White Paper, www.bitpipe.com/rlist/term/ERP.html, accessed July 3, 2007.

Figure 4.6, page 41, Google Analytics, www.google.com/analytics, accessed July 13, 2007.

Figure 4.7, page 41, Google Analytics, www.google.com/analytics, accessed July 13, 2007.

Figure 4.8, page 42, Supply Chain Metrics.com, www.supplychainmetric.com/, accessed June 12, 2007.

Figure 4.9, page 43, Kaplan, Robert, Norton, David, "The BSC: Translating Strategy into Action" (Vintage Books: 1998) The Balanced Scorecard Institute, http://www.balancedscorecard.org/BSCResources/AbouttheBalancedScorecard/tabid/55/Default.aspx. Adapted from **The Balanced Scorecard** by Kaplan & Norton, accessed May 15, 2007.

Figure 5.5, page 50, Scott Berimano, Take the Pledge, www.cio.com, accessed November 17, 2003.

Figure 5.8, page 53, Computer Security Institute.

Page 57 (left): Getty Images.

Page 57 (center): Royalty-Free/Corbis.

Page 57 (right): Royalty-Free/Corbis.

Page 59 (left): The McGraw-Hill Companies, Inc./John Flournoy, photographer.

Page 59 (center): Steven Brahms/Bloomberg News/Landov.

Page 59 (right): PRNewsFoto/Bank of America/AP/Wide World Photos.

P 2.1A, page 73, Digital Vision/Getty Images.

P 2.1B, page 73, BananaStock/PictureQuest.

P 2.1C, page 73, Jason Reed/Getty Images.

Figure 7.4, page 92, Webopedia.com, www.webopedia.comTERM/d/database.html, accessed May 15, 2007; Wikipedia, The Free Encyclopedia, en.wikipedia.org/wiki/Wiki, accessed May 22, 2007; Oracle Database, www.oracle.com/database/index.html, accessed May 17, 2007; www.sitepoint.com/article/publishing-mysql-data-web, accessed May 16, 2007.

P 2.2A, page 107, PhotoLink/Photodisc/Getty Images.

P 2.2B, page 107, Jack Star/PhotoLink/Getty Images.

P 2.2C, page 107, Oleg Svyatoslavsky/Life File/Getty Images.

P 2.3, page 109, Photo courtesy of Cray, Inc.

Page 119 (all): Courtesy of Linden Labs.

P 9.1, page 131, Alexander Heimann/AFP/Getty.

P 9.2, page 131, AP/Wide World Photos.

P 9.3, page 131, © Jeff Greenberg/Photo Edit.

Figure 12.3, page 159, Exact Software, "ERP-II: Making ERP Deliver On Its Promise to the Enterprise", jobfunctions.bnet.com/whitepaper.aspx?docid=144338, accessed July 25, 2007.

Figure 12.4, page 159, Exact Software, "ERP-II: Making ERP Deliver On Its Promise to the Enterprise", jobfunctions.bnet.com/whitepaper.aspx?docid=144338, accessed July 25, 2007.

P 3.2A, page 167, C. Sherburne/PhotoLink/Getty Images.

P 3.2B, page 167, Digital Vision/Getty Images.

P 3.2C, page 167, Ryan McVay/Getty Images.

P 3.2D, page 169, AP/Wide World Photos.

P 3.2E, page 169, Scott Olson/Getty Images.

P 3.2F, page 169, PRNewsFoto/Harley-Davidson/AP/Wide World Photos.

13.1A, page 181, Getty Images.

13.1B, page 181, Getty Images.

13.1C, page 181, Getty Images.

Figure 13.1, page 185, http://www.internetworldstats.com/stats.htm, accessed January 15, 2005.

Figure 13.8, page 189, Tim O'Reilly, "What Is Web 2.0: Design Patterns and Business Models for the Next Generation of Software", 9/30/2005.

Figure 13.9, page 189, Tim O'Reilly, "What Is Web 2.0: Design Patterns and Business Models for the Next Generation of Software", 9/30/2005.

Figure 14.9, page 197, Ecommerce Taxation, www.icsc.org/, accessed June 8, 2004.

Figure 15.10, page 212: Cartesia/PhotoDisc Imaging/Getty Images.

Figure 15.11, page 213: © Tom Grill/Corbis.

P 4.2A, page 224, Creatas/PunchStock.

P 4.2B, page 224, Dynamic Graphics/JupiterImages.

P 4.2C, page 224, PhotoLink/Getty Images.

P 4.2D, page 225, ThinkStock/SuperStock.

P 4.2E, page 225, The McGraw-Hill Companies, Inc./ John Flournoy, photographer.

P 4.2F, page 225, BananaStock/PictureQuest.

17.1A, page 241, Getty Images.

17.1B, page 241, Royalty-Free/CORBIS.

17.1C, page 241, Royalty-Free/CORBIS.

Figure 18.2, page 259, *Information Week.*

Figure 19.1, page 264, Common Outsourcing, www.cio.com, accessed June 15, 2004.

Figure 20.1, page 271, www.expedia.com, www.apple.com, www. dell.com, www.lendingtree.com, www.amazon.com, www.ebay. com, accessed October 13, 2004.

Figure 20.3, page 272, 2005 SCOnline.com, accessed January 2005.

P 5.2A, page 277, Tetra Images/Getty Images.

P 5.2B, page 277, Lars Niki.

P 5.2C, page 277, The McGraw-Hill Companies, Inc., Christopher Kerrigan, photographer.

P 5.2D, page 279, Getty Images/Blend Images.

P 5.2E, page 279, Stockbyte/Getty Images.

P 5.2F, page 279, Ingram Publishing/AGE Fotostock.

Figure B2.6, page B2.7, Michael Hammer. *Beyond Reengineering, How the Process-Centered Organization Is Changing Our Work and Our Lives, New York:* HarperCollins, Publisher, 1996.

P B3.1A, page B3.3, Royalty-Free/CORBIS.

P B3.1B, page B3.3, Stockbyte/Punchstock Images.

P B3.2, page B3.4, SimpleTech Inc.

P B3.3A, page B3.4, Getty Images.

P B3.3B, page B3.4, Daisuke Morita/Getty Images.

P B3.4A, page B3.4, © Stockbyte/PunchStock.

P B3.4B, page B3.4, © Stockbyte/PunchStock.

P B3.5A, page B3.4, Courtesy of Panasonic

P B3.5B, page B3.4, Courtesy of Dell Inc.

P B3.6A, page B3.4, Getty Images.

P B3.6B, page B3.4, Royalty-Free/CORBIS.

Figure B3.3, page B3.5, "Chip Wars," *PC World,* August 2005.

Figure B3.11, page B3.12, Ricadela, Aaron, "Seismic Shift," Information Week, March 14, 2005.

Figure B4.1, page B4.2, *Business Week,* January 10, 2005.

Figure B4.4, page B4.5, *Information Week,* August 9, 2004.

Figure B5.4, page B5.5, www.pcmagazine.com, accessed October 10, 2005.

Figure B6.3, page 303, www.ey.com, accessed November 25, 2003.

Figure B6.4, page 304, "The Security Revolution," www.cio.com, accessed June 6, 2003.

Figure B6.6, page 307, "Spam Losses to Grow to $198 Billion," www.cio.com, accessed August 9, 2003.

Figure B7.10, page 322, Paul Roberts, "Report Span Costs $874 per Employee per Year," www.computerworld.com, July 2, 2003, accessed March 9, 2004.

Figure B7.11, page 323, AMA Research, "Workplace Monitoring and Surveillance," www.amanet.org, April 2003, accessed March 1, 2004.

Figure B10.1, page 365, "ERP Knowledge Base," www.cio.com, accessed June 2005.

Figure B11.9, page 387, www.w3.org, W3C Security resources, accessed June 2005.

Figure B12.2, page B12.3, "50 Trends Shaping the Future," *2003 World Future Society Special Report,* April 2004.

Figure B12.3, page B12.4, Ibid.

Figure B12.4, page B12.5, Ibid.

Figure B13.1, page B13.3, Datz, Todd, "Outsourcing World Tour," *CIO Magazine,* July 15, 2004, pp. 42–48.

Figure B21.3, page 528, AP/World Wide.

## INDEX B3

**(Please note Index B3 is on the OLC – www.mhhe.com/bdt4e)**

## INDEX B4

**(Please note Index B4 is on the OLC – www.mhhe.com/bdt4e)**

## I

IBM, 10, 16
IDC, 16–17
Identity Theft, 6
Information Architecture, 3, 6–7, 14
    Enterprise, 4
    Solid, 2
Information Backup, 4
Information Security, 3–4, 6, 15
Information Security Plan, 6
Information Technology, 2
Infrastructure, 6, 9–10
Infrastructure Architecture, 2–3, 7, 14–15
Integration, 10–11
Interface, 11
Internet, 9–12, 15, 17
Interoperability, 11, 14

## L

Linux, 13, 15–17
Lydian Trust, 12

## M

Metrics, 9–10
Microsoft, 7, 16–17

## N

Networks, 5–7, 9, 11
Northern Ohio Power Company, 5

## O

Open Source 3, 16–17

## P

Patches, 6–7, 16
    Applying, 7
    Critical, 7
Performance, 3, 7–8, 10, 14, 18
Performance Measures, 10

## R

Recovery, 3–6, 14–15
Reliability, 3, 7–9, 14, 18

## S

Scalability, 3, 7–9, 14, 18
Servers, 5, 7, 12, 14

## T

T-Mobile, 3, 12

## U

Unavailability, 5–6
Union Bank of California, 6

## V

Verizon, 11

## W

Web Server, 12
Web Service, 2–3, 10–12, 14–15

# INDEX B5

(Please note Index B5 is on the OLC – www.mhhe.com/bdt4e)

## A

Analog Signaling, 8
Application Integration, 10
Application Layer, 7
Application Processes, 7
Architecture, 3–4, 18

## B

Bandwidth, 14–15, 18
Bank of America, 20
Barclay's Bank, 20
Baud, 14
Bits, 14–15
Bps, 14–15
Broadband Technology, 2, 15–16
BUS Topology, 6
Business Application Integration, 12

## C

Client/Server Architecture, 4
Client/Server Network, 4, 18
Coaxial Cable, 9, 15, 18
Computers, 2–6, 8, 11–12, 16, 18, 20
    Distributed, 4
    Personal, 8
Corporate Network, 4, 15, 17

## D

Data Packets, 7
Devices, 4, 6–7, 20
    Electrical, 9
    Handheld, 19
    Slower, 7
    Wireless Networking, 10
Dial-Up Access, Traditional, 15
Digital Subscriber Line (DSL), 14–16

## E

Encryption, 16–17
Ethernet, 3, 5–8, 18

## F

Fiber-Optic Cable, 9–10, 15
File Transfer Protocol (FTP), 8

## G

Gigabit Ethernet Technology, 5

## H

Hertz, 14
Hybrid Topology, 6
Hypertext Transfer Protocol, 8

## INDEX B12

**(Please note Index B12 is on the OLC – www.mhhe.com/bdt4e)**

## INDEX B13

**(Please note Index B13 is on the OLC www.mhhe.com/bdt4e)**

## BUSINESS DRIVEN TECHNOLOGY CASES

*Business Driven Technology* offers over 70 cases on current companies ranging from Apple to Wikipedia. Unit opening cases have questions spread throughout the unit to help students analyze the case according to material. Each chapter has a smaller case that focuses on specific chapter content. Unit closing cases are in-depth cases covering all unit material. Each business plug-in has two cases that explore the plug-in topics further. Cases include:

- 3Com Optimizes Product Promotion Processes
- Apple—Merging Technology, Business, and Entertainment
- Autonomic Railways
- Banks, Banking on Network Security
- Battle of the Toys—FAO Schwarz is Back
- Business 2.0: Bad Business Decisions
- Business Subject Matter Experts–The Project Manager You Need to Know About *BusinessWeek* Interview with Michael Porter
- Calling All Canadians
- Campus ERP
- Can You Find Your Customers?
- Change at Toyota
- Changing Circuits at Circuit City
- *Chicago Tribune's* Server Consolidation a Success
- Clearwire
- Collective Innovation
- Confusing Carbon
- Creating a Clearer Picture for Public Broadcasting Service (PBS)
- Defense Advanced Research Projects Agency (DARPA) Grand Challenge
- Dell's Famous Supply Chain
- Disaster at Denver International Airport
- eBay's Grid
- eBiz
- Electronic Breaking Points
- Enterprise Content Management at Statoil
- E-espionage
- Executive Dilemmas in the Information Age
- Failing to Innovate
- Fear the Penguin
- Fighting Cancer with Information
- Global Governance
- Got Milk? It's Good for You–Unless it is Contaminated!
- Hacker Hunters
- Harrah's—Gambling Big on Technology
- How Do You Value Friendster?
- How Levi's Jeans Got into Wal-Mart
- Improving Highway Safety Through Collaboration

- Innovative Business Managers
- Intelligent Business: Is It an Oxymoron?
- Invading Your Privacy
- It Takes a Village to Write an Encyclopedia
- Katrina Shakes Supply Chains
- Keeper of the Keys
- Listerine's Journey
- Loopt
- Made-to-Order Businesses
- Mail with PostalOne
- Major League Baseball–The Real Competitive Advantages
- Mining the Data Warehouse
- Mobil Travel Guide
- Outsourcing Brew
- PepsiAmericas' Enterprises
- Political Microtargeting: What Data Crunchers Did for Obama
- Reducing Ambiguity in Business Requirements
- Revving Up Sales at Harley-Davidson
- RFID—Future Tracking the Supply Chain
- Sarbanes-Oxley: Where Information Technology, Finance, and Ethics Meet
- Searching for Revenue—Google
- Second Life: Succeeding in Virtual Times
- Shell Canada Fuels Productivity with ERP
- Social Networking
- Software Developing Androids
- Staying on Track—Toronto Transit
- Streamlining Processes at Adidas
- Tata's Nano $2,500 Car
- The Brain Behind the Big, Bad Burger and Other Tales of Business Intelligence
- The Digital Hospital
- The Ironman
- The U.S. Open Supports SOA
- Thinking like the Enemy
- The World is Flat–Thomas Friedman
- Twitter
- UPS in the Computer Repair Business
- Watching Where You Step—Prada
- Women in Technology
- Wireless Electricity
- Wireless Progression